THE CESARE LOMBROSO HANDBOOK

The Italian criminologist Cesare Lombroso (1835–1909) is the single-most important figure in the founding of criminology and the study of aberrant conduct in the human sciences.

The Cesare Lombroso Handbook brings together essays by leading Lombroso scholars and may be said to focus on four major themes. Initially, it examines the range and scope of Lombroso's thinking; the mimetic quality of Lombroso; his texts and their interpretation. A second theme explores why his ideas, such as born criminology and atavistic criminals, had such broad appeal in the United States and elsewhere. Developing this, the anthology includes articles that considers the manners in which Lombroso's ideas spread across borders; cultural, linguistic, political and disciplinary, by including essays on the science and literature of opera, *La donna delinquente* and 'Jewish criminality'. The final chapters of *The Cesare Lombroso Handbook* investigates examples of where, and when, his influence extended and explores the reception of Lombroso in Britain, France, China, Spain and the Philippines.

This text presents interdisciplinary work on Lombroso from academics engaged in social history, history of ideas, law and criminology, social studies of science, gender studies, cultural studies and Jewish studies. It will be of interest to scholars, students and the general reader alike.

Paul Knepper is Professor of Criminology in the School of Law at the University of Sheffield, UK.

P. J. Ystehede works as a research officer at the Department of Criminology and Sociology of Law, University of Oslo, Norway.

THE CESARE LOMBROSO HANDBOOK

Edited by Paul Knepper and P. J. Ystehede

Routledge
Taylor & Francis Group
LONDON AND NEW YORK

First published 2013
by Routledge
2 Park Square, Milton Park, Abingdon, Oxon, OX14 4RN

Simultaneously published in the USA and Canada
by Routledge
711 Third Avenue, New York, NY 10017

Routledge is an imprint of the Taylor & Francis Group, an informa business

© 2013 Paul Knepper and Per Ystehede for selection and editorial matter; individual contributors their contribution.

The right of Paul Knepper and Per Ystehede to be identified as the authors of the editorial material, and of the authors for their individual chapters, has been asserted in accordance with sections 77 and 78 of the Copyright, Designs and Patents Act 1988.

All rights reserved. No part of this book may be reprinted or reproduced or utilised in any form or by any electronic, mechanical, or other means, now known or hereafter invented, including photocopying and recording, or in any information storage or retrieval system, without permission in writing from the publishers.

Trademark notice: Product or corporate names may be trademarks or registered trademarks, and are used only for identification and explanation without intent to infringe

British Library Cataloguing in Publication Data
A catalogue record for this book is available from the British Library

Library of Congress Cataloging-in-Publication Data
A catalog record has been requested for this book

The Cesare Lombroso handbook/
[edited by] Paul Knepper and Per Ystehede.
   p. cm.
Includes index.
1. Lombroso, Cesare, 1835–1909. 2. Criminologists–Italy. 3. Criminology. 4. Criminal anthropology. I. Knepper, Paul. II. Ystehede, Per.

HV6023.L6C464 2012
364.92–dc23   2012024091

ISBN: 978-0-415-50977-0 (hbk)
ISBN: 978-0-203-08336-9 (ebk)

Typeset in Bembo
by Sunrise Setting Ltd

Printed and bound in the United States of America by Publishers Graphics, LLC on sustainably sourced paper.

CONTENTS

List of Illustrations   viii

Contributors   x

Acknowledgments   xii

    Introduction   1

1 Lombroso and his school: from anthropology to medicine and law   8
  Renzo Villa

2 Cesare Lombroso, prison science, and penal policy   30
  Mary Gibson

3 *Gli Anarchici* and Lombroso's theory of political crime   47
  Trevor Calafato

4 Demonizing being: Lombroso and the ghosts of criminology   72
  P. J. Ystehede

5 The Lombroso Museum from its origins to the present day   98
  Silvano Montaldo

6 Caesar or Cesare? American and Italian images of Lombroso   113
  Patrizia Guarnieri

7   New natural born killers? The legacy of Lombroso in
    neuroscience and law   131
    Emilia Musumeci

8   From subhumans to superhumans: Criminals in the
    evolutionary hierarchy, or what became of Lombroso's
    atavistic criminals?   147
    Simon A. Cole and Michael C. Campbell

9   Lombroso and Jewish social science   171
    Paul Knepper

10 The melodramatic publication career of Lombroso's *La
    donna delinquente*   187
    Nicole Rafter

11 Lombroso's *Criminal Woman* and the uneven development of
    the modern lesbian identity   201
    Mariana Valverde

12 In search of the Lombrosian type of delinquent   214
    Daniele Velo Dalbrenta

13 Lombroso and the science of literature and opera   226
    Jonathan R. Hiller

14 A hidden theme of Jewish self-love? Eric Hobsbawm, Karl
    Marx, and Cesare Lombroso on "Jewish criminality"   253
    Michael Berkowitz

15 The methods of Lombroso and cultural criminology   268
    Dina Siegel

16 Lombroso in France: a paradoxical reception   281
    Marc Renneville

17 Lombroso in China: Dong Xue Wei Ti, Xi Xue Wei Yong?   293
    Bill Hebenton and Susyan Jou

18 Lombroso but not Lombrosians? Criminal anthropology in
    Spain   309
    Ricardo Campos and Rafael Huertas

19 The influence of Cesare Lombroso on Philippine
    criminology   324
    Filomin C. Gutierrez

20 Lombroso and the 'men of real science': British reactions, 1886–1918 342
   Neil Davie

Index 361

ILLUSTRATIONS

0.1	Cesare Lombroso painted by an unknown artist on a palette, (1872 ca)	2
0.2	Statue of Lombroso by Leonardo Bistolfi	3
1.1	Lombroso together with his daughter, Gina Lombroso Ferrero. Pastel on paper, (Durio, 1910)	13
1.2	The Sixth Criminal Anthropology Congress in Turin in 1906	22
2.1	Lombroso's replica of the Philadelphia penitentiary at Cherry Hill	40
3.1	A photo sent by the Queen of Romania, Carmen Sylva, to Lombroso when researching latent suicide	55
3.2	Lombroso's portrait of Sante Geronimo di Caserio	56
3.3	Lombroso's correlations between the different seasons and the upsurge of political violence in different epochs and countries	61
3.4	Lombroso's mapping of the increase in seditions and revolutions in relation to the hot temperatures in Europe between 1791 and 1880	62
4.1	Cesare Lombroso at a spiritist séance (1908)	73
4.2	The medium Eusapia Palladino in a trance	77
4.3	Spirit manifestation created by the medium Linda Gazzera (1909)	87
5.1	The museum of Psychiatry and Criminology of Torino at the beginning of the twentieth century	99

5.2	Recreation of Lombroso's office at the Museum – the furniture of the study that Lombroso and subsequently Carrara had used in the apartment in Via Legnano	106
5.3	The museum was reopened to the public on 27 November 2009 in conjunction with the 100th anniversary of Lombroso's death	107
10.1	Watercolor of a woman suffering from hypertrichosis (end of the nineteenth century)	192
13.1	Image of a typical thief in *The Criminal Man*	236
13.2	Giuseppe Verdi and Arrigo Boito, *Otello*, Act III: "Fuggirmi io sol non so"	246
13.3	Pietro Mascagni and Nicola Daspuro, *L'amico Fritz*, Act I: Beppe's Violin Entrance	248
15.1	Hall of skeletons of criminals from Lombroso C. (1906) "Il mio museo criminale," L'Illustrazione italiana	271
17.1	Portraits of Chinese emigrants. Staits Settlements (British Colonies in South-East of Asia, 1930)	294
19.1	A series of images showing seven notable anomalies in the skull of a Bilibid prison inmate convicted of murder based on the clinical analysis of Sixto De Los Angeles	333
19.2	A sampling of cranial anomalies of criminals based on the autopsies of 44 deceased convicts	334

CONTRIBUTORS

Michael Berkowitz is Professor of Modern Jewish History, University College London.

Trevor Calafato is an Assistant Lecturer at the Department of Criminology at the University of Malta and a PhD fellow at the University of Sheffield.

Michael C. Campbell is Assistant Professor, Department of Criminology and Criminal Justice, University of Missouri-St. Louis.

Ricardo Campos is Tenure Scientist of the Institute of History of the Center for Human and Social Sciences CSIC Spain.

Simon A. Cole is Associate Professor of Criminology, Law and Society, University of California Irvine.

Neil Davie is Professor of British History at the University of Lyon 2.

Mary Gibson is Professor of History at John Jay College of Criminal Justice.

Patrizia Guarnieri is Professor of Modern History at the University of Firenze.

Filomin C. Gutierrez is an Associate Professor of Sociology at the University of Philippines Diliman.

Bill Hebenton is a faculty member in the Centre for Criminology and Socio-Legal Studies, School of Law, and a Research Associate of the Manchester Centre for Chinese Studies, University of Manchester.

Jonathan R. Hiller is Assistant Professor of Italian in the Department of Languages, Literatures and Cultures at Adelphi University.

Rafael Huertas is Professor at the Centre for Human and Social Sciences, CSIC, Spain.

Susyan Jou is Professor, Graduate School of Criminology, National Taipei University.

Paul Knepper is Professor of Criminology in the School of Law at the University of Sheffield.

Silvano Montaldo is Professor of Modern History, University of Turin, and Director of Museo di Antropologia criminale "Cesare Lombroso".

Emilia Musumeci is researcher at the University of Catania.

Nicole Rafter is Professor at the School of Criminology and Criminal Justice, Northeastern University.

Marc Renneville is Senior Researcher at the Alexandre Koyré Center for the History of Science and Technique (Paris).

Dina Siegel is Professor of Criminology at the Willem Pompe Institute for Criminal law and Criminology, Utrecht University.

Mariana Valverde is Professor of Criminology at the Centre for Criminology and Sociolegal Studies, University of Toronto.

Daniele Velo Dalbrenta is Associate Professor at the Department of Law, University of Verona.

Renzo Villa Historia, MD, former researcher at the Institute of criminal anthropology at the University of Turin. Author of '*Il deviante e i suoi segni*', Milano, 1985.

P. J. Ystehede is research officer at Department of Criminology and Sociology of Law, University of Oslo.

ACKNOWLEDGMENTS

One of the great pleasures with conducting research on Cesare Lombroso is to meet and be in contact with people who share both their knowledge, but also a mutual fascination with his work and legacy.

We could not have completed this volume without the help of friends and numerous colleagues. First of all we would like to thank the contributors: Michael Berkowitz, Trevor Calofato, Michael C. Campbell, Ricardo Campos, Simon Cole, Daniela Velo Dalbrenta, Neil Davie, Mary Gibson, Patrizia Guarnieri, Filomin Guitierrez, Bill Hebenton, Jonathan R. Hiller, Rafael Huertas, Susyan Jou, Silvano Montaldo, Emilia Musumeci, Nicole Rafter, Marc Renneville, Dina Siegel, Mariana Valverde, and Renzo Villa. We feel truly lucky that so many Lombroso scholars have been gracious enough to spend their time participating in this project.

Especially we would like to thank Professor Nicole Rafter, Northeastern University, for her support from the very inception of this project. We would also like to thank Professor Silvano Montaldo, University of Turin and Director of the Lombroso Museum of Criminal Anthropology, who not only contributed with an article but also generously provided us with access to material and photographs from the museum collection some of which have never before been published. We would like to express our gratitude to the two anonymous reviewers for their encouragement and insightful suggestion as well as our publishers at Routledge, Tom Sutton, and Nicola Hartley.

Also, we would like to thank for their invaluable help: Cristina Cilli, Museo di Anatomia Umana "Luigi Rolando", Jane Dulllum, University of Oslo, Turid Eikvam, University of Oslo, Kjersti Ericsson, University of Oslo, Elena Gay, the Lombroso Museum of Criminal Anthropology, Turid, and Svein Ystehede.

INTRODUCTION

Paul Knepper and P. J. Ystehede

Enrico Ferri (1856–1929) once remarked that with the death of Cesare Lombroso (1835–1909): the criminal sciences had lost its imagination and luster (Ferri 1912). No longer having Lombroso there to guide, provoke, or initiate discussions suggesting new perspectives and avenues of thought, Ferri thought that Lombroso and those scientists following him in the early stages of criminal anthropology had exhausted and covered most of the aspects as to how to understand the tropes of crime.

After the death of Lombroso in 1909, one project was to raise funding for a statue to commemorate the founder of the Italian school of criminal anthropology. The process was administered by an executive Italian Committee and an International subcommittee. Represented was Austria, Belgium, Brazil, Chile, Cuba, Denmark, Ecuador, France, Germany, Greece, Great Britain, Japan, Luxembourg, Mexico, Norway, Holland, Portugal, the Argentine Republic, Romania, Russia, Scotland, Serbia, Spain, United States, Switzerland, Sweden, Trieste (at the time under Austrian rule), Hungary, and Venezuela. Though the names listed on the International committee almost reads like a who's who list with regard to key players and mayor influences on the sciences of crime at the time, the ceremony itself was to be primarily an Italian affair. The inauguration of the statue of Lombroso by Leonardo Bistolfi (1855–1933) had been much delayed by the Great War. Finally, in the city of Lombroso's birth, Verona, on Sunday September 25, 1921, it was time. Meeting at 9.45 a.m. the attendants walked in a procession down Via Lombroso to Piazzo Santo Spirito. In the crowd in the courtyard one found members from the Lombroso family, academics from universities throughout Italy or visiting from abroad, and people from the city of Verona itself. At the ceremony of the glorification of a son of Verona, his school, the Italian nation and its contribution to the advancement of humanity, one also found representatives of the political life of Italy: Socialists, Christian Democrats, Liberalists, and Fascists. Just after 10 a.m. the

2 Introduction

FIGURE 0.1 Cesare Lombroso painted by an unknown artist on a palette, (1872 ca)

Source: Museo di Antropologia criminale "Cesare Lombroso" dell'Università di Torino (Italia).

first speaker, the politician, lawyer and academic Agostino Berenini (1858–1939) mounted the podium. Addressing the crowd, Berenini asked: "Who was really Cesare Lombroso?":

> Anthropologist? Psychologist? Psychiatrist? Criminologist? Hygenicist? Sociologist? Philosopher? I do not know. The culture of these specialist disciplines all have in them the master, as the earth of Ellade in Homer, as Dante exists in every piece of Italy's soil … I feel in Cesare Lombroso – a benefactor of humanity.
>
> (Berenini quoted in *Le Solenni Onoranze*, 1922, 14)

After the speeches from Agostino Berenini, representatives of the Italian Government, and the Major of the City of Verona, Ferri together with four distinguished visitors from abroad unveiled the statue. Afterward, the crowd started to leave the courtyard, some to partake in a dinner reception, where more speeches were held to honour Cesare Lombroso, his science, and the glory of Italy.

One month after the inauguration of the statue, the Blackshirts (Squadristi) marched on Rome. On October 29, 1921, Mussolini became the new leader of Italy.

FIGURE 0.2 Statue of Lombroso by Leonardo Bistolfi

Source: Archivio storico del Museo di Antropologia criminale "Cesare Lombroso" dell'Università di Torino (Italia).

Raising modern ruins – reconstructions and depictions of Cesare Lombroso

> When he asked me why I had made a drawing of their fortress, I said modestly that I had not realized that these ruins were a fortress. I pointed to the ruinous state of the tower and the walls, the lack of gates, in short, to the general defenceless condition of the whole place, and assured him it had never crossed my mind that I was drawing anything but a ruin. He answered: If it were only a ruin, why was it worth noticing? ... they probably knew, I said, that a great many travelers came to Italy only to see ruins ...
>
> (Goethe 1992, 44–45)

Who was Cesare Lombroso? One way to begin to answer this question is similar to Berenini (1922), emphasize Lombroso's Italian connection. From the age of Johann Wolfgang von Goethe (1749–1832) and onwards, making an Italian journey has been considered the *Bildung* – or the ultimate "education of the self" par excellence. Thus, per chance it is more than apt and appropriate for an anthology on one of the key intellectual thinkers in criminology to start, namely, in Italy.

Lombroso spent the majority of his professional life in Turin, so an inquiry into Lombroso will eventually lead many to visit this former capital of Italy and the place of birth of the science of the born criminal – some will claim – the science of criminology. For a first time visitor to the city and Italy it may take some time to shake preconceived notions and ideas of what Italy is, and has to offer. A sentiment noted and put most eloquently by Henry James (1843–1916) who wrote in *Italian Hours*: "Turin is no city of a name to conjure with, and I pay an extravagant tribute to subjective emotion in speaking of it as ancient" (James 2007, 124). Turin might be said to be a city not so much representing the Italy of the old or ancient philosophers, nor the Renaissance period praised by so many travel writers from Goethe, James, Dickens (to mention a few) and to the present – but rather its modern history. Turin is a city saturated with monuments celebrating the unification of the Italian states and the Risorgimento. It is a city whose buildings and ruins more tell stories of events from the nineteenth century than it conjures "ghosts" from its Roman Imperial past. Turin is the city of Lombroso, of Garibaldi, of Nietzsche – the latter who descended into madness and mentally collapsed in the heart of the intellectual quarters of Turin on Piazza Carlo Alberto. It is a city of the turmoil of the unification, of national romanticism, of decadence and decay, of modern and Fascist architecture.

Turin is also still the home of the Lombroso Museum.[1]

To Lombroso, his museum was, among other things, a manifestation of great battles – a war – physically, literally, and symbolically; collected and fought for in the trenches in the Italian Wars of Independence, the countryside and rural areas of the South, and in the villages and the city streets, in the political and academic quarters and chambers. His museum stands there, according to Lombroso, filled with trophies, weapons, documentation, the heroes and the victims of a global war – of evolution. It stands there to demonstrate and be of service – for posterity – to those who wish to understand the questions of crime, the criminal and its science (Lombroso 1906). For a long time the Museum was reminiscent more of a forlorn, deserted shrine from the wastelands of criminal anthropological and criminological history – but was recently renovated and made more accessible to the general public. When visiting the Lombroso Museum, one should allow oneself to ponder not only on the perhaps more antiquarian aspects of Lombroso's thought, but its complex relationship to the here and now. For a criminologist, the collection might seem not only puzzling, but totally alien. For what do the wax masks and all the other paraphernalia belonging to the Founding Father of Criminology, for instance, have to do with present-day criminological research? Today, visiting the Lombroso Museum, one bridges a time continuum that seemingly has created a series of logical oxymorons. For example; from being a science on "monsters," Lombroso's science has now metamorphosed into what some saw, and still see, as a *monstrous science*. Both the statue of Lombroso in Verona and the Lombroso Museum in Turin have become visual manifestations of the question: by laying down his principles for a new science, what did Lombroso take part in, and contribute, to bring into being?

In the late nineteenth century, Lombroso popularized the body-centered social-scientific study of aberrant behavior – criminality, pathology, madness, and violence. His explanation of "criminal man" swelled from a short book into a multi-volume work; the 5th edition reflects his desire to achieve a comprehensive understanding. More than a hundred years later, he remains enormously popular, and yet, large sections of his writing have yet to be systematically examined. During the past decade, there has been a surge of interest in Cesare Lombroso. A significant body of revisionist scholarship is emerging within criminology and other disciplines across the human sciences. New translations of Lombroso's most widely known works by revisionist pioneers such as Mary Gibson and Nicole Rafter have both fostered and coincided with a re-thinking of his ideas and influence throughout the world, creating the need for a substantial volume of the latest Lombroso scholarship.

The Cesare Lombroso Handbook presents interdisciplinary work on Lombroso from scholars engaged in social history, history of ideas, law and criminology, social studies of science, cultural studies, and Jewish studies. Cesare Lombroso is the single-most important figure in accounts of the founding of criminology and the study of aberrant conduct in the human sciences. There is an emerging body of work calling for a new understanding of his theories and research in the criminal sciences. However, Lombroso appeals to a wide variety of interests other than criminological. Lombroso wrote predominantly about criminality, but also about anarchism and madness, music, literature, spirituality, and sexuality. There is a need for an "interdisciplinary" treatment because contemporary analysis of his work extends to discussions of Italian socialism, sexuality, the body, colonialism, racism, anti-Semitism, social medicine, anarchism, mental illness, criminal identification, museum studies, and photography. Much recent scholarship has appeared in Italian, Spanish, and German. There is a need for a forum in which English-speakers can encounter this work. Although many English scholars cannot access work in Spanish, German, and Italian, many scholars from each of these language backgrounds read English. This is one of the reasons why we are very happy to include articles from authors throughout the world – many who rarely publish in English; this in addition to articles with the most recent research by long-standing Lombroso scholars.

The Cesare Lombroso Handbook brings together essays by leading Lombroso scholars and may be said to focus on four major themes. The main theme in the first chapters may be summarized by the question: "What did Lombroso have to say?" These chapters are preoccupied with the range and scope of Lombroso's thinking; the mimetic quality of Lombroso; his texts and their interpretation.

In Chapters 5 to 9, one will see explored why his ideas had such a broad appeal, whereas Chapters 10 to 15 are articles which shows some of the ways in which Lombroso's ideas spread across borders; cultural, linguistic, political, and disciplinary. The final chapters (16 to 20) provides examples of where, and when, his influence extended. Especially, the geographical diffusion of Lombroso's thought and his role in the emergence of criminology is exemplified.

None of the articles falls neatly into these "boxes," and many could justifiably have been placed in more than one part and under more than one thematic heading. Furthermore, the reader will find that the authors differ regarding how to consider Lombroso's work, influence and influences, legacy, key interests, and how to categorize his research (for instance its relation to positivism). Thus, many of the authors disagree on a number of issues. This we consider as one of the strengths of this anthology. The contributors' different analyses may be traced back, and explained by such factors as differing academic traditions and philosophies of science. Most importantly, we would argue, these differences bring attention to questions of historical methods. What do we do when we write history? What are the consequences by choosing one form of historical narrative instead of another? How should one perceive, trace, and understand "influences" and "developments" when dealing with historical matter? For instance, how shall we consider the relation between Lombroso's thought and the atrocities committed during World War II? To provide yet another example: by positioning Lombroso as the Founding Father of Criminology and at the beginning of the history of the science of criminology, how does this influence, and relate to, how one conceives of Lombroso, the discipline of criminology, and the ontological and epistemological fabric of present-day criminological projects? In other words, make the reader reflect on historical methods and the use of history and historical narratives as "building blocks" in criminological and social research.

Many of the contributions in this volume belong to what may usefully be called *revisionist historians*. By revisionist historians we mean criminologists and historians who contest the traditional, mainstream view presented of Cesare Lombroso – who has been mired in one or another stereotype – and aims to explore Lombroso and criminology from new perspectives. One may argue that to criticize the presentation of the history of criminology is nothing new, and as such, all too easy. It may be, and has been, charged with being written by (and for) a male, white audience, for being sexist, a discipline of the West, Orientalist, and homophobic. Though "criminology" has been called all of these things, above all, however, what perhaps was one of the main problems was simply the lack by criminologists to go *ad fontes* and consult original sources. Though the revisionist historians (may) disagree on a number of issues, what they share is advocating the importance of new historical research for understanding the history of crime, criminology, and the criminal justice system. For a long time, and unfortunately still, the presentation of the history of the science of criminology is in large parts based on, at best, secondary sources. This, unfortunately, has led to a somewhat mythopoeic presentation of its development. Thus, the presentation of the history of criminology is littered with sweeping remarks which, considering the references provided, cannot be supported – leaving the aforementioned evaluations as mere claims, which as such might be neither rejected nor accepted. As Gibson and Rafter puts it: "Misunderstandings of Lombroso's work are so widespread as to constitute a distinct mythology" (Gibson and Rafter 2004, 5).

The Cesare Lombroso Handbook aims to contribute to the process of revising and rectifying earlier omissions, if not settling debates. We also hope to have conveyed to the reader a glimpse into the richness of Cesare Lombroso's, and others', early research on crime. Our biggest regret with this anthology is that Lombroso himself was not available to write the concluding chapter, thus adding his reflections to the heterogeneous voices coming from the historical revisionist historians presented in this volume. Instead, we leave this to the reader. Hopefully, this volume will be part of explaining why Lombroso still fascinates and creates disagreements, and similar to other Italian ruins, holds a romantic sway over the criminological imagination (see also Rafter and Ystehede 2010).

In more than one way, the image of Lombroso on an artist's palette on the opening page provides a meaningful representation. Lombroso has been painted in so many different ways. Scholars in many fields of study, in so many countries, discuss his influence. The swatches of paint on the sides suggest that the portrait has yet to be finished, and this seems appropriate. More than a century after his death, scholars continue to find something of interest in his work. The comprehensive portrait has yet to emerge. Lombroso himself had much to do with this. The artist of the palette portrait is unknown. Lombroso had many friends, so many who found inspiration in his work, it could be someone known otherwise, or someone completely new. Perhaps it is a self-portrait. It is easy to imagine Lombroso with a paintbrush, creating yet another image of himself to add to all the images he created in his writings.

Note

1 Lombroso's collection of body parts is by no means the only one – neither in Italy nor the world. In Italy, you will find among others the Museum of Human Anatomy in Bologna, the Museo della Specola in Florence, and the Anatomical theatre in Padua. The latter museums were all created with papal consent, another testament to the interest of the relationship between the body and the soul in Judeo-Christian dogma. For more information on the Lombroso Museum, see Silvano Montaldo's article in this volume.

References

Ferri, E. (1912) Il Congresso Internationale di Antropologia Criminale a Colonia. Milano: Società Editrice Libraria.
Gibson, M. and Rafter, N. H. (2004) "Editor's Introduction," *Criminal Man*. Durham: Duke University Press, pp. 1–36.
Goethe, J. (1992) *Italian Journey: 1786–1888. Et in Arcadia Ego*. London: Penguin Books.
James, H. (2007) *Italian Hours*. Fairfield: World Library.
Le Solenni Onoranze a Cesare Lombroso in Verona. La inaugurazione del Monumento (1922) Torino: Fratelli Bocca, editori.
Lombroso, C. (1906) "Il mio museo criminale," *L'Illustrazione Italiana* 13, April 1: 302–6.
Rafter, N. and Ystehede, P. (2010) "Here Be Dragons: Lombroso, the Gothic, and Social Control," in M. Deflem (ed.) *Popular Culture, Crime and Social Control*. Bingley, UK: Emerald, pp. 263–84.

1

LOMBROSO AND HIS SCHOOL

From anthropology to medicine and law

Renzo Villa

Cesare Lombroso was officially appointed to the chair of Forensic Medicine and Public Hygiene at the University of Turin by Royal Decree of the 4 January 1876. The Faculty Board went on to approve the separation of Forensic Medicine from Public Hygiene 'at his request'. This was the price that the 40-year-old professor from Verona was prepared to pay for Jakob Moleschott's crucial help in attaining the chair. Lombroso venerated the Dutch *maestro*, 'not just as a disciple but as a novice' (Patrizi 1930, 230). The right gesture had been made, but it was a hard one. Far more than forensic medicine where his contributions had been somewhat desultory, public hygiene had actually been Lombroso's chosen field of study throughout his career, from his graduate dissertation. It was also the battlefield for fiery and bitter disputes over the pellagra issue.

The 30-year-old Luigi Pagliani, who had graduated only seven years before and was promptly appointed assistant in the experimental physiology laboratory, was immediately called to take up the public hygiene teaching post. Pagliani would take the new chair's prestige to great heights. In a mere ten years, he received an invitation to Rome from Crispi to organise the entire national health system. With public hygiene gone, at least psychiatry might have been the subject where Lombroso could count on putting his original methods and research into practice, thereby realising the ambitions he had brought with him to Turin. But this was not to be. The university only granted him an optional course in clinical psychiatry to be held in the newly finished prisons, while clinical teaching was entrusted to the elderly, but well-deserving, Giovanni Stefano Bonacossa. He, at the very least, died the following year.

This event illustrates the heights reached by the clash between the 'experimental' and clinical approaches in psychiatry. The Turin University world was in fact deeply divided between traditionalists, who advocated a passion-related, medical-psychological approach, and the physiopathologists, who gathered around

Moleschott, the standard bearer of a materialism that hegemonised theoretical subjects. Consequently, Lombroso endured a bad reception from his colleagues, who knew him solely via the controversies relating to the research he conducted on toxins produced by rancid corn, and regarded his method of inquiry as little more than superficial. In addition, he was considered little more than an 'original' in relation to the many subjects he was interested in, from the relationship between genius and insanity to the anthropological identity of criminals or the origin of phrenosis. For this and more, the man from Verona enjoyed neither special favour nor attention.

Also his *L'uomo delinquente*, a no-longer-original collection of material from previously published articles, was largely ignored owing to poor sales in the troubled and hectic year of the first Depretis government. The fact that he came from a Jewish family but did not associate with this influential community, openly proclaimed free-thinking beliefs and declared his interest in studying unfortunates (to put it gently), meant he was marginalised by the circles that counted. Life in Turin was not initially a happy one for Lombroso and his family, who crowded into a small flat on the third floor of via della Zecca 33. So, the biography prepared by Lombroso's daughters, Paola and Gina (distributed to the participants at the Sixth Congress of Criminal Anthropology), recalled that the chair had been won due to 'the least important of all of his scientific activities'. They explained that

> the first year that he spent in Turin ... was one of despair, due to the change in his life which had been so unexpected and to our father's attachment to those old walls of Pavia's in spite of everything ... he particularly missed the Lunatic Asylum with its living material and patients renewed every day.
> (Lombroso 1906, 82–3)[1]

Luckily for him, the group of materialists had been growing. Giulio Bizzozero was the general pathologist: extremely precocious (he was a professor in Pavia at 21 years of age, under the auspices of Paolo Mantegazza), Bizzozero embodied Rudolf Virchow's insights in the best possible way. He distinguished himself as one of Italy's top scientists, among the foremost innovators as a methodologist; he became rector in 1885 and senator from 1890 on. After Bizzozero, Lombroso and Pagliani, Angelo Mosso, another formidable exponent of experimentalism, arrived. He occupied the Moleschott's chair, after his transfer to Rome. Mosso had graduated from Moritz Schiff's laboratory in Florence and specialised in Leipzig with Carl Ludwig: a highly gifted physiologist, a famous and brilliant populariser in great demand with publishers. Mosso's great popularising skills and Pagliani's organisational abilities enhanced the quality of the physiological experimentalism. These 'four musketeers', exceptional in so many ways, formed not only prestigious schools of physiology, pathology and public hygiene, and fortified with internationally renowned journals and research, but also moulded generations of doctors inspired by a common intellectual mind-set and corresponding public hygiene programme. In his inaugural lecture of the 1875/76 academic year, Giacinto Pacchiotti exhorted his audience to fight for a social commitment, to be defined more precisely over the following years: by tackling and solving the water, sewerage and energy problems of a rapidly expanding industrial city, and by the creating a true prophylaxis and prevention model, with children particularly borne in mind.

All of the musketeers extolled the pre-eminence and prestige of the scientific vision. Starting from 1877 with Michele Lessona's rectorship,

> the progress of science and lay morality, based on the fundamental values and 'emancipators' of labour, saving and education, came together and empathised. Neither was the notion of utility, which contained forms of anti-metaphysical, observational and experimental knowledge, alien to that alliance.
> (Pogliano 1988, 33)[2]

Famed for his *Volere è potere* (1869), one of the very first *best-sellers*, Lessona was Darwin's translator and populariser. He became a powerful advisor to Loescher and Pomba (the most important publishers in Turin), and from 1892, a senator.

Now the wind had changed. From the 1880s to the end of the century, Lombroso created his own national and international reputation by forming a school that rewarded him with loyalty, esteem and personal affection, even though he was certainly not on a scientific par with his colleagues, and actually occupied a marginal position on the faculty. The school resulted from special meetings and occasions linked to university activities; from the city's scientific, industrial and cultural climate; and not least, from the *maestro*'s energy for controversy. A tireless worker, he had a gift for attracting young people, for arousing enthusiasm and stimulating research. His provocative arguments, and the speed at which he was able to write, meant his articles quickly became a regular fixture in newspapers and journals. He thereby procured entry into Turin's social and intellectual life, although his 'furies and rash words', his support of socialism, and his often spectacular interventions in well-known judicial and criminal cases, meant that he was never completely accepted. From the end of the century on, when the so-called crisis of positivism had become evident, Lombroso managed to become a regular contributor to international rather than national dailies and journals; editors outside Italy received him with favour and curiosity, partly due to his new exploits, not least of all spiritualism.[3] And it was just these freelance journalistic activities, for which he was well paid, that together with his political excesses, lowered his status in the eyes of the university world.

He knew how to inspire and stimulate talent, especially among the youngest and most ambitious such as Ferri, but even more so in the case of the sharper-witted and more impatient Guglielmo Ferrero, and also in the case of the methodical, precise and analytic Mario Carrara. Ferrero and Carrara became his sons-in-law, as well as guarantors of the relationships and personal cult nurtured in particular by Gina Lombroso Ferrero, but also by Paola Lombroso Carrara. Lombroso's family represents the primary reason for Lombroso's lasting fame, together with the 'mythical' criminal anthropology museum. By comparison, Raffaele Garofalo, the first person to write a *Criminologia* text, who publicised and acquired recognised status for the subject, and Ferri, authentic founder not just of criminal sociology, but also of the multi-subject criminological approach, missed their chance at posthumous fame, not only because of their support of fascism, but perhaps even more by the absence of custodians and devotees of family icons.

That Lombroso's reputation had been wrought in the intellectual environment of a special city is absolutely essential to an understanding of the emergence of criminal anthropology. If criminal anthropology was to be studied outside this particular, extremely Italian cultural context, and if Lombroso's fame was not seen as the powerful outcome of a school, we would confirm the claims of his disciples who proclaimed him a 'genius'. We would accord him 'national glory' during the patriotic claims distinguishing the start of the twentieth century, thereby creating a myth parallel to that of the other Cesare: Beccaria. In the case of Lombroso, this myth was created during his lifetime by the *festschrift* that was *L'opera di Cesare Lombroso nella scienza e nelle sue applicazioni*. The second edition of 1908, for which Lombroso himself supplied the preface, should be studied with an eye to rhetorical analysis; it provides a model for panegyrics, with its profusion of superlatives and grandiose phrases; dramatisation of the obstacles, dangers and defences needed to affirm his own theories, not to mention the evidence and the unpredictability of the discovery (remember Villella). This book pursued a commemorative reasoning adorned with an ornamentation suitable for an 'apostle' of 'Italianate superiority'; a figure worthy of 'great palpitations' and 'religious trepidation'. Such deceptive and emphatic hyperbole was to suggest that the foundation of the School, built onto the praises of its own disciples, was utterly 'memorable'.

The 'Lombrosian myth's' main creator had been Enrico Ferri, a man of personal glamour with tremendous appeal as a conference speaker. On the occasion of Lombroso's death, he announced that 'the sole scientific goods to be exported, that conferred glory on the name of Italy in the world', had disappeared and, yet again, 'at that admirable time Darwin, Spencer, Pasteur, Charcot and Virchow were the giants of international science and like them, armed with the science of the nineteenth century, Lombroso had represented the marvellous ascent of contemporary human thought' (Ferri 1909, 548). During the unveiling celebrations in 1921 of the monument to Lombroso in Verona, he would proclaim even more nationalistically: 'He is an Italian thinker, as well as a universal scientist', thus placing him alongside Galileo and Volta (Onoranze 1921, 723). Privately, however, say, as Leon Radzinowicz recalled in his *Adventures in Criminology*: 'But always remember that Lombroso was a genius without talent.' And also:

> he was a genius at guessing, but when he had to expound, to demonstrate, he was lost. You had to know him personally, intimately. I saw him for the first time in 1878. I had just published my graduation dissertation, containing daring statements regarding the renewal of the criminal justice system, and he wrote to me with that goodness of heart which was the most precious of the gems in his many-sided personality .... When I went to Turin for the

first time, I was like a believer going to his Mecca. But, to be honest, I was disappointed by his lessons and saw that other disciples shared the same feeling.
(Onoranze 1921, 729)

For young Ferri in 1878, Lombroso was the author of the *Uomo delinquente*, the second edition. He was the scientist who had put together the gains of phrenology, forensic medicine and psychopathology; and linked them to a simplified evolutionary anthropology, enriched by a relatively original study of cultural expressions, from argot to tattoos, along the lines of folk psychology. The text offered an anthropology in the Vichian and linguistic sense, derived by Paolo Marzolo, but also an anthropology in the vaster and more generic sense of a naturalistic vision where the human being is an organism genealogically intertwined with other living creatures and subject to the effects of heredity, an object to be studied 'using the methods of the physical sciences' as he himself would attempt to do. This criminal-centred anthropology could not have arrived at a better time, offering as it did the readiest and most easily acceptable answer to a public appetite increasingly interested in criminal phenomena.[4] With its apparently scientific language, completed with anatomical measurements, numbers and terminology, Lombroso's writings appeared to be a perfect match with the conventions surrounding 'scientificity': that is, the implementation of a positive science's programme and assumptions. The fascination by the professor also derived from the topics he dealt with: insanity, crime, geniality, abnormal and borderline psychological manifestations. He contributed to the discovery of a world that the literature of the time, from Verism to the Scapigliatura movement, was exploring and thus orienting the taste of a vast constituency. Nor should it be forgotten that one of the reasons both for Lombroso's fame and popularity in Turin accrued from his appearances as an expert in some of the most notorious local and national trials; relived and celebrated in the news for weeks on end, and discussed passionately especially by the city's middle classes. Due to the *Gazzetta piemontese* and *La Stampa* newspapers, and to the illustrated crime literature, his name became extremely popular.

In any case, the fortunes of Lombroso and his criminological approach must be seen within the more specifically Italian context. In a country where modernisation processes required longer times and were more difficult compared with other nations, and where institutions were often immobile and unmovable, any talk about crime, criminals and punishment that aspired to the status of scientific knowledge by defining itself as criminology, was a basic reply (however partial) to a criminal question which drew through fierce debates the attention of an emerging middle class in a newly unified Italy. In order to understand the dynamics of crimes, the motives of perpetrators, and the effectiveness and limits of punishment, many people committed themselves to reforming practices that were possible, in accordance with the laws governing society, to the principles of realism and to social defence, thereby laying the foundations for one of the most lively and versatile criminological theories, which was always intended to be rational, rigorous and anchored on the certainty of facts.

FIGURE 1.1 Lombroso together with his daughter, Gina Lombroso Ferrero. Pastel on paper, (Durio, 1910)

Source: Archivio storico del Museo di Antropologia criminale "Cesare Lombroso" dell'Università di Torino (Italia).

The sciences of crime followed a national path where three paradigms – legal, medical-anthropological, economic-sociological – alternated and intertwined, marked by the complex relationship with a delinquency polarised between organised crime, intimately and necessarily related to the management of the state, and criminal policies. The transformation of banditry into a public order issue and into a manifestation of primitivism, the *mafioso* evidence in the Notarbartolo case, the early scandals involving the Banca Romana, and the study of the popular origins of the *camorra*, provided the materials for a criminal anthropology. The chief merit of this lay neither in arguments nor in research methods, often already outdated, but in the will to investigate, in a recognition of that 'criminal nation' which we still find exactly the same a hundred years later in an inextricable web formed between organised crime and politics; in the most spectacular and unpunished financial corruption; in the eco-mafias; and in the unscrupulous use of crime as a vehicle of political consensus. In short, the country of today, where deaths due to wars between and within criminal organisations far exceed the number of common murders, and where domestic violence, which constitutes the greater part of violent crime, appears unchanged from generation to generation.

But, more than anything, Lombroso had demolished the passage of penal science which had been established by Beccaria on some certainties. An undisputed implication derived from the utilitarian approach: people who commit crimes are independent and rational individuals, able to calculate the consequences of their actions, and therefore capable of choice. This is a necessary presupposition if law and punishment are to be the same for everyone, thereby denying the existence of inequality and *libero arbitrio*, 'free will'. Like Beccaria, penal science theoreticians avoided any reference to criminals as socially and historically pre-determined individuals: but in his *Sul governo e sulla riforma delle carceri in Italia: Saggio storico e teorico* (1867) Martino Beltrani-Scalia had already concluded that prison did not 'regenerate fallen men' and that crime was a 'fault of will'. So that

> in order to prevent people not born criminals from becoming so due to the pernicious contact with perverse people correctional institutions (have to be set up) in order to eradicate the criminal germs, before they have the chance to take deep root in young hearts, these are the true and the sole means by which the ever increasing invasion of criminality can be contrasted.
> (Beltrani-Scalia 1867, 434)

Man naturally strove to be good but 'given the individual and social conditions, he is not always able to subjugate his passions to reason' (Beltrani-Scalia 1867, 22). Immediately after unification, many others also recognised that industrialisation and urbanisation had generated a spectacular increase in property crime, while reports of crimes against morality and the family, the fruit of new sensibilities, increased as well. Meanwhile, an endemic, professional criminality, linked to prostitution, to sleight-of-hand theft and to gambling had been fomented by new marginality and new migrations. Juvenile delinquency became ingrained through repeated offences, and organised crime captured the space formerly occupied by banditry in the news and social attention. The previous theories of Petitti di Roreto on the 'good governance of beggary' were now swept away by completely different crimes and social tensions, causing the youthful Italy to feel completely disarmed, without any instruments except for those useful in widespread and violent repression. The situation of prisoners and prisons in the post-unification decades is sufficiently well known for its classist nature and its undeniable evidence of repression.

In the thirty years that Lombroso worked there, Turin also underwent a transformation. No longer the capital of a small but European-ranking state, with the impulses of a political and moral centre during the *Risorgimento* period when it became the refuge of intellectual exiles from all parts of the peninsula, the city had been forced to change after the autumn of 1864. The capital moved temporarily to Florence. Suddenly Turin found itself without ministries and civil servants, the central bodies, the military orders or a lively press. It survived, but was reduced and reconstructed. It was still traditional but it already had plans. There was the old

> city, slightly slow, slightly leisurely, the earthly paradise of the clerks and pensioners who populated the arcades in the winter and the avenues in summer and the new city, industrious, modern and progressive. Its blue-blooded aristocracy kept up its traditions and its barriers, which separated them from the middle classes. The upper classes with their new, rapidly-made fortunes had still to emerge as a force and class consciousness was just beginning to stir instinctively among the lower classes.
>
> (Zini 1973, 326)

The city's answer to the marginalised devotees of forms of illegality and to 'villains' was to strengthen the police force and install a swift-moving, particularly harsh justice system. Out of a hundred criminal sentences at the Turin Court of Assizes in 1874, almost half were for theft. For the taking of 'four hens', 'thirty bottles of wine', 'sixteen sheets and fourteen shirts' and 'a velvet coat' or 'thirty metres of cloth for military use', the takers spent up to three years in prison. There were many wilful knifings, often leading to death as well as brawls and vendettas, and an unsettling number of rapes against children and young girls: a tragic world of everyday violence, endured by the subjects of social assistance, workers' education and the interventions of public institutions. And then there were the charities, that considered the 'Piccola Casa' of Giuseppe Cottolengo, a sort of anomalous city as a model; while the other 'social saint', Giovanni Bosco, and his followers dealt with precisely those most marginalised classes, with the children where the seed of violence could take root.

But in 1879, Turin was also the town that erected a monument in the form of a grand pyramid surmounted by Lucifer, the bearer of the light of science, to an essential international link, the Frejus tunnel. This furnished stone and bronze testimony to Progress: the vital individual and collective impulse in its heroic form. And it was also 'positive' culture's manifesto: popular, scientist, Masonic. Again in 1884, it was Turin that played host to the grandiose Italian Exposition, a most remarkable undertaking that would leave an incredible philological but nobly built Disneyland in the Valentino park in the form of a medieval-styled, Borgo and Rocca design, by D'Andrade and friends. The exposition's demonstration of superior artisan skills inspired the senator Tommaso Villa with the idea of a 'science city'; the concrete and permanent monument to the popular idea of progress, the superiority of which the city exalted. This was not only in its architectural ornamentation and town planning, but also what was achieved in the 1890s: new industrial enterprises, and the multiplication of workshops, factories, mills and building sites, greatly extended the city's quarters. From 1896 on, the Laboratory of Legal Medicine, and the Psychiatric and Criminological Museum, certainly the most Lombrosian result of criminal anthropology, were finally housed in the Anatomical Institutes Building, one of 'science city's' most eagerly awaited and significant constructions.

While the professor's idea of a faculty was one able to impose itself in popular and experimental terms, the legitimisation of his research benefited from the university's unparalleled scientific prestige.[5] One of the stars of scientific research, he was the incarnation of the positive, experimental spirit and a passionate supporter of the workers' movement. He appeared as one of the champions in the controversies against the backwardness and the injustices of the penal system: a great reformer, against imprisonment, the advocate of alternative measures; in any case, a star in an intense intellectual life which found an outlet in specialised journals and a series of predominantly scientific publications as well as in a highly popularised literary output.

In Turin the scientific interest increased: a score of scientific periodicals existed in a city of three hundred thousand inhabitants, which could boast of an enrolment of two thousand at the university. In 1876, the *Archivio per le Scienze mediche* appeared; in 1881, the *Rivista di Filosofia scientifica*; in 1890 the *Rivista di Igiene e di Sanità Pubblica* and also the *Archives Italiennes de Biologie*: these were just some of the most prestigious. One editor, in particular, Giuseppe Bocca Jr, the third generation member of a family of bookseller-publishers, became a constant supporter of the Lombrosian school. In just thirty years Bocca would follow the entire flow of that experimental and materialistic scientism which later was to flounder in the spiritualistic, esoteric magma. It demanded ever more space from the publisher, passing through the great twenty-year pathography success and the incursions of psychiatrist and anthropologist doctors into the literary genius. The book production desired and promoted by the scion of a typical Turin dynasty provided recognition of his entrepreneurial energy in the form of the *Biblioteca di Scienze moderne*. Leaving Loescher – the publisher of Bizzozero's and Canestrini's *Archivi* and the *Giornale Storico della Letteratura Italiana* founded in 1883 by Arturo Graf, Novati and Renier – Lombroso found a publisher in Bocca that allowed him to publish with others, but who would print and sustain the double series of volumes of the Biblioteca antropologico-giuridica. Together with the *Archivio di psichiatria scienze penali ed antropologia criminale per servire allo studio dell'uomo delinquente*, this was the most credible part of the entire school's output. The Biblioteca, in particular, should be explored and studied carefully since it contains the most significant results of the research of Lombrosian school.

During all his intense activities as researcher, forensic doctor and psychiatrist, the central issue for Lombroso remained criminogenesis. He advanced various causes – atavism, moral insanity, degeneration, epileptoidism – which he saw as coherent with each other, differentiating between them in the editions of his major work. Always he dealt with the origin of criminal behaviour in rigorously naturalistic terms, heavily deterministic and in accordance with a reductionist programme which considered criminals organically constituted as such. The series of anthropological anomalies, discovered through a careful objective examination using simple measuring instruments, would then allow criminals to be classified by 'type'. This would enable – theoretically and also preventively – identification of those due to organic predisposition, distinguishing them from the insane or from occasional criminals, or victims of passion or desire. The conclusion of a similar process, where criminal activity was reduced to the behaviour of primitive man and criminals were regarded as throwbacks, would lead to several paradoxes: as, for example, the case of economic crime. Lombroso and Ferrero concluded that French and Italian perpetrators of serious financial fraud did not have criminal characters (perhaps just 'a hint of it'), and therefore 'they are not born criminals, but criminaloids, differentiating very little from honest people' (Lombroso and Ferrero 1893, 193). Fraudsters presented healthy and normal individuals who were victims of the moment, of the fascination of money; because, the authors determined, financial fraud was nothing more than a sort of civil evolution of law, devoid of any cruelty. They did not represent any danger, therefore; in actual fact, they were not even really guilty: since finance needed absolute control over political and legislative life, members of parliament would all be potentially prone to opportunism and corruption. And having fought for centuries to curb the privileges of kings and priests, warriors and nobles, Lombroso and Ferrero asked: 'shall we maintain the most extraordinary privileges of more than six hundred kings with the fixation of an alleged liberty?' Anti-parliamentarism was thus the conclusion of a brilliant absolution for simple 'criminaloids', fallen into the greed and wealth traps set for members of parliament.

Lombroso found the way to progressively disengage atavism from the more evident anatomic anomalies, by drawing on a neurological symptomatology and returning the brain to primitive expectations. But Lombrosian criminology was not just about criminogenesis, the collection of a chaotic mass of observations, making deep incursions into the territories of what were to become the social sciences; nor was the Lombrosian school just about its *maestro* or Italian criminology reducible to Lombrosism. The professor's role was to supply ideas, launch controversies, provoke fierce discussions, move unexpected interests. In thirty years' activity at the University of Turin he managed to attract great talents and personalities, doctors of high scientific standing and outstanding scholars, a small school of trusted and loyal students and then the extraordinary luck of a daughter, Gina. She became an authentic custodian of her father's interests, the one who made sure his publications remained accessible for decades, and who amplified his image in a continual and inexhaustible production of memoirs and biographies. His sons-in-law, Guglielmo Ferrero and Mario Carrara, did their part too: Ferrero, one of the best known and most frequently read intellectuals in Europe; Carrara, of proven scientific competence and indisputable moral standing. And finally the skilful supporter, instigator and prompter, responsible for the organization of his very thoughts: Enrico Ferri, without whom he would not have been able to create his typology.[6] While at first forensic science travelled the roads mapped by Bertillon and then by Galton, with the methodical and independent application of scientific procedures, Lombroso found a new direction by provoking controversial reactions which in turn generated new research and new classifications, in the common belief that studying crime and criminals scientifically afforded one of the most promising fields of knowledge.

His private life seemed to track the progress of his notoriety and his social position: after six years in a third-rate building yet again close to the University, in via Vanchiglia 6, an area where all classes lived side by side and sometimes on top of each other, from 1886 on Lombroso took up residence in a more prestigious building in corso Oporto 43, today's corso Matteotti. Here Paola and Gina grew into lively adolescents, and met and learned to love Anna Kuliscioff, the *Signora*, who was completing her medical studies and was already the companion of Filippo Turati, the one who referred to his passion for the young ladies ironically. The presence of this emancipated and brilliant woman of European culture was to be essential for their development and intellectual independence and probably also for their father's orientation. Finally in 1892, the family moved definitively to via Legnano 26, a lovely building near a large tree-lined avenue, decidedly more suitable to an acclaimed professor. Here Professor Cesare and consort, the young ladies and Doctor Ugo, held a salon; and here the young Ferrero couple took up residence from 1901 on. In the same year after a longed-for second degree in medicine, following unenthusiastic studies engaged in the literature and after an almost ten-year long engagement, Gina, declared in no uncertain terms to her husband, that she would never move more than a step away from her adored *Papà*.[7] He had finally been accepted to work in the Royal Asylum in via Giulio, and become professor of psychiatry after Enrico Morselli's transfer to Genoa. The Asylum administration and the doctors, originally against Morselli, opposed Lombroso even more and attempted to thwart in any way possible the creation of a department where he could hold lessons. Professor of psychiatry and psychiatric clinical practice from 1896, he continued to teach legal medicine reluctantly; he did not build any research relationships with his faculty colleagues as they were scientists of a completely different fibre. This was also why Lombroso increasingly turned to the other faculty where he held an optional course in law. Both Ferri and Ferrero had graduated in law and here he would be followed not only by aspiring jurists, but also by young students of letters. His law lectures attracted an adoring public especially among Arturo Graf's students. One of them, Zino Zini, recalled:

> Lombroso's lessons in the old amphitheatre of the Istituti di via San Francesco da Paola were infinitely more interesting. Subject: criminal man. This expression created by the psychiatrist from Verona was on everyone's lips. A varied, intrigued and convinced throng packed the hall for a weekly show. Lombroso was the most original individual that I had ever known; I will have the chance to recount and talk about the good and the bad that this real magician of thinking did to our generation, and to some of us in particular, who, as are all magicians, was always in precarious balance between the prodigy and the swindler. The genial Lilliputian entertained his listeners with an affable eloquence made up of a half-scientific and half-dialectal jargon, encrusted with Latin-German-French and words from the Veneto-Piemonte regions. . . . There certainly wasn't much reliability in these alleged positive and experimental methods. We students were easy to please . . . we felt heads, we measured

craniums with great conviction. It's best not to say anything about the progress gained from these studies; let's leave the responsibility for the results in the hands of Lombroso.

(Zini 1973, 339)

Zini's memoirs continued describing comical episodes, similar to those reported by Augusto Monti and other local men of letters, useful for not taking the man and the scientist too seriously.

The Lombrosian story also remains linked to a very specific stage in Turin's cultural history. Gina's intellectual adventure illustrates how the sudden end of Lombroso's fortunes coincided with a turning point in the history of the city. After the reflections on the advantages of degeneration and on creative and sentimental alterity in women, she moved to Florence with Guglielmo, who had inhaled for too long the provincial air of Turin and felt he was misunderstood. In Florence, she was to develop a freer line of thought that would end with refuge in Switzerland, where she wrote in her will to her friends: 'I believe, after considerable reflection and research begun when I was fifteen years old and pursued up to the present, that the evils suffered by mankind are to a large extent caused by the great industries'.[8] The rejection of a civilisation based on machines, which was symbolised by Turin can be interpreted in many different ways. It includes the inability to overcome a deterministic reductionism which constituted Lombroso's most outdated legacy and which would make him decidedly old for the generation forming by the end of the century. They looked out onto the new century with its crises of certainty and unease of modernity.

In the 1890s, when the professor adopted the ways of Turin, not just in terms of his teaching and profession but also of his lifestyle and social relationships, the ties weakened with Raffaele Garofalo, who would always be distant and cold, refusing anything to do with him, now become 'socialist'. The meetings with Ferri, a socialist leader, who had left Paris for Turin where he had become professor of criminal law, only to transfer immediately to Bologna and then to Pisa, were continual and respectful, but necessarily occasional. The close relationships Lombroso formed with socialist circles through him intensified after he had been elected to the Town Council in Turin in 1902, with over eight thousand votes, more than anyone else on the list. Among his closest friends there were Salvatore Cognetti de Martiis, Achille Loria and Zino Zini, but especially Gaetano Mosca and also Roberto Michels, who was the only one actually to leave any personal memories of his warm hospitality (Michels 1911, 362), while others can be deduced from correspondence.[9] It should be noted, however, that it was Michels himself who assessed the relative weight of the professor when he observed: 'Cesare Lombroso (an anthropologist in Turin) and Achille Loria (an economist in Turin) – without doubt the intellectual world's most famous name abroad – refused the socialist candidature offered them solely because overloaded with scientific work'.[10] But in Lombroso's salon there were also artists such as Leonardo Bistolfi, already attracted by spiritualism, and young men such as Giovanni Cena, a great friend of Bistolfi's, one of Graf's students and an enthusiastic author of poetry and novels drenched in social sensibility.

In 1893, Alfredo Frassati, deputy editor of the *Gazzetta Piemontese* (and future owner and editor of *La Stampa*), invited a talented group of economists and new criminal scientists to work together with him: not only Mosca, Einaudi and Jannaccone, but also Lombroso and Niceforo. Lombroso's journalistic activities and his choice of field, the 'conservative socialism of professors', guaranteed that his figure and his research would arouse further, often naive and passionate interest. The same year, Salvatore Cognetti de Martiis was to found the Laboratory of Economics while preparing fortnightly editions of *La Riforma Sociale*, edited with Luigi Roux and Francesco Saverio Nitti. Together they fashioned a concrete, moderate public opinion, soundly informed and open to modernisation, able to deal pragmatically not just with the growing conflicts, but also with new consumer and lifestyle demands. Lombroso therefore belonged to a very precise intellectual and social group, which made its appearance among others in many initiatives such as the foundation of the 'Società di Cultura', a circle which hosted conferences, debates and discussions and also had a reading room with subscriptions to periodicals. This was one of various lively institutions aimed at founding 'technical industrialism and a varied humanistic culture' which animated the town's cultural life (Bergami 1980, 14).

The 'heroic' years of the school of criminal anthropology were those between the Exposition of 1884, where a small collection of skulls and casts was exhibited, and 1900 when a 'school' generation arrived which would be defined in later years in terms of its different skills and roles. The strong personalities of Ferrero and Carrara were naturally pre-eminent and welded together family occurrences, organizational skills and prestige, as witnessed by the numerous letters in Lombroso's private study mentioning Ferrero's fame, which was such as to bring him within a step of the Nobel prize in the immediate aftermath of World War I. Ferrero's contributions to criminology were increasingly rare after his youthful proof of erudition alongside that of his future father-in-law, in *La donna delinquente, la prostituta e la donna normale*; Carrara proposed an initial systematic exposition of the corpus of his father-in-law's, in an academically acceptable and digestible form, with the volume *Criminal Anthropology* beginning in 1901. Carrara had married Paola in 1899, and returned to Turin in 1903 to occupy his father-in-law's chair of legal medicine, which he was to hold until his refusal to swear allegiance to the National Fascist Party. Again in 1903, Antonio Marro, a psychiatrist very close to Lombroso, although strictly speaking not his student, was appointed director of the Turin Lunatic Asylum. Meanwhile, Salvatore Ottolenghi, one of his assistants from 1887 to 1893, first qualified as a lecturer in Cagliari, then in Siena and finally in Rome, where he would become the central figure in criminal sciences and form the successive generation of criminologists, beginning with Benigno Di Tullio. As for Camillo Tovo, Edoardo Audenino and Alberto Cougnet, and also Eugenio Tanzi, they came to constitute the youngest generations later linked to Carrara, while the lawyer Virgilio Rossi, the attorney Scipio Sighele and the criminologist and statistician

Alfredo Niceforo emerged from other professional carriers. At times they attracted international fame, as in Sighele's case of *La coppia criminale* (1909) which became the reference text for many years (and is still drawn on today for its method and many intuitions beginning with the relationship between incubus and succubus). With *La folla criminale* (1891), Sighele scored an absolutely outstanding success in France, and collective psychology would be his debtor for the research methods and paths that lasted well beyond his relatively early death. Mariano Luigi Patrizi, Moleschott's son-in-law and Lombroso's successor, also played a role in Lombroso's progress to professorship, but second to that of the Lombroso daughters.

This was a time of the great organisation of ideas and subjects, the reference texts of which are *Criminologia* (1885) by Raffaele Garofalo and *Sociologia criminale* (1891) by Enrico Ferri. The criminological approach proposed in Garofalo's manual, and immediately translated into French, was especially well received in Europe. By rejecting the codification of the criminal 'type', he merely recognized the psychological and moral character of the criminal; his positive punishment criterion depended on the lesser or greater fear of the criminal, based in turn on the offence against the sense of humanity or compassion or, on the other hand, on the sense of integrity or justice. Simultaneously, a profusion of studies threw open doors onto little-known situations: from Ferrero and Sighele's *Mondo criminale italiano* to Napoleone Colajanni's *Nel regno della mafia*, from Antonio Marro's *I caratteri dei criminali* to Ettore Fornasari di Verce's *La criminalità e le vicende economiche d'Italia dal 1873 al 1890*. Many works documented the perception of crime at the end of the century with analyses of specifically Italian manifestations known to the authors. Ettore Fornasari di Verce studied crime trends in the years of the industrial boom. While reported crimes rose around 6–7 per cent, there was a net fall in armed robberies, extortion and other robberies, alongside a significant rise in theft, fraud and embezzlement. Murders were on the decline, but the beatings, brawls and knifings which bloodied Turin's nights flourished alongside alcoholism and prostitution. The crimes of defamation and slander were on the rise in a society where social control was disintegrating, and reports of many minor crimes multiplied, confirmation of an implicit trust in the forces of law and order. Colajanni had already observed how the 'black number' was distributed proportionately among the various social classes: if part of the crimes perpetrated by the wealthy classes was concealed behind social relations, part of the crimes perpetrated by the poor went unmentioned. This was 'either due to their lack of moral sense', as was the case of all crimes against morality, chiefly in families, or because their detection was impossible. He added: 'many serious crimes are also not reported if committed by members of some dangerous classes, such as between *Camorristi, Mafiosi*, scoundrels' (Colajanni 1889, 540).

The new criminological approach broke down the door of the certainties of the liberal tradition in criminal law: if crime was a natural and not a social occurrence, that is, independent of any variation of positive law, or necessarily changeable conventional definitions, the whole of criminal law had to be reconstructed. It would be based on some individuals' presupposed 'dangerousness', that is on their

FIGURE 1.2 The Sixth Criminal Anthropology Congress in Turin in 1906

Source: Archivio storico del Museo di Antropologia criminale "Cesare Lombroso" dell'Università di Torino (Italia).

'natural' proclivity for crime. The uncontested leading figure in this battle in criminal sciences was to be Enrico Ferri. The long controversies and the subtle distinctions that were put into the field had the merit of clarifying the differences between the liberal conception and the social defence ideology. The dispute between the 'positive school' and those they defined as 'old school' or 'classics' (mockingly, in Luigi Lucchini's opinion) was to assume quarrelsome and purely ideological tones, partly due to the fact that Francesco Carrara was not at the head of a homogeneous school. It was the sum of 'metaphysical, eclectic, later utilitarian tendencies, trusting in the divine origins of criminal law, of Tuscan liberalism or Neapolitan empiricism, of lay or catholic fundamentalist spiritualism or of the contractualist defence of civil rights' (Sbriccoli 1990, 537). Under attack as a group, the various members ended up finding common ground in the pre-eminence of the value of individual liberties to be protected in all their various expressions; in the certainty of procedural guarantees, the obligation of binding terms and in the principles of the certainty and inevitability of punishment. The principle of free will in committing crimes was defended by all. Criminal responsibility was therefore based on the idea of liability, and punishment was meted out as retribution in order to reconstruct the legal order which had been violated. Francesco Carrara's principle, by which crime was a body corporate equipped with precise structural elements, was thus reaffirmed. On the other hand, the famous shift of attention from crime to the criminal, regarded by Ferri as Lombroso's definitive scientific victory, was after all based on a subject classified as a criminal by the same legal regulation, abstract body, or historically given law that they wished to deny.

By denying liability-based criminal responsibility, the positive school substituted an unspecified social dangerousness to which the punishment would be proportional and transformed into a security measure for an indefinite length of time, aimed at prevention and social protection. If the measure of punishment was the fear of the criminal, the classification of criminals became decisive and the criminologist was transformed into the sole judge meting out the punishment substitutes. An expert in sociology and psychology, the judge-criminologist would decide on the provisions which were to replace the punishment: from curbs on freedom of movement and immigration, to the development of roads and railways, to the multiplication of porter's lodges in tenements! Totally casual substitutes, Lucchini found them frankly ridiculous, liking them to 'the abolition of kings in order to prevent regicides'. When occupying his chair in Siena in 1882, Ferri had expressed his wish of launching a new penal doctrine cycle on a scientific basis, where crime would be identified in terms of its naturalness, and investigated in terms of three categories made up of anthropological, physical and social factors. This lead to the classification of criminals as 'insane criminals; born criminals, incorrigible; criminals by acquired habit; occasional criminals; criminals by passion'. The essence of the answer to crime would therefore be: prevention, reparation, repression and elimination. He concluded:

> The incomplete idea, expressed by some jurist and by Lombroso himself, that this new school is nothing but a partial, congenial alliance between criminal law and criminal anthropology, needs to be done away with: no, this is something more and has a far greater scientific and practical value: this is how the experimental method is applied to the study of the crimes of the punishments and therefore, as such, while it brings the breath of the new observations not only from criminal anthropology, but also from statistics, psychology and sociology into the enclosure of abstract legal technicism, it truly represents a new stage in the evolution of criminal science.
>
> (Ferri 1883, 53)

A few years later, in a study titled 'Sulla scuola positiva del diritto penale in Italia', published in the *Rivista Penale*,[11] Aristide Gabelli examined once again the charges against positivists, and received for his effort a special volume containing the unanimous reply of the entire official triad – Lombroso, Ferri and Garofalo. Gabelli was to confirm the wholly historical dimension of criminal law versus the claim of unhistorical scientificity advanced by the emerging human sciences. He rebutted the claim for any basis of social dangerousness when, after all, it was only possible to act after a crime, and also spoke ironically of the demand for a criminological classification of offenders.

On the occasion of the commemorations to Lombroso, in the thirtieth year of the *Uomo criminale* and the *maestro*'s scientific teaching and after the many law- and anthropology-related trials and controversies, the school sought recognition. The Sixth Criminal Anthropology Congress in Turin in 1906 was seen as a victory over the many enemies who had ruined the festivities in Paris in 1889, but ended up being a manifestation in isolation. Paul Topinard had demolished criminogenesis in France by developing those criticisms that were to become the supporting wall of the reaction of French scientific circles. He had used physical anthropology to demolish the possibility of the formulation of a 'criminal type' and therefore

> The name of criminal anthropology has no reason to exist, ... There has been no objection to the title of criminal sociology, but this has been adopted, without doubt to exploit the popularity of the word anthropology, without any authorisation.
> (Topinard 1887, 690)

The Turin congress witnessed the school's last attempt to defend its proposal of a medical-anthropological point of view of penal doctrine, in order to modify the theory of the retribution of the punishment and intervene with alternative measures. Once defeated, this fundamental objective would remain solely in the memory of the commemorations. It reappeared in a supplement to the *Archivio* at the time of Lombroso's death in 1909 accompanied by numerous memorial ceremonies: Ferri in Verona, Bianchi in Bologna, Sighele in Florence, Roncoroni and Berenini in Parma, Antonini in Udine, Cappelletti in Venice, Zerboglio in Reggio Emilia and Alessandria, Agostini in Perugia, Tamburini in Rome, Guglielmo Ferrero in Turin and Morselli in Genova – proof of a vitality and a public still well disposed towards the subject and its founder. Finally, during the unveiling ceremony of the monument by Leonardo Bistolfi in Verona, 25 September 1921, the celebration presided over by Leonardo Bianchi was attended by everyone by this point recognised in the widest sense as 'Lombrosians': Enrico Ferri, Augusto Tamburini, Sante De Sanctis, Antonio Marro, Enrico Morselli, Giovanni Mingazzini, Salvatore Ottolenghi, Mariano Luigi Patrizi and Giuseppe Sergi. This was the last chance they would have to meet as a school, as such, of which Antonio Marro had written:

> The geniality of the social significance of studying the criminal, the constant and indomitable perseverance in defending and championing it and the intensity of the work brought to bear on it, were without doubt extremely powerful factors, in our country no less than in others, in the consideration acquired by criminal anthropology in public opinion, the subject of international conferences, with more or less direct contributions from different Governments, the origin of much research and disputes between scientists and the subject of many special publications or periodicals, the undoubted forerunner of radical legislative and social processes.
> (Opera 1908, 218–19)

These are the times when the rhetorical work of students defending an idea of science and criminology unravels.

The legacy was now shared equally: Mario Carrara took it back to its origins, to legal medicine. His own particular criminological technology dialogues with legal psychiatry on one hand, and on the other offers its experience to forensic toxicology and the various components of criminal sciences. This path would also bear academic and professional fruits in the form of university publications and manuals, although with no original theoretical developments. The attempt to keep clinical criminology alive, which was able to renew itself with respect to the most simple Lombrosian hypotheses and therefore be compared on one hand with Pende and Di Giovanni's bio-typology and endocrinology, and on the other with the neurological acquisitions and the most recent psychiatric nosography, would be pursued almost entirely alone by Benigno Di Tullio. He was one of Salvatore Ottolenghi's most loyal students, with a consistency and stubbornness which would lead to the organisation of the Fifth International Criminology Congress in Rome in 1938. Di Tullio's report *Sul metodo e sulle finalità della criminologia clinica* would present both the centrality of the research into the personality who designed, prepared and perpetrated the crime, and the characteristics of the observation which had to proceed on parallel (but independent) lines of the legal investigation aimed at ascertaining the existence of the crime. This was the anthropological investigation 'aimed at discovering the personality' of the criminal. By identifying occasional criminals, on one hand, and the insane, on the other, it was possible to isolate 'constitutional criminals', in terms of their hypoevolutive, psychoneurotic and psychopathic orientations, in accordance with the 'medicine's constituzionalist-orthogenetic-biotypological dictates'. The imbalance in the psychopathic personality determined a conflict between impulse and will, feeling and intelligence, profound impulses and rational ability, which appeared a decisive factor in triggering many crimes. After the 1940s, Di Tullio had a significantly important role in the orientation of clinical criminology within medical faculties. For many years his vast production would also constitute the essential reference work for the Società Italiana di Criminologia founded, and then headed by himself, in 1957. In 1960, his *Principi di criminologia clinica e psichiatria forense* was still recognised as a university reference, and some of his ideas inspired the first theories concerning the relationship between personality and crime, as in the case of the Belgian Etienne De Greeff's crimino-dynamics.

The other part of the criminological research legacy concerns Garofalo and Ferri's guiding principles, or research into the concomitant causes, into the intentionality of the criminal act, and also into the social aspects of crime. Filippo Grispigni, Ferri's student and Director of the Rome Institute of Criminology, attempted to provide a consistent theoretical classification of the totality of the causes of criminal behaviour, resulting in the identification of criminology with criminal policy, which would have proposed suitable means of prevention and repression based on the conclusions of anthropological and sociological analysis. During the Second International Course of Criminology in Paris in 1953, he revealed his substantial acceptance of criminology as a synthesis of sociological and anthropological-psychological knowledge, thereby also reconfirming a distinction and an independence from criminal law. Meanwhile, Agostino Gemelli, one of the most persistent critics of the founding principles of criminology, which he described as an 'inorganic heap', confirmed the obvious rejection of any naturalistic idea of crime. But he ended up sustaining the widening of the study of the criminal's personality to 'the criminal's organism, his constitution and the influence of those factors on the criminal man's actions' alert to the 'phenomenology of psychic activities in order to determine the mechanism of the crime' (Gemelli 1948, 35; 232).

But more than these criticisms, it was the distancing of a reductionist research horizon, the revival of idealism and spiritualism, that would condemn the members of the positive school, marginalised from the 1920s on. Lombrosian lines of research continued, as in the case of Giovanni Lombardi's *Sociologia Criminale* (1942), that proposed to solve the issue of crime by affirming that 'primitive law is based on force, on reprisal, on vendetta or on parasitical control of the weak and the defeated' (Lombardi 1944, 186) or, in that so-called 'atavistic psychic legacy' to be found in the uses and customs of the working classes, where everyday violence lurked and was committed on a greater scale. Criminal sociology had a hard time between the 1920s and the 1950s. Its survival depended on Alfredo Niceforo, who also enjoyed the reputation of a professor of statistics and demographer and, naturally, of the criminologist who had taught for forty years at the Legal-Criminal School of the Faculty of Law at the University of Rome. Marginalised and under suspicion in the postwar period as a result of his clear role in the development and affirmation of Italian racism, Niceforo was certainly the most radical in indicating the existence of 'two Italies' one of which, with its *camorra*, banditry and mafia represented 'a perfect social atavism'. He should be seen as an example of a frequent tendency in Italy's national culture, however, but also credited as one of the most active collectors of data, which provided examples of vast areas of social malaise, although often heterogeneous and badly interpreted. In an extremely abundant summary and explanation of his research, together with a voluminous bibliography provided by the author, Niceforo demonstrated his encyclopaedic vision of criminology. He repudiated the results of *La delinquenza in Sardegna* of 1897, but substantially confirmed what he had proposed in that and various other studies on criminality in the Mezzogiorno, that is, the recognition of a

> specificity of violent crime to the most backward Regions in the South and a specificity of fraud to the Regions of the North, at the same time invoking a sort of 'law' which would govern the transformation of crime from the backward and barbarous societies to those more imbued with a modern-type civilisation, or from 'barbarous' violence-based crime, to 'civilised' fraud-based crime.
>
> (Niceforo 1953, 63)

He had no difficulty in defending himself in the 'new' debate on regionalism, in accordance with the decisions of the Republican Constitution: it appeared obvious to him that regional differences would always be recognised and analysed, and that the correspondence between criminality and birth, mortality and education rates demonstrated the social diversity in Italy's territories. While he sustained correlations and covariations, he also affirmed the impressiveness of the social and economic progress made against those who 'invoke, not a reasonable administrative decentralisation, but actually a regional devolution of a federal or quasi federal nature' affirming that 'any economic and cultural elevation of the populations' was solely a result of national unification. On the subject of his research he concluded bitterly, however, that:

> the wayfarer's road was a long one and accompanied by the anxiety to reach his destination – the exact knowledge of the facts considered and studied – which moved farther and farther away and which was never reached . . . . A light was sought . . . and it wasn't found.
>
> (Niceforo 1953, 331)

This is a passage all the more disconsolate since described by an extremely active individual, who had personally edited and checked many items of the *Dizionario di Criminologia* published by Vallardi in 1943, a significant work whose authors repeated they were expounding with pride and certainty the main items of the subject that was 'Italian science'. Besides Niceforo, the other editors were Nicola Pende, who guaranteed that the constitutionalist doctrine would be grafted onto the stem of the bio-anthropological tradition, and Eugenio Florian, who had founded the *Rivista di diritto e procedura penale* in 1909 together with Zerboglio, Berenini and Garofalo, later merged in 1921 with Ferri's Scuola positiva. The authors affirmed that conceptual unity was guaranteed by the 'impartial naturalistic-scientific orientation in the study of the criminal and of crime', the conclusions of which would have juridical, procedural and penal applications. The *Dizionario* came out at the worst possible time, right in the most tragic months at the end of the 1920s and Niceforo wanted to return to his own organisation of the subject with his *Criminologia* published by Bocca, which had grown to five volumes published between 1949 and 1953: a sum of knowledge, of various subjects and various approaches, extending up to endocrinology and psychoanalysis, always departing from an anthropological conception in its widest sense, that is, of crime as a subject for natural investigation. His influence was significant, however: the 'multi-factorial' trends which allegedly still justify criminology as a study and still focus on the individual criminal originated in Niceforo, after all.

These late songs of ageing sirens were not to have the desired effect, however. The university and academic world would demolish Lombrosism's errors and limits, using both its ideas of punishment and its criminological orientations to marginalise it, and also by seeking out and favouring other subject and theoretical approaches, and focusing on the still open and ever present, 'criminal question'.

Notes

1 For the documentation relating to Lombroso's university activities, where the suspicious gaps relating in particular to the controversial competition are underlined, see the result of Paola Novaria's diligent research in, 'Cesare Lombroso professore a Torino. Un percorso tra i documenti dell'Archivio storico dell'Università', in Silvano Montaldo, Paola Novaria (2001) *Gli archivi della scienza. L'Università di Torino e altri casi italiani*. Milan: Franco Angeli, pp. 40–55.

2 Claudio Pogliano has produced a pioneering work from the point of view of the dimensions of its perspective, in a study that should always be referred to: 'Mondo accademico, intellettuali e questione sociale dall'Unità alla guerra mondiale', in Aldo Agosti, Gian Mario Bravo (dir.) (1979) *Storia del movimento operaio del socialismo e delle lotti sociali in Piemonte, vol. 1*. Bari: De Donato, pp. 477–544. Reminiscences of those years in: Michele Lessona (1880) *Confessioni di un rettore*. Torino: Roux and Favale.

3 Very interesting observations by Mauro Forno, 'Scienziati e mass-media: Lombroso e gli studiosi positivisti nella stampa tra Otto and Novecento', in Silvano Montaldo (ed.) *Cesare Lombroso. I scienziati e la nuova Italia*, cit., pp. 207–32.

4 Three recent volumes have proposed different approaches, useful for a first idea of Lombroso and the state of the relative studies: Silvano Montaldo, Paolo Tappero (eds) (2009) *Cesare Lombroso cento anni dopo*. Torino: UTET; Silvano Montaldo, Paolo Tappero (eds) (2009) *Il Museo di Antropologia criminale 'Cesare Lombroso'*. Torino: UTET; Silvano Montaldo (ed.) (2011) *Cesare Lombroso. Gli scienziati e la nuova Italia*. Bologna: The Mulino.

5 The reference text on Turin's science faculties, in terms of internal events and cultural context, is by Silvano Montaldo, 'L'università e le accademie: le Scienze antropologiche, biologiche, fisiologiche, naturali, matematiche; la Medicina; la Fisica; la Chimica', in Umberto Levra (ed.) (2001) *Storia di Torino VII, Da capitale politica a capitale industriale (1864–1915)*. Torino: Einaudi, pp. 727–91.

6 Not to be ignored on the entire subject, the incredible edition for schools by Carlos Maria Landecho, S. J. (2006) *La tipificación Lombrosiana de delincuentes. Tomo II*. Madrid: Universidad Nacional de Educación a Distancia.

7 Still unsurpassed is Delfina Dolza's (1990) work, *Essere figlie di Lombroso. Due donne intellettuali tra '800 and '900*. Milano: Angeli.

8 'Je crois, après longues reflexions et recherches commencées lorsque j'avais quinte ans et poursuivies jusqu' à présent, que les maux dont souffre l'humanité sont en grande partie causés par la grande industrie'. 'Hommage à Gina Ferrero Lombroso', *Bulletin de the Societé des amis de Leo Ferrero*, avril 1944 (duplicated). A copy exists at the Fondazione Einaudi in Turin.

9 The general description of Lombroso's figure at the University, in generous tones, however, has appeared in various essays by Angelo d'Orsi, in particular (2002): *Allievi e maestri. L'Università di Torino nell'Otto-Novecento*. Turin: Celid.

10 Quoted in Corrado Malandrino 'Affinità elettive e sotterranee divergenze. Il rapporto Loria-Michels tra accademia e politica attraverso il carteggio inedito (1905–1936)', in Angelo d'Orsi (ed.), *Quaderni di Storia dell'Università di Turin*. 3. 'Achille Loria', 4, 1999, 3, p. 249. Volume valuable for discovering a personality who Engels also argued violently with. In the same volume the important: Luciana Giacheri Fossati, 'Un'amicizia in tempo. Giovinezze parallele di Achille Loria e Enrico Ferri', pp. 215–44.

11 Journal which 'constitutes on its own a mirror reflecting decades of history described so fully, completely and persuasively, that they can be reconstructed – on the legal front and

in terms of the penal policies in this country – simply from its pages'. Mario Sbriccoli (1987) 'Il diritto penale liberale, la "Rivista Penale" di Luigi Lucchini 1874–1900', in *Quaderni fiorentini per la storia del pensiero giuridico moderno*, XVI. Milan: Giuffrè, pp. 105–83 (pp. 106–7). Also see the unsurpassed 'Caratteri originari e tratti permanenti del sistema penale italiano (1860–1990)', in Luciano Violante (ed.) (1998) *Storia d'Italia, Annali, 14, Legge, Diritto, Giustizia*, Torino; and 'Le mani nella pasta e gli occhi al cielo. La penalistica italiana negli anni del fascismo', in *Quaderni Fiorentini per la storia del pensiero giuridico moderno*, 28, 1999, II.

References

Beltrani-Scalia, M. (1867) *Sul governo e sulla riforma delle carceri in Italia: Saggio storico e teorico*. Torino: Tip G. Favale, p. 434.
Bergami, G. (1980) *Da Graf a Gobetti. Cinquant'anni di cultura militante a Torino (1876–1925)*. Centro studi Piemontesi: Torino, p. 14.
Colajanni, N. (1889) *Sociologia criminale*, vol. II. Catania, p. 540.
Ferri, E. (1883) *La scuola positiva di diritto criminale: prelazione al corso di diritto e procedura penale nella R. Università di Siena pronunciata il 18 novembre 1882*. Siena, Torrini.
Ferri, E. (1909) *Cesare Lombroso*, 'Archivio di antropologia criminale, psichiatria, medicina legale e scienze affini', p. 548.
Gemelli, A. (1948) *La personalità del delinquente nei suoi fondamenti biologici e psicologici*. Milano: Giuffrè, pp. 35, 232.
Lombardi, G. (1944) *Sociologia criminale*. Napoli: Novene, p. 186.
Lombroso, C. and Ferrero, G. (1893) 'Sui recenti processi bancari di Roma e Parigi', *Archivio di Psichiatria, scienze penali ed antropologia criminale per servire allo studio dell'uomo alienato e delinquente*, (XIV), p. 193.
Lombroso, P. and Lombroso, G. (1906) *Cesare Lombroso. Appunti sulla vita*. Torino: Bocca, pp. 82–3.
Michels, R. (1911) 'Cesare Lombroso. Note sull'uomo politico e l'uomo privato', *Archivio di antropologia criminale, psichiatria e medicina legale*, p. 362.
Niceforo, A. (1953) *Avventure e disavventure della personalità e delle umane società, Comitato per le Onoranze ad Alfredo Niceforo*. Roma: Bocca, p. 63.
Onoranze (1921) 'Le solenni onoranze a Cesare Lombroso in Verona', *Archivio di antropologia criminale, psichiatria e medicina legale*, p. 723.
Opera (1908) *L'Opera di Cesare Lombroso nella scienza e nelle sue applicazioni*. Torino: Bocca, pp. 218–19.
Pacchiotti, G. (1875) *Il programma dell'avvenire della medicina in Italia*. Torino: Loescher, 1875.
Patrizi, M. L. (1930) *Addizioni al 'Dopo Lombroso'*. Milano: Società editrice Libraria, p. 230
Pogliano, C. (1988) 'Michele Lessona', in Roy Porter (a cura di), *Dizionario Biografico della Storia della Medicina e delle Scienze Naturali*. Milano: Franco Maria Ricci, vol. III, p. 33.
Sbriccoli, M. (1990) 'La penalistica civile. Teorie e ideologie del diritto penale nell'Italia unita', in Aldo Schiavone (a cura di), *Stato e cultura giuridica in Italia dall'Unità alla Repubblica*, Roma-Bari 1990, ora in: Mario Sbriccoli, *Storia del diritto penale e della giustizia. Scritti editi e indeiti (1972–2007)*. Milano: Giuffré, 2009, vol. 2, p. 537.
Topinard, P. (1887) 'Compte rendu de 'L'Homme Criminel', *Revue d'anthropologie* (anno XVI, 1887, fasc. 6, pp. 658–91).
Zini, Zino (1973) *Appunti di vita torinese, a cura di Giancarlo Bergami, 'Belfagor'*, p. 326.

2
CESARE LOMBROSO, PRISON SCIENCE, AND PENAL POLICY

Mary Gibson

> Common people and even the scientific world believe in good faith that the prison, especially the cellular penitentiary, is a silent and motionless organism, deprived of a tongue and hands, because the law commands it to be quiet and to keep still. But ... this organism speaks.
>
> (Lombroso 1888, 5)

With these words, Cesare Lombroso introduced his little-known book of 1888, *Prison Palimpsests*, which reproduced almost a thousand examples of prisoner writing and art. He began publishing examples of prisoner subculture as early as the first edition of *Criminal Man* (1876), which featured chapters on the jargon and poetry of inmates as well as illustrations of their apparent mania for drawing on their bodies (tattoos).[1] In the much-expanded fifth edition of *Criminal Man* (1896–7), an entire volume was devoted to images, many of which had been produced by incarcerated men and women. Such a heavy reliance on prison artifacts points to the dominant role that Italy's penitentiary system played in the construction of Lombrosian criminology. It is perhaps not too bold to suggest that without the close ties that he developed with state institutions of punishment, Lombroso might have failed, or at least been severely crippled, in his attempts to elaborate his new school of criminal anthropology.

Lombroso developed his positivist approach as a young man who came of age during the last years of the Risorgimento, the movement for Italian unification.[2] In his mid-twenties, when war broke out in 1859 to throw off Austrian rule in northern Italy, he volunteered as a military physician in the Piedmontese army. As a non-practicing Jew, he patriotically supported the new Kingdom of Italy, which declared its independence in 1861 and whose parliamentary system promised religious tolerance, secular laws, and cultural modernization, especially in the sciences. Trained in medicine at universities in both Italy and Vienna, he was dedicated to solving social problems in his homeland and overcoming its perceived backwardness compared to northern Europe. In a young state desperate to staff its new national bureaucracies with men of professional expertise, Lombroso was typical of a generation whose members found great opportunities for the advancement of both their careers and their ideas. Thus Lombroso was successful in obtaining not only a series of university posts, most importantly the chairs of legal medicine (1876), psychiatry (1896), and criminal anthropology (1905) at the University of Turin, but also medical positions in several mental hospitals (Pavia, Pesaro, and Reggio Emilia) and in the central jail of Turin (1885).

As both a professor and prison doctor, Lombroso thus defies any attempt to label him as solely an elite theoretician or a lowly practitioner. He was both, and his institutional posts were vital to the development of his innovative theory of criminal anthropology. Based on claims of empirical objectivity, criminal anthropology required the extensive collection of data; because it taught that the object of study should be the criminal rather than the crime, this data had to regard persons. For Lombroso, these persons were prisoners, to whom he had access as a prison doctor, facilitated by his close contacts with national prison administrators in the capital, Rome. Lombroso's energetic and almost compulsive quest to wrest information from prisons and artifacts from prisoners was made possible not only by his growing scholarly reputation but also by his series of administrative posts in state institutions. Poised between theory and practice, Lombroso thus exemplified the dialectical combination of power and knowledge (*pouvoir/savoir*) so brilliantly exposed by Michel Foucault.[3] As an employee of the national prison administration, Lombroso was free to use the prisons as his laboratory for constructing an innovative and influential criminological theory. That theory, in turn, influenced the manner in which Italy's wide array of institutions of confinement classified and disciplined their inmates. After examining Lombroso's close relationship to the Italian prison system, this essay will focus first on the "knowledge" about criminality that he derived from inmates and second on the "power" that he wielded by developing a positivist policy toward incarceration. His research on prisoners resulted in rich but deeply flawed data that he used to elaborate a complex and sometimes contradictory policy toward punishment.

Lombroso in prison

From the beginning of his medical career, Lombroso depended on state institutions for the raw data of his research. His genius, in fact, rested on the realization that captive populations could be measured, observed, and interviewed for the purpose of formulating theories based on biological and psychological "facts." Because these facts could be assembled into statistical tables, Lombroso claimed to be elevating penology from an abstract and old-fashioned philosophy to an exact and modern science. His research methods, which remained similar throughout his lifetime, were developed early in his career when, as a young military doctor, he began to measure recruits and compile statistics on their physical characteristics. As a middle-class northerner, he was struck by the generally bad health of many soldiers, caused by the widespread poverty and economic underdevelopment of the peninsula. Conditions were even worse in the southern province of Calabria, where he was posted in 1862 and, in addition to his military duties, collected information on the medical problems among the local population. After returning to civilian life in the north, he applied this same approach to his patients as director of a series of mental asylums. He utilized much of the resulting information in the first volume of *Criminal Man*, where "the insane" constituted the major control group for his data on criminals. Thus by the time he gained the post as prison physician in 1885, he had perfected a strategy of using an institutional population as the empirical basis for constructing theories about more general categories such as "southerners," "the insane," and now "criminals."

That Lombroso drew much of his data from prisoners and, in turn, was an important voice in policy debates about "prison science," has received little attention from scholars. This is partially the fault of Lombroso himself, who rarely identifies where he located the subjects of the many anecdotes and statistical studies that fill his writings. It is also the result of his periodic laments, that have been picked up by some biographers, about his difficulties in gaining access to Italian prisons. For instance in *Criminal Woman*, Lombroso complains that he was not allowed to photograph female convicts (Lombroso and Ferrero 2004, 135). Historians have also repeated a colorful story told by his daughter Gina, who wrote a sympathetic biography of her father shortly after his death. She recounts that during his early years at the University of Turin, Lombroso was reduced to sending his servant out on the streets and into bars to find "criminals" because he could not get permission to enter Italian prisons. He paid these vagabonds and drunks to be measured and interviewed both in his laboratory and in front of the students who flocked to his first classes in criminal anthropology (Lombroso-Ferrero 1915, 198). Yet both claims are partially suspect. To gather the material for *Prison Palimpsests*, Lombroso had access to prisoners in two men's jails and one women's penitentiary, as he explains in the preface (Lombroso 1888, 6). As for Gina's reminiscences, they go on to recount her father's delight in being subsequently appointed as medical officer of the Turinese jail in 1885, a post he occupied continuously for twenty years.[4] According to Gina, Lombroso went "every morning to *his prison*, even when he was sick, tired, or even melancholy because *his prison* always had the power to restore excitement and joy to his life" (Lombroso-Ferrero 1915, 247–8: emphasis in the original). From that moment, Lombroso did not lack human material for his experiments.

Even if denied access to local prisons during his early career, Lombroso nevertheless relied heavily on data collected from inmates by other criminologists in Italy and indeed throughout Europe. As illustrated by the long list of contributors to his journal, the *Archive of psychiatry, criminal anthropology, and legal medicine* (hereafter *Archive*), and his voluminous footnotes in *Criminal Man* and *Criminal Woman*, Lombroso corresponded with a large network of positivist criminologists, many of whom were themselves doctors in prisons or had access to their own captive populations for purposes of research. Anthony Marro, for example, collected so much data during his tenure as a prison doctor that he published an award-winning book in 1887 titled *The Characteristics of Criminals: An Anthropological-Sociological Study*. Lombroso frequently cites Marro, as well as other colleagues such as Enrico Ferri and Salvatore Ottolenghi to bolster his arguments. Of course, by combining the results of such heterogeneous studies, without clearly indicating the nature of each sample population, Lombroso made a mockery of his scientific pretensions. For instance, in the introduction to the Fourth Edition of *Criminal Man*, he combines the results of over thirty different studies as support for his theory of the born criminal (Lombroso 2006, 234). Although this methodology lacks any rigor by contemporary standards in the social sciences, what is significant is the centrality of prisons as the source for much of the primary material used by his colleagues both in Italy and abroad. In addition, Lombroso was frequently the recipient of the primary materials themselves, as when he received gifts of crime weapons, examples of inmate art, and even the skulls of dead prisoners from fellow positivists – often former students – who held positions in penal institutions across the peninsula.[5]

Lombroso's access to prisons was strengthened by his close ties to the upper echelons of the national prison administration in Rome. His new positivist approach to the study of crime was particularly admired by Martino Beltrani Scalia, who held the position of Director General of Prisons for most of the period between 1879 and 1898. In 1871, when he was rising in the administrative bureaucracy and occupied the post of national prison inspector, Beltrani Scalia founded the *Journal of Prison Sciences* (*Rivista di discipline carcerarie*, hereafter *RDC*) that combined an official bulletin of government regulations with a much longer "non-official" section containing articles by jurists, politicians, and scholars on issues of crime and punishment.[6] A firm champion of policies based on "facts," Beltrani Scalia characterized Lombroso as a "distinguished psychiatrist" in 1875 when the *RDC* began publishing installments of the first edition of *Criminal Man* even before it came out in book form (*RDC* v. 5 1875, 113–26; 375–95; 441–8; 516–22). During the next few decades, the *RDC* hosted a large number of articles by Lombroso, most of which were clinical diagnoses of prisoners based on physical measurements and psychological interviews. That Beltrani Scalia believed that the positivist method should be generalized across the prison system was clear from his preface to an article by Lombroso on the frequency of left-handedness among criminals in which he urged prison doctors to look for the same atavistic trait in their own inmates (*RDC* v. 14 1884, 126–30). In 1891, the *RDC* proudly boasted about its role as "the cradle of criminal anthropology ... searching for truth guided solely by the incontrovertible facts" (*RDC* v. 21 1891, 611–61).

In 1892, Lombroso received, in the words of his daughter, "an unexpected fortune" of prison artifacts, including physical remains, inmate art, and models of prison cells, which had been assembled by Beltrani Scalia in the Roman jail of Regina Coeli (Lombroso-Ferrero 1915, 361). According to Gina, Lombroso rushed to Rome to take possession of this new treasure trove, which joined the private collection that he had been accumulating since his military service. In the same year, the Interior Minister encouraged prison directors throughout Italy to send similar objects to Lombroso. (*Musee* 1906, 4). Encouraged by this governmental recognition of the importance of Lombroso's collection, the University of Turin began to fund further acquisitions and make plans for an official "Museum of Psychiatry and Criminology" to house it (Montaldo 2009, 9). Inaugurated in 1898, the museum remained primarily a research institute for scholars except for special events such as the International Congress of Criminal Anthropology, held in Turin in 1906. Feted at the congress for his life's work, Lombroso in turn regaled the participants with a tour of his museum as well as the Turinese jail, where he demonstrated how to identify a born criminal (Villa 1985, 31–3). In 2009, on the centenary of Lombroso's death, his collection was catalogued, restored, moved to larger quarters, and opened to the public.

Knowledge of prisoners

It is not surprising that Lombroso took advantage, as have many criminologists, of the availability of a captive population of prisoners to generate his data. But if the prison constituted the "special theater" for criminal anthropology, in the words of legal historian Guido Neppi Modona, then Italian inmates provided the model for Lombroso's archetypal figure, the born criminal. (Neppi Modona 2009, 83). Rather than abstractions, Lombroso's criminal types were based on flesh-and-blood individuals who inhabited a specific historical period and had been frequently brutalized both by poverty and the conditions of their incarceration. Lombroso's "knowledge" about the criminal body and psychology in fact pertained particularly to the Italian lower classes or to Lombroso's preconceptions about the poor in his nation.

However, it would be wrong to characterize Lombroso's theories as based solely on the bodies and artifacts of inmates. Notorious for throwing together heterogeneous types of sources, he often complemented his observations from prisons with historical anecdotes, anthropological findings, popular sayings, literature, and even paintings. For example, in his chapter in *Criminal Man* on the "Anthropometry and Physiology of 6,608 Criminals," Lombroso, in addition to his own statistical measurements, uses proverbs about gray hair, a bust of the wrinkled face of a female poisoner from Naples, and a painting by Goya of a brigand with a receding forehead as evidence of biological anomalies (Lombroso 2006, 305–12). Nevertheless, prisons constituted the primary laboratory for measuring, observing, and interviewing criminals as a basis for the myriad tables that characterize both *Criminal Man* and *Criminal Woman*. Without the rich resource of the prison, it is doubtful that Lombroso could have ever developed his multi-faceted portrait of the "criminal type," better known as the born criminal. Although only one of the positivist categories of lawbreakers, the born criminal was the most important for criminal anthropologists because it constituted the standard against which others were defined. Thus the occasional criminal possessed only a few anomalies while the criminaloid lay halfway between the two on the scale of dangerousness. Even as he increased his coverage of the occasional criminal over the many editions of *Criminal Man*, Lombroso nevertheless continued to delight more in analyzing atavism, moral insanity, and epilepsy than the environment in his search for the etiology of delinquent behavior.

The profile of Lombroso's born criminal, or more properly the Italian inmate, is most well known for its long list of biological stigmata. These anomalies included small heads, already held to be indications of inferiority before the publication of *Criminal Man*, as well as low foreheads, wide cheekbones, protruding chins, large jaws, and jug ears. Lombroso went beyond the head, the traditional focus of the earlier school of phrenology, to identify atypical traits on the rest of the criminal body, including small stature, dark hair, wide arm spans, malformations of the hand and foot (including monkey-like prehensile toes), a high frequency of wrinkles, slightly elevated armpit temperature, high rates of heart and liver disease, deformed genitals, and left-handedness. According to Lombroso's theory of atavism, such deformities illustrated the proximity of criminals to their "savage" ancestors and thus their evolutionary failure.

While women of the criminal type shared many characteristics with their male counterparts, their biological role in both "primitive" and modern societies left differing marks on their bodies. Asserting that prostitution was typical of early human society, Lombroso identified sexual deviancy, rather than the violence found in criminal men, as the key to identifying atavism in women. Sexual deviancy could take many forms from the hyper-femininity of nymphomaniacs to the masculinity – and even frigidity – of many prostitutes and female born criminals. Whether lascivious or cold, criminal women and prostitutes shunned maternity, the natural biological role of women according to Lombroso's social Darwinist framework. Thus a masculine physiognomy immediately marked women as criminal, a trait so self-explanatory to Lombroso that he simply presented a series of photographs in *Criminal Woman* to clinch his argument (Lombroso and Ferrero 2004, 139–43). Somewhat contradictorily, he admitted that young born prostitutes often appeared beautiful and even feminine. Such beauty, however, was just the effect of make-up, which prostitutes used to hide their anomalies for the purpose of attracting male customers. Old age, however, revealed their fundamental atavism because "when youth vanishes, those jaws, those cheekbones and sharp angles hidden by adipose tissues emerge and the face becomes virile, uglier than that of a man" (Lombroso and Ferrero 2004, 143).

Perhaps most indicative of Lombroso's approach, which correlated physical disfigurement with mental deficiency, was his measurement of sensitivity using a variety of machines including an algometer, which sent electric shocks to the body. According to Lombroso, algometer readings confirmed his intuition that criminals feel little pain, a phenomenon also demonstrated by their fondness for tattoos. Reversing the common perception that women were more sensitive than men, his experiments revealed an extreme dullness of touch in female born criminals and prostitutes. True to its assumption that external physical abnormalities mirrored internal weakness, criminal anthropology taught that criminals' dullness of touch was correlated with moral insensitivity and their tendency to lie and steal. For women, moral insensitivity was interpreted as primarily sexual, that is as an absence of modesty and maternal feelings, two traits that had slowly developed with evolution and now characterized "normal" women. That criminals were particularly insensitive was confirmed by Lombroso's research on blushing, which occurred rarely among prisoners even when reprimanded about their crimes.

Aside from the sensitivity tests, the psychology of criminals was less easy to measure than their physical bodies. Lombroso took a clinical approach, subjecting prisoners to lengthy interviews about their understanding of their behavior as well as their habits, childhood, and relatives. Lombroso published many transcripts of these interviews, conducted for research and as a basis for his expert testimony in criminal trials, in professional journals or as appendices to *Criminal Man*. Each transcript included a list of physical anomalies, a family history, the answers of the inmate, and Lombroso's positivist analysis of the case. For example, when examining and questioning a young man named Giovanni, who killed his father in 1877, Lombroso and his colleague L. Perotti found in addition to "defects of the ... skull" and "an unusual tactile insensitivity to pain" a "history of insanity" accompanied by a refusal to hide his crime or express remorse (Lombroso 2006, 157). They attributed his mental illness to heredity ("he had insane relatives") and to his diet of moldy polenta, thought by Lombroso to cause pellagra. His close work with prisoners convinced Lombroso that their psychology was marked by vanity, vindictiveness, ferocity, cupidity, laziness, and a passion for sex, alcohol, and cards. In the criminal woman, "masculine" traits such as ferocity and lasciviousness made her a "true monster"; she represented a "double exception" to the natural order because her inferiority as a woman was compounded by her unnatural rejection of the feminine virtues of domesticity, maternity, passivity, and religion (Lombroso and Ferrero 2004, 185). Thus for Lombroso the psychological anomalies of criminals recalled the typically gendered traits of their atavistic ancestors who had been vindictive murderers in the case of men and immodest prostitutes in the case of women.

Less well known than Lombroso's physical and psychological portrait of the born criminal was his study of prisoner art. As Gina wittily remarked, her father was a "born collector," and the results of his energetic but undisciplined mania was most evident in *Prison Palimpsests* (Lombroso-Ferrero 1915, 355). Based on four years of concerted research in the jails of Turin and Alessandria as well as a female penitentiary, *Prison Palimpsests* reproduced 809 examples of writing by male prisoners plus a much smaller number by women. To locate so many words of prisoners, Lombroso was resourceful and innovative: he copied down the lyrics of prison songs; graffiti on prison walls, furniture, and water pitchers; scribbles on the margins of books in prison libraries; tattoos on inmates bodies; and embroidery on their clothes. Characterizing himself as a paleographer of the prison, Lombroso promised "a serious and experimental study" of these traces, or palimpsests, of prison life (Lombroso, 1888, 6). Like biological anomalies, prisoner writings offered "precious evidence of the real psychological constitution of this new, wretched race," which was unable "to speak the language of honest men (Lombroso 1888, 6; 7). Despite his denigration of prisoner artifacts as signs of atavism, Lombroso, as Pierpaolo Leschiutta has pointed out, must be seen as a pioneer of urban anthropology. While early Italian folklorists were scouring rural villages for vestiges of supposedly pure popular traditions, Lombroso instead focused on collecting products of a criminal culture in the process of urbanization and modernization (Leschiutta 1996, 4–5).

Despite the extreme heterogeneity of the 809 examples of male prisoner writing collected in the *Palimpsests*, Lombroso pretended to turn them into scientific data by dividing them into statistical categories. According to his computations, 21.5 percent of them referred to the inmate's crime, 18.3 percent to his fellow prisoners, 15.2 percent to his punishment, and 10.1 percent to his fate and future.[7] In total, 65 percent of the writings expressed the preoccupation of inmates with their legal travails. These scribblings included protestations of innocence ("I've been in prison for two months without being told my crime"), imprecations against informers and police ("I'm inside because of a lying informer. Death to all informers and police"); and complaints about prison life ("In this cell, it is hard for those who do not have money") (Lombroso 1888, 10; 14; 25). Only 11.8 percent referred to either "lust" or "other vices" and only 2.4 percent were "dirty." In a semblance of scientific methodology, Lombroso compared these numbers to a "control group" of writings collected by his assistants from "walls, public toilets, military barracks, and finally books" outside of prison (Lombroso 1888, 256). Of course the "external" writings dealt little with criminal justice but to Lombroso's surprise contained many more "dirty" comments than those by prisoners. Nevertheless, despite his own evidence that only a small minority of prisoners exhibited depravity in their writings, Lombroso continued to insist that prisoners were "a species of earthly demons" (Lombroso 1888, 7).

As was typical of Lombroso, his general condemnation of inmate subculture was often contradicted by a more nuanced evaluation of individual artifacts. For example, he openly admired the following poem cited in *Criminal Man*, finding it to be worthy of Petrarch, in its delicate ode to love:

When I saw you and heard you speak

The blood froze in my veins

And my heart wanted to escape from my breast ...

Every word when she speaks

Attracts, ties, pierces, nay, wounds.

(Lombroso 2006, 79–80)

Similarly, he praised a drawing by the prisoner Sighetti, which imagined the scene of his future death by a firing squad. Lombroso found the composition, in which the execution was framed by trees on the sides and a balcony of spectators at the back, to be well balanced, although he could not refrain from interpreting the drawing as a sign of Sighetti's criminal vanity (Lombroso 2006, 147).

Lombroso's methodology for studying the "signs" of deviancy can be criticized in many ways, several of which relate directly to his use of prisoners as data. First, he elided two categories assuming that prisoners accurately represented the larger universe of criminals. This was inexcusable even in Lombroso's era, when Italian statisticians understood that many crimes go undetected, a phenomenon they called "latent delinquency" and modern criminologists call the "dark figure" of crime (Bosco 1903, 216). Yet Lombroso never questioned whether Italy's prisoners were representative of criminals in general in terms either of their physical/psychological characteristics or their types of offenses. His failure to define carefully the category of "criminal" is particularly puzzling in light of his frequent and caustic criticism – along with his positivist colleagues Ferri and Raffaele Garofalo – of Italy's criminal code, court procedures, and policies of punishment. How could such a flawed system, based on the traditional and – in the opinion of Lombroso – outdated "classical" school of penology produce a population of prisoners who were, by positivist criteria, in fact criminals? Lombroso's radical rejection of reigning legal practices should have made him think much harder about the definition of his object of study.

Secondly, Lombroso fails to make distinctions between prisoners awaiting trial and those serving a sentence of punishment. Because Italian laws of penal procedure denied "conditional release" (with or without bail) to the majority of prisoners, and the courts worked remarkably slowly, suspects often endured long periods of pre-trial detention. Held in large urban jails (*carceri giudiziarie*), these inmates were available for academic study by Lombroso and his positivist colleagues and, in the case of heinous crimes, subjects of their expert testimony (*periti*). As a physician in a jail – rather than a penitentiary for long-term punishment (*casa di pena*) – Lombroso therefore conducted his voracious search for criminological data among a population that included a large number of suspects who would later be declared innocent.

Finally, Lombroso's methodology was most fundamentally flawed in its claim to have discovered a universal criminal type when at most it simply described the traits of marginalized and incarcerated Italians during the first decades after unification. A reverse image of the ideal citizens of the newly united nation, Lombroso's born criminals were short, dark, and disfigured. Barely literate, they wrote graffiti in dialect and decorated their bodies and water jugs with pictures (or primitive pictographs as Lombroso called them) rather than words. Often resorting to prostitution to survive, female offenders failed to blush when reminded of their "crimes." Graffitti on jail walls and jottings in the margins of prisoners' books revealed resentment against police, the courts, and prison guards as well as anxiety about their families. In fact, many traits of the "born criminal" were traits of the Italian poor, and in some instances the southern poor, during the first decades after unification. Malnourished, ravaged by diseases such as malaria, tuberculosis, and pellagra, living in often appalling conditions, and working at heavy labor, large numbers of lower-class Italians would have failed Lombroso's many physical and psychological tests for normalcy. Of course, no simple correlation exists between the born criminal and the Italian prisoner, because Lombroso's research was mediated by his preconceptions, faulty methods, and fallacious hypotheses. But his voluminous statistics, interviews, anecdotes, and collections of artifacts potentially tell us more about the lives and perspectives of the Italian poor than about the fictitious category of the born criminal.

Power over prisoners

Despite his view of prisoners as deceitful, violent, and lascivious, Lombroso was a major critic of imprisonment as a useful or even just form of punishment. In his conclusion to *Prison Palimsests*, he admits that most readers would assume him to be a proponent of the cellular prison, which enforced the strict separation of inmates both day and night. In Italy, and throughout Europe, lively and sometimes acrimonious debates occurred throughout the nineteenth century over the merits of two rival penal models named after pioneering institutions in America: the Philadelphia system of cellular confinement and the Auburn or "silent" system that required separation at night and work in common – and in silence – during the day. That Lombroso had a large replica of the Philadelphia penitentiary at Cherry Hill in his office, and subsequently in his museum, seemed to signal his approval of the continual separation of prisoners to prevent the kinds of communication that he catalogued in *Prison Palimpsests*. Instead, as Silvano Montaldo has pointed out, the model was probably built for the International Prison Congress held in Rome in 1885 and then sent by the Minister of the Interior to Lombroso in 1892 (Montaldo 2009, 103). In any case, Lombroso argues in the conclusion to *Prison Palimpsests* that while the cellular isolation of inmates "seems theoretically completely correct, and I myself have advocated it in [past] books, if you go from my tables to real life, you see that it is mostly an illusion!" (Lombroso 1888, 312).

For Lombroso, "real life" meant that of a prison doctor who understood the impossibility of preventing communication among prisoners. The sly ability of inmates to evade not only legal but also architectural barriers meant that the diffusion of information among inmates in cellular prisons was "damaging (especially for the judicial process) because it was unforeseen" (Lombroso 1896–7, v. 3, 455). As Lombroso knew from his daily visits to the Turinese jail, one of the few cellular prison in Italy, the graffiti on the walls of prison passageways constituted "a type of daily newspaper." Even foggy windows or the pavement of the exercise yard, covered with sand or snow, provided surfaces for the composition of inmate messages (Lombroso 1896–7, v. 3, 456). In addition to scribbling in the margins of books from prison libraries, inmates took advantage of the requirement to attend mass for circulating information. This information came from various sources: outside contractors who organized prison labor, defense lawyers meeting with their clients, administrators in whose office the most educated prisoners worked as copyists,

FIGURE 2.1 Lombroso's replica of the Philadelphia penitentiary at Cherry Hill

Source: Archivio fotografico del Museo di Antropologia criminale "Cesare Lombroso" dell'Università di Torino (Italia).

and, of course, prison guards who were easily bribed. After witnessing all of these avenues of communication, Lombroso declared that "nothing is secret in prison; instead, I can prove that in prison you often learn things that are still unknown on the outside" (Lombroso 1896–7, v. 3, 456). Therefore, Lombroso aligned himself with the opponents of cellular prisons who argued that, in addition to their enormous costs, they failed to reform inmates.

Lombroso also believed incarceration to be inhumane, and he quoted prisoners' laments about the injustice, discomfort, loneliness, and inutility of their punishment. Demonstrating again his contradictory evaluation of inmate artifacts, Lombroso used their words as data to support his policy proposals without ceasing to denigrate them as signs of atavism. Yet his humanitarian sympathies, which led him to joining the nascent Italian Socialist Party, are clearly with the author of the following graffiti: "Poor inmates! They are considered beasts; they are shut up like white bears and then it is claimed that they have been reformed!" Another prisoner complained that "In penitentiaries, you learn to hate society; none of them turns a thief into an honest man; they are universities of thieves where the old teach the trade to the young" (Lombroso 1896–7, v. 3, 453). A more graphic protest against internment as punishment was painted on one of the many water jugs that Lombroso collected from prison cells. In vivid pictures, an inmate predicts his future suicide by hanging accompanied by the following poem titled "Cellular Prison":

Hope is a chimera

The world is an empire ruled by Egoism

God ... Religion! Justice! Grand words!

I ask pardon of those who love me

I give pardon to those who wish me wrong

Tired of suffering, I have decided to die!

Better than the life of a slave on a crooked path.

(Lombroso 2006, 102)

Based on the large number of similar cries of desperation, many reproduced in his *Prison Palimpsests*, Lombroso warned that incarceration would degrade most prisoners, turning them into automatons unable to adapt to normal life upon release.

Instead of inflicting pain on the criminal, Lombroso saw the purpose of punishment to be the protection of society, a prescription that differed little from classical penology. More controversial was his belief that "punishment should be proportional less to the gravity of the crime than to the dangerousness of the criminal" (Lombroso 2006, 341). Because "crime is like an illness that requires a specific remedy for each patient," Lombroso recommended that criminal anthropologists, with their medical expertise, examine lawbreakers and recommend appropriate punishment to the courts. (Lombroso 2006, 341). Thus Lombroso's policy on punishment was filtered through his elaborate categorization of criminals based on their number of anomalies. For born and habitual criminals, he admitted that social defense demanded their elimination or isolation from society because they were not susceptible to rehabilitation. Members of organized crime or repeat and violent recidivists deserved the death sentence, a measure that Lombroso defended as equivalent to the Darwinian struggle for existence among animals but which the Italian parliament abolished in 1889. As an alternative, he strongly lobbied for the establishment of "prisons for incorrigibles," located preferably on islands, where inmates would serve lifetime sentences doing road building, land reclamation, and other projects useful to the nation. Far from population centers and not likely to be released, born criminals need not be confined to cells because their moral contagion would never infect "honest" citizens.

If the state insisted on retaining prisons for lesser offenders – those who fit into his categories of the criminal by passion, criminaloid or occasional criminal – Lombroso rejected the Pennsylvania and Auburn models in favor of the "Irish" or progressive system. Under this model, inmates would first endure a period of cellular isolation after which they would proceed through several stages of increasing comfort, privileges, and finally early release based on their accumulation of merit points for good behavior. According to Lombroso, the progressive system held out a possibility of reform because "liberty is the prisoner's dream and constant preoccupation .... For release from prison, they will do what is right. And because repeated actions become second nature, they might even get used to it" (Lombroso 2006, 143). Reform would be affected through work and moral education not through exaggerated force, which "may crush criminals and, instead of correcting them, induce anger and hypocrisy" (Lombroso 2006, 143). Even the requirement of silence, a hallmark of the Auburn system, might hurt prisoner morale. Instead the Irish system was most consonant with "criminal psychology," although Lombroso warned against the illusion it would effectively solve the problem of recidivism.

Preferable to incarceration were a series of alternatives to prison or, as his colleague Ferri dubbed them, "penal substitutes." He agreed with Ferri that "a few days in jail, usually served alongside habitual criminals, does little to intimidate [the criminal] ... but instead has disastrous effects" by taking away his sense of honor and introducing him to corrupt companions (Lombroso 1896–7, v. 3, 531). For minor criminals who displayed few anomalies and therefore might be reformed, Lombroso suggested a variety of punishments including legal warnings, house arrest with corporal punishment (restricted diets or cold showers), and forced labor without imprisonment. He supported the increased use of fines, which could be proportioned to both the seriousness of the crime and the economic status of the criminal. House arrest and forced labor (a type of community service) would restrict liberty without exposing a relatively honest and possibly repentant lawbreaker to the indignity and contamination of jail. Lombroso was also an enthusiastic proponent of probation and offered a detailed description of its workings in Massachusetts as well as several European nations. Appropriate for first-time offenders, probation was successful, according to his statistics, in preventing recidivism for minor crimes such as theft, drunkenness, and assaults. He therefore strongly recommended its adoption in Italy.

Other groups that deserved special treatment were the mentally ill and juvenile delinquents. For the first, Lombroso was an early and vigorous supporter of the establishment of criminal insane asylums (*manicomi criminali*) to house inmates who were either warehoused in prisons without treatment or in municipal mental hospitals where they posed a danger to other patients. A psychiatrist himself, Lombroso allied with other prominent colleagues in this young field to lobby for these specialized institutions, which would be directed by doctors but staffed by prison guards. Juvenile delinquents also deserved individualization of punishment, something Lombroso believed impossible in the Italian reformatories of his day. Instead, he advocated institutions based on Elmira Reformatory in the United States, which Lombroso claimed had incorporated his theories. Its director, Zebulon Brockway, was said to measure each young man every month to determine a suitable amount of work and program of education. Despite his delight in an institution that employed his biological approach, Lombroso warned that reformatories would have little effect on juvenile born criminals, who were ultimately incorrigible. His glowing support of Elmira also contrasted with his more general advice to find alternatives to prison for young occasional offenders.

Lombroso's prescriptions for the overhaul of Italy's prisons, and more generally its policies of punishment, were widely shared by other positivist criminologists and gained the ear of statesmen and administrators.[8] Prisons were an issue of contention in Italy during the decades after unification because of the notorious conditions of incarceration endured by political prisoners in the old regime states. Usually located in dungeons, towers, forts, and convents unsuited to their purpose, the old prisons were portrayed in political memoirs as places of torture where inmates lived in dank, dark, and insect-infested cells and were forbidden from reading or writing. Such graphic descriptions of human misery aroused public opinion against the monarchs of the peninsula whose repression of civil and political rights was epitomized by the prisoner in chains. So embarrassing was this portrait of barbaric punishment that unification brought immediate calls for prison reform.

Thus Lombroso joined a lively debate about how to modernize punishment, and specifically prisons, in the new state when he began to offer policy prescriptions in the early editions of *Criminal Man*. His recommendations enjoyed only partial success. Despite his close ties to Beltrani Scalia, he understandably failed to convince the director of prisons of the general uselessness and even iniquity of incarceration as a form of punishment. And indeed the Parliament retained prison as a major form of punishment in the new Penal Code of 1889. Against his recommendations, the code abolished the death penalty and only later was probation introduced. He was more successful in bolstering Beltrani Scalia's project to reorganize the system of long-term penitentiaries along the Irish model; the prison reform bill of 1890 accomplished this in theory even if implementation lagged in practice. Juvenile reformatories, while never replicating Brockways' model, adopted education as a primary goal by the early twentieth century and markedly improved condition for boys (but not for girls).[9] Most notably, Beltrani Scalia established several criminal insane asylums during his tenure, an experiment that was later made permanent by Parliament.

While Lombroso's success in shaping legislative policy was limited, he wielded a more subtle but pervasive influence through the penetration of his criminological theory into institutional practice. Criminal anthropology was wildly popular among prison directors and doctors, who regarded Lombroso as the father of a new scientific approach that had restored Italy to legal preeminence. Both the *Archives* and the *RDC* were filled with articles by administrators in jails, penitentiaries, and insane asylums who emulated Lombroso's scientific methods using their inmates as data. Positivist criminologists and their allies in the prison administration – such as Ferri, Garofalo, and Beltrani Scalia – served on parliamentary committees and represented Italy at the international congresses. Lombroso's image of the born criminal – and the fear that modern society was deluged by the dangerous classes – permeated literature and public opinion even if the subtleties of his theory were often misunderstood.

Conclusion

Foucault's insight that the prison is a privileged locus for the extraction of knowledge and the exercise of power offers a new perspective on Lombroso's life work.

Lombroso relied on the Italian prison system for knowledge; that is, the data with which to construct his criminal categories, most importantly that of the born criminal. He subsequently used his positivist theories to argue for specific policies of punishment and thus assert power over those same prisoners who had constituted his data. Yet the circularity of power/knowledge was not as seamless as Foucault has led us to believe. Because of the complexity of the political process in Italy and the existence of rival schools of criminology, Lombroso's proposals for penal reform were only partially adopted. Even more fundamentally, there was some disjuncture between Lombroso's criminal anthropological theory, which emphasized the monstrous nature of the criminal, and his advocacy of relatively nuanced and liberal policies of punishment. Perhaps his dedication to the liberal Risorgimento, and later the socialist party, explains the humanitarian impulse to favor alternatives to incarceration for most categories of criminals. More importantly, the practical knowledge derived from his daily work as a prison physician made him suspicious of rigid models for the ideal penitentiary. Attentive to the specific weaknesses in the Italian prison system and the particular characteristics of Italian prisoners, Lombroso prescribed a flexible range of punishments for all but the most dangerous criminals. Ironically, if the Italian government had fully implemented his proposals for diverting criminals from incarceration, Lombroso might have lost what his daughter had dubbed "*his prison*," and therefore one of the birthplaces of criminal anthropology.

Notes

1 To see how Lombroso's coverage of prisoner subculture expanded over the five editions of *Criminal Man*, see Appendix 2 ("Illustrations in the Five Italian Editions") in Lombroso, 2006, 364–9.
2 For English accounts of Lombroso's career, see Wolfgang (1972) and Gibson (2002). In Italian, see Bulferetti (1975), Villa (1985), Baima Bollone (1992), Frigessi (2003), and Velo Dalbrenta (2004).
3 See Chapter 3 ("Panopticism"), of *Discipline and Punish: The Birth of the Prison*, although this entire work constitutes a long exegesis of the relationship between power and knowledge. Historians have not been entirely uncritical of Foucault's theory of the origins and function of the prison as an instrument of punishment. For an overview of historiographical reactions to Foucault, see Gibson (2011).
4 Lombroso apparently already had access to prisoners in the Turinese jail, since it was previously directed by Antonio Marro, one of his assistants. He hastened to apply for the job of prison doctor, for which he was overqualified, only when Marro moved on to become the director of the mental asylum in Turin.
5 According to Italian law, the bodies of dead prisoners remained the property of the state. Only their material possessions were returned to their families.
6 The *Rivista di discipline carcerarie* (1871–22) was published by the Division of Prisons within the Ministry of the Interior and edited during its first thirty years by Beltani-Scalia.
7 Lombroso was assisted in the statistical section of his book by V. Rossi, whose handwritten tables are reproduced between pp. 272 and 273 (Lombroso 1888).

8 The major exception was Lombroso's advocacy of the death penalty, a position rejected – as he himself admitted – by most other criminal anthropologists (Lombroso 2006, 145).
9 Reformatories for girls were all administered by nuns, who escaped close oversight by the national state and ignored most of the reforms that were implemented in public reformatories for boys.

References

Baima Bollone, P. L. (1992) *Cesare Lombroso ovvero il principio dell'irresponsabilità*. Turin: Società Editrice Internazionale.
Bosco, A. (1903) *La delinquenza in vari stati d'Europa*. Rome: Reale Accademia dei Lincei.
Bulferetti, L. (1975) *Cesare Lombroso*. Turin: UTET.
Colombo, G. (1975) *La scienza infelice: Il museo di antropologia criminale di Cesare Lombroso*. Turin: Boringhieri.
Foucault, M. (1979) *Discipline and Punish: The Birth of the Prison*. New York: Vintage.
Frigessi, D. (2003) *Cesare Lombroso*. Turin: Einaudi.
Gibson, M. (2002) *Born to Crime: Cesare Lombroso and the Origins of Biological Criminology*. Westport CT: Praeger.
Gibson, M. (2011) "Global Perspectives on the Birth of the Prison," *American Historical Review*, 116: 1040–63.
Guarnieri, L. (2000) *L'Atlante criminale: Una scriteriata di Cesare Lombroso*. Milan: Mondadori.
Horn, D. (2003) *The Criminal Body: Lombroso and the AnatoyAnatomy of Deviance*. New York: Routledge.
Leschiutta, P. (1996) *Palimsesti del carcere: Cesare Lombroso e le scritture proibite*. Naples: Liguori.
Levra, U. ed. (1985) *La scienza e la colpa*, Crimini, criminali, criminologi: Un volto dell'Ottocento. Milan: Electa.
Lombroso, C. (1896–7) *L'uomo delinquente in rapporto alla antropologia, alla giurisprudenza ed alla psichiatria*. Turin: Bocca.
Lombroso, C. (1888) *Palimsesti del carcere: Raccolta unicamente destinata agli uomini di scienza*. Turin: Bocca.
Lombroso, C. (2006) *Criminal Man*, Trans. by Mary Gibson and Nicole Hahn Rafter. Durham, N.C.: Duke University Press.
Lombroso, C. and Ferrero, G. (2004) *Criminal Woman, the Prostitute, and the Normal Woman*, Trans. by Nicole Hahn Rafter and Mary Gibson. Durham, N.C.: Duke University Press.
Lombroso-Ferrero, G. (1915) *Cesare Lombroso: Storia della vita e delle opere narrata dalla figlia*. Turin: Bocca.
Marro, A. (1887) *I caratteri dei delinquenti: Studio antropologico-sociologico*. Turin: Bocca.
Montaldo, S. (2009) "Il carcere di Filadelfia," in Silvano Montaldo and Paolo Tappero, *Il museo di antropologia criminale "Cesare Lombroso"*. Turin: UTET, pp. 99–105.
Montaldo, S. and Paolo, T. (2009) *Il museo di antropologia criminale "Cesare Lombroso"*. Turin: UTET.
Le Musée de psychiatrie et d'anthropologie criminelle dans l'Université de Turin (1906) Turin: Bocca.
Neppi Modona, G. (2009) "Quali detenuti per quali reati nel carcere dell'Italia liberale," in Silvano Montaldo and Paolo Tappero, *Cesare Lombroso Cento Anni Dopo*. Turin: UTET, pp. 83–97.
Portigliatti Barbos, M. (1993) "Cesare Lombroso e il Museo di antropologia criminale" pp. 1441–60 in Valerio Castronovo, *Storia illustrata di Torino*. Turin: Elio Sellino.

Velo Dalbrenta, D. (2004) *La scienza inquieta: Saggio sull'antropologia criminale di Cesare Lombroso*. Padua: CEDAM.
Villa, R. (1985) *Il deviante e i suoi segni: Lombroso e la nascita dell'antropologia criminale*. Milan: Franco Angeli.
Wolfgang, M. E. (1972) "Cesare Lombroso, 1835–1909" in Hermann Mannheim, *Pioneers in Criminology*, 2nd Edition. Montclair, NJ: Patterson Smith, pp. 232–91.

3

GLI ANARCHICI AND LOMBROSO'S THEORY OF POLITICAL CRIME

Trevor Calafato

After more than a hundred years of condemnation due to its incoherence, methodological errors and hasty non-empirical opinions, the work of Cesare Lombroso still attracts the attention of numerous intellectuals. Being a prolific writer, in different languages, Lombroso explored various aspects and issues related to numerous criminal characteristics ranging from the physiognomy to the criminal, to medical and social aspects and eventually the spiritual dimension. Amongst these different issues the violence expressed by anarchist actors caught Lombroso's attention and this interest reflected in writings like the *Tre tribuni studiati da un alienista, Il delitto politico, L'uomo di genio, Delitti vecchi e delitti nuovi, Crime: Its Causes and Remedies, The Criminal Man* (5th edition), and the two editions of *Gli Anarchici*. Though these studies were mainly written in Italian, Lombroso published his research on anarchism around the world in different languages, amongst those in English: 'The Physiognomy of the Anarchists', 'Anarchistic Crimes and Their Causes', 'A Study of Luigi Lucheni: Assassin of the Empress of Austria' and 'Some Aspects of Crime'.[1]

Lombroso inquired into *il reo politico* (the political crime) and *il delinquente politico* (the political criminal) in a number of works. Various aspects of the political criminal find reference to *Il Delitto Politico*, an ambitious book that embarked on the exploration of socio-political issues that lured political actors to engage in violent behaviour causing political disruptions envisaging sudden changes in the government administration. With continuous reference to *Il Delitto Politico* amongst other works, in 1894 and 1895 Lombroso published two different editions of *Gli Anarchici* with just a few months in between. In this book, made up of about 150 pages, Lombroso presented theories on the root causes of the political violence expressed by anarchist actors and inquired into the psycho-social factors that encouraged extreme acts of violence such as regicide. In this chapter, I provide an overview of *Gli Anarchici*, covering the different theories expressed by Lombroso; the research methods he used; and his conclusions and recommendations in dealing with, controlling and preventing the occurrence of political violence and terror.

Lombroso's *Gli Anarchici*

The second edition of *Gli Anarchici* includes eleven chapters. This edited version of the first issue included numerous amendments and additional material.[2] In the preface of the first edition (also included in the second edition), Lombroso declared the inspiration to undertake this work, the *Tre Tribuni*, *Antisemitismo* and *Il Delitto Politico*, came from the political parties that divided unified Italy. Lombroso expected that this work would influence the ill will of the anarchist; bring an end to the anarchist dagger challenging the authorities and stop the authorities using capital punishment as an arbiter of criminal justice in political cases.

> *il miglior premio che io possa desiderare, come quello che suggellerà in modo fin troppo sperimentale l'imparzialità del metodo psichiatrico-antropologico applicato alle più ardenti questioni attuali, ch'io ho tentato seguire qui come nelle alter opere, e che vorrei restasse come un faro elevato al di sopra di quelle caduche sempre e spesso ignobilissime preoccupazioni politiche, che il tempo e gli interessi d' un tratto disperdono.*[3]
> (Lombroso 1895, 4)

In September 1894, only two months after the first edition, Lombroso signed the preface of the second edition and explained that on examining the criticism received for the first edition he decided to publish an improved second edition. Amongst the criticism Lombroso wanted to address, he provided his retort to Professor Angelo Majorana, author of the book *Teoria sociologica della costituzione politica* (Sociological theory of the political constitution) who asked 'how and why does a person who in another time and space would be a brigand, a pirate or a good person, is now an anarchist in the worst sense of the word?' (Lombroso 1895, 6). Lombroso explained that the first chapter inquired into the conditions, which societies lived in, surrounded with lies, and economic hitches, which produced delirium. Lombroso explained how the insane and criminals existed in every era but before they became part of antimonarchic insurgent factions, these rebels had been controlled by religion and declared martyrs of crusades and their beliefs. Since 'these altruistic fanatics, especially in the Latin races, arise because they do not find any possible channels to express themselves in their world, find this passage in the social and economic issues' (Lombroso 1895, 8).

Ferrero, Lombroso's co-author and son-in-law, reflected a parallel explanation in the *Idea Liberale* (Liberal Idea), stating 'religion recruits thousands of fanatics, who under diverse theories react feverishly to save human souls from perdition of bad habit'[4] (Lombroso 1895, 8). Ferrero deduced that religion provided activities and venues for recruitment grounds. As a disciplinary institution with strict rules, religion created armies based on obedience and subordination. Lombroso (1895, 8) described religion as a 'lightning conductor of fanaticism'[5] and pointed to the case of Sante Geronimo Caserio as the perfect example of how a religious and disciplined person turned into an active political fanatic and a revolutionary. In this preface, Lombroso considered London as the capital of philanthropic fanatics: movements made of men and women from different social statuses and backgrounds, aimed at curing the social disease of misery life. These rebels wrote journals, made speeches and urged humanitarian reforms rather than instigating political fanaticism resulting in violent behaviours.

Anarchist factions made people believe that their radical movement provided the solution to overcome misery. 'If an energetic fanatic is part of this group and participates in this fight, this individual will be involved with such an intense and extraordinary passion that s/he can bring love or hate to the most extreme consequences' (Lombroso 1895, 11). Extreme behaviour occurred even in religious factions where people turned to be assassins but if an 'epileptic has a predisposition [to extreme violence], this predisposition is magnified thanks to our classical education which makes of violence the most heroic dowry' (Lombroso 1895, 11). Anarchists used these qualities to transform farmers into cold-blooded assassins.

On answering issues raised in the Italian journal *Fanfulla*, Lombroso correlated the inheritance of epilepsy and the disease of pellagra with the possibility that an individual became an extremist. These conditions 'predispose the brains for the most excessive tendencies raising the ordinary feelings to an exponential threshold, concentrating and polarising it in a special direction' (Lombroso 1895, 13) explaining how a farmer becomes a 'violent sectarian' and why punishment should be tailor-made for those involved in anarchism rather than being treated like any other criminal, consequently excluding capital punishment. As a final comment of the preface, Lombroso ridiculed the journalists that got entangled in such a short book and accused the positivists of 'declaring all anarchists epileptics' (Lombroso 1895, 14).

Posizione e cause dell'anarchia

In '*Posizione e cause dell'anarchia*' (The Situation and Causes of Anarchy)[6] Lombroso (1895, 15) encapsulated the social, historical and political issues of decadence and the consequential rise of this anarchist wave with the natural science dictum *multa renascentur quae jam ceciderunt*.[7] The privileged class believed that the rest of the world had their same economic status but intellectuals like 'Tolstoy, Richet, Sergi, Hugo, Zola, Nordau, De Amicis, they will tell you this seems a very sad fin de siècle'[8] (Lombroso 1895, 16). The socio-politico-economic situation, including legislation, favoured the privileged class and ignored the problems of the poor, the majority of the population. Misery lured people to radical campaigns 'fading religious, family, patriotic, church, caste and spiritual ideals in front of our eyes'[9] (Lombroso 1895, 17). The arrogance of the first two Estates (clergy and royalty), experienced in feudalism and hypocrisy of religion, caused the third Estate to react. In Lombroso's eyes the anarchists voiced the protests of those people living in wretchedness. Most of the anarchists were not poor. In fact, Lombroso found that in Paris these actors were employed in a variety of jobs such as journalists, printers, proof readers and propagandists, and amongst the followers there were tailors, shoemakers, labourers in food factories, cabinet makers, barbers, mechanics, masons and professions like architects and stockbrokers (Lombroso 1895).

A violent approach was alluring because it was glorified from classical history (for example, Aristogeiton and Brutus)[10] to the *Risorgimento*, a few decades before the publication of this work. In support of this theory, Lombroso echoed Ferrero's *Riforma Sociale* (Social Reform) (1894) and mentioned a poet, described as a representative of the morals of the new united Italy, who wrote:

> *Ferro e vino voglio io* ... (Iron and wine I want)
>
> *Il ferro per uccidere i tranni*, (Iron to kill the tryants)
>
> *Il vino per celebarne il funeral* (Wine to celebrate their funerals).
>
> (Lombroso 1895, 23)

Violent behaviour was so much ingrained in Italian culture in the late nineteenth century that it won praise for being an appropriate response to conditions. For instance, the clerics praised the stabbings of Ravaillac; the conservatives eulogised the mass shooting of the communards and the republicans lauded the bombings of Orsini. Lombroso considered it normal that violence cropped up from time to time when society was imbibed with violence and considered it 'sacred'. Inspired by Machiavelli, Lombroso stressed that violence, dishonesty and profiteering could be the seeds of destruction in the Italian Government but this did not justify the use of violence. In fact, Lombroso (1895, 23) stated '*la violenza è sempre immorale, anche quando è rivolta a respingere la violenza*'.[11]

Anarchist political ideologies

Condemning the *modus operandi* of anarchist did not hinder Lombroso from discussing some anarchist ideas under the caption '*Idee giuste di alcuni anarchici*' (Good Ideas of Some Anarchists). The veil of despotism in Italy after the unification set the context for protests against the government as exposed by anarchist theoreticians Francesco Saverio Merlino and Peter Kropotkin. Discontentment and frustration were expressed only through violence and the government either used brutal force or reduced the means of subsistence to control and deter. With such political power, Lombroso (1895, 27) deduced that 'a police force that has no crimes to investigate and no criminals to arrest, will invent crimes and criminals, or the police will cease to exist'.[12] Later on, French sociologist Emile Durkheim (1964) stated that in a 'society of saints' where if there would be no form of crime:

> Faults which appear venial to the layman will create there the same scandal that the ordinary offense does in ordinary consciousness. If, then, this society has the power to judge and punish, it will define these acts as criminal and will treat them as such.
>
> (Durkheim 1964, 100)

Consequently, governments created laws and were empowered to use force so that people respected these regulations. On getting accustomed to these laws and the imposed limitations, the government controlled intelligence and free will making people believe that they lived thanks to such restrains. Such tactics meant many people feared any change: workers believed they could not live without their masters and revolutions against the government and the prevailing classes would determine their existence. The most comprehensible ideological theories of anarchists concluded that 'all extrinsic impediments imposed by society or intrinsic moral hurdles should be considered fictitious and that are the cause of our unhappiness and sorrow'[13] (Lombroso 1895, 30).

Lombroso criticised the anarchist ideologies for failing to deliver a viable political programme: very few aimed at attainable objectives since they merely aspired to create a kind of utopia. Lombroso (1895, 32) criticised Kropotkin's principles that 'people should be left free to organise themselves jumping on a heap, like a pack of wolves over a prey'[14] as this lead to crime. Lombroso considered anarchist ideology that is detached from reality as irrelevant and inapplicable. He was convinced that any social reform should take place at a slow pace so that no antecedent work would be destroyed or reduce the force of counter-forces of new thoughts, which Lombroso called *misoneismo* (misoneism). Violence against the established old order is perceived as a crime as it hurts the views of the majority of the people, what Durkheim called the 'collective conscience or representation'. Lombroso (1890a, 435) described the political crime as a 'violent act that breaks the law constituted to maintain and respect the political, social, economic, which it sought by the majority'.[15]

Lombroso gave misoneism a prominent place in his study of the anarchists and dedicated a chapter on the matter called '*Neophilia*'.[16] Lombroso (1895, 33) proposed that 'misoneism reigns over everyone and everywhere, in customs and in religion, in morality and science, in art and politics'.[17] Even geniuses, he said, fight for their ideas and resist change. Echoing English sociologist Herbert Spencer, Lombroso expressed that any progress is an obstacle for the progress to come and some actors resort to aggressive means to impose their evolutionary reforms. However, this perspective varies according to who is the actor of the violent attack. 'An act is considered antisocial, or a crime, only when it is committed by the minority. When the majority of the people approve it, such actions become normal'[18] (Lombroso 1895, 34). Decades later this was translated in the famous aphorism 'one man's terrorist is another man's freedom fighter'. Political crime become unpopular when innocent victims suffer assassinations and consequently repel the faction rather than luring new recruits to join their 'just cause'.

'*La rivoluzione è l'espressione storica dell'evoluzione*',[19] Lombroso (1895, 35) wrote: a gradual revolutionary movement led by a mastermind, rather than a born criminal guarantees success. This evolution through revolution was considered a natural process for the progress of humankind, similar to the turbulent, yet inevitable period of adolescence. Lombroso considered this metamorphosis an important step for better living and distinguished revolution from seditions where 'criminals and madmen are involved because of their morbidity and pathology'[20] (Lombroso 1895, 36), and committed criminal acts that did not influence the dominant ideologies.

Criminality in anarchists

Physiognomy, jargon, tattoos and lyrics were criminal traits Lombroso found in *L'Uomo Delinquente* and reflected in the study of anarchist political actors. Lombroso speculated that anarchists were either criminals or lunatics or sometimes both, though there were exceptions like Henrik Ibsen, Élisée Reclus and Pyotr Alexeyevich Kropotkin. Starting from physiognomy, Lombroso indicated that revolutionaries like Corday, Mirabeau, Cavour and the nihilists such as Ossinski and Michailoff[21] had normal physiological features, sometimes even more beautiful than the normal type. In support of this argument, Lombroso (1895, 37) quoted Spingardi, an esteemed lawyer, who stated 'I never saw an anarchist who was not debilitated or lame or hunchback or without an asymmetric face'.[22] Moreover, Lombroso gathered the percentages of criminal type actors found in the different anarchist groups around the world, which were as follows: 31 per cent of the 41 anarchists in Paris; 40 per cent of the 43 anarchists in Chicago; 34 per cent of the 100 anarchists in Turin. From 320 revolutionaries the criminal type was reduced to 0.57 per cent less than the norm (2 per cent) and 6.7 per cent of the Russian nihilists. As was his frequent habit, Lombroso never specified the methodology used in acquiring these percentages.

In the article 'The Physiognomy of the Anarchists' (1890b), Lombroso highlighted the differences between the political criminal and the born criminal. Such an investigation into the anarchists should 'furnish us with the juridical basis of political crime', a basis the jurists failed to consider or acknowledge (Lombroso 1890b, 25). Referring to *Il Delitto Politico*, Lombroso indicated that initiators and leaders of revolutionary movements had great scientific intellect; Garibaldi, Mazzini and Pisacane had managed to excite and bring about true progress in humanity. In contrast, he found 'anarchists of Turin and of Chicago are frequently of the criminal type' and presented more violent characteristics and hereditary traits than other criminals or the insane (Lombroso 1890b, 28). Anarchists were not true or common criminals because they were attracted to novelty. In consequence, Lombroso (1890b, 30) limned them as 'innovators [and] apostles of progress' that revolted against the surrounding misery. Lombroso considered these extreme political actors more valuable than law-abiding individuals as they examined and questioned the system, found weak points and contributed to improve it.

In addition to the physiognomic aspect, Lombroso (1895) examined the jargon and lyrics used by anarchists and, like criminals, they had a particular jargon such as *copain* instead of *compagnons* (comrade). Other similarities with born criminals had been witnessed in anarchist movements in London where the actors had tattoos of hearts, skulls, crossed bones, anchors amongst others. Lombroso also said that the absence of moral or ethical sense facilitated assassinations and bombings of innocents from the bourgeois class. Ravachol[23] and Pini embodied 'the most comprehensive type of born criminal'[24] (Lombroso 1895, 42). He made deductions from facial characteristics, their criminal acts, the pleasure in evil-doings, and deficiency in the ethical sense together with the hatred of the family and human life. He considered Ravachol as case of degeneration, indicating a morbid inheritance from his grandfather Koenigstein and his great-grandfather, both of whom had been hanged for arson and brigandage. Pini never boasted of his infamy despite being, at 37 years of age, one of the anarchist heads in Paris. However, Pini considered stealing thousands of pounds from the bourgeoisie 'a legitimate expropriation of the expropriated'[25] (Lombroso 1895, 44).

Criminality marked politics in different epochs. Some examples of how criminality helped to change politics were the following: in Greece, the Clephts (thieves in peace time) helped their country to obtain independence; in 1860, when the Pope and the Bourbons joined forces against the party and national army; and in Sicily when the mafia joined Garibaldi (Lombroso 1895).

Mental illnesses and indirect suicides[26]

Apart from physiognomic anomalies Lombroso inquired into particular mental anomalies in anarchists like epilepsy and hysteria,[27] insanity,[28] mattoids[29] and indirect suicides.[30] Theorising that congenital criminal traits of *epilepsy* and *political hysteria*[31] affect anarchist actors, Lombroso (1895) listed vanity, religiosity, hallucinations, megalomania and intermittent geniality as fundamental traits of an innovative person. Muhammad and Felico[32] (Felix) portrayed some, if not all, of these traits.

Gori (a lawyer) identified a kind of anarchist called the *bisognisti*[33] (the 'needists'). The *bisognisti* felt the 'need to steal or kill and claim their actions as legitimate and *needed* [sic] to be done'[34] (Lombroso 1895, 54). According to Lombroso, examples of the *bisognisti* were Caserio (to be discussed shortly), Salvador and Ignazio. Santiago Salvador, a Spanish anarchist who killed about twenty people with a bomb, confessed 'I was dominated by a force that drove me for a desire that I could not repress'[35] (Lombroso 1895, 54). Monges Ignazio suffered epileptic fits after he fell and hit his head, and decided to kill general Rocha without any premeditation or preconceived criminal idea (Lombroso 1890a, 304).

Auguste Vaillant was an example of what Lombroso referred to as hysteric. Vaillant did not present physiognomic features that recalled the born criminal like Pini or Ravachol but was *'un vero fanatico appassionato'*[36] (Lombroso 1895, 53). According to Lombroso, three distinctive bases of fanaticism were: congenital traits from degenerate parents; unhappiness of life through social issues and misery; and education. The anarchist personality of Valliant was the combination of the education provided by priests and fanatic socialists, together with vanity and exaggerated altruism. Lombroso (1895, 53) quotes Vaillant (in French) stating

> society forced me to do it. I found myself in a miserable state. I was hungry. I regret only one thing: my mockery. But it doesn't matter, I am happy, it is good I'll go under the guillotine; I will start again in about eight days.[37]

In this case Lombroso also showed the importance of the press. Vaillant attacked the French Chamber of Deputies in 1893 to revenge the execution of Ravachol.

He took photos of himself in front of the building before the explosion and distributed these for publication in newspapers and journals. As a result of this event the French authorities issued the *lois scélérates* ('villainous laws') which restricted the freedom of press aiming to mitigate the anarchist 'propaganda by deed'. It was the execution of Vaillant that instigated the actions of Émile Henry and Caserio.

Pazzi politici (insane politicians) were anarchist political actors that acted alone and targeted government representatives. 'Most of the time, these people are an echo of the unworthy struggles between the parties on the political or religious conditions of the times'[38] (Lombroso 1895, 55). Religious fanaticism was one of the main catalysts that instigated François Ravaillac in murdering Henry IV, though Ravaillac suffered from delusions of persecution. Similar cases of regicides or attempted regicides were recorded in England; for instance, Margaret Nicholson assaulted the king and Mooney was an Irishman involved in the London bombings. Lombroso declared these individuals to be mad or insane.

Mattoids[39] appeared during revolutions and insurgences and did not have any physiognomic or intelligence anomalies. Lombroso reasoned that mattoids were remarkably cunning and possessed various abilities, as some of them become physicians, parliamentarians, military leaders and teachers. Amongst these characters Lombroso identified Passanante who was a cook and became a policy-maker. One of the distinguishing marks of mattoids was prolific writing. Passanante used reams of paper because publications were the priority in his life. Lombroso specified that in their writings and speeches mattoids projected their exaggerated ideas.

Criminal acts committed by mattoids 'express less evil and minor energies when compared to those committed by born criminals, as they completely lack the practice and the evil shrewdness'[40] (Lombroso 1895, 61). They committed their criminal acts in public with a pretext of public righteousness; they did not show premeditation or create an alibi; they did not have accomplices. Rather than explosives, they used non-lethal methods of attack, such as kitchen knives, stones or boxes with harmless liquid. The major significance of their actions was that they had been reported in prominent newspapers. Lombroso reasoned that though having a moral sense mattoids did not feel guilty for their criminal acts and boasted about their actions believing they did something to help humankind. According to Lombroso, mattoids like Passanante were frequently writers in anarchists' manuscripts and journals.

Indirect suicides was another theory Lombroso incorporated in examining political crimes. Assassinations or attempted killings of heads of state had been punished with capital punishment. Lombroso theorised that the assassins committed these acts because they did not have the courage to take their own lives, even though they had been thinking of suicide. This theory echoed the theories of European psychologists, specifically Maudsley, Esquirol and Krafft-Ebing, who detected an indirect suicide in the death of Karl Nobiling. Nobiling shot at the emperor in 1878 and then tried to commit suicide with the same weapon. Lombroso identified degenerative traits, even though Nobiling had acquired a university degree in philosophy and published a booklet concerned with improvement of the rural

FIGURE 3.1 A photo sent by the Queen of Romania, Carmen Sylva, to Lombroso when researching latent suicide

Source: Lombroso 1895, 75.

economy. On similar lines, Frattini threw a bomb in a square and injured a number of people to protest against the feudal status quo. In court, Frattini did not care any more about his freedom or life and stated 'indeed taking it [his life] (*sic*) would be the greatest benefit for me'[41] (Lombroso 1895, 67).

Further, Lombroso pointed out the research of the Queen of Romania, Carmen Sylva, who investigated the latent suicide issue in political assassinations. The example brought from this researcher described a 30-year-old man who attempted to kill the king by shooting from the street through the lit windows. During the search of his room there were photographs of him armed like a bandit, and one portrayed him in the act of committing suicide while being stopped by his lover (see Figure 3.1). Suicide ambitions and the attempt on monarchs could be elucidated as an indirect suicide and Lombroso believed Henry, Vaillant and Caserio portrayed this attitude.

Crimes of passion and indoctrination

Lombroso dealt extensively with crimes of passion, a topic that comprises the lengthiest chapter of this book. Nowadays, crimes of passion are associated particularly with criminal acts of aggression and violence in conjunction with jealousy or heartbreak. Lombroso associated crimes of passion not only with adultery but also with the fanatic political ideals that included economic and social issues which evolved violent urges into criminal acts. Lombroso described criminals of passion as the antithesis of the born criminal. Physiognomically, these political actors[42] were beautiful and had a peaceful look, similar to nihilists and Sante Geronimo di Caserio (see Figure 3.2).

Lombroso's profile of anarchists indicated females as more prominent in these kinds of crimes especially those aged between 18 and 25 years. Quoting Desmarets (1833), Lombroso indicated that the Napoleonic police watched vigilantly youths aged between 18 and 20 years as their enthusiasm and altruism was considered an illness. Accomplices rarely accompanied the actors, and their political fanaticism was believed to be congenital. Lombroso also declared that anarchists exaggerated their honesty, for instance, French revolutionary Charlotte Corday.

Corday was a representation of the honest woman. She studied Plutarch, Montesquieu and Rousseau but also assassinated Jacobin Jean Paul Marat. When questioned about the killing she answered, 'anger, (indication of the violent passion), inflated my heart and taught me the way to pierce his heart'[43] (Duchess d'Abrantés 1838 cited in Lombroso 1895, 71). Dostoyevsky impersonated anarchist

FIGURE 3.2 Lombroso's portrait of Sante Geronimo di Caserio
Source: Lombroso 1895, 75.

figures in the characters of his novels who considered 'suffering a good thing' (Lombroso 1895). These characters transmitted the idea that pain is sweeter if suffered for an ideal. Devotion expressed by nihilists and the Christian martyrs influenced the ideologies and the inclination for martyrdom. In an improvised speech, one of the 50 nihilists accused in Saint Petersburg stated:

> *Ma per quanto io sia colpevole, voi, giudici, contro me siete impotenti; sì, io sono inaccessibile a qualunque pena, perchè io ho una fede, che voi non avete, nel trionfo delle mie idee. Voi potete condannarmi a vita, ma il mio male, come voi vedete, mi renderà corta la pena. Io morrò, pieno il cuore di questo grande amore, e gli stessi carnefici, buttando a terra la chiave del carcere, scoppieranno in singhiozzi, pregando al mio capezzale.*[44]
>
> (Lombroso 1895, 72)

Martyrdom was alluring and made political actors believe more in their cause and ideology. Through the French philosopher Rénan, Lombroso showed that suffering for a cause can make people believe that martyrdom is the way to realise their beliefs. The Bab's martyrdom in Persia was still a popular argument in Tehran years[45] after its commission: 'Though years have passed by, one can notice that feelings of admiration and horror are still attached to these mishaps when people speak of it'[46] (Lombroso 1895, 73). Crimes of passion became so strong that actors revealed themselves to be fearless of torture and execution. This distinguished the outlook of the criminal of passion from the born criminal's indifference towards life. Lombroso highlighted that some anarchist actors never had a criminal record but a *nevrosi ereditaria*[47] that facilitated the escalation of fanaticism and pure passion for their ideals.

Lombroso described Caserio's family as poor, but his father was a peasant and a boatman, sustaining an acceptable standard of living. The father suffered from epilepsy after he was arrested by Austrian soldiers for smuggling goods. In the region where Caserio's family lived people suffered from pellagra[48] and 'the proletariat standard of living was worse than that of Roman slaves'[49] (Lombroso 1895, 78). Lombroso described Caserio as having a gentle and kind look with a beautifully shaped skull and body and that he never had criminal tendencies apart from those vented by politics. Caserio's brother revealed 'his [Caserio's] dream was to enter the seminary and become a priest, an apostle. He would be angry if his friends stole an apple from the fields'[50] (Lombroso 1895, 76).

Caserio was interested in reading and discussion rather than getting drunk, womanising or gambling. The vocation towards anarchism grew after Caserio received '*i germi dell'anarchismo*'[51] from a workmate (Lombroso 1895, 76). On becoming a fervent anarchist, Caserio read books and papers on anarchy and promulgated anarchist teachings amongst the loutish peasantry. He did not disclose this interest to his employer or his family, except for his brother who reprimanded him before ending their relations. Caserio was arrested for distributing anarchist leaflets and in court acknowledged affiliation and being active in anarchism.

Initially, Caserio manifested extreme fanaticism in religion and later on in politics. In small villages away from the centre and modern influences, the first fanaticisms could only be religious because farmers did not have other ideals apart from religion; for example, Henry, Vaillant and Faure. Caserio could have opted to stay away from this reality as his family had better living conditions but he did not want to turn his back on the suffering of his peers. Caserio became an anarchist but never showed characteristics found in the born criminal. Lombroso compared Caserio's behaviour as reported in the newspapers with the prisoners conducts recorded in the *Prison Palimpsests*.[52] Contrary to indifference to pain of others and their own of born criminals, Caserio wanted to escape his execution and appeared trembling and cried like anyone facing a premature death. However, Caserio's ideology was strong enough to overcome fear; true to type, he did not confess, repent or mention any accomplices.

Lombroso methodically examined Caserio's handwriting, and from this refuted the claim, made by a priest, that Caserio was a proud person. Caserio showed affection towards his family, especially his mother, and when sentenced to death he wrote her a letter.[53] In a few lines, Caserio justified his deed as he was tired of living in a dreadful world where people cannot find work and children ask for bread that they cannot have. Caserio witnessed lot of suffering in life. He occupied a world in which his 8-year-old niece worked fifteen hours a day, and peasants died of pellagra, while the elite lived in luxury. These experiences drew him to the anarchist ideology. A journalist of *Tribuna* (1 August 1894) reported that when Gori, Caserio's lawyer, had asked his client if he had sexual relations, the answer was 'before yes I had, but from when I married the idea I did not frequent more women'[54] (Lombroso 1895, 142). This behaviour distinguished Caserio's genuine anarchist character even from criminal-anarchists like Vaillant who was in a relationship with his friend's wife.

Caserio was a special case for Lombroso that led to inquire whether the punishment given fitted the political crime. The intensity of the punishment for a political crime varied according to the context, and in the case of Caserio, the assassination of the President was considered an outrageous act that evoked the execution of capital punishment. Lombroso disagreed with capital punishment for Caserio because the man was a religious fanatic who had lived in circumstances that lured him to become a fanatic anarchist. Lombroso was convinced that Caserio's ideology could have been moulded into something positive. He could have been rehabilitated because he was not a born criminal; his social background was not veiled by fanaticism and he was still young. Hence the capital punishment of Caserio was less justified than that of Pini and Ravachol. But 'if justice is not a sentence in proportion to a demerit but varies to the satisfaction of the public, even if this is less fair [sic], then Caserio could not be spared from the death sentence'[55] (Lombroso 1895, 143).

Caserio enticed Lombroso to inquire how indoctrination can make a law-abiding person a fanatic and extremist of an ideology. Lombroso (1895, 79) recalled the assassins of the Old Man of the Mountain[56] who with single-minded ideologies rushed with an overwhelming momentum to obtain the perceived goal without thinking of the probable obstacles. Epilepsy stimulated the indoctrination of ideologies and contributed to a mania leading to politically aimed violent acts. Anarchism used the epileptic nature of the calm Caserio and turned him into an assassin (Lombroso 1895). Lombroso also associated hyperesthesia and hypermnesia to explain this shift in attitude. Hyperesthesia is excessive sensitivity for the sufferings of others, while hypermnesia is an exceptional vivid memory associated with mental illness that explains the outstanding clear mind while committing a cold-blooded assassination. Lombroso projected these medical issues on Caserio assassination and stated:

> a few moments before the hour of the murder, which he believed to be his last hour as well, in cold blood he continued to observe accurately and collected any information that might suit him in committing the crime. He even thought how to cross the street because in official processions the important persons sit on the right of the carriage.
>
> This is the single-minded fanatic and such were the messages of the Old Man of the Mountain. The only difference is that his old man was Bakounin and the mission from which he would gain his ticket to paradise was the elimination of the ... alleged tyrant!![57]
>
> (Lombroso 1895, 83)

Altruism and other characteristics

Exaggerated altruism was associated with the personality of extremist political actors both by Lombroso (1895) and by more concurrent recent researchers. Militants of extreme political violence and terrorist actors were said to follow goals of which their surrounding society should be the beneficiary, foreshadowing the modern terrorist.[58] Lombroso dedicated a chapter[59] on altruism, contrasting the selfishness of the ordinary criminal (*delinquente nato*) and the anarchist political criminal found in Vaillant, Henry and Caserio. As examples, Lombroso mentioned Galileo Palla, Sergei Spetniak[60] and Augustin Frederic Hamon. Hamon wrote 'interviewing the unfortunate people in hospital, had a fearsome effect on me; I comprehended the need of solidarity and became an anarchist'[61] (Lombroso 1895, 87), portraying exaggerated altruism and morbid sensitivity for the troubles of others (Lombroso 1895).

Radical altruism was expressed in the speeches of anarchists in the court following the announcement of their executions. Lombroso considered these verbal communications the product of pure enthusiasm and believed that fanaticism made even the most ignorant and uneducated man an orator like Ravachol. In *Gli Anarchici* Lombroso included substantial parts of the speeches of Ravachol and Henry. Ravachol blamed society for his criminal acts as individuals had to compete against each other and wrongdoings were the only option to survive. Facing all this misery around him, Ravachol stated (in 1892) 'I preferred to make myself a trafficker in contraband, a counterfeiter, a murderer and assassin. I could have begged, but it's degrading and cowardly, and even punished by your laws, which make poverty a crime'[62] (Lombroso 1895, 89). Ravachol claimed that the jury used the death penalty to secure a safe society rather than improve policies to reduce poverty. This lack of control over misery and poverty led to crime and without appropriate precautions 'there will always be criminals, because today you destroy one, but tomorrow ten will be born'[63] (Lombroso 1895, 90).

The political passion expressed by Ravachol justified criminal acts exposing traits of the born criminal. On the contrary, Henry (1894) recognised his responsibility in the bombings. Henry explained, 'I was told that life was easy and that it was wide open to those who were intelligent and energetic'[64] but reality disproved this belief (Lombroso 1895, 92). Inequalities in social institutions and social misery drew Henry at first to socialism, but the inefficiency of this movement made Henry embrace anarchism and 'the voice of dynamite' (Henry 1894). The rationale behind the bombs at the Carmaux and the Café Terminus was to hit the bourgeois classes or if the police found the explosive, the police station. Police and other institutions including the newspapers, defended bourgeois interests, while 'the anarchist, was no longer a human but a ferocious animal that had to be exterminated'[65] (Lombroso 1895, 93). This annihilation entailed seizing anarchist publications, abrogating the right to meet and employing different capital punishments in Europe and the Americas. However, it is difficult to destroy anarchy because as Henry said it 'is born in the heart of a rotting and deteriorating society'[66] (Lombroso 1895, 94).

Vengeance for the suffered injustices is another aggravation.[67] Going back to primeval instincts, vengeance is the right to do justice. Lombroso believed that classical education contributed in this appraisal of bloodthirsty political assassins. He theorised that when fanaticism was engaged with cruelty the result was a ferocious born criminal. '[T]he more bizarre and absurd an idea is, the more mad, mattoids and hysterics will it drag behind it',[68] luring fanatics from religion and politics (Lombroso 1895, 98). Lombroso concluded that the political criminals killed for a just cause and demanded vengeance every time that the *lex talionis* is applied against them. Considering this mentality and unstable psychology of the political criminal, Lombroso recommended that authorities should consider these issues when creating new policies that mitigate these violent acts.

Other influences

Recalling the elaborate work of *Il Delitto Politico*, Lombroso correlated the number of recorded revolts to particular issues, for instance meteorological, geographical, ethnical and economic matters. The number of revolts and related crimes was higher in the hot season. As shown in Figure 3.3, Lombroso deduced that an upsurge of violence was predominant in the month of July in a number of European countries particularly those countries found in the south.

Lombroso mapped (Figure 3.4) the correlation between geography and climate influences with the riots in Europe between 1791 and 1880. This highlighted the increase in seditions according to the heat and the number of revolutions

	Evo antico	Evo medio	Evo moderno America	Europa (2)
Primavera	31	14	76	142
Estate	44	28	92	167
Autunno	20	18	54	94
Inverno	20	16	61	92

(1) Vedi *Il delitto politico e le rivoluzioni*, di LOMBROSO e LASCHI, Parte I, 1890.

(2)	Spagna	Italia	Portogallo	Turchia d'Europa	Grecia	Francia	Belgio e Paesi Bassi	Svizzera	Bosnia, Erz., Serbia e Bulg.	Irlanda	Inghilterra e Scozia	Germania	Austria-Ungheria	Svezia, Norv. e Danimarca	Polonia	Russia d'Europa
Primavera	23	27	7	9	6	16	7	6	7	6	5	7	3	4	6	3
Estate	38	29	12	11	7	20	8	5	3	3	9	11	6	4	1	0
Autunno	18	14	4	5	3	15	6	3	1	3	5	4	7	2	2	2
Inverno	20	18	6	3	3	10	2	10	4	3	4	3	2	2	1	1

FIGURE 3.3 Lombroso's correlations between the different seasons and the upsurge of political violence in different epochs and countries

Source: Lombroso 1890a, 49; Lombroso 1895, 104.

per 10 million. In this inquiry Lombroso separated Italy in three regions pointing that the southern of Italy had almost five times more revolutions than the north. Lombroso indicated difficulties in recovering data from Switzerland and Ireland.[69]

Lombroso theorised that people living on mountains tend to be more rebellious and progressive than others like the Tibetans and the Afghan Yusuf. Other geographical points, for instance valleys, converge various populations in the same place while accumulating different moral, political and industrial needs together. Such concoctions of diverse ethnic groups form assemblies of innovative and revolutionary liberal ideologies that fuel revolt machinations. Lombroso linked ethnic groups to networks that found progressive groups recalling the evolutionary process of Charles Darwin and George Romanes.

Apart from the socio-evolutionary aspects, Lombroso observed the bad administration of governments. Citing Machiavelli and Benjamin Franklin, Lombroso explained how government mismanagement is another potential catalyst of violent political actions. Machiavelli stressed 'a Government that neglects the public welfare and persecutes the honest people, becomes the cause of revolts and revolutions. Persecutions mutate ideas into feelings'[70] (Lombroso 1895, 111); while Franklin's script 'Rules by which a great empire may be reduced to a small one', presumed that the main causes of government mismanagement brought seditions in America because troops provoked the crowds in revolts using bullets and bayonets (Lombroso 1895). According to Lombroso, political reforms reduce the number of riots if they fulfil people's aspirations and desires. For instance, the unification of Italy marked undeniable progress but did not take into consideration the customs of the different regions as explored in *Tre Tribuni* (1887) and *Troppo Presto* (1888b).

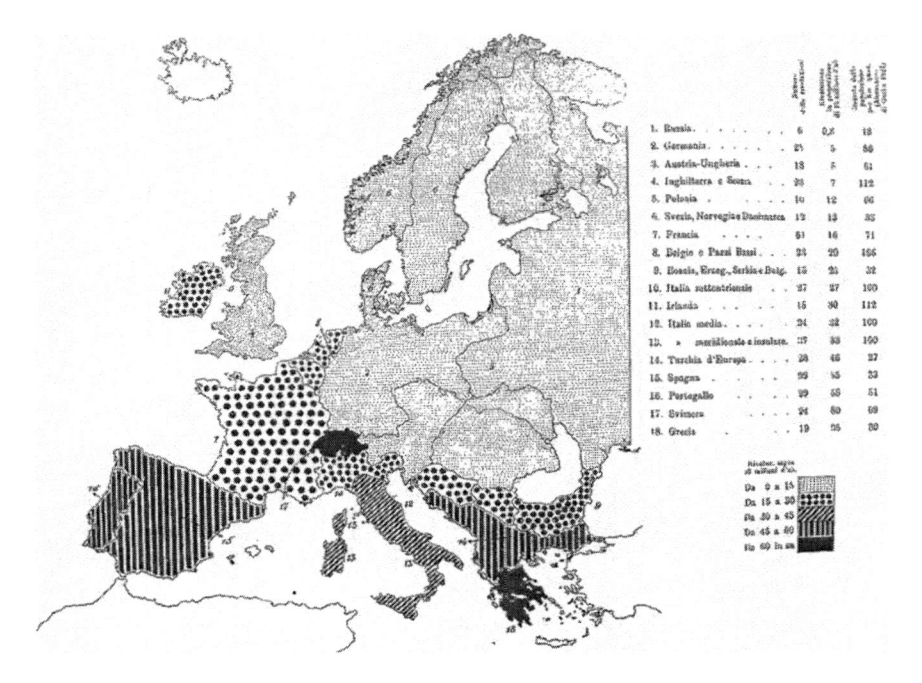

FIGURE 3.4 Lombroso's mapping of the increase in seditions and revolutions in relation to the hot temperatures in Europe between 1791 and 1880

Source: Lombroso 1890a; Lombroso 1895.

Preventions and recommendations

After exploring various traits of the political criminal aiming at a better comprehension of the roots of the anarchist ideology, Lombroso outlined a number of policies to control this phenomenon. Energetic reactions were ineffective against anarchists causing serious repercussions. Considering most anarchist actors insane while being extremely altruist, Lombroso suggested, rather than prison or being given the death sentence, they had to be cured in asylums.

Capital punishment was rendering a service to anarchist actors that aimed for indirect suicide (Lombroso 1895). Lombroso's colleague Enrico Ferri (1894) identified inadequate education and excessive feelings as causes of opportunity crimes, crimes of passion, and for this reason, such crimes should be excluded from capital punishment. In this document, Ferri also considered the relative young age of the actors. The death sentence increased the praise of violent actors and Lombroso (1895) believed that by avoiding capital punishment, the government would smother the idea of martyrdom. The outcome of the extreme stances of Spain and France against anarchists produced a crescendo in the attacks. England and Switzerland repudiated violent penalties against political criminals and anarchists, and hampered these extremist factions without extravagant damages. Harshness acclaimed more fanaticism and portrayed actors like Ravachol as a god or demigod inspiring sympathisers to sing hymns like *la Ravachole*.

Martyrs incited the fantasies of delusional fanatics attracted to martyrdom to express their political choices while showing the vigour of their political dogma (Ferrero 1894). For instance, after Vaillant was executed, he became a martyr; legends about him lured more sympathisers. Lombroso (1895, 116) compared this phenomenon with an 'anarchist hydra'[71] because when heads are cut new ones emerge.[72] Through time, anarchism passed through a purification process and rather than attracting the criminal type, like Ravachol, anarchism allured more law-abiding militants, like Caserio. Lombroso (1895, 116) maintained that 'anarchy used to recruit its heroes among prison candidates, but now heroes are recruited among honest individuals'.[73]

Lombroso also recorded changes in the *modus operandi*, passing from the anonymous commission of a crime to a cold-blooded bartering of the actor's life with that of the target. Ravachol placed the bombs leaving enough time to flee and tried not to be easily identified. On the contrary, Vaillant and Henry did not attempt to escape or shield their identities. Lombroso's theory was that these changes are a natural process and the result of the continuous persecution of anarchism. His rationale was that when politics and personal morality end up in conflict people react violently. Born criminals are the first to react violently as honest individuals are reluctant to respond with such ferociousness. However, the extreme reactions of authorities aiming at the extermination of every anarchist actor and publication vented rage and martyrdom also in honest individuals. Adopting a fanatic and passionate approach, honest individuals conveyed extreme altruism, solidarity and indifference in their criminal acts without fleeing or safeguarding themselves. This explained the attempts to assassinate Italian Prime Minister Francesco Crispi, who permitted the employment of violent methods against political actors while numerous politicians like Depretis, Cavour and Gladstone were never targeted or in any danger. The government is a powerful, rich and educated institution that should set an example of calm and reasonable decision-making. Employing the guillotine haphazardly created martyrs and urged the spirit of struggle and resistance in factions. The outcome was a vicious cycle of violence where the government blamed the anarchists and in turn the anarchists blamed the government and the upper classes.

Considering these distinctive traits of the political criminal from the born criminal, Lombroso proposed punishments that fit the circumstances of every individual case. This section of *Gli Anarchici* refers to the recommendations found in *Il delitto politico* where Lombroso (1890a, 459–461) proposed twelve punishments to repress these political crimes:

1. In case of murder or serious injury of the head of state of Italy or abroad, as a political offence, the punishment should be deportation or confinement, and should be isolated from common criminals. The duration of such penalty should be the same, as that for a common murder or injury.

2. For treason and espionage the punishment should be deportation and confinement without a determined period.
3. For insurgencies and the formation of armed gangs against the government, religion or social force, the penalty should be deportation and confinement. Leaders or instigators of factions should be punished for an indeterminate period.
4. In case of executive acts or conspiracies of criminal directed against the political, social or religious forms of the State, that do not enter the above mentioned categories and the punishment should be an indefinite exile period.
5. For simple injuries of a head of State, the punishment is imprisonment with solitary confinement for a specific period.
6. The same punishment applies for those who participate in insurrections or armed revolts but did not command or instigate the attack. Those who desist as soon as the revolt has begun should be exempted from punishment. Minors should have a lower penalty, while complete drunkenness not for the purpose of criminal conspiracy should reduce responsibility. In case the motive was profit, a fine should be applied pro rata to the assets of the guilty and the loss of political rights. Public officers should be suspended from their office.
7. If state secrets or issues on the government administration are revealed to the public, the punishment should include the loss of the office, revocable pecuniary punishments.
8. Insults to the King and Parliament, through the press, are often a safety valve of the public opinion especially when expressed by men of talent who intend to help the State by revealing the weaknesses. In cases these publications were prompted by personal grievances or depressed feelings, pecuniary penalties should be enough. As for a verbal offence, a mild pecuniary penalty should be enough.
9. The offences of religions that occur in religious practices and rituals should be punished in barbarian countries (colonies), but this cannot take place in civilized countries, except when religion comprises a serious threat to the integrity and the peace of the country.
10. Strikes are allowed only if not armed, punishing only disorders and injuries as common crimes.
11. If parliamentary Deputies committed common crimes, they shall be punished as anyone else. Only after a special request parliamentary offence should go to a parliamentary prison, as happens for the military.
12. Finally, if political crimes attack the freedom to vote should be punished by a fine and temporary suspension from office and political rights.

In *Gli Anarchici*, Lombroso discussed that the punishment of political criminal, excluding the insane and the born criminals, should be temporary and revocable every five years after a parliamentary vote and the public opinion changes stripping them of their criminal nature. The positivist school opposed trials by jury for common crimes except for political crimes because a jury represents the general public. Other regulations, like the French *lois scélérate*, aimed at controlling the freedom of press, but since the anarchists pamphlets arrived from abroad, this law did not deter anarchist publishers and activists. Lombroso advocated greater freedom of speech as writing and printing distracted anarchists and minimised sensational violent attacks. Lombroso (1895, 123) described the press as 'the Proteus of modern life'.[74]

According to Lombroso (1895), the anarchists did not have a hub to target. This made the enactment of international laws futile and made it difficult for police to arrest such dangerous political actors. Government administration varied in every country, and countries enforcing milder laws and following a good administration were less likely to be affected by anarchists. Such countries avoided association with countries that implemented draconian laws to avoid the risk of becoming the target of political insurgents. Lombroso encouraged collaboration between different countries to hinder anarchism through non-violent methods such as: taking photographs of militants; reporting the whereabouts of dangerous persons; and sending anarchist epileptics and mattoids into asylums. Transportation was to be used against the most dangerous individuals.

Superior civilisations or societies managed to control violence without engaging in violent tactics (Lombroso 1895). Lombroso perceived that the English government, administered by Gladstone, was a good example of how reforms heal ethnical, social and economics wounds. The English government trusted the moral strength of the people and did not use aggressive methods to suppress hostilities. Lombroso insisted that this example of treating the extremist anarchist ideology should be reflected in all Europe. More opportune preventive measures should address the social aspect rather than the individual. Lombroso aspired to cure the malaise of anarchism from its roots to control the facilitators that create a fertile ground for this ideology. Thus, where violence is praised in classical education, it should be replaced with science and languages.

Lombroso suggested that to eradicate political, religious and economic fanaticism and related violent actions, it was necessary to decrease the excessive centralisation of property, wealth and power. Socialism, he believed, was the preventive measure against anarchism, even though numerous politicians had categorised socialism as ally of anarchism (Lombroso 1895, 129). However, the ferocious attacks of anarchist press against socialism substantiated the divergence between them, and anarchy had disappeared from Germany, Austria and England after the spread of socialism. Socialists took their rationale from positive studies of society, and history would show the working class that this ordeal was created by the economic system, not by the elite classes. Thus, the solution would be a gradual change in the system modifying the constitution without the use of bombs and daggers.

Conclusions

This brief overview of *Gli Anarchici* shows how Lombroso pursued a thorough and wide-ranging analysis of the political crimes and anarchist political actors. Undoubtedly, the uncertainties of his research methods raise numerous questions, and leave the basis on which he arrived at his generalisations on the root causes of anarchist militants open to criticism. Yet it is evident that Lombroso, contrary to what those who dismiss him as the author of *L'Uomo Deliquente*, did not restrict himself to physiognomic or medical issues. Walter Laqueur, the historian of terrorism, observes that 'Lombroso saw a connection between bomb throwing and pellagra and other vitamin deficiencies among the maize-eating people' (Laqueur 1977, 2). Lombroso took into consideration the wider context that affected the anarchist actors, including political, economic, cultural and social issues. Though Lombroso considered various mental states and diseases that affected these militants, he highlighted that most of these actors had a good level of education and were also employed, sometimes in prominent jobs. The aim of the anarchist actor was to champion the aspirations of people who lived in poverty. By upsetting the status quo, the individuals at the centre of *Gli Anarchici* could not be classified as criminals, whether born criminals or otherwise. Although, as Lombroso pointed out, from a socio-psychological perspective, revolutionary change was not an effective strategy for reform. Even a progressive-minded scientist would resist it.

Lombroso challenged the government; he criticised the authorities for their mismanagement of the situation. He opposed the capital punishment inflicted on caught anarchist actors as this fuelled the sympathisers even more. The opportunity to idolise the dead as martyrs helped these extremist actors to attract further recruits and indoctrinate them for future attacks. Laqueur (1977, 2) misinterpreted this work when he says that 'Lombroso had doubts from the beginning about the efficacy of international cooperation against anarchist terrorism'. In fact, Lombroso was in favour of international cooperation and suggested standardised punishments, treatments and monitoring of the movements of political criminals. However, Lombroso expressed that countries employed different administrations, policies and tactics to control anarchism, and this influenced the severity of the anarchist problem at national level but also international cooperation.

Lombroso should be regarded as a pioneer in the study of terrorism and political violence, but numerous academics had dismissed him (and continue to) without reading what he actually wrote on this subject. *Gli Anarchici* provided a concise study of political violence and anarchist terrorism suggesting a temperate response. It leads to the question: How would the understanding of terrorism be different if researchers did not judge the book simply because the name 'Cesare Lombroso' appeared on its spine?

Notes

1 Hornton and Rich (2004) have brought a number of these together for their collection of Lombroso's work in English. Many of these works can be found on the world wide web.
2 This edition included two additional chapters: '*Mattoidi*' (Mattoids) and '*Altre influenze: meteoriche, etniche, economiche*' (Other Influences: Meteorological, Ethnicity And Economic). Also, material on the case of Caserio and a map indicating the revolutions in Europe between 1791 and 1880. It is important to note that I translated the book from the original source since there is no official English translation. Due to continuous reference to previous works in order to tackle appropriately the issues discussed in *Gli Anarchici* there were occasions where I referred to the same works mentioned in the original text to complete this work.
3 This paragraph was translated as follows: 'The best prize that I might wish, is the application of an all experimental impartiality of the psychiatric-anthropological method to the most current hot issues, that I have tried to follow here as in my other works, of which I would like to remain a reference point, high above those outrageous political concerns, that time and interest often dispersed.'
4 *la religione recluta migliaia di fanatici, che sotto i nomi e le teorie più diverse si agitano febbrilmente per salvare le anime umane dalla perdizione del vizio.*
5 *la religione non può che molto meno essere un parafulmine del fanatismo.*
6 Chapter 1 of Lombroso, C. (1895) *Gli Anarchici*. Torino: Bocca.
7 This Latin phrase, attributed to the poet Horace (65–8 BC), can be translated as 'many that have fallen into decadence or were slain will be reborn'.
8 *Tolstoi, p. es., Richet, Sergi, Hugo, Zola, Nordau, De Amicis, essi vi diranno che la nostra fine di secolo appare ben triste.*
9 *gli ideali religiosi, famigliari, patriottici, quelli di campanile, di casato, di spirito di corpo o di casta andaronsi sotto i nostri occhi dileguando.*
10 Harmodius and Aristogeiton were pederasts in ancient Athens. The two lovers became known as the Tyrannicides after they killed the Peisistratid Hipparchus. After their death they were fashioned into a potent symbol of Athenian democracy, though their motivation in the assassination was initially personal revenge.
11 Violence is always immoral, even when it is directed to counter violence.
12 *Una polizia dove non ci sieno delitti da scoprire e delinquenti da arrestare, provocherà, inventerà i delitti ed i delinquenti, o cesserà di esistere.*
13 *Tutti i freni estrinseci o sociali, intrinseci o morali, sono fittizi, e devono essere considerati come la causa della infelicità e tristizia umana.*
14 *lasciare al popolo libertà di fare le divisioni di quanto gli occorre, di gettarsi sul mucchio, così come un branco di lupi sulla preda.*
15 *ogni lesione violenta del diritto costituito della maggioranza, al mantenimento e al rispetto dell'organizzazione politica, sociale, economica, da essa volute.*
16 '*Neofilia*'– Chapter 9 of Lombroso, C. (1895) *Gli Anarchici*. Torino: Bocca.
17 *il misoneismo impera su tutti e dovunque, nei costumi e nella religione, nella morale e nella scienza, nell'arte e nella politica.*
18 *prima perchè un atto sia antisociale, vale a dire un delitto, è ch'esso sia l'opera d'una minoranza. Quando la maggioranza lo approva esso diviene un'azione normale.*
19 Revolution is the historical expression of evolution.
20 *i delinquenti ed i pazzi vi partecipano in maggior copia spintivi dalla loro morbosità a pensare.*

21 It is important to note that the names are copied exactly from the book. This does not exclude that there are mistakes in the spelling of the names as were spelt in Italian of the late nineteenth century.
22 *Per me non ho mai visto un anarchico che non fosse segnato o zoppo, o gobbo, con faccia asimmetrica.*
23 The real name of Ravachol was François Claudius Koenigstein but he adopted the name of his mother (Marie Ravachol) after his father abandoned the family when he was only 8 years old, retrieved from http://www.marxists.org/reference/archive/ravachol/biography.htm, accessed on 8 August 2011.
24 *il tipo più completo del criminale-nato.*
25 *espropriazione legittima degli espropriati.*
26 *Suicidi indiretti.*
27 '*Epilessia ed isteria*' – Chapter 3 of Lombroso, C. (1895) *Gli Anarchici*. Torino: Bocca.
29 '*Pazzi*' – Chapter 4 of Lombroso, C. (1895) *Gli Anarchici*. Torino: Bocca.
29 '*Mattoidi*' – Chapter 5 of Lombroso, C. (1895) *Gli Anarchici*. Torino: Bocca.
30 '*Suicidi indiretti*'– Chapter 6 of Lombroso, C. (1895) *Gli Anarchici*. Torino: Bocca.
31 In this case both 'epilepsy' and 'political hysteria' are italicised even in the original text (Lombroso 1895, 48) because their meaning is not the same is not the usual meaning found in dictionaries or medical literature. The meaning of these two words is modified to what Lombroso identifies as the traits that fit subjects he examined. These issues are examined in more detail in *L'Uomo Delinquente*, Vol. II, Part 1 and *Il Delitto Politico*, Part 3.
32 Felico, a member of a group of anarchists in Naples was charged 12 times for attempted murder, strike, defamation and epilepsy.
33 The word *bisognisti* is derived from the word *bisogno* that means need or necessity. For the purpose of this research this word will be used in Italian as in the original text though the closest translation would be the 'needists'.
34 *esempio sente il bisogno di rubare qualche cosa, di ammazzare qualcuno: vi provano che la cosa è lecita e che bisogna farla.*
35 *spinto da una forza che mi dominava, per un desiderio elle non potei reprimere.*
36 a true fanatic enthusiast.
37 '*La société m'a forcé à le faire. J'étais dans une situation misérable. J'avais faim. Je ne regrette qu'une chose: ma gausse. Mais c'est égal, je suis content, et on fera bien de me guillotiner; je recommencerais dans huit jours.*'
38 *il piu delle volte un'eco indegna delle lotte dei partiti, delle condizioni politiche o religiose del loro tempo.*
39 Chapter 5 was added in the second edition of *Gli Anarchici*, 1895.
40 *vi spiegano minore crudeltà e minore energia dei rei-nati, mancando completamente in loro la pratica e l'astuzia nel male.*
41 *Che anzi togliermi questa [sic] sarebbe il più gran benefizio che farmi si potesse.*
42 Lombroso studied the physiognomies of Italian revolutionaries Dandolo, Porna, Porro, Schiaffino, Fabrizi, Pepe, Paoli, Fabretti and Pisacane from their effigies.
43 *L'ira, rispose (e così indicava la violenta passione), aveva gonfiato il mio cuore e mi insegnò la via per giungere fino al suo.*
44 Although I am guilty, you judges are powerless against me. Yes, I am impervious to any sentence, because I have a faith in the triumph of my ideals that you do not have. You can condemn me for life imprisonment, but as you see my sickness will shorten the sentence. I will die with my heart full of love and even the executioners throwing the prison keys on the floor will burst into tears, praying at my deathbed.

45 The martyrdom of the Bab took place at noon on Sunday, the twenty-eighth of Sha'ban, in the year 1266 AH, July 9 1850 AD retrieved from http://bahai-library.com/books/dawnbreakers/chapters/23.html accessed on 3rd August, 2011.
46 *Quando il discorso, oggidì ancora, cade su quel fatto, si può giudicare dall' ammirazione mista ad orrore che la folla provò e che gli anni non hanno schemata.*
47 Hereditary neurosis.
48 Pellagra is a disease resulting from malnutrition, showing a sign of poverty.
49 *Dove il proletario è in peggior condizione degli schiavi romani.*
50 *Sognava d'entrare in seminario e diventare un prete, un apostolo. S'irritava coi compagni se rubavano anche una mela pei campi.*
51 The germs of anarchism.
52 Lombroso, C. (1888a) *Palimsesti del Carcere.* Torina: Bocca.
53 *Lione, 3 agosto 1894,* 'Cara madre, Vi scrivo queste poche righe per farvi sapere la mia condanna è la pena di morte. Non pensate (s'intende: non pensate male) o mia cara madre di me?
Ma pensate che se io corressi questo fatto non è che sono divenuto (s'intende : un birbante) e pure molto vi dirano che sono un assassino un malfattore.
'No perchè voi conosciete il mio buon quore, la mia dolcezza che avevo quando mi trovavo presso di voi? Ebbene anche oggi è il medesimo quore: se ò comesso questo mio fatto è precisamente perchè ero stanco di vedere un Mondo così infame' (Lombroso 1895, 141).
54 *Prima sì. Ma, dacchè ho sposato l'idea non bazzico più donne.*
55 *se la giustizia dev'essere non tanto l'applicazione di una pena ad un demerito, quanto la soddisfazione di un sentimento pubblico* anche meno che giusto*, allora non poteva risparmiarsi la condanna di morte a Caserio.*
56 'Medieval Europeans, who remained ignorant of Muslim beliefs and practices ... transmitted a number of inter-connected tales about the secret practices of the Assassins and their leader, a mysterious Old Man of the Mountain' (Daftary 2008, vii).
57 *... a pochi momenti da quell'ora che crederà l'ultima anche per sè, continua ad essere l'osservatore il più preciso, il più indifferente d'ogni particolare, e raccoglie ogni dato che possa preparargli*
più sicura l' azione triste che compirà: riflettere a pochi secondi dal misfatto come bisogna attraversare la strada, perchè è a dritta che i personaggi importanti seggono in carrozza nei cortei ufficiali.
Tale è il fanatico monoideizzato : tali erano i messi del Vecchio della Montagna: solo che il suo vecchio era Bakounine e la missione che gli doveva guadagnare il Paradiso era di spegnere iI ... presunto tiranno.
58 For example, Hoffman (2006. 37): 'not pursuing purely egocentric goals; he is not driven by the wish to line his own pocket or satisfy some personal need or grievance. The terrorist is fundamentally an *altruist*: he believes that he is serving a 'good' cause designed to achieve a greater good for a wider constituency – whether real or imagined – that the terrorist and his organization purport to represent.'
59 Later on the some of these theories of extreme altruism were translated in English and published. The publication was, Lombroso, C. (1901) 'Some Aspects of Crime', *Humanitarian* 19: 316–19.
60 Sergius Michaelovitch Kravchinski known in nineteenth-century London revolutionary circles as Stepniak or Sergius Stepniak, was the Russian who killed the chief of that country's secret police with a dagger in the streets of St Petersburg in 1878.
61 *... ad interrogare gli infelici dell'Ospedale dove io era. Fu spaventoso l'effetto: compresi il bisogno della solidarietà e divenni anarchico.*
62 *... ho preferito farmi contrabbandiere, falso monetario, ladro e uccisore, assassino. Avrei potuto mendicare, ma ciò è degradante e vile: e ancora è punito dalle vostre leggi, che fanno un delitto della miseria.*

63 ... e sempre vi saranno dei delinquenti, perchè oggi voi ne distruggete uno, domani ne nasceranno dieci.
64 Mi si era detto che la vita era facile e largamente aperta alle intelligenze ed alle energie.
65 L'anarchico non era più un uomo, era una bestia feroce alla quale si dava la caccia da ogni parte e della quale la stampa borghese, vile schiava della forza, domandava in tutti i toni lo sterminio.
66 essa è nata nel seno di una società putrescente e che si sfascia.
67 Silke (2003, 36) recognised the psychology of vengeance as a cause of political violence.
68 ... quanto più strana e assurda è un'idea, tanto più trascina dietro a sè matti, mattoidi e isterici.
69 Switzerland was going through changes in its constitutions and was swapping from aristocracy to democracy while in Ireland the socio-political conditions were so dire that citing Gabriel Tarde, Lombroso (1895, 106) proposed that the only ways out were emigration or suicide.
70 Un Governo, in cui il benessere pubblico sia negletto e gli onesti perseguitati, è causa di rivolte e di rivoluzioni. Le persecuzioni vi mutano le idee in sentiment.
71 ... idra anarchica.
72 Decades later Arquilla and Ronfeldt (2001) described terrorism as an 'acephalous (headless) and polycephalous (hydra-headed)'.
73 ... prima l'anarchia reclutava i suoi eroi tra i candidati alla galera, ora li trova tra gli individui onesti.
74 Proteo della vita moderna.

Bibliography

Arquilla, J. and Ronfeldt, D. (2001) *The Advent of Netwar (Revisited)*, retrieved from http://www.rand.org/pubs/monograph_reports/MR1382/MR1382.ch1.pdf, accessed on 1 July 2009.
Daftary, F. (2008) *The Assassin Legends: Myths of the Ima'ilis*. London: I.B. Tauris & Co. Ltd.
Desmarest, (1833) 'Témoignages historiques, ou quinze Ans de haute police sous Napoléon', in Lombroso C., 1895, *Gli Anarchici: seconda edizione con aggiunte*. Torino: Bocca, p. 70.
Duchess d'Abrantés Laure Junot (1838) *Vite e ritratti delle dame celebri d'ogni paese*. Milano.
Durkheim, E. (1964) *The Rules of Sociological Method and Selected Texts on Sociology and its Method*, translated by Halls W. D. Mueller. New York: Free Press.
Ferrero, G. (1894) 'La Riforma Sociale' in Lombroso C., 1895, *Gli Anarchici*. Torino: Bocca.
Ferri, E. (1894) 'Discorso Parlamentare', (7th July), in Lombroso C., 1895, *Gli Anarchici*. Torino: Bocca.
Henry, E. (1894) *Émile Henry's Defense*, The Anarchist Library, retrieved from http://theanarchistlibrary.org, accessed 15 February 2010.
Hoffman, B. (2006) *Inside Terrorism: revised and expanded edition*. New York: Columbia University Press.
Horton, D. and Rich, K. (eds) (2004) *The Criminal Anthropological Writings of Cesare Lombroso Published in the English Language Periodical Literature During the Late 19th and Early 20th Centuries. With Bibliographical Appendices of Books and Periodical Literature Pertaining to Lombroso and Criminal Anthropology*. New York: Edwin Mellen Press.
Laqueur, W. (1977) 'Interpretations of Terrorism: Fact, Fiction and Political Science', *Journal of Contemporary History* 12: 1–42.
Lombroso, C. (1887) *Tre tribuni studiati da un alienista*. Roma: Fratelli Bocca.
Lombroso, C. (1888a) *Palimsesti del Carcere* Torino: Bocca.
Lombroso, C. (1888b) *Troppo Presto: Appunti Al Nuovo Progetto Di Codice Penale*. Torino: Bocca.

Lombroso, C. (1890a) *Il delitto politico e le rivoluzioni in rapporto al diritto, all'antropologia criminale ed all scienza di governo*. Torino: Fratelli Bocca.

Lombroso, C. (1890b) 'Illustrative Studies in Criminal Anthropology: III. The Physiognomy of the Anarchists', *Monist*, vol. 1: 336–43.

Lombroso, C. (1894) *L'uomo di genio in rapporto alla psichiatria, alla storia e all'estetica*. Torino: Bocca editore.

Lombroso, C. (1895) *Gli Anarchici: seconda edizione con aggiunte*. Torino: Bocca.

Lombroso, C. (1900) 'A Paradoxical Anarchist', *Popular Science Monthly*, vol. 56: 312–15.

Lombroso, C. (1901) 'Some Aspects of Crime', *Humanitarian*, 19: 316–19.

Lombroso, C. (1902) *Delitti vecchi e delitti nuovi*. Torino: Fratelli Bocca.

Lombroso, C. (1911) *Crime: Its Causes and Remedies*, translated by Horton, H.P. Boston: Little Brown & Co.

Lombroso, C. 2006 [1896–7] *Criminal Man*, translated by Gibson, M. and Rafter, N. H. Durham, NC: Duke University Press.

Majorana, A. (1894) *Teoria sociologica della costituzione politica*. Torino: Fratelli Bocca.

Ravachol (1892) *Ravachol's Forbidden Defense Speech*, The Anarchist Library, http://theanarchistlibrary.org, accessed 17 October 2009.

Silke, A. (2003) *Terrorists, Victims and Society: Psychological Perspectives on Terrorism and its Consequences*. Chichester: John Wiley.

4

DEMONIZING BEING

Lombroso and the ghosts of criminology[1]

P. J. Ystehede

> In speaking of haunted houses, I have had occasion, previously, to remark how curious it may appear that we can now report such facts, and in such numbers and so well attested, when almost whole centuries have passed without anyone taking notice of them, except among the lower classes, who are not, so to speak, in communication with the educated classes . . . . For my part, if I may have been wrong in denying these facts before studying them, I have not, at all events, thought myself bound to deny them because I did not succeed in explaining them.
> (Lombroso 1906, 302)

> ghost stories do yield scientific material of a very valuable sort . . . . The fact is, the belief in ghosts, in witchcraft, in second-sight, and all the rest of it is a continuous inheritance of our race from every remote and savage period. Even among the relics of the cave men, certainly among the relics of the later stone-age men, there are numerous objects which point back clearly to the existence of ghost theory . . . . It is impossible that a belief so ancient, so universal, and so constantly should not have produced profound modifications in the brain and the whole psychical mechanism of the entire human race ... it may perhaps be considered as innate in the evolutionary sense, with the vast majority of mankind; a sort of blank form answering to the concept of ghost must most probably be potentially present in almost every human brain.[2]

In what has been called "the heyday of the middle class ghost" (Fincane 1988), Lombroso also spent his time behind velvet curtains observing supernatural phenomena, such as going around town on the lookout for ghosts. In one of his articles, Lombroso describes some of the haunted houses he had visited during the last two decades. In most cases, he had only got to investigate ex post facto, but he also had first-hand experience of these hauntings; one incident being, *the case of the haunted cellar*. In 1900, to the misfortune of a family of merchants, their spirit and wine

FIGURE 4.1 Cesare Lombroso at a spiritist séance (1908)

Source: Archivio storico del Museo di Antropologia criminale "Cesare Lombroso" dell'Università di Torino (Italia).

cellar seemed to be under attack from invisible entities. The situation was becoming so unbearable, both morally and financially, that the family realized this had to end either "by love or by force" (Lombroso 1906, 367). Lombroso then saw it as up to himself to visit the family Fumero.

> I presented myself at the wine shop on November 21st without giving my name and asked for information as to the asserted phenomenon, I was much surprised to hear the master of the house declare that the events of which I spoke had readily happened, but that, very fortunately "Professor Lombroso had come, and since then the disturbances had ceased." Greatly puzzled by this reply, since I had never even set foot in the house before, I made myself known and asked for an explanation, desiring to find out whether someone had made use of my name, for purposes which I intended to discover later on, if necessary. M. and Mme. Fumero then confessed that having heard that I was to visit the house, the idea had occurred to them of declaring that my appearance had put to flight the "spirits"! They thus managed to free themselves from the annoyance caused them by gossips and the police; for this purpose they saw no harm in attributing to me the powers of the Grand Exorciser! But these good people then informed me that the mysterious phenomena were unfortunately still going on, and perhaps I might have the opportunity of seeing them with my own eyes, if I would take the trouble to go down into the cellar.
>
> (Lombroso 1906, 367–8)

Lombroso gladly accepted the offer and went down into the cellar to give the wine bottles a closer examination. After having checked the shelves for strings, Lombroso started waiting. He did not have to wait for long. Much to Lombroso's astonishment – even though he had lit six candles supposing this would make the spirit phenomena cease in the part of the cellar he was sitting – the bright light did not forestall the bottles from falling and spirit fingers from moving. At the time Lombroso left the wine cellar, 15 bottles had met their sad demise. Lighting of candles was just one of the many precautionary measures recommended by the spirit researcher. Ghost hunting was a serious and risky business, an activity incorporating discipline, control, surveillance, and strict monitoring. To be able to safely and scientifically observe supernatural phenomena required the governance of strict procedures, protocol, and methodological principles (Fincane 1988).

Lombroso's turn to "occultism" is by later Italian intellectual biographies mostly dated to the mid-1880s, starting with his studies on hypnotism and magnetism. This research was part of the trajectory of nineteenth-century discourse on mesmerism, which by the end of the century held a controversial yet prominent role in the discourse on crime (Crabtree 1993; Winter 1998). The disagreement was mainly on the question of who could be hypnotized and the ramifications this had on human will and autonomous agency. The two main positions may be summarized as follows: (1) that of the *Salpetrie* School who argued that hypnosis merely could be employed on, and was part of the illness of (mainly female) hysteric patients; (2) that of the *Nancy* School, who maintained that everyone in given circumstances might be hypnotized. This had important legal consequences, since it raised the issue of whether a person could be hypnotized into committing criminal acts. However, this discourse had much wider effects in the later discourse of the criminal sciences – for how to understand the role of "influence" and "suggestion" on human will and behavior (?) This led to a discussion of whether there were degrees of hypnotic and trance-like states performing "suggestion" and "influence" on the individual (Lawrence and Campbell 1988).

Especially, the advent of photography and film addressed these dilemmas and brought into being an awareness of other psychical anomalies; because, what did these shadows on the screen reveal?

> The positivists' documentaries seem ... to deliver to these images, magical details. The body became apparent for everyone to see, to the pupils of the eye – similar to the cinematographic machine – wherefrom came a procession of inner ghosts. In other words – being a séance that had become a collective one. A journalist, who witnessed the event, reports the disquietude of those present when: "*a white cinematic screen, transformed into a vertical, anatomical table*". On the white screen, the inside of the mediumistic body was exhibited, like the outside. This autopsy, as Lombroso called these imprinted traces, at that moment retrieved a posthumous, spectral life.
>
> (Viola 2005, 56–7)

The study of various forms of spectral life would be an explicit focus for his research in the last two decades of his life. According to Paul Tabori, Lombroso came to accept the spiritualist doctrine comparably late (Tabori 1972). In Italy, one finds followers of spiritualism and attending séances with mediums from the late 1840s – the Italian spiritualist movement seems to have been mainly followers of, and informed by, the spiritualist doctrines of Allen Kardec (1804–69) – the founding father of French spiritualism (Biondi 1988). Though calling Lombroso a spiritualist follower of Kardec, per se, is misleading, since a fundamental tenant of Kardecian spiritualism is a belief in reincarnation, which Lombroso does not argue for. Rather, he came to accept the spiritualist claim of the existence of ghosts; that spirits had a will and agenda of their own.

This loss of time in becoming aware of the supernatural, seems to have been amended by the energy he put into research of these questions. For a long time, it may not have been the case that Lombroso did not succeed in providing explanations, as he did not choose to publish them. *It was not until the end of his life, Lombroso openly embraced the magic that his science later has been said to discourage.* According to him, the final focus and stage of the evolution of the Italian school of criminal anthropology was to understand the biology of spirits (Lombroso 1909). Lombroso's ambition was not only to prove the existence of the world of spirits, but to scientifically prove that crime also had its roots in the possession of such things as malign and evil spirits and demonic forces, though this issue in his work is stated in a minor key, because the prime objective was to gain acceptance for the very existence of the supernatural. This may be one of the reasons why Lombroso's, and the criminal sciences', interest in spirits and ghosts is a part of his/their research that various historiographies on the criminal sciences development have chosen, it seems, to ignore. This research is never mentioned in any of the intellectual historiographies of the discipline of criminology. In counterview, the entire tradition of narration on the history of criminology bases its historiography on that the beginning of the historical development of the discipline has its roots in the very rejection of demonological and spiritual explanations for understanding criminality. Though Lombroso spent, at least, two decades of his career studying ancient and modern witchcraft – judging from these historiographies – one may initially conclude that this was an interest of minor importance. Furthermore, when considering Lombroso's understanding of crime, this interest in the supernatural is of no relevance to the sciences on the tropes of crimes' later development. This research, somehow, stands apart from what is seen as Lombroso's main thought and legacy; i.e. one will not find a questioning of whether this interest should be considered to belong on the margins of the rise of criminal sciences. However, I would argue this marriage of science and "ghost theory" is of fundamental importance when aiming to understand aspects of the genesis of Lombroso's science, its duration, and its legitimacy, such as the later scientific and conceptual metamorphosis. By this is meant the process of rationalization on the tropes of crime and the creation of the new politics of scientific and magical visions; namely, what gradually, and presently, can be said scientifically to be visible and scientific in the discourse on the tropes of crime and the criminal. In this perspective, the legacy of Lombroso on the modern criminological imagination is also to be found in paper trails wherein is employed (gothic) monsters and doubles to understand the scientific realities of crime, the history thereof, the individual criminals, and the criminogenic society. In fact the impact of Lombroso's visit to the wine cellar – this cave analogy for the theoretical developments of criminology and the criminal sciences of the twentieth century – is rather astonishing. This spirit research was not a discontinuity of his earlier works, but accepting his claim, was the next step for his science – and the criminal sciences. In this last work, having imbued meaning and understanding of the dangers found in life, from the micro-level, the smaller life forms to the evolution of humanity, in society and its institutions, in history and culture – he now extended his grand narrative to incorporate the dangers from the beyond.

As with the criminal types – the born criminal and the criminal of passion – Lombroso's discovery of the unknown has its origin story. In 1882, in Turin, Lombroso was called to aid the daughter of a family friend. This 14-year-old girl, Lombroso at first believed suffered from hysteria brought on by the start of menstruation. The girl had the ordinary symptoms of hysteria such as vomiting, dyspepsia, somnambulism, and fatigue. However, he soon discovered that he had to re-evaluate his initial diagnosis. What seemed different from normal hysteria, was that this girl was able to see into and predict the future (she could see weeks in advance when she would have new fits), as well as tell what people she knew were doing in other places far away (she could state the exact time her older brother, attending university in another city, went to bed). She was also able to see, read, and smell with other parts of her body.

> when I approached a finger to her ear or to her nose, or made as if I were going to touch it, or, better still, when I caused a ray of light to flash upon it from a distance with a lens, were it only for the merest fraction of a second, she was keenly sensitive to this and irritated by it. "You want to blind me!" she cried, her face making a sudden movement like one who is menaced.
> (Lombroso 1909, 3–4)

Experiencing periods of blindness, this made her other senses even more acute. Though being blind, and blindfolded by Lombroso, nevertheless, the girl could read any text he brought before her. This was the beginning, according to Lombroso, of his research into the occult. Now, his archives of criminal anthropology acquired a shadow cabinet. It may peradventure be thought that this body reading, and others, somewhat re-invigorated Lombroso's dissolving faith in anthropometry. When comparing the first spirit photographs which appeared in the 1840s,[3] with those taken later in the century one may notice that in the beginning the spirits are often found as a multitude of heads spurting from the frame – making the human form resemble the hydra of Greek mythology. This posed new challenges for Lombroso to combat. On the other hand, the machines which created these pictures, in the hands of science opened up the possibility for readings of the

FIGURE 4.2 The medium Eusapia Paladino in a trance

Note: The photo was taken on 12 July 1906 in Genova (Italy).

Source: Archivio storico del Museo di Antropologia criminale "Cesare Lombroso" dell'Università di Torino (Italia).

invisible anthropometry of Man. Not only were there photographs and moving pictures, but, for example, the discovery of X-rays in 1895 by Wilhelm Röntgen (1845–1923) was yet another machine creating incertitude and that centered the criminal anthropologists' attention on the nature and extent of mechanic exposure (Hessenbruch 2001).

Lombroso has in later historical narratives also been called one of the founding fathers of what at the end of the 1940s would be known as parapsychology (Tabori 1972). Here Lombroso, as in the criminological historiographies, is considered to be among the first who scientifically studied the tropes of the paranormal. As with the later criminological tradition, Lombroso has been highly criticized for his methods of research and conclusions. The most critical voices have in both traditions arguably been on the sexism found in his work; a sexism duly noted by Feminist parapsychologists such as Nancy Zingrone, who has analyzed the relationship between Lombroso and the psychic medium Eusapia Paladino (1854–1918):

> In Lombroso's description of her characteristics, both as medium and as woman, however, one can almost see Paladino shuffling up and down the evolutionary continuum as Lombroso listed each new attribute: down a peg because she was "populana" (a peasant); up a peg because she was keen enough in intellect to flatter his "genius" ... down a peg because she was orgiastic in her trance convulsions and had a tendency to "*fly at her adversaries and beat them*"; and up a peg because she was generous and often gave her money to the poor and the sick.
>
> (Zingrone 1994, 116)

In the following discussion of Zingrone's lecture, several participants note that the tradition of Lombroso led to a complete disregard of women's personal experiences, and an inconsiderateness of women's experience of the paranormal one also found in the later development of its research program. By the weight given to quantitative and positivist research to secure parapsychology to gain acceptance as a science – "parapsychologists" such as Lombroso had violated, neglected and abused those somehow in touch with spirits. The question of the individual's own experience – either as the perpetrator of crime or victim thereof – is a concern one also finds gradually becoming of central importance for criminology, especially the tradition of critical criminologists in their discussion on the value of, and relationship between, quantitative and qualitative research. For the latter research tradition (somewhat similar to the former), the main methodological question became as such the concern of how the researcher should relate to her or his doubles, and how to respect the others' sensibilities. Lombroso and his tradition were considered to be somewhat insensitive in these matters. Lombroso was not the first thinker who scientifically or otherwise addressed the question of the supernatural and its relevance on the tropes of crime. Rather he should be seen as the first to found a school which most persistently and scientifically addressed the nature of ghosts and its relation to crime and the criminal. The study of the unknown invisible worlds, evidently not only a study to understand those individuals who claimed to be able to communicate with the invisible worlds, not just to understand what some thought of as mere parlor tricks, but also seen as a possible useful tool to be employed in criminal investigations (Wilson 1985). When Lombroso participated in his second recorded séance in 1892 in Naples, he was in quite a distinguished company to bear witness and to examine what Paladino was supposedly able to materialize from thin air. The host of the séances (17 in total), Enrico Morselli (1852–1929)

> tied Eusapia Paladino to a camp bed in the way that he would tie a dangerous maniac. Yet in fairly good light six phantoms presented themselves in

succession in front of the cabinet, the last one being a woman with a baby in her arms. Each time after the phantom retired, Morselli rushed into the cabinet and found the medium as he left her ... Indeed, according to Richet, "more than thirty very skeptical scientific men were convinced, after long testing, that there proceeded from her body material forms having the appearances of life."
(Fodor 1934)

According to Lombroso, the biology of the spiritual world could be scientifically proven; in this case if not set into motion or shown by a medium, the spiritual world was also invisible to most scientists – even for Lombroso who prided himself on being able to detect what the majority of people could not. The problem with studying the medium, as with the criminal, seems to have been that they were seldom docile or cooperative. As with many of the criminal types they were prone to lying, cheating, stealing as well as displaying other forms of indecent behavior. To Lombroso, this unbecoming nature was analogous to the unbecoming nature of the criminal types. This judgment he based not solely on the medium's (or those somehow in touch with the unknown) acts but on a reading of their bodies and its history. Lombroso argued that it was through their very atavism and this force manifestations – the medium Paladino being in a unique position – making her a conduit for the criminal anthropologists to examine and gain access to knowledge of the world of spirits. This otherworld he believed influenced the land of the living. Since atavism was a source prevalent in both the criminal and the genius, he found both groups to be in this unique situation; that they were in fact visited by the invisible world, and that these visitations left traces that could influence their acts, i.e. both to commit horrible crimes and/or to create great wonders. These traces he found in history and fiction, from personal accounts by Dante's son – Jacopo Alighieri – being told in a dream by his recently deceased father the whereabouts of lost cantos, in stories by Shakespeare such as Hamlet, and by Goethe. There were also stories told by nameless people in Italian institutions, and Lombroso's own experiences which he wrote down as scientific proofs of having communicated through Paladino with his own mother and other dead relatives. For those that still might harbor some doubts of the existence of the spiritual world, Lombroso brought a wealth of scientific evidence such as measurements of the body of Paladino, studies of her family history, and a large number of machines to make visible to the reader that which had been invisible (Lombroso 1909).

Perhaps, what mostly caught the eye were the spirit photographs – pictures that made it even more apparent than the criminal photographs – that mankind truly was possessed by unknown forces of nature. The spirit doubles that Lombroso was able to see in the criminal photographs, would with the spirit photographs now fortunately become accessible to everyone. But there were those who were skeptical. As with the criminal photographs, one finds from their first occurrence a discussion and a questioning of their status as scientific proof. These phantoms, some claimed, were merely the result of their makers double exposure. The scientists were not in control of their craft or aware of their senses being deceived. As in the case of the scientific photographs of criminals, these pictures of ghosts were as such used as scientific evidence to prove Lombroso's claims, though it is important to recognize that their employment (again, as with the criminal photographs) went beyond that of being mere quantifiable visualization's of truths. To Lombroso, as others later would argue, such critics were missing a vital point. Because even when shown to be fake, this did not necessarily make the images less real. The question in need of scientific study was whether the phantoms might be classified as spirit or psychic reflections – the latter "produced" as a result of the collaboration between the disembodied and embodied consciousness of the photographer and the object. Concordantly, even if the photographer intended to create fakes these fakes might as such be genuine since one could presuppose that the photographer was not in total control of himself or his object, his environment or his medium. As Harvey has noted, both alluding to the semblances between nineteenth- and early twentieth-century discourse on psychic/spirit photography and physical sciences – and the present horrible sublime scientific concerns with the consequences for our humanity with the advent of the internet:

> Psychic investigators . . . looked into a world beyond appearances (but none the less real for that). Likewise they claimed to have observed the elemental . . . and witnessed the metamorphosis of spirit substance into a physical phenomenon. The construction and transformation of this substance, to produce an "extra," took place, they believed, within a domain (a "psychicyber space," as it were) which was independent of spatial scale and beyond temporality, by a network of participants (wherein the distinctions between the sender and the receiver, and observer and participant, and artifact and artificer, were obfuscated), who were connected and communicated across the common boundary of consciousness and at unimaginable distances, swiftly and using the interface of photography technologically.
>
> (Harvey 2004, 122)

To Lombroso, the existence of poltergeists and ghosts was by no means in any conflict with his materialist and evolutionist orientation. Ghosts could be measured and weighted by science, he argued, given their radioactive qualities (Lombroso 1909, 188–90). The problem resided often in that when a soul became disembodied, especially if it had been so for a prolonged period of time, it was very confused. Thus, the challenge was to make reason and science of the spirit communication coming from the medium. This was even more of a challenge if the ghost happened to be insane (Lombroso 1909, 185). As he earlier had argued that to accept the laws of socialism did not contradict the laws of evolutionist science – relying on, amongst others, the psychic research of Alfred Russell Wallace (1823–1913) – Lombroso now argued that when giving a proper scientific account of the grand schemes of things one should scientifically recognize that our material existence was not just a question of *the survival of the fittest* – but also *the survival of the fittest spirits*.

It seems at first glance that of the researchers on the tropes of crime, it is those focusing, or showing a particular interest in the abnormal and criminal psychology of the individual, who seem to most often be inclined in the academic public at times to extend their interests into the "para" part of psychology and crime. Perhaps the most famous criminologist after Lombroso was Donald West – one of the leading scholars on legal psychiatry and criminology in Great Britain – who held the presidency of the Society of Psychic Research from 1963 to 1965. In England – as in Italy – this was research conducted with great scientific and methodological agility. As West commented in his inauguration speech at the Society of Psychic Research, the study of the paranormal was a thorny issue, fraught with methodological concerns. The psychology of the mediumship should be of central concern to the researcher. Moreover, the possible influence and control the medium might hold over the psychology of the scientist needed to be considered as a factor influencing the final picture. Furthermore, another central concern should be the psychology and control of the scientists themselves, over the data.

> the visions, that some persons are able to induce by gazing into a crystal ball are created in their own subconscious minds and do not come from outside themselves. The explanation is, of course, equally applicable to those visions of sleep, which we call dreams, as well as to the hallucinations and delusions of the insane .... The interposition of a habitual spirit guide provides an easy excuse for deficiencies in the spirit communication .... Psychiatrists have ceased to regard states of hysterical mental associations with much respect. If ... came to the notice of a doctor today, the first question would be what drove him into this escape mechanism. Did he, for example, have a nagging wife? A shot of pentothal or even a little "shock" treatment would soon bring back his lost memories.
>
> (West 1963)

Even with the help of modern medicine, West found it important to consider the historical, social, and cultural context which might explain the delusion prior to considering the presence of the supernatural. Thus, even if the scientists did not consciously intend to create errors of judgment, these phenomena seen as genuine might as such be fake since one might presuppose that the scientist was not in complete control of himself, his environment, his object or his medium.

In all fairness, Lombroso was not totally averse to at times questioning his medium's relation to this otherworld. For instance, he found it strange that his mother speaking to him through Paladino used terms of endearment he had not heard her call him when she was among the living. However, he blamed these mishaps of transmission and deceits on the bad filter of Paladino – and on the nature of her psychic atavism. A similar logic as with the spirit photography's seems to have been applied – the more Lombroso and others found evidence of Paladino having lied or cheated this merely proved to Lombroso that she was truly a genuine medium. To Lombroso, to show that ghosts existed, that this was the next step for his science, was not a mere question of scientific or personal integrity, but more grandiose – a duty to mankind:

> It seemed to me a duty that, up to the very last of the few days now remaining to me, I should unflinchingly stand my ground in the very thick of the fight .... But note this well, however doubtful each separate case may appear, in the ensemble they form such a compact web of proof as wholly to baffle the scalpel of doubt .... In psychical matters we are far from having attained scientific certainty. But the spiritistic hypothesis seems to me like a continent incompletely submerged by the ocean, in which are visible in the distance broad islands raised above the general level, and which only in the vision of the scientist are seen to coalesce in one immense and compact body of land, while the shallow mob laughs at the seemingly audacious hypothesis of the geographer.
>
> (Lombroso 1909, v–vii)

One may wonder if Lombroso, in this paragraph, was not only recounting psychic research, but also his science on the born criminal – his status on the scientific skyline at the time being that of a fading star. Employing the language and metaphors of the Italian Renaissance men of medicine, Lombroso asked the scientists to blunt their Occam razors – acknowledging that part of this journey still would have to be undertaken on fraternal trust. In contrast to Lombroso's self-acclaim, for some later commentators, Lombroso's science was not the Promised Land it purported to be but the early sighting and premonition of the rise of a new leviathan.

To Lombroso, the face of death became literally the final frontier of his science – as it literally had been the beginning. In a similar fashion, Shelley's Dr Frankenstein argued that: "To examine the causes of life, we must have recourse to death. I became acquainted with the science of anatomy: but this was not sufficient" (Shelley 2004, 50). No longer was the truth for Lombroso found merely in the reading of dead bodies, but in a reading of dead souls – this time talking back. What was Lombroso's favorite key to unlock the mysteries of the unknown, "atavism", this time in the medium Paladino – and the criminal anthropologists' unique ability to speak to and understand the unknown – whether being famous spirit guides such as John King, his dead mother or dead children, was once again the mystical force of nature for prosperity and knowledge as a source to forces up to no good.

When reading this scientific literature of Lombroso and other criminal scientists, as Warner reminds us, it is important to reflect that:

> The air was growing ever more crowded, yielding up all manner of mysteries to new instruments devised to detect and inventory its components. But these findings continually interplayed with metaphysics and were brought to bear on psychic forces as well as physical forces. Mesmeric theories were woven

into concepts of electricity ... the discovery of radio waves and the subsequent invention of the wireless, of telegraphy, of the telephone produced a fevered – and delighted search – to penetrate the unseen .... It is difficult from our inured vantage point today to imagine how exciting, fascinating, and extreme seemed the possibilities that the new instruments opened up for their first users .... Radio waves could not be grasped by the human senses, only the effects of the new methods of transmission .... Visible verification surrendered its hegemony to other warranties of presence – acoustic and haptic .... In the absence of natural sensory means to verify the principle at work, a dependence on second-order technological proof of hidden energy arose, translating touch into sight, as in the photograph .... The extension of the word "medium" itself in the early 1850s, to someone with paranormal powers reveals the parallelism perceived between the vehicle – the aether – and its products.

(Warner 1999, 120–1)

The science of Lombroso had from the beginning been dependent on machines in the creation of its techno–horror. These machines were producing results and phenomena that would mystify and amaze many a scholar. No longer would Lombroso, as in earlier centuries' medical science, merely deconstruct the boundaries between the human and the animal – the body and its parts – but also the boundaries between the human and the new automatons. The human being was not only at peril quite literally in all possible interpretations one might conceive – of physical and spiritual miscegenation and technogenation – but also visual, haptic, and acoustic enation and contamination. Though rarely considered as relevant to the development of the sciences on the tropes of crime, the advent of the twentieth century saw the coming of a new "loud." Scientists now found black noise, white noise, city noise, degenerate noise, all of which if the circumstances were right, might be "suggestive," "influencing," dangerous, and crime-inducing noise. At the time, Loos wanted to rid the city of atavistic decorum – Viennese composers of classical music were on a quest for a pure sound – a music free from the atavistic sound of music. The dangers to the individual were now somehow coming from the very physical scenery of the city – through the eyes and air waves. This was not only a concern for natural scientists, architects, and composers – or cultural critics of Max Nordau's (1849–1923) distinction, but also for other philosophers and writers who are most often not associated with or perceived as intellectually mingling with, the "Lombrosian crowd." The modern age with the coming of all that jazz struck fright into Theodor Adorno (1903–69), who found even the rhythm and heart of modernity to be dangerously off beat (Steinert 2003).

The born criminals were by far not the only monsters of the nineteenth-century scientific imagination. In the second half of the nineteenth century, there was not only a rise of a scientific and diagnostic culture categorizing a variety of criminal types, but one also finds elephant men and human telephones. The latter group was made up of individuals having the qualities of the telephone scientifically proven by their ability for automatic writing. The possible uncanny potentials of the telephone and telegraph had been a source of some debate since the first occurrence of this phenomenon. For example, in the Guiteau trial – Guiteau assassinated the US president James A. Garfield (1831–81) – some commentators believed that if Guiteau was not possessed by the Devil himself then he certainly was by one of his demonic inventions. Notwithstanding Guiteau's own conviction, he repeatedly stated that he had not been in the service of the National Phone Company, but Jesus Christ and Company Ltd (Rosenberg 1968). Karl Marx (1818–83) was not the only political activist to find the world growing more *alien* – one all too often forgets that not only did Lombroso live in an age which largely redefined space, time, and sound, his was a science at the frontier, with a stated program of defining the dangers. Never before seen in the narratives of the scientists had the body, the human form, and human identity ever been at such peril as in Lombroso's age. They risked degenerating back into an apish past, developing into decadent, effeminate moral monsters or turning into life forms resembling the new machinery and technological equipment. There was now no complete security to be found for either the living or the dead in the view of science from the world or the cosmos. Lombroso was by no means the only one concerned with strange phenomena such as ghost lights in the sky over Turin – so were people and scientists all over the world. The strange was a focus of narratives in science and fiction. Now, in the wake of the rise of natural science, gothic fiction also seemed scientifically credible as in Franz Kafka's story of an individual one morning waking up to find himself having overnight metamorphosed into, or at least having attained the self-realization of being, a big bug. The possibilities and wonders of what the human agent in the nineteenth and early twentieth century might be possessed by (or turn into) seem in retrospect almost limitless – at least until one tries to formulate the limits of what it is possible, scientifically, or fictionally speaking, for an individual to be dangerously "possessed" by today.

It is easy to join Warner and others in their enthusiasm with these scientific investigations. One may conclude, in the light of these scientific narratives by Lombroso, that truly victorious was fantasia over mimesis, imagination over empiricism. Though, as often seems to be the case, this research and quest for scientific enlightenment into the nature of ghosts – some have argued – had a somewhat volatile quality. These later investigations, instead of following Walt Whitman's lead and sing the body electric and as the Futurists embrace the speed and noise of the twentieth century, have like Lombroso centered their attention on where one may find ample "currents" for concern. Undoubtedly, in the context of the history of a science on crime and the criminal, "this fevered and delighted search" yielded what some see as somewhat of a tragedy. As the development of a photograph needed the contrast of light and dark, the study of spirits has been seen as casting shadows. Those not having the luxury or fortune of indulging in their time of leisure in the new, strange, and bizarre were not necessarily to be celebrated at parties of the privileged, or to be the belles of the ball, but examined in institutions by men of science hungry for new knowledge and to dissect this new, yet perceived as ancient, magic residing in the world of moderns (Owen 2004). Though at times the belief in ghosts was merely discarded as superstitious nonsense of the uneducated, by the end of the nineteenth century, experiencing not only what reason and science understood as being there, but also not being there, was to be considered a symptom of a sick, delusional, and criminal mind in the need of treatment. As Sigmund Freud (1856–1939) would argue "an illusion would be to suppose that what science cannot give us we can get elsewhere" (Freud 1989, 71). Where earlier seeing ghosts and spirits or what the enlightenment medical professionals could not credit being there had been crucial in categorizing people as mad and insane, the psychiatrists and criminal scientists of the late nineteenth and twentieth centuries were now seeing, and believing, in ghosts. Lombroso seems very much aware of this, but he argued that the new science, the unquestionable integrity of the researchers, and the machines proved that ghosts were more than mere hallucinations.

Scientists who did not believe in ghosts, poltergeists, etc. saw it as their duty to study and shed light on these things that, supposedly, went bump in the night. The last decades of the nineteenth and the early decades of the twentieth century were the years for "ghost trials" throughout the world. How to define what constituted modern age, reason and science was now in every sense of the word a spiritual thriller. These trials – as the question of hypnosis, "suggestion," and "influence" on the human will and behavior – did really pose quite a few challenges for those in the legal profession; for example – in the spirit of law – how to establish the subjective guilt of mediums. Again, here could criminal anthropologists, criminal scientists and so on be of invaluable service when classifying, scientifically, the nature of the respective accused ghosts in question. In their discourse on the psychology of mediumship and the existence of ghosts, the skeptics used the same science – the same strategies of knowledge as those who tried to make their existence scientifically evident. Physicians with similar methods as Lombroso went to work to get rid of what they saw as potentially dangerous and superstitious nonsense – once and for all setting the matter of Zeitgeist in order. As Lombroso argued that the physical constitution enabled mediums, criminals, and geniuses to see the spirit world, one critical commentator noticed that these delusions were mostly prevalent among women. He then argued there had to be something wrong with their womanhood – the scientist found that the vagina and the womb of the mediums not being in the position they naturally ought to be (Wilkes 1982). What perhaps all the dissenting voices, whether believers of spiritualism, ghosts or not, gradually agreed upon was that certainly these largely unexplained phenomena showed the need for further research. The critics did not voice an ontological questioning of the existence of ghosts, or the longevity of the human soul for that matter, just like they did not ontologically question Lombroso's claim of born criminality. Nor did they question that at times these mediums produced unexplainable phenomena. As William James (1842–1910) argued: even though he did not see scientific evidence for the existence of ghosts, there were ghostly apparitions. These ghostly apparitions, he believed as with other psychologists such as Freud, were often telepathic manifestations. Cornelius Tabori, in an interview with Sigmund Freud on 21 July

1935 in Vienna, asked Freud his opinions on the occult:

> And do you think that these are convincing proofs of telepathy or clairvoyance," I asked. "Oh no," he said. "I admit that neither of these offer proof. But you know that I do not believe in accidents. The transference of thought, the possibility of sensing the past or the future cannot be merely accidental. Some people say," he smiled, "that in my old age I have become credulous. No ... I don't think so. Merely all my life I have learned to accept new facts, humbly, readily. I believe that telepathy is a psychical event in one man causing a similar psychical event in another man. It can be presumed that the connection between these two psychological phenomena is physical – perhaps similar to the receiver and the speaking tube of a telephone.
>
> (Tabori 1951, 218–19)

These powers of the mind were believed to somehow travel through space to influence and form the minds and behavior of others. Moreover, he claimed that this somehow communicated influence from the mind's "ghostly creations" – might guide the mind and human behavior in a negative manner. These phantoms were so deeply imbedded in the psyche that the human sciences were still only at the beginning of understanding what he saw as being still beyond scientific reason; that science was only on the verge of grasping how these phantom faculties harmed, or alternatively, could be put into servitude.

As with museums and collections dedicated to criminals and their scientists, in the early twentieth century one saw also museums popping up all over the world dedicated to ghosts and their scientists – the two often being one and the same. The museums had the strangest, as well as the most ordinary, on display. For example, as Tabori discovered, when visiting one of these museums in Budapest, in the spring of 1931:

> The third cupboard holds a glass container which is filled with flour. "We had some lady sitters on that séance," smiled Chengery Pap. "They were all good housewives – so the spirit sent us some flour." "A most polite gesture," I said. "Extremely polite," agreed the doctor.
>
> (Tabori 1951, 141)

Pap was just one of the many self-proclaimed new experts on crime and the paralegal. In the wake of Dr Lombroso – and, one may add, Mr Holmes and Dr Watson – one saw new generations of largely gentlemen scholars and private entrepreneurs traveling to the seats of learning bringing back information on crime that these had to offer. The criminal sciences created spaces wherein the criminal scientists and their objects could also establish relationships and focus on mutual interests they found fun and exciting. For example, these séances were places where people of different ages, background, gender, and class met in twilight to hold hands in the dark and exchange bodily and spiritual fluids. Embracing, crying, sweating,

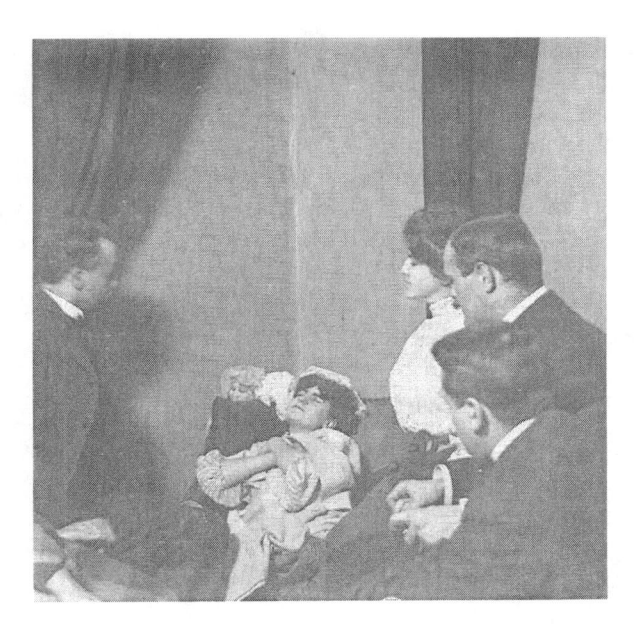

FIGURE 4.3 Spirit manifestation created by the medium Linda Gazzera (1909)

Note: From the photographic album of the doctor Enrico Imoda (1908 ca).

Source: Archivio fotografico del Museo di Antropologia criminale "Cesare Lombroso" dell'Università di Torino (Italia).

vomiting, hemorrhaging, kissing (not necessarily in that order), etc. – mediums bodies swaying back and forth – were perceived as degenerate, atavistic, primitive, painful, seductive, erotic, terrifying, ridiculous, orgasmic, and orgiastic trance-like states, as creating matter to excite and aghast scientists and people in general.

As with the International Congresses of Criminal Anthropology, the researchers interested in the "occult" also gathered in international fora – the first was in Paris in 1892 – which Lombroso also attended. The attendance list, of approximately 400, "reads as a virtual who's who of the new experimental psychology" (Treitel 2004, 47). Many of these scientists, when attending séances with mediums, when studying mesmerism, hypnotism, telekinesis, telepathy, second sight, prophetic dreams or ectoplasm, would have strongly disagreed with the suggestion that they were conducting research into the occult. In fact, these interests had nothing whatsoever to do with the occult or magic, but were merely uncharted territories for science. Freud posed the question to Tabori – *can there really be anything that is occult to science?* (Tabori 1951, 218). As this discourse develops, one also finds the gradual realization among some scientists that the powers of the mediums may not belong merely to some (foremost female) hysteric mediums, but was a blank form somehow present in every human brain.

Ghosts had now become an explicit scientific legitimate double to be found in historical evolution, as the evolution of the individual psyche – answering to civilization and its discontents. As Freud stated the matter, the double:

> was originally an insurance against death of the ego, an "energetic denial of the power of death" as Rank says: and probably the "immortal soul" was the first "double" of the body ... when this stage has been left behind, the double takes on different a aspect. From having been an assurance of immortality, he becomes the ghastly harbinger of death.
>
> (Freud quoted in Miller 1985, 135)

Still to be found among hysterics, neurotics, and so on, this redistribution of ghostly apparitions to the humanity at large, this scientific realization seems to have come as quite a relief to many scientists. As James noted in his presidential address to the Society of Psychic Research of 1896:

> It is pleasant to turn from phenomena of the dark-sitting and rat hole type (with their tragi-comic suggestion that the whole order of nature might possibly be overturned in one's own head, by the way in which one imagined oneself, on a certain occasion, to be holding a tricky peasant woman's feet) to the "calm air of delightful studies."
>
> (James quoted in Thurswell 2001, 31–2)

In the discourse on psychic research, one sees the development of a hierarchization of what was to be considered the proper occult objects and phenomena for scientific study. This development, and the conclusions drawn from it, were not that dissimilar to those gradual realizations found in the discourse on crime and the criminal. Time and again, the object was to determine the substance of, and what framed, free will. Though the criminal sciences of the early twentieth century would for the most part gradually cast off the name "born criminal," if not the belief in crime as also being rooted in pathological preconditions of various force and power, they were on a similar quest as Lombroso's discoveries and research on criminals and ghosts. They were on a journey to understand, to try to capture and encapsulate in science what in the 1930s German criminology would be coined *Dämmerzustand der Menscheit*. As the German criminal scientist Dr Bischoff tried to explain this to the journalist Tabori:

> In many people this strange disposition to this twilight, transitional condition is quite evident, easy to observe – with others it remains hidden for a long time until some external event intervenes and its sudden effect triggers off the slipping or sliding into the Dämmerzustand. In such a condition a person might commit actions which, once the twilight period is over, fills him with the greatest horror, despair and regret. Of course, such a condition has a thousand different manifestations and there are many transitory stages between the actual twilight, befogged state, and other disturbances and fluctuations of consciousness. Most of the people who are obedient slaves of their visionary twilight

condition are recruited from the ranks of epileptics, hysterics and other physically or mentally handicapped people.

(Tabori 1974, 244)

These ranks were to be found growing ever more numerous, as their illnesses were made ethereal. Those who called this "befogged," misty condition that somehow was believed to exist within and outside the body and the world – leaving traces and taking possession of man and the world by some of their ancient addresses, holding on to the peasant woman's feet – were to be severely criticized.

Lombroso's great opus on the biology of the spiritual world, published posthumously got a somewhat mixed reception as with most of his research. To some, this work was seen as another testimony to the unscientific character of Lombroso's inquiries, whereas devout followers such as Hans Kurella (1858–1916) saw that Lombroso's otherwise genius and brilliance had misguided him in this case (Kurella 1910). Kurella was just one of many concerned with the consequences of inviting the occult into criminal science – both in respect to the status thereof, and the science itself. To many of Lombroso's critics and fellow scientists on the tropes of crime, these people who claimed to see ghosts were often merely sick; not possessed by a sick spirit, but spiritually sick. The counterclaim was partly based on the Enlightenment rationalist tradition of discourse that ghosts are merely figments of the imagination. This view on the matter one also finds among the early Italian romantic writers. As Giacomo Leopardi (1798–1837) noticed in the 1830s, though the advent of reason had shown that these ghosts and specters were not real, he still found his fellow countrymen less than sober in these matters and concluded that even in the most enlightened societies in Europe, such as Italy, people were still insisting on seeing and believing in spirits (Leopardi 2003). Notwithstanding the condemnation of many of the Enlightenment philosophers, even the romantically inclined and the condemnation of later thinkers throughout the nineteenth century until the present, these phantoms of yore gradually became legitimate objects for scientific study. After Lombroso, ghosts were now also to be found in criminal science.

The lack of historical interest in Lombroso's research into ghosts, poltergeists, telepathy, not forgetting levitation, and the spiritual and psychic investigations of other criminal anthropologists and criminologists in general, is as such understandable. Considering the moral sentiment of much of the research on Lombroso, one may claim that there are other more present pressing concerns in respect to the discourse on crime and punishment and its sciences. One may neatly label Lombroso's and others' enquiries into psychic phenomena as being just another part of his scientific romanticism (as with the born criminal), or an epistemological recoil, not to mention the inevitable nervous breakdown of an extreme belief in scientific materialism. Of course, one could merely conclude that this was another problematic aspect of the scientists' and/or science's attempts at self-empowerment, or of exerting their powers on the world around them. This obvious new potential for, and abuse of, power is certainly an important aspect with these spirit (and psychic) investigations. Yet such an emphasis may take the attention away from considering this discourse in relation to the later criminological discourse and diagnostics of risk and danger, whether the critique and historical representations of Lombroso's science and what has been perceived as his main scientific legacy, the power of its "influence" and "suggestion" – as what later criminological perspectives have seen as dangerous "influences" and "suggestions" in the discourse on crime. Perhaps this perspective may pose the question: when Lombroso or other men or women of knowledge in general or criminal scientists talked about spirits and zeitgeists, what were they actually talking about? This, of course, is a problematic point to raise because when the natural scientists, the sociologists or the great philosophers talk of, for example, spirits and ghosts, they can't talk about actual ghosts, alternatively ghostly apparitions – can they? This was a question of great importance to Lombroso and other psychic researchers and scientists at the end of the nineteenth and the beginning of the twentieth century – a time when even Socrates himself showed up as a medium's spirit guide (Wilkes 1982). According to the *Pall Mall Gazette*, quoted at the beginning of this chapter, at the end of the nineteenth century Germany also had become the country of geists. Despite whatever Georg W.F. Hegel (1770–1831), alluded to in the text, had intended – the view that is presented claims that Hegel most likely would also have had ghosts on his mind when writing his work on *The Phenomenology of Spirit*. In Lombroso's work this seems to have been the case with quite a few of the earlier great philosophers, scientists, and writers – as it also was with criminals. Of course, one would argue today that there are quite important distinctions, scientifically and philosophically speaking, between "geists" and "ghosts," which should be mentioned, whether the ghost or geist in question, is Hegel's or others. The point is that in Lombroso's criminal anthropology and the scientific discourse at the end of the nineteenth century – and the later social discourse on crime and the criminal – these distinctions – if not totally eroded – radically altered. As Jacques Derrida (1930–2004) has noticed, when Marx wrote "*Ein Gespenst geht um in Europa*" there are quite a few ways in how this was and can be read (Derrida 1994). Derrida, one may presume, realized the polemical aspects of Marx's arguments on the ghost of communism and the vampires of capitalism. The invocation of monsters in political and scientific discourse is a very powerful mode of organizing thought – of which Lombroso's criminal anthropology may be, if not the sole, then one of the best examples. Furthermore one should be careful in employing Derrida's understanding, whose texts seem in modern philosophy to be more haunted than most (Castricano 2001). However, he had an important point when he argued that ghosts (and one may add gothic monsters) in nineteenth-century and in modern thought became somewhat topical.

The study of the biology of the spiritual realm seems at first glance to be a declaration or command from its master beyond the grave that the criminal anthropological and later criminological traditions did not heed. Rather, as the story goes the discipline gradually developed away from instead of focusing on criminal types or biological determinist causes to criminal behavior. Instead it turned to predominantly more psychological or social explanations to understand crime and the criminal. As the scientific narratives on the tropes of crime develop into the current academic discourse, the mode of narration becomes not only a question of studying the individual human "beast" but also her or his habitat. The dangerous forces that were believed to induce crime were now more and more to be found in the threats coming from the city, society, in dreams, the system, and the culture, which were seen as containing brews and concoctions with possible dangers that might somehow "possess" the individual and lead it astray.

The dawn of the twentieth century did not only see the rise of the science on ghosts as a natural phenomenon, but the rise of a science on ghosts as a social phenomenon. Prior to this stigmata were seen as a religious and medical distinction of the body. At present it is also viewed as an act of the social (Goffman 1963; Becker 1963; Lemert 1967). In the criminological intellectual historiographies the development of the tradition of scientifically addressing the tropes of crime in the context of the social is traced back to Durkheim. Though it is uncertain whether Lombroso ever read the works of Durkheim – though they corresponded by mail – Durkheim did certainly read Lombroso.[4] This is also the case in Durkheim's study of criminals, spirits, and ghosts. In *The Elementary Forms of Religious Life*, Durkheim's ambition is to explain religious man, or rather modern man. Like Lombroso he tried to show modern man by contrasting him with his atavistic double – primitive man. This view one finds in Lombroso and other (criminal) anthropologists' work. As the Australian aborigine was the most primitive of the races, Durkheim argues that their religion is the most primitive of Mankind. Thus, it might by the study of their religion be possible to find the genesis to the religious life of more civilized societies. Durkheim uses Lombroso's research in *Criminal Man* to make the practice of tattooing not only analogous to totemism – but its *raison d'etre*. Durkheim argued that tattoos testify to both the individual as well as the moral life of groups. In other words, as symbols may serve to create religious sentiments, they may also serve to create criminal sentiments. One of the distinctions between these two was that whereas Lombroso had earlier argued that the criminal subjectivity was related to internal (and external) physiological forces, and in his final work argued that criminal subjectivity could also be created by spiritual contagion, Durkheim's emphasis was on the latter: as an act of contagion by the collective representative may make an object sacred, it also can through an act of contagion make an individual into a criminal. Rather than maintaining a distinction between religion and science, Durkheim even argued that such a distinction was unscientific because the supernatural was real – being part of human and material reality. Thus, he argued – as Lombroso argued for the possibility of creating a biology of spiritual life – that it was possible to extract principles, or elementary forms of spiritual life, i.e. making a sociological science of the world of spirits (Durkheim 1995). Whereas Durkheim largely transformed Kantian metaphysics into metapsychology (Schmaus 2004) and though his was no argument for inborn criminality, Durkheim's perspectives on Man and his relation to the world of spirits, unequivocally left the question of human will and autonomous agency in quite an ambivalent position. The individual was, once again, caught between the totem and its taboos. Durkheim's thesis on the supernatural as real one will also find partially echoed in Max Weber (1864–1920):

> principally, there are no mysterious incalculable forces that come into play, but rather one can, in principle, master all things by calculation. This means that the world is disenchanted. One need no longer have recourse to magical means in order to master or implore spirits, as did the savage, for whom such mysterious powers existed. Technical means and calculation perform the service. This above all is what intellectualisation means.
>
> (Weber 2004, 12–13)

This, among the most widely commented paragraphs of Weber, is a statement making many later thinkers pose questions such as: does magic really cease to exist merely by making a distinction between magic and modern technical reason? What is the soundness of, in principle, the very perspective of considering magic as only being the reason of children and savages? Sometimes, it was even considered if perchance modern technical reason conjured some magic of its own? Lombroso, Freud, Durkheim, and Weber were just a few among the many scientists who turned to the study of what they saw as primitive cultures and magic to understand the world and reason (or lack thereof) of moderns. In their respective manners, they were all arguing that the objective of science was to understand spirits. What they all shared seems to be a belief that science, in the end, was a form of safeguard against wizardry – or for the scientist to be perceived as a wizard, or becoming one, whether perceived by scientists or others in the need – or fear – of Grand Exorcisers.

There is not only an interest in the supernatural among the scientists on crime and the criminal, but there is also a displaced supernaturalism and gothicism (see especially Rafter and Ystehede 2010) in the nineteenth- and twentieth-century scientific vocabulary and language on crime and deviance that one seldom take time to consider. As Castle has noticed, the language of the post-Enlightenment mental experience is suffused by a displaced supernaturalism (Castle 1995), not only found in the narratives of Lombroso, but also other criminal scientists. According to Castle, that these "spectral others," or ghosts, were gradually incorporated in the world of thought has to many become so self-evident that this is a historical development one seldom takes time to consider. Furthermore, what may have been the consequences of this development of relocating ghosts to being internal and part of the imagination? Castle argues that this, what she calls "*spectralization of the other*" – ghosts becoming to be seen as internal properties of the individual – was part of, or an effect of, the project of Enlightenment rationalism.

> The belief that ghosts and specters are only products of imagination – that they come from within the mind itself – is in fact ... a relatively recent notion, one that has emerged in a definite form in Western Europe only over the

past two hundred and fifty years .... After 1700, however, with the breakup of traditional communities, the growing challenge to religious orthodoxy, and the popularization of new scientific attitudes, a more skeptical and mechanistic view gradually came to prevail: that ghostly apparitions were "things of the mind" – figments, or phantasmata, produced by a disordered or overwrought brain. Which isn't to say, I hasten to add, that men and women in earlier periods either failed to recognize or denied the delusion making powers of the imagination .... What is new in the eighteenth century – and particularly the second half of the eighteenth century is the particular sense of urgency that begins to attach to such psychological speculations. Because traditional beliefs regarding the "Invisible World" no longer seemed plausible – the ancient beliefs in spirits and demons Enlightenment rationalist like to argue, had been utterly exploded – apparitions had to be reinterpreted as coming from within.

(Castle 1995, 170)

In her study she focuses on the early gothic narratives as reflecting what she calls: the modern invention of the uncanny. This she sees as created by the gradual relocalization of ghosts and the monstrous into becoming part of the physical and mental geography of the individual. Castle points out that this discourse has led to the self-contradictory modern conclusion that ghosts, on the one hand, do not exist; whereas, on the other hand, are now found as a prerequisite in science for being able to see the modern world, physically, through the science of Newtonian optometry calling the visual lens on the eye a "specter." The eighteenth-century discourse on ghosts as only things of the mind, this displacement of ghosts into becoming internalized in the mental fabric and seen as part of the imagination, or as delusions of the insane, has according to Castle led to paradoxical consequences for modern science and thought. Today, there is a sentiment and also a scientific acceptance that an individual might somehow be "haunted" by his or her mind and body's and senses' experiences of reality – and history. In the context of the criminal sciences and criminology, a modern scientific understanding that an individual might somehow be haunted by crime – and its science – developed. Not only do we at present legislate against criminals, but also against their ghosts – whether of the past or future, whether these invisible entities are perceived as holy or wholly scientific. Also Castle belongs to this tradition, and is among those expressing a concern with the consequences of this:

The problem with displacing the supernatural "back" into the realm of psychology, however, is that it remains precisely that: only a displacement. The unearthliness, the charisma, the devastating noumenon of the supernatural is conserved. One cannot speak in the end, it seems to me, of a "decline of magic" in post – Enlightenment Western culture, only perhaps of its relocation within the new empire of subjectivity itself. The apparition writers in the decades around 1800 took on the traditional world of spirits, and like sorcerers' apprentices performed on them the very act of magical metamorphosis that Freud would later celebrate – the transformation of metaphysics into metapsychology. But the effect was to demonize the world ... we continue to speak – innocently perhaps but also with subtle anxiety – of being "haunted" by our own thoughts and persuaded by "ghosts" inside our head. We fear (and legislate against) the madness of the phantom world within. Until it is possible to speak of ghosts inhabiting, as it were, the mind of rationalism itself, this sense of being haunted is likely to remain – far more than any nervous fear of the police – the distinctive paranoia of modern world.

(Castle 1995, 189)

Whether one places the tropes of crime in the "empire of subjectivity" or in the "empire of the social," to employ Castle's terms alluding to these historical processes of the scientific colonialization of the modern mind and world, according to her, they remain in science and narrative just displacements. Basically, they are nothing more than displacements of ghostly apparitions. Though her main focus is the ramifications on the individual, she also briefly mentions that the individual was not the only entity which would be filtered through a language of gothic reverie; one also finds the Ghost of Society and the Ghost of Modernity itself. Gothic metaphors are found in the grand narratives on the development of individuality, as they are in the descriptions of historical progress. Certainly, what has received scant attention and reflection from the critics of Lombroso's born criminals, is that these scientists did not only make the individual potentially dangerous, but also what resides outside of the individual. What had been familiar and secure through the scientific narratives of Lombroso and the later tradition of scientists on crime and the criminal was made uncanny. Even more, that was how, in general, law abiding individuals could easily be seduced to descent into twilight states. Individuals were no longer the only dangerous elements of the world, but now also where they roamed, where ever more parts of their habitat and habitus were taken into account. Certainly the individual and the world had been viewed as dangerous before, perhaps from time immemorial, but this had not been spirit visions given such a credence by science. As José Monleon argues: "This definite internalization of otherness, this final inclusion of unreason within the parameters of reason implied not only that monstrosity was 'real', but that it actually formed part of reason. The monsters were possible because 'we' were the monsters" (Monleon 1990, 27).

Now Lombroso's research and science on spirits are considered to be on the margins, in the re-appropriation of the terminology of explaining and understanding spirits of yore to the new criminal sciences. Even so, some of the cultural associations of old remained. They lingered on, so to speak – and took part, as new terms were added, in the form-shaping-ideology of criminal anthropology and later criminology. This scientific gothic imagination leads back to Lombroso and Lombrosian discourse – his legacy found in narratives whether by Lombroso's critics in criminology or by the later scientists on the individual criminal. One will find the zealous critics reverting, as Lombroso once did, to fiction, also gothic fiction or turn to the gothic tradition, when narrating science. Such discourse is also found in contemporary attempts of scientific rejuvenation and enlightenment – to ward off disenchantment. It is my opinion, as opposed to the early discourse of criminal anthropology, we now find ourselves in, perhaps, the fortunate, more enlightened paranoid position to celebrate that "crime" (and its ghosts) can be the property of everyone. The spirit of Lombroso is at present predominantly envisioned in these scientists on the individual criminal – the paranoid fear of his ghost seems also to haunt the minds of his critics. Let us not forget the objects of his science, who still in the discourse on crime are more "visited" than most. This seems to have been the case with the psychic medium Carmine Mirabelli (1889–1951) who – despite the fact that Lombroso had died from a heart attack in 1909 – continued to communicate to the Cesare Lombroso Institute of Psychic Research (founded in Sao Paolo in 1919) new scientific results and suggestions for criminal policies, from the criminal anthropologist throughout the 1920s (Da Silva Mello 1960). One may add that, as strange as it may appear, there are still people, even in the most enlightened criminological societies in Europe, insisting on seeing and believing in spirits. As one will discover, there is still also the feeling of "hantise," expressed by critics of Lombroso's legacy – finding the ghost of the scientist, at times, a bit too close for comfort.

Notes

1 This article is a revised version of an article earlier published in Norwegian. See Ystehede, P. J. (2007) "Lombroso og den nye vitenskapen for praktisk magi. Betraktninger om opprinnelsen og utviklingen til modern kriminologi" in *Materialisten* 3.
2 Leader Comment, "Psychical Research," *Pall Mall Gazette* (21 October 1882), in Ledger and Luckhurst (2000, 278–9).
3 The invention of spirit photograps is most often attributed to William H. Mumler (1832–84), see Clouthier (2004).
4 To mention a few examples, see Durkheim 1997a, 115, 116 ,125, 257; Durkheim 1997b, 104, 113, 116, 340, 345; Durkheim 1995, 234.

References

Becker, H. S. (1963) *Outsiders. Studies in the Sociology of Deviance.* New York: The Free Press.
Biondi, M. (1988) *Tavoli e medium. Storia dello Spiritismo in Italia.* Roma: Gremese.
Castle, T. (1995) *The Female Thermometer. 18th-Century Culture and the Invention of the Uncanny.* New York: Oxford University Press.
Castricano, J. (2001) *Cryptomimesis: The Gothic and Jacques Derrida's Ghost Writing.* Montreal: McGill-Queen's University Press.
Clouthier, C. (2004) "Mumler's Ghosts", in Cheroux, C., Fischer, A., Apraxine, P., Canguilhem, D. and S. Schmit (ed.) (2004) *The Perfect Medium. Photography and the Occult.* New Haven: Yale University Press.
Crabtree, A. (1993) *From Mesmer to Freud: Magnetic Sleep and the Roots of Psychological Healing.* New York: Yale University Press.

Da Silva Mello, A. (1960) *Mysteries and Realities of this World and the Next*. London: Weidenfeld & Nicolson.
Derrida, J. (1994) *Specters of Marx*. USA: Routledge.
Durkheim, E. (1995) *The Elementary Forms of Religious Life*. USA: The Free Press.
Durkheim, E. (1997a) *The Division of Labour*. USA: The Free Press.
Durkheim, E. (1997b) *Suicide. A Study in Sociology*. USA: The Free Press.
Fincane, R.C. (1988) *Appearances of the Dead. A Cultural History of Ghosts*. New York: Prometheus Books.
Fodor, N. (1934) *These Mysterious People*. http://www.survivalafterdeath.org/books/fodor/chapter19.htm.
Freud, S. (1989) *The Future of an Illusion*. London: W.W. Norton and Company.
Goffmann, E. (1963) *Stigma*. New Jersey: Prentice Hall.
Harvey, J. (2004) "The Photographic Medium: Representation, Consciousness, and Collaboration in Early-Twentieth- Century Spiritualism," in *Technoetic Arts* (2004), Volume 2.
Hessenbruch, A. (2001) "Science as a Public Sphere. X-rays Between Spiritualism and Physics," in Goschler, C. (ed.) (2001) *Wissenschaft und öffentlichkeit in Berlin, 1877–1930*. Stuttgart: Franz Steiner Verlag.
Kurella, H. G. (1910) *Cesare Lombroso als Mensch und Forscher*. Wiesbaden: Bergmann.
Lawrence, J.-R. and Campbell, P. (1988) *Hypnosis, Will and Memory: A Psycho-Legal History*. New York: The Guilford Press.
Ledger, S. and Luckhurst, R. (ed.) (2000) *The Fin de Siècle. A Reader in Cultural History c.1880–1900*. New York: Oxford University Press.
Lemert, E. (1967) *Human Deviance, Social Problems and Social Control*. New York: Prentice-Hall.
Leopardi, G. (2003) *Thoughts*. USA: Hesperus Press.
Lombroso, C. (1906) "The Haunted Houses which I have Studied," in *The Annals of Psychical Science*.
Lombroso, C. (1909) *After Death – What? Spiritistic Phenomena and Their Interpretation*. Boston: Small, Maynard & Company.
Miller, K. (1985) *Doubles. Studies in Literary History*. Oxford: Oxford University Press.
Monleon, J. B. (1990) *A Specter is Haunting Europe: A Sociohistorical Approach to the Fantastic*. New Jersey: Princeton University Press.
Owen, A. (2004) *The Darkened Room: Women, Power, and Spiritualism in Late Victorian England*. Chicago: University of Chicago Press.
Rafter, N. and Ystehede, P. (2010) "Here Be Dragons: Lombroso, The Gothic, and Social Control" in M. Deflem (ed.) *Popular Culture, Crime and Social Control*. Bingley, UK: Emerald, pp. 263–84.
Rosenberg, C. (1968) *The Trial of the Assassin Guiteau. Psychiatry and Law in the Guilded Age*. Chicago: The University of Chicago Press.
Schmaus, W. (2004) *Rethinking Durkheim and His Tradition*. Cambridge: Cambridge University Press.
Shelley, M. (2004) *Frankenstein*. USA: Simon and Schuster.
Steinert, H. (2003) *Die Entdeckung der Kulturindustrie. Oder: Warum Professor Adorno Jazz – Musik nicht ausstehen konnte*. Münster: Westfälisches Dampfboot.
Tabori, C. (1951) *My Occult Diary*. London: Rider and Company.
Tabori, P. (1972) *Pioneers of the Unseen*. USA: Taplinger Publishing.
Tabori, P. (1974) *Crime and the Occult. How ESP and Parapsychology Helped Detection*. Great Britain: Latimer Trend & Company.

Thurswell, P. (2001) *Literature, Technology and Magical Thinking, 1820–1920*. Cambridge: Cambridge University Press.
Treitel, C. (2004) *A Science for the Soul. Occultism and the Genesis of the German Modern*. USA: The John Hopkins University Press.
Viola, A. (2005) "Storie di fantasmi per adulti: Lombroso e le tecnologie dello spettrale," in Turzio, S., Villa, R. and A. Viola (2005) *Locus Solus. Lombroso e la fotografia*. Milano: Bruno Mondadori.
Warner, M (1999) *Spirit Visions*. The Tanner Lecture on Human Values, Yale University, http://tannerlectures.utah.edu/lectures/documents/Warner_01.pdf.
Weber, M. (2004) "Science as a vocation" in Weber, M. (2004) *The Vocation Lectures*. Indianapolis: Hackett Publishing Company.
West, D. (1963) *The Psychology of Mediumship*, http://www.survivalafterdeath.org/articles/west/mediumship.htm
Wilkes, C. (1982) *The Psychic Detectives. Paranormal Crime Detection, Telepathy and Psychic Archaeology*. San Francisco: Mercury House.
Wilson, C. (1985) *The Psychic Detectives: The Story of Psychometry and Paranormal Crime Detection*. San Francisco: Mercury House.
Winter, A. (1998) *Mesmerized: Powers of the Mind in Victorian Britain*. New York: Yale University Press.
Zingrone, N. L. (1994) "Images of Woman as Medium: Power, Pathology and Passivity in the Writings of Frederic Marvin and Cesare Lombroso," in Coly, L and White, R. A. (ed.) (1994) *Women and Parapsychology. Proceedings of an International Conference held in Dublin, Ireland*. September 21–22 1991. New York: Parapsychology Foundation Inc.

5
THE LOMBROSO MUSEUM FROM ITS ORIGINS TO THE PRESENT DAY

Silvano Montaldo

According to the testimony of Lombroso himself, the collection began when he was still a university student around the middle of the 1850s. It expanded in 1859 during the Second War of Independence, in which he participated as a voluntary doctor in the Piedmontese army, being able to 'craniologically measure thousands of Italian soldiers and also collect skulls and brains' (Lombroso 1906a, 302). The search for anthropological material continued after he was discharged. As his daughter Gina would later write, Lombroso 'was a born collector' (Lombroso Ferrero 1921, 355). 'Not a day went by', echoed her father, 'whether in Pavia, Pesaro or Turin, without me trying to expand my collection of madmen and criminals who had died in mental hospitals or in prison'. As early as 1864, the year in which for the first time he combined clinical teaching with that of anthropology, Lombroso on occasions made his students produce portraits, plaster casts or wax models of the faces of the dead bodies upon whom autopsies had been performed at the Hospital of Pavia. In many cases, they were people who had been struck by pellagra, but evidence has also been found indicating an interest in criminology. After that, a clinical and prosopographic method was drawn up through which he constructed the histories of those criminals that played such an important role in his scientific career. The Hospital of Pavia's post-mortem table also gave rise to his most famous find, namely the skull of 'bandit' Giuseppe Villella. For Lombroso it had become a genuine scientific relic, sufficient to give credence to the theoretical construction of the *Uomo Delinquente*, and to attribute value and meaning to the entire collection, that over a period of ten years 'had gradually grown by both fair means and foul', including the profanation of cemeteries in Sardinia, Lombardy, Tuscany and Piedmont (Lombroso 1906a, 302). This collection could not help but reflect the serious inconsistencies in Lombroso's experimental methodology, but it also brought the benefits of a wide variety of perspectives, with the search for new exhibits, of differing meanings and nature (Villa 1985, 136; Portigliatti Barbos 1985a, 231–6).

FIGURE 5.1 The museum of Psychiatry and Criminology of Turin at the beginning of the twentieth century

Source: Archivio fotografico del Museo di Antropologia criminale "Cesare Lombroso" dell'Università di Torino (Italia).

The first steps

In 1876, when Lombroso moved to Turin, the collection had become so large that it posed him significant logistical problems, initially forcing him to use his own home for storage. Life in that small space, 'cluttered with skeletons and Museum crates', was hard for the family (Lombroso Ferrero 1921, 193). The situation improved the following year when the collection was moved to two sites in the ancient convent of San Francesco da Paola in Via Po, which the university had assigned to him as the Laboratory of Forensic Medicine and Experimental Psychiatry. It was a great relief for his relatives and neighbours, but it was not an acceptable solution for the scientist, who was not able to create a display inspired by scientific or exhibitive criteria (Lombroso Ferrero 1921, 196, 363, 366). It was merely a storage space for anthropological material that, from time to time, would be taken and used for a lesson, experiment or research with a view to publication. It was an educational and scientific collection, not an exhibition designed to illustrate the thoughts of a criminologist, who had in the meantime published the first edition of *Uomo Delinquente*.

The collection was presented to the public for the first time in 1884, as part of the Anthropology Exhibition held at Turin's *Esposizione Generale Italiana*. The scientists claimed significant exposure in the event that celebrated Italy's early stages as a unified nation, designed and organised to show Italian and international public opinion the results achieved by unification. It was no coincidence that, when the exhibition closed after registering nearly three million visitors, the organisers stressed the ideal continuity between the event and the new higher education institutions that would spring up soon afterwards. Lombroso's criminal anthropology was perfectly in tune with those who had created the exposition. Lombroso, intent on promoting the modernisation of the state's fundamental structures through the application of a scientific theory that proclaimed itself to be avant-garde, was not about to miss the opportunity to give greater exposure to his suggestions. Indeed, the Exposition was also supposed to host the first Congress of Criminal Anthropology, but it was postponed due to an outbreak of cholera. However, this was not the case with the anthropological exhibition, which therefore represented the true meeting of Lombrosism with the general public after the success of the second edition of *Uomo Delinquente*, in 1878, and the appearance in 1884 of the third edition, which would remain incomplete. 'Rich and extremely interesting', to the point where it always attracted 'a lot of people', the anthropological section was a triumph of craniology, boasting at least a thousand skulls which were 'interesting from a number of physiological and moral perspectives' (Pettinati 1884, 282). A year later, in Rome, under the aegis of the III World Penitentiary Congress, the congress postponed in 1884 was finally able to take place, and the first International Exposition of Criminal Anthropology was held. With anthropologist Giuseppe Sergi and psychiatrist Enzo Sciamanna, Lombroso had sent an appeal to prison doctors, psychiatrists, asylum directors and anatomical pathologists, asking them to 'send to Rome skulls, brains, photographs of criminals, moral madmen, epileptics and their work' (Lombroso *et al.* 1885, 237). The Veronese scientist, acknowledged as the founder of the new science, but already on the receiving end of considerable criticism for his organicism on the part of French anthropologists, thus attempted to provide an exhaustive demonstration of the validity of his interpretations of deviance (Severi and Lombroso 1886, 5–6). In the seventeen days during which the exhibition was open, as part of a wider exposition on prisons, 17,803 paying visitors were recorded and, enhanced by 'the most precious documents from their collections' that the 'best scientists in Europe' had sent to Rome, 'powerfully showed – according to Lombroso's devoted daughter – the alliance of the theory with the facts' (Barini 1885, 605; Lombroso Ferrero 1921, 250). It was also the first official appearance of the new school of criminal law, which had long been planned by jurists, who had begun to accept the ideas of the Veronese criminologist, in order to propose to the political class a radical reform of the punitive system. These were ambitious aims that aroused extensive international support but also a strong resistance which marked the beginning of a downward curve for Lombroso's theories (Frigessi 2003, 208–14). The following year, when presenting an account of the exhibition, Lombroso made a significant admission: based on his experience, he was inclined to believe that criminal anthropology was capable of attracting the masses and igniting the public imagination, but for those who were not familiar with the theory of criminal atavism and therefore unable to 'read' skulls, brains and death masks, these demonstrations would remain completely incomprehensible; 'like a museum of Assyrian inscriptions' (Severi and Lombroso 1886, 14).

Lombroso also showed his collection to the general public on the occasion of the II International Congress of Criminal Anthropology, which took place in Paris during the exposition marking the centenary of the French Revolution. The anthropologists reserved the honour of the opening speech to the maestro, but criticism from his French colleagues was harsh and dismissive, as they united in emphasising that the environment, circumstances and other conditions more significantly influenced crime (Frigessi 2003, 218–22).[1]

The academic institutionalisation

For Lombroso and his disciples, it was time to close ranks, extend research, systematically apply all physical analysis tools to their bodies of deviants and expand the collection. All this was foreseen in the programme of the new Institute of Forensic Medicine which was due to open in 'science city', in Turin, according to a model which was common to other disciplines, and which foresaw a strong connection between the laboratory, museum, library and school. The first projects date back to the end of the 1870s, but the new headquarters of the institute was only inaugurated in October 1898, on the occasion of the I National Congress of Forensic Medicine. Meanwhile, Lombroso set to work on expanding his collection, which despite his efforts, as well as those of collaborators and admirers, 'still remained poor' (Lombroso 1906a, 302). It was at this time that the true foundation of Lombroso's museum took place, and it was institutionalised as a museum at the University of Turin. In 1889, the scientist had been given permission by the *Ministero di Grazia, di Giustizia e dei Culti* to move all the bodies of evidence lying in the chancellery of the City Court to Via Po. Three years later, Home Office Minister Nicotera granted him access to an abundance of criminological material that had been gathered in Regina Cœli prison. Furthermore, he was promised the cooperation of the directors of a number of penal institutions. Again in 1892, the administrative commission of the Torinese University Consortium, finally 'praising the proposal to found a Museum of Psychiatry and Criminology', wrote him an extraordinary cheque for 500 lire (Annuario 1900, 69–70). The first purchases with these funds were made in December of that year.[2] In 1896, the notably larger collection was moved to new premises by Mario Carrara (1866–1937), the most rigorous student to have developed under the guidance of Lombroso, whose daughter Paola he married. It was he, following the example of what had been done for the human anatomy, pathology and forensic medicine collections in Turin and in Wien, that brought order to a chaotic mass, 'making it usable', as Gina remembers.

In other words, he transformed the collection into a museum, although it remained above all a scientific laboratory and was not intended to be frequented by the general public (Lombroso Ferrero 1921, 397; Carrara 1897). Carrara was also almost certainly responsible for a long article which appeared in French in 1906 during the celebrations of the maestro's thirty years of academic teaching, organised in conjunction with the VI International Congress of Criminal Anthropology (Cini 1906). His was the most precise description of the museum ever carried out, almost as if Carrara intended to use it to make up for the lack of a real catalogue. Firstly, the creation and the main purpose of the museum founded by Lombroso was outlined, that of being 'the plastic and undeniable document supporting its conception about the man considered into madness and into crime' *(le document plastique et irréfutable à l'appui de ses conceptions sur l'homme considéré dans la folie et dans le crime)* (Musée 1906, 3). It was not, and nor was it intended to be, a museum of crime, but rather of museum of criminal anthropology, its history, its direction and its choices (Villa 1985, 29–30). The museum certainly reflected Lombroso's ideas, but it was also the fruit of Carrara's dedication, who designed the exhibition in a period during which Lombroso's theories were under severe attack from all sides and when Lombroso himself was attracted to research into spiritism. On the one hand, the museum ensured the preservation of scientific material on which Carrara and his fellow-disciples continued to work. On the other hand, the layout given to the exhibition played on visual effects in order to impress and persuade (Musée 1906, 16). On the occasion of Lombroso's jubilee, between 28 April and 3 May 1906, an Exposition of Criminal Anthropology and Forensic Policing set up in the museum and in other premises in the *Palazzo degli Istituti anatomici* (Bovero 1908, 655–67), was opened to the public. Those attending the congress judged the museum to be 'unique: because well-known scholars and unknown admirers had sent documents and illustrative material on delinquents and madmen from all over the world' (Carrara 1910, 209). As a preview to the event, a shorter article written by Lombroso himself had appeared with an extensive set of images in *Illustrazione Italiana*, a popular current affairs and culture periodical. A Spanish version, 'Mi museo criminal', appeared in two Iberian magazines and in an Argentinean magazine on psychiatry, criminology and forensic medicine, while the English translation was published by *The New York Times* (Lombroso 1906a, 302–6; Lombroso 1906b, 288–94; Lombroso 1907a, 67–72; Lombroso 1907b, 15–22; Lombroso 1907c).

Evidently, Lombroso and his collaborators had also decided to put forward the criminal anthropology collection in the clash between supporters and critics of the theory of the 'born delinquent', an issue which had been dominating the field of positivist criminology. Resorting to periodicals and daily newspapers in order to raise the museum's profile leads one to think that Lombroso and his collaborators were trying to communicate with the general public as well as those with a professional interest in the subject, perhaps in an attempt to encourage the donation of new material. At the end of the exhibition, some of the exhibits on display became a permanent part of Lombroso's museum, enhancing its heterogeneity. Three years later, a circular from the *Ministero di Grazia, di Giustizia e dei Culti* ordered the chancelleries of the kingdom to send to the Court of Turin all those bodies of evidence that, after lying in storage for a few years, would have been destroyed as objects not suitable for sale; the chancelleries were required to deliver such material to the Lombrosian museum in order to expand 'a kind of experimental collection, which lends light and assistance to the research of scholars of the world of crime', putting it on an equal footing with the museum of criminology founded in Rome by Salvatore Ottolenghi (Ministro 1909).[3]

There were another two reasons why it was necessary to take the step up from a university collection to an actual museum. The first is that psychiatrists and criminologists had begun to collect exhibits in Italy and abroad and display them in temporary or permanent exhibitions in hospitals, universities, prisons or police stations. Pasquale Penta, the first tenured professor of an official criminal anthropology course at the University of Naples, which started in 1896, had developed a private collection which was subsequently extended to include a second collection put together by Angelo Zuccarelli, his successor in 1904. The two collections converged into a single museum, which Zuccarelli accompanied with a 'display room and school of criminal anthropology' (Florian 1943, 580). The materials relating to post-unification banditry were shown to the general public during the *Mostra di ricordi storici del Risorgimento meridionale d'Italia*, organised in Naples for the fiftieth anniversary of Italian unification (Giammattei 2011, 153–9). While Penta and Zuccarelli were gathering these materials, the Reggio Emilia mental hospital had instituted a Museum of Psychiatric Anthropology, formed by a collection of skulls and a set of drawings and other work done by inmates, as well as a Museum of Antiquity, dedicated to the history of immobilisation equipment (Vaschide 1900, 135–6). Other, lesser-known collections were almost certainly being formed, since in 1889 the Zanardelli code had foreseen the possibility of acquiring body parts from deceased prisoners for scientific research purposes. Abroad, the situation was no different: between the end of the 1800s and the new century, museums of criminology or psychiatry were appearing in Lyon, Berlin, Hamburg, Dresden, Graz, London, Havana, St Petersburg and Wien (Gross 1896, 74–94; Carrara 1913; Finzi 1914, 492–5; C.D.G. 1922, 3; Finzi 1925, 50–7; De Castro et al. 1930; Borzacchiello 1997, 29–70; Regener 2003, 43–56; Morehead 2011, 109–10). Furthermore, these collections were no longer aimed exclusively at scholars. In October 1905, *Je Sais Tout*, a widely read French magazine, published a portrait of Auguste-Armand Marie – at the time the director of the Villejuif mental hospital in the Île-de-France, and already translator of *Gli anarchici* and *L'antisemitismo e le scienze moderne* into French – accompanied by some of the works of art from the Torinese museum and by an article written by the psychiatrist himself, in which he put forward the idea of instituting a museum of madness.[4] It was therefore crucial to reiterate, as the extraordinary publicity hype of 1906–7 confirmed, the supremacy of the Torinese school in the field of anthropological, criminal and psychiatric museology. The second reason was partly a consequence of the first: since 1885, during the course of the first international congress of criminal anthropology in Rome, Sergi launched a proposal to institute an Italian national museum in this discipline (Actes 1886–7, 21). Projects aimed at creating central scientific museums for natural history, ethnography or geology had circulated in the Italian scientific community after unification, often running aground against the difficult equilibriums existing between the various centres, exasperating rivalries (Puccini 2011, 563; Canadelli 2011, 873–4). The proposal put forward by Sergi, who had started teaching anthropology in Rome the year before, was approved on the basis of Enrico Ferri's agenda, but it was not followed up on, partly due to the strong opposition of Lombroso, who aimed to achieve such recognition for his creation and feared that this idea joined with the intentions of the prison administration, which, after the plundering carried out by the Verona scientist in 1892 of the material gathered in the Regina Cœli, had planned to found its own museum of criminology (Borzacchiello 2006, 5). Lombroso, in 'Il mio museo criminale', made no secret of the rivalry unleashed by this initiative, which threatened to remove precious exhibits from the Torinese collection. One of his pupils, Judge Donato Costanzo Eula, during the inauguration of the new headquarters of the Lombrosian museum in the *Palazzo degli Istituti anatomici*, had echoed Sergi's proposal, being careful, however, to state that he did not intend to discuss the matter of which city should host the central museum of criminal anthropology (Eula 1898, 339–40). The expected recognition for the museum that he had created never arrived, since at the beginning of the 1900s the Prison Administration moved to generate popular interest in the results obtained in the fields relating to the study of delinquency and the new penitentiary policy (Polidori 1913, 170–1). Nonetheless, Lombroso wanted to donate his body to science, in line with a widespread custom among positivist scientists. In accordance with his last will and testament, Lombroso's body was moved to the institute on 20 October 1909, the day after he died, while students and pupils held vigil. On 21 October an autopsy was performed, and the brain, face, heart and skeleton were taken and preserved in the museum.

Mario Carrara as director

After the death of the *maestro*, Carrara continued to oversee the development of the institution, with the exception of a period between 1911 and 1913, when Mariano Patrizi, professor of physiology at the University of Modena, was hired on a temporary basis to teach criminal anthropology. On 21 March 1912, the Faculty of Medicine and Surgery authorised, upon Patrizi's request, the creation of the Institute of Criminal Anthropology, in the context of which he initiated a 'technical specialisation course for the natural history of crime and for penal magistery'.[5] Patrizi's project foresaw the strengthening of the Laboratory of Criminal Anthropology in order to add 'experimental demonstrative means' to the skull and skeleton section as well as to the museum's collections, with the aim of introducing 'the exact methods of physiology and experimental psychology' to the curriculum. However, at the end of that year Patrizi had already asked the Ministry of Public Education to be exempted from his mission at the University of Turin due to what he defined as the 'special conditions in which the professorship and the teacher find themselves', or rather the lack of a laboratory, equipment, an assistant and an attendant, and the difficulties encountered by the decree of appointment to the post of professor of criminal anthropology. Soon afterwards, Patrizi returned to Modena[6] and the teaching post was assumed by Carrara, professor of Forensic Medicine, on an unpaid basis. Carrara continued until the beginning of 1932 when he was expelled from the university for refusing to pledge allegiance to the fascist regime, which four years later abolished the professorships of criminal anthropology in all the universities in Italy (Martucci 2009, 297).[7] He had maintained a link between his studies – with which he had attempted to renew criminal anthropology, opening it up to new research into endocrinology – and the museum. Carrara gave a personal influence to the organisation of the museum, accompanying Lombroso's own sectors of interest with others that were more strictly related to the developments of scientific policing and forensic medicine. This led to the formation of a second museum, partly thanks to private donations, constituted by photographs and anatomical preparations relating mainly to traumatology and forensic asphyxiology (*Il Piemonte* 1924, 4; Carrara 1928).

A long decay

When Carrara was forced to abandon teaching and the management of the museum, it appeared that the Home Office Minister intended to move the Lombrosian collections to Rome. This was, perhaps, a reprisal against the blatant anti-fascism of the principle heirs and successors of Lombroso's work (Dolza 1990, 159–64).[8] In the capital, Lombroso's collections would have enhanced the criminal museum, opened in 1931 by the General Direction for the Institutes of Prevention and Punishment, by order of Minister *Guardasigilli* Alfredo Rocco (Vozzi 1931, 13–52). The dean of the Faculty of Medicine in Turin sent a letter of protest to the Ministry, while Gina Lombroso Ferrero wrote to Princess Maria José, wife of Umberto of Savoy, appealing for an intervention to try and stop the operation.[9] It is not known whether the reactions of the faculty and of the Lombroso family were enough to prevent the moving of the museum, or whether a compromise had been struck with the transfer of part of the collection to the capital, as the presence of certain objects of Piedmontese origin in Rome's current criminology museum may suggest. The majority of the Lombrosian collections, however, remained in Turin, in the *Palazzo degli Istituti anatomici*, having been entrusted to Ruggero Romanese (1886–1969). He was one of Carrara's pupils and collaborators and had returned to Turin from Parma, where he had been awarded the professorship, in order to teach forensic medicine in November 1933. Without there being the possibility of further additions to the collections, since the authorisation of the Ministry of Justice in relation to the bodies of evidence deposited in the chancelleries of the courts had been revoked in favour of the museum in the capital, Romanese planned to reorder all the materials in view of a transfer to

FIGURE 5.2 Recreation of Lombroso's office at the Museum – the furniture of the study that Lombroso and subsequently Carrara had used in the apartment in Via Legnano

Source: Archivio storico del Museo di Antropologia criminale "Cesare Lombroso" dell'Università di Torino (Italia).

a new headquarters (Romanese 1943, 581–2).[10] The transfer of both the Lombrosian museum and that of forensic medicine, now considered separate entities, did not take place until 1948, when the Forensic Medicine Institute building was constructed in Corso Galileo Galilei. On this occasion, the Carrara family donated the furniture of the study that Lombroso and subsequently Carrara had used in the apartment in Via Legnano 26 (see Figure 5.2).[11] Romanese continued to direct the museum until 1962 when he was succeeded by Sergio Tovo (1916–2011), also one of Carrara's collaborators. Under the management of Tovo, the museum was in favour of forging a stronger relationship with the public, allowing the introduction of guided tours and access to exhibits for observation on the part of a wide range of scholars. This was the period when a documentary, *Criminalità-disperazione*, was produced by director Paolo Saglietto, concentrating on Lombroso and the concept of deviance, followed in 1975, three years later, by a book by Giorgio Colombo entitled *La scienza infelice*: two initiatives that focused attention on the museum as a testimony to an era, and as an extraordinary collection of cultural heritage, while interest in Lombroso's work increased further due to the publication of his first scientific biography, written by Luigi Bulferetti.

A museum for the history of science and society

In 1983, when Tovo retired, the management of the museum was taken over by Mario Portigliatti Barbos, who had in the meantime become the director of the

Institute of Medical and Forensic Sciences, which derived from the unification of the Institutes of Forensic Medicine and of Criminal Anthropology. Under his leadership, plans for the transfer and renewal of the museum began to take shape, and the first step was the systematic cataloguing of all the exhibits, which took place between July 1990 and September 1994. Earlier, the exhibition in Turin entitled '*La scienza e la colpa. Crimini, criminali, criminologi: un volto dell'800*', organised in 1985 by Portigliatti Barbos, Umberto Levra and Renzo Villa, achieved great public acclaim and attracted international attention to the Lombrosian collections, which began to be sought after for exhibitions in Italy and abroad (Portigliatti Barbos 1985b; Levra 1985; Rizzo 1985; Gallino 1985)[12]. In 1998, Portigliatti Barbos retired and was succeeded by Paolo Tappero, who, in the context of the university project 'Museum of Man', coordinated by Giacomo Giacobini, continued to collaborate in arranging the transfer of the museum to other premises. The idea was to design an exhibition with a layout which was more suitable for use by a public that was not necessarily made up experts on Lombroso and criminal anthropology, and who would therefore need adequate information in order to correctly interpret the theories of the scientist and to understand, despite the fallaciousness, the importance of the historical, cultural and social context of the period (Giacobini *et al.* 2008, 21–31).

The latter is currently the main aim of the Lombrosian museum which is again present in the *Palazzo degli Istituti anatomici*, the headquarters chosen to house the museum collections of the University of Turin relating to the 'human sciences'.

FIGURE 5.3 The museum was reopened to the public on 27 November 2009 in conjunction with the 100th anniversary of Lombroso's death

Source: Archivio fotografico del Museo di Antropologia criminale "Cesare Lombroso" dell'Università di Torino (Italia).

The museum was reopened to the public on 27 November 2009 in conjunction with the 100th anniversary of Lombroso's death (see Figure 5.3). The event enjoyed significant coverage in the main national daily newspapers and on the television news, contributing to a renewed focus of attention on the scientist from Verona on the part of scholars and the general public.[13] The renewed interest in Lombroso has been fed by the publication of a growing number of studies carried out throughout the world, by conferences and by the reissuing of his main works.[14] The new museum, which has received great acclaim in prestigious magazines and which has aroused the interest of artists and writers of international renown, had been visited by 38,988 people up to May 2011, of whom one in five were not residents of Turin (Abbot 2010, 300; Becker 2010, 56–8).[15] The opening of the Lombroso Museum has also led to an increase in interest in the other two museums linked to the University of Turin, and further attention has been attracted towards Lombroso's collections from the organisers of some of the most important international exhibitions.[16] According to the results of the questionnaire given to visitors asking them for their opinions, the museum has met with almost unanimous consensus, with 96 per cent of people stating they were either quite or very satisfied with the experience (Mangiapane *et al.* 2011). Furthermore, a look at the visitors' book, positioned at the end of the exhibition, confirms the positive impressions made on the public: 81 per cent of the people who left a comment expressed an explicitly positive assessment. It is also necessary to state, however, that the reopening of the Lombroso Museum has been strongly contested by minority groups who have been active on the Italian scene for some time now, proponents of a prejudicially hostile interpretation of the National unification process in which nostalgia emerges for the ancient pre-unification states, as well as catholic traditionalism and southern pretensions (Galasso 2010, 345–9; Montaldo 2012). Political parties such as *Per il Sud*, following a line of repulsion/imitation of the *Lega Nord*, identify the Veronese scientist with the ideology of a racist vision towards those from the south of Italy, with a somewhat contrived interpretation of the past and against objective reality. Thus, they see in the present museum a new unabated proposal of Lombroso's theories, feeding controversy which has been echoed in local newspapers and in the support of members of the Italian Parliament who were part of the majority that sustained the last Berlusconi government.

Notes

1 This did not prevent Émile Durkheim from asking Lombroso in 1895 to participate with a number of examples of his research in an exhibition on the social sciences which he intended to organise in Bordeaux. Archive of the 'Cesare Lombroso' Museum of Criminal Anthropology (henceforth AMAC), letters from Durkheim to Lombroso, 10 February, 9 March, 4 and 16 May 1895.
2 AMAC, *Inventario delle proprietà mobili del Consorzio universitari esistenti nel Museo Psichiatrico e Criminologico.*

3 The circular of 25 June 1909, n. 1643, was not inserted in the '*Bollettino ufficiale del Ministero di Grazia e Giustizia e dei Culti*', but was observed by some chancelleries, who sent bodies of evidence to the Lombroso museum.
4 On Marie's initiative, which influenced the artistic avant-garde, see Morehead 2011, 103–5.
5 Historical Archive of the University of Turin (henceforth ASUT), Minutes of the Council of the Faculty of Medicine and Surgery, 21 March 1912; *Registro degli esami del Corso di perfezionamento per la Storia naturale del delitto e Magistero penale, Corso di perfezionamento in Criminologia (1912–1914)*.
6 Central State Archive, Rome (henceforth ACS), Ministry of Public Education, Directorate General for Higher Education, personal, teaching and administrative files, II deposit, file 118, letter from Patrizi to Luigi Credaro, 30 December 1912; ASUT, Minutes of the Council of the Faculty of Medicine and Surgery, 8 February 1913.
7 ASUT, personal file of Mario Carrara, sf. teaching positions (1922–32); sf. Dispensation from service liquidation of pension (1931–2).
8 ACS, Central political records, files 1112 (Mario Carrara); 2033 (Guglielmo Ferrero); 2034 (Leo Ferrero).
9 AMAC, letter from Gina Lombroso Ferrero to Maria José, March 1932. A few months earlier, Gina's son, Leo Ferrero, had been received by Albert I, King of Belgium and father of Maria Josè, as is evident from a second letter written by Gina and addressed to a member of the Belgian royal family, dated 16 March 1932.
10 Born in Pergine, Trentino, Romanese graduated in Turin in 1910 and in Berlin he specialised in bacteriology and forensic medicine. ASUT, personal file of Ruggero Romanese, sf. certificates of service, non-European assignments, other certificates.
11 Institute of Forensic Medicine, University of Turin, Correspondence, Letter written by Enrico Carrara, 30 June 1947.
12 Listed here a some of the most signigicant exhibitions in which items of the Lombrosian collections were displayed from 2005 to 2009: 'Wunderblock', Wien, 1989; 'Bunuel – Auge des Jahrhunderts', Bonn, 1994; 'Darwin und darwinismus', Dresden, 1994; 'L'âme au corps: arts e science 1973–1993', Paris, 1993–4; 'Identità e alterità', Venice, 1995; 'Bunuel – La mirada del siglo', Mexico City, 1996; 'Police Pictures: The photograph as evidence', San Francisco, 1997; 'Spectacular bodies', London, 2000; 'La memoria della scienza', Turin, 2004; 'Evoluzione. Le vie della vita', Dresden, 2005; 'Die Anatomie des Bösen', Schaffhausen, 2008; 'Arte genio e follia. Il giorno e la notte dell'artista', Siena, 2009.
13 See: Massimo Novelli, 'Il ritorno di Lombroso. Il museo della crudeltà' *La Repubblica* 27 September 2009; Umberto Galimberti, 'Un uomo normale e la sua ossessione' ivi; Ernesto Ferrero, 'Super Cesare dicci chi è il delinquente' *La Stampa* 17 October 2009; Mario Baudino, 'Lombroso, un crimine per ogni faccia' *La Stampa* 18 October 2009; Lara Ricci, 'Nel museo degli errori' *Il Sole 24 ore* 1 November 2009; Giuliano Galletta, 'Il marchio criminale' *Il secolo XIX* 27 November 2009; Oddone Camerana, 'Criminale voglio guardarti in faccia' *Osservatore romano* 13 December 2009; Gaetano Prisciantelli, 'Cesare Lombroso. Un museo per lo scienziato che giudicava i criminali dal naso' *Il Venerdì di Repubblica* 20 November 2009, pp. 74–6; Roberto Barbolini, 'Con quelle facce un po' così' *Panorama* 26 November 2009, pp. 181–2. Alberto Angela made a documentary at the museum entitled, *Il volto dell'assassino. Le teorie di Lombroso*, broadcast on *Superquark*, RaiUno, on 16 June 2011 and on *Passaggio a Nord-Ovest*, RaiUno, 4 February 2012.

14 Lorenzo Picotti and Francesca Zanusso (eds), *L'antropologia criminale di Cesare Lombroso: dall'Ottocento al dibattito filosofico-penale contemporaneo. Atti del Convegno internazionale svoltosi in occasione del primo centenario della morte presso la Facoltà di Giurisprudenza dell'Università degli Studi di Verona (16–17 ottobre 2009)*, Napoli: ESI 2011; Silvano Montaldo (ed.), *Cesare Lombroso. Gli scienziati e la nuova Italia*, Academy of Science of Turin – University of Turin, Museum of Criminal Athropology 'Cesare Lombroso', 5–6 November 2009, Bologna: il Mulino 2011. See: Cesare Lombroso and Guglielmo Ferrero, *La donna delinquente, la prostituta e la donna normale*, introduction by Mary Gibson and Nicole Hahn Rafter, Milano: et al./edizioni 2009; Cesare Lombroso, *In Calabria*, introduction by Luigi Guarnieri, Soveria Mannelli: Rubbettino 2009; Id., *Ricerche sui fenomeni ipnotici e spiritici*, with foreword by Giorgio Colombo, Milano: et al./edizioni 2010; Id., *L'uomo delinquente studiato in rapporto all'antropologia, alla medicina legale e alle discipline carcerarie*, edited by Lucia Rodler, preface by Dario Melossi, Bologna: il Mulino 2011.

15 On Paul Auster and Art Spiegelman's visits to the Lombroso Museum, see: Guido Tiberga, 'Lombrosiani a New York' *La Stampa* 20 January 2012.

16 From November 2009, the Lombroso Museum has collaborated in the following exhibitions: 'Crime & Châtiment. De Goya à Picasso', Paris, Musée d'Orsay, 15 March to 27 June 2010; 'Tre il dire e il fare. Unità d'Italia e unificazione europea: cantieri aperti', Turin, State Archive, 28 January to 16 April 2011; 'Images of the Mind. Bildwelten des geistes aus kunst und wissenschaft', Dresden, Deutsches Hygiene-Museum, 22 July to 30 October 2011, then transferred to the Moravian Gallery in Brno (Czech Republic) until February 2012; 'Banditi dell'Arte', Paris, Halle Saint Pierre, currently in progress; 'Faces', Athens, Onassis Cultural Centre, currently in progress.

References

Abbot, A. (2010) 'Turin's Criminology Museum,' *Nature* 463: 300.
Actes (1886–7) *Actes du premier congrès international d'anthropologie criminelle. Biologie et sociologie (Rome, November 1885)*. Turin, Rome and Florence: Bocca.
Annuario (1900) *Annuario della R. Università di Torino 1899–1900*: 69–70.
Barini, G. (1885) 'III Congresso penitenziario internazionale. Esposizione industriale carceraria', *Rivista di discipline carcerarie* 15: 677–83.
Becker, P. (2010) 'Buon giorno, Professore! Visiting the Museo di Antropologia criminale "Cesare Lombroso"', *Il mestiere di storico, Annale SISSCO* 1: 56–8.
Borzacchiello, A. (1997) 'I Musei criminali e l'ideologia del delinquente: raccolte ed esposizioni dall'Ottocento a oggi', *Rassegna penitenziaria e criminologica* 1: 29–70.
Borzacchiello, A. (2006) 'Le "raccolte criminali" sul finire dell'Ottocento. La nascita dei musei criminali e di polizia scientifica', in Ead (ed.) *Museo criminologico*. Roma: Ministero della Giustizia, Dipartimento dell'Amministrazione penitenziaria, pp. 5–17.
Bovero, A. (1908) 'Exposition d'anthropologie criminelle et de police scientifique', in *Comptes- rendus du VI e congres international d'Anthropologie criminelle, Turin, 28 avril–3 mai 1906*. Turin-Milan and Rome: Bocca, pp. 655–67.
Bulferetti, L. (1975) *Cesare Lombroso*. Torino: Utet.
Canadelli, E. (2011) 'I musei scientifici', in Francesco Cassata and Claudio Pogliano (eds) *Scienze e cultura dell'Italia unita, Storia d'Italia, Annali*, vol 26 Torino: Einaudi, pp. 867–93.
Carrara, M. (1897) 'I periti medici e lo studio della medicina legale all'estero', *Riforma medica* 13 (2): 7–12.
Carrara, M. (1910) 'Cesare Lombroso', *Annuario della R. Università di Torino 1909–1910*.

Carrara, M. (1913) 'Un museo per la criminalità infantile', *Archivio di antropologia criminale, psichiatria e medicina legale* 34: 697–703.
Carrara, M. (1928) 'Institute of Legal Medicine and Criminal Anthropology Royal University of Turin', *Methods and Problems of Medical Education*: 105–15.
C.D.G. (1922) 'Nel 30° anno di fondazione dell'Istituto di Antropologia Criminale "Giambattista della Porta" ', *Il giornale universitario*, November 1–15.
Cini, R. (1906) 'Il sesto Congresso d'antropologia criminale. Il giubileo scientifico del prof. Cesare Lombroso', *La Stampa* 118, April 29, p. 3.
Colombo, G. (1975) *La scienza infelice. Il Museo di antropologia criminale di Cesare Lombroso*. Torino: Boringhieri.
De Castro, R., Blanco Errera, J., Castellanos, I. and Valdés Castillo, E. (1930) *El museo de la catedra de medicina legal de la universidad de La Habana*. La Habana: Imp. El Universo.
Dolza, D. (1990) *Essere figlie di Lombroso. Due donne intellettuali tra '800 e '900*. Milano: Franco Angeli.
Eula, D. C. (1898) 'Come potrebbe essere praticamente istituito un Museo di Antropologia criminale', *Rivista mensile di Psichiatria forense, Antropologia Criminale e Scienze affini* 1: 339–42.
Finzi, M. (1914) 'Il museo criminale di Berlino', *Rivista penale* 79: 492–5.
Finzi, M. (1925) 'Il museo criminale di Lione', *Nuova Antologia* 322: 50–7.
Florian, E. (1943) 'Musei criminali', in Eugenio Florian, Alfredo Niceforo and Nicola Pende (eds) *Dizionario di criminologia per opera di numerosi autori* vol 2, Milano: Vallardi, pp. 579–81.
Frigessi, D. (2003) *Cesare Lombroso*. Torino: Einaudi.
Galasso, G. (2010) 'Centocinquant'anni', *L'Acropoli* 4: 345–9.
Gallino, L. (1985) 'Delitti in vetrina. Criminali e criminologi dell'800', *La Stampa* April 17, p. 3.
Giacobini, G., Cilli, C. and Malerba, G. (2008) 'Il Museo dell'Uomo di Torino. Un progetto in corso di realizzazione', *Museologia scientifica* 2 (1–2): 21–31.
Giammattei, E. (2011) *Mostra di ricordi storici del Risorgimento meridionale d'Italia*. anastatic reprint edited by E. Giammattei, Napoli: Edizione Comune di Napoli.
Gross, H. (1896) 'Das Kriminal-Museum in Graz', *Zeitschrift für die gesamte Strafrechtswissenschaft* 16: 74–94.
Levra, U. (1985) 'Alla ricerca di un marchio biologico', *La Stampa – TuttoScienze* March 6, p. 1.
Lombroso, C. (1906a) 'Il mio museo criminale', *L'Illustrazione italiana* 13, April 1: 302–6.
Lombroso, C. (1906b) 'Mi museo criminal', *Archivos de psiquiatria y criminologia aplicadas a las ciencias afines* 5: 288–94.
Lombroso, C. (1907a) 'Mi museo criminal', *Protocolo medico-forense* 9: 67–72.
Lombroso, C. (1907b) 'Mi museo criminal', *Revista frenopática española* 5: 15–22.
Lombroso, C. (1907c) 'My Museum of Criminal Psychology', *The New York Times* February 17.
Lombroso, C., Sciamanna, E. and Sergi, G. (1885) 'Congresso ed esposizioni d'Antropologia Criminale', *Rivista di discipline carcerarie* 15: 237–8.
Lombroso Ferrero, G. (1921) *Cesare Lombroso. Storia della vita e delle opere* (2nd edn). Bologna: Zanichelli.
Mangiapane, G., Spanu, L., Cilli, C., Malerba, G. and Giacobini, G. (2011) 'I visitatori del Museo di Antropologia criminale "Cesare Lombroso" dell'Università di Torino. Un primo bilancio dopo un anno di apertura al pubblico', *Museologia scientifica* 5 (1–2), currently being printed.

Martucci, P. (2009) 'Un'eredità senza eredi. L'Antropologia criminale in Italia dopo la morte di Cesare Lombroso' in Silvano Montaldo and Paolo Tappero (eds) *Cesare Lombroso cento anni dopo*. Torino: Utet, pp. 291–300.

Ministro (1909): 'Il ministro Orlando ed il Museo Antropologico Criminale di Torino', *Archivio di antropologia criminale, psichiatria, medicina legale e scienze affini* 30: 542.

Montaldo, S. (2012), 'La "fossa comune" del Museo Lombroso e il "lager" di Fenestrelle: il Centocinquantenario dei neoborbonici', *Passato e presente*, currently being printed.

Morehead, A. (2011) 'The *Musée de la folie*. Collecting and Exhibiting chez les fous', *Journal of the History of Collections* 23: 101–26.

Musée (1906) *Le Musée de Psychiatrie et d'Anthropologie criminelle dans l'Université de Turin*. Torino: Bocca.

Pettinati, N. (1884) 'L'esposizione dei morti', *L'Esposizione italiana* 36: 282.

Il Piemonte. Quotidiano di Torino (1924) 'Il Museo d'Antropologia', 23–24 January, p. 4.

Polidori, C. (1913) 'Il museo criminale penalogico italiano', *Rivista di discipline carcerarie e correttive* 28: 169–71.

Portigliatti Barbos, M. (1985a) 'Scienza e crimine nell'Ottocento: la risposta medica' in Umberto Levra (ed.) *La scienza e la colpa. Crimini, criminali, criminologi: un volto dell'800*. Milano: Electa, pp. 231–8.

Portigliatti Barbos, M. (1985b) 'Criminologia oggi che cosa c'è di nuovo', *La Stampa – TuttoScienze* March 6, p. 1.

Puccini, S. (2011) 'A casa e fuori: antropologi, etnologi e viaggiatori', in Francesco Cassata and Claudio Pogliano (eds), *Scienze e cultura dell'Italia unita*, Storia d'Italia, Annali, vol 26. Torino: Einaudi, pp. 547–73.

Regener, S. (2003) 'Criminological Museums and the Visualization of Evil', *Crime, History & Societies* 7: 43–56.

Rizzo, R. (1985) 'Uomini e fantasmi', *La Stampa* March 9, p. 14.

Romanese, R. (1943) 'Museo di Antropologia criminale (Università di Torino)', in E. Florian, A. Niceforo and N. Pende (eds), *Dizionario di criminologia per opera di numerosi autori* vol 2. Milano: Vallardi, pp. 581–2.

Severi, A. and Lombroso, C. (1886) *La prima esposizione internazionale di Antropologia criminale a Roma*. Torino: Bocca.

Vaschide, N. (1900) 'Organisation scientifique: l'Institut psychiatrique de Reggio', *Revue de psychiatrie* 4: 135–6.

Villa, R. (1985) *Il deviante e i suoi segni. Lombroso e la nascita dell'antropologia criminale*. Milano: Franco Angeli.

Vozzi, R. (1931) *Museo Criminale*. Roma: Ministero della Giustizia.

6

CAESAR OR CESARE?

American and Italian images of Lombroso

Patrizia Guarnieri

As a seasickness

Reading Lombroso's works is a demanding undertaking, because his vast production as scientist and columnist appears heterogeneous, frantic, and intentionally without conceptual order. It is a production that is built on progressive accumulation of material, apparently without an orderly selection of what Lombroso had written or noted before, and without making distinction between his own thoughts and those he had gotten from other authors. One can for instance reflect on how much the publication *L'uomo delinquente* (Criminal Man) grew from the 255 pages of its 1st edition to the four large volumes of the 5th edition. "Reading it was a psychic experience equivalent to feeling seasick" whispered a French colleague of Lombroso in 1990, obviously with the intention of criticizing him (Mesnil 1900, 628). Others thought the same way. Almost one century later, even the Italian scholars who wished to present him in a non-judgmental manner, had to admit the existence of inconsistencies in Lombroso's writings and hence the difficulty to structure his publications in terms of themes addressed, which they attempted anyway to do in a collection of his works published in 1995 (Lombroso 1995).

Understanding Lombroso in translations to foreign languages may be even harder. How and what was exactly translated when in 1911 *Criminal Man* appeared for the first time in English? Rather briefly summarized, or based on a French translation of only one of the four volumes of the 5th edition of 1896–97. A similar difficulty was faced by Mary Gibson and Nicole Rafter, respectively authors of *Born to Crime* (2002) and *Creating Born Criminals* (1997), who issued a translation based on selected parts of Lombroso's Italian editions (Lombroso 2006). Much more than for other authors, the renditions of Lombroso's works in the various translations have been heavily affected by the cultural context, expectations, and needs which they have addressed – at Lombroso's time as well as today. This must be taken into consideration in order to understand the Lombroso phenomenon, including his undeniable fame, which many have pondered on since Mesnil (1900).

A number of questions arise when one looks at how Lombroso's work was received: what has his work meant for the scientific community and for the public during the course of time? Even in the enormous literature that refers to him, one can observe the same inconsistent accumulation that characterizes his own production. Opposite opinions seem to co-exist: when critics seem to liquidate his work as "pseudo-science," the appreciation arises for the precursor of modern as well as earlier scientific theories.

The recent 100-year anniversary of Lombroso's death has been an occasion of debate among scholars as well as among the public – at least in Italy, and an opportunity for some deliberation. Giorgio Israel, a scholar in science, fascism, and Jewish history, has identified in the debate a lack of critical originality. It ranged from the "condemnation of Lombroso as champion of a brutal and extreme anthropology, or from his classification as father of modern racism, to the opposite end where he rises as the great scientist who anticipated the modern naturalistic view of man" (Israel 2010, 145).

In the latter regard, Peter Becker has shown how, in recent years, appreciative references to the "inventor" of criminology have grown into a debate about neuroscience, extending to magazines for the general public dealing with neurobiological topics (Becker 2010). Images of Lombroso as a precursor are repeatedly drawn, both for theories and ideologies that are well appreciated, such as the neuroscientific ones, as well as for those that are denigrated, like the biological theories of crime, or the inequalities of race or gender. It seems to me that these images overlap with each other and build on the same mistake or methodological ingenuity – in the context of history of science – regardless of the different opinions on theories for which Lombroso was seen as a precursor.

The enthusiasm for Lombroso as a leader in neuroscience has not eliminated the execration of Lombroso as the father of scientific racism. This accusation – that Israel considers "more than exaggerated ... simply ridiculous" (Israel 2010, 145) – in fact is not supported in the current scientific debate. Yet it still lingers, whenever new studies are undertaken. So when, in 2003, a new biography about Lombroso was released (Frigessi 2003), there were press critiques of the very fact of having paid attention to the founder of criminal anthropology, a figure who was glorified by the totalitarian fascist regime (a statement which is historically unfounded and in fact unsustainable).[1] In 2009, during the conference that was organized to celebrate Lombroso's 100-year anniversary, in the Italian congress someone again alluded to his alleged responsibility in anti-semitism, provoking indignation from a direct descendant of Lombroso, who was present and whose family had suffered from anti-semitic persecution and had been forced to emigrate or to hide, after the fascist laws of 1938.[2] As another example, a street protest organized by a so-called "civil insurgence movement" against the reopening of the Museum of Lombroso in Turin. In Calabria, in the village where the "brigante" Giuseppe Villella was born, on whose head the anthropologist had found the stigmata of the "born criminal," there has been claims for his rehabilitation as a victim of pseudo-scientific racism (Guarnieri 2010, 238).

Even today, current issues are discussed with approaches that reinforce a negative image of Lombroso. One finds this in the press as well as in parliamentary debates and not only in Italy. At the French *Assemblée Nationale*, in January 2008, during a discussion on a draft law on security arrest, the proposing Minister had been accused of being a follower of Lombroso and "his positivist philosophy, which had produced the worst of Nazi Germany" (Renneville 2009, 211). These are ridiculous opinions as Giorgio Israel commented; or historical contradictions, as observed by Marc Renneville.

Should Lombroso be left in peace, rather than improperly pulling him into all sort of debates on current issues? Although those judgments are not shared by today's historians, their unwieldy presence cannot be disregard, a presence which has been lasting and which the past history has contributed to build in a more or less direct fashion. As known, the image of Lombroso as inspirer of the Final Solution, racist, pseudo-scientific in relation to criminals as well as to women, has emerged in the late 1970 and onwards. This judgment is expressed in several books on the history of racism published in the United States – from *Toward the final solution* by George Mosse (1978) to *The Mismeasure of Man* by Stephen J. Gould (1981) – which were written and read in a "heated" political and cultural climate, and which were translated, well received, and much used in the condemnation of Lombroso. By virtue of these publications, the Lombroso debate restarted in Italy, in a sudden and negative fashion, after a long silence that still needs to be explained.

The way an author is received can reveal much about the needs and concerns of the community that exalts, blames, censures, or forgets him. The Lombroso centenary celebration seems to me to have resulted in a better knowledge of how wide the circulation of his ideas was, although variously interpreted, in different European, American, or Asia countries. Galileo and Leonardo apart, Lombroso is the only Italian scientist who has enjoyed much international fame, a fame that was mainly positive outside Italy. Hence, it is surprising that a negative image has prevailed and in fact is the only one remaining in the general public.

At this point, I would like to focus on the development of the reception and view on Lombroso in two different countries, i.e. United States and Italy, considering the repercussions of these on one and the other side of the ocean. The choice of this comparison allows one to investigate significant questions such as: what happens when scientific ideas circulate on a world basis? When they migrate elsewhere and return transformed? And how these transformed ideas are received back in a context that in the meantime has changed? What about if they don't come back at all? In natural sciences the migration to different national contexts occurs on the basis of a commonly shared language; but for human sciences things are more complex because of various types of interactions, contamination, misunderstandings which affect the way theories are transformed and became socially acceptable. Lombroso addressed serious questions that very much reflected the interest of the society at that time, and for which politicians and ordinary people wanted to have urgent answers. It was also believed and hoped that science could provide the solutions that were needed. But how and under what conditions these solutions could actually be used was a matter of debate, the content of which varied depending on the context in which the debate itself occurred.

Fascination and Americanization

Lombroso himself expressed his view *On the dissemination of criminal anthropology* (Lombroso 1890). His presentation was supported by the circle of his associates and appears reliable, certainly interesting. While Europe "was fighting even for its name" (and the strongest opponents were among his fellow psychiatrists), America welcomed the criminal anthropology with ovation. Not only in the countries of South America, Argentina in particular, as he wrote for a book first published in Buenos Aires in 1888 and then in Turin (Lombroso 1890, xxxiv–xxxv), but also in the United States. As he recognized in 1909, America gave to an increasing extent "a warm and sympathetic reception to the ideas of the Modern School which they speedily put into practice" (Lombroso 1911b, xix).

Lombroso was comparing the generosity of the new world to the ungratefulness of the old one, and the American ability of putting ideas into practice with the European defect of wasting time in sterile debates, mostly animated by academic or professional rivalry. Lombroso complained a lot about this. He really suffered from the isolation and the attacks that came from across the Alps, the explicit and harsh accusations from the French "cousins" as well as the misunderstandings of the Germans. He was especially suffering for the strong criticism raised from the area of Italian positivism, a complicated, heterogeneous cultural and scientific movement, as the series of specialist research since the 1980s on the history of Italian scientific culture on the nineteenth and twentieth centuries has demonstrated.[3] In the absence of an authoritative leadership as was the case for other national positivisms in Europe, the Italian culture cultivated more souls.

Certainly, Italian positivism did not have a single direction; therefore, placing Lombroso within a framework defined by rigid associations among organicism, determinism, positivism, etc. does not help understanding of either his polyhedral figure or the changing context around him. Since 1903, the inexorable criticisms of Benedetto Croce and Giovanni Gentile on *La Critica* were regularly directed against all the positivists – historians, philosophers, anthropologists, psychologists, pedagogues; but even before the dominant neo-idealism proclaimed "the end of positivism" (Gentile 1917, ed 1969, 308–316), Lombroso was attacked from within, not from the adverse part as he stressed even to his American audience. A colleague, Enrico Morselli, who was almost twenty years younger and who had been appointed instead of Lombroso the professorship and the position of asylum director in Turin, coined him – without respect – "the steelyard psychiatrist" (Morselli 1906; Guarnieri 2002). The founder of the Italian society of anthropology, the famous evolutionist Paolo Mantegazza, with whom good relations were ruined due to the disagreement over atavism, thought Lombroso was obsessed with numbers, but "unable to handle the scale and the rule" (Mantegazza 1888, 71). Contemporary scientists complained about the absence of independent checking, the small number of cases observed, the crudeness of its statistics, and the simplicity of its deductions; the criminologists and criminal lawyers noted that his approach did not sufficiently acknowledge the social and the psychological factors of crime. The list of critical quotes might be made long, confirming what many researchers have documented: the Italian cultural context cannot be seen as having been favorable to Lombroso. This was certainly the case in the scientific arena, as well as in the field of practices and their social acceptability (Giacanelli 1995).

In the court room, modern science was not prevailing against the philosophy of free will shared by magistrates; nor was it able to convince public opinion which generally wanted severe punishments for murder crimes. That a murderer should not be sentenced because experts identified on his face and body the stigmata of his pre-determined attitude to crime was not acceptable, not even when the physical aspect was most suitable to the application of the Lombrosian categories, which in any case were not able to explain the specificity of each case: such as, in the internationally quoted case of the child murderer Carlo Grandi, who was malformed, dwarfish and with twenty-one fingers, and whose autobiographical manuscript Lombroso framed in his museum. Tried in Florence in 1876, he was found guilty and sentenced, and after twenty years released and put in an asylum, but the process was a mess, and appeared like an offense inflicted on modern science (Guarnieri 1993).

Lombroso often felt that he was misunderstood. He showed self-criticism for some errors he made and is well known that in further reviews of *Criminal Man*, he gave space to the social factors. But some of the criticisms were difficult to swallow for Lombroso, especially the accusation of having neglected the psychology: he was grateful to America and to those who do not acknowledge this criticism and thought he was also a psychologist. For the compilation that was issued in his honor – *The Work of Cesare Lombroso in Science and its Applications* – he would have preferred the title *Synopsis of my Findings and Mistakes in Sociology, Criminal Anthropology, Forensic Medicine and Psychiatry* (Lombroso 1908, xv). It is remarkable that even in 1906, during the celebrations made in his Turin, at over 70 years of age and at the end of his career, Lombroso was not spared from heavy criticisms, which made him expressing pessimism about the future of criminal anthropology in Italy after him: "a legacy without heirs" as it is called (Martucci 2009, 291).

At the same time, Americans were enthusiastic about him and his science. Lombroso said it himself; he was glad about it and yet mildly perplexed. He felt their "almost fanatical adherence" to his ideas, even before his major work had appeared in English (Lombroso 1911a, xi). According to recent studies, his reputation in USA peaked in the last decade of the nineteenth century and early twentieth century. Although, some degree of criticism was not lacking: "His work is by no means perfect: he is apt to jump at conclusions too rapidly, to accept date too lightly [. . .]. Still, when all is said and done, his work is undoubtedly epoch-making," concluded Helen Zimmern, a writer of German Jewish origin who did a lot to make

Lombroso known to British and American readers[4] (Zimmern 1898, 348). Those who believed in the necessity of scientific criminology scrutinized him: an Italian had inspired a new science in the USA (Rafter 2009, 281). At the time, he was respected as a scientist (more than among his Italian countrymen), and as a columnist. Between 1891 and 1912, many English-language magazines, especially American ones, published about forty of his articles (Horton and Rich 2004). In conclusion: in the US, not just specialists, but "large audiences [were] hungry to read what he had to say on almost any subject" (Rafter 2009, 283).

This is somewhat surprising, especially when keeping in mind the negative image of Lombroso that later emerged in the United States, and then bounced with resonance in Italy. As Mary Gibson (2010, 354) has recently pointed out, that negative image emerged, in the popular and militant Gould publication of 1981, written in the first year of the Ronald Reagan presidency, which was translated into Italian in 1985 (by a publisher close to the Italian communist party), and then reprinted again and again. How can one explain that sort of fascination for Lombroso, while he was alive, followed by so much condemnation?

The Americans at that time, before "statistics was taught in schools [...], were unlikely to notice [his] methodological flaws that jump out today" (Rafter 2009, 1). Nicole Rafter who together with Gibson has provided English readers with a meaningful portrait of Lombroso as an intellectual, and replaced a cartoon image of him, seems to explain his popularity in America with the scientific ignorance prevailing at that time. This, however, is not a convincing explanation. As mentioned above, Lombroso was immediately scolded for methodological errors by many of his contemporaries in Europe; and also they had not learned statistics at school. Any scientist can be criticized on the basis of subsequent knowledge but this constitutes a methodological error – the so-called "presentism" – in the history of science but not only there, which for the case of Lombroso's work has been recurrent. In any case the scientific merits of a theory judged retrospectively does not explain its success, or lack of it, at the time when it was created.

Another, and more provocative, hypothesis may be that perhaps Americans liked Lombroso simply because they had not read his books. This is not entirely true, but not completely wrong either. While Lombroso was alive, only one of his books appeared in an abridged American edition: *The Female Offender*, which was released in 1895 just two years after the original was issued. Written together with his future son-in-law, the journalist and writer Guglielmo Ferrero, the book was considered "one of Lombroso's less important books" (Parmelee 1911, xii) within the circle of the American criminologists who admired him and wanted his work to become known.

Whereas in 1909 Cesar Lombroso was universally known, as the Northwestern University criminologist John Wigmore kindly wrote, the "English speaking world is acquainted with his theories largely through hearsay" (Parmelee 1911, xii–xiii). His fame in the USA was more due to "frequent appearances in popular American periodicals" (Simon 2005–06, 2164) than through knowledge of his scientific work. This knowledge came late, was not thorough, and was not without misunderstandings, starting from the quality of the translation of the posthumous edition of 1911 for "The Modern Criminal Science Series," which left all non-English authors more or less dissatisfied (Petit 2007, 851).

This did not prevent, however, the American reception of Lombroso to be very favorable, supportive and, I might add, full of unpredictable developments – not at all similar to the developments for which he was condemned nearly a century later. Even in the history of ideas, fascination implies a projection of wishes on the object that fascinates us. What counts is not so much knowing it well – especially at the beginning it is the opposite that helps – but having us believe in the realization of a project. In the late 1800s and early 1900s, educated Americans knew that the science was European, and that the best research was done in the ancient universities of the old world. To study in Berlin, Paris, Vienna was itself a credential, as it happened for example to William James, who after attending the Wundt laboratory in Leipzig, had obtained the chair of Psychology at Harvard, even though he had returned from Germany as a confirmed anti-Wundtian, something that James did not find convenient to say at the beginning of his career.

American culture was primarily geared to putting ideas into practice, the can-do spirit. But the search for new ideas was occurring in Europe and in order for the US to cast off their feelings of inferiority, they needed to learn, liberate the disciplines from the empiricism in which they were embedded, and look at overseas models. The project, as declared and pursued, was twofold: to import the scientific ideas from Europe, but adapt them according to the needs of their young nation, which did not renounce pragmatism, making use of practical ideas, especially those that could best fit their needs.

It was in this process that the fascination for "Caesar" Lombroso as "the inventor of scientific criminology" occurred. *A modern man of science*: this is how he was presented in the first biography about him which appeared in English in 1911, written the year before by the German neurologist Hans Kurella and translated into English with the help of Havelock Ellis. The fact that it was first released in Germany was at the time an excellent reference for the cultivated part of the American audience in search of science, since Germany with its twenty-one state universities was seen as the epitome of scientific excellence.

For criminology and for modern criminal justice, however, the primacy was Italy. It is "the glory of Italy, the land where Roman law, the foundation of modern law, was born" – a German-American author pointed out – "that it has proceeded to the study of this problem [of criminality] by the only truly scientific method" (Zimmern 1898, 342). The first American Institute of Criminal Law and Criminology, founded in Chicago in 1909, decided to inaugurate "The Modern Criminal Science Series," translating the best European scholars of the field. Three were Italians: Lombroso was of course the first, followed by the sociologist Enrico Ferri, and by the jurist Raffaele Garofalo.

Lombroso did not oppose his "Americanization." Indeed, he deliberately contributed to it by distributing paternity titles to various Americans, which he publicly acknowledged as those which best applied his ideas. Unlike other European academicians, he did not worry that his thought could be contaminated; for him, what counted above all was that his work was considered useful. In this sense, the attraction between him and America was reciprocal, more intensely and less ambiguously than it has been in other cases.

Americanization in fact always entailed new and unpredictable outcomes, unrecognizable in the initiation context, that responded to the needs of mobility and development of the new world. Hence, ideas that in Europe were not considered scientific enough, had success when re-adapted for American society. Lombroso knew the fortune that phrenology by Franz Joseph Gall and Johann Spurzheim, or the magnetism of Franz Mesmer had in the United States. Lombroso certainly knew of the American psychical researchers who had wanted to meet the medium Eusapia Paladino from Puglia (his favorite), while he for the same reason had been derided by his Italian colleagues. Perhaps he learned about the reception that Americans gave to Freud: a triumphal one, unthinkable in Europe at the time, and full of misunderstandings which very much tormented the Austrian professor.

It is worth noticing that the Americanization that separately involved both Cesare Lombroso and Sigmund Freud, produced decades later recurrent comparisons between their ideas, which they personally never initiated. The two physicians had in fact no interest for each other. Despite the proximity of their respective locations and the affinity of their disciplines, they never met, never wrote to and never quoted each other in their respective publications, although these were numerous. But on the other side of the ocean they were acknowledged at the same time with an extraordinary success. Their ideas were widespread in different ways, then revised in subsequent waves, then banned. Their names were associated or confronted, especially with regard to Jewish science and nazism. Their theories on specific research topics such as childhood, sexuality, and delinquency were compared among scholars – in Italy, for example, by the Jewish psychiatrist Marco Levi Bianchini (Levi Bianchini 1921) and in the UK and the United States primarily among European Jewish psychoanalysts who had fled from Nazism.

Recently, both Lombroso and Freud were reappraised in relation to new investigations in neuroscience. The encounter and the clash that took place between them, who died with thirty years difference from each other, in 1909 and in 1939, are part of the paths and of the unpredictable outcomes of certain ideas seen in different contexts, beyond the intentions of the protagonists, who in fact never met.

Developments and losses

Freud landed in New York on August 21, 1909, to travel to Worcester, Massachusetts where the psychologist Stanley Hall, a scholar of adolescence, had invited him for a meeting at the Clark University. Also Lombroso should have gone to the United States in 1909. John Wigmore, dean of the Law School at Northwestern University had even visited him at his home in Turin, in May 1908, to invite him and to appoint him as Harris lecturer in 1909–10 (Parmelee 1911, xiii). At the age of 74, Lombroso declined due to health and old age. Nevertheless, "during his final illness," he managed to write the introduction to the book *Criminal Man, According to the Classification of Cesare Lombroso, Briefly Summarized by his Daughter Gina Lombroso Ferrero*; G.P. Putnam's Sons published it in 1911 in New York and London in "The Science Series."

What did Lombroso want to say to his American readers? He defined the essential core of its science and its practical purpose, that it was "the study not of crime in the abstract, but of the criminal himself in order adequately to deal with the evil effects of his wrong-doing" (Lombroso 1911b, xi–xii). He asserted the process by which, slowly and with doubts, he had come to his *Criminal Man* based on observations and on the experimental method that he had applied first to the sick in the asylums, then to the inmates of prisons (he recalled the cases of Villella, Verzeni, and Misdea) to investigate the differences rather than the similarities between them and normal individuals. Although the clinical studies had confirmed the anthropological observations, all his

> attempts would have been sterile had not a solid phalanx of jurist, Russian, German, Hungarian, Italian and American, fertilized by correcting the germ and hasty conclusions one side, suggesting appropriate reforms and applications and, most important of all, applying my ideas on the offender to his individual and social prophylaxis and cure (Lombroso 1911b, xvii).

Lombroso spoke then of criminal anthropology as a composite building which many after him together had contribute to build, a stone upon a stone. He used the plural: *they* or *we* had raised it, expanded and improved it – firstly Enrico Ferri who had added the two criminal types: "occasional criminal" and "criminal by passion." They strengthened and defended the building they built. At the beginning, the school of criminal anthropology was attacked from all parts of Europe with "calumnies and misrepresentations which always follow in the train of audacious innovations." They were accused of excessive indulgence towards criminals, of pursuing criminals' impunity and release, of considering criminals merely and eternally slaves of their instincts.

We can notice that these allegations were significantly different from the nearly opposite ones that the leftists raised in the late 1970s and 1980s against biological determinism of which they believed Lombroso was the founder. In 1909, he claimed that criminal anthropology "on the contrary, gave a powerful impetus to the labors of statisticians and sociologists." The science had matured, also thanks to them. One nation, however – America – had understood it and "speedily put into practice, with [...] brilliant results." The Reformatory at Elmira, the probation system, the juvenile courts, and the George Junior Republic were the "achievements", were the realizations he wanted to mention in the 322 pages of the summary of his work, composed by his daughter Gina who had "shared in my anxieties, insults, and triumphs" (Lombroso 1911b, xix–xx).

Maybe that list was used to win the favor of the American public – but not only for that. Lombroso had already written about the above-mentioned American institutions several years earlier in texts aimed at European readers. In his work on *Les applications de L'anthropologie criminelle* of 1891 he included the probation system as he did in the Italian edition of *Criminal Man*. In the third volume, which Lombroso considered as the most important of his work, he illustrated at length the "excellent preventive institution for minor age or occasional offenders," which was in force in the USA and which was extended to adults in Massachusetts from 1878. He had above all commended the correctional facility of New York, from which he claimed to receive and read the weekly newsletter written by the convicts. In Elmira he saw "the first practical and serious application of my studies," because the fixed penalty corresponding to the crime committed was replaced by the indeterminate sentence, which was each time adapted to the individualized study and treatment of the indicted (Lombroso 1897, 538–43).

Both the probation system and the Elmira reformatory dated back to the 1870s. Elmira was opened in 1876, when the first version of *Criminal Man* was issued. The enunciation of criminal types and especially the occasional criminal had yet to come. Believing like Lombroso did, that an Italian book had inspired American institutions, seems less likely than Havelock Ellis had stated in 1891: the founders of Elmira "seem to have been guided purely by practical and social considerations and to have had no knowledge of the scientific movement that was arising in Europe"; where, on the other hand, criminologists had worked "purely as scientific investigators" (Ellis 1891, iv).

The distinction between the practical and the theoretical was in reality less sharp, at least based on what the founder of criminal anthropology told himself. American commentators insisted perhaps to show a mutual convenience: "in the future, there is now good reason to hope, these two currents of scientific advance and practical social progress will be united" (Ellis 1891, iv). While the US certainly needed European science, the latter could benefit from the US interest. It "is now essential that these reforms should be studied in the light of this new science of criminology and that they should be given a sound scientific basis. European science and American practical reform should be brought together," argued the sociologist Maurice Parmelee (Parmelee 1908, 6).

The intent was to import European scientific ideas and adapt them to America (or "Americanize"), in a planned fashion (Petit 2007; Pifferi 2009): first, by translating for the American public, or better by summarizing and presenting in a digestible way the European treaties on criminology. Lombroso's work was part of this. His major work appeared in the United States in two versions – not translations – in the same year and, as already said, more than three decades after the only abridged edition of one of his minor books was issued. What audience were the publishers G.P. Putnam's Sons and Little, Brown and Company aiming at? To understand this parallel editorial operation one would need to know the intentions of those who had promoted it (and now we have some background of one of the two), and whether they succeeded or not.

Obviously, the American readers did not engage themselves in a comparative analysis between the volumes of 1911 that apparently were proposing to be the same work. Such comparative analysis has not been made, nether between the two nor with the original third volume of the fifth edition, which is the main one where non-biological aspects are addressed, and to which both American editions make explicit reference. What interests us here is how each volume was presented to the American public. Certain differences are evident.

The volume of 322 pages published as the 27th in "The Science Series" was edited by the zoologist F. E. Beddard and by the Columbia University psychologist Edward Lee Thorndike, who in 1912 was about to be appointed chairman of the American Psychological Association. In *Criminal Man, According to the Classification of Cesare Lombroso*, he had written only the introduction which I mentioned above. The author was in reality Gina Lombroso Ferrero, as stated on the title page. Lombroso's collaborator and daughter writes in the first person, explicitly distinguishing in the text what she referred to as "my father and his disciples" from her own observations, including the large space dedicated to crime prevention. Gina Lombroso Ferrero devoted an entire chapter to this subject, where she insisted on the "preventive institutions for destitute adults" and in particular on the work done by the Salvation Army, which "from what I was able to observe in America, seems to me the best organized" (Lombroso G. 1911, 167). One could say that her work sort of flirted with America ("*americaneggiasse*"); combining what appeared to be the most useful end of Lombroso's ideas with the actual practices organized in various parts of the United States. I believe she did it well aware that her father was altogether in favor of an effective American "contamination" of the ideas he had developed in Italy.

The other volume instead, published with the support of the American Institute of Criminal Law and Criminology of Chicago, had the now deceased Lombroso as author and bore the title *Crime: its Causes and Remedies*, translated from the French edition *Le crime; causes et remédes* (1899) and less close to the original *Uomo delinquente*. The choice of the title was not the best, because the great merit of Italian criminal anthropology consisted of abandoning the study of crime as an abstract entity, and focusing on the concreteness of criminal individuals – and especially the American commentators stressed this merit. A common preconception that Lombroso recognized but one type of criminal, the atavistic one, wasn't true and Lombroso had indeed rejected it, claimed sociologist Maurice Parmelee, who noticeably had been in charge of the introduction (Parmelee 1911, xxviii). This came in addition to the translated preface which Lombroso had written in 1906 and devoted to Max Nordau, wherein the author rejected the accusation "of having neglected the economic and social caused of crime and of having confined [...] to the study of the born criminal."

"Strange to say" but Lombroso was ignorant in biology and especially in inheritance, which he mixed up with atavism, observed Parmelee, who emphasized the transition from a mainly naturalistic and anthropological approach toward a growing recognition on the social causes of crime. The first biological approach could not avoid to be challenged, but after he had greatly modified his sociological conception and "whatever may have been his faults, Lombroso was the great pioneer [...] in the great movement towards the positive, applications of the inductive methods of modern science to the problem of crime" (Parmelee 1911, xxxii). That's why the American Institute of Criminal Law and Criminology had chosen his most mature work to make him known in the US. Parmelee was alluding to a convergence of intents, when he quoted a long passage in a letter from Lombroso to his fellow Wigmore, concerning the next National Conference on Criminal Law and Criminology in Chicago, which "will mark a new era in the progress of criminal law." It included a number of recommendations to his American colleagues:

> if I could offer any suggestion to a so competent a body of men, it would be to emphasize the importance of apportioning of mestizos, not according to the offence, but according to the offender. To this end the probation system, which it is the great credit of America to have introduced, should be extended so as to suit the offender's type and individuality. It is futile to fix a term of imprisonment (novel) for the born criminal; but it is most necessary to shorten to the minimum the term for the emotional offender, and to modify it for the occasional offender, and to place the latter under the supervision of a judge, and not to let his fate be so fixed that it amounts merely to a modern form of slavery (Lombroso to J.H. Wigmore, Turin, May 3, 1909 quoted by Parmelee, 1911, xiii).

The Italian scientist expressed his appreciation of the American penal reforms: it was what they wanted. The initiatives of the American Institute, starting from the Conference of the 1909 series, were all actions of "propaganda of the Science of Criminology among the American legal profession, who are hitherto quite deaf to its appeal," explained its President Wigmore to Enrico Ferri, another Italian who got involved in the mission (Wigmore to E. Ferri, January 16, 1909 in Petit 2007, 877). With the edition of the works of Lombroso, Ferri, and Garofalo, and a few other Europeans, the Committee on translations for the modern criminal science series had the "purpose of reaching the lawyers," and for this they had chosen a law publishing house – Little, Brown and Co, Boston. "The treatises need not to be the very latest"; the important thing was that the works would become accessible to that public and for that each author was to grant permission to revise the texts as they felt appropriate (Wigmore to the President of the Committee W.W. Smithers, June 15, 1909, in Petit 2007, 889).

Crime: its Causes and Remedies was admittedly not a translation, but an English version which was in turn based upon the "French version" published in 1899, mainly based on the third volume of the last Italian edition (which, however, was of 1896–7), warned the translator Henry P. Horton who benefitted of the German 1902 translation by Kurella and Jentsch, from which he cut "few notes and other details interesting to Italians only" (Horton 1911, xxxvii). The result was a mess.

For the permission to print, now that the author had died, Wigmore had to ask Gina Lombroso Ferrero. Her letters of protest, recently published, reveal her opposition: in her view, from that edition presented to the American public, they could not understand what Lombroso had really written. She asked that the missing parts be at least summarized, like she had done for Putnam's. Gina Lombroso Ferrero did not need to bother, replied Wigmore by insisting on his request. "Will you, therefore, fill out the documents of consent accordingly? As to the preface, we can arrange for it ourselves, instead of asking you to do it." In the future, was his vague promise, perhaps one could hope "of translating Professor Lombroso's entire book. But no publisher in this country would undertake it at present" (Wigmore to Gina Lombroso, April 19, 1910, in Petit 2007, 895). In other words, take it or leave it: and Gina Lombroso Ferrero gave up.

It's ironic that the blame for the incorrect reception of Lombroso's work in the US was later put on her. To remedy the poor translation, Mary Gibson and Nicole Rafter issued new American editions of two criminology books by Lombroso, which had appeared in the US during his lifetime, or shortly after. There was another paradox: the good "translations" (the new *Criminal Man* is a fairly elaborate synopsis of various versions) came out when his reputation was not good anymore. Starting from the late 1970s, criminal anthropology has become quite an easy target for controversies and has been under many attacks: from Mosse, Gould, and dozens of critical and radical criminologists. But when did the American fascination with him finish?

According to the criminologist Nicole Rafter, "his reputation went into an eclipse from which did not recover for nearly a century" (Rafter 2009, 286); that is, until today. Jonathan Simon, Professor of Law at Berkeley, has another opinion. In 2006, he released a brilliant and very detailed essay on a specialist journal to show "How the inventor of scientific criminology who died at the beginning of the twentieth century continues to haunt American crime control at the beginning of the twenty-first." Therefore, in his opinion, the influence of Lombroso, far from being eclipsed by his death, persisted and still persists in the United States.

Even the periodization of the judgments of these two American scholars are very far apart, Rafter's sources go no further than 1912 and regarding "American criminal anthropologists" she limits herself to a list of nine authors and books published between 1893 and 1910 (Rafter 2009, 280, quoting Rafter 1992). William Healy with his *Individual Delinquent* of 1915 is missing, although his work represents the best-known criminology treaty made by an American author until the 1950s. Further, Healy's work has often been related to the individual-approach of the Italian criminologist, as mentioned below.

Simon provides quantitative evidence of Lombroso's prominence in American legal thought from 1891 to 1990 by the number of quotes made in specialized American magazines over a century, and comparing them to the citations of Healy, Ernest Burgess (of the famed Chicago School of sociology), and Sheldon Glueck, a criminologist at Harvard Law School. Simon's conclusions contradict those of

Rafter when he stresses that for most of the period considered the presence of Lombroso is the highest – and a constantly growing one (Simon 2005–6, 2143–4).

Concluding remarks

But why these different conclusions regarding Lombroso's reception in America? Evidently there must have been two different "Lombrosi." Rafter insists on a criminologist with a strong profile in biology (insomuch that she envisages him rehabilitated "today [...] when biological explanations of behavior again prevail"), which seems to be the motivation for her polemical attitude toward Lombroso (Rafter 2009, 286). Simon instead distinguishes between various versions of Lombroso's thought and its effects, such as the rejection by the European jurists and the enthusiasm of the American lawyers. The influence of positivist criminology appears to be related to the enthusiasm about rehabilitation in the American criminal justice, in contrast to the use of punishment as a deterrent. Simon also points to Italian positivist criminology in America in analyzing historical trends in crime control theories and policies.

If these studies are not compared with each other, the thesis of criminologist Shafter seems to confirm that in Italy the consensus has been mainly to condemn Lombroso, without historical context – after the long decades of silence in which the Italian scientist most known outside Italy was buried There was not such silence in the United States, as Simon's research has shown. The initiative of the American Institute of Criminal law in 1909 to import the European science of crime – "but always in an American perspective" – has apparently been successful. The publication of William Healy, who like many American intellectuals had come to study in Europe, in London, Berlin, and Vienna where he tried to get in touch with Freud, was hailed as a breakthrough comparable to that of the Italian inventor of criminology. Healy closed one era of criminology to open the next. This was comparable to the reception of Lombroso more than a century before, said a well-known history book of American criminology (Fink 1938).

The time-periodization was sort of rough; just four years had passed between *The individual Delinquent* of 1915 and the translation of *Criminal Man*, twenty years if one considers the expanded (and the less organic) edition of 1895 to which both American publications of 1911 had referred to, and less than fifty years from the very first skinny original version of 1876. In any case, it had not passed a century as it seemed instead to Arthur Fink in his work of 1938.

The date 1938 brings us back to the tragic events in Italy. With the introduction of the racial laws of 1938 Jews were forced to hide or escape. The "Measures for the defense of the race in fascist schools" dismissed all the Jewish teachers and students from Italian schools, universities, and academies. Only a very few returned after the war: the forced migration of displaced scholars always resulted, in Italy, in difficulty in returning – or no return at all. The consequences of fascism for Italian culture have been long-lasting and deep. One reflects on the small number of teachers who refused to pledge allegiance and give an oath to fascism in 1931, or on the many that in 1938 were expelled and replaced, and almost never reinstated after the war. Together with their names and academic positions, their ideas as well were erased, discredited, or ignored, given the Jewish origin of the authors. Ideas that had circulated internationally, which elsewhere were fertilized and transformed, did not return, nor were they inserted into contexts now different from those in which they were developed.

Something similar happened in Italy to the theories of Lombroso, much discussed within positivism, devalued by neo-idealism, and then decidedly rejected by fascism. In 1931, Mario Carrara, son-in-law of Lombroso and his successor to the chair of criminal anthropology, had to leave this position because he refused to swear the oath of allegiance, together with only 11 other professors out of 1200. Given that even "the mathematical sciences, if cultivated by a Jew cannot be anything else than Semitic," so much more were the human sciences of Lombroso and Freud condemned. In 1939, the President of the National Institute of Fascist Culture, a distinguished jurist, declared that the positivistic school of law was to be totally rejected because, similar to the classical school of Beccaria, it had been unable to conceive a criminal law based on race. The racist concept of law would henceforth constitute the basis of fascism (Maggiore 1939, 144).

Silence fell on Lombroso; certainly nothing was admitted about reforms which, rightly or wrongly, seemed inspired by him, especially those regarding rehabilitation and prevention. Questions on the non-return to Italy of ideas that elsewhere had led toward innovative paths as it happened to criminal anthropology *the American way* also means having to deal with the anti-semitism and opportunism of an academic culture of which also Lombroso's science became a victim.

Acknowledgments

I wish to thank Paula Fass, Michael C. Grossberg, Michele Pifferi, Edward Shorter for their comments and suggestions, and Per Jørgen Ystehede for his patient assistance with the translation.

Notes

1 See "Lombroso – a totalitarian?" *Sole 24 Ore*, Suppl. Sunday, May 11, 2003, p. 30 under the title, letters of N. Erba and the response by A. Massarenti accused of having positively reviewed the biography of Lombroso by Delia Frigessi (2003).
2 Response made by Luigi Carrara, in reaction to the words spoken by Pietro Rossi, the President of the Academy of Sciences of Turin, at a conference on "Cesare Lombroso scientists and the new Italy" (November 5–6, 2009), published later in a volume, edited by S. Montaldo (2010). During the Fascist period, the persecution which struck Lombroso's family circle was motivated by politics and race. If we limit ourselves to "scientific repercussions" and the forced brain drain that occurred, one can mention that in 1931 Mario Carrara married to Lombroso's daughter Paola, lost his professorship and was expelled from the University of Turin because he refused to swear an oath of loyalty to the fascist regime. He died the year before the racial laws of 1938 were issued. Moreover, because

of these laws, Lombroso's son Ugo was expelled from the University of Genoa where he taught physiology and had to emigrate to Paris.
3 About Italian secondary sources of the 1980s on Italian positivism, see at least Poggi (1987, 261–7).
4 On the important relationship between Cesare Lombroso and Helen Zimmern, see Knepper (2011, 360–1). Simon describes her attitude toward Lombroso as "typical of the American response." Her articles first appeared in the popular *Science monthly*, and then reprinted in the magazine *The Green Bag*, patronized by the Legal Realists (Simon 2005–2006, 2145).

References

Becker, P. (2010) 'Lombroso come luogo della memoria della criminologia', in S. Montaldo (ed.) *Cesare Lombroso. Gli scienziati e la nuova Italia*. Bologna: il Mulino: 33–51.
"Disposizioni urgenti sull'Istruzione superiore", r. decr. n.1227, 28 August 1931, art. 18.
"Provvedimenti per la difesa della razza nella scuola fascista", r. decr. n.1390, 5 September 1938.
Ellis, H. (1891) *The New York State Reformatory in Elmira*. London: Stanley Paul.
Fink, H. (1938) *Causes of Crime: Biological Theories in the United States, 1800–1915*. Philadelphia: University of Pennsylvania Press.
Frigessi, D. (2003) *Cesare Lombroso*. Torino: Einaudi.
Gentile, G. (1917, 2nd edn 1925) 'Le origini della filosofia contemporanea in Italia', in G. Gentile (1969) *Storia della filosofia italiana*, a cura di E. Garin, vol. 1. Firenze: Sansoni.
Giacanelli, F. (1995) 'Il medico, l'alienista. Introduzione', in C. Lombroso, *Delitto Genio e follia. Scritti scelti* a cura di D. Frigessi, F. Giacanelli, L. Mangoni. Torino: Bollati Boringhieri: 5–43.
Gibson, M. (2002) *Born to Crime. Cesare Lombroso and the Origins of Biological Criminology*. Westport-London: Praeger; Ital. trans. (2004) *Nati per il crimine. C.L. e le origini della criminologia biologica*. Milano: B. Mondadori.
Gibson, M. (2010) 'Uno sguardo americano su Stephen Jay Gould', *Contemporanea*, 13:354–9.
Gould, S. J. (1981) *The Mismeasure of Man*. New York: Norton; Ital. trans. (1985) *Intelligenza e pregiudizio*. Roma: Editori Riuniti.
Guarnieri, P. (1993) *A case of child murder. Law and science in nineteenth-century Tuscany*. Cambridge and New York: Polity Press.
Guarnieri, P. (2002) 'Morselli, Enrico', in F. M. Ferro e C. Maj (eds) *Anthologies in Italian Psychiatry*. New York: World Psychiatric Association: 177–86.
Guarnieri, P. (2010) 'Il caso Lombroso', tavola rotonda in S. Montaldo (ed.) *Cesare Lombroso: gli scienziati e la nuova Italia*. Bologna: il Mulino.
Horton, D. M. and Rich, K. (eds) (2004) *The Criminal Anthropological Writings of Cesare Lombroso Published in the English Language Periodical Literature During the Late 19th and Early 20th Centuries*. Lewinston-New York: The Edwin Mellen Press.
Horton, H. P. (1911) 'Translator's note', in Lombroso C., *Crime: its Causes and Remedies*. Boston: Little Brown and Co.
Israel, G. (2010) *Il fascismo e la razza. La scienza italiana e le politiche razziali del regime*. Bologna: il Mulino.
Knepper, P. (2011) 'Lombroso's Jewish Identity and its Implication for Criminology', *Australian and New Zealand Journal of Criminology*, 44: 355–369.

Kurella H. (1911) *Cesare Lombroso a Modern Man of Science*, translated from the German. New York: Rebman Co.
Levi Bianchini, M. (1921), Cesare Lombroso: un grande iniziato', *Archivio generale di neurologia, psichiatria e psicoanalisi*, 2:109–12.
Lombroso, C. (1890) 'Sulla diffusione della antropologia criminale', in L. M. Drago, *I criminali nati*, Torino: Bocca, (or. ed. 1888, *Los ombre de presa*, Buenos Aires).
Lombroso, C. (1891) *Les applications de l'anthropologie criminelle*. Paris: Alcan
Lombroso, C. (1897) *L'uomo delinquente in rapporto all'antropologia, alla giurisprudenza ed alla psichiatria*, 5a ed, vol. 3. Torino: Bocca.
Lombroso, C. (1908) 'Introduzione' in *L'opera di Cesare Lombroso nella scienza e nelle sue applicazioni*. Torino: Bocca.
Lombroso, C. (1911a) *Crime: its Causes and Remedies*, translated by H. P. Horton. Boston: Little Brown and Co.
Lombroso, C. (1911b) 'Introduction', in *Criminal Man According to the Classification of Cesare Lombroso, Briefly Summarised by his Daughter Gina Lombroso Ferrero*. New York-London: G.P. Putnam's Sons.
Lombroso, C. (1995) *Delitto genio follia. Scritti scelti*, a cura di D. Frigessi, F. Giacanelli, L. Mangoni. Torino: Bollati Boringhieri.
Lombroso, C. (2006) *Criminal Man*, translated and with a new introduction of M. Gibson and N. Rafter. Durham and London: Duke University Press.
Lombroso, G. (1911) *Criminal Man – According to the Classification of Cesare Lombroso, Briefly Summarised by his Daughter Gina Lombroso Ferrero*. New York-London: G.P. Putnam's Sons.
Maggiore, G. (1939) 'Diritto penale totalitario dello Stato totalitario', *Rivista italiana di diritto penale*, 11:140–61.
Mantegazza, P. (1888) 'Gli atavismi psichici', *Archivio per l'antropologia* 18:69–82.
Martucci, P. P. (2009) 'Un'eredità senza eredi. L'antropologia criminale in italia dopo la morte di Cesare Lombroso', in S. Montaldo, P. Tappero, *Cesare Lombroso cento anni dopo*, Torino: Utet: 291–300.
Mesnil, J. (1900) 'Le phénomene Lombroso', *Mercure de France*, 11: 627ff.
Morselli, E. (1906) 'Cesare Lombroso e la filosofia scientifica', in *L'opera di Cesare Lombroso nella scienza e nelle sue applicazioni*, nuova ed. Torino: Bocca: 354–84.
Mosse, G. L. (1978) *Toward the Final Solution. A History of European Racism*. New York: H. Fertig; Ital. trans. (1986) *Il razzismo in Europa dalle origini all'Olocausto*. Roma-Bari: Laterza.
Parmelee, M. (1908) *The Principles of Anthropology and Sociology in their Relations to Criminal Procedure*. New York: The Macmillan Co.
Parmelee, M. (1911) 'Introduction to the English Version', in Lombroso C., *Crime: its Causes and Remedies*. Boston: Little, Brown and Co., pp. xi–xxxvi.
Petit, C. (2007) 'Lombroso en Chicago. Presencias europeas en la modern criminal science americana', in *Quaderni fiorentini per la storia del pensiero giuridico moderno*, 36: 801–900.
Pifferi, M. (2009) 'Exporting Criminology: the Individualization of Punishment in Europe and America', in L. Beck Varela, P. Gutierrez Vega and A. Spinosa (eds), *Crossing legal cultures. Yearbook of Young Legal History*, vol.3. Munich: M. Meidenbauer: 439–57.
Poggi, S. (1987) *Introduzione a il positivismo*. Roma-Bari: Laterza.
Rafter, N. H. (1992) 'Criminal Anthropology in the United States', *Criminology*, 30: 525–45.
Rafter, N. H. (1997) *Creating Born Criminals*. Urbana: University of Illinois Press.
Rafter, N. H. (2009), 'Gli Stati Uniti', in S. Montaldo, P. Tappero (eds) *Cesare Lombroso cento anni dopo*. Torino: Utet: 277–86.

Renneville, M. (2009) 'La Francia', in S. Montaldo, P. Tappero (eds) *Cesare Lombroso cento anni dopo*. Torino: Utet: 203–11.

Simon J. (2005–2006) 'Positively Punitive: How the Inventor of Scientific Criminology who Died at the Beginning of the Twentieth Century Continues to Haunt American Crime Control at the Beginning of the Twenty-First', *Texas Law Review*, 84: 2135–72.

Zimmern, H. (1898) 'Criminal Anthropology in Italy', *Green Bag*, 10: 342–9.

7

NEW NATURAL BORN KILLERS?

The legacy of Lombroso in neuroscience and law

Emilia Musumeci

> The question whether the disease gives rise to the crime, or whether the crime from its own peculiar nature is always accompanied by something of the nature of disease, he did not yet feel able to decide.
>
> F. Dostoevsky, *Crime and Punishment* (1866)

The image of Cesare Lombroso in Italy between contempt and *damnatio memoriae*

'They used to call me the "Alienist of the steelyard" [*l'alienista della stadera*] at that time. Well, probably there won't be a trace of my name within a few centuries' (Lombroso 1886, 277). This is what Cesare Lombroso feared in 1886, acclaimed by students and followers, scorned by colleagues and adversaries. Just as quickly as they rose, his theories rapidly sank into oblivion after his passing. Yet today, over a century after his death, the discussion of Lombroso's work still continues (Montaldo and Tappero 2009; Montaldo 2010). Lombroso's words sound strangely and undoubtedly prophetic as we wonder what is the legacy of Lombroso's theories in current Italian criminology and criminal law doctrine. If we analyse the textbooks nowadays used in Italian Universities we immediately notice that Lombroso, who is defined abroad as the 'Father of Modern Criminology' (Wilcox and Cullen 2010, 565) in Italy, is almost totally ignored or dismissed with a few lines in the introduction to the history of criminal law. In particular, criminal law references to Lombroso and his school are found more in detail only on a small number of criminal law handbooks (e.g. Fiandaca-Musco 1995). In other cases, you can merely find, briefly and uncritically, presented the debate between the Classical School and Positivist School and in many cases there is not any mention at all of Lombroso or criminal anthropology. More or less the same picture presents itself when we look at the textbooks used in criminology and sociology of deviance in Italy. With a few exceptions (Melossi 2002; Correra-Martucci 1999), most of the textbooks belittle or ignore altogether the existence of the Positivist School in Italy (Pisapia 2005). For example, the two most widely used handbooks in Italian universities (Bandini *et al.* 2003; Ponti and Merzagora Betsos 2008) provide Lombroso with not more than a few sentences, if they even choose to mention him at all.

Actually, Lombroso and his school fell into oblivion soon after his death in 1909, due to the Catholic Church. In particular, this can be accredited to Father Agostino Gemelli, who wrote the book *Funeral of a Man and of a Doctrine* [*I funerali di un uomo e di una dottrina* 1911], published with the intention of deconstructing Lombroso's work. In addition, the neo-idealist doctrine eminently represented by Benedetto Croce and Giovanni Gentile, probably also contributed to his decline. I do not want to dwell on the reasons for this oblivion, but rather aim to understand what is left of his image and his doctrine, though it is – as we have seen – almost completely ignored in Italy by jurists and criminologists, so as to constitute a sort of *damnatio memoriae* on Lombroso. This is even more evident if we examine quotations in major national newspapers about Lombroso. When mentioning the famous Veronese psychiatrist, or using the term 'lombrosian' it is often referred to as the idea of identifying a criminal from his face; the adjective itself, 'lombrosian', is used as an 'insult' or a 'joke'.[1] In many other cases, Lombroso is ridiculed through regaling curious anecdotes or eccentric statements from his vast work.[2] That Lombroso is seen as an awkward and almost 'cursed' character is shown more and more by the recent controversy triggered by the reopening of the Museum of Criminal Anthropology 'C. Lombroso' in Turin. Despite the fact that this reopening was inspired by the attempt to highlight the scientific and historical errors of Lombroso, it was considered, on the contrary, as an attempt to rehabilitate Lombroso's image. Protesters argued his science had contributed to criminalising the people from Southern Italy. These protests, led by self-styled Southern and *neoborbonici* (New Bourbons) resulted in the creation of a group on the social network Facebook, aimed at obtaining the immediate closure of the museum and the restitution of 'the skulls of the Southern brigands, victims of the ferocity of the Savoys' kept in the museum. This controversy was greatly blown up and politically exploited, as a part of a wider dispute raised in Italy at the time of the 150th anniversary of the Unification of Italy. However, it is also a sign of how the figure of Lombroso, more than a century after his death, is still viewed with strong and contradictory feelings, and of how his legacy, at least in Italy, is a rather peculiar one.

'I'm not guilty – but my brain is': neuroscience and criminal justice

If no jurist or criminologist in Italy today aims at revitalising Lombroso's thesis on the born criminal, one may ask, however, whether the legacy of Lombroso has been picked up by forensic psychologists and neuroscientists. The neuroscientific paradigm, which considers thoughts as a result of synaptic connections, mere brain images (Frith 2007) to be captured by fMRI, is now permeating all areas of knowledge. It is therefore not surprising that these techniques, far from remaining closed in aseptic laboratories, have now entered even the austere courtrooms: love (Bartels and Zeki 2000) or violence (Niehoff 1999; Denno 1990) in fact, according to neuroscientists, can be considered as normal bio-electrochemical reaction. So, faced with the disintegration of the power of psychiatrists and their expertise, now deemed less objective and less certain, in the courts the judges are increasingly choosing to rely on techniques that appear more 'certain' and 'infallible' than others. Despite the several, heterogeneous scientific disciplines that are indicated under the term 'neuroscience', there exists an underlying idea which unites them all; i.e., that it is possible to explain all human behaviours, even the most complex, simply by understanding how the brain works. In other words, for the neuroscientists, 'we are our neurons' because the mind is what the brain does. Nevertheless, is this approach typical of our age, pretentiously defined as Post-human Era or, more emphatically, *Neurocentric Age* (Becker 2010; Dunagan 2010)? When taking a closer look at this research, we can see that it is deeply rooted in the classical neuropsychology which developed in the early nineteenth century, with phrenological studies by Franz Joseph Gall and Johann Gaspar Spurzheim, and neurological ones made by Pierre Paul Broca, Carl Wernicke and Ludwig Lichtheim, the studies conducted by Moritz Benedikt in Austria, by Henry Maudsley in United Kingdom and by Lorenzo Tenchini in Italy. Most importantly, the aim to give a strong significance to biological aspects of crime and, in particular, to the innate diversity of brains and bodies of criminals, inevitably recalls the thesis of 'born criminality' developed in Italy by Lombroso in the second half of the nineteenth century. Re-thinking the studies already made in craniology and phrenology, Lombroso, influenced by positivism, decided to investigate crime by analysing this phenomenon through an experimental method, which accepted as scientific facts only what can be rigorously established, measured and catalogued with scientific means. All of these studies, from Gall to Lombroso, regardless of the different historical backgrounds and the different approaches, with their focus on investigating and studying the brain and the skull, may be considered as foreshadowing modern neuroscience. Not by chance, still today neuroscientists frequently refer to a nineteenth-century case: the incredible story of Phineas P. Gage, a well-known event concerning a man who miraculously survived a terrible accident that irreversibly damaged his brain with reported effects on his personality (Macmillan 2000; Becker 2008). On 13 September 1848, while 25-five-year old Gage was working to build a railroad in Vermont, an iron rod of about four feet long, three centimetres in diameter and weighing six kilograms went through his head, destroying much of his brain's left frontal lobe. The rod was found thrown about thirty metres away from the accident but Gage inexplicably survived. Despite the fact that a few minutes later he was apparently conscious and able to walk, from that moment something in him was definitely changed: suddenly Gage was no longer the polite and amiable person he was before, but he had become sour, violent and totally devoid of inhibitions; in other words, all the symptoms of what is today considered from a medical point of view, an 'acquired sociopathy' (Damasio *et al.* 1994).[3] Although this case was studied at the time (Harlow 1848) it has now become part of the history of neuroscience, especially after it was studied again in 1994 by Antonio Damasio and his team at the University of Iowa. In the research, through neuroimaging techniques, they computer-simulated the path left by the iron bar and localised the brain damage in the ventromedial prefrontal cortex (VMPFC), drawing conclusions about the connection between brain damage and aggressive behaviour (Sapolsky 2006). So, what happens if a New Millennium Phineas Gage commits a murder? Should she or he be held criminally responsible? In other words, the burning issue is the possibility of being convicted or acquitted because of one's own neurons or genes.

During the last decades, especially in the United States, neuroimaging techniques (functional magnetic resonance imaging, positron emission tomography, etc.) and genetic screening have more and more frequently played an important role in assessing criminal responsibility. So, in the courtroom there seems nowadays to be fewer black robes and more white coats: if once new technologies were mostly used during the investigating period preceding the trial, now the possibility of 'reading the brain' of the accused, seems to be a new and unsettling reality of modern trials. Thanks to these techniques, it is indeed possible, to see which brain areas are activated in response to certain stimuli: a positron emission tomography (PET) measures the activation of certain brain areas through the intensity of their metabolism, while a functional magnetic resonance imaging (fMRI), able to examine the blood flows, is required to understand what kind of brain activity is in progress, like a more sophisticated version of the famous *Truth Machine*. Another controversial technique that could be used to retrieve the memory traces of their experiences is that of Brain Fingerprinting, developed in the 1980s by Lawrence Farwell, a neuroscientist at Harvard University; it consists of a device able to probe human memory in search for 'brain fingerprints' revealing memories of events experienced in the past. Certain brain waves, called p300, are detected through electrodes placed on the skull of the person to be tested and the machine measures the electrical activity in the brain subject to external stimulations (Levy 2007). In the US, neurotechnologies in criminal trials have been used since the early 1990s, with the first pioneering decisions on the famous cases of Weinstein and Hinckley and the more recent case of Brian Dugan, a brutal rapist and serial killer. In an attempt to spare Dugan from the death penalty, his defence tried to use the data arising from fMRI of Dugan's brain as a 'mitigating circumstance', showing how the brain of the accused, a psychopath, differs from that of 'normal' people. Kent Kiehl, a controversial neuroscientist at the University of New Mexico and called by some journalists 'the new Lombroso', was used as an expert witness in support of Dugan's defence (Seabrook 2008). Kiehl is the one who, on the basis of the fMRI abnormalities found in prisoners' brains, claims that criminals brains differ from the law-abiding population. The risk behind this case is that the impact of neuroscience on the forensic world[4] could contribute to the creation of the so-called 'CSI effect' (Starrs 2004) or rather, the perception of the omnipotence of forensic science to resolve, by scientific methods, every 'cold case', as it happens in the episodes of the American crime drama television series called *CSI*.

Looking for the evil gene: the Bayout case

Aside from remaining a typical phenomenon of the US courts, the influence of neurotechnologies is also starting to spread throughout Italy. One example of this was the decision at the Court of Assizes of Appeal in Trieste (2009) which granted a reduction of sentence to a man who had already been convicted of murder in the first instance, for having committed the crime in a mental state of partial insanity because he was 'genetically predisposed to an aggressive behaviour'. This decision has been called historical and scandalous, based on scientific paradox, revolutionary and 'Lombrosian'. Moreover, it was the first judgement made in Italy (and perhaps in Europe) in which neuroscientists and geneticists had played a fundamental role. This case, which generated considerable sensation around the world, often has been misunderstood. The superficial conclusion, is that there allegedly was discovered an 'evil gene' or 'violence gene'. The case involved a 40-year-old Algerian citizen, Abdelmalek Bayout, who have been living in Italy since 1993 and was involved in a brawl in Udine with some South American boys in 2007. The row broke out because one of the men began taunting Bayout, who was wearing make-up. Bayout, a Muslim, claimed he wore eye make-up because of religious reasons, but was insulted in public and accused of being a homosexual. In order to avenge the beatings and insults suffered during the brawl, Bayout, a few hours later, purchased a knife and stabbed to death one of the men who had called him gay, a 32-year-old Colombian citizen named Walter Felipe Perez Novoa. In first instance, Bayout, submitted to a psychiatric evaluation, was considered as

> suffering from a serious psychiatric and psychotic-style disorder and, in particular, a type of delusional psychotic disorder in subject with impulsive-antisocial traits and cognitive-intellectual ability below lower limits of normal.
> (Court of Assizes of Appeal in Trieste 2009, 72)

Thus, he was sentenced to twenty-two years and six months in prison, which, given the extenuating circumstances and other mitigating circumstances were in fact, nine years and two months' imprisonment. Bayout's defence, claiming a series of procedural and substantive irregularities, appealed asking for a verdict of not guilty by reasons of insanity (NGRI) or at least a lighter sentence. In the second trial, new findings of the new expertise regarding the existence of *mens rea*,[5] was provided to the Court to consider the 'serious clinical and psychiatric condition' of the accused. For example, some years prior to the murder, Bayout had been subject to treatments based on narcoleptic drugs by the Mental Health Center of Udine. Therefore, the Court's decision should take into account these circumstances.

Faced with the difficulty of deciding on Bayout's state of mind, the judges appointed some experts to analyse the accused through the latest techniques of neuroscience and genetic screening in order to find 'significant genetic polymorphisms to modulate responses to environmental variables including, in this particular case, those concerning the exposure to stressful events and the reaction to the same type of impulsive behaviour' (Court of Assizes of Appeal in Trieste 2009, 74). The experts, Pietro Pietrini, a molecular biologist from the University of Pisa, and Giuseppe Sartori, a cognitive neuroscientist from the University of Padova, conducted a series of tests and found abnormalities in brain-imaging scans with functional magnetic resonance (fMRI) of the accused and in five genes that have been linked to violent behaviour – including the gene encoding the neurotransmitter-metabolizing enzyme monoamine oxidase A (MAOA-A), also called the 'warrior gene' (Lyle 2010; Yong 2010), involved in the metabolism of catecholamines (neurotransmitters that are responsible for modulation of mood). Carrying a low-activity MAOA gene (MAOA-L) Bayout was considered 'more inclined to aggressive behaviour if provoked or socially excluded' or he would suffer from a sort of 'genetic vulnerability'. The Court, agreeing with the findings of the report, argued that the presence of certain genes in the accused's DNA would make him 'particularly aggressive – and therefore vulnerable – in stressful situations'. In addition to this 'genetic vulnerability', the Court argued that 'the alienation resulting from his need to combine the respect for fundamentalist Islamic faith with a Western behaviour pattern' (Court of Assizes of Appeal in Trieste 2009, 73–4) in Bayout created further limitations on his ability to understand the reality and consequences of his own behaviour. Inevitably, this verdict triggered a heated debate.

In newspapers, all over the world, the Bayout decision is referred to as a futuristic possibility of being convicted or acquitted just 'reading' the genetic makeup or through brain scanning. In particular, many Italian and foreign newspapers noticeably emphasised this case for its alleged 'discovery' of the 'murderer gene' or 'violence gene'. For example, the French newspaper *Libération*, in an article provocatively entitled '*Un juge italien découvre le gène du meurtre*' [An Italian judge discovers the murder gene] (Inizal 2009) accused the Court in Trieste of issuing a verdict based on scientific gibberish or expression of some undeclared racial prejudices. The British newspaper *The Times*, published an article with the eloquent title 'The Get Out of Jail Free gene' (Ahuja 2009), and wondered to what extent it is possible, scientifically and ethically, to use DNA as defence in a criminal trial. The sensation caused by the Bayout case did not limit itself, however, to the newspapers, but roused the interest of scientific magazines such as *Nature* (Feresin 2009) and *The New Scientist* (Callaway 2009). The Bayout case has even become the object of a parliamentary interrogation of a PDL's deputy, Souad Sbai, which blamed the Court of Assizes of Appeal in Trieste for having issued a racist verdict decision, in contrast with Italian Constitution, art. 3 and for the risk to recognise the existence of a sort of 'cultural mitigating circumstance' not allowed by Italian Criminal Law (Sbai 2009). But the judges probably did not want to pass a 'racist verdict' because their focus was primarily on the reconstruction of Bayout's clinical diagnosis in order to decide about his criminal responsibility. His clinical history had shown, before the experts' report, that he was affected by serious mental health diseases because he was suffering from episodes of delirium and paranoia and that he had to be treated with psychotropic drugs. So, probably the frantic research by the experts of signs or stigmata attesting abnormality and innate aggressiveness in the brain and in the DNA of the accused, actually had not the assumed nature of 'scientific objectivity', being rather an *ad hoc* construction to show an already pre-set thesis: free will does not exist, therefore, if it is not possible to choose between good and evil; criminals are born, not made. Which better subject, then, to claim a similar thesis, if not an already mentally disturbed man like Bayout and, on the other side, a Colombian boy as a victim as so many others? It is clear that the Bayout case would merely have resulted in some brief paragraphs in the crime news in the local daily paper, if it had not been for the contribution of the neuroscientists. The sentence, already notably reduced due to the verdict of partial insanity and for the procedural reasons, was slightly decreased in the second instance. Probably, considering Bayout's past, it would have been easy to decide for a diminution of responsibility 'simply' through further psychiatric evaluation, without carrying out any brain scan or submitting the accused to complex genetic tests. Such a decision assumes a strong symbolic and ideological meaning, because it represents the wish to impose, also in a juridical field, the neuroscientific paradigm of reducing ideas and thoughts to a series of cerebral images, produced through a synaptic connection among neurons with the inevitable consequence that everything an individual thinks and claims, is not a demonstration of his/her own conscience and his/her own personality, but a mere movement of neurons.

Born to kill: the Albertani case

This approach, previously only sketched, appears to be more powerful after a new Italian case law: the polemics about the Bayout case had just calmed down when another judgement, in some ways similar to that of Trieste, rekindled the discussion about the presence of geneticists and neuroscientists in courtrooms. It was the decision of the Judge for Preliminary Investigations at the Criminal Court of Como of 20 May 2011 (but which motivation was made public 20 August 2011) to use the methods developed by cognitive neuroscience and behavioural genetics to decide on criminal responsibility of Stefania Albertani a 28-year-old woman charged with multiple accounts of aggravated murder of her sister and the attempted murder on her parents. She was sentenced to twenty years' imprisonment, instead of thirty due to being deemed partially insane. Also in this case, the presence of low-activity MAOA-A was found in the genetic make-up of the accused. However, whereas in the first case, the judges openly discussed the issue of 'genetic vulnerability', in the case of Como, perhaps to prevent criticism of being deterministic, the judge, in a decision counting over 60 pages, tried to justify the verdict of diminished responsibility by reason of partial insanity, by invoking many causes. These cases are, however, only superficially similar. The Bayout case is not a premeditated crime committed by a person treated in the past for mental disorders;

the Albertani case, happening in the family sphere, was a murder also motivated by economic reasons. While the Bayout case may be said to fall within the category of 'an ordinary crime', the Albertani case may be compared to a horrific episode of the television series *Criminal Minds*. In order to shift the blame to her sister for the failure of the family company, Stefania killed her after feeding her large amounts of psychotropic drugs (benzodiazepines and promazine as evidenced by the coroner's report), which made her incapable of reacting, and then set fire to her sister's body. Unlike Bayout, Albertani underwent five expert evaluations. Faced with a scenario that brings into play two totally opposite hypotheses (which is not so unusual in Italian criminal trials in which the expertise of the prosecution often affirms a thesis diametrically opposed to that of the defence), the judge surprisingly decided to embrace, for the ruling decision, the thesis of two new experts for the defence, Giuseppe Sartori and Pietro Pietrini, that had already been appointed in the Bayout case. In addition to clinical interviews, the accused was subjected to a battery of neuropsychological tests (the IAT-*Autobiographical Implicit Association Test*, and TARA-*Timed Antagonistic Response Alethiometer*, used to establish whether an autobiographical memory trace is encoded in the accused's brain) to assess both general mental health conditions and individual mental functions, including attention, memory, perception and language, which showed that Albertani had a dissociative identity disorder. Furthermore, Sartori and Pietrini intended to demonstrate Albertani's incapacity to distinguish between right and wrong and control her impulsivity using neuroscientific techniques such as EEG and VBM – Voxel-Based Morphometry. VBM showed a lack of integrity and functionality of the anterior cingulated cortex, linked to obsessive-compulsive disorder and aggressiveness, where the person lacks the capacity to substitute the automatic behaviour with a different one. In addition it was found, as in the Bayout case, the presence of the MAOA gene polymorphism. With this considerable amount of data and results, which were presumed to be objective, Albertani was found guilty, but only partially responsible and recognised as a 'socially dangerous person'. But why all these tests if other experts had already established that Albertani suffered from psychosis? There was a lack of trust in psychiatry which was considered by the judge a too discretionary science to reach 'objectivity and evidence-based data' results, (Judge for Preliminary Investigations at the Criminal Court of Como 2011, 39) such as to provide answers 'less discretionary' as those 'corroborated by the findings of brain imaging and molecular genetics'. The judge asserts that neuroscience today does not have a 'deterministic criteria which automatically infer that some morphological abnormality of the brain achieve certain behaviours and not others' (Judge for Preliminary Investigations at the Criminal Court of Como 2011, 39). Moreover, the judge repeatedly emphasised that the verdict was not influenced by any kind of determinism, by arguing that the morphology of the brain and the genetic factor – given the *probabilistic* nature of medicine – are not causes but only 'risk factors' of crime (Judge for Preliminary Investigations at the Criminal Court of Como 2011, 41), as high cholesterol or blood pressure are for a heart attack or stroke believed by one of the two experts. These statements and clarifications, however, are contradicted by the results achieved. The partial insanity ruling was strongly influenced by the findings of neuroscientific evidence based on a masked determinism. So, this decision hides an aim that goes beyond the single case law and the practical reason (to strengthen the thesis of defence against that of prosecution): to accredit and 'validate the new neuroscientific tools that are the subject of heated debate, especially in the United States' (Ovadia 2011). Maybe there was also a hidden purpose: to have the hegemony in the field of forensic evaluation of insanity in the courtrooms. The 'new' power of neuroscience, relying on a presumed objectivity is trying to undermine the 'old' power of forensic psychiatric, which, for some decades, is in crisis, as is also evidenced by the heated debate triggered from the new publication of the updated version of the *Diagnostic and Statistical Manual of Mental Disorders* (DSM-5), by the American Psychiatric Association (APA), scheduled for May 2013.

To conclude, in the cases of Trieste and Como, it would be easy to achieve similar results regarding the criminal responsibility through 'traditional' methods used by psychiatry, but then these judgements wouldn't have received much publicity in the mass media. Obviously, even the Albertani case, much was published in newspapers and magazines around the world; for example, the headline in *New Scientist* was 'Brain Scans Reduce Murder Sentence in Italian Court' (Hamzelou 2011) and many journalists portrayed Stefania Albertani like a 'born criminal' and the decision as a result of the 'new lombrosianism' (Bencivelli 2011, 9).

Neuro-optimists versus neuro-sceptics

Is it true, therefore, that the judges are bound to be supplanted by neuroscientists who would 'write' the judgements of conviction or acquittal in their place? Besides the various nuances one needs to take into account when evaluating the impact of neuroscience on criminal law, there are two approaches that are competing in the field, which could be called 'neuro-optimistic' and 'neuro-sceptical'.

According to the first approach, with proponents including Joshua Greene and Jonathan Cohen, neuroscience *finally* demolishes all the old certainties of law, such as the existence of free will as the foundation of the right to punish. Not by chance, they say that 'when we look at people as physical systems, we cannot see them as any more blameworthy or praiseworthy than bricks' (Greene and Cohen 2004, 1782). These scholars are part of an extremist group who sees neuroscience as a Copernican revolution intended to sweep out ancient superstitions throughout science, deconstructing *ab imis* our approach to criminal law, tearing the veil of ignorance that prevents us from understanding how illusory the concept of free will can be and consequently, how fallacious a retributivist approach of criminal punishment based on that ephemeral concept is.

Conversely, the 'neuro-sceptics', among whose ranks we can list Stephen Morse (Morse 2004; Morse 2011) whose motto is 'brains do not commit crimes; people commit crimes' (Morse 2006a, 397), states that the techniques supported by neuroscientists, as developed and refined, can never replace the judge in his assessment of criminal responsibility. According to Morse, the problem of the existence of free will, which is relevant on a purely metaphysical level, is absolutely irrelevant for law (Morse 2007) because through the current scientific developments, though advanced, only a few brain abnormalities can be detected in an unmistakable manner so as to eliminate the minimum level of legally relevant rationality for the assessment of responsibility. Conversely, only a true reversal of the concept of *personhood* could cause a real revolution of the entire law system (Morse 2006b). Morse, therefore, not only argues that the hopes and fears caused by the 'neuroscientific revolution' are totally blown out of proportion; he even denounces the attitude of those who emphasise the role of the brain when discussing crime by considering it a real psychosis defined as Brain Overclaim Syndrome (BOS) (Morse 2006a). A 'solomonic' solution is offered by scholars who belong to the more 'moderate' trend of 'soft determinism', i.e. our actions are only partly necessitated and in any case, a space of freedom remains. Among the moderates, Michael Gazzaniga, stands out; he is a famous cognitive neuroscientist who, on the issue of personal responsibility, claims that, despite the fact that the brain is an automatic device, governed by rules and driven by a moral and legal point of view, people are equally responsible of their own actions because they are free to make their own decisions and accept the consequences. This depends on the concept of 'ethical responsibility' adopted by Gazzaniga, as it exists within community and not in the individual who is interrelated with others in society. In short, according to the Californian neuroscientist the 'brain is determined, people are not' (Gazzaniga 2005).

Framing these perspectives, one finds the question of the existence of free will and the tension between determinism and freedom. So, the severest legal and philosophical implication arising from the veiled genetic determinism underpinning these Italian decisions (and more generally, the 'neuro-optimistic' approach) is the impossibility to consider blameworthy the act of murder and, therefore, assign criminal responsibility. Alas, the French astronomer Pierre-Simon Laplace's assertion is carried out in the forensic field, i.e. free will is an illusion doomed to disappear as soon as men recognise they are governed by laws as strict as those regulating the motion of the planets. Since it is not Man who kills, but rather 'her genes' or 'her brain', the criminal responsibility of the accused has to be excluded altogether or diminished, in our legal system. To convict would be similar to punish an animal that is prey to its instincts, or a robot, unable to act differently by design. Another dangerous implication is that against the uncontrollable actions of a 'violent by nature', society can and must protect itself. When facing a bloodthirsty beast or a machine gone bad, one must render them harmless.

Spectres of Lombroso

But is this debate new and/or revolutionary? In the history of criminology and criminal law, there have always been discussions about the philosophical foundations of responsibility and the relationship between freedom and necessity. Just consider the bitter debate concerning free will, between the champion of the

Classical School, Francesco Carrara,[6] who firmly argued in favour of the existence of free will as opposed to the Positivist School of Lombroso who, on the contrary, denied its existence.[7] Now as then, an approach denying free will and claiming determinism is inevitably accompanied by a relief of responsibility, with the ambivalent consequence that it is not possible to punish the offender who, on the one hand, cannot be blamed for actions he did *not really choose to do*, but who on the other hand, is considered as a dark and ominous danger to society, to somehow be neutralised. The most emblematic example of this attitude is given by Lombroso who, through the famous 'discovery'[8] of the median occipital fossa in the skull of the Calabrian brigand Villella in 1870, theorised the differences between criminals and so-called 'normal' individuals, asserted that a criminal is, since birth, 'a miserable variety of man ... more pathological of the insane' (Lombroso 1874, 498).[9] All his life, Lombroso devoted himself to a frantic search of the bodies and faces of prisoners and fools, in order to find the stigmata of deviance, the unmistakeable, irrefutable evidence that a criminal is predetermined to commit evil acts because he is biologically different from any other human being, but more so a monster (Musumeci 2009). In particular, he explained this diversity with *atavism*, reducing criminals to the primitive and savage, and calling them *incorrigible* and dangerous to society. So, if on the one hand Lombroso invoked better prison conditions and a mitigation of punishment – as *ineffective* and therefore unnecessary cruelty – on the other hand, he agreed on the death penalty considering that

> born criminals, programmed to do harm, are atavistic reproductions of not only savage men but also the most ferocious carnivores and rodents. This discovery should not make us more compassionate towards born criminals (as some claim), but rather should shield us from pity, for these beings are members of not our species but the species of bloodthirsty beasts.
> (Lombroso 1889, 23–4)

And again, in another part of his work, Lombroso went back to the problem that seemed to haunt him, that is whether it is right to punish a man who is not free to choose and consequently, where the sense of words like blame, reward, hope and fear, honour and dishonour reside, if this man's actions are driven by nature. Thus Lombroso wondered:

> [W]hy must the thief be punished? How does it happen that a donkey is punished for its stupidity, and why must we kill a hydrophobic dog? Shall we kill those who hurt us? Is the one who kills the rabid dog just? What can the dog do of its rabies?'
> (Lombroso 1893, 385).[10]

Although this may sound strange, those who today insist on praising the 'magnificent and progressive destiny' of neurosciences, are the same scholars and scientists that take the distances from the 'rough Lombrosian determinism', without realising that both approaches are not so different. Over the obvious more accuracy of clinical diagnostics and research between the Lombrosian anthropometry and the actual fMRI studies, both approaches have the same starting point, which can be summarised in a famous Lombroso passage:

> 'unvarying laws govern society more profoundly than written legislation. In sum, statistics as well as anthropological observations indicate that crime is a natural phenomenon – one that philosophers would deem as necessary as birth, death and conception'.
>
> (Lombroso 1896, 68)

Perhaps in a not-too-distant future (and not very reassuring), neuroscientists will be able to uncover the mysteries of human nature, implementing what Philip K. Dick described in his disturbing short story 'Minority Report' (Dick 1956) in which 'Pre-crime' arrests killers before they commit crimes. Beyond sci-fi landscapes, in the immediate future there could be a posthumous revenge by Lombroso about the possibility to 'read' on men's bodies the signs of inborn evil: maybe there's a *fil rouge* linking criminal anthropology and neuroscience today, crossing throughout all biological theories of crime (Gibson 2002; Rafter 2008). It is necessary to point out that rather than continuity or discontinuity between Lombroso and neuroscientists, there is an almost secret and unacknowledged link: far from being an acknowledged relationship between master and pupils, in many cases this cumbersome legacy is seen as an awkward burden which it is necessary to get rid of as hastily and lightly as possible. Nevertheless, the attempt carried out by neuroscientists and geneticists, most often results in failed parricides (Musumeci 2012). Forensic scientists and cognitive neuroscientists, especially in Italy, tried to stray away as much as possible from Lombrosian theories, putting into oblivion wrong or outdated theories, but paradoxically, they just got closer to Lombroso, retracing the same path already beaten by the latter. Where neuroscientists, even with sophisticated research and experiments are bent on denying free will, they are unwittingly Lombrosian. It is not about precursors where there are none, but to find out the real importance of the Lombrosian thesis, leaving the most ridiculous and scientifically questionable aspects of his work that made him infamous all around the world: the attribution of a moral characteristic based on facial features or anatomical structure (i.e. ear length, head shape, etc.), spiritism, misogyny and a veiled racism. Beyond these aspects, the operation implemented by neurosciences today differs from the Positivist School only in the tools used, which are more accurate and more technologically advanced (at least from our point of view).

Today's neuroscientists may be portrayed as the *Angelus Novus* by Paul Klee, masterfully described by Walter Benjamin having a body projected towards the future and with outstretched wings forward, but the face 'turned toward the past' (Benjamin 1940, 392). Whereas they *then* spoke about 'hereditary defect', they *now* speak about 'genetic bent'. Whereas they *then* spoke about 'cranial conformation', they *now* speak about 'brain areas' and so on. Moreover, we do not have to look for possible 'heirs' of Lombroso among the ranks of jurists, but as it was already in his time, we have to search for heirs in the ranks of scientists (Becker and Wetzell 2006). Perhaps no one described Lombroso's methodology better than Enrico Ferri:

> Cesare Lombroso looked for the fact as the hunting dog feverishly looks for the prey. And as he found the fact, his brain lit up and threw out sparks of wonderful insights and the most distant phenomena were explained by his thought on unexpected contact and comparison.
>
> (Ferri 1909, 560)

It is ironic then, that on the one hand, Lombroso is denied and ridiculed, and on the other hand neuroscientists are celebrated as the 'new prophets', even where they adopt the same paradigm as Lombroso's: the empirical method and its claim for objectivity that, now as then, are the link binding the Positivist School of Lombroso and the research of many neuroscientists today.

Is it, so, 'new wine into old wineskins'? In spite of appearances, much has remained but, most of all, the attempt to create an inseparable link between nature and behaviour, in a sort of return to the old, to the birth of criminology, when as we are reminded, in a concise and illuminating way by Nicole Rafter – all theories on crime were biological (Rafter 2008). It is just as if the more neuroscientists try to drive away Lombroso's spectre, the more it reappears, as in one of the séance sessions which so fascinated him during the last years of his life.

Notes

1 See Piperno (2008), Berselli (2009) and Merlo (2010).
2 An example of this attitude is Stella (2009).
3 This research was then developed in the famous trilogy: Damasio A. R. (1994) *Descartes' Error. Emotion, Reason, and the Human Brain*. New York: Putnam; Id. (1999) *The Feeling of What Happens. Body and Emotion in the Making of Consciousness*. New York: Harcourt; Id. (2003) *Looking for Spinoza: Joy, Sorrow, and the Feeling Brain*. New York: Harcourt.
4 See also the interesting dossier about the interrelationship between neuroscience and forensics, 'Specials Nature News – Science in Court', in *Nature*, vol. 464, n. 325, 18.03.2010, available online at http://www.nature.com/scienceincourt and, more recently, Freeman (2011).
5 Bayout was considered as a subject with dependent-negativistic personality disorder with significant anxiety-depression accompanied by delusional and abnormal thinking. Furthermore, he had cognitive difficulties with correctly interpreting situations he encountered, although, his condition was not so severe as to abolish all capacity for making good judgements.
6 According to Carrara: 'For us, followers of the moral sciences, the new thermometers and telescopes are of no use, because the tools of our human knowledge do not benefit from the senses, but only from the study of man's interiority as revealed by his external acts which have always been and will always be the same, until man is, in terms of

psychological faculty, the same man who came out from the hands of the Creator. Telescopes and thermometers do not help in order to judge whether a man is free or not. We must descend into the inner recesses of our minds' (Carrara 1883, 508–9).
7 Enrico Ferri's was the major theoretical effort among the members of the Posivitist School to deny free will – see Ferri (1878).
8 'This was not merely an idea, but a revelation' (Lombroso 1911, xiv).
9 This famous paragraph by Lombroso has also been translated into English by David G. Horn as follows: 'that unhappy variety of humans which is, in my opinion, more pathological than the lunatic: criminal man' (Horn 2003, 32).
10 Here Lombroso repeated Joch's words (agreeing with him) quoted by Alfredo Frassati (1891) in his book *La nuova Scuola penale in Italia ed all'Estero*, who traces the achievements of the Lombrosian School and shows the similarities to such as Franz Joseph Gall, Rondeau and Joch, 'precursors' for the ideals of the 'new criminal school'.

References

Ahuja, A. (2009) 'The Get Out of Jail Free gene', *The Times*, 17 November.
Bandini, T., Gatti, U., Gualco, B., Malfatti, D., Marugo, M. I., and Verde, A. (2003) *Criminologia*, vol. 1. Milano: Giuffrè.
Bartels, A. and Zeki, S. (2000) 'The Neural Basis of Romantic Love', *NeuroReport*, 27.11.2000, vol. 11, n. 17: 3829–34.
Becker, P. (2008) 'New Monsters on the Block? On the Return of Biological Explanations of Crime and Violence', in Hering Torres M.S. (ed.) *Cuerpos anómalos*. Bogotá: Editorial Universidad Nacional, pp. 270–82.
Becker, P. (2010) 'The Coming of a Neurocentric Age? Neurosciences and the New Biology of Violence: a Historian's Comment', *Medicina & Storia*, n. 19–20: 101–28.
Becker, P. and Wetzell, R. F. (eds) (2006) *Criminals and Their Scientists. The History of Criminology in International Perspective*. New York: Cambridge University Press.
Bencivelli, S. (2011) 'Restano i dubbi, lo spettro di Lombroso', *Alias – Il Manifesto*, October, n. 38: 9.
Benjamin, W. (1940) 'On the Concept of History', Id. *Selected Writings, 1938–1940*, vol. 4. Cambridge: Harvard University Press [2003].
Berselli, E. (2009) 'Politici lombrosiani', *La Repubblica*, 19 October.
Callaway, E. (2009) 'Murderer with "Aggression Genes" Gets Sentence Cut', *The New Scientist*, 03 November.
Carrara, F. (1883) 'Libertà e spontaneità. Prolusione al corso di diritto e procedura penale (28 novembre 1882)' in Id. *Reminiscenze di cattedra e foro dell'avvocato Francesco Carrara*. Lucca: Tipografia Canovetti.
Correra, M. M. and Martucci, P. (1999) *Elementi di Criminologia*. Padova: Cedam.
Court of Assizes of Appeal in Trieste, 01.10.2009, pres. ed est. Reinotti, in *Rivista penale*, 2010, 1: 70–5.
Damasio, H., Grabowski, T., Frank, R., Galaburda, A. M. and Damasio, A. R. (1994) 'The Return of Phineas Gage: Clues about the Brain from the Skull of a Famous Patient', *Science*, vol. 264, n. 5162: 1102–5.
Denno, D. W. (1990) *Biology and Violence: From Birth to Adulthood*. New York: Cambridge University Press.
Dick, P. K. (1956) 'The Minority Report', *Fantastic Universe*, January, vol. 4 n. 6: 4–36.
Dunagan, J. F. (2010) 'Politics for the Neurocentric Age', *Journal of Futures Studies*, November, vol. 15: 51–70.

Feresin, E. (2009) 'Lighter Sentence for Murderer with "Bad Genes"', *Nature*, 30 October.
Ferri, E. (1878) *La teorica dell'imputabilità e la negazione del libero arbitrio*. Firenze: Barbera.
Ferri, E. (1909) 'L'opera di Cesare Lombroso', in *Archivio di Antropologia criminale, Psichiatria, Medicina legale e scienze affini*, XXX: 547–60.
Fiandaca, G. and Musco, E. (1995) *Diritto Penale. Parte generale*. Bologna: Zanichelli.
Frassati, A. (1891) *La nuova Scuola penale in Italia ed all'Estero*. Torino: Bocca.
Freeman, M. (ed.) (2011) *Law and Neuroscience*. New York: Oxford University Press.
Frith, C. (2007) *Making up the Mind: How the Brain Creates Our Mental World*. Malden: Blackwell.
Gazzaniga, M. (2005) *The Ethical Brain*. New York/Washington DC: Dana Press.
Gemelli, A. (1911) *I funerali di un uomo e di una dottrina. 3a edizione notevolmente aumentata e completamente rifusa*. Firenze: Libreria Editrice Fiorentina.
Gibson, M. (2002) *Born to Crime: Cesare Lombroso and the Origin of Biological Criminology*. Westport: Praeger.
Greene, J. D. and Cohen, J. D. (2004) 'For the Law, Neuroscience Change Nothing and Everything', *Philosophical Transactions of the Royal Society of London B* (Special Issue on Law and the Brain), vol. 359: 1775–85.
Hamzelou, J. (2011) 'Brain Scans Reduce Murder Sentence in Italian Court', *The New Scientist*, 2 September on http://www.newscientist.com/blogs/shortsharpscience/2011/09/brain-scans-reduce-sentence-in.html.
Harlow, J. M. (1848) 'Passage of an Iron Rod Through the Head', *Boston Medical and Surgical Journal*, vol. 39, n. 20, December 13, 1848: 389–93, now also in *The Journal of Neuropsychiatry and Clinical Neurosciences* 11, 2, Spring 1999: 281–3.
Horn, D. G. (2003) *The Criminal Body. Lombroso and the Anatomy of Deviance*. New York: Routledge.
Inizal M. (2009) 'Un juge italien découvre le gène du meurtre', *Libération*, 28 October.
Judge for Preliminary Investigations at the Criminal Court of Como, 20.05.2011–20.08.2011, available on line at http://static.ilsole24ore.com/DocStore/Professionisti/AltraDocumentazione/body/12600001-12700000/12693249.pdf.
Levy, N. (2007) *Neuroethics. Challenges for the 21st Century*. New York: Cambridge University Press.
Lombroso, C. (1874) 'Deformità cranica congenita in un vecchio delinquente, in Id., Raccolta di casi attinenti alla medicina legale', *Annali Universali di Medicina*, Mar., Ser. 1, Vol. 227, Issue 681: 493–9.
Lombroso, C. (1886) 'Appendice alla Polemica', in Lombroso, C., Ferri, E., Garofalo, R. and Fioretti, G. *Polemica in difesa della scuola criminale positiva*. Bologna: Zanichelli.
Lombroso, C. (1889), 'Troppo presto', in AA.VV., *A ppunti al nuovo codice penale*. Torino: Bocca.
Lombroso, C. (1893), *Le più recenti scoperte ed applicazioni della psichiatria ed antropologia criminale*. Torino: Bocca.
Lombroso, C. (1896), *L'uomo delinquente in rapporto all'antropologia, alla giurisprudenza ed alle discipline carcerarie*, 5^a edizione, vol. II. Torino: Bocca.
Lombroso, C. (1911) 'Introduction' in Lombroso Ferrero G., *Criminal Man, According to the Classification of Cesare Lombroso*. New York and London: G.P. Putnam's Sons.
Lyle, D. P. (2010) *Dangerous DNA: The Warrior Gene*, http://writersforensicsblog.wordpress.com/2010/06/15/dangerous-dna-the-warrior-gene, 15 June.
Macmillan, M. (2000) *An Odd Kind of Fame: Stories of Phineas Gage*. Cambridge: MIT Press.
Melossi, D. (2002) *Stato, controllo sociale, devianza. Teorie criminologiche e società tra Europa e Stati Uniti*. Milano: Bruno Mondadori.

Merlo, F. (2010) 'Garantisti ad personam lasciate stare Sciascia', *La Repubblica*, 12 October.
Montaldo, S. (ed.) (2010) *Cesare Lombroso. Gli scienziati e la nuova Italia*. Bologna: Il Mulino.
Montaldo, S. and Tappero, P. (eds) (2009) *Cesare Lombroso cento anni dopo*. Torino: Utet.
Morse, S. J. (2004) 'New Neuroscience, Old Problems: Legal Implications of Brain Science', *Cerebrum*, Fall, vol. 6: 81–90.
Morse, S. J. (2006a) 'Brain Overclaim Syndrome and Criminal Responsibility: A Diagnostic Note', *Ohio State Journal of Criminal Law*, vol. 3: 397–412.
Morse, S. J. (2006b) 'Moral and Legal Responsibility and the New Neuroscience', in J. Illes, *Neuroethics. Defining the Issues in Theory, Practice, and Policy*. Oxford: Oxford University Press, pp. 33–50.
Morse, S. J. (2007) 'The Non-Problem of Free Will in Forensic Psychiatry and Psychology', *Behavioral Sciences & the Law*, vol. 25: 203–20.
Morse, S. J. (2011) 'Genetics and Criminal Responsibility', *Trends in Cognitive Sciences*, September, vol. 15, n. 9 – special issue 'The Genetics of Cognition', pp. 378–80.
Musumeci, E. (2009) 'Le maschere della collezione "Lorenzo Tenchini"', in Montaldo, S. and Tappero, P. (eds), *Il Museo di Antropologia criminale 'Cesare Lombroso'*. Torino: Utet, pp. 69–76.
Musumeci, E. (2012) *Cesare Lombroso e le neuroscienze: un parricidio mancato. Devianza, libero arbitrio, imputabilità tra antiche chimere ed inediti scenari*. Milano: Franco Angeli.
Niehoff, D. (1999) *The Biology of Violence. How Understanding the Brain, Behavior, and Environment Can Break the Vicious Circle of Aggression*. New York: The Free Press.
Ovadia, D. (2011) *Il caso di Como e le neuroscienze in tribunale*, Blog Mente e Psiche – Le Scienze, on http://ovadia-lescienze.blogautore.espresso.repubblica.it/2011/09/06/il-caso-di-como-e-le-neuroscienze-in-tribunale/.
Piperno, A. (2008) 'Chiara e Kafka: i depistaggi di un omicidio. Il delitto di Garlasco', *Corriere della Sera*, 27 January.
Pisapia, G. V. (2005) *Manuale operativo di Criminologia*. Padova: Cedam.
Ponti, G. and Merzagora Betsos, I. (2008) *Compendio di Criminologia*. Milano: Raffaello Cortina.
Rafter, N. (2008) *The Criminal Brain. Understanding Biological Theories of Crime*. New York and London: New York University Press.
Sapolsky, R. M. (2006), 'The Frontal Cortex and the Criminal Justice System', in Zeki, S. and Goodenough, O. (eds.) *Law and the Brain*. New York: Oxford University Press, pp. 227–43.
Sbai, S. (2009) 'Interrogazione a risposta scritta', *Camera dei Deputati – Resoconti dell'Assemblea*, Atti di controllo, Allegato B, Seduta n. 241, 29 October.
Seabrook, J. (2008) 'Suffering Souls. The Search for the Roots of Psychopathy', *The New Yorker*, 10 November, pp. 64–73.
Starrs, J. E. (2004) 'The CSI Effect', *Scientific Sleuthing Review*, Vol. 28, No. 2: 32–4.
Stella, G. A. (2009) 'Lombroso, il catalogo delle assurdità', *Corriere della Sera*, 28 April.
Wilcox, P. and Cullen, F. T. (eds.) (2010) *Encyclopedia of Criminological Theory*, vol. I. Thousand Oaks: Sage.
Yong, E. (2010) 'Dangerous DNA: The Truth about the "Warrior Gene"', *The New Scientist* 12 April, n. 2755.

8

FROM SUBHUMANS TO SUPERHUMANS

Criminals in the evolutionary hierarchy, or what became of Lombroso's atavistic criminals?

Simon A. Cole and Michael C. Campbell

Background

Cesare Lombroso is famously associated with positing the notion of the "born criminal" (though he did not coin the term) and the very notion of biological causes of crime. Though he may not necessarily have been the first ever to posit this notion, he is with some justification widely known as having originated the fields of both biological criminology and, indeed, criminology itself (Gibson 2002; Pasquino 1991). In turn, Lombroso is widely associated with biological determinism, the notion that some individuals are biologically destined to commit crimes. Recent scholarship has shown that Lombroso's thought was more varied and nuanced than the popular stereotype of him as nothing more than a knee-jerk biological determinist (e.g. Gibson 2002; Gibson and Rafter 2006; Gibson 2006; Bondio 2006). But even notwithstanding this nuance, there is no disputing either the strong biological component in Lombroso's thought or his influence in prompting criminological thought about biological causes of criminal behavior (e.g. Rodriguez 2006; Bondio 2006; Rafter 1992).

Strict biological determinism was, of course, attacked immediately upon its dissemination (Pick 1989; Nye 1984). Nonetheless, Lombroso and his followers' call for attention to be paid to the biological contribution to crime was deeply influential in the late nineteenth and early twentieth centuries (e.g. Rodriguez 2006; Bondio 2006; Rafter 1992), and it led to some now notorious eugenic interventions (e.g. Mucchielli 2006; Rafter 1997; Selden 1999; Kevles 1985; Degler 1991). However, after the Second World War, "Biological theories, tainted by associations with Nazi eugenics, fell into disgrace," and "sociological explanations of crime dominated theoretical work in the academy for the rest of the century" (Rafter 2008, 199). Biocriminology became tainted by the stigmatization of eugenics (which was itself an ironic twist of fate, given that eugenics was itself a stigmatizing movement) (Ramsden 2009). Biological criminology did not begin a resurgence until late in the twentieth century.

> Today [however] it is picking up speed and threatening not to eclipse sociological theories but to break their monopoly. Even though sociological theories remain dominant in criminology departments, biological theories are developing rapidly elsewhere in the academy, enlisting prestigious sciences such as genetics in their cause and generally showing impressive versatility and vitality.
> (Rafter 2008, 199)

This resurgence has been fueled in part by "spectacular advances in the genomic and neurological sciences" (Cooper et al. 2010, 334): the "the cachet of genes" (Hacking 2001, 152), through the Human Genome Project and the general ascendance of genetics as at least a partial explanation for nearly all human disease and behavior (Duster 2006; Marks 2002; Allen 2004; Kerr 2004; Rose 2000; Nelkin 2004) and the development of powerful new brain imaging technologies (Raine 1993; Dumit 2004).

Rafter (2008, 199) uses the term "contemporary biocriminology" to describe this "new" biocriminology which arose beginning in the 1960s and is beginning to flourish today. As Rafter notes, this broad term encompasses a wide variety of researchers, who vary greatly in disciplinary training and orientation, and methodological and theoretical approach, and who often couch their conclusions quite differently, making broad generalizations about "contemporary biocriminology" tenuous. For clarity, Rafter sorts "contemporary biocriminology" into five etiological categories, while cautioning readers that these categories should not necessarily be treated as "discrete and independent": (1) acquired biological abnormalities; (2) cognitive deficits; (3) evolutionary theories; (4) neuroscientific theories; and (5) genetic explanations of crime (Rafter 2008, 203). In this article, we will make claims about a subset of contemporary biocriminologists that do not necessarily apply to the larger group. Our group falls within Rafter's category (3): evolutionary theorists. However, our claims are not about all evolutionary theorists of crime, but a smaller subset still: those who are situated within the discipline of criminology. We distinguish between researchers trained and situated in criminology (e.g. Walsh) and those trained in other disciplines like psychology (e.g. Raine, Moffitt, Caspi). These distinctions can be confusing; Raine, for example, was trained as a psychologist, might be characterized today as a neuroscientist, but is currently employed in a criminology department. In this paper, we are trying to make claims about a small group of individuals trained, and currently situated, in criminology who promote genetic and evolutionary explanations of "crime." It is tempting to use the term "biocriminologists" to refer to this group because that term seems to capture quite well what we are trying to convey: biologically oriented criminologists. However, because Rafter uses the term "biocriminology" to refer to the broader category of researchers from all disciplines exploring all biological explanations of criminal and violent behavior, it would confuse matters for us to use the same term to mean something narrower. In searching for an alternative term, we decided the best course was to use a term that the actors use for themselves: "biosocial criminologists" (Ellis 2003b). Thus, in this article the term "biosocial criminology" will refer to work situated within the discipline of criminology that posits genetic and evolutionary explanations for "crime." The term "contemporary biocriminology," consistent with Rafter's usage, will refer to a broader category of research situated within all disciplines which explores all biological explanations for criminal and violent behavior. In this paper, our strongest claims apply only to "biosocial criminologists"; those claims do not necessarily apply to the broader group of "contemporary biocriminologists."

Despite its recent resurgence, biosocial criminology remains quite marginalized within the discipline of criminology. Biosocial criminologists attribute this state of affairs to "ideology" (Cooper et al. 2010), a misguided, "politically correct" over-reaction to the eugenic excesses of Lombrosian-influenced biological criminology. A review of criminology textbooks concluded, "Sadly, twenty recent books link biological explanations of crime to sexism, racism, and fascism, a common tactic used by some criminologists (especially those embracing critical perspectives) to discredit these arguments" (Wright and Miller 1998, 333). This "ideology" leads to "a selective interpretation and understanding of the data rather than an objective and rational evaluation of the evidence" (Cooper et al. 2010, 345). Criminologists who harbor this ideology,

> "old-guard criminologists" with no background in biology[,] still rule the roost in most departments and try to make sure that new criminologists who are hired think as they do.... Despite all of the efforts to ensure academic freedom in American colleges, teachers who fail to kowtow to the majority perspective in their discipline are still usually passed over when it comes to filling job vacancies.
>
> (Ellis 2003b, 249–51)

This bias is driven by a supposed "taboo" against biological criminology that developed as a reaction to the appropriation of Lombrosian biological criminology by proponents of eugenics, ranging from Nazis to sterilizers of the "feeble-minded." Indeed, the supposed systematic exclusion of biology from contemporary criminology has been dubbed "Lombroso's legacy" (Wright et al. 2008). As one journalist observes, contemporary biological criminology "is far removed from the eugenicist Francis Galton ... but the memory of 20th century history will not easily be shifted" (Rose 2006). The resistance to biosocial criminology, it is argued, is "ideological, driven by social scientists who envision racist and fascist hordes marching in lockstep behind anything remotely connected with the biology of human behavior" (Walsh 2000a, 1098). In invoking "ideology" as an explanation for the unpopularity of biological explanations within criminology, biosocial criminologists are availing themselves of a strategy that dates back several decades in which

Supporters of more radical programmes of eugenic improvement reveled in the process of stigmatization as a source of legitimacy. They cast eugenics as a victim of politics and ideology – population scientists having sacrificed their objectivity in the face of social pressure.

(Ramsden 2009, 857)

For example, William Shockley, a proponent of racial biology, "rapidly adopted the identity of a persecuted minority" and cast himself and eugenics "in the role of 'victim'" (Ramsden 2009, 871). In this sense, biosocial criminologists resemble Lombroso himself who was well aware of the widespread criticism of his ideas and "pictured himself as a beleaguered pioneer, an explorer or hunter struggling bravely onward in search of truth" (Rafter and Ystehede 2010, 266).

From Lombroso to biosocial criminology

Should biosocial criminology be viewed as continuous with Lombrosian criminology, or should it be viewed as severable? What does contemporary biosocial criminology have to do with Lombrosian biocriminology? The two intellectual movements certainly do bear some similarities. Both look to locate the cause of criminality in the body. Both are primarily individualistic in focus, in that their goal is to understand those causes of criminal behavior that may be associated with particular individuals, as opposed to those that may be associated with environments shared by individuals, although there is also some effort to explain differences between groups, such as the sexes. Both focus heavily on the brain, though other somatic entities are studied as well. Both seek somatic "markers" that will serve to "identify" the individuals with criminal propensities. Both are founded upon some notion of innate criminality; though Ferri's term "born criminal" is no longer used, biosocial criminology is nonetheless focused on drawing attention to causes of criminal behavior that emanate from "within" (the body) that have supposedly been historically neglected in favor of those that emanate from "without" (the environment).

At the same time, however, there are vast differences between the biocriminology of Lombroso's time and that of today. As biosocial criminologists argue, "evolutionary theories of criminal and antisocial behavior have in fact reemerged during the past two decades in forms that the 19th century theorists would scarcely recognize" (Ellis and Walsh 1997, 260). "That was then, and this is now" (Walsh 2000a: 1098).

> Those who assert that behavior genetics today is strongly ideological in its directions and focus are inordinately impressed by the facts of the first half of this century and take too little account of developments in genetics that have occurred in the last half century.
>
> (Goldman 1994, 97)

Most obvious, of course, are the differences in technology. Lombrosian criminologists examined and measured skulls using calipers and filled skulls to measure their volume. They used calipers and rulers to take anthropometric measurements. They devised elaborate sphymometers and hydrosphygmometers to measure the pulse and plethysmographs to measure circulation and sensitivity to pain. Craniometers and craniophores measured skull size, dynamometers grip strength, the tachianthropometer a series of anthropometric measurements, the clinometer the angles of the head. Algometers administered electric shocks. This is not to even mention the goniometer, estheiometer, baristesiometer, thermesthesiometer, olfactometer, ergograph, cephalograph, and campimeter. They interpreted tattoos. They compiled composite photographs to elicit the "criminal" physiognomy (Horn 2003, 2006).

The tools of biocriminology have changed. Neuroscientists use cutting-edge brain imaging technologies, including computerized tomography, magnetic resonance imaging, positron emission tomography, and functional magnetic resonance imaging instead of measuring skulls (Rafter 2008, 222). But the most powerful and promising new technology is, of course, genetics. Thus far, biological criminologists have made strong claims only about a single genetic marker, a gene that codes for monoamine oxidase A (MAOA) (Caspi *et al.* 2002). But the hope is that over the next several decades, as the broad genetic research program sparked by the Human Genome Project begins to bear fruit, genetics will yield significant and powerful new insights into criminal behavior. Remarkably, Raine, the leading brain imaging researcher in criminology, suggests that Lombroso simply had the right ideas but the wrong tools (Leslie 2010; Raine 2006). Conceptual tools have changed as well. Lombroso drew on nineteenth-century anthropology and proto-Darwinian thought. Later in his career, he incorporated Darwinism into his theories. Biosocial criminologists draw heavily on later streams of thought within evolutionary theory, primarily sociobiology and evolutionary psychology.

In addition to new tools, there are also several important differences between Lombrosian and contemporary biological criminology in terms of presentation and rhetoric. Many critics see continuities between Lombrosian and contemporary biocriminology:

> Talk of a criminal diathesis – a propensity to commit crimes, which different people may have in different degrees ... is not antiquated. It is alive and well ... the program is not only alive and well, but preserves, to an astonishing degree, the verbal formulations of days so long ago that we all thought they had disappeared.
>
> (Hacking 2001, 150–2)

Well aware of this, contemporary biocriminologists are far more careful in their claims than were their predecessors.

Lombroso and his contemporaries were often sloppy in their reasoning and use of evidence, and flamboyant and inconsistent in their claims (Gibson 2002, 28).

Most contemporary biological criminology is much more careful and cautious in both its use of evidence and its framing of knowledge claims. Another important difference concerns determinism. While recent scholarship has shown that Lombroso was not as strict a determinist as popular mythology held him to be, it is nonetheless fair to read a strong biological determinism in his work and that of many of his followers (Gibson 2006, 144; Bondio 2006, 193). Contemporary biological criminology is consistent and vociferous in its disavowal of biological determinism (e.g. Ellis and Walsh 1997; Walsh and Ellis 2003; Rose 2006; Caspi et al. 2002): "Although genes may increase propensity for criminality, for example, they do not determine it – the preponderance of individuals with the same gene are likely *not* to have engaged in serious antisocial behavior" (Baker et al. 2006: 45, original emphasis). Instead, contemporary biological criminology flies under the banner of "biosocial," a term intended to highlight that explanation is sought, not in biology alone, but in interactions between biology and environment (e.g. Walsh and Ellis 2003; Baker et al. 2006; Walsh 2000a, 1097; Raine et al. 1997; Wasserman 1994). As Rafter (2008, 203) notes,

> the biosocial model has risen to the fore, offering an escape from the endless and unproductive nature-versus-nurture debate ... Biocriminologists themselves now reject out of hand the hard determinism that sociologists (and others) found objectionable in earlier biological theories of crime. In fact, the new work on genetics and crime stresses environment's crucial role in shaping criminal behaviors.

Contemporary claims to explain criminal behavior are framed in terms of gene-environment interactions (sometimes called "GxE") (Baker et al. 2006, 38). Indeed, many biological criminologists seem to assign *primacy* to environment as a causal force. Often they appear to be arguing only for the *inclusion* of biological factors, not their primacy. For example, Caspi and Moffitt's report on what is probably the most persuasive empirical finding of contemporary biocriminology, their findings concerning the MAOA gene, insists that the abusive home environment "causes" violent behavior. The gene's function, for those who have it, is *only* to offer protection against this effect (Caspi et al. 2002; Gillet and Tamatea 2012). This denial of determinism becomes a way to sever biosocial criminology from the Lombrosian notion of the born criminal: "I must strongly emphasize that there is absolutely nothing in the concept of G/E correlation that can in any way be construed as supporting the notion of congenital criminality" (Walsh 2000a, 1083). But note that this rhetorical severing is premised on the historically false claim that Lombroso was solely a determinist and did not himself allow for biology–environment interaction.

Even the GxE metaphor is proving to be far too simple. Recent developments in molecular genetics in general suggest that very little causation can be attributed to single genes. Instead, most causation is believed to derive from correlations between many genes and even from interactions between those genes. So, rather than "GxE," we have "multi-GxE," As Rafter (2008, 234) notes, "future research on genetics and crime is likely to move beyond the study of variants for single genes to investigate how genes and their variants interact with one another and their environments to increase one's risk of antisocial behavior."

Having clearly learned from Lombroso's mistakes, contemporary biological criminologists may yet be more successful than he was at escaping the determinist label. Whether they will be successful in doing so, however, is still unclear. Determinisms are simple explanations with great appeal to the human mind, and it is far from obvious that contemporary biological criminologists' efforts to escape it will be sufficient to overcome the public desire to attribute it to them.

Another major rhetorical difference between Lombrosian and contemporary biocriminology lies in the area of what we might anachronistically call the "criminal justice policy implications" of biocriminology. Reforming law and penal institutions was a central motivation for Lombroso's work, and he was, therefore, not reticent about articulating the logical policy implications of his ideas. Again, in popular mythology, Lombroso has often been misunderstood, having been incorrectly believed to have opposed capital punishment and even to have opposed punishment entirely (e.g. Hacking 2001: 148). In fact,

> Although his practical advice became increasingly specialized over the years, Lombroso's basic philosophy of punishment never changed. In opposition to the Enlightenment principles of Beccaria, he counseled that punishment be tailored to individual criminals rather than to their crimes. He explicitly rejected the principle of moral responsibility, arguing that criminals acted out of compulsion, whether from their innate physical or psychological degeneracy or from the social environment.
>
> (Gibson 2002, 26)

Thus, policy prescription was central to Lombroso's work, and it was openly and unapologetically discussed within it. Indeed, Lombroso asserted "It is the job of criminal anthropology to establish the relationship between criminals and their punishment" (Lombroso 2006, 341), and "demonstrate[d] some awareness of the use of knowledge in society and of the political use to which 'objective scientific analyses' could be put" (Knepper 2011: 367).

Contemporary biocriminology's posture toward policy is quite different. Rather than exploring and expounding upon the policy implications of biological causes of crime, contemporary biological criminology tends to bracket off policy discussions. Instead, it adopts the familiar contemporary scientific rhetorical trope of claiming that it is merely reporting "neutral" scientific findings, from a perspective that is completely agnostic about policy. "Although genetics is not inherently ideological, it can be put to ideological uses, by misinterpretation if necessary" (Goldman 1994, 98).

The danger for public policy is not in the data. The data are just the way things happen to turn out. Instead, the problem is the reflexive, knee jerk medicalization of behavioral genetics, a tendency that is, sadly to say, not limited to our critics.

(Carey and Gottesman 1994, 90)

The caveats issued by Fishbein (1990, 55) are a good example of the cautious posture contemporary biocriminologists adopt toward any possible policy implications of their work (see also Glenn and Raine 2009: 256–7). She urges "caution against the premature application of biological findings" and notes that "The weaknesses in design sampling techniques, and statistical procedures preclude drawing definitive conclusions, and results are frequently contested and unreliable." She goes on to warn against basing "Policies and programs ... on equivocal and controversial findings." Anticipating the accusation that contemporary biocriminology might lead to neo-eugenics, she notes that "care must be taken not stigmatize or otherwise traumatize individuals or groups that are, as yet, innocent of a criminal or civil violation." Fishbein asserts, "we must avoid applying labels to behaviors we do not understand." She notes that any contemplated intervention based on biocriminology "in the absence of a proven violation of law would demand careful consideration." And, she uses the word "transgressions" to describe the possibility of "forced compliance with a 'therapeutic regimen'." How different in tone this is from the readiness and confidence with which Lombroso was prepared to advise governments how they should punish!

In some cases, biocriminologists go even further and suggest that their findings should hardly influence social policy at all – they "have more implications for policy-related research and debate ... than they do for social policy per se" (Cauffman et al. 2005, 162). Others predict that when biocriminological research kicks into gear "nothing much will happen for public policy, but a lot will happen for the psychology and the neurobiology of behavior" (Carey and Gottesman 1994, 89). There are exceptions to this generalization within contemporary biocriminology, most notably the public policy scholar James Q. Wilson (Wilson and Herrnstein 1985). The subfield of biosocial criminology, however, seems especially dismissive of its own potential policy implications. A close reading of the corpus of biosocial criminology would seem to suggest that the primary motivation for biosocial criminology is not policy changes but, rather, contributions to criminological theory (Ellis and Walsh 1997, 260) and the "maturing" of criminology as a discipline (Walsh 2000a, 1099).

Paradoxically, this posture is least apparent with regard to the touchy subject of eugenics. Here contemporary biocriminologists are not agnostic about policy; instead they openly disavow neo-eugenics. In the debate following the notorious canceled 1992 National Institutes of Health conference on genetic research into crime and violence and "Violence Initiative," it was said that "all participants in the debate" agree on "the urgency of preventing human genetic research from being used for eugenic and racist purposes" (Wasserman 1994, 107). "In 1995, genetic data provide the basis for very powerful arguments *against* racism and eugenics" (Goldman 1994: 98, original emphasis). Indeed, at some points biocriminologists go so far as to argue that the policy implications of biocriminology will inevitably be *environmental* interventions (Walsh 2000a, 1098; Fishbein 1994, 93). And, indeed, it is tempting to read the MAOA findings, for example, as inviting social, rather than pharmacological, policy interventions (Taylor 2009, 440).

Contemporary biocriminologists' careful caveats might, however, provoke a certain degree of skepticism among those aware of the long history within criminal justice policy of doing precisely the sort of thing Fishbein warns against: basing "Policies and programs ... on equivocal and controversial findings." Indeed, many criminal justice policies are adopted without any empirical support whatsoever (Zimring *et al.* 2001). Contemporary biocriminologists who have read their history should understand that, like Lombroso himself, if they choose to produce knowledge, they should expect to have very little control over the uses and resulting policies that rhetorically invoke that knowledge as justification.

Lombroso and evolution

An additional, hitherto largely unnoticed, discontinuity between Lombrosian criminology and biosocial criminology forms the main subject of this paper. That concerns the status of the criminal in the evolutionary hierarchy. Lombroso famously emphasized the notion of *atavism*, "the reversion of criminals to a lower state of physical and psychological evolution" (Gibson 2006, 139). For Lombroso, "As atavistic throwbacks on the evolutionary scale, criminals constitute a group that differs from law-abiding citizens and instead resembles 'savages' from less civilized societies" (Gibson and Rafter 2006: 39). Lombroso initially

> identified all born criminals as atavistic .... The ferocity of criminals, for example, was "common to ancient and savage peoples but rare and monstrous today." Atavism even explained the popularity of tattoos among lawbreakers because "tattoos are one of the special characteristics of primitive man and of those in the wild." In short, criminals were "savages living in the middle of a flourishing European civilization," identifiable by their physical and moral anomalies. They represented throwbacks on the evolutionary scale, a freakish reappearance in modern European civilization of its brutish past.
> (Gibson 2006, 145)

The notion of an evolutionary hierarchy was crucial to Lombroso's argument.

> Lombroso's theory was not just a vague proclamation that crime is hereditary – such claims were common enough in his time – but a specific *evolutionary* theory based upon anthropometric data. Criminals are evolutionary throwbacks in our midst. Germs of an ancestral past lie dormant in our heredity. In some

unfortunate individuals, the past comes to life again. These people are innately driven to act as a normal ape or savage would, but such behavior is deemed criminal in our civilized society.

(Gould 1981, 124, original emphasis)

Positivist criminology emerges to offer a scientistic discourse of the subject which avoids the instabilities of the volitional subject and – in association with eugenics and other evolutionary theories derived from Herbert Spencer and Charles Darwin – rearticulates a hierarchical social order which is now founded upon social science rather than class.

(Hutchings 2001, 167)

Evolutionary theory prompted Lombroso to characterize criminals as "quasi-humans," transitional figures "between humans and the 'lower' species" (Rafter and Ystehede 2010, 273, quoting Kelly Hurley in part). This notion of atavism famously recurred repeatedly in Lombroso's writings. "Criminals," Lombroso wrote, "resemble savages and the colored races" (Lombroso 2006, 91). As he summarized:

> Atavism remains one of the most constant characteristics of the born criminal, in spite of, or rather together with, pathology. This book has provided convincing evidence that many of the characteristics of primitive man are also commonly found in the born criminal, including low sloping foreheads, overdeveloped sinuses, frequent occurrence of the medium occipital fossetta, overdevelopment of the jaw and cheekbones, prognathism, oblique and large eye sockets, dark skin, thick and curly head hair, large or protuberant ears, long arms, similarity between the sexes, left-handedness, waywardness among women, low sensitivity to pain, complete absence of moral or affective sensibility, laziness, absence of remorse and foresight, great vanity, and fleeting, violent passions.

(Lombroso 2006, 222)

On some occasions, Lombroso even claimed to be able to quantify the proportion of criminal behavior attributable to atavism: "Up to 35 percent of all criminals are atavistic born criminals who differ physically from normal individuals" (Lombroso 2006, 338).

In proper Darwinist fashion, Lombroso's notion of atavism was not limited to human evolutionary history. Thus, in some of his most curious passages he traced the evolutionary origins of human criminal behavior to that of bees, fish, and carnivorous plants (Lombroso 2006, 168). "From the perspective of atavism, the difference between the instinctively cruel acts of animals, plants, and criminals is very small" (Lombroso 2006, 223). Elsewhere, Lombroso noted his colleague Tonnini's finding of faster healing among criminals. "This recuperative power, in his view, represents an atavistic return to the animalian stage of evolution, in which creatures like lizards and salamanders can reproduce entire limbs. All degenerates, epileptics, imbeciles, and moral madmen possess the ability to heal quickly" (Lombroso 2006, 255). This view led Lombroso to portray criminals, at least metaphorically, as members of different species which in turn justified his approval of the death penalty, albeit used sparingly.

> Born criminals, programmed to do harm, are atavistic reproductions of not only savage men but also the most ferocious carnivores and rodents. This discovery should not make us more compassionate toward born criminals (as some claim), but rather should shield us from pity, for these beings are members not of our species but the species of bloodthirsty beasts.
> (Lombroso 2006, 348)

Lombroso thus characterized capital punishment, in Darwinian fashion, as an "extreme form of natural selection" (Lombroso 2006, 348).

Contrary to popular myth, over the course of his career Lombroso backed off from the notion that atavism was the sole explanation of criminality. This was in part in response to his critics. Lombroso himself noted that "Some adversaries, particularly foreigners, misread or misunderstand me and accuse me of being exclusively atavistophile or epileptophile in my etiology of crime" (Lombroso 2006, 230). The leading competing explanation was *degeneration*, which was advocated by Lombroso's French adversaries (e.g. Pick 1989; Nye 1984, 121; Gibson 2006, 145; Leps 1992). Degeneration differed from atavism in that the criminal decayed backward into a lower evolutionary state, rather than simply being born into that lower state. Crucial, however, for our purposes, both atavism and degeneration placed the criminal below the "normal" individual in the evolutionary hierarchy.

Evolution in biosocial criminology

If we juxtapose the discourse above with biosocial criminology, we find something remarkable: the position of "the criminal" in the evolutionary hierarchy has flipped completely. In a remarkable passage, published in the world's leading criminology journal, Ellis and Walsh (1997, 255) distinguish biosocial from Lombrosian criminology as follows:

> All of the modern evolutionary theories share only a faint resemblance to the first evolutionary theory in criminology proposed over a century ago by Lombroso. The dissimilarities are understandable in part because Lombroso knew nothing of the concept of genetics, nor did he have the benefit of the vast store of research on evolutionary principles developed over the past century or a modern understanding of how brain functioning controls behavior, including learned behavior. As a result, nothing resembling the concept of *atavism* is found in modern evolutionary theories of criminal behavior. In fact, rather than considering criminals throw backs to some primitive human form, most modern evolutionary theories of criminality imply the opposite: that

criminal behavior may mark a special adaptation to life in large impersonal societies. If so, criminal and antisocial behavior may have only been adaptive over roughly the past 10,000 years at most, and only then primarily in urbanized environments.

In other words, "the criminal" is no longer *less* evolved than "normal" law-abiding citizens, but *more* evolved. "The criminal" is no longer a less-evolved creature living among us – "savages, living amidst the very flower of European civilization" (Lombroso 2006: 78) – and preying upon us (as in atavism theory) nor a less-evolved creature who mates with "normal" individuals and thus reverses the progress of evolution (as in degeneration theory). Rather, the criminal is a more evolved creature living among us. The criminal threatens the normal citizenry not because he is an inferior being who, in the frustrations born of his lack of fitness, resorts to violence, but because he is a *superior* being whose superior abilities and adaptation allows him to exploit the normal citizenry. Moreover, we have supposedly built a society for which criminals are adapted. In this formulation, the criminal is portrayed as a sort of superman.

> recent explorations of this possibility have gone far beyond Lombroso's (1896) suggestion that criminals are atavistic throwbacks to some primitive human life form. Not only did Lombroso know nothing of genetics, he also thought criminals were poorly adapted to life in complex industrial societies. Recently, several evolutionary theorists have argued that criminals may actually be better adapted for living in large modern societies than for living in small foraging or horticultural communities.
>
> (Ellis and Walsh 1997, 231)

In this way, biosocial criminologists treat evolution differently than do many psychologists who research psychopathy. Jalava (2006, 425) showed that contemporary psychopathy research echoes degeneration theory in portraying the psychopath as an "evolutionary throwback ... as representing characteristics typical of either an earlier stage of human development (whether child-like or primitive) or an evolutionarily less developed species," characterizing them as "children," "reptilian," "primal," "alien," and "inhuman". Thus, Jalava (2006, 430) argues that "Current psychopathy research is by and large a continuation of" the degeneration research program. Thus, we can see conflicting strains of thought within contemporary biocriminology: psychopathy researchers posit criminals as evolutionarily inferior, whereas biosocial criminologist conceive criminals as evolutionarily superior.

How have biosocial criminologists managed to reorder the evolutionary hierarchy in this way? Their arguments rest in large measure on new, not always entirely compatible, developments in evolutionary theory, such as the field of evolutionary psychology and the "selfish gene" metaphor popularized by Dawkins (1989). Biosocial criminologists argue that in evolutionary psychology's terms, criminals are "cheaters," individuals who have adopted "alternative reproductive strategies"

(Ellis and Walsh 1997, 245). Whereas the "mainstream" strategy is skill at procuring resources through legitimate means like hunting and gathering, the alternative strategies are twofold: first, deceiving females as to one's ability and intention to procure resources, or, second, procuring resources through illegitimate means like what we would today call "crime" (Ellis and Walsh 1997, 245; Ellis 2003a, 26–8; Glenn and Raine 2009: 254).[1]

Biosocial criminologists argue that both the mainstream and the alternative strategies lead to reproductive success; humans' contemporary genotype, therefore, has selected for individuals who apply both strategies. Indeed, game theory is employed to show that a stable population requires an equilibrium between non-cheaters and cheaters (Raine 1993, 29–37).

A second line of argument proceeds more directly from crime to reproductive success:

> According to the evolutionary theory of rape, the male reproductive advantage derived from having multiple sex partners has resulted in natural selection favoring genes promoting brain patterns for "pushiness" in pursuit of sexual intercourse. In some males, genes may carry pushiness to the point of actual force, especially after less violent tactics fail to yield results. In other words, over generations, pushy males will probably be more successful at passing on their genes, including any genes coding for readily learning pushy sexual behavior, than will less pushy males. While these ideas may not be pleasant to contemplate, proponents of the evolutionary theory of rape contend that the dynamics of rape cannot be fully understood without taking into account its reproductive consequences.
>
> (Ellis and Walsh 1997, 234)

Such extraordinary statements have obvious gender implications. As Rafter (2008, 214) writes, when biosocial criminologists (here referring to Thornhill and Palmer (2000), rather than Ellis and Walsh)

> gloss over the social realities of rape with platitudes about evolved male aggression, they themselves are guilty of the naturalistic fallacy. This fault is a direct inheritance from their social Darwinist predecessors, who unabashedly translated their picture of the world as they wanted it to be into "scientific" terms, confusing *ought* with *is*.

Rafter argues the biosocial view of "rape is really an extended rant about what men and women *ought* to be like – females passive and males aggressive."

In terms of explicit assertions that criminals are "more evolved," we have only been able to locate the above statements by two leading biosocial criminologists. Although Ellis and Walsh assert that "several evolutionary theorists have argued that criminals may actually be better adapted for living in large modern societies than for living in small foraging or horticultural communities" (Ellis and Walsh

1997, 231), they offer no citations that indicate which "evolutionary theorists" share this view. As noted above, most contemporary biocriminologists are more cautious in their claims, and, while they may or may not hold such views, we have been unable to find any explicit statements in their writings that would allow us to attribute such views to them. Clearly, this limits us from making strong claims that this view is influential or widely believed among criminologists or even among biocriminologists. However, our justification for discussing it at length in this paper derives not from the supposed prevalence of the view expressed but from its very extraordinariness. We feel that the claim is worth discussing if Ellis and Walsh may be taken at their word that "several evolutionary theorists" share it. However, we also believe the claim is well worth discussing if that is *not* true – if Ellis and Walsh, presumably sincerely, confabulated the belief that "several evolutionary theorists" share this extraordinary claim.[2] The emergence of this claim, whether it emerged from evolutionary theory or from biosocial criminology, may tell us something about the political and cultural context surrounding "crime discourse."

That said, this notion of "the criminal" as superman inevitably evokes the now discredited (Becker 2001), and far better known, notion of the "superpredator" that arose around the same time, during the 1990s period of rising crime rates (DiIulio 1995). While the "superpredator" would seem closely analogous with the sort of evolutionarily superior criminal posited by biosocial criminology, it should be noted that we unable to find any direct connection between the two metaphors. DiIulio, the originator of the "superpredator" notion, was not a biosocial criminologist, and the original superpredator text made no mention of evolution or even biological causation at all (DiIulio 1995). Instead, DiIulio attributed the rise of superpredators to "moral poverty" (a notion that admittedly does seem to evoke Lombroso's notion of "moral insanity," Lombroso 2006, 212), and his ideas would seem to derive more from the notion of psychopathy than from biosocial criminology. Nor have biosocial criminologists sought to invoke the notion of the superpredator. Nonetheless, similarities remain in that DiIulio conceived superpredator as "radically present-oriented," interested in "immediate rewards," motivated by "sex, drugs, money," and "naturally" inclined to "murder, rape, rob, assault, burglarize, deal deadly drugs, and get high" (DiIulio 1995). These attributes are in some ways consistent with the biosocial image of criminals as psychopaths (who are notoriously present-oriented) and as acting out their "selfish genes" short-term reproductive strategies.

Evolution and society

For Lombroso, evolution was an inherently ameliorative process, albeit one that might require some minor social interventions to allow it to function properly. Thus, he argued that if his proposal for lifetime incarceration for "incorrigibles" were adopted, "there would be a return to the process of natural selection that has produced not only our race but the very justice that gradually came to prevail with the elimination of the most violent" (Lombroso 2006).[3] For Lombroso, crime had "social utility" only "among less civilized peoples" (Lombroso 2006, 352), though at other moments he argued that "political crimes" had social utility. Crime was not adaptive at all for civilized societies, and crime could be reduced, perhaps eventually eliminated, merely through the progress of civilization itself: "As social conditions improve, crime will lose its atavistic ferocity" (Lombroso 2006, 354).[4]

Biosocial criminologists thus sound far more pessimistic than Lombroso. Rather than developing a society to which crime is maladapted and thus will eventually wither away, according to biosocial criminologists, we have developed a society for which criminals are *better* adapted and crime should be expected to thrive. The public policy implications for those activities that fall under the general auspices of "social progress" (alleviation of poverty, improved education, improved health care, and the like) of this shift should not be overlooked. One public policy implication of Lombroso's criminology was that social progress would yield its own rewards in terms of reductions in crime, perhaps tempered somewhat by the development of new crimes. For biosocial criminologists, in contrast, the society we have developed – "urbanized," "impersonal," "modern" – provides an ecological niche for which crime is adapted, and they are silent as to what effect, if any, "social progress" might have on that, rather dire, situation. Indeed, biosocial criminologists suggest that individuals with "mutant" criminogenic genes would have a greater chance of reproducing in large, modern societies like those prevalent today than in smaller societies characteristic of earlier human history:

> Consider what might happen if a mutant gene arose in a small foraging society that inclined one of its members to be unusually aggressive toward other group members and/or to be disrespectful of other people's property rights. In a small society, this individual would probably be ousted unless he or she quickly learned to restrain his or her impulses. In a large society, however, this same individual might be able to act upon his or her antisocial impulses repeatedly without detection or ill consequences. Not only would he or she be able to find many more unwary victims in a large society, but the chances of being identified and punished would be less.
>
> (Ellis and Walsh 1997, 244)

The reproductive rates of those labeled "criminals" is of obvious importance in this discussion. As noted, Lombroso himself was generally optimistic in believing that "atavistic" criminals were in the process of dying off, though he allowed that natural selection might need some help in the form of well-crafted policy interventions, like lifetime incarceration for "incorrigibles." Of course, Lombrosian theory was taken up by eugenicists like Galton, Pearson, and Havelock Ellis who were far more concerned than Lombroso had been about higher rates of reproduction among the lower classes. The French degeneration theorists were likewise pessimistic though for the opposite reason: rather than having high birth rates, degenerates were infecting the entire nation with *low* birth rates, thus enervating the body politic. On this dimension, biosocial criminologists seem most like the eugenicists; they are concerned that modern society constitutes an environment in which

> persons who are highly disposed toward crime might be able to reproduce at fairly high rates, at least under certain conditions, such as when the chances of being identified or punished are fairly low (e.g. in large cities as opposed to small communities).
>
> (Ellis and Walsh 1997, 231)

We see then that the biocriminological paradigm has been consistent in viewing criminality as an evolved trait. But over the course of a century, the place of the "the criminal" in the purported evolutionary hierarchy has completely flipped. Biosocial criminology has switched from placing "the criminal" at the bottom of the human evolutionary hierarchy to placing him at the top. In other words, "the criminal" has not merely marginally improved his position in the hierarchy; he has bypassed the entire "normal" human population. In a mere century, the criminal has been transformed from subhuman to superhuman.

Of course, arguing that criminality is an evolved trait does not necessitate arguing that it is *more* evolved, as the counterexample of Lombrosian criminology demonstrates. Raine, a brain researcher, for example, is ambiguous as to whether he shares the view of biosocial criminologists who draw on genetics and evolutionary psychology: he says crime was adaptive in early human history, which would be consistent with Lombroso, but does not say whether he believes it continues to be so (Raine 1993, 28; Rafter 2008, 210). The explanation for why contemporary biosocial criminologists view born criminals as supermen need not, therefore, be sought in the notion of evolutionary theory itself and its consequences for criminology, but, rather may be sought elsewhere. That elsewhere may be, for example, the culture and politics in which contemporary biosocial criminology is produced.

As historians, our interest is, of course, not in the truth value of contemporary biosocial criminologists' claims, but rather in historical explanation for why such claims are made (Garland 2000). Historians explained the French criminologists' theory of degeneration, in which the criminal was viewed as being in a lower evolutionary state, by reference to cultural and political concerns. Nye (1984, xii), for example, attributed anxiety about the "national health" of the body politic following France's defeat in the Franco-Prussian War. Pick (1989, 222) explained the same phenomenon by reference to "a bio-medical conception of crowd and mass civilization as regression." He also explained Lombroso's theory of atavism in the context of the unification of Italy; Lombroso wanted to "make Italians" partly by culling the less evolved (119; see also Melossi 2001, 19). Melossi (2001, 29) suggests that "the representation of crime" is "a way of talking about society and society's ills" and, indeed, about "the moral value of society as a whole." If, as Hacking (2001, 152) suggests, "the targets of [the biosocial] research program are chosen by social values and social fears," then what does the flipping of the born criminal from the bottom of the evolutionary hierarchy to the top tell us about our contemporary social values and social fears?

Explanations

Somewhat to our surprise, we have searched in vain for any comment upon the remarkable elevation of the born criminal from the bottom to the top of the evolutionary hierarchy, even among critical criminologists whom one might expect to be among the first to notice and comment upon this development. (To some extent this would seem to bear out biosocial criminologists' complaint that they are marginalized and ignored in mainstream criminology.) Instead, contemporary criminology tends to characterize biosocial criminology as a "dehumanizing rhetoric" (e.g. Hagan 2010, 114). Taken literally, the term "dehumanizing" is ambiguous as to whether the criminal is portrayed as subhuman or superhuman. A cursory reading of contemporary criminology, however, reveals that biosocial criminology is understood as portraying the criminal as a lower, not a higher, form of life. Garland (2001, 135–6), for example, emphasizes that contemporary biocriminology portrays the criminal as "barely human," "beyond all human understanding," "a human predator," and "a feral, pre-social being." Likewise, cultural criminologists note that contemporary media discourse portrays criminals as "subhuman" (e.g. Meyer 2010, 200), "nonhuman," "semi-human," or "antihuman," that "as animalistic predators, criminals are separated from humanity" (Surette 2007, 204, 208, 219, 221), or even as "abhuman" or "inhuman" (Valier 2002, 330). Arguably, the notion of the criminal as "predator," which implies the normal citizen as prey, imputes a certain biological superiority – the "top" of the food chain – to the criminal. But, at the same time, the "animalistic" connotations of the term "predator" may be seen as denoting a lower place in the evolutionary hierarchy.

In order to find any comment at all on the notion of the criminal as biologically superior, rather than inferior, we must turn to the literature on "gothic criminology" (Picart and Greek 2007b).[5] Gothic criminology's interest in the portrayal of the monstrous would seem particularly germane to our discussion. Just as Rafter and Ystehede have noted vampire imagery in some of Lombroso's most cited writings (2010, 276), Gill's (2007, 152) account of the enormous popularity of vampires in popular culture suggests an uncanny similarity between vampires and the born criminals of biosocial criminology who are programmed by their own "selfish genes" to seek material (and thus reproductive) advantage over others. Indeed, the genetically engineered "mutants" of, for example, the television series *Mutant X* may be read as metaphors for the genetically programmed criminal of biosocial criminology (159).

As far as we have been able to find, only in the gothic criminological literature on serial killer and vampire films is the notion of the criminal as superhuman explicitly discussed. Epstein (1995, 73) noted that serial killers are routinely portrayed as "superhuman." Picart and Greek noted that serial killers and vampires are portrayed as "Übermensches" and serial killers as "superhuman" (Picart and

Greek 2007c, 230–1; see also Epstein 1995). They argued that Steven Grlscz, of the film *Immortality* (1998), was portrayed as "superhuman" (244), Hannibal Lecter, of *Hannibal* (2001), as "the hero, the superior being" (246). To be sure, however, Hannibal Lecter was an exceptional figure, representative of the sort of "criminal genius" who was not unknown even to positivist criminologists of Lombroso's time (Hutchings 2001). We should be cautious about drawing connections between the sort of criminals, like charismatic serial killers, vampires, and "supervillains," represented in popular culture, and the sorts of "ordinary" criminals who are, presumably, the subjects of biosocial criminology.

Even the gothic criminologists, however, with their focus on popular culture rather than on the science of biosocial criminology, did not fully draw the connection between the notion of the criminal as superhuman and the flipping of the place of the criminal in the evolutionary hierarchy in biosocial criminology. Epstein (1995: 75) concluded that the serial killer is represented as at once superhuman and "biologically normal, mortal," whereas biosocial criminology represents the criminal as both mortal and supernormal. And, when Picart and Greek distinguished "the modern serial killer" from "Lombroso's atavistic evolutionary throwbacks," the distinction they drew was that the contemporary criminal's "primitivism" is "unrecognizable by outside physical features." This was not the distinction drawn by Ellis and Walsh, who claimed the contemporary criminal is not atavistic or primitive at all, but "the opposite." Thus, biosocial criminology's portrayal of the born criminal as superhuman was only dimly and ambiguously prefigured in contemporary gothic media representations of criminality. Further explanation, therefore, seems necessary.

One important development between the late nineteenth and late twentieth centuries lies in the nature of discourse about evolutionary theory itself. Lombroso and his school were guilty of an error that was quite common at the time: reading evolution as a hierarchy, a teleological progression from "lesser" to "greater" organisms, and even races, culminating, of course, with Northern European men. Evolutionary theorists emphasize that evolution development is merely change and should not be equated with progress. "Species didn't become better; they became different" (Marks 1995, 18). To be sure such misreadings of Darwinism remain common today, but they have become less common than they were in the late nineteenth century (Marks 2008, 72). Thus, the pains that biosocial criminologists take to disavow any claims that born criminals are lower in the evolutionary hierarchy may simply reflect an increased awareness that evolutionary theory should not be equated with hierarchy.

However, were biosocial criminologists merely reflecting a non-hierarchical reading of evolutionary theory, then we should expect them to have emphasized that the fact that "born criminals" are different from "normals" does not imply that they are worse or better. But that is not what they have written. Instead, they have resurrected a hierarchical view of evolution, but placed criminals above "normal" citizens: criminality is "a special adaptation to life in large impersonal societies" (Ellis and Walsh 1997, 255). Thus, criminals are still "othered" and portrayed as monstrous in biosocial criminology. Elevating criminals above "normals" is as much a mode of "othering" as denigrating them; it does not constitute viewing criminals as "just different." Monsters may be viewed as inferior to "normals" or superior, but they are always "other." Thus, biosocial criminology remains stigmatizing. It, in a sense, stigmatizes without stigma. There are, of course, analogies that might be drawn to other discourses in which groups are stigmatized by being cast as *more*, rather than less evolved. The popular notion of Asians as genetically advantaged comes to mind, as does the attribution of superior athletic ability to Africans (Brooks 2009).

This resurrection of the evolutionary hierarchy with criminals at the top requires further explanation than merely the removal of teleology from evolutionary discourse. What explains this flipping of the evolutionary hierarchy in biosocial criminology? We suggest that what has changed is not criminologists' perception of the criminal, but their perception of society. It seems likely that what has been lost over the past century is social scientists' optimistic view of society as progressing toward an ever more civilized state for which born criminals would be ever more poorly adapted. Lombroso offered an optimistic view in which civilized society could achieve social control by ridding itself of its less evolved members (Rafter and Ystehede 2010, 280). Biosocial criminologists offer a more pessimistic vision. They seem to view society as a brutish jungle – recall that it was NIH scientist Frederick Goodwin's characterization of the urban environment as a "jungle" that made contemporary biocriminology controversial for most of the 1990s – for which criminals are *better* adapted than the rest of us. Criminality is "a special adaptation to life in large impersonal societies" (Ellis and Walsh 1997, 255). Unlike Lombroso, who was able to believe that society would continuously improve simply by allowing the majority of "normals" to follow their biologically programmed urges (except when he argued that "political crime" was necessary for society to improve), biosocial criminology suggests that social order can only be maintained by convincing or coercing "normals" to resist their instincts and act against the interests of their "selfish genes." The homology of this notion with what is perhaps the famous move in recent criminological theorizing – Hirschi's claim that what needs to be explained is, not why individuals commit crime, but why they do *not* commit crime – has not escaped us. But it would also seem to reflect a deep pessimism about the neo-liberal regime that now governs most of the planet. Gill (2007, 152) notes a consistency in popular culture's portrayal of the supposed monstrousness of criminals with the monstrousness of corporations and governments:

> The worst traits of vampires, demons, and the undead, their willingness to use and betray all to satisfy their desires, their determination to perpetuate an inhuman mode of existence, often are played out in, or projected onto, entrepreneurial business ventures, political schemes, or government projects.

Biosocial criminology seems to perceive a similar analogy between criminals' and corporations' ruthless and tireless struggle for advantage. Just as degeneration theory may be read as reflecting anxiety about "mass-democracy and socialism"

(Pick 1989, 218), biosocial criminology may be read as expressing anxiety about neo-liberalism. It is not difficult to understand why biosocial criminologists might see a global economy that for which individualized greed, acquisitiveness, and consumption is supposed to be the engine, a culture in which these values are valorized and celebrated, and a regulatory regime in which the line between celebrated entrepreneur and financial criminal seems razor thin as an environment for which the "born criminal" is supremely well adapted.

As noted above, critical, and even "mainstream" sociologically-oriented, criminologists tend to criticize biosocial criminology as essentially biological determinism and social Darwinism in new clothing. As such biosocial criminology would seem to be complicit in the hegemony of neo-liberalism. And, it may well be. However, our interpretation is more sympathetic in that we read a certain anxiety about neo-liberalism in biosocial criminology. We read biosocial criminology not merely as a discourse bent on employing the newest biological markers to stigmatize the "criminal" population, but also as a discourse that reflects profound anxieties about a contemporary neo-liberal society that seems to provide such a comfortable ecological niche for ruthless, self-interested behavior of all kinds, criminal and otherwise. Whether this anxiety represents the primary motivating force behind biosocial criminology or a fleeting manifestation of lingering doubt within a general commitment to neo-liberalism is not yet clear to us.

Acknowledgments

The authors are grateful to Nicole Rafter, Mary Gibson, Per Ystehede, Troy Duster, Harry Levine, and David Guston for encouragement, suggestions, and assistance. Responsibility for any errors lies with the authors. This material is partially based on work supported by the National Science Foundation under Grant no. SES-0115305 and the National Institutes of Health under Grant no HG-03302. Any opinions, findings, and conclusions or recommendations expressed in this material are those of the author and do not necessarily reflect the views of the National Science Foundation, the National Institutes of Health, or any of the scholars mentioned above.

Notes

1 The curious thing here, of course, is the notion of a clear delineation between "legitimate" and "illegitimate" means of resource procurement that carries across thousands of years of human history and manages to map consistently onto different social contexts. In contemporary society, one wonders about the clarity of the distinction in areas like, for example, financial crime or resource procurement that produces environmental damage.
2 For the record, we believe it is unlikely that evolutionary theorists have made this claim.
3 Despite contemporary biocriminologists' efforts to distance themselves from Lombroso, his latter argument – that the notion of justice itself was "evolved" – is echoed almost precisely in contemporary evolutionary psychology (see, for example, Walsh 2000b).

4 Interestingly, Lombroso suggested that this reduction in crime would be accompanied by a shift away from violent crime and toward what we would today call "white-collar" or financial crime: "fraud, swindling, and bankruptcy."
5 "Gothic criminology"' is a term that has been used in somewhat inconsistent ways. For example, Rafter and Ystehede (2010), writing as historical criminologists, have described the work of the criminologist Lombroso as "gothic." Theirs is a claim and stance quite different from that of the contributors to Picart and Greek (2007b), who conceive of *themselves* as "gothic criminologists": critical criminologists who document and critique gothic themes in popular cultural discourse about crime. Even within this volume, however, the use of the term diverges: Picart and Greek (2007a, 28) note that one contributor, Surette (2007), uses "gothic criminology" to mean "the opposite of what we mean by the term" because it "assumes an uncritical engagement with the proliferation of Gothic images in popular culture."

References

Allen, G. (2004) "DNA and Human Behavior Genetics: Implications for the Criminal Justice System," in D. Lazer (ed.) *The Technology of Justice: DNA and the Criminal Justice System*. Cambridge: MIT Press, pp. 287–314.
Baker, L. A., Bezdjian, S. and Raine, A. (2006) "Behavioral Genetics: The Science of Antisocial Behavior," *Law and Contemporary Problems* 69: 7–46.
Becker, E. (2001) "As Ex-Theorist on Young 'Superpredators,' Bush Aide Has Regrets," *The New York Times* (Feb. 9): A19.
Bondio, M. G. (2006) "From the 'Atavistic' to the 'Inferior' Criminal Type: The Impact of the Lombrosian Theory of the Born Criminal on German Psychiatry," in P. Becker and R. F. Wetzell (eds) *Criminals and Their Scientists: The History of Criminology in International Perspective*. Cambridge: Cambridge University Press, pp. 183–206.
Brooks, S. N. (2009) *Black Men Can't Shoot*. Chicago: University of Chicago Press.
Carey, G. and Gottesman, I. I. (1994) "Genetics and Antisocial Behavior: Substance Versus Sound Bytes," *Politics and the Life Sciences* 15: 88–90.
Caspi, A., Mcclay, J., Moffit, T. E., Mill, J., Martin, J., Craig, I. W., Taylor, A. and Poulton, R. (2002) "Role of Genotype in the Cycle of Violence in Maltreated Children," *Science* 297: 851–4.
Cauffman, E., Steinberg, L. and Piquero, A. R. (2005) "Psychological, Neuropsychological and Physiological Correlates of Serious Antisocial Behavior in Adolescence: The Role of Self-Control," *Criminology* 43: 133–75.
Cooper, J., Walsh, A. and Ellis, L. (2010) "Is Criminology Moving Toward a Paradigm Shift? Evidence from a Survey of the American Society of Criminology," *Journal of Criminal Justice Education* 21: 332–47.
Dawkins, R. (1989) *The Selfish Gene*. New York: Oxford University Press.
Degler, C. N. (1991) *In Search of Human Nature: The Decline and Revival of Darwinism in American Social Thought*. New York: Oxford University Press.
DiIulio, J. J. (1995) "The Coming of the Super-Predators," *The Weekly Standard* 1: 11 (Nov.): 23.
Dumit, J. (2004) *Picturing Personhood: Brain Scans and Biomedical Identity*. Princeton: Princeton University Press.
Duster, T. (2006) "Comparative Perspectives and Competing Explanations: Taking on the Newly Configured Reductionist Challenge to Sociology," *American Sociological Review* 71: 1–15.

Ellis, L. (2003a) "Genes, Criminality, and the Evolutionary Neuroandrogenic Theory," in A. Walsh and L. Ellis (eds) *Biosocial Criminology: Challenging Environmentalism's Supremacy*. New York: Nova Science Publishers, pp. 13–34.

Ellis, L. (2003b) "So You Want to Be a Biosocial Criminologist? Advice from the Underground," in A. Walsh and L. Ellis (eds) *Biosocial Criminology: Challenging Environmentalism's Supremacy*. New York: Nova Science Publishers, pp. 249–56.

Ellis, L. and Walsh, A. (1997) "Gene-Based Evolutionary Theories in Criminology," *Criminology* 35: 229–76.

Epstein, S. C. (1995) "The New Mythic Monster" in J. Ferrell and C. R. Sanders (eds) *Cultural Criminology*. Boston: Northeastern University Press, pp. 66–79.

Fishbein, D. H. (1990) "Biological Perspectives in Criminology," *Criminology* 28: 27–72.

Fishbein, D. H. (1994) "Prospects for the Application of Genetic Findings to Crime and Violence Prevention," *Politics and the Life Sciences* 15: 91–4.

Garland, D. (2000) "The New Criminologies of Everyday Life: Routine Activity Theory in Historical and Social Context," in A. Von Hirch, D. Garland and A. Wakefield (eds) *Ethical and Social Perspectives on Situational Crime Prevention*. Oxford: Hart, pp. 215–24.

Garland, D. (2001) *The Culture of Control: Crime and Social Order in Contemporary Society*. Chicago: University of Chicago Press.

Gibson, M. (2002) *Born to Crime: Cesare Lombroso and the Origins of Biological Criminology*. Westport, CT: Praeger.

Gibson, M. S. (2006) "Cesare Lombroso and Italian Criminology: Theory and Politics," in P. Becker and R. F. Wetzell (eds) *Criminals and Their Scientists: The History of Criminology in International Perspective*. Cambridge: Cambridge University Press, pp. 137–58.

Gibson, M. and Rafter, N. H. (2006) "Editor's Introduction," *Criminal Man*. Durham: Duke University Press, pp. 1–36.

Gill, P. (2007) "Making a Killing in the Marketplace: Incorporation as a Monstrous Process," in C. J. Picart and C. Greek (eds) *Monsters In and Among Us: Toward a Gothic Criminology*. Madison, NJ: Fairleigh Dickinson University Press, pp. 142–63.

Gillett, G. and Tamatea, A. J. (2012) "The Warrior Gene: Epigenetic Considerations," *New Genetics and Society* 31: 41–53.

Glenn, A. L. and Raine, A. (2009) "Psychopathy and Instrumental Aggression: Evolutionary, Neurobiological, and Legal Perspectives," *International Journal of Law and Psychiatry* 32: 253–8.

Goldman, D. (1994) "Interdisciplinary Perceptions of Genetics and Behavior," *Politics and the Life Sciences* 15: 97–8.

Gould, S. J. (1981) *The Mismeasure of Man*. New York: Norton.

Hacking, I. (2001) "Degeneracy, Criminal Behavior, and Looping," in D. Wasserman and R. Wachbroit (eds) *Genetics and Criminal Behavior*. Cambridge: Cambridge University Press, pp. 141–67.

Hagan, J. (2010) *Who Are the Criminals? The Politics of Crime Policy from the Age of Roosevelt to the Age of Reagan*. Princeton: Princeton University Press.

Horn, D. G. (2003) *The Criminal Body: Lombroso and the Anatomy of Deviance*. New York: Routledge.

Horn, D. G. (2006) "Making Criminologists: Tools, Techniques, and Production of Scientific Authority," in P. Becker and R. F. Wetzell (eds) *Criminals and Their Scientists: The History of Criminology in International Perspective*. Cambridge: Cambridge University Press, pp. 317–36.

Hutchings, P. J. (2001) *The Criminal Spectre in Law, Literature and Aesthetics*. London: Routledge.

Jalava, J. (2006) "The Modern Degenerate: Nineteenth-century Degeneration Theory and Modern Psychopathy Research," *Theory & Psychology* 16: 416–32.

Kerr, A. (2004) *Genetics and Society: A Sociology of Disease*. London: Routledge.

Kevles, D. J. (1985) *In the Name of Eugenics: Genetics and the Uses of Human Heredity*. Berkeley and Los Angeles: University of California Press.

Knepper, P. (2011) "Lombroso's Jewish Identity and its Implications for Criminology," *Australian & New Zealand Journal of Criminology* 44: 355–69.

Leps, M.-C. (1992) *Apprehending the Criminal: The Production of Deviance in Nineteenth-Century Discourse*. Durham: Duke University Press.

Leslie, I. (2010) "Arrested Development," *London Times* (Feb. 4).

Lombroso, C. (2006) *Criminal Man*. Durham: Duke University Press.

Marks, J. (1995) *Human Biodiversity: Genes, Race, and History*. New York: Aldine de Gruyter.

Marks, J. (2002) *What It Means to Be 98% Chimpanzee*. Berkeley and Los Angeles: University of California Press.

Marks, J. (2008) "Great Chain of Being," in J. H. Moore (ed.) *Encyclopedia of Race and Racism*. Detroit: Macmillan, pp. 68–73.

Melossi, D. (2001) "Changing Representations of the Criminal," in H.-J. Albrecht, A. Koukoutsaki and T. Serassis (eds) *Images of Crime: Representations of Crime and the Criminal in Science, the Arts and the Media*. Freiburg: Edition Iuscrim, Max-Planck-Institut für Auslänisches und Internationales Strafrecht, pp. 9–44.

Meyer, A. (2010) "Evil Monsters and Cunning Perverts: Representing and Regulating the Dangerous Paedophile," in M. Deflem (ed.) *Popular Culture, Crime and Social Control*. Bingley, U.K.: Emerald, pp. 195–217.

Mucchielli, L. (2006) "Criminology, Hygienism, and Eugenics in France, 1870–1914: The Medical Debates on the Elimination of 'Incorrigible' Criminals," in P. Becker and R. F. Wetzell (eds) *Criminals and Their Scientists: The History of Criminology in International Perspective*. Cambridge: Cambridge University Press, pp. 207–30.

Nelkin, D. (2004) "God Talk: Confusion between Science and Religion," *Science, Technology, and Human Values* 29: 139–52.

Nye, R. A. (1984) *Crime, Madness, and Politics in Modern France: The Medical Concept of National Decline*. Princeton: Princeton University Press.

Pasquino, P. (1991) "Criminology: The Birth of a Special Knowledge," pp. 235–50 in G. Burchell, C. Gordon and P. Miller (eds.) *The Foucault Effect: Studies in Governmentally*. London: Harvester Wheatsheaf.

Picart, C. J. and Greek, C. (2007a) "Introduction: Toward a Gothic Criminology," pp. 11–43 in C. J. Picart and Greek, C. (eds) *Monsters In and Among Us: Toward a Gothic Criminology*. Madison, N.J.: Fairleigh Dickinson University Press.

Picart, C. J. and Greek, C. (eds) (2007b) *Monsters In and Among Us: Toward a Gothic Criminology*. Madison, N.J.: Fairleigh Dickinson University Press.

Picart, C. J. and Greek, C. (2007c) "The Compulsions of Real/Reel Serial Killers and Vampires: Toward a Gothic Criminology," in C. J. Picart and C. Greek (eds) *Monsters In and Among Us: Toward a Gothic Criminology*. Madison, NJ: Fairleigh Dickinson University Press, pp. 227–55.

Pick, D. (1989) *Faces of Degneration: A European Disorder, c. 1848-c. 1918*. Cambridge: Cambridge University Press.

Rafter, N. H. (1992) "Criminal Anthropology in the United States," *Criminology* 30: 525–45.

Rafter, N. H. (1997) *Creating Born Criminals: Biological Theories of Crime and Eugenics*. Urbana-Champaign: University of Illinois Press.

Rafter, N. (2008) *The Criminal Brain: Understanding Biological Theories of Crime*. New York: New York University Press.

Rafter, N. and Ystehede, P. (2010) "Here Be Dragons: Lombroso, The Gothic, and Social Control" in M. Deflem (ed.) *Popular Culture, Crime and Social Control*. Bingley, UK: Emerald, pp. 263–84.

Raine, A. (1993) *The Psychopathology of Crime: Criminal Behavior as a Clinical Disorder*. San Diego: Academic Press.

Raine, A. (2006) *Colloquium*. Department of Psychology & Social Behavior, University of California, Irvine.

Raine, A., Brennan, P., Farrington, D. P. and Mednick, S. A. (eds) (1997) *Biosocial Bases of Violence*. New York: Plenum Press.

Ramsden, E. (2009) "Confronting the Stigma of Eugenics: Genetics, Demography and the Problems of Population," *Social Studies of Science* 39: 853–84.

Rodriguez, J. (2006) *Civilizing Argentina: Science, Medicine, and the Modern State*. Chapel Hill: University of North Carolina Press.

Rose, D. (2006) "Lives of Crime," *Prospect* 125 (Aug.).

Rose, N. (2000) "The Biology of Culpability: Pathological Identity and Crime Control in a Biological Culture," *Theoretical Criminology* 4: 5–34.

Selden, S. (1999) *Inheriting Shame: The Story of Eugenics and Racism in America*. New York: Columbia Teachers College Press.

Surette, R. (2007) "Gothic Criminology and Criminal Justice Policy," in C. J. Picart and C. Greek (eds) *Monsters In and Among Us: Toward a Gothic Criminology*. Madison, NJ: Fairleigh Dickinson University Press, pp. 199–226.

Taylor, P. J. (2009) "Infrastructure and Scaffolding: Interpretation and Change of Research Involving Human Genetic Information," *Science as Culture* 18: 435–59.

Thornhill, R. and Palmer, C. (2000) *A Natural History of Rape: Biological Bases of Sexual Coercion*. Cambridge: MIT Press.

Valier, C. (2002) "Punishment, Border Crossings and the Powers of Horror," *Theoretical Criminology* 6: 319–37.

Walsh, A. (2000a) "Behavior Genetics and Anomie/Strain Theory," *Criminology* 38: 1075–107.

Walsh, A. (2000b) "Evolutionary Psychology and the Origins of Justice," *Justice Quarterly* 17: 841–64.

Walsh, A. and Ellis, L. (eds) (2003) *Biosocial Criminology: Challenging Environmentalism's Supremacy*. New York: Nova Science Publishers.

Wasserman, D. (1994) "Research into Genetics and Crime: Consensus and Controversy," *Politics and the Life Sciences* 15: 107–9.

Wilson, J. Q. and Herrnstein, R. J. (1985) *Crime and Human Nature*. New York: Simon & Schuster.

Wright, J. P., Beaver, K. M., Delisi, M., Vaughn, M. G., Boisvert, D. and Vaske, J. (2008) "Lombroso's Legacy: The Miseducation of Criminologists," *Journal of Criminal Justice Education* 19: 325–338.

Wright, R. A. and Miller, J. M. (1998) "Taboo until Today? The Coverage of Biological Arguments in Criminology Textbooks, 1961 to 1970 and 1987 to 1996," *Journal of Criminal Justice* 26: 1–19.

Zimring, F. E., Hawkins, G. and Kamin, S. (2001) *Punishment and Democracy: Three Strikes and You're Out in California*. Oxford: Oxford University Press.

9

LOMBROSO AND JEWISH SOCIAL SCIENCE

Paul Knepper

The formation of social science as a means of enquiry in the late nineteenth century coincided with emergence of anti-Semitism. Its proponents referred to themselves as 'anti-Semites' to demonstrate they were not opposed to Jews as a matter of religion, but because of racial characteristics. In Germany and Austria, anti-Semitic political parties contested elections, and in France, the Dreyfus affair exposed a reservoir of anti-Jewish sentiment. In the United Kingdom and the United States, anti-Semitic rhetoric accompanied discussion over immigrants seeking to escape the pogroms in Russia and the growth of Jewish communities in leading cities. The combination of social-scientific analysis and anti-Jewish agitation produced a 'scientific anti-Semitism'. A flurry of pamphlets, articles and books drew on an emerging race science which made Jewish characteristics the object of study. By the end of the First World War, there was enough anti-Semitic material to fill a small library. It was in one of these libraries in fact, at the National Socialist Institute in Munich, that Adolf Hitler read Houston Stewart Chamberlain's *Foundations of the Nineteenth Century* and Henry Ford's *The International Jew* (Ryback 2009, 50).

One group of Jewish intellectuals responded with a Jewish-oriented social science. Joseph Jacobs, Arthur Ruppin and Maurice Fishberg, among others, generated a literature that has come to be known as 'Jewish social science' or 'Jewish statistics'. Many within this group originally trained as medical doctors, and acquired social science training either through apprenticeship or self-study. They worried that anti-Jewish statements derived from social science would prove more harmful than the one-sided rants of anti-Semites, and they sought to counteract this new threat with 'objective' research of their own. Looking back, many of their methods and statements have a dissonant quality. Jewish social scientists measured skulls, noses and chests; prepared distributions of eye, hair and skin colour; and looked for trends in statistics of birth, marriage, suicide and crime. They made statements about Jews as a race, using the term in the sense of 'ethnicity' but also in the sense of a biological category of humanity (Efron 1994; Endelman 2004; Hart 1999, 2000).

To what extent did Lombroso contribute to Jewish social science? At first glance, he fits the profile. He was born into a Jewish family and trained in medicine. He appreciated anthropometric analyses, relished statistical information, and took an interest in Jewish questions. Lombroso addressed Jewish issues in his books on crime, genius and other subjects, and published a series of articles and a short book about anti-Semitism. Further, the founders of Jewish social science knew of Lombroso's work, and he knew of them; Jacobs, Fishberg and Ruppin cite Lombroso and he cites their work. Lombroso contributed, in fact, to key debates within Jewish social science: whether Jews represented a pure or mixed race; what explained patterns of Jewish crime; whether the solution to anti-Semitism was to be found in Zionism or assimilation.

The Jewish race

Before the Holocaust, Jewish intellectuals did not avoid racial language in reference to the Jewish people. Jewish social scientists tended to accept definitions of Jews as a race and accepted the value of race science as a means of inquiry. What they rejected was the implications of racial distinctions proposed by anti-Semites and the linking of characteristics as immutable features of inheritance. Essentially, Jewish social scientists made use of the concepts and methodology of race science to manufacture their own explanations of Jewish outlook and behaviour. It provided them, as John Efron (1994, 29) puts it, with a 'liberating discourse'.

One of the primary debates within Jewish social science had to do with the constitution of the Jewish race. Joseph Jacobs advanced the rather startling view of a pure Jewish race undiluted over the centuries. Jacobs was born in 1854 in Australia, and after schooling in Sydney and London, completed a degree at Cambridge. He first attracted public notice with articles in *The Times* in which he drew attention to persecution of Jews in Russia. This led to the formation of the Russo-Jewish Committee, of which Jacobs served as secretary until he emigrated to the United States in 1900 to become an editor of the *Jewish Encyclopedia*. He sought to acquire specialised training in race science, and during the 1880s, worked alongside Francis Galton. Jacobs took exception to claims that Jews amounted to a degenerate, inferior race, insisting that the 'remarkable similarity of the Jewish physiognomy all over the world' implied racial purity. The comparative anthropological evidence pointed to a race with 'superior mental capacity', and this was confirmed by the prevalence of persons with Jewish blood in European dictionaries of eminent persons. Racial homogeneity was evident in Jewish features and expression. The similarity of Jewish physical features suggested to the 'ordinary mind' an 'absolute proof unity of race'. The telling signs of Jewish identity included a typical nose and eyes – what Jacobs referred to as 'Jewish nostrility' and the 'Jews' eye' (Jacobs 1899, 502–11). Max Nordau, influential author and Zionist leader, who agreed with Jacobs about the reality of a Jewish race, remarked that Jewish features were so obvious that any 'street loafer' could tell when a Jew walked by; it required 'scientific diagnosis' to deny that Jews constituted a 'variety' or at least 'sub-variety' of mankind (Fishberg 1911, 474).

Maurice Fishberg took the opposite view. Trained in medicine, Fishberg emigrated from Russia to the United States in 1889. From his position as chief medical examiner for the United Hebrew Charities of New York, he had access to large numbers of Jewish immigrants from Eastern Europe for anthropometric study. Fishberg argued that Jews amounted to a mixed population; the anthropological evidence had falsified the notion of Jewish racial purity. He found no differences between Jews and Christians that resulted from 'racial causes' or 'hereditary transmission'. The physical characteristics of modern Jews indicated that they did not present the homogeneity of a physical type. Both 'Jews and other Europeans', Fishberg (1911, 550) maintained, 'consist of conglomerations of various racial elements blended together in a manner that makes it impossible to disentangle the components'. Jewish characteristics resulted from the environment, and particularly, the similarity of social conditions in which they were forced to live. Fishberg scoffed at the idea that a passing glance on a street was sufficient to determine Jewish identity. 'It is an undeniable fact that the cast of countenance depends as much, probably more, on the social *milieu* than on the anthropological traits' (Fishberg 1911, 513).

At the centre of this disagreement, there was the matter of skulls, and Lombroso furnished essential evidence. Anthropologists regarded the skull as the most telling characteristic for making racial distinctions, given that, in theory, it retained its size and shape and was least receptive to influence of environmental change and social selection. They favoured the 'cephalic index', the ratio of a skull's length to its breadth, for racial categorisation. Specifically, they termed human populations with round heads as 'brachycephalic', and populations with long heads, 'dolichocephalic' (Fishberg 1903a). Evidence from the cephalic index appeared to present a problem for Jacobs. Because Jews had descended from ancient Hebrews, and they were Semites, why did modern Jews not have dolichocephalic skulls, as did present-day Arabs? He turned to Lombroso who had produced the only study to yield measurements of ancient Hebrew skulls. Lombroso had obtained five specimens from the catacomb of Saint Calixtus in Rome, dating from a time when racial mixing was not thought to have taken place. Lombroso found two to be brachycephalic and three mesocephalic, leading to the conclusion that the ancient Hebrews, like their modern counterparts, were primarily brachycephalic (Efron 1994, 86).

Fishberg also found support for his theory in Lombroso. He cited Lombroso's study of 112 Italian Jews, in which he had concluded that they represented a mixed race. Comparing Lombroso's result to similar studies, Fishberg noted general agreement about the prevalence of the brachycephalic type. He also cited Lombroso's findings concerning the Hebrew skulls from the catacomb of Saint Calixtus, and suggested that while no conclusion ought to be drawn from a sample of five, he was prepared to concede that the results were consistent with the brachycephalic argument (Fishberg 1902, 686). Fishberg, however, went on to insist that the matter of Jewish racial purity would not be settled by skulls alone, but other indexes, that is pigmentation – colour of skin, hair and eyes. Based on his review of this evidence, Fishberg suggested modern Jews had some infusion of non-Jewish blood. He examined whether pigmentation was influenced by climate or a fixed trait, that is, a characteristics transmitted by heredity. He concluded that while the ancient Hebrews had dark complexions, intermixing with people over the centuries meant Jews did not maintain themselves in a state of 'extreme purity' but took on 'blood traits' by influsion of non-Jewish blood into blood lines of Jews (Fishberg 1903b).

In shifting the discussion away from skull, and towards skin, Fishberg accessed a key strategy of Jewish racial science. To transform race science into a liberating discourse, Jewish intellectuals tended to rely on Lamarck's theory of environmentalism over Weismann's theory of 'germ plasm' and the basis of inheritance. French naturalist Jean-Baptiste Lamarck explained evolutionary development as a direct response to environmental conditions. In order to adapt to environmental changes, species will adapt, using limbs more or less frequently, and developing new body parts to meet new conditions. The anatomical and physiological changes accompanying this process, he taught, were heritable. An altered cell structure, induced by environmental influences, would be passed on to future generations. This approach allowed Jewish intellectuals to construct their own narratives of the Jewish race and offer rival explanation of Jewish characteristics with respect to health and disease, capitalism, and so on (Hart 2000, 11–12).[1] Nordau, for example, taught that Jews constituted a degenerate race, meaning, that their bodies had deteriorated as a consequence of generations of persecution. Centuries of existence in crowded, filthy conditions behind ghetto walls had left Jews in a degraded physical condition. And, invoking Lamarck, Nordau warned that this would become a permanent feature of the Jewish race unless they made a revolutionary change in their manner of living. He sought the renewal of the Jewish body in physical exercise, escape from the cities, and a return to agriculture (Falk 1998, 594).

Lombroso, too, adhered to Lamarck in his theorising about Jews. Drawing on his study of Hebrew skulls in antiquity, Lombroso claimed that characteristics of modern Jews had been inherited from thousands of years ago. This racial legacy included a distinctive set of physical characteristics, including tenacity of purpose, clannishness, intolerance, ethical passion and a spirit of rebellion. These traits explained the prominence of Jews in religious and social revolutions. Owing to climatic causes and race mingling, many of the physical characteristics had disappeared, so that Jews in modernity corresponded with their fellow citizens (Lombroso 1897a, 204). At the same time, new Jewish traits had emerged. Jews displayed excessive activity and curiosity, in political and scientific areas, 'making the Hebrew the born reporter and journalist of the modern world'. Further, Lombroso claimed, 'avidity of gain is a characteristic that has now become almost hereditary among the Hebrews'. The modern series of acquired physical characteristics was due to climatic influences, such as migration to colder countries, but more specifically to 'selection by persecution'. Only by the appearance of meanness and sordidness – acquired physical characteristics that had become hereditary – could the Jews save themselves from the fierce persecutions. Qualities such as courage, generosity and boldness would have been more harmful than useful under such pressures (Lombroso 1897a, 206).

Methods of race science

The practitioners of Jewish social science relied on techniques of investigation used in race science. Craniometry and anthropometry signified that establishing racial categories of humankind was not something that could be successfully undertaken by ordinary people, but only trained experts with specialised instruments and procedures. Statistics as well signified access to technical knowledge that enabled objective, scientific statements by neutral observers of the human condition. The texts of Jewish social science are filled with declarations of mathematical proofs; columns, charts and graphs; rates, percentages and proportions (Morris-Reich 2010; Soffer 2004). It was a style of analysis that Lombroso would use to propel him to fame in criminology (Horn 2006).

The twelve-volume *Jewish Encyclopedia,* published in New York from 1901 to 1906, contains entries for births, blindness, complexion, craniometry, deafness, expression, eyes, hair, insanity, marriage, morbidity, noses, pathology, sex and suicides. As Jacobs explained in the entry for anthropology, 'much turns upon the preliminary question of whether contemporary Jews are of the same race as those mentioned in the Bible'. He included a discussion of anthropometry in which he noted that Jews displayed darker complexions than surrounding peoples of Europe. Jews had darker hair as well: on average, 15 per cent of Jews had black hair compared to only 3 to 4 per cent of other Europeans. Jews tended to have the longest and narrowest noses, at 77 millimetres and 34 millimetres, respectively. He noted that the characteristic shape of the Jewish nose is the nostril, so often represented with a 'figure 6' formation in caricatures (Jacobs 1901, 619–20).[2]

The range of methodological strategies in Jewish social science can be seen in Jacobs's work. To argue for the purity of a Jewish race, Jacobs marshalled demographic statistics, anthropometric data, historical evidence and photographic analyses. He compared 'vital statistics' for Jews and non-Jews, including rates for marriage, birth and death. He discussed the incidence of diseases and ailments, from diabetes to haemorrhoids; the prevalence of insanity; the portion of Jews affected by deafness, blindness and colour-blindness. He reviewed anthropometric data: height and width; head size and shape; colour of hair, eyes and complexion. Jacobs included figures for the length and shape of the nose, facial expression and gait. 'There is probably something distinctive about the gait of Jewish women' Jacobs surmised. 'Here in England, at any rate, most Jewesses can be distinguished at once by their swaying walk, due to their walking from the hip, not from the knee'. He was unsure whether this reflected a habit imported from the Continent, or whether it extended from ancient times, as mentioned by the prophet Isaiah (Jacobs 1886a, 51).

To investigate facial expression, Jacobs turned to the technique of composite photography devised by Francis Galton. Galton was born in Birmingham, the son of a successful banker who enjoyed scientific instruments. He was related through his mother's family to the Darwin family and remained on good terms with his cousin, Charles Darwin. He completed his education at Trinity College, Cambridge, before making a study tour of southern Africa. After returning to England, he established a laboratory for analysing the human body; he measured heads, noses, arms, legs, hair colour, breathing power, reaction times and the frequency of yawns. He was made Fellow of the Royal Society in 1856.[3] Galton coined the word 'eugenics', a concept that had some appeal to Jews in the early twentieth century. According to the *Jewish Chronicle*, eugenics consisted of efforts to ensure children were born without physical defects due to the imperfect health or physique of their parents. From the days of Moses, Jews had been eugenists in the sense that hygienic laws and devotion to their children had contributed to a sturdy race. The editors were pleased when Galton agreed that hygienic regulations with the Mosaic code had contributed to the fitness of the Jewish race. But they were dismayed by his 'somewhat startling view' that persecution over the centuries had contributed relatively little to the quality of Jewish descendants (*Jewish Chronicle* 1910).

Jacobs persuaded the headmaster of the Jews Free School in Bell Lane, London, to allow him to make a series of portraits of the boys. The evidence from facial expression enabled Jacobs to confirm his conclusion that there had been little mixture of Jewish blood, by challenging the view of the long Jewish nose and the Jewish eyes as set closer together. In 1886, he shared his findings on the 'racial characteristics' of modern Jews with an audience at the Anthropological Institute of Great Britain and Ireland. He relied on the photographs 'to confirm the conclusion I have drawn from history, that there has been scarcely any admixture of alien blood amongst the Jews since their dispersion'. Essentially, he affirmed Galton's photographic technique as supplying the 'best definition of the Jewish expression and of the Jewish type' but reversed his conclusion; Jacobs did not see in the photographs evidence of the 'cold calculation' Galton detected. 'There is something of the dreamer and the thinker than the merchant', Jacobs concluded, and this despite the fact that the young fellows 'had to fight a hard battle of life' and an early age. At the conclusion of Jacobs' presentation, Britain's chief rabbi, Dr Hermann Adler, affirmed his conclusion with a number of references from scripture (Jacobs 1886a, 52–6).

Jacobs found inspiration in Galton's *Heredity Genius* for a study of Jewish ability. Essentially, Galton had calculated the number of eminent men within particular areas (celebrity, art, science and practical life) within each million of the general population. Jacobs pursued this strategy to compare proportions of genius among English and Jews, using an imaginative system of graphs and diagrams. He explained the superiority of the Jewish intellect in many fields as a feature of the tendency to live in cities, to love their children and solidarity against persecution. 'The contemporary Jews are the survival of a long process of unnatural selection which has seemingly fitted them excellently for the struggle for intellectual existence.' Jacobs acknowledged that some might question the conclusions of a Jewish statistician who had placed Jews at the top of the racial hierarchy in intellectual achievements. Questions had been raised when a great Swiss naturalist, de Candolle, had written a long book to show the superiority of Swiss naturalists. But, Jacobs protested, he would had handed over the work to a non-Jewish researcher had he found one with the patience to classify 30,000 Jewish names (Jacobs 1886b, 365–6).

In 1890, Jacobs completed another project inspired by Galton's methods. He carried out anthropometric measurements on English Jews along the lines of Galton's experiments at the International Health Exhibition in 1885. Together with a colleague, Jacobs made measurements at the Jewish Working Men's Club, Great Alie Street, in London's East End. They replicated the apparatus Galton had set up in South Kensington, and for several weeks, subjected men and women to the 'somewhat wearying process of being tested and measured'. They then moved their laboratory to the West End where a number of Jews volunteered to sit for the research. The tests and measures assembled information about height, eyesight (colour, distance), hearing, breathing, hand strength (grip, pull), weight, chest circumference, and colour of eyes and hair. Altogether, they made 21 measurements on 423 individuals to yield a grand total of 8,863 statistical facts. Their study was meant to isolate the effect of nurture, given that both groups, East End Jews and West End Jews, derived from the same race. 'The general result is tolerably clear' they concluded, 'English Jews in general compare unfavourably in almost all anthropological measurements with the class of Englishmen who visited the Health Exhibition'. However, comparing the West End Jews alone to the Health Exhibition population, 'the inferiority vanishes entirely'. The study demonstrated the effect of generations of 'bad nurture' within particular preconditions established by race (Jacobs and Spielman 1890, 81).

Theorising about Jews and crime

Crime, a subject on which Lombroso claimed particular expertise, was a staple theme for Jewish social science. Fishberg, Jacobs and Ruppin all discuss criminal behaviour among Jews. Essentially, they refuted claims to racial differences as explaining different patterns of crime among Jewish populations.

It had been claimed that Jews were inferior in ethics, morals and character, Arthur Ruppin recounted. Whether this was true could not be answered with individual cases but required a survey of criminal statistics. Born in the Prussian province of Posen in 1876, Ruppin studied law at the University of Halle and University of Berlin. In 1904, he became founding director of the Bureau for Jewish Statistics where, along with his assistant Jakob Thon, he produced studies of demography, economics, education and criminality. *The Jews of Today*, which first appeared in 1904, defined the field of Jewish social science. He compared crime figures for Jews and Christians in Germany (1903–6), Austria (1898–1902), Hungary (1904) and the Netherlands (1902). The analysis revealed the differences between the criminality of Jews and non-Jews was due 'solely to difference in social conditions'. The patterns of crimes committed by Jews had to do with greater prosperity and higher education of the Jews, their restriction from agriculture, their concentration in trade and industry, and large towns. There was no question of racial differences, Ruppin emphasised, unless the prevalence of alcoholism among Christians, which was responsible for so many criminal acts, and 'greater cunning' displayed in crimes committed by Jews, were regarded as 'dispositions of race'. Ruppin did not avoid a racial definition of Jewishness, but denied its relevance to the explanation for criminal behaviour: 'The more one studies the question, and investigates the causes of crime, the more clear does it become that those who would account for the differences between Jewish and Christian criminality by inborn qualities of race are deceiving themselves', he explained; 'If one goes to the root of things, one finds that social conditions are everywhere responsible for criminality' (Ruppin 1913, 220–1).

Ruppin did not think Lombroso's theory of atavistic criminality was particularly helpful to Jewish social science. The question of Jewish-Christian differences in criminal behaviour, he insisted, was 'quite apart' from the question raised by Lombroso and his school as to whether some individuals were born criminals or not. The born criminal was not a person who resorted to stealing, forgery or inflicting bodily harm, that is, the crimes that claimed the greatest attention; but was rather a person devoid of feeling, one who could not restrain himself from sexual immorality, robbery and murder. 'Such men may exist, but they are as rare among criminals as are the insane among the sane'. The numbers of atavists were simply too small for atavism to explain criminality. 'It would be too absurd to attribute those delinquencies in which Jews are more strongly represented than Christians (these are in Germany, usury, bankruptcy, failures in business, falsification of documents, evasion of military service, fraud and libel) to inborn criminal disposition'. They are the results of 'recent changes in social life' (Ruppin 1913, 221–2).

The originator of atavistic criminality, however, was not consistent in the application of his theory. To explain patterns of Jewish crime, Lombroso relied on environmental influences rather than hereditary or biological factors (Gibson 2002, 106). In the second edition of *L'uomo delinquente*, Lombroso contrasted the criminality of Jews and of gypsies. Race influenced crime among the two populations, but in opposite directions. Statistics revealed the level of Jewish criminality in several countries to be lower than other residents of these countries, and this level would have been even lower but for the tendency of Jews to gravitate towards professions of shop-keeping and manufacturing which had higher rates of crime among all groups. Lombroso acknowledged 'generations of swindlers and thieves' among Jews based on the prevalence of Jewish names among those charged with such crimes in France and the Yiddish vocabulary of receivers of stolen property used in England and Germany. But, he proposed that Jewish involvement in these crimes represented an acquired behaviour learned over the centuries in reaction to systematic persecution: desperate poverty, exclusion from public jobs and a hedge against violence. 'Perhaps it was to avoid being massacred that Jews decided to become accomplices to feudal lords as receivers of stolen goods'. If so, Lombroso reasoned, it was surprising Jewish crime rates were not even higher. Instead, these rates declined with emancipation and entry of Jews in public life (Lombroso 2006, 118–19).

Lombroso's explanation of patterns of crime found among Jews resembled Fishberg's. So many contradictory statements had been made about the criminality of Jews, Fishberg declared in 1911, it was important to limit the discussion to statistical evidence. To begin with, statistics of crime in various countries 'seem to confirm the assertion that the Jews are less likely than Christians to get into conflict with the law'. He compared rates of crime for Jews and Christians in Germany (1899–1902), Holland (1898–1902) and Austria (1898–1902) to show less involvement of Jews. He emphasised that to draw firm conclusions about 'Jewish crimes' it was necessary to examine differences for particular crimes over a longer period of years and that factors related to place of residence, occupation and education had immense influence. The convictions for fraudulent bankruptcy in Germany (1899–1904) were seven times higher for Jews than for Christians. 'All this indicates that, considering the large proportion of Jews engaged in banking and in commercial pursuits, there is little wonder that a larger number of failures are shown among them' (Fishberg 1911, 407–11).[4]

Lombroso pursued an identical tack in reference to alcoholism. In general, Lombroso saw alcoholism as a principal cause of certain types of criminality. He proposed that in its acute and chronic form, it led to a type of criminal madness, which led to particular types of injuries. In addition, he maintained that the genetic inheritance transmitted by alcoholic parents had an organic character (Cottino 1985). In an interview with *The New York Times*, he said he knew of no more direct cause of insanity than alcoholism. In a typical asylum, at least 55 per cent of the patients would have become insane through alcoholism. But Jews displayed a remarkable freedom from alcoholism. The director of the Jewish lunatic asylum in Amsterdam had informed him that he had not found a single case of insanity caused by alcohol among his residents (*The New York Times* 1908). His comments concerning Jews and alcoholism, as well as mental illness, match the view expressed in the *Jewish Encyclopedia*. While alcoholism prevailed around the world, among Jews it remained an unknown affliction (Gottheil 1902).

Lombroso offered a similar explanation for alleged links between Jews and mental illness. He pointed to Jews as an example of the links between race and heredity on genius and insanity. As a race, the Jews of Europe demonstrated a proclivity for 'more precocious and extended mental work' than Jews of Africa and the East. European Jews had even surpassed Aryans, Lombroso insisted, citing Jacobs's study of 'The Comparative Distribution of Jewish Ability'. This achievement was due to the 'bloody selection of medieval persecutions' and the 'influence of a temperate climate'. Lombroso allowed that Jews possessed 'more than enough priests and dogmas', and if there were no great scientists, it was because 'they have not yet completed their ethnic evolution'. The mental achievement and capacity for genius came at a price, however; that of a neurotic tendency that Jacobs had chosen to overlook. Jewish elements within the population produced five or six times as many lunatics as the rest of the population. While this fact had so far escaped the notice of anti-Semites in Germany, Lombroso said, they might be less irritated by the successes of the Jewish race if they bothered to acknowledge the cost of it. The anti-Semitic movement threatened to deprive Jews of contributing their talents, as did laws and prohibitions prior to emancipation (Lombroso 1911, 133–7).

Gilman characterises Lombroso's view of psychopathology among Jews as 'one of the most articulate answers to those anti-Semites who called on medical studies to prove the degeneracy of the Jews'. Lombroso's work compared favourably with Martin Englander's *The Evident Most Frequent Appearances of Illness in the Jewish Race* (1902). Both Lombroso and Englander attributed mental illness in Jews to pressures of the marketplace and effects of persecution (Gilman 1984, 154).

Zionism and anti-Semitism

Essentially, Jewish social science had to do with an attempt by Jewish intellectuals to create a new 'scientific' paradigm and agenda of Jewish self-definition and self-perception (Efron 1994, 5). Jewish social science was divided over questions about the place and future of Jews in Europe. Emancipation had led many Jews to turn their back on a religious tradition and pursue opportunities in modern society. But what was left of Jewish identity once Judaism had been discarded? Could Jews expect to participate in wider society? What was the best response to the rising surge of anti-Semitism?

Lombroso shared with Jacobs, Fishberg and Ruppin a commitment to defending Jews from anti-Semitic attacks. Lomboso turned his criminal anthropology against scientific anti-Semitism. Having tackled problems of genius and crime, Lombroso said that he was prepared to attack the problem of anti-Semitism 'with the new instrument which I have introduced into the scientific world'. This instrument, he assured his readers, has 'guaranteed me also against the perils of partiality' (Lombroso 1897b, 1). The anti-Semitic movement, which first broke out in Germany, constituted a sociological phenomenon. It could not be about the dissimilarity of races, Lombroso insisted, because greater dissimilarity of races could be found in history where races later fused. It was not about the accumulation of wealth by Jews, because other religious groups, who accumulated wealth, were not hated. Rather, the anti-Semitic movement derived from two reasons 'both of them atavistic'. The first had to do with the 'feeling of superiority' which had accompanied nationalism, and the second with 'stratification of memory', the longing of Christian peoples to suppress those who refused to concede to them in political and religious terms over the centuries (Lombroso 1897b, 4–5).

Lombroso also brought his criminal anthropology to an analysis of the Dreyfus affair. 'With the ideas of criminal anthropology at hand, in fact, it is easy to decide who are the genuine criminals in the Dreyfus case', he declared. To begin with, there was Esterhazy. While he displayed few anatomical signs, the physiological signs of the born criminal were 'patent and complete'. Esterhazy displayed precocity, impulsiveness, excessive sensuality and megalomania; he offered his nephew a prostitute in marriage and habitually used slang expressions. The other obvious accomplice, Paty du Clam, was 'plainly, a criminal and a hysterical subject to boot'. He persisted in doing evil for evil's sake. It was possible to understand the complicity of the generals, who determined to hide their treachery, and the stupidity of others, Cavialgnae, Méline and Faure, who continued the mistake for fear of being exposed as incompetent. Using this same analysis affirmed the innocence of Dreyfus. Dreyfus appeared 'to be precisely an average sort of man, without too much virtue or too many vices'. Dreyfus was vain without megalomania, longed for his family, and reluctant to see evil even where it existed (Lombroso 1899, 1674–5).

Lombroso went on to offer his own theory of how the Dreyfus affair had come about. The 'secret spring' behind the case was that of 'the Jesuit party' who launched an anti-Semitic movement in Vienna, Rome and other European cities. The Jesuits did not plant the case against Dreyfus, but encouraged its fermentation, in an effort to destroy esteem for Jews in public places. Lombroso admitted he had no 'documentary proofs' of a Jesuit plot. Finding such evidence was difficult given their ability 'to cover up their traces'. But there were signs of Jesuit involvement, including squandering of large sums of money, by Esterhazy, on journalists. The church had sided with the army, as seen in the sermons of Father Didon, who declared that French society ought to sacrifice everything for its soldiers (Lombroso 1899, 1676). Lombroso's explanation is telling. It could be argued that anti-Semitism represented an application for Lombroso's approach; that having settled on atavism as an explanation for criminality that received intense and sustained criticism, Lombroso sought opportunities to demonstrate its value. But having promised a demonstration of his atavistic theory in the Dreyfus case, he proceeded to walk away from it. In seeking to defend Jews, he abandoned any pretence of scientific objectivity or statistical evidence. Lombroso could be accused of resorting to conspiracy theory in his comments on Dreyfus, but not adhering to his favourite theory.

Lombroso would appear to part company with Jewish social science in at least one crucial point. Mitchell Hart (2000, 19) argues that the tradition of Jewish social science was 'conceived at the intellectual and institutional levels primarily as a Zionist project, although a strong-non-Zionist involvement can adduced' (see also, Hirsch 2009). For Ruppin, Zionism was a logical extension of his view of an active universal humane *Weltanschauung* rather than the fulfilment of a teleological history of the Jewish people. He considered Jews as comprising a national entity on the basis of biological, historical, cultural and religious grounds (Falk 1998, 592–3). Because he believed it served wider human interest to maintain individuality, as well as societies, as diverse as possible, it served wider human interests to maintain Jews as a biologically and culturally distinct entity rather than allow them to disappear through assimilation. 'Just as it would be absurd to destroy specific kinds of fruit in order to produce one general kind, so it is equally absurd to wish to wipe out national differences', Ruppin taught, 'Mankind of today aims not at uniformity, but at making use of individuality of every nation for the common good' (Ruppin 1913, 217–18).

Contemporary observers are less sure. Nancy Harrowitz contends that *L'antisemitismo e le scienze modern* contributed more to the cause of anti-Semitism than anti-defamation. She calls Lombroso to task on positive remarks about the scarcity of Jews and assimilation as a strategy for avoiding negative reaction. 'We must ask ourselves why a scientist would make such as statement [about the scarcity of orthodox Jews] if he in fact did not share the prejudices from which he claims to defend them'. As for Lombroso's favourable comments about assimilation, Harrowitz concludes: 'In attempting to defend the Jews from the racist rhetoric of anti-Semitism, Lombroso adopted the equally racist logic of the erasure of difference' (Harrowitz 1994, 45, 50). David Forgacs says that Lombroso's work 'falls into the wider pattern of this period of Jewish disientification, or, if one prefers, Jewish self-hatred'. Lombroso argued that anti-Semitism was not a scapegoating of Jews, as if they had been arbitrarily selected for blame, but was motivated in part by the actions of Jews themselves. Lombroso claimed that Jews' experience in commerce left them with a habit of craftiness, remained vulnerable to mental illness, displayed strange attachment to old customs, and displayed a weak character' (Forgacs 2003, 98–9).

What is clear is that Lombroso's analysis of threat of anti-Semitism led him away from nation-building as a solution. 'The proposal that the Jews should retire to Palestine is impracticable for many reasons' Lombroso insisted, 'If there is to be emigration it should be to directly towards modern centres, such as Australia or North America'. The 'pseudo-idyllic colonies' in Palestine would be suitable only for this 'old fanatics of the Slavonic lands' who remained 'impenetrable to modern ideas' and still dreamed of a 'reign of Zion upon the earth' (Lombroso 1897b, 10). Lombroso favoured complete equality. Experience had shown that where Jews had been allowed to enter any career they wished, their 'usurious customs and capitalistic excesses disappear'. In return for grant of full equality across political, social and economic spheres, Jews should recognise that many of the rites pertained to the past and were no longer useful or desirable (Lombroso 1897b, 10). In his comments about persecution leading to progress in Jewish civilisation, Lombroso said that in warm climates, Jews had 'not progressed a step beyond their fellow-countrymen'. This was true of Jews in Abyssinia, as well as in Judea, despite having been 'objects of peculiar care from their devout coreligionists of all Europe' (Lombroso 1897a, 205–7).

But as Hart suggests, there were contributors to Jewish social science who argued for assimilation. The point of Fishberg's *The Jews: A Study of Race and Environment* was to demonstrate the case for assimilation. 'The Western Jews prove that there is nothing within the Jew that keeps him from assimilating with his neighbours of other creeds'. As soon as political and civil disabilities imposed on Jews were removed, Jews adapted themselves successfully to their new surroundings. Further, emancipation from legal disabilities led Jews to set aside practices which had promoted their isolation. Western Jews could not be distinguished from their fellow citizens in dress, language, manners and customs. Fishberg welcomed secularisation and inter-marriage with non-Jews. If present trends continued in Holland and Prussia, within a few generations, Dutch and Prussian Jews would cease to exist. 'Lombroso was right in his statement that if all Jews were baptized, their descendants, after two or three generations, would probably not exhibit any peculiarities' (Fishberg 1911, 552).

Conclusions

Should Lombroso's name be placed alongside that of Jacobs, Fishberg and Ruppin? Was Lombroso a practitioner of Jewish social science? The historians who have identified Jewish social science as a distinct tradition of scholarship do not say. John Efron and Mitchell Hart mention Lombroso, but allow his status to remain ambiguous. Sander Gilman frames Lombroso as a Jewish thinker, but others, like David Forgacs, would seem to maintain some reservations.

It is clear that Lombroso contributed to debates within and around Jewish social science. He appreciated the investigative techniques of Jewish social scientists, agreed with their interpretations of particular issues, utilised common conceptual analyses, and even shared their motivation and commitments. To judge solely from the body of work Lombroso produced about Jews, he should be considered as making a substantive contribution to Jewish social science. This is particularly true if we situate Lombroso in his own time, the world in which Jewish social science emerged. A nineteenth-century world threatened by anti-Semitism, but without knowledge of where it would lead in the twentieth century; a world before the Holocaust of European Jewry. Lombroso defended Jews, and while many disparaged Zionism, Judaism, and traditional forms of Jewish life, others within the frame of Jewish social science were not far away. The problem is that Lombroso did not write only about Jewish issues. He produced a large body of work about crime, mental illness and other topics. It is hard to reconcile his views of Jewish issues with his statements in these other areas. Even judged by the standards of his own time, his views of race contributed to colonialist and imperialist ideologies. Lombroso was also an inconsistent and contradictory writer, which makes it challenging to locate his core principles and values. During the last two decades of his life, Lombroso increasingly relied on writing to generate an income, which meant that he became even more of a polemicist than he already was.

But understanding Jewish social science, and Lombroso's relationship with it, is significant, because it provides a hedge against genealogical interpretations of his work. Lombroso can be taken as 'the father' of biological criminology or other ills within contemporary outlooks. But this ignores the reality of his concepts and methods as contributing to more than one stream of ideas. The legacy of Jewish social science demonstrates that even the dubious methods of anthropometry could be read more than one way, both as a means of oppression and a means of opposition to oppression.

Notes

1 So much so, in fact, that Lamarckism came to be identified as a Jewish theory. In Germany, the National Socialists dismissed Lamarckism as the product of 'liberal-Jewish-Bolshevist science' (Slavet 2007, 39).

2 Maurice Fishberg, who prepared the entry for 'craniometry', reviewed the debate of cephalic index, in which he came down on the side of purity consistent with Jacobs, his editor (Fishberg 1903a, 333–5).
3 One of his more curious projects consisted of a 'beauty map' of the British Isles. By making pin holes in a piece of paper hidden in his pocket, Galton classified the girls he met on the city streets as 'attractive, indifferent or repellent'. London, he discovered, ranked highest (Newman 1988, 1143); a finding that might have been explained – had he discussed his findings with Jacobs – by the greater portion of Jewish women with a pleasing walk.
4 In a sense, Fishberg allowed more of a biological element in Jewish crime than Lombroso. In New York city, Fishberg said, patterns of crime had changed in Jewish neighbourhoods. While in the 1880s, it was rare for Jews to commit murder, several Jews had been convicted of this crime in recent years. The change may have been due to the increased consumption of alcohol, or to acquisition of knowledge of the importance of physical force. The appearance of several prize fighters from among the Jewish immigrants, Fishberg suggested, 'shows that they have of late begun to cultivate their muscles, which have been neglected for centuries' (Fishberg 1911, 417).

References

Cottino, A. (1985) 'Science and Class Structure: Notes on the Formation of the Alcohol Question in Italy (1860–1920)', *Contemporary Crises* 9: 45–53.
Efron, J. (1994) *Defenders of the Race: Jewish Doctors and Race Science in Fin-de-Siècle Europe*. New Haven, Connecticut: Yale University Press.
Endelman, T. (2004) 'Anglo-American Scientists and the Science of Race', *Jewish Social Studies* 11: 52–92.
Falk, R. (1998) 'Zionism and the Biology of Jews', *Science in Context* 11 (1998): 587–607.
Fishberg, M. (1902) 'Physical Anthropology of the Jews I—The Cephalic Index', *American Anthropologist* 4: 684–706.
Fishberg, M. (1903a) 'Craniometry' in *The Jewish Encyclopedia*. vol 2. New York: Funk and Wagnalls, pp. 333–6.
Fishberg, M. (1903b) 'Physical Anthropology of the Jews II—Pigmentation', *American Anthropologist* 5: 89–106.
Fishberg, M. (1911) *The Jews: A Study of Race and Environment*. London: Walter Scott.
Forgacs, D. (2003) 'Building the Body of the Nation: Lombroso's *L'antisemtismo* and Fin-de-Siècle Italy', *Jewish Culture and History* 6: 96–110.
Gibson, M. (2002) *Born to Crime: Cesare Lombroso and the Origins of Biological Criminology*. Westport, Connecticut: Greenwood.
Gilman, S. (1984) 'Jews and Mental Illness: Medical Metaphors, Anti-Semitism, and the Jewish Reponses', *Journal of the History of the Behavioral Sciences* 20: 150–9.
Gottheil, W. (1902) 'Alcoholism' in *Jewish Encyclopedia*, vol 1. New York: Funk and Wagnalls, pp. 333–4.
Harrowitz, N (1994) *Antisemitism, Misogyny and the Logic of Cultural Difference: Cesare Lombroso and Matild Serao*. Lincoln, NE: University of Nebraska Press.
Hart, Mitchell B. (1999) 'Racial Science, Social Science, and the Politics of Jewish Assimilation', *Isis* 90: 268–97.
Hart, M. (2000) *Social Science and the Politics of Modern Jewish Identity*. Stanford, California: Stanford University Press.

Hirsch, D. (2009) 'Zionist Eugenics, Mixed Marriage, and the Creation of a "New Jewish Type"', *Journal of the Royal Anthropological Institute* 15: 592–609.

Horn, D. (2006) 'Making Criminologists: Tools, Techniques and the Production of Scientific Authority', in Peter Becker and Richard Wetzell, *Criminals and Their Scientists: The History of Criminology in International Perspective*. Cambridge: Cambride University Press, pp. 317–36.

Jacobs, J. (1886a) 'On the Racial Characteristics of Modern Jews', *Journal of the Anthropological Institute of Great Britain and Ireland* 15: 23–62.

Jacobs, J. (1886b) 'The Comparative Distribution of Jewish Ability', *Journal of the Anthropological Institute of Great Britain and Ireland* 15: 351–79.

Jacobs, J. (1899) 'Are Jews Jews?' *Popular Science Monthly* 55: 502–11.

Jacobs, J. (1901) 'Anthropology' in *The Jewish Encyclopedia*. New York: Funk and Wagnalls, pp. 619–21.

Jacobs, J. and I. Spielman (1890) 'On the Comparative Anthropometry of English Jews', *Journal of the Anthropological Institute of Great Britain and Ireland* 19: 75–88.

Jewish Chronicle (1910) 'Eugenics and the Jew' (20 July), p. 16.

Lombroso, C. (1897a) 'The Heredity of Acquired Characteristics', *The Forum* 24: 200–8.

Lombroso, C. (1897b) 'Concerning the Anti-Semitic Movement', *To-Morrow* 3: 1–11.

Lombroso, C. (1899) 'The Secret Spring in the Dreyfus Case', *The Independent* 51 (22 June): 1674–6.

Lombroso, C. (1911) *Man of Genius*. London: Walter Scott.

Lombroso, C (2006) *Criminal Man*, Mary Gibson and Nicole H. Rafter, trns. Durham, NC: Duke University Press.

Morris-Reich, A. (2010) 'Circumventions and Confrontations: Georg Simmel, Franz Boas, Arthur Ruppin and Their Responses to Antisemitism', *Patterns of Prejudice* 44: 195–215.

Newman, J. (1988) *The World of Mathematics* vol 2. Redmond, Washington: Tempus Books.

The New York Times (1908) 'Free of Alcoholism' 4 October, p. 11.

Ruppin, A. (1913) *The Jews of Today*. London: Bell and Sons.

Ryback, T. (2009) *Hitler's Private Library: The Books That Shaped His Life*. London: Bodley Head.

Slavet, E. (2007) 'Freud's "Lamarckism" and the Politics of Racial Science', *Journal of the History of Biology* 41: 37–80.

Soffer, O. (2004) 'Antisemitism, Statistics, and the Scientization of Hebrew Political Discourse: The Case of *Ha-tsefirah*', *Jewish Social Studies* 10: 55–79.

Wyrwa, U. (2007) 'Antisemitism in Europe and the Italian-Jewish Response: The Coverage of the Journal *Il Vessillo Israelitico* (1879–1914)', *Studia Judaica*.

10
THE MELODRAMATIC PUBLICATION CAREER OF LOMBROSO'S *LA DONNA DELINQUENTE*

Nicole Rafter

Few texts have had so melodramatic a publication career as Lombroso's *La donna delinquente* (Lombroso and Ferrero 1893). The theatrical stops and starts of its publication history doomed it for years to misunderstanding and scorn, although this same rollercoastering trajectory eventually led to the work's rescue, restorations of its reputation, and happy endings. In the twists and turns of its publication history, *La donna delinquente* reflects, more than any of Lombroso's other works, his own career, which was also characterized by sudden reversals and extremes in public and scientific opinion. More generally, it reflects changing attitudes toward the place of women – and studies of women – in society.

La donna delinquente exists in four versions, each reflecting quite different social circumstances but together tracing a melodramatic arc replete with stock characters (a villain with a knife, a damsel in distress, and sisterly saviors) and a hammy plotline. Its original authors hoped to expose the female criminal as "a true monster," "more terrible than any male counterpart" (Lombroso and Ferrero 2004, 185, 183). Its first English translation (Lombroso and Ferrero 1895) flayed the text, excising every hint of sex or sexuality and reshaping the book to fit a Victorian morality. A new, if partial, English translation (Lombroso and Ferrero 2004) rescued the text from its mutilated state; and a recent Italian version (Lombroso and Ferrero 2009) restored the complete original, making it once again accessible in its pristine state. From mutilation through rescue to restoration, *La donna delinquente* has traversed the plotline of a gothic romance.

In what follows, I describe the first version of *La donna delinquente* (1893) as a text, examine the cultural circumstances in which Lombroso produced it, and assess its impact in Italy. Next, I turn to the chopped-up English translation, *The Female Offender* (1895), describing ways in which it differed as a text, the cultural circumstances in which it appeared, and its cultural impact in England and the United States. In the third section, I go through the same steps for *Criminal Woman* (2004), also speaking about my odd experience of participating in the restoration of this classic text. The final section describes the new edition of 2009, commenting on its significance.[1]

La donna delinquente (1893)

L'uomo delinquente or *Criminal Man* (Lombroso 1876), the book in which Lombroso first put forth his theory of the atavistic born criminal, was 17 years old when he started working on *La donna delinquente*. Although Lombroso had revised *L'uomo delinquente* several times, critics continued to attack it. Some complained that he had not used a control group; thus he decided to test his born-criminal theory on a new group[2] – women – and to compare female offenders with "normal" women. Lombroso invited Gugliemo Ferrero, a 19-year-old law student, to assist him with the book and, with characteristic generosity, credited Ferrero with co-authorship. The book's full title is *La donna delinquente, la prostituta, e la donna normale*.

The original text of *La donna delinquente* (1893) consists of 640 pages organized into four parts with a total of 31 chapters, plus illustrations and a preface in which Lombroso speaks anxiously about the hostile reception he anticipates for this study. One of the chapters is titled "Sexual Sensitivity (Lesbianism and Sexual Psychopathy)," and elsewhere, too, Lombroso spends a good deal of time discussing female sexuality and sexual deviance. (My reasons for mentioning this will become clear in a moment.) The book was apparently reprinted in Italian twice, in 1894 and 1903, before being reissued in 1913 in a new edition by his daughter Gina Lombroso-Ferrero.[3] A 1915 edition (perhaps identical with that of 1913) was reissued in 1923 and 1927. Until very recently, when the original was fully reprinted, it was almost impossible to get a clear idea of its scope and nature. Working in the United States on the translation of 2004, Mary Gibson and I found it difficult even to obtain a microfilmed copy of the first edition.

In what ways was *La donna delinquente* shaped by the cultural circumstances in which it was written? It shows the impact of a number of nineteenth-century trends and enthusiasms: one was the growing prestige of science, especially Darwinism; another was a reaction against Enlightenment legal theories, premised as they were on the assumption of free will; yet another was the nineteenth-century fondness for consumer-oriented displays (Benjamin 1999), a predilection reflected in Lombroso's spread-sheet photographs of criminal women and graphs of their anomalies. I will focus here on three influences that seem to me to have been particularly important: the movement for female emancipation; the birth of sexology; and the public debate in Italy over prostitution.

Lombroso and Ferrero produced *La donna delinquente* during a period when Italian feminists, paralleling first-wave feminism in the US and UK, were starting to establish formal organizations. Activists in the women's movement were demanding access to education, entrance to the professions, equality within the family, and the right to vote. Lombroso, who was politically liberal and a friend of the feminist Anna Kuliscioff, did not oppose all changes in women's legal status. But he was profoundly troubled by the prospect of a fundamental restructuring of gender roles, as shown by his allocation of the first major section of *La donna delinquente* to proofs of the inferiority of even normal women. Lombroso argued that women are doomed by evolution to be inferior to men – emotionally, intellectually, morally, and physically. By ridiculing intellectual women as masculine and by insisting on maternity as the natural and sole goal of all women, he scientifically affirmed the wisdom of traditional gender roles and undercut efforts for female emancipation.

While the women's movement was unsettling the outer world, it was also working mischief in Lombroso's own home. At the time he embarked on *La donna delinquente*, Lombroso's two daughters, Paola and Gina, were both approaching the age of 20 and growing more independent. Moreover, while he was working on the book, Anna Kuliscioff spent a great deal of time with Lombroso's family, dining with them almost nightly and slipping the girls a copy of J. S. Mill's *The Subjection of Women* (Dolza 1990). Arguments within the family over women's roles, together with the women's movement that Kuliscioff represented, probably inspired passages in *La donna delinquente* where he speaks of educated women with annoyance and even trepidation. The book's biological "proofs" of female inferiority were part of a reaction against transformations in women's status (Gibson 1982; Gibson 1990; Horn 1995).

The advent of sexology, another aspect of the cultural context in which Lombroso worked, also leaves its mark on the pages of *La donna delinquente*. Although he was never as focused or systematic in his study of human sexuality as Richard von Krafft-Ebing, whose work he greatly admired, Lombroso was nonetheless a transitional figure between Victorian prudery and the celebrations of sexual freedom that came to characterize sexology in the early twentieth century. Lombroso shared many views with earlier nineteenth-century moralists. In keeping with the bourgeois ideology of separate spheres for men and women, he points to the mobility of sperm and immobility of the egg to justify male public activity and female domestic passivity. Claiming that "primitive" women, including born criminals and born prostitutes, are characterized by an unbridled and masculine sex drive, he heralds monogamy and the sexual modesty of bourgeois women as valuable products of evolution. And he proudly reports that white European women no longer desire sexual intercourse except for procreation, the defining act of womanhood.

Yet Lombroso resembled contemporary sexologists in his curiosity about a variety of sexual practices and his interest in cataloguing them. *La donna delinquente* devotes sections to adultery, frigidity, lesbianism, masturbation, and premarital sex. In a long section on the history of prostitution, Lombroso enumerates its many purposes in the past: to celebrate the gods, to entertain guests, and, in the case of Greek and Renaissance courtesans, to unite beauty and learning. Two chapters analyze the causes and characteristics of contemporary prostitution. Even though Lombroso is sometimes prurient and always anxious to reinforce female chastity or monogamy, his approach contrasts with his contemporaries' silence about sexuality.

A third influential aspect of the cultural context in which Lombroso worked was the Italian debate over whether prostitution should be prohibited or regulated. Rapid growth of the Italian population had caused mass migration to the cities of both North and South, swelling the ranks of the so-called dangerous classes. A central figure in the iconography of the dangerous classes was the prostitute, a woman seemingly no longer bound by family or morality. To middle-class observers, the hordes of homeless and unemployed women on urban streets were indistinguishable from prostitutes (Gibson 1986/1999). Actual prostitutes, blamed for the spread of venereal disease, were placed under police supervision and required to live in state-regulated brothels. Under these circumstances, it is not surprising that Lombroso found the prostitute even more threatening and atavistic than the criminal woman. Indeed, a central thesis of *La donna delinquente* is that "prostitution is closer than criminality to woman's primitive behavior" (Lombroso and Ferrero 2004, 149).

What sort of an impact did *La donna delinquente* have in Italy? Recent criminologists have sometimes dismissed Lombroso as a ridiculous figure whose writings had little impact on larger policy debates, but in fact he was the leader of a large group of lawyers, physicians, and psychiatrists who constituted the so-called Positivist or Italian School of criminology, and whose theory of the born criminal dominated debates on criminal justice through the fascist period (Gibson 2002). Moreover, Lombroso wrote for the popular press as well as professional journals. He and his followers were social activists, eager to influence legislation and public policy.

Mary Gibson (2004) argues that *La donna delinquente* had a significant impact on a range of Italian women, including prostitutes, criminal women, "normal" women, and lesbians. By maintaining that prostitution is the female equivalent of male crime, Lombroso both criminalized prostitution and sexualized female criminality. Raising the specter of the atavistic born prostitute, his book helped perpetuate the Italian government's policy of restricting prostitutes to licensed brothels. His positions contributed to the defeat of the feminist abolitionist movement, which had worked to free prostitutes from state control.

La donna delinquente also reinforced the belief that all female behavior, including female criminal behavior, is governed by women's sexual organs. For generations to come, not only prostitution but also women's offenses like murder and even theft were analyzed in sexual terms. In prisons in the US and Europe, Lombroso's arguments strengthened the emphasis on moral rather than economic training for female offenders. And they undergirded the view that even "normal" women lose their self-control during menstruation, pregnancy, nursing, and menopause – a sequence that leaves little time for female self-governance. Only lesbians may have been in some ways shielded by Lombroso's book, and that only because he classified them as a subset of prostitutes, thus helping to keep them invisible. Gibson writes (2004, 100–1):

> By subsuming lesbianism under prostitution, Lombroso may have diverted attention away from lesbian behavior and life outside of brothels and prisons, thus minimizing any 'moral panic' about the possibility of normal society being affected by this vice. In this way lesbians in Italy may have remained unnoticed and in some sense freer because of the displacement of anxiety on to prostitutes.

The female offender (1895)

The Female Offender (1895), excerpted from *La donna delinquente* and translated by someone who remains unidentified, runs to 313 pages, about half the length of the original. Nowhere does it indicate that it is only a partial translation; readers could not have known that they were reading excerpts from a much longer whole.

Nor, of course, could readers have understood *how* the English version related to the Italian original. Organized into 18 chapters, *The Female Offender* covers roughly the same ground as Parts III and IV of *La donna delinquente*. It omits Lombroso's preface, all of Part I on The Normal Woman, all of Part II on Female Criminology, and, in Part IV, chapters on "Sexual Sensitivity," "The Born Prostitute," and "The Occasional Prostitute." Because the material on Normal Woman had been cut, no one could realize – no one could *possibly* realize – that to reach his conclusions about criminal women, Lombroso had in fact used a control group of "normal" women. Without notice, *The Female Offender* also omits shorter passages on breasts and genitals, menstruation, sexual precocity, fecundity, female eroticism, and virility. Again without notice, *The Female Offender* shifts the final chapter of *La donna delinquente* (1893), "Hysterical Offenders," to an earlier position in the book.

Taken together, these omissions and switches mutilate the original, hacking it in two and pruning its text. The edition's major drawback, however, is that it simplifies Lombroso's arguments, making it impossible for readers to grasp the complexity of his thought.

Where it does cover the original, *The Female Offender* translates Lombroso literally but listlessly into sanitized and sometimes confusing English prose. Lombroso's original – hastily written like most of his work – presents many problems of interpretation; instead of confronting these problems, the translator of *The Female Offender* (who evidently had no criminological background) reproduces them, for example by translating an Italian pronoun of ambiguous reference into an equally ambiguous English pronoun. Worse yet, *The Female Offender* drains even short phrases of sexual content. In a passage describing a woman referred to as "M.R.," for instance, it reports that she "resisted the profligate designs of her father" (Lombroso and Ferrero 1895, 198). But the original clearly states that M.R. "resisted her father, who wanted to rape her" (*stuprarla*) (Lombroso and Ferrero 1893, 474). As a result, *The Female Offender* is a pedestrian, bowdlerized, and sometimes incomprehensible text.

Originally published by the Unwin company in London and Appleton in New York, *The Female Offender* replaced Lombroso's own preface with an introduction by W. Douglas Morrison, an English cleric; it has almost nothing to do with the book. This English edition was reprinted 14 times between 1897 and 1980, after which a New Mexico press brought out a "new and expanded edition" (Lombroso 1983) which was actually one-third the length of the Appleton original. More mutilation.

FIGURE 10.1 Watercolor of a woman suffering from hypertrichosis (end of the nineteenth century)

Source: Archivio storico del Museo di Antropologia criminale "Cesare Lombroso" dell'Università di Torino (Italia).

In what ways was *The Female Offender* shaped by the cultural circumstances in which it was written? Two seem particularly relevant: the Anglo-American world's thirst for scientific explanations of crime and its attitudes toward sexuality.

In England and the United States in the early 1890s, a shift away from free will accounts of criminal behavior and toward positivist explanations created a demand for scientific criminology. Some proto-Lombrosian work had been produced in England (Maudsley 1874; Thomson 1870; also see Davie 2005) and in the United States (Dugdale 1877; also see Rafter 1997). Articles on Lombroso's work were turning up in the popular press, and readers' hunger was further stimulated by the 1890 publication of Havelock Ellis's *The Criminal*, the first English-language book on criminal anthropology. However, men and women who read only English as yet had no access to a full-length book by Lombroso, nor would they until 1911 (Lombroso 1911; Lombroso-Ferrero 1911). The desire for something substantive by Lombroso himself about the criminal may, ironically, have led to the cuts in *The*

Female Offender. The publishers may have simply decided that material on normal women and prostitution would be far less interesting to English and American readers at this point in time than the hardcore, criminal-anthropological material on anomalies and atavisms.

Moreover, the translator and publishers seem to have been exceedingly anxious to avoid mentioning either normal or deviant sexuality. Krafft-Ebing's *Psychopathia Sexualis* was not published in English until 1892, and Havelock Ellis's first book on human sexuality, *Man and Woman*, did not appear till 1894. The reading public in England and America, whatever they might have been doing in private, were perhaps not yet ready for Lombroso's anecdotes of nymphomania and Sapphic prison orgies. If the publishers deemed the book's sexual content too racy for this audience, they may simply have decided to excise it. From today's perspective, however, this was close to the literary equivalent of genital mutilation.

As for *The Female Offender*'s cultural impact in England and the United States,[4] no other book has ever rivaled its influence on thinking about women and crime. Lombroso bequeathed four interrelated (albeit sometimes contradictory) concepts to subsequent understandings of female criminality. The first concerned the nature of female crime, which according to Lombroso is fundamentally biological in origin. While he was not the first to equate female deviance with sexuality, he powerfully reinforced the association by confirming it "scientifically." The effects reverberated throughout Anglo-American criminal justice systems: psychiatrists explained female crime such as shoplifting in terms of sublimated sexuality (O'Brien 1983), and in many jurisdictions girls arrested for delinquency were automatically given vaginal exams to determine their virginity (Chesney-Lind 1973). (These effects, of course, flowed less from Lombroso than from the ancient equation of female deviance with sexuality on which he drew; it was he, however, who seemed to prove that the equation was right.) Related to Lombroso's emphasis on the biological nature of female criminality is the notion that female criminals are less evolved than both male criminals and law-abiding women, an idea that throughout the twentieth century reinforced infantilizing programs in women's prisons – treatment and disciplinary measures that treated inmates as errant children (Rafter 1990).

A second major part of Lombroso's legacy to the Anglo-American world is the idea that criminal women are more masculine than law-abiding women. This concept reemerged with considerable fanfare with the publication of Freda Adler's *Sisters in Crime* (1975), a work arguing that women's crime rates are on the rise because women (especially women of color) are becoming more like men. Closely related to the masculinity thesis is the criminological tendency to conceptualize female criminality as what Frances Heidensohn (1996, 114) calls "a beauty contest," in which the prize of being deemed "reformable" is awarded to the most feminine (meaning, among other things, Caucasian) offenders.

A third facet of Lombroso's legacy in English-speaking countries is the idea that not only criminal women but also "normal" women are inherently deviant, bundles of pathology that can at any moment explode into criminality. This pathologization

Lombroso, by way of contrast, was committed to assimilation. He was prepared to go to extreme lengths to insist that Jews had a place in Europe and should expect to make a future there. He was anti-Zionist, rather than non-Zionist. In the 1890s, Jean Finot challenged Lombroso to write a response to anti-Semitic claims. Finot (born Finkelhaus) was a Polish journalist who became a French citizen and founded a journal, *La Revue des Revues*. Lombroso's response was to produce *L'antisemitismo e le scienze modern* (Anti-Semitism and Modern Sciences) published in Turin in 1894. A German translation appeared a year later. In this short book, Lombroso set out to refute claims of 'scientific anti-Semitism' that Jews comprised a degenerate sub-class of humans. Lombroso began with a counter-attack against arguments by Edmond Picard and Renan. Picard wrote about the threat of Jewish wealth and excessive concentration of capital. Ernest Renan claimed Semitic peoples lacked the mental variety and breadth needed to achieve perfection, that is to say, they were less highly evolved and less capable of progressive evolution. He dismissed the Semitic contribution to civilisation as negligible, insisting their innovations in politics, art, science and philosophy had been surpassed by others (Forgacs 2003, 96–7).

In the middle of *L'antisemitismo e le scienze modern*, Lombroso took the view that there was no single Jewish race. Jews represented a mixture of races, including Aryans and Indians, and Jews tended to share the physical characteristics as other people living in the same region. He pointed out that among European Jews, there was great variation in colours of hair and eyes, head sizes and shapes. In a series of appendices, he offered statistical proof to substantiate these claims. Lombroso welcomed this hybridism as a good thing because, as with grafting, it tended to produce evolutionary movements (Forgacs 2003, 98). However, before delivering his argument of Jewish race mixture, Lombroso maintained that the anti-Semitic movement did not result from the arbitrary prejudice of non-Jews but reflected in part the actions of Jews themselves. He gave five reasons for this. (1) The Jews long practice of commerce had given them a habit of craftiness and tendency to lie. (2) In-breeding had produced genius but also neurotics. (3) Jews clung to old customs, such as the 'savage practice of circumcision' and 'stupid rites of the Passover matzah' which aroused ridicule and repugnance. (4) Jews displayed a weakness of character. They were more obstinate and inflexible than others, which gave them a 'moral inferiority' and (5) their petulance and impatience which produced a tendency to lord over others (Forgacs 2003, 98–9).

Flaminio Servi, rabbi of Casale Monferrato, welcomed Lombroso's defence against anti-Semitic attacks. He published and edited *Il Vessillo Israelitico* (Hebrew Banner), an Italian monthly newspaper founded in Vercelli. In 1881, Lombroso published an article in the paper about race and insanity in which he pronounced anti-Semitism as a disgrace. Servi was also familiar with *L'antisemitismo e le scienze modern*; he appreciated Lombroso's method and conclusions. Although Lombroso allowed certain objectionable statements about Judaism to enter into his work, Servi concluded, he managed nonetheless a substantive critique of prejudices against Jews (Wyrwa 2007, 200).

of ordinary womanhood authorized physicians and other normalizers to intervene more frequently and deeply in women's lives than in those of men. Additionally, it made female sexuality automatically suspect.

Fourth and finally, in English-speaking countries Lombroso's work on the female offender helped define "normality" itself as, in part, the absence of criminal tendencies (see also Horn 1995). This standard has been applied to male behavior as well, but there remained alternative ways of thinking about male deviance (heroic rebellion, for example, or the sowing of wild oats). Female lawbreaking, on the other hand, almost always ran the risk in England and the United States of being labeled abnormal and hence pathological. This put law-abiding women, too, in peril, for any woman who threatened the status quo could be deemed abnormal.

In many respects, *The Female Offender*'s legacy in English-speaking countries paralleled the impact of *La donna delinquente* on Italian thinking about women's nature and female criminality. But in Anglo-American countries, much more so than in Italy, Lombroso eventually became a whipping-boy for feminist criminologists. Dorie Klein (1973), Carol Smart (1976), and others used Lombroso's pronouncements on women to expose the sexist biases in criminology in general. In Italy, the reaction against Lombroso was more muted, but this had less to do with differences between the two texts than with international differences in the women's movement and in the goals of criminology itself (Rafter and Heidensohn, eds. 1995; Pitch 1995). Moreover, Italians had reason to be proud of Lombroso, a man whose work was respected worldwide (e.g. Rafter 2010).

Criminal woman (2004)

The purpose of the new translation of *Criminal Woman* (2004), as of its companion volume *Criminal Man* (Lombroso 2006), was twofold: to provide, for the first time, an adequate English translation of one of Lombroso's major criminological works and to lay foundations for an emerging new generation of Lombroso scholarship. The new editions aimed at facilitating Lombroso scholarship in fields as diverse as anthropology, art history, criminology, and rhetoric; Italian and European history; the history of science, medicine, and psychiatry; law and legal history; and studies of gender, race, and ethnicity.[5] Mary Gibson and I were especially anxious to produce books that our students – college graduates and undergraduates – would find readable and interesting. Our introduction to *Criminal Woman* (Rafter and Gibson 2004) examines in depth one of the issues I've looked at briefly here: the impact of Lombroso's work on subsequent theory and practice in the area of women and crime in the English-speaking world. However, Gibson and I were less interested in trying to answer questions than in providing materials for others to use in answering long-standing questions about Lombroso's work and formulating new ones.

To select material for inclusion in the new edition (Lombroso and Ferrero 2004), we developed three guidelines. First, we aimed at completely translating Lombroso's theoretical arguments and adhering to the order in which he presented them. Second, we aimed at clearly representing his scientific procedures, including his use of tables, illustrations, and citations. Third, we needed to reduce the size of the 1893 original to make the new edition readable and affordable. Indeed, our contract with Duke University Press specified that we would submit a manuscript no longer than 97,000 words; this meant that we had to squeeze the original 640 pages of *La donna delinquente* into a book of 300 pages while at the same time adding our substantial Editors' Introduction, appendices comparing our edition with the two previous volumes, notes explaining difficult passages in Lombroso's text, a glossary, and references – all this while also remaining true to the first two guidelines. About half of the new edition is given over to previously untranslated material from *La donna delinquente*, while the other half consists of a compressed and retranslated version of the material covered by *The Female Offender*.

Reducing *La donna delinquente* (1893) to a manageable size while retaining the original Parts and chapter structure involved cutting pages, paragraphs, and – within single sentences – words that seemed unnecessary. We eliminated two sorts of material: repetitions and examples. Lombroso seems to have been untroubled by repetitions and indeed, he often presents material over and over again, approaching it from new angles or combining it in new ways with other topics. We did away with most of his overlaps. We also eliminated many of the examples Lombroso presents in support of his positions. To Lombroso as a scientist, a wealth of examples was important because it signified a wealth of scientific evidence for his theory. The sheer quantity of evidence mattered less to us, however. From today's point of view, moreover, the "science" of Lombroso's examples is often dubious or even ludicrous. (Some of his contemporaries shared this opinion.) Our policy for each of Lombroso's new points was to translate one or two of the more vivid or clarifying examples but to omit the rest.

Our cuts created two "translation effects" – meaning changes that flowed from our translation policies. First, they minimize Lombroso's long-windedness and clarify sentences that, in the original, were tangled or obscure. In this respect, our translation somewhat distorts the original; it is, if I might say so, easier to read. Second, by cutting some of the book's outlandish examples, our translation may, ironically, make the text seem more rational and scientific than it in fact was. In this respect, too, our cuts may slightly "improve" Lombroso's original.

Lombroso wrote in formal, scholarly Italian, using medical and scientific terms that are today obsolete. To twenty-first-century Italians whom we used as consultants, Lombroso's language is old-fashioned, difficult, and at times even incomprehensible. However, its datedness is in part an effect of the passage of time. To his educated contemporaries, Lombroso's language would have seemed appropriately learned, and among non-scientists, his obscure terminology might actually have had a credentialing effect, increasing his credibility.

Because one of our goals was to make Lombroso's work accessible, we translated obscure words into more familiar terms. We also tried to relax his prose style a bit, making it slightly more colloquial. Our rule-of-thumb was to write for our audience, not his. On the other hand, we did not aim at fully colloquial English. We attempted to make his prose comprehensible to modern readers while preserving some of its formality.

In working on this translation, we occasionally flinched at reproducing Lombroso's gaffs and missteps – his sloppy use of statistics, uncritical examples, unsophisticated generalizations, internal contradictions in the text, and overall incoherence. Our temptation here was akin to what translation theorists call "ennoblement" – the temptation, confronted most often by poetry translators, to make translated material more flowery or elevated than it was originally. But if our temptation was similar to that of ennoblers, it was certainly not the same: few translators can have had to cope as we did with outright foolishness on the part of the source-author.

In our view, Lombroso's work is historically valuable despite its scientific and logical naiveté. In fact, it is valuable partly *because* it so clearly reveals scientific and scientistic vulnerabilities, making them available for study. For better or worse, one outstanding quality of Lombroso's work is its magnificent tangle of brilliance and nonsense, the way it combines what a recent biographer calls Lombroso's "encyclopedic ambition, his characteristically extreme mental adventuresomeness, and his titanic failures" (Guarnieri 2000: 14). Our key concern was to produce a full (if abbreviated) and accurate translation, a concern that led us to explicitly resolve to include the warts. We still flinched, but having recognized the temptation to hide Lombroso's faults, we were better able to resist it.

Mary Gibson and I have been asked why we decided to undertake new translations of Lombroso's work. We did so because as criminological historians, we found it impossible to get along without them. Separately, while doing research on nineteenth-century criminology, we had often been frustrated by our inability to trace the development of Lombroso's ideas over time due to the lack of materials. *La donna delinquente* (1893) was all but inaccessible in the Italian original, and we suspected that the 1895 English translation was misleading.[6] We were also frustrated by apparent misstatements about Lombroso that appeared in standard criminological texts. We saw an opportunity to rescue a text that had been mutilated in translation, and we took it. Had we realized at the start that the project would take eleven years, we might never have begun; but we were able to work individually on other projects as well during that time (we took turns translating, editing, preparing indices, and so on), and the Lombroso translations have indeed enabled us to write much more authoritatively about the development of nineteenth-century criminology.

The process of translating *La donna delinquente* and writing hundreds of explanatory footnotes was long and sometimes tedious, but it was also pleasurable. Much of my pleasure came from working with Mary Gibson, from whom I learned a great deal about the history of Italian women, Italian criminology, and the Italian language. Another part of the pleasure came from my odd sense of colleagueship with Lombroso himself. Although I disagreed with him at almost every turn, I enjoyed the intimacy I inevitably acquired with his thought processes. I got to know the structure of his ideation and his intellectual habits, including his tendency to go limp and vague when he sensed that he was approaching a logical contradiction. Lombroso cared passionately about his work, and he would have loved knowing that this book is still of interest over a century after he produced it – although he would have been astonished that those who produced it as a new scholarly text were women.

La donna delinquente (2009)

Completing the cycle from rescue to restoration, in 2009 a small Italian press called *et al.* republished the complete original of Lombroso and Ferrero's work under the original title: *La donna delinquente, la prostituta e la donna normale*. Initiative for this new edition came from an Italian feminist scholar, Ombretta Ingrasci, who had read and reviewed the 2004 English translation for *History Workshop Journal* (Ingrasci 2006). Ingrasci's interest had begun with her research on mafia women, a topic covered in Lombroso and Ferrero's 1893 study. She wanted to make Lombroso's original available to Italian scholars and also to contribute new material to the Italian "debate on the female question during the male chauvinist Berlusconi era" (Ingrasci 2011). Ingrasci found it very difficult to find a copy of the Italian original in good enough condition to be reproduced but finally located a copy in the Biblioteca di Cremona.

Ingrasci contacted Mary Gibson and myself, along with Duke University Press, to see if we would agree to prefacing the new work with an Italian translation of our introduction to the 2004 edition (Rafter and Gibson 2004). She was anxious not to republish the work without a critical, analytical introduction, for otherwise she would risk the appearance of merely celebrating Lombroso (Ingrasci 2011). Gibson and I gladly agreed to her request, and Gibson somewhat revised our introduction to locate the new edition in the context of, first, Italian criminology and its almost complete indifference to issues of sex and gender and, second, the growing international interest in Lombroso's oeuvre. The new edition appeared in time for a 2009 international Lombroso conference commemorating the centennial of his death. At last, scholars around the world had access to *La donna delinquente*'s original text.

****

Does the melodrama end here? *La donna delinquente*'s publication history leaves it safely out of harm's way, but that history is already unfolding beyond the tale told here. In 2010, Nabu Press – a company that specializes in reprinting books with expired copyrights[7] – issued a reprint of *The Female Offender* (1895). Subsequently Mary Gibson and I heard from Professor Kyung Jae Lee of the Korean Institute of Criminology, who in 2010 had published a Korean translation of our *Criminal Man* (2006); now he was asking permission to translate our *Criminal Woman* (2004) as a companion volume. Soon, then, there will be a Korean translation of our English translation of Lombroso and Ferrero's Italian original! While the publishing history of *La donna delinquente* will no longer resemble a melodrama, it clearly has sequels to come.

Acknowledgments

Thanks to Ombretta Ingrasci for information on the publication history of the 2009 Italian edition of *La donna delinquente*; to Michael McCullough of Duke University Press for information on sales of the 2004 edition of *Criminal Woman*; and to Mary Gibson for updates on her 2004 article and for all she has taught me over the years about Italian social history.

Notes

1 This article expands and updates Rafter 2011, an article written in 2003 (although not published till much later) and thus in need of updating with several important new publication events.
2 Even in the first (1876) edition of *L'uomo delinquente*, Lombroso included data on criminal women as well as criminal men – a truly innovative step, considering that most US and UK criminologists did not follow suit for over a century. However, not until *La donna delinquente* (1893) did Lombroso attempt an extended comparison of female with male criminals. *La donna delinquente* also makes three-way comparisons among female criminals, prostitutes, and "normal" women.
3 It is difficult to get clear information on the various early editions and reprints of Lombroso's work. The information given here came from a combination of sources: The National Union Catalog, the Library of Congress's WorldCat listing, and, especially, Renzo Villa's study (1985) of *Il deviante e i suoi segni*.
4 Much of what I say here applies to Anglophone Canada and Australia as well.
5 According to data from Duke University Press (McCullough 2011), *Criminal Woman* (2004) has been adopted as a text in such diverse courses as Sociology of Gender, Detective Fiction, Women's History, and "Modern Spectacles."
6 It was even more difficult to do research on *L'uomo delinquente*, which went through five Italian editions, the last of them four volumes long (Lombroso 1876, 1878, 1884, 1889, 1896–1897). No one knew how the two partial English translations of *L'uomo delinquente* (Lombroso 1911; Lombroso-Ferrero 1911) related to Lombroso's originals or which edition they derived from. How could we hope to make intelligent generalizations about a body of work so large, confusing, and inaccessible? The answer was obvious, if daunting: we couldn't unless we translated it ourselves.
7 See http://wiki.answers.com/Q/Who_and_where_are _Nabu_Press (downloaded July 24, 2011).

References

Adler, F. (1975) *Sisters in Crime*. New York: McGraw-Hill.
Benjamin, W. (1999) *The Arcades Project*. Cambridge, MA: The Belknap Press of Harvard University Press; translated by Howard Eiland and Kevin McLaughlin.
Chesney-Lind, M. (1973) "Judicial Enforcement of the Female Sex Role: The Family Court and the Female Delinquent," *Issues in Criminology* 8 (2): 51–69.

Davie, N. (2005) *Tracing the Criminal: The Rise of Scientific Criminology in Britain, 1860–1918*. Oxford, UK: Bardwell.
Dolza, D. (1990) *Essere figlie di Lombroso: Due donne intellettuali tra '800 e '900*. Milan: Franco Angeli.
Dugdale, R. L. (1877) *"The Jukes": A Study in Crime, Pauperism, Disease and Heredity; also Further Studies of Criminals*. New York: G. P. Putnam's Sons.
Ellis, H. (1890) *The Criminal*. London: Walter Scott.
Ellis, H. (1894) *Man and Woman: A Study of Human Secondary Sexual Characters*. London: Scott.
Gibson, M. (1982) "The *Female Offender* and the Italian School of Criminal Anthropology," *Journal of European Studies* 12: 155–65.
Gibson, M. (1990) "On the Insensitivity of Women: Science and the Woman Question in Liberal Italy, 1890–1910," *Journal of Women's History* 2 (2): 11–41.
Gibson, M. (1986/1999) *Prostitution and the State in Italy, 1860–1915*. Columbus, OH: Ohio State University Press.
Gibson, M. (2002) *Born to Crime: Cesare Lombroso and the Italian Origins of Biological Criminology*. Westport, CT: Praeger.
Gibson, M. (2004) "Labeling Women Deviant: Heterosexual Women, Prostitutes, and Lesbians in Early Criminological Discourse," *Gender and the Private Sphere in Italy*, ed. Perry Willson. London: Palgrave-Macmillan.
Gibson, M. and Rafter. N. (2009) "Introduzione" to C. Lombroso and G. Ferrero, *La donna delinquente, la prostituta e la donna normale*. Turin: et al.
Guarnieri, L. (2000) *L'atlante criminale: vita scriteriata di Cesare Lombroso*. Milan: Mondadori.
Heidensohn, F. (1985/1996) *Women and Crime*. London: MacMillan Press.
Horn, D. G. (1995) "This Norm Which Is Not One: Reading the Female Body in Lombroso's Anthropology," in J. Terry and J. Urla (eds) *Deviant Bodies*. Bloomington, IN: Indiana University Press, Chapter 4 (pp. 109–28).
Ingrasci, O. (2006) "'Anomalous Females': Cesare Lombroso and Guglielmo Ferrero, *Criminal Woman, the Prostitute and the Normal Woman*," *History Workshop Journal* 61: 264–7.
Ingrasci, O. (2011) Email communication of August 27, 2011, to Nicole Rafter, about the origins of the 2009 Italian edition of *La donna delinquente*.
Klein, D. (1973) "The Etiology of Female Crime," *Issues in Criminology* 8 (2): 3–30.
Krafft-Ebing, R. von. (1892) *Psychopathia Sexualis*. Philadelphia: F A. Davis Co.
Lombroso, C. (1876) *L'uomo delinquente studiato in rapporto alla antropologia, alla medicina legale ed alle discipline carcerarie*. Milan: Hoepli.
Lombroso, C. (1878) *L'uomo delinquente in rapporto all'antropologia, giurisprudenza e alle discipline carcerarie*. Turin: Bocca.
Lombroso, C. (1884) *L'uomo delinquente in rapporto all'antropologia, giurisprudenza ed alle discipline carcerarie. Delinquente-nato e pazzo morale*. Turin: Bocca.
Lombroso, C. (1889) *L'uomo delinquente in rapporto all'antropologia, alla giurisprudenza ed alle discipline carcerarie*. 2 vols. Turin: Bocca.
Lombroso, C. (1896–1897) *L'uomo delinquente in rapporto all'antropologia, alla giurisprudenza ed alle discipline carcerarie*. 4 vols., including *L'atlante*, Turin: Bocca.
Lombroso, C. (1911) *Crime: Its Causes and Remedies*. Boston: Little, Brown, and Company.
Lombroso, C. (1983) *Basic Characteristics of Women Criminals*. New and expanded edition. Albuquerque: The Foundation for Classical Reprints.
Lombroso, C. (2006) *Criminal Man*. Translated and with a new introduction by M. Gibson and N. H. Rafter. Duke University Press.

Lombroso, C. and Ferrero, G. (1893) *La donna delinquente, la prostituta e la donna normale.* Turin: Roux.
Lombroso, C. and Ferrero, W. (1895) *The Female Offender.* With an introduction by W. D. Morrison. London: Unwin; New York: Appleton.
Lombroso, C. and Ferrero, G. (2004) *Criminal Woman, the Prostitute, and the Normal Woman.* Translated and edited by N. H. Rafter and M. Gibson. Durham, NC: Duke University Press.
Lombroso, C. and Ferrero, G. (2009) *La donna delinquente, la prostituta e la donna normale.* Prefazione di M. Gibson e N. H. Rafter. Turin: *et al.*
Lombroso-Ferrero, G. (1911) *Criminal Man, According to the Classification of Cesare Lombroso, Briefly Summarised by his Daughter Gina Lombroso-Ferrero.* New York and London: G. P. Putnam's Sons.
McCullough, M. 20 July 2011. Email communication to Nicole Rafter from Duke University Press re sales of *Criminal Woman* (2004).
Maudsley, H. (1874) *Responsibility in Mental Disease.* New York: D. Appleton and Company.
O'Brien, P (1983) "The Kleptomania Diagnosis," *Journal of Social History* 17: 65–77.
Pitch, T. (1995) "Feminist Politics, Crime, Law and Order in Italy," in N. H. Rafter and F. Heidensohn, eds. *International Feminist Perspectives in Criminology: Engendering a Discipline.* Buckingham, UK: Open University Press, Chapter 5 (pp. 86–106).
Rafter, N. H. (1990) *Partial Justice: Women, Prisons, and Social Control.* 2d ed. New Brunswick, NJ: Transaction.
Rafter, N. H. (1997) *Creating Born Criminals.* Champaign, Ill.: University of Illinois Press.
Rafter, N. H. (2010). "Lombroso's Reception in the United States." in D. Downes, D. Hobbs, and T. Newburn (eds) *The Eternal Recurrence of Crime and Control.* Oxford: Oxford University Press, pp. 1–15.
Rafter, N. H. and Gibson, M. 2004. "Editors' Introduction." in C. Lombroso and G. Ferrero, *Criminal Woman, the Prostitute, and the Norman Woman.* Durham, NC: Duke University Press, pp. 3–33.
Rafter, N. H. and F. Heidensohn (eds.) (1995) Introduction to *International Feminist Perspectives in Criminology: Engendering a Discipline.* Buckingham, UK: Open University Press.
Rafter, N. (2011) "Lombroso's 'La Donna Delinquente': its Strange Journeys in Italy, England and the USA, Including Scenes of Mutilation and Salvation," in D. Melossi, M. Sozzo, and R. Sparks (eds.) *Travels of the Criminal Question: Cultural Embeddedness and Diffusion.* Oxford: Hart Publishing, pp. 147–60.
Smart, C. (1976) *Women, Crime, and Criminology: A Feminist Critique.* London: Routledge & Kegan Paul.
Thomson, J. B. (1870) "The Psychology of Criminals," *Journal of Mental Science* 17: 321–50.
Villa, R. (1985) *Il deviante e i suoi segni: Lombroso e la nascita del'antropologia criminale.* Milano: Franco Angeli.

11
LOMBROSO'S *CRIMINAL WOMAN* AND THE UNEVEN DEVELOPMENT OF THE MODERN LESBIAN IDENTITY

Mariana Valverde

The paper that follows is not the one I set out to write. When I heard Nicole Rafter talk about her new translation of Lombroso's *La donna delinquente*, and was told that this would include the sexological chapter that had been left out of the old translation, I thought I could put the proto-lesbians in Lombroso's text in the context of the history of sexual discourses and thus make a contribution to the collective enterprise.

On first reading, it seemed that this task would be relatively simple. The word "lesbian," used both as a noun denoting a type of person and as an adjective specifying an erotic activity, appears several times in the chapter in question. It even appears in the title of the chapter – "Sexual sensitivity (lesbianism and sexual psychopathy)." However, it quickly became apparent that Lombroso's text cannot be firmly located within any one of the established sexual knowledge paradigms – and, more importantly, it cannot be properly understood as either "a mix" of X and Y or "a transition" from X to Y.

The peculiar relation that Lombroso's text has to the genealogy of scientific knowledge of human variation requires discussion, even in a short paper, because without such a discussion it is impossible to make sense out of the text. Thus, I will comment on Lombroso's knowledge practices generally before going on to a substantive (and philological) discussion of his treatment of female-female eroticism. The paper will conclude with a historiographical reflection that calls for a de-centering of "crime" in favor of approaches that pay close attention to the actual dynamics of knowledge formation within the human sciences.

Junkyard epistemology

Lombroso's notorious lack of rigor and consistency is at one level hardly unusual or surprising, given what we know about the knowledge practices found throughout the whole array of late nineteenth century knowledges of vice, crime, disease, and degeneration (Pick 1989; Russett 1989; Showalter 1990; Garland 1985; Valverde 1991, 1992, 1998, chapters 2 and 3). Whether in the more extreme version popularized by the Max Nordau version (Nordau 1895) or in its attenuated and reasonable Havelock Ellis version, the degeneration paradigm treated human variation as simultaneously cultural, psychic, and bodily, with writers showing what we would today describe as a cavalier lack of concern for drawing the line between nature and culture (Latour 1993). In addition, the cause-effect relation was often thought of as very fluid.

But while arguing about the relative weight of various factors, men and women of science agreed (more often implicitly than explicitly) on what had to be eliminated from scientific discourse.[1] Krafft-Ebing, Havelock Ellis and Freud disagreed on many key substantive points: but none of them regarded folk sayings and proverbs as "evidence" on a par with physiological and behavioral observations, as Lombroso did.

Havelock Ellis is worth mentioning here by way of contrast, since he did a great deal to popularize Lombroso in the English-speaking world, and he presents many of his own observations (on criminality at any rate, not so much on sexuality) as drawing upon Lombroso's pioneering project (Ellis 1901). Now, Ellis's work (especially that on criminality) happily mixes physiological and anatomical observations with psychological interpretations of life histories and inner feelings. But while content to not draw much of a line between nature and culture, the physical and the psychic, the inherited and the acquired, he certainly drew a sharp line between science and other forms of knowledge. In discussing criminality he attempts to verify and authenticate the "facts" he is borrowing from Lombroso, in standard scientific manner. And when discussing "sexual inversion" (Ellis and Symonds 1897), he relies almost exclusively on case histories collected by physicians and scientists (by contrast with Lombroso, who is happy to use biographical information about people who are long dead gleaned from popular histories and orally transmitted stories).

Remarking that Lombroso does not use scientific methods for collecting and evaluating data, however, does not help us to understand what is going on. Instead of criticizing Lombroso for what he did not do it is more useful to explain just what he *is* doing. What he does is that instead of using the filter of science, which scrutinizes evidence carefully and allows only certified facts into the knowledge process, Lombroso works in the manner of a junk dealer, by pawing through a heterogeneous collection of knowledge claims that includes popular folklore, legal texts, anthropological measurement charts, psychological case histories, observations made by doctors in prisons and brothels, photographs of Russian prison inmates, concepts taken from the latest psychiatry, methods borrowed from the phrenology of the 1840s, and the letters of Madame de Stael. Old bits of used knowledge are thus gathered and recycled by an author who claims to be speaking with the voice of science, but who in his writing practice exhibits a child-like passion for collecting odd bits of broken knowledge objects and idiosyncratically arranging them in interesting shapes.

The specific dynamics of Lombroso's knowledge production are evident even in the title of chapter on sexual deviance – "Sexual sensitivity (lesbianism and psychopathy)." First of all, if we are in the 1890s, why is sexual sensitivity, a purely physiological entity or indicator, given such prominence? This object of inquiry is reminiscent of but not in fact measurable with the "algometer" that Lombroso elsewhere advocates as a tool for measuring pain sensitivity. But however it is measured, how can this entity shed any light on women's libidinal object choice or on women's gender/sexual identity?[2] One response would be to state that the fascination with the surfaces of the body shows that Lombroso is "stuck in the past," that he is "really" an anthropometric enthusiast. But if he were "really" a physical anthropologist, why the second half of the chapter title? Why shift, without a pause, from the physiological register favored at the time that Lombroso went to medical school (1850s) to the much newer register of psychic identities and degenerate families which the term "sexual psychopathy," taken directly from Krafft-Ebing, suggests?

There is no real answer to this question – there cannot be an answer, in fact, since the question was not one that Lombroso would have asked. As Rafter and Gibson point out in their introduction, in one of his very few reflexive comments Lombroso first critiques his own previous love of anthropometric measurements, then claims that it was not him but others who "abused" this approach, and lastly (illogically) concludes that anthropometry is a (or perhaps the?) scientific method. Rafter and Gibson (2004, 13) conclude that "what began as self-criticism becomes self-congratulation." Scientists are institutionally obliged to think that new research should be used to critique earlier theories: thus, if encountering new data, they have to either change the theory or show that their new findings are at bottom consistent with previous theories. Remarkably, Lombroso simply ignores this imperative. He finds it quite possible to both disagree with his own earlier work and to totally agree with it, at the same time.

If we presuppose the traditional evolutionary model of the human sciences that recent work in the history of science has taught us to question (Poovey 1998; Foucault 1971, 1980; Latour 1993), we would explain Lombroso's contradictions as symptoms of a transitional phase, the transition from descriptive natural history approaches (including physical anthropology) to twentieth-century bio-psychological sciences of human variation. But if we don't presuppose an evolutionary model of the human sciences, we can consider the hypothesis that the peculiarly Lombrosian textual move that Rafter and Gibson sensitively describe as produced by "conflicting impulses – ambition, scientific integrity, exasperation with critics, inertia, a sense of superiority, and simple annoyance at the need to acknowledge past mistakes" (Rafter and Gibson 2004, 13) performs not an evolutionary transition but rather an almost postmodern anything-goes eclecticism, within which inquiries into the provenance of the bits of knowledge one uses are simply not deemed worthwhile.

One curious element of the chapter title is the use of the parenthesis: "Sexual sensitivity (lesbianism and psychopathy)." In keeping with postmodern rhetorical practice, the parenthesis is not used grammatically: lesbianism and psychopathy (linked by a mere "and" rather than by a logical connection) do not here combine to form either a subordinate clause or a digression from a main argument about physiological sensitivity, which are the two main grammatical uses of the parenthesis. Skin sensitivity is merely the first topic covered in the chapter; it is not the main theme. Thus, the parenthesis does not serve to organize the text logically and hierarchically: on the contrary, it simply juxtaposes paradigms, research methods, and governing rationalities without logically linking them. Indeed, the postmodern slash (not yet invented) would have suited Lombroso's rhetorical practice wonderfully: the ontological ambiguity that postmodern texts intentionally produce by the use of the slash is exactly the effect that Lombroso's misleading parenthesis actually produces.

Eclecticism is hardly unusual, of course, even in scientific texts: but it would be difficult to find a scientific writer who so openly, almost joyously embraces eclecticism, without any guilt. Havelock Ellis's measured reading of Lombroso is telling in this regard: as we shall see shortly, Ellis's restrained, above-the-fray stance – a stance totally in keeping with the academic habitus of today – stands in sharp contrast to Lombroso's obvious delight in prowling the junkyard of the human sciences, collecting every bit that strikes his fancy, and using not the scientific method but bricolage to create new texts that are clearly, without apology, made up mainly of recycled stuff.

We now (finally) get to the third term of the chapter title, namely lesbianism.

Sapphists, tribades, masculine women, Urnings, and their relations

On first seeing the word lesbianism in the title, anyone familiar with the history of female sexuality would think it peculiar that Lombroso, in so many ways stuck in the natural-history paradigm of the 1840s, should be so far ahead of his time as to use the word "lesbian" (Chauncey 1989; Faderman 1981; Doan 2001). In the 1890s, medical and scientific texts were much more likely to use the words "congenital invert" or "homosexual" to refer to the persons with the sex/gender deviant identity, while using terms such as "unnatural vice" or "tribadism" to refer to the erotic practices.

But this apparent leap forward in time, something like the opposite of atavism, in Lombroso's text is due only to the translators' choice to use today's term (lesbian) instead of sticking to Lombroso's usage. The glossary at the back of the book informs us that neither lesbians as a group of women nor lesbianism as an activity are actually much discussed. Most of the time, when the English text has "lesbianism," the original has "tribadism." (Indeed, one of Lombroso's publications has "*tribadismo*" in its title.)[3]

The glossary also informs us that occasionally Lombroso uses an equally archaic but not particularly scientific term, "sapphism." This is very rarely found in the nineteenth-century medical discussions of "tribadism"; it appears to have been more common in the erotic novels (mainly in French) that sexologists sometimes used and sometimes denounced.[4]

And as if this semantic instability were not confusing enough, Lombroso also uses the term "Urning," invented in the 1860s (before the word "homosexual" was coined) by the first gay scientific writer, Karl Henrich Ulrichs. Ulrichs' term – variously translated into English as "Uranian" or "Urning" – which is arguably more relevant to the genealogy of gender identity than to that of sexual orientation, was no longer in wide use in the 1890s. By that time, homosexual and invert were the most common scientific terms used to describe the type of person, while perversion, homosexuality, sodomy, unnatural vice, tribadism, and (less often) lesbianism were used to denote the activity within scientific discourses.

A brief comparison of Lombroso's discussion with two influential texts on the same subject by important contemporaries will suffice to give a sense of Lombroso's "distinction" in the field of knowledges of female sexuality. The first point of comparison will be the great sexologist Richard von Krafft-Ebing, often regarded as the key author of the modern homosexual identity. In *Psychopathia sexualis* (whose 1892 edition Lombroso cites at length in *Criminal Woman*), Krafft-Ebing famously endeavors to separate those people who engage in same-sex erotic vice for specific reasons (such as being deprived of heterosexual contact in prisons or being seduced by others) from the true "inverts," the congenital or born inverts whose nature it is to seek individuals of the same sex for erotic satisfaction (Krafft-Ebing 1965). What would soon come to be called homosexual desire is called "antipathic sexual instinct" or "contrary sexual instinct." And what would soon become homosexuality as an act is here called "perversion" (as distinct from the identity, which is "inversion").

Krafft-Ebing's text is important for Lombroso's work on female deviance because several of Lombroso's case histories are taken directly from *Psychopathia sexualis*. Now, the evidence regarding female sexual perversion that gets through Krafft-Ebing's scientific filter consists almost wholly of individual case histories, either in the form of written autobiographies or in the form of medical case histories related by authoritative physicians. Both of these kinds of data are woefully scarce in respect to women, Krafft-Ebing complains, in part because women's intimate friendships seem to flourish without being scrutinized, and in part because women, much to Krafft-Ebing's dismay, do not confide in their (male) doctors. In addition, because sex among women is not illegal (in Germany as in England), court records are not generated. Thus, "Science in its present stage has but few data to fall back on, so far as the occurrence of the homosexual instinct in woman is concerned as compared with man" (Krafft-Ebing 1965, 262).

In a knowledge move repeated later by Otto Pollak in his well-known theory of "the dark figure of female crime," Krafft-Ebing uses this scarcity of accounts as a datum to conclude that the absence of good data does not mean women are less likely than men to suffer from congenital inversion: it simply means there is a dark figure of female homosexuality:

> I have though long experience gained the impression that inverted sexuality occurs in woman as frequently as in man. But the chaster education of the girl

deprives the sexual instinct of its predominant character [i.e. genital expression]. ... All of these circumstances work in her favour, often serve to correct abnormal inclinations and tastes, and force her into the ways of normal sexual intercourse. We may, however, safely assume that many cases of frigidity or anaphrodisia in married women are rooted in undeveloped or suppressed antipathic sexual instinct.

(Krafft-Ebing 1965, 262–3)

Krafft-Ebing did not argue that one can always separate women who have had erotic relations with other women into two distinct groups, the occasionally perverse and the congenitally inverted or homosexual. He included social and cultural factors in his analysis, showing that the sharp analytical line between perversion and inversion is more analytical than empirical. One of the several stories of gender and sex inversion that he collected (an autobiographical one) contains a passage that describes the relation between inversion and perversion in terms consistent with his theory:

I was born a girl, but a misdirected education forced my fiery imagination early into the wrong direction. ... The reading of French novels and lascivious companions taught me all the tricks of perverse erotics, and the latent impulse became a conscious perversity. Nature has made a mistake in the choice of my sexuality and I must do a life-long penance for it, for the moral power to suffer the unavoidable with dignity is lost.

(Krafft-Ebing 1965, 277)

Described as a highly cultured lady who loved sports and wore masculine clothes, this writer reads her deviance sociologically; but she simultaneously spreads the blame in two other directions: "nature" for having implanted the perverse impulse, and herself, for having lacked the willpower to resist "this abnormal impulse."[5]

While admitting that in any one person's life congenital degeneracy, education, opportunity, and willpower were all intertwined, Krafft-Ebing still maintained a very sharp analytical separation between the born invert and the casual or weak-willed pervert, and to that extent greatly contributed to the formation of the modern homosexual identity (here including the lesbian identity). The extent of his influence is a matter of much debate, with historians of sexuality today being rather skeptical of the empirical accuracy of Foucault's well-known account of the transition from the act-based governance of sex performed by the criminal law and by religious codes to modern knowledges of identity (Foucault 1980); but taking sides in this debate is unnecessary here.

It is very clear that Lombroso had available to him, in Krafft-Ebing's work, a scientific model that carefully organized and explained not only sexual behavior but also inner feelings about identity: but he did not choose to adopt this model. He plunders Krafft-Ebing's text, recycles a few good stories, and, more creatively, he re-formats data found in that book to construct a chart that tabulates all the sexual deviations (including fetishism, sadism, and so forth) attributed to particular women throughout the whole of Krafft-Ebing's volume.

Now, you will recall that Krafft-Ebing had complained about the scarcity of data on women's perversions. He did not present his small collection of stories as quantitatively significant data. Lombroso, however, counts up instances of female sexual perversion in Krafft-Ebing's text – and, forgetting the rather large gap between Krafft-Ebing's second-hand anecdotes and real life, he draws the conclusion that sexual vices are *in fact* rarer among women than among men. He does not mention Krafft-Ebing's thesis about the dark figure of female sexual vice.

This maneuver is just one example of Lombroso's deliberately perverse use of scientific data – a feature of Lombroso's text that many subsequent social scientists have denounced, but which I would here like to consider not as a negative (lack of scientific rigor) but rather as a positive choice, as effecting an epistemology that I have earlier described as "postmodern." Let me justify the "postmodern" label a little more.

Postmodern architecture is characterized by the simultaneous use of motifs and esthetic codes from diverse historical periods, a wilful juxtaposition of classical and modernist elements without syntheses or even transitions. Similarly, we have seen that Lombroso's evident interest in the *content* of the latest psychological science (Krafft-Ebing's concept of the congenital invert, for example) in no way implies a commitment to the scientific method and the scientific habitus. In particular, the born invert – instantiated in the "cases," mainly borrowed from Krafft-Ebing, featuring masculine women with an erotic interest in other women – makes a rather fleeing appearance in Lombroso's text. But most of the space devoted to female-female eroticism in the relevant ten pages or so of the current translation features not modern lesbians or even late nineteenth-century inverts or Urnings but rather two entities of much older provenance. These are "tribade" and "tribadism." A few words about the history of this now forgotten word are necessary before turning to Lombroso's own use of it.

The tribade, in ancient Greek culture, was the woman who challenged the hierarchy thought to be inherent in sex as such by assuming the masculine position in her erotic life. She did not possess anything like a distinct sexual identity; her rebellion was a social and political one, the same as that of a male slave daring to take the active role in sexual encounters. But with the rediscovery of ancient Greek texts in the Renaissance, the word "tribade" became available to describe female-female eroticism, now seen not so much as a challenge to hierarchy as such but rather to gender roles (Laqueur 1990).

"Tribade" and "tribadism" seem to have been used in French sources much more than in English sources, and not just in the French "erotic novels" constantly denounced by English scientists.[6] Whether Lombroso's preference for these terms is due to his reading of French sources or to an autonomous Italian philological development I cannot tell, but the French connection, whether determinative or not, is certainly present.

In the chapter under discussion, German sexology is treated with much respect, but pride of place goes to a wonderful book — never translated into English — produced in the 1830s by the indefatigable public health doctor A.J.B. Parent-Duchatelet, who, after gaining public renown with his rational plan for the sewers of Paris, turned his attention to what he called moral sewage, namely, prostitution. Parent-Duchatelet painstakingly collected information about 5,000 prostitutes, mainly from police, prison officials, philanthropic ladies, and the medical authorities who tested women and gave out licenses. Most of what Lombroso says about prostitutes' penchant for "tribadism" is taken from this massive book. However, Lombroso uses Parent-Duchatelet's data to arrive at the opposite conclusion — as he did with Krafft-Ebing's data on female sexual perversion.

Parent-Duchatelet is a careful scientist of the 1830s, that is, in the natural history mold: thus, one of his key concerns is to compare subspecies of prostitutes. He shows that Paris prostitutes who come from the provinces are demographically distinct from native-born women, and he performs careful calculations that show that the average age at which women enter the trade differs by geography and by social and family condition. But Paris prostitutes being divided mainly into official brothel workers, on the one hand, and "filles libres" or freelancers, on the other, his investigation of female-female eroticism has as its key research question whether "tribadism" is more prevalent in brothels or among freelancers (Parent-Duchatelet 1857, vol. I, 160–2).

Tribades as a group and tribadism as a practice are not sharply differentiated, incidentally; living in a time just before degeneration and well before psychology, for him all illicit sex is a matter of vice, habit, and customs. Vice is visible; vice can be described, and its incidence mapped onto the streets of the city. In the early Victorian paradigm of vicious customs — the paradigm that gave us Henry Mayhew's compendium of London slum characters — eroticism appears not as the truth about the self (Foucault 1980) but rather as but one part of the social-moral life of the underclasses. Asking if a particular relationship is evidence of homosexual behavior or of homosexual identity would not make sense. The discourse of the vices and habits of the urban nomads and exotic slum dwellers deconstructs (or ignores) the binary opposition of act vs. identity that became so crucial in the 1890s.

Parent-Duchatelet states that the vast amount of information he has about brothel life — information based on the constant inspections carried out by his own Bureau of Public Hygiene — suggests tribadism is relatively rare. The only form of tribadism one regularly finds in brothels, he states (giving numerous examples), consists in fictive marriages, often between the madam of a brothel and a younger woman. These relations take place mainly in middle age or old age and are mainly about love and support. Insofar as a sexual activity is concerned, Parent-Duchatelet tells us that sex between women, rare among young brothel workers, is by contrast very common among freelance prostitutes. Why? Because they are the ones that go to prison (since they are liable to prison terms, not for prostitution itself, of course, but for operating without a license). Prisons are the breeding grounds of that historically specific form of eroticism that is tribadism.

Havelock Ellis's work on criminality repeats some of the Parent-Duchatelet findings (significantly using the by then anachronistic word "tribade" in doing so). And yet, Ellis is known to us mainly as the most important sexologist in the English speaking world, and specifically as the English-speaking writer who "provided perhaps the most comprehensive description of female sexual inversion" (Chauncey 1989, 91; see also Bland 1995, 256–7). Even more rigorously than Krafft-Ebing, Ellis turned away from the quasi-anthropological documentation of vicious or criminal behavior in the slums in order to pursue the study of inner sexual identity (mainly among the educated). And unlike Krafft-Ebing, he had an evident sympathy for those individuals he encountered (mainly in his friendship circles, significantly, rather than in asylums or even in private medical practice) who said that they had been born different, born inverts.

Ellis's work on sexual inversion is primarily concerned with "the Oscar Wilde type" and its female equivalent; in it we read about the inner moral struggles of educated men and women who fought with their demons and had their whole sense of self rendered criminal by the law (Ellis and Symonds 1897). To that extent it is an excellent example of modern sexology. But it is absolutely crucial to the effect that this work had on later sexology and later sex radicalism,[7] I argue, that Ellis suddenly states that he will not discuss the information he has about same-sex erotic behavior in prisons. Now, the scientifically careful Ellis would be the last person one would expect to discard a whole field that had in the past produced much data on deviance of every kind, including "tribadism." But that's exactly what he does:

> In prisons and lunatic asylums in Europe, homosexual practices flourish among the women fully as much, it may probably be said, as among the men. There is indeed some reason for supposing that these phenomena are here even more decisively marked than among men. Such manifestations are often very morbid, and doubtless often very vicious: *I have no light to throw upon them* and I do not propose to consider them.
>
> (Ellis and Symonds 1897, 82; emphasis added)

Why does Ellis refuse to even consider a sizeable collection of data which he had himself used in his work on criminals?

In this paragraph we can see a key switch point in the genealogy of European knowledges of deviance. At the time Ellis might not have known just why it felt wrong to include prison perversion tales in his work on inversion. But with the benefit of hindsight we can see that Ellis's exclusionary move foreshadows what would happen in the course of the following two or three decades. From the 1910s and 1920s onward, expert knowledge of prisons – and of working class deviance generally – would take a diverging path, and result in the formation of the criminology of the 1930s and 1940s, the criminology of the Gluecks' *Five Hundred Delinquent Women*. Such works (as Rafter and Gibson point out in the introduction) are curiously out of step with the advances of twentieth-century sexology and psychology.

In the mid-twentieth century, women offenders continued to be examined by a criminological gaze concerned with menstruation (and tattoos, another hobby horse of physical anthropology). But educated masculine women with a taste for lesbianism (the ladies who in Lombroso's text are thrown in, pell-mell, with the prison inmates), disappear from criminological discourse. Correspondingly, scientific and sex-radical knowledges of "born inverts" proceeded as if Vita Sackville-West, Gertrude Stein, and Radclyffe Hall exemplified the lesbian identity as such rather than a particular kind of upper-class lifestyle.

The educated invert who can write her or his own story in eloquent prose, and who, while always afraid of being blackmailed (see McLaren 2002), does not feel like a criminal and is rarely treated as a criminal is nowhere to be found in Ellis's Lombroso-influenced discussion of criminality. Ellis's criminal women include Parent-Duchatelet and Lombroso's tribades, but not the middle- and upper-class proto-lesbians of Ellis's own pioneering work on sexual inversion.

Female-female eroticism among uneducated women in prisons (and among prostitutes) was left for future criminologists to investigate. There seemed to be absolutely nothing in common between possibly perverse women of the lower classes, on the one hand, and the Gertrude Stein-type lesbians who traveled in literary and artistic circles. This largely class-based break in the history of knowleges of female deviance would have long-lasting consequences on both sexology and criminology.

Knowledges of sexuality and the history of criminology

The history of criminology has been written as a more or less self-contained story in which one theory of crime replaces another. This method (which reads into the past the highly specialized division of academic labor that we have today) is firmly rejected in David Garland's important *Punishment and Welfare* (Garland 1985). Garland locates the rise of criminology in is actual context, that is, a time in which eugenic projects to improve "the race," psychological projects to identify and treat mental illness, and political experiments with social welfare and social security, which were not then very distinct from one another, in turn surrounded and shaped the emerging discourses and practices regarding crime and criminals. Eugenics, criminal justice reforms regarding habitual offenders and inebriates, and early social welfare measures are properly seen as branches of a single tree – a tree that I would like to label with the admittedly ambiguous double title, "social defense/social hygiene."

One important branch of the social defense/social hygiene project, and one that is barely mentioned in Garland's ambitious work, is that concerned with the study and management of sexualities and sexual desires. This branch is not made up of "sexology" only. Today's scholarship tends to suggest that contrary to Foucault's presentation of "sexology" as *the* modern discourse on sexuality, sexology was only one and not always the most important element in a knowledge network in which claims about sexual desire and sexual identity (and the often undifferentiated question of gender identity) preoccupied many people and institutions not primarily concerned with sex. This is as true in regard to lesbianism as in regard to homosexuality. Laura Doan's groundbreaking book shows that claims about female-female eroticism were deployed in the England of the First World War to discredit the self-appointed women's police force led by Mary Allen; to attempt to sink a 1920 Criminal Law Amendment Act mainly concerned with child abuse; to further a right-wing campaign against German sympathizers including Mrs Asquith; and to ridicule (straight) women's fashion experiments (Doan 2001). If governing urban order, colonial order, gender relations, and personal character can be done "through" alcohol (Valverde 1998, 2000), so too the importance of sexual discourses as a dimension of contemporary politics lies in the fact that much has been governed "through" sexuality.

I could now end with a ringing call, in the traditional feminist rhetorical style that begins the last paragraph of the article with the phrase, "We must ..."; for example, "criminologists must begin to take the history of sexuality into account." But it is my hope that I do not need to climb on any soapbox. It is my hope that by locating Lombroso's comments on tribades and sapphists in the context of the history of sexual discourses, the paper itself has persuaded you that including the history of sexuality within the purview of criminological research and teaching will not only add to our education but will change the way we understand discourses of crime and deviance.

Notes

1 When I say "women of science" I do not mean only the first generation of women physicians; I include intellectuals like Charlotte Perkins Gilman, Jane Addams, and Beatrice Webb, who were not medical or natural scientists but used scientific paradigms and (in Webb's case especially) scientific research methods. For more on first-wave feminism and scientific knowledges of sexuality and race, see Valverde 1992 and Valverde 2000.
2 The discourses on the contemporary lesbian identity (envisaged as largely psychic and largely unrelated to physiology) that emerged in the late 1920s in England and France and somewhat earlier in Germany rarely mention physiological factors at all, but when they do the interest is more in heredity or internal processes that would later come to be called "hormonal." Measuring the skin's sensitivity to pain or pleasure would not have been seen as relevant to understanding "lesbianism" in this modern sense. [cites – Doan, Faderman, D'Emilio and Freedman ...]
3 The late nineteenth century Larousse *Grande Dictionnaire Universel* defines "tribade" as "femme dont le clitoris a pris un développement exagéré et qui abuse de son sexe," a definition that highlights anatomy, not psychic identity. "Tribadism" is then defined as "habitudes vicieuses des tribades," a definition very much in keeping with Lombroso's ambiguous usage. The modern *OED* does not capture this genealogy at all. Giving sixteenth-century France as the site of the modern (non-Greek) invention of the term, it defines a "tribade" as "a woman who engages in sexual activity with other women; a Lesbian." Two citations are given, the first from Ben Jonson (1601), "Light Venus ... with thy tribade trine, invents new sports," a quote that does not shed much light on the anatomy vs. psychic identity debate, and the second a quote from Havelock Ellis's

work on criminality. In the quoted passage, discussing the prevalence of tattoos among convicts, Ellis states that "such emblems are common among pederasts and tribades." It is impossible to determine whether Ellis chose somewhat obscure Greek words instead of "homosexual" and "lesbian" in order to avoid obscenity charges and/or to exclude readers without a classical education (elsewhere in the same text Ellis gives long racy quotes from Lombroso's collection of prison graffiti in Italian only, explicitly to exclude all but the highly educated readers) or whether he is simply using Lombroso's own antiquated usage because that was the book in front of him as he penned those words.

4 In his chapter "Sexual inversion in women," Havelock Ellis has a very long footnote which begins with Diderot's well-known racy novel *La religieuse*, in which unnatural vices in convents are described so as to fuel anticlericalism, and ends with the fin-de-siecle "degenerate" writings of Swinburne, Guy de Maupassant, Zola, Lamartine, and Verlaine (Ellis and Symonds 1897, 78, n1). This arguably literary tradition is said to have spawned "a large number of novels, which I have not read, and some of which are said to touch the question with considerably less affectation of propriety." As is well known, Ellis's attempt to be scientifically inclusive and mention all representations of female sexual inversion, while still maintaining English propriety by claiming that his reading of French erotic writing was limited to works of "higher rank," failed: Ellis's work (said in the first edition to be co-authored with Ellis's recently deceased friend John Addington Symonds) was prosecuted as obscene and its distribution was halted, despite Ellis's careful precautions (e.g. prior publication in medico-legal journals of most of the chapters in the book).

5 This may have been the story that Radclyffe Hall had in mind when she has the heroine of her famous 1928 lesbian novel *The well of loneliness*, Stephen Gordon (who had been encouraged to dress and act as a boy by a foolish but scientifically learned father) shown as going into her father's library, taking Krafft-Ebing's volume from the shelf, and suddenly (in a flash of lightning, as Lombroso would say) seeing her inner truth, her sexual identity, in black and white. On Hall's use of Krafft-Ebing see Doan 2001.

6 The most thorough study of lesbian life in the mid-twentieth century, based on numerous oral histories and paying close attention to language issues, does not find "tribade" or "tribadism" being used by women themselves or by authorities talking about lesbians. The authors themselves occasionally use "tribadism" as a neutral academic synonym for what their informants called "dyking" (Kennedy and Davis 1993).

7 The impact of Ellis's work on sexual inversion in England itself was somewhat delayed, due to the prosecution of the first edition, but hundreds of self-described inverts of both sexes who read in the newspapers about the prosecution wrote to Ellis (Bland 1995, 262) and may well have sought out the somewhat later US edition.

References

Bland, L. (1995) *Banishing the Beast: English Feminism and Sexual Morality*. London: Penguin.

Chauncey, G. (1989) "From Sexual Inversion to Homosexuality: the Changing Medical Conceptualization of Female Deviance," in K. Peiss and C. Simmons (eds.) *Passion and Power: Sexuality in History*. Philadelphia: Temple.

D'Emilio, J. and Freedman, E. (1988) *Intimate Matters: a History of Sexuality in America*. New York: Harper and Row.

Doan, L. (2001) *Fashioning Sapphism: the Origins of a Modern English Lesbian Culture*. New York: Columbia University Press.

Ellis, H. (1901) *The Criminal*. London: Walter Scott.

Ellis, H. and J. A. Symonds (1897) *Studies in the Psychology of Sex, vol. 1 Sexual Inversion.* Watford: The University Press.
Faderman, L. (1981) *Surpassing the Love of Men.* New York: HarperCollins.
Foucault, M. (1971) *The Order of Things: an Archaeology of the Human Sciences.* New York: Pantheon.
Foucault, M. (1980) *The History of Sexuality, vol. I.* New York: Vintage.
Garland, D. (1985) *Punishment and Welfare.* London: Gower.
Kennedy, E. and Davis, M. (1993) *Boots of Leather, Slippers of Gold: the History of a Lesbian Community.* New York: Routledge.
Krafft-Ebbing, R. von (1965) *Psychopathia Sexualis* [Translated from the 12th German edition]. New York: Stein and Day.
Laqueur, T. (1990) *Making Sex: Body and Gender from the Greeks to Freud.* Cambridge: Harvard University Press.
Latour, B. (1993) *We Have Never Been Modern.* Cambridge: Harvard University Press.
McLaren, A. (2002) *Sexual Blackmail: a Modern History.* Cambridge: Harvard University Press.
Nordau, Max (1895) *Degeneration.* New York: D. Appleton and Company.
Parent-Duchatelet, A. J. B (1857) *De la prostitution a la ville de Paris.* Paris, Bailliere [2nd enlarged edition]. 2 vols.
Pick, D. (1989) *Faces of Degeneration: a European Disorder, 1848–1918.* Cambridge: Cambridge University Press.
Poovey, M. (1998) *The Making of the Modern Fact.* Chicago: University of Chicago.
Rafter, N. H. and Gibson, M. (2004), "Introduction" to Cesare Lombroso, *Criminal Woman.* Chapel Hill, NC: Duke University Press.
Russett, C. (1989) *Sexual Science: the Victorian Construction of Womanhood.* Cambridge: Harvard University Press.
Showalter, E. (1990) *Sexual Anarchy: Gender and Culture at the Fin de Siecle.* New York: Viking.
Valverde, M. (1991) *The Age of Light, Soap and Water: Moral Reform in English Canada 1880s–1920s.* Toronto: McClelland and Stewart.
Valverde, M. (1992) "'When the Mother of the Race is Free': Race, Reproduction and Sexuality in First-wave Feminism" in F. Iacovetta and M. Valverde (eds.) *Gender Conflicts: New Essays in Women's History.* Toronto: University of Toronto Press.
Valverde, M. (1998) *Diseases of the Will: Alcohol and the Dilemmas of Freedom.* Cambridge: Cambridge University Press.
Valverde, M. (2000) "'Racial Poison': Drink, Male Vice and Degeneration in First-wave Feminist Discourse," in I. C. Fletcher, L. E. Mayhall, and P. Levine (eds.) *Women's Suffrage in the British Empire.* London: Routledge.

12
IN SEARCH OF THE LOMBROSIAN TYPE OF DELINQUENT[1]

Daniele Velo Dalbrenta

Lombroso yesterday, today ... and tomorrow

I would like to introduce my reflections with a quotation from *Hitchcock Presents*, a well-known anthology series on thriller movies which was produced a few decades ago: the famous director narrates how a criminologist convinced him about the soundness of Lombroso's Criminal Anthropology. Among other arguments, the criminologist – according to Hitchcock's narration – explained to him how camuse-snub noses, prognathism, sparse facial hair, cranial asymmetry and insensitivity to pain undoubtedly are indicators of criminal attitudes. As they went together to a wrestling match, both Hitchcock and the criminologist noticed – as a proof of the above stated considerations – that the supporters of the 'evil', unfair and 'ready to all' wrestler, had snub noses and prognathous jaws; on the contrary, all those who supported the 'good' one did not have such type of physical characteristics. Hitchcock and his friend were naturally supporting the 'good' wrestler, when suddenly the 'evil' wrestler was thrown outside of the ring, falling right on the director's friend, who was injured. The criminologist, who refused any medical assistance – although his nose was clearly tumid and his jaw had become prognathous – started to support the 'evil' wrestler, yelling rude insults, never caring about his injuries. Just a look at his friend, formerly known to be a rather polite and respectful person, convinced Hitchcock that Lombroso was indeed right: now his friend – snub-nosed and square-jawed – had become as evil as never before (Hitchcock 1970, Introduction).

Through this apologue (that could inspire further reflection), Hitchcock offers quite a savoury exposition of the hardest challenge that rests with those who – today like yesterday – are going to face Lombroso's Criminal Anthropology: taking *seriously* – to say, in its deep meaning – the simple yet disruptive idea that sustains this controversial science, instead of easy dealing with it by labelling it like reverie, mental perversion or such. The underlying idea is – namely – the hypothesis according to which some individuals would be *naturally* inclined to crime, due to a biopsychic anomaly.

Such inclination was originally characterised as *atavism* (re-emersion of elements that belong to previous phases of the evolution process) and later on was redefined in various ways which were all in any case provided with an empirical – in other terms, *scientifically analysable* – characterisation.

Apart from the naivety of the initial atavistic formulation, the above-mentioned hypothesis, considering also its radical character, immediately caused strong reactions, which originated from opposed representations of Criminal Anthropology: on one hand, the symbol of the scientific theorisation of any form of discrimination (according to illness, gender, ethnicity, social class, etc.); on the other hand, the foundation of the research line that will later assume the name of criminology.

This writing assumes, instead, that it is possible to mediate between those two opposite representations within a third one which states the common acknowledgement of the *everlasting (archetypical) character* of Criminal Anthropology: beyond any merely 'negative' or antiquary interest, Criminal Anthropology will at last emerge as something that should not easily be taken for granted and that instead continuously opens to critical reflection.

From here on, also the choice of this writing's focus can be easily explained: facing the proverbial and naively understood type of delinquent to whom Lombroso owes his fame, and in which I think it's possible to detect the fundamental characteristic of Criminal Anthropology, to better underline how rich a *discussion* on this theme can be, although such themes appear rather far away from our times (and maybe also from our good conscience).

Adventures and disadventures of the Lombrosian type of delinquent

Before moving to any other consideration, it is now time to introduce the Lombrosian concept of 'type of delinquent'. We can first notice that – although it has been the target *par excellence* of the polemics against Lombroso's theory[2] – the 'delinquential type' has not been traced by the author from the beginning, nor has it ever reached a proper categorical clarity. Such concept, in fact, suffered from those disharmonies, disconnections and incongruities that affected the whole anthropological-criminal system.

More specifically, the first theoretical draft of an *anthropological typology of delinquent* seems to appear, with all the uncertainties of the case, only in the Preface to the third edition of *Criminal Man* (1884),[3] with the connotations of a rational self-evidence: 'in this edition I dedicated much attention to the set of anomalies that form the so-defined "type" and I tried to make the reader autonomously realise it, with the documents at hand'(Lombroso 1884, XIII, my translation).

This is the 'definition' thereby suggested by Lombroso:

> it seems to me that the type ... should be taken with those mental reservations that are used for averages within statistics; – when it is argued that the average length of life is 32 years, and that the deadliest month is December, no-one means that anyone should die in December of the thirty-second year of life.
> (Ibid.)

Now, as everybody knows, Lombroso was rather 'allergic' to definitions, and he seldom undertook philosophical considerations, though there are of course some exceptions, among which, for instance, the prefaces to *Criminal Man*. Therefore, even if one looked for a proper definition of the criminal type, able to represent a point of leverage of the whole Lombrosian criminal-anthropological reflection, it would be hard to find something more than the previously mentioned sentence. The latter, moreover, represents a re-adaptation (which is familiar with Lombroso's habits) of part of the Preface to the second edition of his work:

> And there are also some too subtle critics who, not fully recognizing on the first rascal that they happen to meet *the characteristics that I attribute to the Criminal Man*, they negatively react and denounce the false. But I must let those people understand that any description of mine, albeit grounded on evidence and facts, should be taken with that reservation that should be used for all average data in sociology.
> (Lombroso 1878, 6, my translation)

In other words, as it can be easily deduced from these linguistic alchemies, the characteristics of the delinquent as they have been 'discovered' pre-exist the type for which Lombroso is famous still today (even at the level of the mere small-talk quotation, used to remark on something sinister or ominous in someone's appearance). The type, in fact, is born as an autonomous concept only when passing from the second (1878) to the third (1884) edition of *Criminal Man* – which, by the way, remained incomplete due to a serious 'accident' connected precisely to an underlying 'indecision' about the configuration of the type itself.

Well, what had happened?

Some difficulties had certainly emerged from empirical research: during the new writing of *Criminal Man* Lombroso found himself bound to seriously rethinking and specifying the *delinquent nature* previously characterised in terms of atavism (and then approximately corrected by using the concepts of *degeneration* and *moral madness*). Such rethinking was performed in light of an *epileptoid background* that he had thought to catch sight of, as a principle in which the various characteristics progressively outlined during his research would find a convergence (whose composition would emerge as a causal explanation of crime interpreted as an interruption in the delinquent's development). So the third edition – whose first volume (dedicated to the born-delinquent and to the moral-mad) had just come out – was left aside, and Lombroso found himself writing all over again.

Apart from this, though, we must also notice that between the second and the third editions a different approach to the human 'material' subjected to Lombroso's research was emerging: *descriptive 'naturalism'* which typically belonged to the first phase of the Lombrosian Criminal Anthropology (and which was expressed in the first two editions of *Criminal Man*), rich in moral implications and, meanwhile, sometimes characterised by caricatural traits, was replaced by an approach informed by *statistic seriality*. The latter perspective will be the lens through which the subsequent editions will be conceived, although further breakthroughs will still be bound to highly characterised individualities (the case of soldier Misdea, for instance, which resulted in to interrupting the third edition) (Turzio *et al.* 2005).

Much could be said in this regard, and more specifically about how this different approach started with an increasingly wider (albeit an initial diffidence) use of as cognitive-explicative support: the difference from the famous drawings by Luigi Frigerio appears thereby remarkable.

This said, it must be acknowledged that, as a matter of fact, a full shift from the first perspective to the second never happened. In fact, the Lombrosian type of delinquent emerges as an *ideal tension* between two poles: on one side, the alleged determinisms made 'evident' by the *concrete individual's peculiarities* (physical and psychical traits like, for example, peculiar forms of ears and nose, absence of pain, passion for tattoos, superstition, etc.) and, on the other side, the *statistic average* of anomalies recorded within a certain population (prisoners, prostitutes, alienated people). A tension which is non-resolved, resulting in being theoretically dispersive anytime Lombroso tried (as he actually claimed to do) to enclose and explain all this within *a single universal law* of delinquency (able to keep together all the past, present and future cases of predisposition to delinquency). It obliged therefore Lombroso to continuously outline exceptions and to permanently redesign the whole system.

The evidence of such problems can be found in the continuous proliferation – after any edition of *Criminal Man* – of specific typologies of delinquents whose common (natural) matrix resulted to be hard, or even impossible, to find. Already in the third edition Lombroso had added the figures of the occasional delinquent, the mad delinquent and the alcohol-addicted delinquent: as I remarked above, it is interesting to notice that right in the edition in which Lombroso tried a unitary conception of the phenomenon of delinquency by mean of criminal-anthropological type, the latter was already dissolving, leaving in its place a plurality of typologies (which resulted in being, indeed, rather autonomously characterised).

An attempt to find a remedy to such an embarrassing situation – which stated the uncertain empirical basis of a self-proclaimed one-and-only 'science' of crime – was tried by the trusty Ferri, who, as a lawyer who paid attention to practical implications, had soon concentrated his efforts in outlining a taxonomy of the typologies of delinquents, some of which were introduced in Lombroso's work under Ferri's influence. They were finally reduced to five: born-, mad-, habitual-, -for passion, occasional-delinquent.

This did not lead Ferri to draw from the Lombrosian concept of 'type' some more defined conclusions: in its never-resolved formulation, in fact, the criminal-anthropological type turns out to be nothing else but 'a set of distinctive characters, a sort of average ..., a synthetic expression ..., a sort of fixed point and common centre around which the differences that have been empirically found are like several deviations towards different directions'; so, as Ferri puts it (finding support in many other authors) 'the type is a set of features, but, related to the group that it characterizes, it is also the set of those traits which appear more evident and more frequently repeated' (Ferri 1891, 185).

This is beyond doubt the recognition that the exclusively rational consideration of the statistical aspect is fundamental to the integration of the single case's analysis: in fact, it depends on something much more blurred and shaded, which, exceeding the phenomenical sphere, borders with intuition, if not with metaphysics. So it happens that, getting closer to the fifth and last edition of *Criminal Man*, Ferri is echoed again by Lombroso (intuitive *par excellence*[4]), to state a sort of self-evidence of the type, which would emerge as 'agglomeration' of anomalies:

> the agglomeration of the anomalies found in criminals – and that every day appears more intense – so that if we made a mistake that was just in being too cautious in calculating it – is the safest and most precise demonstration of the type, which is the effect of this agglomeration: therefore it would not be necessary to refine such concept: but, since it is on the criminal type that the battle goes on, intense like in the first days, ... we will need to insist on it.
> (Lombroso 1893, 94, my translation)

It is useless to say that such 'insistence' – by Lombroso and his followers – will ultimately turn into openly showing further criminal statistics, refining anatomical indexes, reporting new anamneses, collecting more data (etc., etc.). Nevertheless, the need of continuously correcting and diversifying the types according to the researchers' results (and the connected, continuous recombination and reformulation of hypotheses), as well as the recognition of anomalies with reference to the type, still *presuppose* an *underlying ultimate hypothesis able to explain the phenomenon of delinquency*. The incapacity of realising such underlying presupposition will affect the whole development of the research conducted by Lombroso and his followers with an insurmountable difficulty, once the atavistic hypothesis had to be discarded for credibility reasons. Still, as previously remarked, the atavistic hypothesis will remain as a sort of 'logical connection factor' of bio-determinism: therefore, Lombroso kept connecting the type of delinquent to atavism until the very end of his research (Lombroso 1894).

Maybe, then, beyond the nominal allegiance to atavism, the decisive element might be what Lombroso more generally recognises in his writings: an indefatigable work of application to *experience* – accompanied by an adequate level of *rational mediation* – which, as it seems, renounces true and real claims of conceptualisation. On the opposite side, the possibility is not excluded of an *instinctive knowledge* of criminal physiognomy (which Lombroso deems to be more developed among women and, following a typical association of his, among children and savage people).[5]

Although our discourse at this point could become longer and enter more detailed argumentation, the limited purposes of this writing suggest a move towards a conclusion by underlining that the Lombrosian type of delinquent – unlike its many precursors (Gibbons 1965, 27; Clinard and Quinney 1967, 6–7) – seems to be something much more *perplex and profound* than what is (usually) commonly understood.[6] It is an ambiguous *mixtum compositum* of reality, fiction and verisimilitude that makes Criminal Anthropology unique (unlike many and sometimes luckier 'imitations') and in the meanwhile represents at best its timeless appeal.

Verifying the ambiguity of the Lombrosian type of Delinquent in Joseph Conrad's *Secret Agent*

Moving from the comprehension that Lombroso himself had of his own idea of criminal type, the following paragraph aims at verifying the ambiguity of the Lombrosian ideal-type of delinquent, with the purpose of showing how this *semi-concept* – that most of all, though unwillingly, indicates the limits of human reason – results in being meaningful: although it is pretty clear that such semi-concepts cannot – as it has been argued so far – aspire to become a scientific explanation of the phenomenon of delinquency, such semi-concepts help to concentrate the attention on biopsychical-behavioural regularities that emerge from the subjective side of the criminal phenomenon.

In order to avoid emotional biases, I will follow a brief itinerary of 'Law and Literature' which appeared to me rather appropriate in catching the idea of an *insuperable complexity of human nature* from which one cannot exclude the presence, in various forms, of a sort of predisposition to deviance (whatever this may mean).[7]

Although it is not rare to find Lombrosian influences in the literature of those times (some of which were explicitly recalled in authors like Zola, but also Dostoevsky and Tolstoy: Gaaker 2005). I would like to focus on Joseph Conrad's *The Secret Agent*, a work which does not receive much attention in the literature on Criminal Anthropology,[8] but which emerges as a very important reference for the purposes and the perspective of this writing. Written in 1907 – when the parabola of Lombrosian Criminal Anthropology had already come to an end – Conrad's work narrates events that happened around the 1880s, right at the time of Criminal Anthropology's climax.

The story could be seen either as rather simple or full of complex implications, depending on the viewpoint. Conrad tries, in fact, to combine rather 'elevated' themes, belonging to political philosophy and to international politics, with events which took shape in the filthy world of London's anarchist clubs and brought about the dissolution of a family. The shadow of a crime creeps on the narrated events, which are pervaded, though – these are words that the Author himself uses in his introductive note – by the consciousness of 'criminal futility of the whole thing' (Conrad 1907–1994, 8).

Let us get closer to the story's plot.

The context, as anticipated, is *fin-de-siècle* London, that provides the stage for a mysterious attack that shakes the conscience of the population. As Conrad himself explains in the introductive note to the book, the story is inspired by an explosion occurring in Greenwich Park, in which a man lost his life, seemingly on his way to make a demonstrative attack inspired by anarchist purposes (Conrad 1907–1994, 8–9).

The plot develops around the shifty figure of Verloc, a secret agent in the service of tsarist Russia – infiltrated in London's anarchist environments, a dealer by way of camouflage – and of his wife Winnie, who found in him – before love – protection for herself and for her family, made up of her mother and her brother Stevie, who has mental problems.

The quiet of the family, which stands on Winnie's mild devotion to her husband, is troubled and then is definitively compromised when, in the wake of the Greenwich Park explosion, Verloc finds himself forced by the anarchists of 'his' club to organise an attack meant to destabilise public order and to consequently provoke a foreseeable reaction from the police forces. Verloc clumsily pursues this task, but also involves in his mission the guiltless and naive Stevie, Winnie's brother, causing his death.

This fact precipitates events and leads Winnie to murder Verloc, once she learns of her husband's responsibility in causing the death of her beloved brother Stevie.

The epilogue describes Winnie taking flight with the anarchist Ossipon, who initially ignores the facts. Although he had been in love with her for a long time, Ossipon, after discovering the truth, abandons Winnie, who will finally commit suicide by throwing herself into the freezing waters of the English Channel.

The story itself has a Lombrosian nuance, and not only for the obsessive, openly displayed care for the description of physiognomic characteristics and of psycho-social connections (an example of the latter we will briefly provide): other specific Lombrosian themes emerge here, for instance, the figure of the delinquent woman and that of the anarchist criminality which had put a strain on Lombroso's anthropological doctrine, to the point of witnessing the problematic nature of the type.

On the other hand, Conrad quoted Lombroso as criminal anthropologist in some parts of his writing; therefore, it is worth briefly focusing attention on these passages. In a first piece, placed at the beginning of the narration, the scene describes the violent reaction of an anarchist named Yundt to the Lombrosian 'diagnosis' of degeneration extemporaneously given by Ossipon – also known as 'the doctor' – about the poor Stevie (who was indeed animated by the exaggerated altruism that Lombroso found in the anarchists):

> 'Lombroso is an ass'. Comrade Ossipon met the shock of this blasphemy by an awful, vacant stare. And the other, his extinguished eyes without gleams blackening the deep shadows under the great, bony forehead, mumbled, catching the tip of his tongue between his lips at every second word as though he were

chewing it angrily: 'Did you ever see such an idiot? For him the criminal is the prisoner. Simple, is it not? What about those who shut him up there – forced him in there? Exactly. Forced him in there. And what is crime? Does he know that, this imbecile who has made his way in this world of gorged fools by looking at the ears and teeth of a lot of poor, luckless devils? Teeth and ears mark the criminal? Do they? And what about the law that marks him still better – the pretty branding instrument invented by the overfed to protect themselves against the hungry? Red-hot applications on their vile skins – hey? Can't you smell and hear from here the thick hide of the people burn and sizzle? That's how criminals are made for your Lombrosos to write their silly stuff about.'

(Conrad 1907–1994, 47)

Here we have, in Conrad's fictional construction, the most radical criticism that could be ever expressed towards Lombroso (and that not many of his adversaries were able to express with equal intensity): to say, not starting – besides what had been assumed – from a self-evident notion of type of delinquent, since this does not exist *in rerum natura*.

In short, Lombroso had not understood that his criminal type had been precisely 'constructed' – and it could not be otherwise – on the base of a series of assumptions that had nothing scientific: in such assumptions, instead, the endoxal or even the accidental dimensions played a fundamental role (e.g. the validity of some legal norms, being subjected to legal action and to criminal process, being judged guilty, being sent to jail, and, more generally, all that was intimately connected to the political and socio-cultural context).

In expressing such criticism, though, Conrad adds, as if it was undividable from it, a shocking element of obscurity connected to the person that said those words – namely the anarchist Yundt – who was a few lines above described (though not with genuinely Lombrosian characteristics) as *intimately* evil (Jacobs 1968):

On the other side of the fireplace, in the horse-hair armchair where Mrs Verloc's mother was generally privileged to sit, Karl Yundt giggled grimly, with a faint black grimace of a toothless mouth. The terrorist, as he called himself, was old and bald, with a narrow, snow-white wisp of a goatee hanging limply from his chin. An extraordinary expression of underhand malevolence survived in his extinguished eyes. When he rose painfully the thrusting forward of a skinny groping hand deformed by gouty swellings suggested the effort of a moribund murderer summoning all his remaining strength for a last stab.

(Conrad 1907–1994, 43)

In another, equally meaningful piece, we find again the anarchist Ossipon, a genuine admirer of Lombroso's, who, after figuring out the murder committed by the one who he had been madly in love with, finally understands that – thanks to Criminal Anthropology – Winnie,

> the sister of the degenerate [Stevie] – [was] a degenerate herself of a murdering type ... or else of the lying type. Comrade Ossipon might have been said to be terrified scientifically in addition to all other kinds of fear.
>
> (Conrad 1907–1994, 233–4)

Ossipon had, as we read a few lines before:

> gazed at it as no lover ever gazed at his mistress's face. ... He gazed at her, and invoked Lombroso, as an Italian peasant recommends himself to his favourite saint. He gazed scientifically. He gazed at her cheeks, at her nose, at her eyes, at her ears ...
>
> (Conrad 1907–1994, 238–9)

Strangely enough, Ossipon himself – free from the fetters of traditional morality yet respectful of the laws of science – is typically characterised by a delinquential appearance, at least according to the original 'version' of the type of delinquent: slant-eyed, with a fuzz, negroid traits, camuse nose, protruding lips, prominent cheek-bone (Conrad 1907–1994, 44–5). We could object that his 'colours' do not belong to the type (he is described as blond, with a red and freckled face), but, as we could easily foresee, this sequence of references could endlessly go on ...

Through these continuous contrasts and overturning of perspective, an effect of estrangement spreads around from the pages of *The Secret Agent*: Conrad thus communicates, maybe better than anyone else, the sense of vertigo that comes from dealing with a *discourse on the limit* of the comprehensibility of life itself, or, in other terms, with a *discourse on life's mystery*.

This could even imply, considering that little or nothing we can know about the essence of things, the 'reliability' of the criminal-anthropological doctrine – though, as we know, such reliability could never be demonstrated in scientific terms and modes ...

A non-conclusion

At the end of this brief re-reading of the Lombrosian ideal type of delinquent, I hope I have been able, as I wished, to show glimpses of the non-obviousness of Criminal Anthropology.

I most especially hope that this itinerary succeeded in underlining that the type of delinquent – emblematic vessel of Criminal Anthropology – represents a real, complex and stimulating philosophical-penal problem (and, in any case, something very different from what is usually intended when, in more or less facetious words, someone mentions a 'lombrosian type' referred to someone else who has a 'primitive' appearance). This should help avoiding the continuous and often fully unconscious return of the negative aspects of Lombroso's doctrine.

That said, I still keep the uneasy sensation that I managed to transmit just a part of the deepness of this 'superficial' author. I guess I should have adequately remarked that Lombroso always pursued the 'substantisation' of his ideal type of delinquent through concepts – like, mostly, atavism, degeneration, moral madness and epilepsy – which were closely influenced by the cultural *milieu* in which Lombroso's work had been nurtured. Yet, the research on these concepts was driven by an obsession that was absolutely non-scientific.[9] This could have given me the opportunity of underlining the uneasy, restless nature of Criminal Anthropology. Such discipline – which claimed to be a 'science' – was in fact tormented by the impossibility of answering in a scientific way the 'metaphysical' questions that it had the strength and courage to state, with a clarity that can be rarely found in the time of the 'twilight' of metaphysics. But this was not the main focus of this writing which I am going to conclude:[10] on the contrary, here I tried to face the Lombrosian challenge of testing the soundness of the ultimate hypothesis on which the whole building of Criminal Anthropology is grounded – the possibility of scientifically characterising the delinquent by mean of signs resumed in an ideal-type. A hypothesis, the latter, which unites genius and madness (just to recall another theme that Lombroso was fond of[11]) and results in being overarching, unsustainable by men, mostly by scientists. Yet, as Borges puts it (Borges 1956–1995, 120),[12] hypotheses – unlike the 'naked' reality – cannot exempt themselves from the obligation to be interesting ...

Notes

1 This writing represents a partial translation of the text that I had presented at the International Conference *The Criminal Anthropology of Cesare Lombroso: From Nineteenth Century to Contemporary Criminal- Philosophical Debate* (Verona, 16–17 October 2009).
2 See, among others, Falcone 1891, where it is clear the intention of criticising the 'heart' of Lombroso's Criminal Anthropology by hitting the type.
3 This does not mean, of course, that the evolution of the anthropological-criminological type should be researched only and merely in the evolution of *Criminal Man* as a book: on the contrary, the latter emerges as a remarkable indicator of a broader and much more complex process. See also Villa 1985.
4 As it's commonly recognised: see, e.g. Lombroso Ferrero 1921; 433 ss., Rühl 1910, 14; Zerboglio 1925, 16 and ff.
5 This idea appears in *Criminal Man* since its third edition: Lombroso 1884, 288. See also the final edition: Lombroso 1896–7, I, 310 and ff.
6 It must not surprise, therefore, that the most complete study to date available about the Lombrosian type of delinquent was aimed at demonstrating a substantial lack of understanding of the Criminal Anthropology among both its sustainers and detractors. See Landecho 2004–6.
7 It is interesting to notice that the Italian penal positivism left a large heritage of writings which someway anticipate perspectives and sensitivities which now typically belong to a 'Law and Literature' approach. See, on this point, my recent writing: Velo Dalbrenta 2010.
8 See however Pick 1989, 109–110.
9 It is, by the way, well known that, in his last years, Lombroso had undertaken various researches on spiritualistic phenomena (Lombroso 1909).

10 See, for further considerations on the paradoxical Lombrosian metaphysics, Velo Dalbrenta 2004.
11 Genius and madness: according to some biographies such a theme plays a central role in Lombroso's interests (even more than criminal-anthropological arguments): see, for example, Toffoletto 1944.
12 The novel I am quoting is *Death and the Compass*.

References

Borges, J. L. (1956) *Ficciones*. Buenos Aires: Emecé Editores. (See, for the Italian translation, Borges, J. L. (1995) *Finzioni*. Torino: Einaudi.)

Clinard, M. B. and Quinney, R. (1967) *Criminal Behavior Systems. A Typology*. New York: Holt.

Conrad, J. (1907) *The Secret Agent. A Simple Tale*. London: Methuen & Co. (See, for a new English edition, Conrad, J. (1994) *The Secret Agent. A Simple Tale*. London: Penguin Books.)

Falcone, G. (1891) *Esame critico del tipo criminale*. Palermo: Tip. Del Giornale di Sicilia.

Ferri, E. (1891) 'Il tipo criminale e la natura della delinquenza', *Archivio di psichiatria, scienze penali ed antropologia criminale per servire allo studio dell'uomo alienato e delinquente* 12: 185–215.

Gaaker, J. (2005) 'The art to find the mind's construction in the face'. Lombroso's Criminal Anthropology and Literature: the Example of Zola, Dostoevsky and Tolstoy, *Cardozo Law Review*, 26(6): 2345–77.

Gibbons, D. C. (1965) *Changing the Lawbreaker*. Englewood Cliffs, NJ: Prentice-Hall.

Hitchcock, A. (1970) *Murders on the Half-Skull*. New York: HSD.

Jacobs, R. G. (1968) 'Comrade Ossipon's Favorite Saint: Lombroso and Conrad,' *Nineteenth-Century Fiction* 23: 74–84.

Landecho, C. M. (2004–2006) *La tipificación lombrosiana de delincuentes I-II*. Madrid: UNED.

Lombroso, C. (1878) *L'Uomo delinquente in rapporto all'antropologia, alla giurisprudenza e alle discipline carcerarie*, 2nd edn. Torino: Bocca.

Lombroso, C. (1884) *L'Uomo delinquente in rapporto all'antropologia, giurisprudenza ed alle discipline carcerarie. Delinquente-nato e pazzo morale*, 3rd edn. Torino: Bocca.

Lombroso, C. (1893) *Le più recenti scoperte ed applicazioni della psichiatria ed antropologia criminale*. Torino: Bocca.

Lombroso, C. (1894) 'Il tipo criminale nei rei selvaggi', *Archivio di psichiatria, scienze penali ed antropologia criminale per servire allo studio dell'uomo alienato e delinquente* 15: 571.

Lombroso, C. (1896–1897) *L'Uomo delinquente in rapporto all'antropologia, alla giurisprudenza ed alle discipline carcerarie*, 5th edn, I-III. Torino: Bocca.

Lombroso, C. (1909) *Ricerche sui fenomeni ipnotici e spiritici*. Torino: UTET.

Lombroso Ferrero, G. (1921) *Cesare Lombroso. Storia della vita e delle opere*, 2nd edn. Bologna: Nicola Zanichelli.

Pick, S. (1989) *Faces of Degeneration: A European disorder, c.1848–c.1918*. Cambridge University Press.

Rühl, K. (1910) *Cesare Lombroso*. Halle a. S: Carl Marhold.

Toffoletto, E. (1944) *Lombroso*. Brescia: La Scuola.

Turzio, S., Villa, R. and Violi, A. (eds.) (2005) 'Lombroso e la fotografia', *Locus Solus* 2.

Velo Dalbrenta, D. (2004) *La scienza inquieta. Saggio sull'Antropologia criminale di Cesare Lombroso*. Padova: CEDAM.

Velo Dalbrenta, D. (2010) 'La finzione più vera. Studi sugli archetipi letterari della devianza nel pensiero penalpositivistico italiano', in P. Mittica (ed.) *Diritto e letteratura. Prospettive di ricerca*. Roma: Aracne, pp. 321–39.

Villa, R. (1985) 'La tipologia lombrosiana e la classificazione dei delinquenti', in Umberto Levra (ed.) *La scienza e la colpa. Crimini, criminali, criminologi: un volto dell'Ottocento*. Milano: Electa, pp. 283–7.

Zerboglio, A. (1925) *Cesare Lombroso*, 2nd edn. Roma: A. F. Formíggini.

13

LOMBROSO AND THE SCIENCE OF LITERATURE AND OPERA

Jonathan R. Hiller

The porous barrier between science and literature in Lombroso's Italy

To say that Cesare Lombroso was interested in studying works of literature and music in addition to his anthropological-criminological pursuits is to make a distinction between these two fields of inquiry that Lombroso himself would have scarcely recognized. The worlds of science and works of art, real-life delinquents and fictitious characters, primitive "palimpsests" scrawled by prisoners and canonical works of European literature are inextricably intertwined in the very fiber of Lombroso's works. When Lombroso's ponderous tables and graphs failed to make a point as emphatically as he would have liked, a mélange of literary examples always served to achieve the desired rhetorical effect. For instance, in his 1893 *La donna delinquente, la prostituta e la donna normale*, Lombroso cites passages from the works of Flaubert, Schopenhauer, Zola, Molière, and Stendhal to bolster his conclusion that women are inveterate liars. Never mind if a passage might have been intended ironically or if the words were the narrator's or a character's – if it appeared in an important cultural work, it counted as evidence. As Nancy Harrowitz has rightly observed of this technique, "There is no distinction made between quotations from literary creations of these authors and direct statements from the authors themselves. Lombroso's use of such cultural expressions to make a 'scientific' point is the most unscientific part of his method" (Harrowitz 1994, 32). While distinguishing between "scientific" and "unscientific" in Lombroso is generally futile, the preponderance (and what is more indiscriminate use) of cultural works in Lombroso's anthropological texts is doubtless a primary feature to be found therein.

On the other hand, as Lombroso argued in 1899, the producers of culture themselves were no less impervious to the clarion call of scientific discoveries than Lombroso and his school were to works of culture. The marriage of the scientific and the literary, according to Lombroso, was the defining feature of late nineteenth-century European poetics. Writing in one of Italy's leading journals, *Nuova antologia*, Lombroso argued that works exploring the delinquency and insanity catalogued so painstakingly in his scientific works had exploded in contemporary literature. Leafing through the pages of Europe's finest contemporary authors, Lombroso sees overwhelming evidence that the literary world has taken notice of his scientific discoveries. Lombroso remarks,

> We have reached a point where one can be certain, turning to one of Ibsen's latest masterpieces, of seeing, at least three or four madmen and rogues (if not the entire cast), each of whom has such specific characteristics that they seem virtually sculpted by an alienist or a criminal anthropologist.
> (Lombroso 1899, 665)[1]

Dostoyevsky, Lombroso likewise observes with pride, "paints with those characteristics which I attempted to define, statistics in hand, in my works" (667).

In this chapter, I shall highlight the salient aspects of Lombroso's extensive relationship to literature and opera. Lombroso's was an era where the boundaries between scientific and cultural works were particularly permeable, and as such the exchanges between criminal anthropology and men of letters was anything but unidirectional. Beginning with an explanation of why it was that late nineteenth- and early twentieth-century Italy proved such a receptive intellectual environment for such interdisciplinary exchanges,[2] I shall proceed to outline the two sides of this bilateral borrowing; first, the principal aspects of Lombroso's engagement with literature, and then those of the literary community's assimilation of positivist criminological ideas. I shall conclude with an analysis of Lombroso's relationship to opera. In all, Lombroso's hegemonic position among Italian intellectuals at the close of the nineteenth century led his writings to exert a totalizing vision of Italian society which could not help but express itself in the pages of the Italian novels and scores created during his ascendancy.

Criminal anthropology's unique appeal to the makers of culture in Italy and beyond

"Positivism," writes Alan Mallach, a scholar of Liberal Italy, "was a doctrine made to order for a body of people who, having overthrown the old order, were determined to build a new society on its ruins" (Mallach 2007, 10). Following this architectural metaphor, Lombroso was the planner whose blueprints would shape the way in which this new society was conceived. As is well known, Italy, politically united by a serious of serendipitous events between 1859 and 1861, faced the fundamental challenge of building national identity almost from the ground up, oftentimes, in the words of one historian of the period, despite "an indifferent or even hostile populace" (Seymour 2006, 96). Cobbling together a cohesive national state out of a patchwork of seven variegated kingdoms and provinces proved a primary concern among the new Italy's ruling class. Due to its precarious finances, its initial reliance upon foreign powers' good graces, and perhaps most of all its less-than-stellar military performance during the 1860s (in particular the ignominious defeats to Austria at Custoza and Lissa in 1866), the early years of Italian statehood are characterized by what Suzanne Stewart-Steinberg has called "a language that posited marginalization and powerlessness as fundamental aspects of what it meant to be modern Italians" (Stewart-Steinberg 2007, 3).

Crucial to this conception were the writings of the Neapolitan politician and academic Francesco De Sanctis, whose masterpiece, the 1870–1 *History of Italian Literature*, attempted to retroactively construct an Italian literature back to the Middle Ages (no mean feat since Italy, of course, did not exist as such in previous epochs) as a way of educating patriotic young citizens. The work is part of De Sanctis's larger program, which embraced the values of diligence, temperance, and self-denial for the good of the fatherland – again, to borrow Stewart-Steinberg's turn of phrase, a "project of creating the great nation-school through the act of self-limitation" (58). Limping into the 1870s with the somewhat anti-climactic capture of Rome, the Italian élites seemed unable to provide a more convincing notion of what it meant to be Italian than this essentially negative conception. Using metaphors likening Italy to a sick patient, politicians bemoaned Italy's inferiority and the apparent lack of a remedy for it. Parliamentary lethargy eventually led to the 1876 ouster of the Historic Right, when the nation looked to the Left to breathe new life into what many worried was a stillborn state. Thus, the 1870s were a propitious moment for a new man with fresh ideas to emerge. Lombroso proved the transitional figure, a medical doctor (in the literal sense) whose theories could provide a remedy for Italy's (figurative) ailments. A large part of this remedy involved a re-envisioning of the connection between Italian literature and Italian society.

Lombroso, whose early works were written for a relatively restricted and primarily scientific audience, broke through in the politically momentous year of 1876 with *The Criminal Man*, a bestseller which was expanded to several times its original size by its fifth edition, released twenty years later. Its key concepts of the "born criminal" and of physiognomic diagnosis of this type soon spread to the whole of the peninsula and beyond; translations soon appeared in the major European languages and Lombroso became an international celebrity with a following of respected scientists across the disciplines. As Mary Gibson has observed, Lombroso kept his place as an intellectual to be reckoned with through endless self-promotion in popular journals: "Tireless in his mission to popularize his ideas," Gibson writes, "Lombroso published over a thousand articles during his life in at least seventy journals, many of them, like *Nuova antologia*, aimed at the general educated public" (Gibson 1998, 99). Literature constituted one of the most fertile common grounds Lombroso could rely on when presenting his ideas to the non-scientific community. Allusions to literature are therefore in no way secondary in accounting for Lombroso's success; his facility with Boccaccio, Shakespeare, or Daudet was in the end extremely helpful if not vital in reaching the minuscule reading public, far more effective than adopting an unalloyed scientific idiom.

It is beyond doubt that Lombroso and his followers were particularly successful in infiltrating the literary sector. As Gibson and Nicole Hahn Rafter note, the positivist scientists' sphere of influence gradually began to encompass the literary world: "Enthusiasm for positivism swept Italy in the last half of the nineteenth century, spreading from the sciences to social theory and even to humanistic research in history and literature" (Lombroso 2004, 17). The school's general tendency to publish wherever possible was particularly evident in the pages of literary journals. Lombroso, notes Andrea Rondini, author of the 2001 *Cose da pazzi: Cesare Lombroso e la letteratura*, was himself particularly adept at presenting his scientific findings in literary magazines, where he sought to become a "popularizer of his own theories" (Rondini 2001, 12). How and to what end Lombroso and his followers blended the scientific and literary in their criminological texts will occupy the next section.

Literature as scientific evidence: universal delinquency and timeless genius

Literature, broadly speaking, has two functions in the scientific treatises of criminal anthropology, each linked to a major Lombrosian theory. The first is the use of literary texts (generally through the use of illustrative "sound bites") as proof or reinforcement for the existence of analogous types of criminal behavior. These literary citations are taken as vessels of valid scientific insight. To give an example, Lombroso, in *The Criminal Man*, claims that educating people will not necessarily lower the probability of their committing criminal acts. Instead, he argues that the "born criminal" will simply commit different types of crimes depending on the means provided by his education. Educating prisoners, Lombroso argues, may thus have no effect other than to contribute to increased society among men who will then band together to commit crimes. Consequently, Lombroso writes, "I dare say that, in part, prison schools contribute to the growth of criminality ... observed in many administrative regions" (Lombroso 1878, 191). Having scored this point, he calls in Canto XXXI of Dante's *Inferno* as corroborating evidence:

> Here I will take courage from Dante's opinion: "Che dove l'argomento della mente/S'aggiunge al mal voler ed alla possa,/Nessun riparo vi può far la gente [for where the mind's acutest reasoning/is joined to evil will and evil power,/there human beings can't defend themselves[3]]."
>
> (Lombroso 1878, 191)

In *The Criminal Woman*, Lombroso wishes to make the point that a woman's maternal instincts are stronger than her affection toward her husband. To prove this, he rattles off five literary examples of how easily widows remarry, including Shakespeare, who, "in *Richard III*, describes the facility with which a widow, after scorning and hating him, marries the murderer of her beloved husband" (Lombroso 1903, 125).

By using such literary examples, Lombroso has "translated" scientific points about delinquency into terms which any educated person would have been expected to understand. Beyond this, Lombroso's methodology has achieved another significant aim. If centuries-old words of wisdom substantiate Lombroso's findings, then it stands to reason that the theories Lombroso and his followers are proposing are universally true. If it was true that in Dante's time, education did not bring with it the benefit of curbing criminal behavior and that the Shakespearean widow Anne jumps into Richard III's arms, the underlying points these examples represent have always been valid. Thus, Lombroso's theories take on an air of authority underscoring that his scientific findings, despite their revolutionary new way of observing the world, have a continuity with the great authors of the past. All that was needed to make these collective truths ironclad science was Lombroso.

The second major usage of literature in criminal anthropological texts is similar to the first, but has significant differences owing to its application to a different theoretical problem. Lombroso's twin fascination alongside criminality was his lifelong investigation into the linkage between genius and madness, an evolutionary condition which he viewed as related to if categorically distinct from criminality. Whereas criminals commit crimes because of their biological anomalies, biological anomalies instead *permit* men (and, far more rarely, women) of genius to achieve greatness. However, these anomalies, Lombroso cautions, must necessarily be compensated for in physical and mental deficiencies, these in proportion to the magnitude of a genius's gift. In making the case for this reading of genius, Lombroso and his followers used subjects who were both widely regarded as geniuses while at the same time thought of as being flawed: the giants of world literature (and, as I shall discuss later, music). Again, Lombroso is banking on the fact that such artists' notoriety would help a general readership to make sense of his science. Everyone knew, for instance, that the Renaissance poet Torquato Tasso spent much of the latter stages of his life in forced seclusion due to repeated violent outbursts. In more recent times, Lord Byron's erratic, scandalous behavior had shocked all upstanding Europe. Thus, to use such men as test subjects was a way of using commonplace references to ground convincing arguments about the nature of a (presumably) complex subject such as genius. Any biographical particulars (and, as in so many other cases, Lombroso and his colleagues were none too picky about the reliability of such information) were fair game in diagnosing degeneracy in its myriad forms. The majority of subjects chosen in such studies were deceased, which conveniently meant that no direct rebuttals would be forthcoming. In criminal anthropological studies of geniuses, literary citations did not serve to reinforce conclusions drawn from data; rather, they *were* the data. What better way to prove that a given author was a degenerate than to demonstrate that degeneracy in the output of the author's diseased mind? Rondini has eloquently summarized this methodology, writing:

> Literary works are considered as documents exhibiting and confirming a pathology already fully present and operating at the corporeal and mental state. An artwork possesses no autonomy of meaning, no added aesthetic value. It

is devoid of any polysemy; it is a pathway toward the physical person of the author.

(Rondini 2001, 53)

As in criminological arguments, the effect on Lombroso's audience was to make criminal anthropology's writings on genius part of a continuum of progress, the ultimate scientific proof of concepts which everyone intuitively credited. The positivist scientists thus achieved a key objective of their larger program through these investigations into the lives and works of great authors.

The seesaw of genius and degeneracy: the smear campaign against Giacomo Leopardi

By the end of the nineteenth century, Lombroso and his disciples had turned their analyses of geniuses' pathological conditions into a kind of cottage industry. Publishing monograph after monograph, the positivists, for a time, succeeded in infiltrating superseding traditional literary criticism. As Rondini remarks,

> The great impact of Lombroso's ideas on the culture of the late nineteenth century has among its corollaries the birth of a school formed by scholars who apply the theories of the master to literary works, taking up his principles and approach.
>
> (Rondini 2001, 66)

Several traditional critics, sensing the direction the wind was blowing, began to incorporate scientific findings into their works, including august figures the likes of Arturo Graf (1848–1913), a student of De Sanctis and a respected man of letters. Meanwhile, the criminal anthropologists heaped scorn on those critics who followed a traditional approach. One of Lombroso's trusted associates, Giuseppe Sergi (1841–1936), had the following choice words for such critics:

> we find ourselves in front of ignorant plebs who curse science and who would stone us if they could. I am told that these critics make such a din because they dislike scientists who occupy themselves with art and literature. Scoundrels! They should thank, indeed venerate us. Here Goethe's phrase comes to mind, that men despise that which they don't understand.
>
> (Sergi 1899, 29)

To get a sense of the breadth of the studies of the literary arm of Lombroso's school, one need only look at works published between 1896 and 1898, which include Enrico Ferri's *Delinquents in Art* (1896), Luigi Roncoroni's *Genius and Madness in Torquato Tasso* (1896), Giuseppe Ziino's *Shakespeare and Modern Science* (1897), Paolo Bellezza's *Genius and Insanity of Alessandro Manzoni* (1898), Alfredo Niceforo's *Criminals and Degenerates in Dante's* Inferno (1898), and Giuseppe Antonini and Luigi Cognetti De Martiis's *Vittorio Alfieri: Psychopathological Studies* (1898).[4]

What, then, was the larger aim of this new offshoot of Lombrosian theory? Certainly, to discredit the old guard, steeped in the (primarily Hegelian) philosophy of the day, which to criminal anthropologists was so much metaphysical claptrap. Beyond this, the types of authors the scientists targeted most frequently reveals something more about what they hoped to accomplish. Disproportionately represented among the studies are the authors and texts of Romanticism and post-Romanticism. The sixth edition of Lombroso's urtext *The Man of Genius*, for instance, includes substantial analyses of the following authors: Alfieri, Balzac, Beethoven, Baudelaire, Burns, Byron, Foscolo, Heine, Hoffmann, Hugo, Keats, Leopardi, Manzoni, and Wagner (Lombroso 1894b, 720–3). This targeting of the Romantics is no coincidence. The criminal anthropologists, after all, thought of themselves as the heirs of the Enlightenment who generally believed in the scientific method's ability to explain all natural phenomena (and to explain all phenomena, including literature, as natural). Romanticism's focus on the sentimental, the intangible, and the mystical seems to have struck Lombroso's school as a step backward on the path of progress. Conversely, De Sanctis's newly minted concept of Italian literature is remarkable for embracing the Italian Romantics, in particular Foscolo and Leopardi.

In particular, Leopardi (1798–1837) was, from the point of view of a positivist criminologist, an ideal laboratory subject. Famous for his idiosyncratic habits, his anguished family and sentimental life, and his physical deformities (including a hunchback), Leopardi's biographical data were compellingly pathological. In the 1870s and 1880s, many of his diaries and letters were published, providing a plethora of sources from which new "discoveries" could be brought to light. Leopardi was profoundly pessimistic about the prospects for a united Italy, which, from the perspective of a scientist writing after thirty years of unification, seemed as good an indicator as any of mental illness. The fact that he had been dead for decades made him rather unlikely to protest any aspersions cast on his legacy. Most importantly, Leopardi's poetry, much of it profoundly autobiographical, was intensely gloomy. That De Sanctis's had singled Leopardi out as one of the greats in his *Study on G. Leopardi*, published after De Sanctis's own death in 1885, would only make matters worse for the poet. And so Lombroso's school set out to knock the poet off his lofty pedestal with gusto.

Between 1896 and 1899, criminal anthropology produced four significant analyses of Leopardi. These works highlight the techniques and strategies employed by Lombroso's school to quickly, effectively, and lastingly damage a perceived enemy's reputation within the Italian intellectual community. In the first, M. L. Patrizi's 1896 *Psycho-Anthropological Essay on Giacomo Leopardi and His Family*, the author establishes the parameters by which Leopardi would be judged scientifically. His point of departure is that Leopardi's family is full of lunatics and criminals, getting the poet off to a bad evolutionary start. Patrizi paints Leopardi's father as an irascible tyrant and his mother is a woman defined by a lack of maternal instincts, indications of psycho-moral deficiencies (Patrizi 1896, 50, 64). Leopardi's genetic disadvantage manifests itself in a case of rickets, giving him the hunchbacked appearance for which he became well known (95). For poor Leopardi, rickets is just the beginning of a laundry list of physiological disorders. Patrizi cites low appetite (95), sensitivity to physical contact, amblyopia (i.e. dimness of vision due to tissue deterioration) along with impaired hearing (97), and finally fatigue (105) as symptoms of "cerebro-spinal neurasthenia," (111), i.e. nervous system exhaustion. This neurasthenia in turn determines Leopardi's poetics.

For Patrizi, Leopardi's poetry is the ineluctable result of his genetic, physical, and mental deficiencies, what the scientist terms a "specific product of his bio-psychology" (132). To prove this, he discusses Leopardi's works themselves in a manner laughably amateurish to a modern reader, but devastatingly convincing in its day. To give one example, Patrizi claims that Leopardi's "overblown self-esteem" can be proven through a reading of the poem "The Approach of Death." Five rather nondescript lines of "The Approach of Death," Patrizi seems to think, serve to close the case (169).

In *Genius and Degeneration* (1897), Lombroso himself chimes in, endorsing and condensing Patrizi's arguments, making them more palatable for the general reader. Finding Patrizi's diagnosis adequate, Lombroso is interested in plumbing the depths of Leopardi's psychosis. Repeating little more than hearsay, Lombroso paints the portrait of a truly bizarre subject. He dwells on the poet's obsessive fear of illness and hypersensitivity to light (Lombroso 1897, 61), and then moves on to anecdotes, at which point things get downright zany. Lombroso writes that

> An eccentricity of Leopardi, one which made quite an impression on his friends, was that during the winters in Bologna, he would curl up in a bag of feathers for hours on end, coming out covered in down, such that he seemed a wild man to those who saw him.
> (Lombroso 1897, 62)

Lombroso cites evidence that when his avian fancies passed, Leopardi was prone to bashing his head against walls and falling to the ground, convulsing (64). Another "well-known" (yet uncited) fact, according to Lombroso, was "how he had become hunchbacked by overindulging in masturbation from a tender age" (67).

Paolo Bellezza's "On the Superlative in Leopardi," which appeared in the *Giornale storico della letteratura italiana* in 1899, constitutes a significant escalation of the positivists' campaign against Leopardi. A professor of literature by trade, Bellezza was in fact one of the most diligent literary critics associated with Lombroso's school. Whereas Patrizi and Lombroso at least rhetorically cast themselves as outsiders to literary criticism proper, Bellezza's analysis of Leopardi is that of an insider. Bellezza, as a respected literary scholar publishing in a literary journal, added an authority that neither Patrizi nor Lombroso could claim. This paved the way for subsequent critics of Leopardi to blend scientific pathology and conventional literary analysis. Though Bellezza's literary argument is a feeble one, in essence that Leopardi's overuse of superlatives demonstrates that his poetry produces a kind of hyper-reality (Bellezza 1899, 102–3), his article is another step on the way to making the Lombrosians' vision of Leopardi increasingly hegemonic.

Bellezza's final remarks in his essay call for his fellow literary critics to write works that reflect the scientific truths about Leopardi that have been proven beyond a doubt. "Let the new work come in which this true Leopardi might find new life!" cries Bellezza (105). Using a metaphor in which a shrouded figure of Leopardi is held up to the light, Bellezza envisions a new study. "How much greater would he be before us," Bellezza muses, "if we saw him in his entirety and only in his truest light!" (105). The last major work of positivist criticism on Leopardi, taking Bellezza's lead, attempts to carry out this project, adopting the same metaphor in its title.

Giuseppe Sergi's *Leopardi in the Light of Science* (1899) is the culmination of the positivists' efforts, a work which combines scientific and literary sensibilities, directly engages literary critics (including De Sanctis), and provides a compelling, totalizing vision of Leopardi's neurosis and its effect on his poetry. A major novelty of Sergi's study is his choice to open a polemic with literary critics directly. His primary target is naturally De Sanctis (already dead fifteen years at the time of writing), whom Sergi lambasts for his hopelessly unscientific reading of Leopardi. The *Study on G. Leopardi*, Sergi argues, is an uninformed, fanciful, even idiotic work. The main point that Sergi takes issue with in De Sanctis's work is the claim that Leopardi had a keen perception of nature. The psychologist-cum-philosopher spares no expense in proving De Sanctis wrong, dedicating eight pages to demolishing his adversary's analysis, claiming that De Sanctis deliberately ennobles Leopardi (Sergi 1899, 6–13). Sergi perorates this condescending (but rather insubstantial) argument by calling De Sanctis's entire argument simply "inconceivable" (13). From there, Sergi embarks upon a lengthy analysis of over a dozen of Leopardi's poems, finding, to no one's surprise, that pathology trumps prosody. Hampered by "an extremely poor chromatic sensibility," Leopardi can only represent a dim, depressing shadow-world (55).

Having definitively trounced De Sanctis and proved Leopardi's poetry to be color-blind, all that remained for Sergi to do was nominate a different champion of Italian poetry. He chose Giosuè Carducci (1835–1907), who, ironically, was a champion of Leopardi's works and the first editor of Leopardi's collected philosophical writings, the *Zibaldone*, which appeared in 1898. Carducci already enjoyed widespread acclaim as the prophet of the new Italy, and his outspokenly progressive views and general belief in Italy's destiny[5] coincided with the beliefs of the majority of the members of the Lombrosian school. Sergi refers ebulliently to Carducci as a "superior and strong man" (47), just the man to replace the decrepit Leopardi.

For the moment, Carducci would be viewed as the better poet in large part thanks to the continued positivist anti-Leopardi crusade, taking the Nobel Prize in Literature in 1906. However, Sergi would be displeased to learn that the hunchback of Recanati would ultimately re-emerge as Italy's greatest modern poet, while Carducci's fame has waned in recent years.

Lombrosian literature: the geniuses talk back

In a critical study surveying contemporary trends in Italian literature at the close of the nineteenth century, the famous literary critic Téodor de Wyzewa wrote that "of twenty Italian books published at present, at least ten are manifestly inspired by Lombrosian doctrines" (cited in Rondini 2001, 16). While we can only guess if Wyzewa's estimate was accurate, the statement indicates how widely Lombroso's theories had circulated among Italian writers. While Lombroso and his cohorts were writing literary works of science, Italian writers were, at the same time, experimenting with the narrative possibilities offered by the latest scientific discoveries. As Andrea Carli has argued, Lombroso's ideas appealed to writers for two related reasons: first, because Lombroso "knows how to package the immense potential of grotesque pathologies and of real monsters authorized by science," and also, more broadly, "because he exemplifies modern, scientific stylistic trends, which are engaging and sometimes even narrative" (Carli 2004, 213). It is from this point of departure that we can begin to explore the various types of inspiration that a remarkably diverse group of literary figures took from the works of criminal anthropology. Many borrowed the criminals and degenerates lurking in Lombroso's criminological texts. Others would borrow Lombroso's racial theories in support of patriotic or colonial agendas. Still others instead borrowed positivist scientific style, using somatic traits as shortcuts for character, or converting the narrator into a sort of scientific observer of events. Lombroso's works, in short, proved elastic enough to provide a generation of writers with new models, creating a new trajectory for literature that coincided with the retroactive modifications Lombroso's school had made to literary criticism itself.

In 1886, Edmondo De Amicis (1846–1908) published one of the definitive children's novels of the era, *Heart*, which chronicles a year in the life of schoolboy Enrico Bottini, an average if good-natured student from the northern city of Turin. Designed to instill civic virtue, the novel chronicles the ups and downs of Enrico's year, including such inspirational events as a rally at which Enrico gets to behold King Umberto. In creating this idyllic, patriotic world, De Amicis faced a problem relating to his readership: to make the work appeal to all Italians and not just those from the north, he needed to find a way to acknowledge regional difference. To achieve this aim, De Amicis created characters from Italy's other regions, lifting Lombroso's writings on north/south difference to do so.

Not long into the school year, a new student arrives in Enrico's class. The boy comes from Reggio di Calabria, which, as the narrator points out, is over five hundred miles from Turin. The novel makes it clear that this boy, named Coraci (a southern surname), is not at all like his classmates. His physiognomy is radically different from his Torinese schoolmates. If we compare his description to that of Lombroso's descriptions of a typical southern Italians found in *The Criminal Man* and *The White Man and the Man of Color*, the source of this pseudo-racial difference becomes evident. Speaking of the inhabitants of Sicily, for instance, Lombroso writes that the area around Palermo was "where the rapacious tribes of the

Berbers and Semites had their first and most tenacious settlements and where the anatomical type, customs, politics and morals retain an Arab imprint" (Lombroso 1878, 245). What, then, do the Berbers look like? "A real midway point between Negroids, Semites and Whites," Lombroso writes in *The White Man and the Man of Color* (Lombroso 1871, 177). They tend to exhibit certain features of the "true" African races, Lombroso continues, similar to their cousins, the Abyssinians, who have "skin between black and copper, [and] dark, ... frizzy, on rare occasions wooly hair" (178). Turning to *Heart*, we see that De Amicis could easily have found his Calabrian subject in such texts: "Yesterday evening ... the principal came in with a new pupil, a very dark faced boy, with black hair, with large, black eyes" (De Amicis 1894, 6). Another feature links Coraci to Lombroso's archetypal thief, who, according to *The Criminal Man*, has "thick, interconnected eyebrows" (6). Lombroso presents a cartoonish image of just such a man right below this description, to associate a face with his criminological construct (reproduced in Figure 13.1).

De Amicis's southern subject has similarly "thick eyebrows, conjoined on his forehead" (De Amicis 1894, 6).

That Coraci plays a minor and unobtrusive role in the novel, despite seemingly to come from another species entirely, is ultimately demonstrative of De Amicis's solution to the racial issue he has brought up. De Amicis seems willing to acknowledge that northerners and southerners are different races, but does not, in the end, accept the implications of this hypothesis. Interestingly, Enrico's class does have a genuine "born criminal," but it is not Coraci. Instead, a Torinese boy named named Franti is ultimately expelled for repeated infractions (155). Nonetheless,

FIGURE 13.1 Image of a typical thief in *The Criminal Man*

Source: Lombroso 1878, 47; author's reproduction of original.

Heart, Italy's most successful book of childhood formation after Collodi's *Adventures of Pinocchio*, bespeaks a disturbing trend linking patriotic education to certain ideas about biological difference among Italian citizens.

Lombroso's ideas about north/south difference would be of crucial importance to writers of grown-up fiction as well. Giovanni Verga (1840–1922), among Italy's finest nineteenth-century novelists, offers an intriguing case of criminal anthropology's resonances in literature. Verga, a member of the Sicilian gentry, began his career writing in the typically Romantic style so popular in post-unification northern Italy. Finding little success or satisfaction with this Romanticism, Verga turned his imagination back to his native Sicily and, by the end of the 1870s, had elaborated a new literary style inspired by the tribulations of the impoverished Sicilian peasantry. His new works featured a nearly invisible narrator, an innovative use of vernacular expressions, and the manifestation of passions in their elemental form. This style, dubbed *verismo*, was, as Verga famously put it in a sort of manifesto for the movement, concerned "with the naked and pure fact" (Verga 2006, 202). In this manifesto, Verga declares his interest in pursuing his craft with "scientific meticulousness" (203). The result of his new approach, Verga argues, is to understand "The science of the human heart" (203).

If Verga's interest in unlocking the scientific truths of human experience sounds similar to Lombroso's desire to explain the material causes of certain types of behavior, this is not coincidental. Verga's greatest literary works were written between 1874 and 1890, just as Lombroso's ideas were spreading throughout Italy. An analysis of one of Verga's most famous short stories, his 1878 "Rosso Malpelo," (literally "Red Badhair") will serve to illustrate how much criminal anthropology was on Verga's mind. "Rosso Malpelo" is the tale of an impoverished sulfur miner working under Mount Etna, disliked by all on account of his red hair. Subjected to back-breaking labor and abused by his fellow workers, Malpelo's life is an endless succession of toil, cruelty, and danger. Hopeless and friendless, Malpelo ends up perishing in one of the cave-ins that so frequently occur in the mines.

Within this framework, Lombroso and his criminal archetypes figure prominently. The physical descriptions of the protagonist leave little doubt on this score. Lombroso identifies redheads in general and the Sicilian subset of this group in particular as likely criminals in *The Criminal Man*. Citing a table on the hair color of criminals throughout Italy, he notes that it is, "in Emilia and in Sicily[,] those with red hair" who exhibit a disproportionate tendency to commit crimes (Lombroso 1878, 53). In Verga's tale, Malpelo's red hair is clearly a negative indicator. "They called him Malpelo," the tale begins, "because he had red hair; and he had red hair because he was a malicious and evil boy, who promised to turn out a flower of wickedness" (Verga 1900, 119). In an excellent article on the links between literature and positivist science, Sandra Puccini points out that "Rosso Mapelo" follows criminal anthropology stylistically in this *incipit*. She writes, "The opening sentence could have been taken from a scientific work of the time: for example, from the biography of some 'born' killer, of a brigand, or perhaps of an anarchist or country prophet" (Puccini 2004, 67).

Along with inauspicious red hair, Malpelo's "scowling grey eyes" (Verga 1900, 151) also bespeak his wickedness. Grey-eyed criminals, Lombroso argues in *The Criminal Man*, make up a disproportionately large percentage of the criminal population and are furthermore singled out for the ferocity of their crimes (Lombroso 1878, 54–5). The narrator makes it clear that Malpelo's actions conform to his atavistic physicality. Malpelo, like so many of Lombroso's born criminals, is compared to a savage, a sort of beast: "He was truly an ugly mug, grim, snarling and *savage*" (Verga 1900, 120, emphasis mine). Malpelo spends his spare time gratuitously inflicting pain on pack animals and abusing his only friend (127–9).

What makes Verga's short story a masterpiece is the internal tension that threatens to entirely undo this apparent acceptance of Lombrosian physiognomy. Malpelo is the tale's hero. Universally hated and forced to risk (and ultimately lay down) his life to serve the economic interests of an unfeeling capitalist machine, Malpelo meets his fate with resignation and dignity. In perhaps the most majestic phrase in the entire story, Verga suggests that Malpelo may not be a born criminal at all – he may simply be play-acting. Midway through the tale, we read: "Aware that he was *malpelo*, he resigned himself to being the worst one possible" (127). Here, the verb used to mean "resign oneself" also carries the meaning "to dress up." Thus, the entire logic of difference which informs the tale risks, like the walls of Malpelo's sulfur mines, collapsing. We should not forget, however, that Lombroso's presence is the linchpin which holds the narration together.

Lombroso's presence within the works of the other of the two major theorists of *verismo*, Luigi Capuana (1839–1915), shows just how versatile the scientist's theory could be. Capuana, like Verga, was very interested in using scientific examination as a way of reinvigorating literature. In a university lecture of 1902, Capuana advocates the comprehensive application of a methodology of positivist inquiry to literature. He envisions a world where art is viewed as a substance to be viewed like a sample in a test tube, in which "it too is a sort of physical secretion, like sugar or phosphorous coursing through the human body" (Capuana 1902, 10). He calls for a new discipline to study and create this art, the "Science of literature" with a capital S, a science which will replace the tired, empty ideas of rhetoric and aesthetics: "What we can now, without ambition or vanity, call *Science of literature* or science of art ... has come to replace what was once called rhetoric and also aesthetics. ... The revolution that this method produces is radical" (17, emphasis original).

Capuana was fascinated by the possibilities opened up by exploring the links between science and literature. Even his first short story, "Dr. Cymbalus," published in 1867, demonstrates a clear fascination with matters scientific. This Naturalist-inspired tale centers around a lobotomy performed by one Dr Cymbalus, the world's "greatest living physiologist," whose "discoveries about the nervous system are the most extraordinary conquests of modern science" (Capuana 1988, 76). The particular scientific thread that linked Capuana to Lombroso was not, as in Verga's case, an exploration of Lombroso's theories on criminality. Rather, it was the examination of spiritualistic phenomena. Capuana dabbled in scientific experiments involving mesmerism, hypnosis, and the supernatural, penning two essays on the subject, the 1884 *Spiritualism?* and the 1896 *World of the Occult*. This interest in scientific exploration of the spirit world soon put Capuana on a collision course with Lombroso, who spent the last years of his career in a relentless examination of this very subject.

Lombroso and Capuana began an association that was to endure for the remainder of Lombroso's life in 1884, when Lombroso wrote Capuana two letters commending him for *Spiritualism?* (Di Blasi 1968, 151). They soon became friends, frequently exchanging ideas on both science and literature. From the mid-1880s until Lombroso's death, Capuana would write many short stories which were essentially literary *mises-en-scène* of Lombroso's latest scientific findings on the spirit world. Tales of clairvoyant visions, revenants, and haunted houses abound in these gothic tales,[6] so disparate from Verga's Darwinian struggles for survival that it is at first blush difficult see the two novelists as scions of a coherent school.

Over the course of their long friendship, Lombroso and Capuana would argue for years over one point regarding spiritualistic phenomena: were they composed of matter, or were they truly ethereal, disembodied from the corporeal world? Lombroso, the consummate materialist, contended that sprits must be made of matter like everything else, while Capuana was unconvinced. This bone of contention led the latter to fashion the crown jewel of the Lombroso-Capuana connection, the short story "A Vampire," which first appeared in the *Corriere della Sera* in 1904 and was later published on its own in 1907, this time with a dedication to Lombroso himself. Capuana praises Lombroso in this dedication, wishing to "pay you reverent homage, to add my writer's little voice to the unanimous acclamations of the Scientists of the entire world" (Capuana 1995, 5). In the tale, Capuana dramatizes the debate over the material nature of spirits in a narrative featuring an autobiographical protagonist and a scientific antagonist.

Capuana uses "A Vampire" to prove that spirits cannot be confined to the realm of the material. In the tale, the protagonist, Lelio Giorgi (like Capuana a man of letters), is haunted by the vampiric revenant of his wife Luisa's first husband, a ghostly visitor who feeds on the life-force of Giorgi's son. In desperation, Giorgi summons his friend, the great scientist Mongeri, who according to one critic is an Italian Van Helsing (Del Principe 1995, 15), to help him exorcise the vampire. The scientist reacts by scoffing at Giorgi's claim: "How do you expect me not to laugh? ... I don't believe in spirits!" (Capuana 1995, 9). Hallucination or subconscious suggestion, Mongeri is certain, can explain away this seemingly supernatural situation. Mongeri is pedantic and self-assured to the point of arrogance. He makes constant appeals to science, of which he considers himself to be a paladin. At one point he even says, "You'd like a scientific explanation? Very well, in its name, I shall answer you" (10). Mongeri is made to appear very foolish when it turns out that science cannot solve Giorgi's vampire problem.

Capuana's scientist is a cleverly wrought parody of Lombroso. In a ingenious moment, he mimics Lombroso's tendency pepper his scientific analysis with proverbs such that the resemblance is unmistakable. Mongeri advises Giorgi and Luisa to leave town to break the spell of their mutual hallucination, citing a characteristically Lombrosian proverb to back the idea: "The only way to overcome certain fixed impressions," Mongeri lectures, "is to seek diversion, to superimpose stronger impressions, removing oneself from the places that contributed to producing them. 'One devil chases away another': a most wise proverb" (11–12).

Events in the climactic scene in "A Vampire" allow Giorgi to wipe the smile off Mongeri's (and Lombroso's) condescending face. Mongeri presumes to interrupt the vampire's visits by his mere presence; naturally, his plan fails. The vampire returns at its appointed hour, and Mongeri's attempts to control its actions are laughable. The vampire, to spite this presumptuous scientist, proves that non-matter can indeed be substantial but not material, slapping Mongeri on the shoulder: "He felt an invisible hand rap twice on his shoulder, and in the same instant he saw, in the light before him, a greyish hand, half transparent, almost as if made of smoke" (33). Mongeri and Lombroso's materialist position are thereby discredited. Thus, the end of Capuana's dedication, in which he entreats Lombroso to "Accept [this tale], Illustrious friend, with your usual bonhomie" (5) is less of a formulaic closing than an apologetic disclaimer, lest his friend take this parody too personally.

The Decadent movement, with its frequent explorations of abnormal, macabre subjects, was certainly fertile literary soil in which to plant Lombrosian ideas. Its finest poet and novelist, Gabriele d'Annunzio (1863–1938), like Verga, reached artistic maturity just as Lombroso's ideas were at their most dominant. As literary critic Derek Duncan has argued, d'Annunzio and Lombroso "share a common repertoire of ideological assumptions" (Duncan 2006, 20), and d'Annunzio's works are full of Lombrosian figures: "D'Annunzio writes about the kind of men Lombroso cautions against. They worry his readers," Duncan writes (20). Perhaps the best example of this can be found in d'Annunzio's second novel, *Giovanni Episcopo*, published in 1892. This novel's plot seems almost to have been lifted from Lombroso's chapter on crimes of passion in *The Criminal Man*, in which we learn of a certain Milani, who

> suspecting his wife of adultery . . . is made nearly certain . . . by being insulted as a cuckold. . . . Returning home, he hears it mentioned by his daughters, takes a knife, runs to the café and, stabbing his rival, says to him, "This is how to defend one's honor."
>
> (Lombroso 1878, 135)

Giovanni Episcopo's eponymous protagonist, a workaday Roman clerk, is dominated by Giulio Wanzer, a personification of pure delinquency who epitomizes viciousness, sadism, and duplicity. While Wanzer is fleeing the long arm of the law, Episcopo marries Ginevra, a faithless woman whose loose morals leave the paternity of their son, Ciro, in doubt. Years later, Wanzer resurfaces and begins carrying on with Ginevra in front of Ciro, leading a crazed Episcopo to brutally murder the nefarious criminal.

The most extraordinary link between Lombrosian science and *Giovanni Episcopo* is found in the novel's curious framework. Written from Episcopo's point of view in the first person, the narrative voice makes repeated references to an interlocutor to whom Episcopo tells his story. While we never hear this interlocutor speak, Episcopo reacts throughout to unheard prodding from this voice. From the way in which Episcopo reacts to this invisible figure, it becomes clear that he is being interrogated. Curiously, his interrogator is not interested in establishing his guilt, since we learn early on that Episcopo was discovered with knife in hand over Wanzer's slain body, (d'Annunzio 1892, 22). The mysterious interviewer, we are to understand, is interested in making a scientific case study of this intriguing murderer. From the outset, this unseen scientist is probing Episcopo to get a complete picture of his physical and mental makeup. The first lines of the novel respond to the interrogator's request to spare no details: "So, you want to know ... What do you want to know, signore? What must I tell you? What? –Ah, *everything!*–It will be necessary for me to tell you everything, from the beginning" (17; ellipses, italics and punctuation original). The narrator is aware of the invisible criminologist's penetrating, analytical gaze: "Do you think me mad? Oh, no? I thought I read it in your eyes" (21). At one point during these interactions, the shadowy figure diagnoses Episcopo's mental state: "A hallucination, yes, nothing more. Well said. Oh yes, yes, yes, well said ... Thank you, signore" (49). One would be hard pressed to find a novel which makes such innovative use of the criminal-anthropological mode of inquiry.

The anthropological format of the novel is certainly not the only apparent connection to Lombroso. For purposes of concision, suffice it to say that the primary characters in d'Annunzio's novel correspond very neatly to types of criminals in *The Criminal Man*. The malicious Wanzer is a "born criminal"; Episcopo, the "occasional criminal"; Ginevra, the archetypal prostitute; Ginevra's father Battista, the pathological alcoholic. As I consider such characters in depth elsewhere in this chapter, let us now move on to the last of the novelists I shall discuss, Alfredo Oriani.

Oriani (1852–1909) is among Italian literature's lesser-known figures. A prophet of the *ennui* of the modern condition, Oriani is most likely to be remembered because his greatest admirer was a journalist-turned-politician from his native Romagna, Benito Mussolini. This alone makes the study of this unjustly forgotten figure inherently compelling; the fact that Mussolini's idol wrote and was active during the same period as Lombroso (they died within a day of each other in October 1909) even more so. Oriani was an iconoclast who spent his entire career attempting in vain to convince the literary establishment of his worth, exhibiting what one biographer has called "a lasting monomania ... he considered himself a genius, ... an artistic personality of extraordinary stature" (Cortesi 2001, 27).

His *The Hereafter*, published in 1877 and purchased by few, is the most overtly Lombrosian of his novels. At the novel's core is a love quadrangle involving two wealthy young men and two women, a situation untangled by a shocking lesbian love scene at the novel's conclusion. We need go no further than the first few pages of the text to show Oriani's debt to Lombroso. To introduce his two male protagonists, Oriani delivers page-length Lombrosian physiognomic observations, which border on the absurd in their attention to detail. The following is an excerpt from the description of just one of these two characters:

> Giorgio gave off the air of a privileged, unfulfilled, perhaps even wretched nature; one might have said that the ghastly pallor of his face was washed away in its very lividness, while the vivacity of his large, black pupils contrasted strangely with his drawn in, very thin, and painfully sarcastic mouth. Was this a result of nature or of habit? Probably of both, and probably this drawing in of the lips and eyes was also present in his head and heart. If the artist had a special class of man, as if from another race, one would at first glance have identified him as such.
>
> (Oriani 1890, 23–4)

This description is remarkable for how explicitly it ties in so many of Lombroso's ideas in one paragraph. We have before our mind's eye a bizarre physical specimen whose anomalies establish a physiognomic bio-determinism. We have a meditation on the source of the subject's sorrow (Lombroso, of course would have opted for the genetic answer). We conclude with an unequivocal classification of the man into an inferior race – Oriani made this character a born criminal all but in name. That Mussolini selected Oriani of all men as his "official" novelist should give us pause to reflect on how seriously we should take the regime's official stand on Lombroso, who, for several reasons,[7] was disparaged and vilified as the Fascist years went on.

Criminal anthropology's final frontier: positivism and opera

In 1894, writing in an article for the newly created *Rivista musica italiana*, Lombroso declares audaciously: "Even music, that art form which seemed to be inspired by feeling and by the most complete subjectivity, has entered into a completely scientific phase" (Lombroso 1894a, 117). Lombroso is convinced that the music of his day, no longer inspired by the sublime and unquantifiable, has begun to show the influences of a positivist cultural model of unequivocal, scientifically quantifiable expression. The article in which this statement appears, "The Most Recent Scientific Inquiries Into Sounds and Music," is a sort of call-to-arms for positivist scientists to wade into the murky waters of music. The journal, printed by one of Lombroso's primary editors, Fratelli Bocca, was from the outset a positivist outpost. One need only peruse the titles of other musicological studies it published, for instance Carlo Jachino's article which dares the reader to ask, "Is Wagner a Degenerate?" to get a sense of the journal's worldview.

In a later article in the 1894 *Rivista musicale* (Lombroso wrote three articles for the journal's inaugural edition) entitled "On the Mental Effects of Music," the good doctor concedes that he lacks the musical training necessary for technical musical analysis, but asserts that this is an advantage rather than a drawback:

> I am a layman concerning the musical arts – if on the one hand this makes my work imperfect, on the other I hope that this can provide new insights, which,

neglected by the technically adept, might be of use to whosoever wishes to set about studying various questions in greater depth (526).

In each of the three articles, Lombroso apprises his readers of the latest findings on neurological reactions to music, including supposedly universal listener responses to given composers (from the old masters to Arrigo Boito) and physiognomic analyses of composers altogether consistent with his writings on genius. In "Deafness Among Musicians," he offers a brief physiognomic analysis of Beethoven which "definitively" explains the composer's famous deafness. Always the etiologist, Lombroso attributes Beethoven's deafness to idiosyncratic bathing habits: "After the exertion of a composition, he would plunge his head into a basin of freezing water" (526). A recurring point in the articles is that each work of music produces the same effect in every listener. Operatic composers are specifically indicative of this trend. For instance, in "The Mental Effects of Music," he writes:

> Wagner offers a restless amusement . . . and this comes through regardless of the individual listener's differing intelligence, sex and state of mind. . . . From Heine to the humblest amateur, everyone is struck by an air of gay laughter found even in Rossini's most dramatic moments (529).

The relationship between the positivist school of criminal anthropology and music is one of its lesser-studied aspects. While Lombroso concedes that musical analysis is largely beyond the skill set of the positivist anthropologists, this did not stop the school from producing a series of analyses of composers and librettists. Composers' idiosyncrasies provided endless fodder for scientists looking for cases-in-point of geniuses' pathological behavior. Indeed, Lombroso claims that "in no other branch is *inspiration*, which is to say *genius*, so essential" (cited in Frigessi 2003, 316; emphasis original). Thus the aforementioned Beethoven and Wagner were among the school's favorite targets, the latter often being cast as the musical embodiment of degeneration, an unsurprising stance given Wagner's pronounced (and enduring) unpopularity on Italian soil.[8]

Italian composers soon took notice and duly reciprocated science's interest in music. This tendency is most prominent among operatic composers, who were the most highly respected and visible subset of the Italian musical community in Lombroso's lifetime. Following Lombroso's rise to prominence, the Italian operatic stage witnessed a shift in dramatic sensibility that undoubtedly reflects the new epistemological mindset of criminal anthropology. Gone were the mannered costume dramas, noble sentiments, and Romanticism which had inspired the generation of Rossini, Donizetti, and Verdi. Instead, crimes of passion, degenerate prostitutes, madmen, cities' underbellies, and "oriental" subjects were the order of the day, a clear extension of the subjects that Lombroso and his followers were so diligently cataloging and diagnosing contemporaneously. Composers of the Italian *giovane scuola* (sometimes imprecisely referred to as *verismo* composers), beginning with Pietro Mascagni and his landmark *Cavalleria rusticana* (1890), were particularly fascinated by such unsavory topics. From *Cavalleria*'s vengeful mafioso Compare Alfio, to the insane, murderous Canio of Leoncavallo's *Pagliacci* (1892), to the prostitutes of Neapolitan slums in Giordano's *Mala vita* (also 1892), the operas of this era indisputably demonstrate a desire to scrape up and animate the criminal dregs of society. Here, I shall offer several examples of operas where criminal anthropology is most clearly present. As will become evident, the *giovane scuola* composers are remarkable for the variety of positivist criminological ideas they incorporated into their operas; they dexterously adapt divergent scientific ideas to suit different types of operas.

The first major opera in which criminal anthropology figures prominently is Verdi and Arrigo Boito's 1887 *Otello*. This opera, which premiered only days after the Battle of Dogali, Italy's first major colonial defeat at the hands of the Ethiopians,[9] bears unmistakable signs of Lombroso's writings on race, and the opera's protagonist is cast as a scientifically inferior savage in consequence. Boito was a transitional figure between the older and younger elements in nineteenth-century opera, both Verdi's last librettist and a composition professor at the Milan Conservatoire who counted Puccini, Mascagni, Catalani, and others of the *giovane scuola* among his pupils. The multitalented Boito (a journalist, poet, and short story writer as well as a composer and librettist) was deeply interested in scientific theories of racial difference. As I have discussed elsewhere (Hiller 2009, 17–22), Boito published a remarkable short story in 1867, in which a black man and white man square off at chess, demonstrating a thorough understanding of contemporary theories on racial difference. The gestation period for the *Otello* libretto, from about 1879–87, was, of course, Lombroso's heyday in Italy and abroad, and we have much circumstantial evidence that Boito knew Lombroso's works and quite possibly knew Lombroso personally (23). Both the text and music of *Otello* indicate that Boito was a careful student of Lombrosian theory.

The most important physical description of Otello shows how strong this Lombrosian influence is in the opera. In his 1871 *The White Man and the Man of Color*, Lombroso singles out thick lips as a key indicator of black men's innate savagery, writing: "he has jet-black skin … sunken eyes, thick and protruding lips" (23). These lips are one of the few traits that Boito chooses to include in his libretto, when Jago sings, "the lovely Desdemona,/… Will soon come to dislike the dark kisses/Of that savage with swollen lips" (Boito 1975, 429). While there is a Shakespearean precedent for this racial slur "What a full fortune does the thicklips owe/if he can carry't thus!" (*Othello* I, i, 67–8) the modification to "swollen" and the addition of "savage" are editorial additions to the opera demonstrative of Boito's nineteenth-century understanding of African inferiority.

Otello has a fainting spell at the end of the opera's third act, a moment which provides key musical reinforcement for Boito's textual depiction of a the protagonist as a savage. In this scene, Otello is unable to control himself due to the African blood which courses through his veins, and as a result loses his capacity to reason. As I have written, "Lombroso characterizes blacks as being unable to govern the passions that well up in their blood, leading to violent outbursts. … The opera's protagonist makes explicit reference to this hegemony of his blood" (Hiller 2009, 24). That Otello sings "Only I cannot escape from myself! ... Blood! Ah! ... It grieves me!" (Boito 1975, 500) indicates the librettist's full absorption of this scientific idea. By now, Otello is singing "convulsively, raving" (501). The descending chromatic pattern in Verdi's score is an ingenious device used to represent Otello's loss of reason and sinking descent into madness, confirming the textual point (see Figure 13.2). Such is a very fitting end to an act in which the Moor has given in to what Boito (and Lombroso) would view as the inevitable result of Jago's successful effort to make Otello's savage blood tell.

A few years after *Otello*'s premiere, the 26-year-old Pietro Mascagni would take the operatic world by storm with his 1890 *Cavalleria rusticana*, a tale of passion, jealously and murder adapted from Verga's eponymous short story and drama. This opera, one of the most commercially successful in the history of Italian opera, launched a career that would bring the Tuscan composer to international prominence until his death in 1945. *Cavalleria*, a lightning-paced thriller which made novel use of elements not often seen in grand opera, was to radically alter the direction in which the *giovane scuola* composers would take for years to come. New operas, imitating *Cavalleria*'s novel approach, would be gritty, violent, and short. What critics have failed to see in this change of trajectory is just how much Lombrosian criminal anthropological texts inform these operas. While the *giovane scuola* composers would ultimately go in different directions as they matured, a cluster of operas from the early 1890s is rife with characters who seem to spring forth from the pages of criminological taxonomies – murderers, prostitutes, and everything in between.

Beginning with Mascagni, the 1891 comedy *L'amico Fritz* is a prime example of how much Lombroso "haunted" the composer. Mascagni wrote this lighthearted and charming comedy (with libretto by the serviceable if undistinguished Nicola Daspuro) to prove that his pen could produce something completely different from the coarse realism of *Cavalleria*. Nonetheless, it shows a surprising reliance on Lombroso's writings on race in creating one of its characters. The rather trite plot, based on the French tandem Erckmann-Chatrian's novel and play *L'Ami Fritz* (of 1864 and 1877, respectively), concerns a confirmed bachelor, Fritz, who, egged on by the kindly rabbi David, ultimately falls for a peasant-girl, the comely Suzel. The action takes place at Fritz's birthday party, at which his assorted friends attempt to convince him of the evils of bachelorhood. In this entourage is Joseph, a gypsy. While this character is something of a non-entity in the source material, his adaptation for the lyric stage is painted with a distinctly Orientalist brush, a sort of conduit for the exotic vein which made *Cavalleria* so distinct. That Mascagni should single out a gypsy as the locus of exoticism in this opera is more understandable if we look at Lombroso's writings on gypsies, articulated most clearly in *The Criminal Man*.

Lombroso was a key figure in re-imagining the terms by which this ethnic group was examined. As historian Thomas Acton observes, in the nineteenth century, "The explanation of [the gypsies'] social exclusion and the nomadism ... no longer needed to be their wickedness ... [C]riminology itself, culminating in Lombroso,

FIGURE 13.2 Giuseppe Verdi and Arrigo Boito, *Otello*, Act III: "Fuggirmi io sol non so"

Source: Verdi and Boito 1887, 319–20.

began to adopt geneticist explanations" (Acton 2005, 105). In *The Criminal Man*, Lombroso writes that the gypsies "are the living image of an entire race of criminals, who exhibit all the passions and vices thereof" (Lombroso 1878, 249). Dishonest and cruel, their dislike of hard work is legendary. They are alcoholics and baby-killers, swindlers and prostitutes, a group which Lombroso demonizes, a cocktail of "the recklessness of the savage and of the criminal" (249).

The strongest evidence that Mascagni and Daspuro may have integrated Lombroso's writings on gypsies is the character's surprising sensuality and effeminacy. By the criteria set in *The Criminal Man*, such traits are expected. Gypsies, Lombroso writes, "are seen walking in bare feet, and yet wearing gallooned or gaudy clothes; other times without stockings but with yellow boots," exotic clothing presumably more suitable to women than to civilized men (249). Fearful of manly combat, the gypsies "gave awful proof" of their cowardice when made to fight in the Austrian army. Mascagni chooses to cast his gypsy, Beppe, as a travesty role (i.e. a cross-dressing female singer). That Mascagni and Daspuro might have had Lombroso in mind provides a possible explanation to this otherwise mysterious revival of a gender-bending tradition not often employed since the days of Mozart and Rossini.[10]

Beppe's entrance in the opera, a violin solo evocative of stereotypical "gypsy" fiddling, is a neat embodiment of his scientifically informed ethnic difference. It is in essence a musical announcement of the player's "othered" background. Beginning on an arpeggio of an A major chord for several measures, it then ascends with a sensuously exotic melisma up to an implied D minor (see Figure 13.3). The rabbi David makes direct reference to the titillating quality of the music, declaring that the notes from the violin "are like kisses!" (Suardon 1900, 9).

Beppe, as far as the other characters are concerned, is an insufferable character, further highlighting his (or her) racial difference. Beppe's invitation to Fritz's party is contingent upon a musical contribution to the event – he is made to sing for his supper. Fritz is bored by Beppe's aria, establishing a far more adversarial relationship between the two characters than is to be found in the source material. "Will you finish up?" sings Fritz, according to the stage directions "with spite" (9). Clearly, the presence of a gypsy offends the prejudiced sensibility of Mascagni and Daspuro's country squire.

Umberto Giordano's *Mala vita* and Ruggero Leoncavallo's *Pagliacci*, which both premiered in the first half of 1892, pay due homage to Mascagni's *Cavalleria* in their dynamic construction, but also to criminal anthropology in their respective uses of physiognomy to convey character. *Mala vita* (whose verses, like those of *Fritz*, are by Daspuro) is an opera set in the bowels of an impoverished Neapolitan quarter, the Basso Porto. The opera hinges on a love triangle in which the aptly named Vito Amante, stricken with tuberculosis, vows to marry a prostitute after divine providence cures his illness. His none-too-pleased current lover, the unhappily married Amalia, vows to prevent Vito from carrying out his plan to wed his fallen woman of choice, Cristina. While the choice of setting for the opera might owe something to the assorted positivist texts of Lombroso's school dealing with problems of urban

FIGURE 13.3 Pietro Mascagni and Nicola Daspuro, *L'amico Fritz*, Act I: Beppe's Violin Entrance

Source: Mascagni and Suardon 1891, 26.

crime, the connections run deeper than this. In particular Amalia, by far the opera's most interesting character, greatly resembles Lombroso's born prostitute.[11]

Amalia's key character traits that link her back to Lombroso are her adulterous rejection of her husband and her pathological attachment to her lover Vito. In *The Criminal Man*, Lombroso claims that prostitutes, the female equivalents of male criminals (Lombroso 1878, 220), display both of these traits. He writes, "if many prostitutes completely dissolve all family bonds ... Then they have a true, excessive passion for their lovers," after which he offers several graphic examples (109). When Vito first makes his vow, Amalia immediately sniffs out the danger and, according to the stage directions, "places herself face-to-face with Vito," demanding "What vow have you made?" (Giordano and Daspuro 2003, 42). In the opera's second act, Amalia viciously defends her territory, threatening Cristina in an effort to keep her lover. While her declaration that "in my heart/I have agony, death .../I need nothing else/In the world: I have lost everything!/Peace, hope, honor! .../I live, I burn for this love!" might at first blush seem like the usual operatic hyperbole, the fact that she is willing to defend that love by "crying out in rage, [flinging] herself to seize a knife on the table," (60) gives the scene an unmistakably Lombrosian feel.

Pagliacci's most Lombrosian character is its murderous protagonist, Canio, who, having discovered his wife's infidelity, kills her in cold blood and stabs her lover for good measure. Leoncavallo (who, following the example of his idol Wagner, wrote his own verses) was the son of a Calabrese magistrate, making it likely that he would have had at least some familiarity with Lombroso's works, so hotly debated by Italian jurists. The way in which the opera's protagonist "snaps" at the opera's conclusion demonstrates Leoncavallo's debt to Lombroso. Canio follows what Lombroso argues is the typical pattern of behavior for crimes of passion, maintaining his cool until events push him over the edge, at which point he springs to action at with uncontrollable rage.

In the chapter in *The Criminal Man* on crimes of passion, Lombroso characterizes such crimes as qualitatively different from crimes committed by born criminals. The preponderance of cases that Lombroso cites in the chapter have to do with husbands who murder adulterous wives upon discovering their infidelity. "Offended honor," Lombroso writes, is a key trigger for such crimes. Once a man is so dishonored, his rage is uncontrollable: "The passions which stimulate the impulsive criminal are not of the type which one can restrain" (Lombroso 1878, 133). "Not only do they procure no alibi," Lombroso writes of such criminals, "not only do they not hide their crimes," but they murder "right in front of their friends" (132–3). Canio, like his "class of 1892" companion Giovanni Episcopo, follows this formula closely. At the opera's climactic moment, Canio avenges his besmirched honor, singing: "Man retakes his rights, and his heart, which bleeds/Desires blood to wash the dishonor, accursed hussy!" (Leoncavallo 1958, 28). Canio then stabs his wife in front of an entire crowd of spectators "in a paroxysm of rage," after which he locates her lover in the crowd, "spins like a beast, leaps on him and in an instant stabs him" (28).

Of course, these few examples are only a sampling of the sorts of borrowings of Lombroso's theories that would persist on the lyric stage well into the twentieth century. Alberto Franchetti, another *giovane scuola* composer, would write the opera *Cristoforo Colombo* in late 1892 to commemorate the 400-year anniversary of Columbus's expedition. The third and fourth acts of *Colombo*, which chronicle the Spanish conquest of the Americas, reflect certain findings from *The White Man and the Man of Color*, which had appeared in its second edition a few months before the opera's premiere. Indeed, Lombroso's statement that "family bonds are neither so sacred nor as close as ours are ... there is no word for *marriage* ... among the Indians" (Lombroso 1892, 77) may well have inspired the plot for these acts, in which the Indian queen Anacoana runs off with the Spaniard Don Roldano without a thought for her family (Franchetti and Illica 1903, 251–380). Indeed, it is hard to conceive of Puccini's Tosca, who murders Scarpia with such *sang-froid*, without Lombroso's *Criminal Woman* having envisioned this particular type of woman. As it currently stands, there is much room for further research in the links between science and opera, an opening which with any luck will be taken given the increasing interest in opera from this crucial period in music history.

Notes

1 Unless otherwise noted, all translations in this chapter are my own.
2 For concision, I will generally limit myself to discussing Lombroso's impact within Italy, where the effects of his writings were clearest and most pronounced. This is not to

say that Lombroso's writings did not also have a profound effect abroad, as can be attested to by the constellation of important cultural figures (and, of course, other scientists) who fell under Lombroso's spell. To give only a few examples, Lombroso's ideas figure significantly in the works of Zola, Stoker, and Conrad (see Kern 2004: 227–36).

3 Here I have used Allen Mandelbaum's translation (Alighieri 2004: 285).
4 For more on these works, see Rondini's excellent section on "Stile e psichiatria" (Rondini 2001: 64–78).
5 After unification, both Carducci's Republican beliefs and progressive ideology subsided somewhat. His later poems in fact tend toward a more conservative political stance and a less rosy view of modernity. While Carducci's youthful reputation was called into question by his ultimate decision to set aside Republican values and reconcile himself to the monarchy, by then the myth of Carducci proved larger than the man.
6 The Capuana 2007 *Novelle del mondo occulto* (listed in the References) is an excellent collection of such works.
7 Not the least of which was his Jewish background.
8 As Alan Mallach notes, Italy's musical community exhibited a visceral aversion to Wagner (Mallach 2007, 16).
9 At Dogali, five hundred Italian soldiers were taken by surprise and annihilated by a much larger Ethiopian force.
10 Even Alan Mallach, Mascagni's most sympathetic biographer, has difficulty justifying this choice dramatically. He writes: "The opera's weakest link is Beppe the gypsy violinist, implausibly cast as a trouser role" (Mallach 2002, 82).
11 While Lombroso would not release *The Criminal Woman*, his definitive treatise on the subject of female delinquency, until the year after Giordano's opera premiered, one must keep in mind that *The Criminal Woman* is on the whole a repackaging of ideas already present in Lombroso's assorted writings leading up to 1893. Thus, *Mala Vita*'s usage of a "born prostitute" is by no means anachronistic.

References

Acton, T. (2005) "Modernity, Culture and 'Gypsies': Is there a Meta-Scientific Method for Understanding the Representation of 'Gypsies'? And do the Dutch really exist?" in N. Saul and S. Tebbutt (eds) *The Role of the Romanies: Images and Counter-Images of "Gypsies"/Romanies in European Cultures.* Liverpool: Liverpool University Press, pp. 98–116.
Alighieri, D. (2004) *Inferno*, trans. Allen Mandelbaum. New York: Bantam Classics.
Bellezza, P. (1899) "Della forma superlativa presso il Leopardi," *Giornale storico della letteratura italiana*, 33: 83–105.
Boito, A. (1975) *Otello*, trans. and ed. W. Weaver in *Seven Verdi Librettos*. New York: Norton.
Capuana, L. (1902) *La scienza della letteratura: Prolusione*. Catania, Italy: Giannotta.
Capuana, L. (1988) *L'aldilà*. Catania, Italy: Tringale.
Capuana, L. (1995) *Un vampiro*. Florence: Passigli.
Capuana, L. (2007) *Novelle del mondo occulto*, ed. A. Cedola. Bologna, Italy: Pendragon.
Carli, A. (2004) *Anatomie scapigliate: L'estetica della morte tra letterature, arte e scienza*, Novara. Italy: Interlinea.
Cortesi, P. (2001) *Il letterato del villaggio: Vita di Alfredo Oriani*. Cesena, Italy: Società Editrice "Il Ponte Vecchio."
D'Annunzio, G. (1892) *Giovanni Episcopo*. Naples: Pierro.

De Amicis, E. (1894) *Cuore: libro per ragazzi*. Milan: Fratelli Treves.
Del Principe, D. (1995) "Misbegotten, Unbegotten, Forgotten: Vampires and Monsters in the Works of Ugo Tarchetti, Mary Shelley, Bram Stoker, and the Gothic Tradition," *Forum Italicum*, 29.1: 3–25.
De Sanctis, F. (1885) *Studio su G. Leopardi*. Naples: Morano.
Di Blasi, C. (1968) *Luigi Capuana: originale e segreto*. Catania, Italy: Giannotta.
Duncan, D. (2006) *Reading and Writing Italian Homosexuality: a Case of Possible Difference*. Burlington, VT: Ashgate.
Franchetti, A. and Illica, L. (1903) *Cristoforo Colombo: Dramma Lirico in Quattro Atti ed un Epilogo*, vocal score. Milan: Ricordi.
Frigessi, D. (2003) *Cesare Lombroso*. Turin: Einaudi.
Gibson, M. (1998) "Biology or Environment? Race and Southern 'Deviancy' in the Writings of Italian Criminologists, 1880–1920," in J. Schneider (ed.), *Italy's Southern Question*. London: Berg, 99–115.
Giordano, U. and Daspuro, N. (2003) *Mala vita*, audio CD with libretto, perf. P. Di Gregorio, M. Miccoli, M. Graziani, cond. A. Cavallaro. Bologna, Italy: Bongiovanni.
Harrowitz, N. (1994) *Antisemitism, Misogyny, and the Logic of Cultural Difference: Cesare Lombroso and Matilde Serao*. Lincoln, NE: University of Nebraska Press.
Hiller, J.R. (2009) "'Eppure è un negro': Reflections of Cesare Lombroso's Social Darwinist Racial Theories in *Otello*," *La Fusta*, 17: 17–32.
Kern, S. (2004) *A History of Causality: Science, Murder Novels, and Systems of Thought*. Princeton: Princeton University Press.
Leoncavallo, R. (1958) *Pagliacci*, bilingual libretto, trans. George Mead. New York: F. Rullman.
Lombroso, C. (1871) *L'uomo bianco e l'uomo di colore*, 1st edn. Padua, Italy: F. Sacchetto.
Lombroso, C. (1878) *L'uomo delinquente studiato in rapporto alla antropologia, alla medicina legale ed alle discipline carcerarie*, 2nd edn. Turin: Fratelli Bocca.
Lombroso, C. (1892) *L'uomo bianco e l'uomo di colore*, 2nd edn. Turin: Fratelli Bocca.
Lombroso, C. (1894a) "Le più recenti inchieste scientifiche sui suoni e la musica," "La sordità fra i musicisti," and "Sugli effetti psichici della musica." *Rivista Musicale Italiana*, 1: 117–30, 524–6, 526–31.
Lombroso, C. (1894b) *L'uomo di genio in rapporto alla psichiatria, alla storia ed all'estetica*, 6th edn. Turin: Fratelli Bocca.
Lombroso, C. (1897) *Genio e degenerazione: nuovi studi e nuove battaglie*. Palermo, Italy: Remo Sandron.
Lombroso, C. (1899) "Il delinquente e il pazzo nel dramma e nel romanzo moderno," *Nuova Antologia*, 79.163: 665–81.
Lombroso, C. (1903) *La donna delinquente, la prostituta e la donna normale*. Nuova edizione economica. Turin: Fratelli Bocca.
Lombroso, C. (2004) *Criminal Woman, the Prostitute, and the Normal Woman by Cesare Lombroso and Gugliemo Ferrero*, trans. N. Hahn Rafter and M. Gibson. Durham, NC: Duke University Press.
Mallach, A. (2002) *Pietro Mascagni and His Operas*. Boston: Northeastern University Press.
Mallach, A. (2007) *The Autumn of Italian Opera: From Verismo to Modernism, 1890–1915*. Boston: Northeastern University Press.
Mascagni, P. and Suardon, P. [N. Daspuro] (1891) *L'amico Fritz*, vocal score. Milan: Casa Musicale Sonzogno.
Oriani, A. (1890) *Al di là*, 3rd edn. Milan: Giuseppe Galli, 1890.

Patrizi, M. L. (1896) *Saggio psico-antropologico su Giacomo Leopardi e la sua famiglia*. Turin: Fratelli Bocca.
Puccini, S. (2004) "I selvaggi tra noi. Ignoti predecessori, infelicissimi fratelli nostril," *Lares*, 70.1: 59–98.
Rondini, A. (2001) *Cose da pazzi: Cesare Lombroso e la letteratura*. Pisa, Italy: Istituti editoriali e poligrafici internazionali.
Sergi, G. (1899) *Leopardi al lume della scienza*. Palermo, Italy: Remo Sandron.
Seymour, M. (2006) *Debating Divorce in Italy: Marriage and the Making of Modern Italians, 1860–1974*. New York: Palgrave Macmillan.
Stewart-Steinberg, S. (2007) *The Pinocchio Effect*. Chicago: University of Chicago Press.
Suardon, P. [N. Daspuro] (1900) *L'amico Fritz, Lyric Comedy in Three Acts*, bilingual libretto, trans. Frederic Lyster. New York: F. Rullman.
Verdi, G. and Boito, A. (1887) *Othello: A Lyrical Drama in Four Acts*, vocal score. New York: G. Schirmer.
Verga, G. (1900) *Cavalleria rusticana ed altre novelle*. Milan: Fratelli Treves.
Verga, G. (2006) *Tutte le novelle*. Milan: Mondadori.

14

A HIDDEN THEME OF JEWISH SELF-LOVE?

Eric Hobsbawm, Karl Marx, and Cesare Lombroso on "Jewish criminality"

Michael Berkowitz

Dedicated to the memory of Professor Domenico Sella, 1926–2012

Since the appearance of Jeremy Boissevain's *Friends of Friends: Networks, Manipulators, and Coalitions* (1974), scholars are increasingly sensitive to the ways that people work together generally, as well as to the means by which knowledge is transmitted contemporaneously and over time. Almost any professional and academic field that attempts to apply universal standards and respects precedents reveals the existence of networks. This is transparent in preface and acknowledgment sections of books and articles, in addition to routine references. But along with skeletons and sinews of epistemology, supports and connections that are known and admitted, there also are pathways operating beneath the surface. Sometimes the constituents of, and those effected by, these chains are oblivious to the structures of which they are a part, of how they come to think and operate as they do. This paper contends that Karl Marx and the historian Eric Hobsbawm belonged to a network concerning views about Jews and crime that includes Cesare Lombroso and Moses Mendelssohn – all of whom except for Mendelssohn were largely oblivious to this as a Jewish construct, as well as squeamish about revealing their own connections to Jews.

The relationship between Hobsbawm and things Jewish is complicated, to say the least. On the May 10, 2005, to commemorate the 50th anniversary of the founding of the Leo Baeck Institute, an august learned society dedicated to the study of German-speaking Jewry, Eric Hobsbawm delivered its major annual lecture at University College London. Much anticipated and well attended, scores were turned away at the door. By academic standards it was a sensation – in large part simply because Hobsbawm agreed to participate in an overtly Jewish forum. I do not know why he accepted. Possibly it was due to the fact that the invitation had come from Peter Pulzer, with whom Hobsbawm has a long-standing and respectful relationship; perhaps he wished to pay homage to the venerable Leo Baeck Institute.

Similar to the failure of Hobsbawm's quest in 1996 to locate his mother's grave in the Vienna Central Cemetery (Hobsbawm 2003, 42), this foray into a Jewish fold produced little result.

Hobsbawm's address, "Enlightenment and Achievement: The Emancipation of Jewish Talent since 1800," which appeared as "Benefits of Diaspora" in the *London Review of Books*, was pedestrian (Hobsbawm 2005). Nothing new or interesting was expressed in this superficial survey, and his cryptic, mild jibe at Israel at the end was abrupt and disjointed. As much as I had hoped to be enlightened, or at least not bored, I was not terribly surprised that the lecture was a disappointment. I appreciate Hobsbawm as a scholar and critic, and sympathize, to a large measure, with his views. Yet his attempts to make sense of (or even describe) his Jewish identity are excruciating, and his historical work is remarkable for ignoring Jews. For example, Hobsbawm's history of banditry omitted "Jewish robber bands" in Central and Northern Europe (Hobsbawm 2000). I do not believe that he was unaware of their existence. As a social historian his avoidance of European Jewry renders his work far less nuanced that it might be. He seems deeply uncomfortable, even anguished by the fact that he was born a Jew. Throughout his autobiography he exerts strenuous effort to proclaim his lack of identification with Jews, and self-consciously distances himself from what may be perceived as Jewish concerns.

Early in his autobiography, he ruminates:

> What would have been my life if [my mother], Fraülein Grün, aged eighteen, one of three daughters of a moderately prosperous Viennese jeweller, had not fallen in love with an older Englishman, fourth of eight children of an immigrant London Jewish cabinet-maker, in Alexandria in 1913? She would presumably have married a young man from the Jewish Mitteleuropean middle class, and her children would have grown up Austrians. Since almost all young Austrian Jews ended up as emigrants or refugees, my subsequent life might not have looked very different – plenty of them came to England, studied here and became academics. But I would not have grown up or come to Britain with a native British passport.
>
> (Hobsbawm 2003, 2–3)

One of the greatest British historians either is mad, delusional, or intellectually dishonest. He knows, of course, that it is absurd to assert that "almost all young Austrian Jews" got out of the country. He has not, or could not, come to grips with the fact that they were murdered in the Holocaust, a word he cannot even utter.

There is, however, at least one item in Hobsbawm's body of work in which he indulges something akin to a Jewish defense, and reveals a perverse pride in associating with a tiny segment of Jews. In a business-oriented, conservative journal in 1955, *The Quarterly Review*, Hobsbawm explored what he termed "The Economics of the Gangster." The author assumed it would be "unread" (Hobsbawm 2003, 394; Hobsbawm 1955). It is in large part a middle-brow apologia, giving gangsters credit, if not kudos, for being productive and exploiting the contradictions of capitalism for their own ends. My impression is that Hobsbawm enjoyed writing it. I believe it represents a rare instance in which he published something "positive" about Jews, who are vaguely referred to as the "ghetto immigrants" from which gangsters originate (Hobsbawm 1955, 255). Although the crooks he addresses were not exclusively Jews, their cohort certainly included a fair number, including Moe Annenberg and Bugsy Siegel, and Hobsbawm writes that "Sidney Hillman of the Amalgamated Clothing Worker's used gangsters" as an instrument of union politics (Hobsbawm 1955, 240). It may be said that Hobsbawm was following a distinctly Jewish trajectory of indirectly dealing with Jews through their historical association with criminality — and letting them off the hook by virtue of their circumstances. In a tone reminiscent of Horatio Alger (who happened to be Jewish as well), Hobsbawm concludes that "the ambitious young man in the big city will still be able to make up for an initial lack of resources and training with muscle, a good sense of leadership, and a good native head for figuring out the odds" (Hobsbawm 1955, 256).

At nearly the same moment, but in a less self-effacing manner vis-à-vis the Jewishness of his subject — which one might expect from the United States — sociologist Daniel Bell (1919–2011) published what became one of his classic pieces, "Crime as an American Way of Life: A Queer Ladder of Social Mobility" (1953). Now part of the anthology *The End of Ideology* (Bell 1967), like Hobsbawm's piece it is largely a non-scholarly survey of organized crime, focusing on the succession of ethnic groups that seemed to dominate different periods. Bell likewise normalizes and romanticizes the attraction to unlawful pursuits as part-and-parcel of a strategy aiming ultimately for inclusion and respectability. Yet similar to Hobsbawm he obscures the unabashed greed that underscores the lust for wealth, as well as the legacy of violent crime — including that perpetrated by Jews — by sharply differentiating between gambling and other crimes.

Notably, Bell places Moses Annenberg, father of multi-billionaire and Jewish philanthropist Walter Annenberg, in the category of "gamblers." Hobsbawm is slightly more accurate on this, acknowledging Annenberg's career as a "slugger" while nevertheless failing to mention the possibility of his culpability in murder. Although it is true that Annenberg amassed the bulk of his fortune through monopolizing information and the transmission of news concerning horseracing, he had originally established himself, along with his brother, Max, as an "enforcer" for William Randolph Hearst. In contrast, however, to Bell's inference that the price Moe Annenberg paid for his crimes was more severe than warranted, contemporary accounts speculate that he was guilty of scores of crimes to which he was never called to account, including murder (Rockaway 1993, 201). What is unmistakable, however, is that the family's means of doing business involved violence. Both Hobsbawm and Bell, while clearly having access to reliable information, chose to turn a blind eye to heavy Jewish involvement in contract killing, which especially gainsays Hobsbawm's characterization of this group as a "businessmen" like a "company lawyer" or "chartered accountant" (Hobsbawm 1955, 244, 245) and that "all necessary killings were carried out in the most efficient and inconspicuous manner" (Hobsbawm 1955, 256). This is a far cry from the swath of flamboyant murders detailed by Turkus and Feder in *Murder, Inc.* a main source for Hobsbawm and Bell (Turkus and Feder 1952).

I believe that both Hobsbawm and Bell were following a tradition established by none other than Karl Marx. Marx's polemics explicitly on Jews are among his most misunderstood works which appear only at a particular moment of his career (Fischer 2007, 56–102). However, he did manage to write about Jews in the context of other groups and social problems. One of these occurs in a discussion of crime in *Das Kapital*. In order to illuminate the association of Jews and criminality in Marx's time, we must revisit the origins of the discourse on Jews and criminality beginning with the era of Jewish emancipation.

Moses Mendelssohn, the harbinger of the Jewish Enlightenment movement or *Haskala*, sought to debunk the mythical distinction, within the emancipation debate, between so-called "producers" versus "consumers." Jews were typically cast as non-or anti-productive, capable of only consuming and re-selling, the latter of which sometimes was deemed illegal. In 1782 Mendelssohn wrote:

> Not only making something but doing something also, is called producing. Not he alone who labors with his hands, but, generally, whatever does, promotes, occasions, or facilitates anything that may tend to the benefit or comfort of his fellow-creatures, deserves to be called a producer; and, at times, he deserves it the more, the less you see him move his hands or feet.
>
> (Mendelssohn 1782, 45)

As has been discussed by Mordecai Breuer, Klaus Berghahn, and others, intellectual positions regarding Jews and crime were articulated in debates concerning Jewish emancipation and the extension of Jewish rights in the German States. Christian Wilhelm von Dohm's "Über die bürgerliche Verbesserung der Juden" (Dohm 1791) reveals the widely accepted view that Jews were "guilty of a proportionally greater number of crimes than the Christians; that their character in general inclines more toward usury and fraud in commerce." Still, Dohm contends, "Everything the Jews are blamed for is caused by the political conditions under which they now live, and any other group of men, under such conditions, would be guilty of identical errors" (Dohm 1791, 31). In his attempt to undermine Dohm's plea to enhance the standing of the Jews, Johann David Michaelis responded that:

> We can see, principally from reports of investigations of thieves, that the Jews are more harmful than at least we Germans are. Almost half of those belonging to gangs of thieves, at least those of whose existence is known to us, are Jews, while the Jews are scarcely 1/25th of the total population of Germany. If this 1/25th part supplies the same number of riff-raff as the whole German people, or even more, then one must conclude that at least in respect to thievery,

which I consider to be the lowest of the vices, the Jews are twenty-five times as harmful or more than the other inhabitants of Germany.

(Michaelis 1782, 42)

Moses Mendelssohn was prompted to address the issue, which he did by ascribing the deeds of Jewish criminals to their abominable social position, and by seeing the Jews' connection with stealing as a transitional, rather than permanent aspect of their vocation.

It is true that quite a number of Jewish pedlars deal in stolen goods; but few of them are outright thieves, and those, mostly, are people without refuge or sanctuary anywhere on earth. As soon as they have made some fortune they acquire a patent of protection from their territorial prince and change their profession.

Hence a "queer ladder of social mobility." Mendelssohn continues

This is public knowledge; when I was younger I personally met a number of men [Jews] who were esteemed in their native country after they had elsewhere made enough dubious money to purchase a patent of protection. This injustice is directly created by that fine policy which denies the poor Jews protection and residence, but receives with open arms those very same Jews as soon as they have "thieved their way to wealth." Although he is inspired by Scripture, Herr Ritter Michaelis seems to have a bias against poverty. Among the Jews, however, I have found comparatively more virtue in the quarters of the poor than in the houses of the wealthy.

(Mendelssohn 1783, 48)

Mendelssohn was aware that "a number of Jews existed in Central Europe who supported themselves by both stealing and trading."

These thieves benefited from both activities that mutually reinforced each other. Salesmen on the roads seem to have found ample opportunities to steal, and stealing augmented some traders' meager income. Such Jews were frequently recent immigrants from Eastern Europe, who had not yet secured the right to live in a city. As a result, they attempted to earn a living on the road by trading, begging, and sometimes stealing. Banditry provided an alternative for the poorest of the poor Jews who had difficulties sustaining themselves in low-income, or irregular occupations.

(Sanders 1993, 12)

Or to enable them to gain a permit to engage in lawful business. To accuse the Jews of immorality, Mendelssohn lamented, was to "confuse cause and effect" (Mendelssohn 1783, 48; Wolf and Salomon 1817, 141).

It is not surprising then, that Gotthold Ephraim Lessing chose the stereotype of the Jewish thief as the basis for undermining the myth that the Jews were unvirtuous in his play, "The Jews" (1853). The history of the Jews in Lübeck and Moisling of 1898 includes a 28-page response, by Gabriel Riesser, to what was termed a spiteful article and lecture by F.C.B. Ave-Lallemant, which propounded the "fantasy" of Jewish preponderance in crime (Riesser 1842; Carlebach 1898). In Britain, as the right of Baron Rothschild to sit in Parliament was debated, it was asserted that Jews "have never, in any age or any country, been prevalent in crime." But the phrase that follows is telling: "their crimes have mostly been the result of the degraded position to which they have been reduced, the degraded pursuits into which they have been compelled" (Van Oven 1848, 15).

Within the Jewish world, as early as the eighteenth century, the notion was articulated that crime and criminals exist as something contingent, situational, and transitional – relative to the established order. Did not the Jews' contributions to society far outweigh any damage wrought by Jewish crooks (Wolf 1864, 97–9)? There are even moments when Jewish writers come close to arguing that crime and criminals are "socially constructed," at least a century before such a term would come into intellectual parlance (Wolf 1861, 189). In a word, this could not be more different than the view that criminality represents an innate trait (Rylands 1889, 76). Criminals among themselves were not typically seen by Jews as extraordinary or evil individuals, but mainly as "unfortunates" (Wolf 1861, 189).

Karl Marx's illustrations of the economic construction and function of criminality was not simply derived from the Young Hegelians. It was filtered through the discourse of Jewish emancipation, especially as Marx obtained much of his insights about criminals, the law, and society from his teacher, Eduard Gans (Melamed 2001, 23–9; Wasczek 1987, 167–78l; Avineri 1967, 36–56; Avineri 1985, 199–208), who before his conversion and Professorship in Law at the University of Berlin had been one of the founders of the *Wissenschaft des Judentums*, the society for the academic study of Jewry and Judaism. Gans, like his *Wissenschaft des Judentums* colleague Heinrich Heine, was well aware of the legendary Jewish robbers (Heine 1976, 32), and was extremely critical of the police and penal institutions. Otto Ulbricht writes that

> After 1830, Jewish banditry began to disappear, and after the middle of the century nothing more was heard of it. When full legal emancipation was finally reached in Imperial Germany in 1871, the Jewish crime rate was considerably lower than the Christian one.
>
> (Ulbricht 1995, 70)

Yet Herbert Reinike's demonstrates the unfortunate coincidence of the institutionalization of modern criminal statistics, in the 1840s with the last decade of significant Jewish criminal activity (Reinke 1990, 1992).

Although recent scholarship on Marx has described his exposure to the legal theorist F. K. Savigny to be of great consequence, I believe that Gans had more influence on the young Marx, and Marx's musings about crime poked fun at both Savigny and Gans — but display an ironic detachment closer to the spirit of Gans. This appears in the unedited manuscript *Theorien über den Mehrwert*, sometimes referred to as the fourth volume of *Kapital*, which Marx wrote between January 1862 and July 1863. The material was first published by Kautsky in a controversial edition between 1905 and 1910:

Digression: On Productive Labour

A philosopher produces ideas, a poet poems, a clergyman sermons, a professor compendia and so on. A criminal produces crimes. If we take a closer look at the connection between this latter branch of production and society as a whole, we shall rid ourselves of many prejudices. The criminal produces not only crime but criminal law, and with this also the professor who gives lectures on criminal law and in addition to this the inevitable compendium in which this same professor throws his lectures on to the general market as 'commodities.' ... The criminal moreover produces the whole of the police and of criminal justice, constables, judges, hangmen, juries, etc.; and all these different lines of business, which form just as many categories of the social division of labour, develop different capacities of the human mind, create new needs and new ways of satisfying them. Torture alone has given rise to the most ingenious mechanical inventions, and employed many honourable craftsmen in the production of its instruments. The criminal produces an impression, partly moral and partly tragic, as the case may be, and in this way renders a 'service' by arousing the moral and aesthetic feelings of the public. He produces not only compendia on Criminal Law, not only penal codes and along with them legislators in this field, but also art, belles-lettres, novels, and even tragedies, as not only Müllner's "Schuld" and Schiller's "Räuber" show, but "Oedipus" and "Richard the Third." ... The effects of the criminal on the development of productive power can be shown in detail. Would locks ever have reached their present degree of excellent had there been no thieves? Would the making of banknotes have reached its present perfection had there been no forgers? And if one leaves the sphere of private crime, would the world market ever have come into being but for national crime? Indeed, would even the nations have arisen? And has not the Tree of Sin been at the same time the Tree of Knowledge ever since the time of Adam?

(Marx 1975, 306–10; Wheen 1999, 308–9)

At times Jews have been fascinated, and even enthralled, by the real and mythical exploits of Jewish crooks — which is not synonymous with an internalization of the anti-Semitic discourse on Jews and crime (Gilman 1986). Marx was probably moved by Spiegelberg's boast in Schiller's *Rauber* that he was "restoring the fair distribution of wealth, in a word bringing back the golden age ..." (Schiller 1979, 41).

The case also may be made that the inception of the "positive" or "positivist" school of criminology that emerged around Cesare Lombroso was closer to the spirit of Marx than is often assumed. Joseph Conrad, in his 1923 play and novel *The Secret Agent*, exclaims through a foul-mouthed radical: "Lombroso's an ass!" Eighty years later, most comment on Cesare Lombroso (1835–1909) corroborates this crude remark. To be sure, Lombroso is widely credited with elevating criminology as a discipline in its own right, distinct from law and sociology. Yet he is not held in high esteem due to his espousal of what are now seen as retrograde or half-baked ideas, which tie too directly a person's outward appearance and psyche (Spectacular Bodies 2000–1). As a notable Italian Jew, discussions of Lombroso by scholars such as Martin Kemp and Marina Wallace, Daniel Pick, Nicole Rafter, Mariacarla Gadebusch, Mary Gibson, Sander Gilman, and Nancy Harrowitz, usually stress how his theories of the "born criminal" and "degeneration" contributed to anti-Semitism, racism, "Jewish self-hatred," and institutionalized misogyny (Harrowitz 1994, 63–80). Despite the fact that these analyses are illuminating, especially from the perspective of literary history, I would argue that Lombroso is in many respects under-appreciated for his influence on criminology – and this has impeded comprehension of relationships between his experience as a Jew and his criminological thought.

Lombroso was the first physician/anthropologist to rip thought about criminality away from its "classical" mooring (Drähms 1900, vii–viii) – such as the school of "judicial idealism" represented by A.F. Thiele in Germany and Arthur MacDonald in England, that distinguished between separate Jewish and Christian spheres of morality (Thiele 1841–3; MacDonald 1911–19) – toward a more detached, religion-blind socio-economic and anthropological view. Furthermore, Lombroso's theories strongly dissented from contemporary nationalistic policing ideology and practice – from which Jewish immigrants from Eastern Europe to Central and Western Europe often received the sharp end (Aschheim 1999). Law enforcement officials tended to categorize Jews (along with gypsies) as a criminal menace, as was propounded by F.C.B. Ave-Lallemant (Ave-Lallemant 1858).[1]

Ave-Lallemant, about whom little is written, was the most prolific German expert on crime in the mid- to late nineteenth century, who was resurrected by the Nazis – despite the fact that he avoided "racial science" per se (Ave-Lallemant 1882: xvi). As opposed to the old guard, Lombroso was more willing to accept the importance of situational forces than is usually understood – especially the socio-economic milieu of the criminal, and he observed that Jews were actually far less likely to be criminals than their Gentile counterparts. Despite conceding that Jewish prostitutes constituted a social problem, and that Jews were disproportionately involved in some types of shady business practices in contrast to Gentiles, Lombroso usually did not think it worthwhile to focus much attention on Jews in criminological discussions (Lombroso 1894). Jews were distinguished, Lombroso thought, for producing men and women of genius and degenerates – but not thieves and murderers. His own people seemed to frustrate the hell out of him, due to their simultaneous embrace of modern and outlandishly outmoded ways (Lombroso 1895).

It is with a great deal of thought that Sir Leon Radzinowicz,[2] a preeminent criminologist throughout the twentieth century, begins his weighty autobiography by recalling one of his early meetings with Ernico Ferri, the leader, after Lombroso, of "the positive school of criminology." In an opening section called "The maestro," Radzinowicz relates:

> "What are you reading, young friend?"
> "Cesare Lombroso's *L'Uomo Delinquente*."
> "Very good. But always remember that Lombroso was a genius who lacked talent."
>
> This was one of my first conversations with Enrico Ferri. It took place ... in September 1927, at his Institute of Criminology in Rome. He must have attached importance to his comment for a few months later, while talking to me in his splendid villa about the work of Lombroso, he pointed to Lombroso's bust on his desk and said: "My young friend, do not make the mistake common to so many of Lombroso's detractors, and always remember that he was a man of genius though he was without talent."
>
> (Radzinowicz 1999, 3)

Ferri and his protégé Radzinowicz are more discerning judges than Conrad. Lombroso was, above all, a radical universalist who fervently believed that "Nature, the pitiless leveller, teaches us all to be humble and modest" (Lombroso 1895, 49). In a similar vein, Sigmund Freud wrote that "we hate the criminal and deal severely with him because we view in his deed, as in a distorting mirror, our own criminal instincts" (Freud 1985: 450). From early modern times to the present, Jews have been made aware of their identification by non-Jews with a propensity to criminality, yet its impact on Jews have not been thoroughly examined.

From the substantial entry on "Criminology" in the *Encyclopaedia Judaica* (Hermon 2007) we learn that Jews have made signal contributions to the field. There remain, however, many aspects of the Jewish role in the emergence and evolution of criminological discourses that are underexplored. It should not be dismissed as merely coincidental that many (if not the clear majority) of the founders of the discipline, and a disproportionate number of leaders in the field up through the mid-twentieth century were European Jews, or "of Jewish origins," as the coarse euphemism runs. Jews have played a seminal role in the creation and propagation of modern, and now mainstream, liberal criminological discourses. Ferri's thought also is distinguished by its radical secularism, and total rejection of religious concepts of individual morality, which remain cornerstones of the discipline.

I would go so far as to say that criminology was almost as much a secular "Jewish sect" as was the psychoanalytic movement (Klein 1985). A few caveats, however, must be added: first, that the leaders of criminology were not so much a contemporary cohort as they were related diachronically – a succession of figures; second, as Jews, many of them Italians, their relationship with the non-Jewish world was not as embattled as was fin-de-siècle Central Europe for Freud and his circle; and third; it was less difficult for criminology to find a home in faculties in law and social science, especially anthropology, than for psychology and psychiatry in faculties of medicine. Not surprisingly, there is substantial cross-over between the psychoanalytic and criminological movements. Although it was well known that Lombroso and many of his followers were Jews, criminology was not perceived as a Jewish enclave – it was apparently much more inclusive. None of this, however, detracts from the fact that it held special significance for Jews. Little wonder, then, that Sir Leon Radzinowicz of Cambridge and Dr Max Greenhüt of Oxford, who began their lives as Jews, and Hermann Mannheim, of the London School of Economics, put the field on the map in post-World War II Britain – as Jews helped establish the field in the United States, Germany, Norway, Denmark, Belgium, Indonesia, and Argentina (Hermon 2007).

From the mid-nineteenth century to the 1920s, Jews were drawn to discussions of criminality, which impinged on the role of Jews, due to the historical legacy of Jews involved in crime and the prominence of Jews as a special category in criminological controversies. This was especially apparent in Germany, where the euphemistically termed *Kriminalstatistik* debate, over the relationship of Jews to crime, never abated from the 1848 to 1945, and possibly beyond. Generally speaking, such controversies about Jews and crime ran counter to a pro-Jewish emancipatory discourse that attempted to rationally explain, and then overcome the problem of Jewish criminality, and hence assist in attaining the full inclusion of Jewry in European civil society. With the rise of right-wing regimes in Germany and East Central Europe between the world wars, Jews were increasingly drawn to criminology when it became apparent that "the lofty principles of 'social defence' could be effortlessly distorted into cruel patterns of 'social aggression,' and that the Nazis intended to push their version of crime and punishment as far as they could" (Radzinowicz 1999, 76). But decades before the Nazi rise to power, Jews tended to move criminology toward favoring social and environmental explanations as opposed to essentialist constructions that pre-determined Jewish difference – akin to the role of Franz Boas in anthropology, as is discussed by John Efron and David Hollinger (Efron 1994; Hollinger 1996).

Although the biographies of Lombroso emphasize his privileged background, born into a notable Northern Italian Sephardic family, it is reasonable that the legacy of Jewish criminality in Italy, and Europe generally, played a part in his development and choice of intellectual and professional concentration. A great deal of Italian Jewish history, especially that of the Jews of Venetia, revolved around accusations of Jewish criminality. The fear that Jews were procurers of prostitutes was raised as early as 1409 (Calminani 1985, 10); even one of the elite founding Jewish families of Venice, the Meshullams, were accused of fencing stolen goods around 1533 (Calimani 1985, 34). Early modern Italian history includes swashbuckling Jewish outlaws (Calimani 1985, 77), like the members of the "robber bands" in Central Europe. Smuggling, kidnapping, and arson became common charges against Jews in the mid-sixteenth century (Calimani 1985, 88), Leon da Modena, "the most famous and controversial of all Venetian rabbis," was known through his autobiography to have been obsessed with gambling (Calimani 1985, 152); he was drawn into a scandal involving stolen goods in 1636 (Calimani 1985, 162). More important, probably, was the influence of Simone Luzzatto (1583–1663), author of the *Discorso circa il stato de gl'Hebrei: et in particolar dimoranti nell'inclita Citta di Venezia* (Discourse on the situation of the Jews, especially those in the City of Venice) "an effort to convince his readers of the usefulness of the Jewish presence in Venice," by focusing on material realities rather than philosophical and religious ideals. He is credited with "working out an original theory of economics," (Calimani 1985, 179) and Jews and crime writ large in his world view. Historian Riccardo Calimani, following the lead of Moses Schulvass, believes that Luzzatto was prompted to write his *Discorso* after an extraordinary crime in 1635, when a huge cache of valuables

> was stolen in the heart of the city. The event caused a great uproar and when some of the loot was traced to the ghetto, the scandal intensified. The thieves were arrested, and some of them were Jews. ... Some high-ranking particians and judges were also involved in the scandal, suspected of having taken bribes. Between vendettas and unexpected turns of events, the case took on the proportions of a full-fledged affair of state. ... The whole ghetto felt threatened."
> (Calimani 1985, 180–1)

As a result of his effort to placate this conflict, in 1638 Luzzatto wrote that it was not surprising that there should be "some agitators and scoundrels" among the Jews, but this was not grounds for questioning their indefatigable loyalty to the crown. In his defense of the Jewish role in the life of the city, Luzzatto states,

> The crimes of a few among our nation are exaggerated, by some, as intolerable disgrace and unsupportable calamity; but the ordinary benefits, conveniences and profits that derive from our people are overlooked and neglected as imperceptible and unknown things. The Jews bring considerable wealth to the noble city of Venice and should be considered "an integral part of its common populace."
> (Calimani 1985, 182)

The problem, as Luzzatto sees it, derives primarily from the situation imposed on Jewry:

> "In the body civil, the Jew may be likened to the part of the foot that treads the ground, which being inferior to all the other members is a burden to none, but indeed supports them. ... And I say that, since the Jew is forbidden any profession except Trade, he harms people of no condition, neither Artisans,

nor Foreigners, nor is he a great burden even to the Merchant Citizens." The risks of sailing are many and unpredictable. True, there are wealthy merchants, but many of them experience sudden bankruptcy.

In addition, Luzzatto, like Mendelssohn after him, acknowledges the crimes of a minority of Jews as a social problem, but he wishes to bring greater attention to what calls the "utility of trade" to which Jews contribute so substantially (Calimani 1985, 182).

A contemporary of Lombroso stated that his academic positions were "revolutionary" but perhaps more important, he held very little, if any reverence "for what was traditionally established." This was reinforced by the Lombroso family's "loss of fortune, consequent upon the political disturbances in Italy, which lasted until the re-establishment of the Austrian dominion" (Kurella 1911, 3–4). As Enrico Ferri makes clear in his discussion of the history of criminology, Lombroso was the first to take almost nothing for granted, as sacrosanct – starting with assumption that crime has both natural and social causes, and that there is no reason to believe that the prevention of crime can only be attained through punishment, or threat of punishment (Ferri 1913, 124). With his colleagues, Lombroso urged that society could and should take upon itself the responsibility for investigating and eliminating the conditions that lead to crime, that "we must first understand the criminal who offends, before we can study and understand his crime" (Ferri 1913, 15–16). Although "economic misery" is at the basis of much of criminality, the Positive School also asserted that capitalism itself nurtured crime through competitiveness, and often the person who wins out is "the best bargainer" while "the most honest, talented, and self-respecting" often suffer "the pangs of starvation" (Ferri 1913, 74–5). Despite the current reception of Lombroso, the school that he championed asserted that

> in order to be a criminal it is … necessary that the individual should find himself permanently or transitorily in such personal, physical and moral conditions, and live in such an environment, which become for him a chain of cause and effect, externally and internally, that disposes him to crime.
> (Ferri 1913, 22)

It called for nothing less than "a complete and fundamental transformation of criminal justice itself …" (Ferri 1913, 24). As Marx pronounced that the basis of all criticism was the criticism of religion, "Positive" criminology under Lombroso radically and irreparably removed itself from any religious realm. It was the absolute, abject secularism of criminology that helped attract Jews to the discipline. A lingering, ambiguous and almost playful association between Jews and crime is a connecting thread between criminologically-minded Jewish intellectuals from the late eighteenth century to our own time.

Beyond the realm of literature (Roskies 1984; Rubin 2000; Murav 2003) there remain many aspects of the "Jewish" investment in criminological discourses that are unexamined and underexplored. Along with a reconsideration of Cesare Lombroso, Karl Marx's role as a founder of criminology as a discipline, especially through his encounter with the teaching and thought of Edouard Gans, deserves further scrutiny. Marx was more influenced by the associations of Jews with criminality than typically assumed. Similar to Marx's irreverent treatment of criminality in *Kapital*, Daniel Bell (1953) and Eric Hobsbawm (1955) authored notable articles about organized crime that may be better understood in the context of "Jewish" associations with criminality. Both Bell and Hobsbawm's apologetic interpretation of gangsterism was a means for them to defend and positively identify themselves with a "counterhistorical" ethnic-Jewish legacy. Although by no means do I contend that the works of these scholars can be totally explained through focusing on their "Jewish" background, it seems that these remarkably similar analyses stem in part from an unacknowledged engagement with a problem that was part of the intellectual landscape from the mid-nineteenth to the mid-twentieth century. The possibility that there may be ongoing Jewish discourses on criminality has rarely been entertained by scholars. This sharply contrasts the rich mine of sources on the subject that remain ripe for plunder.

Notes

1 Much of this was enmeshed in a fascination for the so-called language of thieves, *Rotwelsch*, which has been examined by Sander Gilman and others.
2 I am indebted to my late colleague Raphael Loewe for informing me about Radzinowicz.

References

Aschheim, S. (1999) *Brothers and Strangers: The East European Jew in German and German-Jewish Consciousness, 1800–1923*, 2nd edn. Madison: University of Wisconsin Press.
Ave-Lallemant, F. C. B. (1858) *Das deutsche Gaunertum in seiner sozial-politischen, literarischen und linguistischen Ausbildung zu seinem heutigen Bestande*. Leipzig: Brockhaus.
Ave-Lallemant, F. C. B. (1882) *Physiologie der deutschen Polizei*. Leipzig: F.A. Brockhaus.
Avineri, S. (1967) "The Hegelian Origins of Marx's Political Thought," Review of Metaphysics 21, 1: 33–56.
Avineri, S. (1985) "Feature Book Review: The Discovery of Hegel's Early Lectures on the Philosophy of Right," *Owl of Minerva* 16, 2: 199–208.
Bell, D. (1953) "Crime as an American Way of Life," *Antioch Review*, 13, 2: 131–54.
Bell, D. (1967) *The End of Ideology: on the Exhaustion of Political Ideas in the Fifties*, rev. edn. New York: Free Press.
Boissevain, J. (1974) *Friends of Friends: Networks, Manipulators, and Coalitions*. Oxford: Wiley-Blackwell.
Calimani, R. (1985) *The Ghetto of Venice*. Translated by Katherine Silberblatt Wolfthal. New York: M. Evans.
Carlebach, S. (1898) *Geschichte der Juden in Lübeck und Moisling, dargestellt in 9 Voträgen*. Lübeck: privately published.
Dohm, C. von (1791) "Concerning the Amelioration of the Civil Status of the Jews," in Jehuda Reinharz and Paul Mendes-Flohr (eds.) (1995) *The Jew in the Modern World*. New York: Oxford University Press.

Drähms, A. (1900) *The Criminal: His Personnel and Environment*. New York and London: Macmillan.

Efron, J. M. (1994) *Defenders of the Race: Jewish Doctors and Race Science in Fin-de-Siecle Europe*. New Haven: Yale University Press.

Ferri, E. (1913) *The Positive School of Criminology: Three Lectures Given at the University of Naples, Italy, on April 22, 23, and 24, 1901*. Translated by Ernest Untermann. Chicago: Charles H. Kerr and Co.

Fischer, L. (2007) *The Socialist Response to Antisemitism in Imperial Germany*. Cambridge: Cambridge University Press.

Freud, S. (1985) In *Forms of Prayer for Jewish Worship, III: Prayers for the High Holidays*, eighth edition. London: The Assembly of Rabbis of the Reform Synagogues of Great Britain (eds.).

Gilman, S. L. (1986) *Jewish Self-Hatred: Anti-Semitism and the Hidden Language of the Jews*. Baltimore: Johns Hopkins University Press.

Harrowitz, N. (1994) *Anti-Semitism, Misogyny and the Logic of Cultural Difference: Cesare Lombrose and Matilde Serao*. Lincoln, NE and London: University of Nebraska Press.

Heine, H. (1976) "The God Apollo," in Klaus Briegleb *et al.* (eds.) *Samtliche Schriften*. Munich: Hanser, vol. VI, p. 32.

Hermon, Z. (2007) "Criminology," in Michael Berenbaum and Fred Skolnik (eds.) *Encyclopaedia Judaica*, Volume 5, 2nd edition. Detroit: Macmillan Reference, pp. 301–4.

Hobsbawm, E. (April 1955) "The Economics of the Gangster," *The Quarterly Review*, no. 604: 243–56.

Hobsbawm, E. (2000) *Bandits*. London: Weidenfeld & Nicolson.

Hobsbawm, E. (2003) *Interesting Times: A Twentieth Century Life*. London: Abacus.

Hobsbawm, E. (2005) "Benefits of Diaspora," *London Review of Books*, vol. 27, no. 20 (20 October 2005): 16–19.

Hollinger, D. (1996) *Science, Jews, and Secular Culture: Studies in Mid-twentieth Century American Intellectual History*. Princeton: Princeton University Press.

Klein, D. B. (1985) *Jewish Origins of the Psychoanalytic Movement*. Chicago and London: University of Chicago Press.

Kurella, H. (1911) *Cesare Lombroso: a Modern Man of Science*. Translated by M. Eden Paul. London: Rebman.

Lessing, G. E. (1754) "The Jews" in Jehuda Reinharz and Paul Mendes-Flohr (eds.) (1995) *In The Jew in the Modern World*. New York: Oxford University Press, pp. 62–4.

Lombroso, C. (1894) *Der Antisemitismus und die Juden im Lichte der modernen Wissenschaft*. Translated by H. Kurella. Leipzig: G. H. Wigand.

Lombroso, C. (1895) "Atavism and Evolution," *The Contemporary Review* 68, July.

MacDonald, A. (1911–19) "Need of University Men to Study Men," in *Studies of Modern Civilized Man* (bound pamphlets by the author), 1911–19, Bodleian Library, Oxford.

Marx, K. (1975) *Karl Marx, Friedrich Engels. Collected Works*. Moscow: Progress Publishers, with New York: International and London: Lawrence & Wishart.

Melamed, Y. (2001) "Leaving the Wound Visible: Hegel and Marx on the Rabble and the Problem of Poverty in Modern Society," *Iyyun* 50, 1: 23–39.

Mendelssohn, M. (1782) "Response to Dohm," in Jehuda Reinharz and Paul Mendes-Flohr (eds.) (1995) *The Jew in the Modern World*. New York: Oxford University Press, pp. 44–8.

Mendelssohn, M. (1783) "Remarks concerning Michaelis' Response to Dohm," in Jehuda Reinharz and Paul Mendes-Flohr (eds.) (1995) *The Jew in the Modern World*. New York: Oxford University Press, pp. 48–9.

Michaelis, J. D. (1782) "Arguments Against Dohm." in Jehuda Reinharz and Paul Mendes-Flohr (eds.) (1995) *The Jew in the Modern World*. New York: Oxford University Press, pp. 42–4.
Murav, H. (2003) *Identity Theft: The Jews of Imperial Russia and the Case of Avraam Uri Kovner*. Stanford: Stanford University Press.
Radzinowicz, L. (1999) *Adventures in Criminology*. London and New York: Routledge.
Reinke, H. (1990) "Die 'Liason' des Strarechts mit Statistik. Zue den Anfängen kriminalistischer Zählungen im 18. Und 19. Jahrhundert," *Zeitschrift für Neuere Rechtsgeschichte/ZNR* 12: 169–79.
Reinke, H. (1992) "Kriminalität also 'zweite Wirklichkeit' von Tätigkeitsnachweisen der Justizverwaltung. Bemerkungen zu Kriminalstatistiken des 19. Jahrhunderts als Materialien einer historisch orientierten Kriminologie," *Unrecht und Rebellion. Zur Sozialgeschichte der Kriminalität und des Strafrechts*, 2. Beiheft der Zeitschrift Kriminologisches Journal: 176–84.
Riesser, G. (1842) "Einiges zur Entgegnung auf den Aufsatz Juden und Dünste," in No. 44–46 der N.L.Bl. vom Jahre 1841", *Neue Lübeckische Blätter*, January 2 1842.
Rockaway, R. (1993) *But—He was Good to His Mother: The Lives and Crimes of Jewish Gangsters*, 6th edn. Jerusalem: Gefen.
Roskies, D. (1984) *Against the Apocalypse: Responses to Catastrophe in Modern Jewish Culture*. Cambridge MA: Harvard University Press.
Rubin, R. (2000) *Jewish Gangsters of Modern Literature*. Urbana: University of Illinois Press.
Rylands, I. G. (1889) *Crime: Its Causes and Remedy*. London: T. E. Unwin.
Sanders, J. (1993) "From Burglars to Businessmen: Jewish Bandits in 18th and 19th Century Germany." Unpublished paper. Waltham, MA: Brandeis University.
Schiller, F. (1979/1781) "The Robbers," trans. F.J. Lamport. *The Robbers and Wallenstein*. London: Penguin.
Spectacular Bodies: The Art and Science of the Human Body from Leonardo to now (exhibition) (2000–1). London; Los Angeles: Hayward Gallery; University of California Press.
Thiele, A. F. (1841–3) *Die juedische gauner in Deutschland, ihre taktik, ihre eigenthumlichkeiten und ihre sprache, nebst ausfuhrlichen nachrichten uber die in Deutschland und an dessen grenzen sich aufhaltenden beruchtigsten judischen gauner* . . . Berlin: Auf kosten des verfassers.
Turkus, B. B. and Feder, S. (1952) *Murder, Inc.: the Story of The Syndicate*. Garden City, NY: Permabooks.
Ulbricht, O. (1995) "Criminality and Punishment of the Jews in the Early Modern Period," in R. Pho-chia Hsia and Hartmut Lehmann (eds.) *In-and-out of the Ghetto: Jewish-Gentile Relations in Late Medieval and Early Modern Germany*. Washington and Cambridge: German Historical Institute and Cambridge University Press, pp. 49–70.
Van Oven, B. (1848) *Ought Baron Rothschild to Sit in Parliament? An Imaginary Conversation between Judaeous and Amicus Nobilis*, 2nd edn. London: Effingham Wilson.
Waszek, N. (1987) "Eduard Gans on Poverty: Between Hegel and Saint-Simon," *Owl of Minerva* 18, 2: 167–78.
Wheen, F. (1999) *Karl Marx*. London: Fourth Estate.
Wolf, G. (1861) *Geschichte der Israelitischen Cultusgemeinde in Wien 1820–1860*. Wien: Wilhelm Braumüller.
Wolf, G. (1864) *Die Juden in der Leopoldstadt im. 17. Jahrhundert in Wien*. Wien: Verlag vom Herzfeld und Bauer.
Wolf, I. and Salomon, G. (1817) *Der Chrakater des Judentums nebst einer Beleuchtung der unlängst gegen die Juden von Prof. Rühsnd Frieserschienen Schriften*. Leipzig: Carl Gottlob Schmidt.

15

THE METHODS OF LOMBROSO AND CULTURAL CRIMINOLOGY

Dina Siegel

The idea that by looking at someone's face one can instantly recognize a genius, a madman or a criminal, or the ability to derive someone's character and state of mind from their external features continues to fascinate us. For generations, scientists have searched for an easy way to identify types of human beings such as geniuses, lunatics and criminals. In *Physiognomica*, a volume ascribed to Aristotle, the link between body and character is described with the assumption that it is possible to 'read' internal character from outer appearance (Vogt 1999). In the Middle Ages, physiognomy and palmistry, which claimed to be able to recognize the character and predict the future of a person through the features of face or palm, were widely popular in Europe. In 1486, Heinrich Kramer (also known as Henricus Insitoris), a German inquisitor of the Catholic Church, published a handbook for witch-hunters, the *Malleus Maleficarum*, which was widely used throughout Europe between 1487 and 1520 (Trevor-Roper 1967). The text distinguished between different categories of witches and the possible damage and misfortune they could inflict on society (Woodworth and Porter 2000, 243).

At the end of the eighteenth and beginning of the nineteenth century, graphology, which focused on a person's handwriting to determine his character and brain activity, and phrenology, which analysed character and temperament on the basis of skull measurements, were used to predict a child's future or the success of a match between partners, and to collect information about potential employees.

It was, however, not before the appearance of criminal anthropology and the numerous publications by Cesare Lombroso that the connection between physical appearance, personality and risks for society, especially risks of crime, was taken up as a serious scientific endeavour. The use of scientific research methods and the presentation of data at various scientific forums contributed to this 'scientific' image.

Today, all these ideas are considered to be 'pseudo-scientific', but the human desire to be able to calculate and predict risks and success is still alive. And even though Lombroso's conclusions were later dismissed as unfounded, the stereotypes and images he presented as scientific findings are still part of our culture (Fleming 2000, 209). In our time, these images and stereotypes are easily recognizable not only in movies and television series, but also in 'criminal profiling', a widely accepted forensic discipline. Criminologists, biologists, anthropologists and physiologists around the world still find it difficult to abandon the dream of being able to recognize, predict and control 'born criminals'. Lombroso's role in history was not only to dream this dream aloud, but also to try and provide evidence for its scientific viability.

In this chapter, I intend to analyse the impact of Lombroso's research methods, which I compare with contemporary methods of cultural criminological research. Even though the Lombrosian and cultural criminological approaches are obviously contradictory and seemingly irreconcilable, this article will demonstrate that they have much in common and that both can contribute to contemporary criminological research and the development of theories. I will also ask how it can be that even after being discredited, Lombroso's works managed to survive and even made a sensational 'comeback' in criminology at the beginning of the twenty-first century: Who were the people behind the process of preservation and promotion of his ideas through the twentieth century?

The research methods of Lombroso

Door meten tot weten[1]
Heike Kamerlingh Onnes (Dutch Nobel Prize winner)

In essence, Lombroso's central ideas are fairly straightforward: a significant percentage of people who commit crimes are 'born criminals'. These individuals do not operate from rational incentives or by choice and their behaviour can be classified as atavistic. From an evolutionary perspective, they rank among the primitive and amoral creatures. Therefore, society has a right to defend itself against these 'savages' as if they were wild animals. The task of the criminal anthropologist is to establish the distinctive external characteristics of the criminal individual and to identify these persons in order to protect the rest of society.

To achieve these purposes Lombroso employed a number of methods, the most prominent of which was anthropometry, the measurement of body parts. He believed that measuring a human body was the way to learn about a person, in this case – a criminal (Harrowitz 1994, 113).

Lombroso did not invent this method. The first attempts to measure skull shapes and their alleged link to a person's character were performed by the German father of phrenology, Franz Joseph Gall (1758–1828). According to Gall, the brain is the source of all mental activity and the measurements of the head indicate the character, temperament and general mental functioning of a person (Heeschen 1994).

Similarly, Samuel George Morton (1799–1851) collected hundreds of human skulls from all over the world in an attempt to classify them into general categories. Morton argued that the size of the brain is dependent on the size of the skull, which in turn is also connected to a person's intellect (1839).

Lombroso also considered skulls and facial features to be indicators of innate genetic criminality. With the help of craniometers and callipers a person's features could be measured and classified, for example jaws, foreheads, cheekbones, noses, ears, lips, eyes, facial hair, arms and others. According to Lombroso (2006), criminal anthropology needed numbers and to him the statistical data of his measurements constituted scientific evidence.

At first glance, therefore, Lombroso could be considered a typical quantitative criminologist, someone who relies mainly on statistical data. He 'believed in the need for first-hand observations and measurement of individual cases instead of philosophical-logical-juridicial speculation and abstraction' (Mannheim 1965, 215). But he was not just a 'producer of facts', he was also convinced that human beings are able to instinctively understand the criminal type (Horn 2003). He sometimes used intuition and imagination himself, and he was even open to compromise regarding some of his ideas. For example, 'he restricted the category of the born criminal to 35 per cent of criminals, recognising in addition the existence of the insane and, in particular, the occasional criminal' (Mannheim 1965, 216).

In addition to pure quantitative method he also applied comparative analysis in his methodology and eventually arrived at the 'universal type', which meant that 'the Italian born criminal showed the same characteristics as, say, the Chinese or English' (Mannheim 1965, 216). From 1866 onwards, Lombroso began to collect skulls, skeletons, brains, tattoos and various other objects, which he stored in his private museum at his home in Turin. To the collection of skulls of soldiers and civilians from various regions in Italy, which he gathered in the course of his career as a military doctor, he later added craniums from foreign countries, as well as the skulls of criminals and lunatics, which he obtained from prisons and asylums (see Figure 15.1).

The prison was his laboratory, where he observed and measured the body parts of the criminals. His books are full of multiple photographs and drawings, produced and collected by him and other scientists in different countries, to illustrate the 'dangerousness' of the criminals and the portray an image of 'the criminal' with quantifiable traces of anomalies and deviations (Horn 2003, 21–2). To prove his arguments he also performed autopsies on dead criminals and employed methods of pathological investigation.

The critics of Lombroso emphasized the flaws in his methods, from the fact that he did not use control groups to the accusation that he manipulated data. Or, in the words of biologist Steven Gould (1981, 126), that he 'performed some mental gymnastics to incorporate it within his system'. One of his critics was Agostino Gemelli (1878–1959), a Franciscan professor of psychology and founder of the Universita Cattolica del Sacro Cuore in Milan, who also pointed to the weakness

FIGURE 15.1 Hall of skeletons of criminals from Lombroso C. (1906) "Il mio museo criminale," L'Illustrazione italiana

Source: Archivio storico del Museo di Antropologia criminale "Cesare Lombroso" dell'Università di Torino (Italia).

of the 'small samples' of Lombroso's research and his ignorance of new biometric methods developed by Francis Galton and Karl Pearson (Gibson 2002, 42).

Despite such criticism, the network of positivist criminologists in nineteenth-century Italy included scientists, lawyers, physicians, psychiatrists and police investigators. The Italian School of Criminology, with Cesare Lombroso, Enrico Ferri and Raffaelo Garofalo as its leaders, tried to parry the attacks of the French sociological approach of Gabriel Tarde, Paul Topinard and Leonce Manouvrier at different international congresses. Although the sociological approach won the debate, the popularity of Italian criminology remained widespread around the world.

Many criminologists have tried to classify and label (potential) criminals on the basis of race, heredity and intelligence, both before and after Lombroso. At the beginning of the twentieth century, the influence of Lombroso's ideas was apparent not only in the Italian, but also in the Dutch and French criminological literature. In the Netherlands, it was Arnold Aletrino who in 1902 emphasized the 'individual factor' as opposed to environmental factors. In his '*Handleiding bij de studie der crimineele anthropologie*' he focused on anatomical, physiological and psychological descriptions of criminals (Fijnaut 1992, 5).

In 1914, the American Gerald Fosbroke published his book *Character Reading Through Analysis of the Features* in which he argued that the physical characteristics of a person's face are a reflection of his character (Turvey 2002, 4). In the 1920s, crimino-biological schools were established in Germany and Italy, and in 1927 Adolf Lenz founded the Criminological Biological Society. In 1923, Erich Wulffen published his *Woman as a Sexual Criminal*, which was based on the idea that female crimes are connected to sexual abnormalities (Turvey 2002, 5). The

German psychiatrist Ernst Kretschmer proposed the existence of four basic body types, including a correlation with criminal potential.

It is important to remember that the German-Italian school flourished against the historical background of the totalitarian regimes of the Soviet Union and Nazi Germany, both of which made claims on its behalf, with the most disastrous consequences during World War II (Manheim, 1965). As a result, the biological approach to criminal behaviour was long considered taboo. The mere mention of biology in criminological work was considered non-scientific, politically charged and insensitive.

It was only in the 1970s–1980s that publications began to appear on bio-psychological and bio-social criminology issues, such as L. Taylor's *Born to Crime, the Genetic Causes of Criminal Behaviour* in 1984, and C.R. Jeffrey's *Criminology; an Interdisciplinary Approach* in 1990.[2] These days, bio-criminological research is flourishing in Europe, while bio-psychological and bio-social criminology are received with a lot of interest from the media and the general public. The new generation of bio-social criminologists is not only trying to identify potential criminals, but also working on the development of tools to 'improve' these people with the help of medication and therapies developed from a biological, bio-chemical, neurobiological or bio-psychiatric perspective (Robinson 2003). In addition, genetics, epigenetics (i.e. the study of the influence of environmental factors on gene expression) as well as evolutionary psychology are now routinely used in various crime prevention policies (Walsch and Beaver 2009).

In 1879, Lombroso published a book entitled *Sull'incremento del delitto in Italia* (On the Increase of Crime in Italy) with practical advice on how to apply criminal anthropology to the Italian criminal justice system. Salvatore Ottolenghi (1861–1934), professor of legal medicine, one of the founders of Scuola di Polizia Scientifica and a great admirer and follower of Lombroso, starting measuring and interrogating prisoners 'live' during his lectures before a class of police officers from the Public Security Force. He claimed that the principles of positivist criminology should be applied in the daily work of the criminal justice system (Gibson 2002, 9–11).

The first steps in the direction of criminal profiling were not only taken in Italy. During the 1888 'Jack the Ripper' murders in Whitechapel, the divisional police surgeon George Philips used so-called 'wound pattern analysis', by examining the victim's wounds and comparing them with the characteristics of offenders (Turvey 2002, 11). Thomas Bond, another British surgeon, tried to compose a criminal profile of Jack Ripper and according to some sources he came to be known as the offender profiler (Newburn *et al.* 2007, 493; Petherick 2005).

Today criminal profiling claims to be a separate discipline in the study of crime and this can be seen as a significant result of the 'comeback' of biological criminology. The core of contemporary criminal profiling is to understand the origins of criminal behaviour and this reminds us of Lombroso's ideas and aspirations. The media play an important role in the growing popularity of criminal profiling. The media's fascination with biological, 'psychic' or supernatural notions, 'police heroes' and the almost magical powers of criminal profilers can be seen as a reflection of the public's hopes and expectations that crimes can be solved on the basis of an analysis of the traits and features of criminals. The crime, fear and terror, mad murderers and the illusory powers of their opponents that dominated the newspapers and literature of the nineteenth century still feature in today's media, in the manifestos of political parties, in the arts and in the entertainment industry (Hutchings 2001). It is therefore no surprise that criminal profilers are often romanticized and 'many profilers have come to enjoy the suggestion that they are among an intellectual elite who have special knowledge and divining powers' (Turvey 2002, xi). These heroic, highly intelligent crime-fighters are apparently involved in a battle with the 'criminal class' of recognizable, predictable, but also incorrigible and unstoppable specimens of *Homo criminalis*.

In the 1970s, FBI special agent Howard Teten introduced a criminal profiling programme called 'applied criminology', which included teaching the abnormal aspects of criminal behaviour (Turvey 2002, 35). The modern profiling community, established in March 1999 and headed by the Academy of Behavioural Profiling, has grown into an international multidisciplinary organization promoting its own scientific methods, terminology and standards. Today, criminal profiling has become strongly associated with law enforcement investigations. It was Lombroso, however, who invented the term 'scientific police' and who predicted that the application of positivist theories would offer police officers respect, honour and prestige (Gibson 2002, 135).

Cultural criminology

The influence of Lombroso on the development of the bio-social school in criminology and the emergence of new forms and methods of criminal anthropology in the twenty-first century is obvious. However, his dream did not become the exclusive property of the bio-social criminologists. It is perhaps paradoxical that some of his research methods came to be appreciated by cultural criminologists, who embody the exact opposite of Lombroso's ideas, namely that criminal behaviour is not hereditary but that socialization and culture are crucial to a person's attraction to crime.

In the mid 1990s, a new theoretical and methodological school of thought, now known as cultural criminology, came to prominence in the United States and the United Kingdom (Ferrell and Sanders 1995). Cultural criminology emerged from the need to look critically at the discipline of criminology and to ask questions about the direction criminologists are going in the twenty-first century. What exactly are criminologists supposed to study, measure, and analyse? The feeling was that too many criminologists were busy with the production of data (what Jock Young called 'voodoo criminology'), instead of looking for in-depth explanations for the criminal events happening around them (Young 2004). The aim of the founders of cultural criminology was to break down the walls of their own discipline and to introduce fresh ideas into existing criminological thought, not just from the traditional sister-disciplines such as sociology, statistics and economics, but also from insights gained in other fields, such as literature, music, art, architecture and philosophy. The main argument of cultural criminologists is that crime is interconnected with 'culture', not with 'nature', as advocated by Lombroso and the modern bio-social criminologists.

Cultural criminology was born in the period of late modernity, which is characterized by high mobility of persons and goods, pluralism of values, materialism, consumerism and marital instability. Static identities, social norms and clear rules are no longer relevant in the social sciences. The dream of a positivist criminology, based on cause and effect, has become impossible in late modernity (Young 2004, 23). The influence of family, race, ethnicity and neighbourhood is no longer that important in an age of fluid identities. 'We need always to remind ourselves that we are not "pieces of nature" but have "become" who we are and therefore subject to change' (Presdee 2004, 44).

Following this line of thought, there seems to be almost no place left for Lombroso in our times. However, several aspects of cultural criminology appear to be directly linked to Lombroso's ideas, especially his research and presentation methods, which are still relevant in the period of late modernity. It is not so much his ideas, but rather his personality that could be the subject of a cultural criminological study. In the course of the twentieth century, the extraordinary scope of his multidisciplinary research methods and his creative explanations for human behaviour, have been pushed into the background. Now he is mostly remembered as a naïve pseudo-scientist. But it was not the power of Lombroso's insight and knowledge that was important, but his role as a 'de-coder' of criminals. He was fascinated with criminals, not with crime. It is important to focus on Lombroso as a person, or in other words, to analyse his work within the framework of a cultural criminological 'case-study of Lombroso', which takes into account his social world, his contacts, his preferences and his fascinations.

In his analysis of the changing representations of criminals in different historical periods, Dario Melossi argues that 'representations of crime and criminality are not random and unpredictable results of creative endeavours (though they are also this). Rather, they are conceptualizations deeply embedded within the main patterns of social relationships in a given society in a given period' (Melossi 2000, 296).

The development of Lombroso's ideas should be considered within the historical context of the Italian Unification of 1861 and the annexation of the southern provinces. The vast differences between the North and the South gave rise to all sorts of images and stereotypes about the differences between human populations. As a medical officer, Lombroso was influenced by these stereotypes. The economic and political difference between the North and the South was such that, according to Melossi (2000, 301): 'it had to be represented in the myth of the heritage of human evolution as this connected with races and individual dispositions'. We can only fully understand the development of Lombroso's ideas when we take into account the socio-economic context in which he found himself at the time.

In 2003, at the congress of the American Society of Criminology, Nicole Rafter suggested that we should reassess the role Lombroso played in criminology, widen our knowledge about his work and try to put stereotypes aside in order to construct a more complete picture of his ideas and contributions. In Italy, various publications have come up with new facts, interpretations and considerations (Villa 1985; Frigessi 2003; Gatti and Verde 2011). These new sources challenge the traditional image of Lombroso and the inadequacy of his findings and explanations.

Lombroso's methods and contemporary cultural criminology

Lombroso used quantitative methods in his research ('anthropology needs numbers'). His statistics were so impressive that he was able to convince the public of the correctness of his arguments. The same is true today: a barrage of graphs and figures is still guaranteed to impress government officials and policy-makers. In fact, many mainstream criminologists seem to spend most of their time producing numbers. In contrast, Lombroso always combined his statistics with qualitative data, which is rare these days, as criminology is still basically divided into 'quantitative' and 'qualitative' schools.

Lombroso's qualitative methods

Lombroso collected material objects and presented them as facts. But he also tried to discover the personal stories of criminals in their arts and crafts, which he hoped would reveal what they thought, desired, experienced or dreamt about. Much like today's cultural criminologists, Lombroso believed that criminals were also engaged in a symbolic performance. Similarly, by incorporating life stories, dreams and their interpretations into criminological research cultural criminologists hope to gain a deeper understanding of crime than cold statistical data will ever be able to provide.

Lombroso argued that the bodies of 'born criminals' revealed their dangerousness to society. It was not just the atavistic 'stigmata', but also other material items that could be useful in recognizing a criminal. Lombroso collected skulls, skeletons, brains, tattoos and various other objects. His criminal anthropology was not unlike 'performance art'. During his lectures, he presented live examples of criminals. He used skulls, tattoos and other material to prove to the audience that it was possible to visually recognize dangerousness (Morrison 2004). Today, similar methods of presentation are regularly used in university lectures and seminars, such as the use of PowerPoint presentations with photos, video fragments or animated images. Lombroso already included images, anecdotes and illustrations of the criminal culture in his writings and lectures. In his presentation at the Congress of Criminological Anthropology in Turin in 1906, he described 'the morning of a gloomy day in December 1870 [when I] found in the skull of a brigand a very long series of atavist anomalies' (cited in Rock 2007, 122).

Lombroso's followers as well as his opponents imitated his colourful language and imagery: 'The cold, wild glance of the murderer, and the restless glance of the thief, are unmistakable' (Kurella 1911, 51). The impact of Lombroso's performance and ideas on Russian culture inspired various art forms, from the literature of Dostoevsky (Gaakeer 2004/5) to the paintings of Kandinsky (McKay 1996).

Lombroso's interpretations of his findings are often questionable, for example when he argued that prison graffiti is comparable to the drawings of primitive cavemen and a result of the criminal's uncivilized drives, but he considered this type of visual evidence an important part of his research. Another example is that of argot and the songs of criminals. He believed that criminals spoke differently from the 'civilized' people of his time, their speech being similar to that of savages, and that their language was therefore easily recognizable. He regarded tattoos as another element of their criminal communication. The bodies of born criminals supposedly revealed their latent social dangerousness, and tattoos were a telling example of their 'visible stigmata'. The practice of tattooing was introduced by sailors returning from the South Pacific and was 'mostly confined to the lower classes' and prostitutes (Fletcher 1971, cited in Morrison 2004, 76). Lombroso considered this practice an atavism, as it came from primitive peoples, and this explained why it was so readily adopted by criminals (Lombroso 1896). In his historical period the distinction between primitive and civilized was widely accepted.

Today, cultural criminologists would explain the same findings (tattoos, graffiti, etc.) differently, mainly as cultural messages, 'criminal language', or even as artistic expressions, but they share Lombroso's fascination with criminal art and craft, sculpture, poetry and songs (Rafter and Gibson 2006). Cultural criminology distinguishes itself from mainstream criminology by its emphasis on the importance of paintings, music, films and other visual art forms as representations of criminal cultures, styles, symbolic codes and rituals. Just like Lombroso studied tattoos, graffiti and prisoners' paintings, post-modern cultural criminologists continue to emphasize the importance of cultural presentations as possible explanations of crime.

Emotions

Dealing with emotions such as pleasure, hatred, passion or boredom is not something one expects from most of today's mainstream criminologists, focused as they are on the increase or decrease of criminality, on crime control and prevention instruments, or on analysing crime from the perspective of rational choice/routine activity theories. The cultural criminological approach is probably unique in its emphasis on the importance of emotions for a better understanding of criminals. 'Cultural criminology ... captures the phenomenology of crime – its adrenaline, its pleasure and panic, its excitement, and its anger, rage and humiliation, its desperation and its edgework' (Young 2004, 13).

Lombroso was concerned about the emotions of criminals. He described them as exhibiting 'certain moral insensitivity', which in combination with 'precipitous passions explain(s) the lack of logic in crimes and the disjuncture between the gravity of a deed and the motive' (Lombroso 2006, 63–4). In other words, nature is cruel and emotionless, and so are criminals. However, as Lombroso himself stated, one category of crimes fell outside the scope of his analysis of criminal insensitivity, namely crimes of passion. 'Unlike the apathetic common criminal, the criminal by passion displays exaggerated sensitivity and excessive affections' (Lombroso 2006, 105). What other emotions did Lombroso detect in criminals? Pride, cruelty, idleness and an exaggerated sense of self-worth. 'A natural consequence of criminals' limitless vanity and inordinate sense of self is an inclination toward revenge for even the pettiest motives, as in the example of the inmate who killed someone for refusing to polish his shoes' (Lombroso 2006, 66).

Multidisciplinarity

The aim of cultural criminology is 'to continue turning the intellectual kaleidoscope, looking for new ways to see crime and the social response to it' (Ferrell et al. 2008, 6). It is no exaggeration to say that Lombroso personified the concept of interdisciplinarity (Gaakeer 2004/5, 2376). He was a psychiatrist, a criminal anthropologist, an anatomist, a philologist, a statistician, a neurologist, a mystic and a political scientist (Kurella 1911). His wide-ranging interests in science, art and literature can be held up as an example to many contemporary criminologists who rarely bother to look beyond their own limited field of study.

Lombroso was willing to travel far from home to look for examples supporting his theories. The encounter between Tolstoy and Cesare Lombroso at Tolstoy's residence Yasnaya Polyana, where the Russian writer spent the last years of his life, still serves as a colourful example of a clash of ideas and as an illustration of the influence of Italian criminal anthropology on Russian literature at the beginning of the twentieth century. In August 1897, Lombroso participated in the Twelfth International Medical Congress in Moscow, where he presented his ideas on the connection between madness and genius using the examples of Kant, Dante and others. In his book *Genius and Madness* (1864) Lombroso argued that a genius is a degenerate whose madness is a form of compensation for excessive intellectual development. Lombroso decided to visit the famous Russian writer Lev Tolstoy, who was at the time considered to be the world's foremost literary genius, in order to observe the 'degenerative' features of the great man. Contrary to his expectations, he found a strong, rustic-looking old man with thick eyebrows and clear eyes, who was relaxed at first but became increasingly irritated when Lombroso expounded on his idea of the 'born criminal'.

Lombroso and Tolstoy were disappointed with each other. The Italian was unable to confirm his theory, while the Russian was angered by the naïve and immoral ideas of the famous criminal anthropologist. When Lombroso claimed that society had every right to defend itself against the 'atavistic' type, even by the imposition of the death penalty, Tolstoy was not prepared to compromise and stated that all punishments, without exception, were criminal (Mazzarello 2001; Rock 2007). Tolstoy's irritation with Lombroso's ideas was later expressed in his book *Resurrection*, in Prince Nekhludov's observation: 'ne vo vlasti odnikh ludei ispravliat drugikh [It is not in the power of some to improve others]' (Tolstoy 1959, 468) The issues they argued over still occupy the minds of intellectuals today.

Coda

Lombroso was an imaginative and provocative thinker, as opposed to many present-day academics, who are often reluctant to take risks, or focus only on producing facts and statistics in aid of policy-making, but rarely come up with innovative, stimulating or thought-provoking ideas. Cultural criminology is the branch of criminology where the ideas of the innovative scholar Lombroso are still being discussed and interpreted. His findings may have been rejected by science, he may have been a naïve pseudo-scientist, a mystic perhaps, but his influence is both undeniable and inescapable and many of the questions he asked a century ago are still waiting for answers.

Notes

1 Lit. 'From measuring comes knowing'.
2 In the Dutch context, the so-called 'Buikhuisen affair' must be mentioned. In 1978 professor Wouter Buikhuisen introduced a biosocial research programme at the University of Leiden. His theory of the etiology of the early starting, chronic offender was met with enormous resistance. The hostile reactions of his colleagues and students contributed to his early retirement and he left the country. To all intents and purposes, Buikhuisen himself was considered by many to be the deviant individual (Van Swaaningen 2009, 467–8).

References

Ferrell, J. and Sanders, C. (eds) (1995) *Cultural Criminology*. Boston: Northeastern UP.
Ferrell, J., Hayward, K. and Young, J. (2008) *Cultural Criminology: An Invitation*. Newbury Park: Sage.
Fijnaut, C. (1992) 'De geboren misdadiger (The born criminal)', *Tijdschrift voor Criminologie*, 1: 3–7.
Fleming, R. B. (2000) *Scanty Goatees and Palmar Tattoos: Cesare Lombroso's Influence on Science and Popular Opinion*. The Concord Review.
Frigessi, D. (2003) *Cesare Lombroso*. Torino: Einaudi.
Gaakeer, J. (2004/05) 'The Art to Find the Mind's Construction in the Face', Lombroso's Criminal Anthropology and Literature: The Example of Zola, Dostoevsky, and Tolstoy, in *Cardozo Law Review*, vol. 26: 6.
Gatti, U. and Verde, A. (2011) 'Cesare Lombroso: una revision Critica', in Picotti, L. and F. Zanuso (red.) *L'antropologia criminale di Cesare Lombroso: dall'Ottocento al dibattito filosofico-penale contemporaneo*. Napoli, Roma: Edizioni Scientifiche Italiane s.p.a.
Gibson, M. (2002) *Born to Crime. Cesare Lombroso and the Origins of Biological Criminology*. Westport: Praeger.
Gould, S. (1981) *The Mismeasure of Man*. New York and London: W.W.Norton.
Harrowitz, N. (ed.) (1994) 'Lombroso and the Logic of Intolerance', in *Tainted greatness: anti-Semitism and cultural heroes*. Temple University Press, pp. 109–26.

Heeschen, C. (1994) 'Franz Joseph Gall (1758–1828)', in Eling, P. (ed.) *Reader in the History of Aphasia. Classics in Psycholinguistics*, 4. Amsterdam: John Benjamin Publishing Company.
Horn, D. (2003) *The Criminal Body. Lombroso and the Anatomy of Deviance*. New York: Routledge.
Hutchings, P. (2001) *The Criminal Spectre in Law, Literature and Aesthetics. Incriminating Subjects*. London and New York: Routledge.
Kurella, H. (1911) *Cesare Lombroso. A Modern Man of Science*. New York: Rebman.
Lombroso, C. (1896) 'The Savage Origin of Tattooing', *Popular Science Monthly* (April): 793–803.
Lombroso, C. (2006) *Criminal Man*, Gibson, M. and N. H. Rafter (trans.). Durham, NC: Duke University Press.
McKay, C. (1996) 'Fearful Dunderheads': Kandinsky and the Cultural Referents of Criminal Anthropology, in: *Oxford Art Journal*, vol. 19,1: 29–41.
Mannheim, K. (1965) *Comparative Criminology*. Part One. London: Routledge and Kegan Paul Ltd.
Mazzarello, P. (2001) 'Lombroso and Tolstoy. An Anthropologist's Unwitting Gift to Literature', *Nature*, vol. 409, February.
Melossi, D. (2000) 'Changing Representations of the Criminal', *British Journal of Criminology*, no. 40: 296–320.
Morrison, W. (2004) 'Lombroso and the Birth of Criminological Positivism: Scientific Mastery or Cultural Artifice?' in Ferrell, J., K. Hayward, W. Morrison and M. Presdee (eds) (2004) *Cultural Criminology Unleashed*. London, Sydney, Portland, Oregon: Glasshouse Press.
Morton, S. (1839) *Crania Americana, or a Comparative View of the Skulls of Various Aboriginal Nations of North and South America*. London: Simpkin, Marchall & Co.
Newburn, T., Williamson, T. and Wright, A. (2007) *Handbook of Criminal Investigation*. Willan Publishing.
Petherick, W. (2005) *Serial Crime: Theoretical and Practical Issues in Behavioral Profiling*. Academic Press.
Presdee, M. (2004) 'The Story of Crime: Biography and the Excavation of Transgression', in Ferrell, J., K. Hayward, W. Morrison and M. Presdee (eds) (2004) *Cultural Criminology Unleashed*. London, Sydney, Portland, Oregon: Glasshouse Press.
Rafter, N. and Gibson, M. (2006) Editors' Introduction, in Lombroso, C., *Criminal Man*, (trans. Hafter, N. and Gibson, M.). Durham, NC: Duke University Press.
Robinson, M. B. (2003) *Why Crime? An Integrated Systems Theory of Antisocial Behaviour*. Upper Saddle River, NJ: Pearson/Prentice Hall.
Rock, P. (2007) 'Cesare Lombroso as a Signal Criminologist', *Criminology and Criminal Justice*, no. 7: 117–33.
Tolstoy, L. N. (1959) *Sobranie sochinenii v 12 tomach (Collection of writings in 12 volumes), Voscresenie (Resurrection)*, vol. 11. Moscow: Chudozhestvennaya literatura.
Trevor-Roper, H. (1967) *The European Witch-Craze: of the Sixteenth and Seventeenth Centuries and Other Essays*. New York: Harper Co.
Turvey, B. (2002) *Criminal Profiling. An Introduction to Behavioural Evidence Analysis*. San Diego: Elsevier Academic Press.
Van Swaaningen, R. (2009) 'Criminology in the Netherlands', *European Journal of Criminology*, vol. 3(4): 463–501.
Villa, R. (1985) *Il deviante e i suoi segni: Lombroso e la nascita dell' antropologia criminale*. Milan: F. Angeli.
Vogt, S. (1999) (trans. and comm.) *Aristoteles: Physiognomonica*. Berlin: Akademie Verlag.

Walsch, A. and Beaver, K. M. (eds) (2009) *Biosocial Criminology. New Directions in Theory and Research*. New York: Routledge.

Woodworth, M. and Porter, S. (2000) 'Historical Foundations and Current Applications of Criminal Profiling in Violent Crime Investigations', *Expert Evidence*, no. 4, pp. 241–64.

Young, J. (2004) 'Voodoo Criminology and the Number Games', in Ferrell, J., K. Hayward, W. Morrison and M. Presdee (eds) (2004) *Cultural Criminology Unleashed*. London, Sydney, Portland, Oregon: Glasshouse Press.

16

LOMBROSO IN FRANCE

A paradoxical reception

Marc Renneville

In 1835, a man charged with raping and dismembering his child victims was convicted and sentenced to death in Turin. After his execution, the body was handed over for public autopsy. The post-mortem examination, conducted amidst scenes of great pomp and ceremony, revealed, according to one report, 'a sinister face; a ginger beard; coarse, thick, reddish hair; an atrophied right eye; thick upper lips and a flattened nose'. The head was subjected to a phrenological examination with the help of a craniometer. The following result was recorded:

> Those present were astonished by the development of the temporal bones covering the organs of cunning (secretiveness), destructiveness (cruelty, carnivorousness), and of the parietal bones corresponding to the organ of circumspection. The organs of religion, benevolence, educational capacity and comparative perspicuity, on the other hand, were comparatively small.

The top of the skull was removed, and the study of the cerebral convolutions within confirmed the initial diagnosis: the frontal lobe was under-developed, while the lateral lobe was abnormally enlarged and the anterior lobe 'smaller than expected' (De Rolandis 1835). Whatever the pertinence of that verdict, for the historian there is a certain symmetry in the fact that it was in this same Italian city that Cesare Lombroso would spend the major part of his professional life, a life that would begin just a few months after the phrenological examination of the Turin rapist and murderer.

Lombroso before Lombroso: criminal anthropology in France, 1878–85

When the first French translation of *L'Uomo delinquente* appeared in 1887, Cesare Lombroso and his theories were already well known in the country. In fact, the idea of applying the methods of anthropology to the study of criminals had made its appearance there some thirty years earlier in the period following the decline of the phrenological movement. In particular, a body of work produced in the 1860s by a small but influential group of researchers inspired by the racial theories of Arthur de Gobineau (1816–82), among them Roujou, Bordier and Orschanski, had advanced an atavistic explanation of criminal aetiology well before the publication of *Criminal Man*. By the end of the following decade, the study of the skulls and brains of murderers had expanded rapidly. For example, Arthur Bordier (1841–1910) presented his research on the skulls of thirty-five guillotined murderers to a gathering of the Paris Congress of Anthropological Science in 1878. Like Lombroso, Bordier drew on the theory of atavism to explain the criminal tendencies of his decapitated subjects, noting their anatomical similarity to Man's prehistoric ancestors. In his view, the subjects under study had been born with 'traits characteristic of prehistoric races; traits no longer to be found in the races of today, and which had reached them by a form of atavism'. For Bordier then, like for Lombroso, the criminal was

> an anachronism, a savage in a civilised country, a kind of monster; something comparable to a wild animal which, born to stock tamed and domesticated long ago, suddenly makes its appearance bearing the stamp of that untameable savagery which characterised its distant ancestors.
>
> (Bordier 1879, 297)

Despite this appeal to atavism, Bordier differed from Lombroso in arguing that criminals were neither 'mesaticephalic' nor 'microcephalic', but on the contrary had a larger than average brain. Between about 1880 and 1890, the *Bulletin de la Société d'anthropologie de Paris*, the organ of the Paris Anthropological Society, together with similar bulletins from anthropological societies in Lyons, Brussels and Bordeaux, published a large body of such work on criminal skulls. Gradually, however, research devoted purely to the measurement of deviant skulls would give way to a concern to identify the various pathologies afflicting the criminal brain.

It is against this background of a well-established tradition of French crimino-anthropological research that the first reactions to Lombroso's work in the country need to be seen. As early as 1879 in fact, Alfred Maury (1817–92) had provided his countrymen with a detailed review of the second edition of *Criminal Man*. Although Maury was a close friend of Lombroso, this did not stop him from expressing certain reservations about atavism. However, it was not until the following decade that a coherent French position on Lombroso and his theories began to emerge. The two men who would come to symbolise this French school of criminology, Gabriel Tarde (1843–1904) and Alexandre Lacassagne (1843–1924), were both initially drawn to Lombroso's theories before adopting what would prove to be a consistently hostile attitude to the Italian's work. Indeed, such a critical stance would characterise the French scientific community as a whole in this period, a community which would forge its own criminological theories out of a thoroughgoing rejection of Lombroso's 'criminal type' and his atavistic conception of criminal aetiology.

Gabriel Tarde was one of the most influential voices in French criminology at the end of the nineteenth century (Renneville 2004a,b). Magistrate, head of the French Justice Ministry's statistical service, *professeur* at the *Collège de France*, and member of the prestigious scientific foundation, the *Institut de France*, Tarde is better known today for his sociological work and his opposition to Durkheim. However, he also played a key role in circulating and discussing Lombroso's ideas in France, probably in the first instance thanks to a suggestion from his friend Alfred Espinas (1844–1922). Espinas had drawn Tarde's attention to Lombroso's work as early as 1879, expressing 'the wish that this book be translated and become a valued reference work for our examining magistrates' (Espinas 1879, 146).

From 1883 onwards, Tarde corresponded regularly with a variety of Italian specialists in the field, among them Filippo Turati, Napoleone Colajanni, Achille Loria and Enrico Ferri, and penned reviews of their work for the *Revue philosophique*. However, as Massimo Borlandi has convincingly argued after a close examination of these Franco-Italian contacts, Tarde's status with his Italian correspondents changed over time, shifting from that of valued ally during the years 1883 to 1888–9, to that of recognised enemy of Lombrosian criminology in the subsequent period (Borlandi 2000). There are signs of this rift as early as 1884 in the pages of Tarde's book, *La criminalité comparée*, where Lombroso's theory of the criminal type is criticised (ch.1); as are the positions of Poletti on the relationship between crime and social development (ch.2); and those of Ferri and Morselli on the question of the law of compensation between murder and suicide (ch.4).

In the first chapter of *La criminalité comparée*, significantly entitled 'The Criminal Type', Tarde provided a closely argued refutation of Lombroso's theory of the born criminal. This chapter had been written in the second half of December 1884, and first appeared in an 1885 issue of the *Revue philosophique*.[1] In this piece, Tarde marshalled anthropological evidence to disprove the existence of a Lombrosian criminal type, arguing that in his view the Italian had confused the characteristics of the criminal, the madman and the savage. Surveying data from a variety of sources on the anatomical, physiological, psychological and sociological bases of Lombroso's 'born criminal', the French magistrate concluded that no such type could be shown to exist. While Tarde stated that the Italian School had over-estimated the importance of anthropological markers of criminality, he was careful to add that his remarks concerned 'only the interpretation given by Lombroso of the physical and other characteristics so frequently exhibited by criminals. They do not in any way seek to deny the existence of the criminal type.' Tarde went on to claim that this criminal type was not in fact 'anthropological' as the Lombrosians argued, but rather 'social', and could in fact be considered a form of 'professional' type, with features derived from a specific occupational background, irrespective of the ethnic origin or physical characteristics of the individual concerned. Certain general features, Tarde went on, were 'present at birth'; others were the result of learned behaviour or imitation, such as tattoos and slang. For Tarde, then, the 'criminal at birth' (*criminel de naissance*, not to be confused with Lombroso's born criminal or *criminel-né*) could only exist in relation to a particular social context. Thus, if that context was right – or rather wrong – any individual could be born a criminal. However, given that such contexts vary over space and time, the specific features associated with the criminal-at-birth-type would also vary. Tarde also stressed that such types were not to be confused with the criminally insane: 'No-one, except certain monomaniacal arsonists or murderers, and some kleptomaniacs, who should not be confused with born criminals, is born programmed to kill, to burn or to steal from his fellow man' (Tarde 1886, 50–8).

Alexandre Lacassagne, professor of forensic medicine at Lyons' Faculty of Medicine, was the acknowledged head of the city's *Milieu Social* School of criminology, the avowed aim of which, as he put it, was 'the study of social problems in the light of modern science' (Lacassagne 1882, 211). In 1886, along with René Garraud, Henri Coutagne and Albert Bournet, Lacassagne founded the *Archives d'anthropologie criminelle et des sciences pénales*, a scientific journal dedicated to circulating the school's views, and stimulating further research.[2] Like Lombroso, Lacassagne considered that the punishment should match the criminal rather than the crime. He was never a card-carrying Lombrosian, however, for at an early stage he began to elaborate his own theory of criminal aetiology, noticeably different from that of the Turin professor. While rejecting firmly the notion of atavism, Lacassagne nevertheless did not hesitate to use the theory of regression to account for the nefarious effects on the individual of such environmental factors as diet, alcohol, education, economic hardship and revolutionary upheaval. The cerebral instability which resulted from the action of such forces led to what he termed an 'inevitable conflict' in the brain in which 'the posterior part of the brain would come to dominate the anterior part'. What this meant was that action and instinct tended to gain the upper hand over the 'cerebral functions'. In this way, there existed in society individuals who were 'the slaves of fatal organic dispositions' which might be either inherited or acquired (Lacassagne 1882, 255).

Throughout his career, Lacassagne would continue to defend the notion that the wrongdoing of certain criminals could be explained in terms of defective heredity, but at the same time as early as the first Congress on Criminal Anthropology at Rome in 1885, he was keen to stress that his own approach differed from that of Lombroso in a number of important respects. He told the Rome delegates that in his view the Italian School constituted an unwarranted deviation from the traditions of Gall, Broussais, Morel and Despine. He also endeavoured to play down the explanatory power of the Italian's theories, implying that the latter had jumped to conclusions on the basis of inadequate data, and urged instead the need for prudence with his calls not to 'go too quickly' and his warnings of 'the dangers of seeking easy and precipitous solutions'. However, Lacassagne's reservations concerning Lombrosian criminology would make little impact on those attending the Rome congress. This derived in part from the fact that the wide-ranging scope of the Lombrosian project made it difficult to refute in its entirety. Also problematic for Lacassagne's line of attack was the fact that the Italian had gone some way to placating his critics with his admission that there existed a class of 'occasional' criminals for whom 'the physical and above all the social environment provides the principal cause and determination of criminal behaviour, because of the weak moral sense and lack of foresight of the individuals concerned' (*Actes* 1887, 126). And then there was the question of the balance of forces at Rome. The fact that most of those present were already won over to Lombrosianism before the congress opened its doors contributed to Lacassagne's failure to win support for his position, but it should also be remembered that the distinctiveness of that position had not yet been fully worked out in the mind of the Lyons professor. However, what was clear to all at the close of proceedings in Rome was that there now existed a body of criminological opinion which rejected outright the relevance of Lombroso's atavistic theory to the explanation of crime.

Anti-Lombrosian criminal anthropology in France, 1885–1909

The theory of atavism would constitute a regular target for Lombroso's critics. For French commentators, atavism was to be understood as a form of 'normal heredity', that is to say as 'the *ensemble* of hereditary forces belonging to a race'. This process of 'heredity in reverse' was considered to take precedence over 'individual heredity', subject to the influence of the social milieu (Lacassagne 1876; Sanson 1893). According to this view, atavism corresponded to the transmission of the oldest, most 'fixed' forms of inherited characteristics; those least susceptible to unpredictable short-term variation. It was on this point that there were important differences of opinion between the French and the Italians. Given a choice between according explanatory primacy to the action of processes of slow, pathological degeneration or the kind of sudden, unpredictable atavism which the Italians claimed to be at work in the minds and bodies of criminals, most French specialists opted unequivocally for the former. As anthropologist Léonce Manouvrier (1850–1927) liked to point out, '*Natura non saltus est*' (Nature makes no leaps). French doctors and scientists were thus unanimous in their refusal to consider atavism as a specific form of degeneration. For French specialists from Lacassagne to Sanson and from Féré to Rabaud, such talk verged on heresy. Had not the great Morel himself specifically ruled out such a notion? Gallic patience was thus sorely tested by Lombroso and Ferri's efforts to argue that the two concepts were perfectly compatible.

The theory of degeneration thus developed in French criminological circles as a counter-proposition; one seen as providing powerful ammunition to challenge Lombroso's theory of atavism. The strategic importance of the degeneration argument explains the profusion of work in this area in the 1880s, all of which focused on the criticism of Lombroso's anthropological 'criminal type'. Even the 'professional type' developed by Tarde, Colojanni and others did not escape censure. For the medical advocates of degeneration theory, accused by their detractors of 'seeing pathology everywhere', there was thus no question of accepting the idea that the existence of a collection of 'anomalies' could justify the identification of a new criminal 'type'.

One of the first of the medical critics to plough this furrow was the alienist Charles Féré (1852–1907). An intern at Paris's Salpêtrière Hospital where he studied under the celebrated neurologist Jean-Martin Charcot (1825–93), Féré became in 1882 the head of pathological anatomy in the hospital's department of nervous diseases, before moving on, five years later, to work in the psychiatric ward attached to the city's *Préfecture de Police*, as well as at the capital's Bicêtre Hospital. A year before the Paris Congress on Criminal Anthropology in 1889, Féré published a short work in which he launched a vigorous attack on the theory of atavism and the criminal type. This book provides in many ways a characteristic example of French objections to the Italian School, and indeed would be frequently cited in this context.

The main thrust of Féré's argument was not to deny the existence of the kind of physical 'stigmata' identified by Lombroso, but rather to draw on them as evidence to shore up the degenerationist case. Thus, hare lips, hernias and the possession of supernumerary fingers or toes were all taken as signs of abnormal embryonic development, rather than evolutionary retrogression. For Féré, moreover, such defects were always markers of *localised* pathology, rather than some 'general organised plan' (Féré 1888, 67). His explanation of crime drew explicitly on the theory of physical and mental degeneration, both of which were seen as having a common origin in the action of such forces as alcoholism, the advanced age of the parents at conception, and insalubrious sanitary conditions – all of which causes could incidentally also be found in Lombroso. The existence of families where crime and insanity alternated over the generations was taken as clear evidence for the nefarious influence of such factors.

The categorical refusal on the part of dyed-in-the-wool degenerationists to countenance anything resembling a 'criminal type', be it anthropological or professional, would turn out to be a powerful weapon for critics of Lombrosian theory. Rather than seeing wrongdoing as the result of a distant phylogenetic inheritance, French critics argued forcefully in favour of a conception of criminal aetiology which emphasised the role of acquired characteristics resulting from morbid ontogeny. Advocates of this view hoped that it would come to vanquish all others as an explanation of criminal behaviour, but before achieving the hoped-for victory they would find themselves under concerted attack from home-grown specialists of the sociological school founded by Emile Durkheim.

Among the advocates of this medicalised approach to criminal aetiology was the physician Charles Debierre (1853–1932) who in 1885 published a study of the criminal skull which challenged Lombroso's conception of the anthropological criminal type. Debierre shared the determinist approach characteristic of the French School of the period, but expressed greater caution on the subject than most, preferring to await the results of future research before committing himself. He had similar reservations about degeneration theory. While a supporter of the approach, he argued that the biological causes of criminal behaviour remained to be fully determined. Despite such equivocation, Debierre's conclusions on the possible existence of a 'criminal skull' left no room for doubt. In his view, there was 'no particular feature, no combination of traits, either of the bones of the skull or of the encephalon' capable of 'identifying the murderer' (Debierre 1895, 459).

Two years earlier, Léon Maupaté had defended a doctoral thesis on criminal anthropology before a panel chaired by Paul Brouardel. Maupaté's research, based on the study of a sample of sixty-five child and adolescent offenders aged between 7 and 21, had set out to explore both the physical and moral aspects of crime. His results were then compared with those from a control sample taken from the same psychiatric hospital as the first group, but this time with no record of criminal behaviour. Each offender was examined from an anthropological and psychiatric point of view, and the physical and mental stigmata of degeneration and crime were noted. Maupaté's thesis was intended in part to test the hypothesis of Lombroso's 'born criminal', but above all to verify the existence of the 'criminal type'. His conclusions, like Debierre's, were unequivocal. In his view, there existed 'no regressive or degenerative stigmata making it possible to identify the criminal, and by sequestering him from childhood, prevent crime' (Maupaté 1893, 224). Ten years later, Lyon-based anthropologist Dr Lucien Mayet (1874–1949) would develop a similar argument (see also Rakowski 1897).

Mention should also be made of alienist Paul Legrain (1860–1939), who likewise drew on degeneration theory to argue that degenerates *could* become criminals, and that certain of their number bore distinctive physical stigmata, but that this did not mean that *all* criminals would be found to be in possession of such incriminatory traits (Legrain 1894, 8–9). One of those who shared Legrain's scepticism was the Belgian Dr Jules Dallemagne, one of a sizeable contingent of like-minded specialists from that country including Heger, Houzée, Warnots and Vervaeck. However, this did not stop Dallemagne from taking Lombrosian theories seriously enough to undertake his own search for the physical defects of criminals (Dallemagne 1896). One last example is worth noting in this context. The influential pathologist Professor Paul Brouardel (1837–1906), referred to above, also rejected the criminal type out of hand. Like many of his colleagues, he was hostile to the concept of an in-born 'criminal nature', and followed Lorain in considering that degeneration resulted in a process of arrested development in the child. However, like Lacassagne and Émile Laurent (1861–1904), Brouardel believed in the existence of a degenerate urban type, who resembled in some ways the 'accidental collective type' described by Paul Topinard (Brouardel 1890).

One final example of degeneration theory applied to the study of crime should be mentioned, and that is the work of alienist Valentin Magnan (1835–1916). In a paper given to the 1892 Brussels Congress on Criminal Anthropology, Magnan distinguished between two principal types of criminals. There were on the one hand the criminally insane and on the other those who were of sound mind, but still abnormal since they were unable to control criminal impulses emanating from what he called a 'morbid criminal obsession' (Magnan 1893, 334–5). This view was shared by Émile Laurent, a follower of Lacassagne, for whom crime was 'no more than an epiphenomenon, an accident in the life of the degenerate, the insane, the epileptic and all those who, in a word, live under the burden of degenerative stigmata'. He went as far as claiming that crime was in reality 'the synthesis of every form of human degeneration' (Laurent 1908, 172).

Lombroso's legacy in France

In an article co-written by Alexandre Lacassagne and his disciple and successor Étienne Martin (1871–1949) in 1905 on the subject of 'the present state of our knowledge in the field of criminal anthropology', it was conceded that virtually every one of the physical stigmata identified by the criminal anthropologists had their basis in fact: 'What is at issue is uniquely the interpretation of those physical anomalies which we have listed at length. Everyone agrees that physical stigmata are to be found in criminals, particularly those weighed down by hereditary defects' (Lacassagne and Martin 1906, 7). In similar fashion, Dr Henri Thulié (1832–1916) noted the following year that while the debate on the born criminal in France had prompted 'eloquent discussions' on the subject, disagreements had been in reality largely a matter of 'squabbling over words' (Thulié 1907, 25).

Even though the influence of Manouvrier and Durkheim would play a major role in weakening the impact of degenerationist medical research on crime and the criminal, the latter only gradually lost ground in the emerging French science of criminology. When one looks beyond the squabbles over words noted by Thulié and Havelock Ellis, there were in reality important lines of convergence between the French medical specialists interested in crime on the one hand and the researches of Cesare Lombroso on the other. After all, was it not the case that Lacassagne's scientific journal *Les Archives* had changed its name in 1893 in order, among other reasons, to give a greater role to the study of what it called 'cerebral physiology'? And had not Jules Dallemagne – as we have seen a stern critic of the Lombrosian school – stated that the study of 'the crime problem' necessitated 'the study of criminal psycho-physiology' (Dallemagne 1896, 208)?

An exhaustive examination of French-language responses to Lombroso is beyond the scope of the present study. While traces of the Italian's influence can be seen in the art and sculpture of Edgar Degas and in the novels of Émile Zola, his theories were never adopted lock, stock and barrel (Becker 2005). Indeed, a critical attitude to Lombroso would remain the dominant response in France, both in literary and in legal circles (Noiray 2005). That being said, the sheer volume of that critical output was not without consequences. By dint of repetition, Lombroso's ideas gained a paradoxical after-life, both in literature and in the collective consciousness, feeding into both Zola's *Bête Humaine* and Bram Stoker's *Dracula*. The way in which the debate on criminal anthropology in France was organised around reactions to a foreign author served, moreover, to conceal certain of the approach's internal contradictions behind appeals to national 'schools'.

Gradually, however, Lombroso was assimilated into the French collective memory as one of the 'founding fathers' of criminology. For example, a 1950 book devoted to criminal tattoos by Jacques Delarue, an inspector in the central bureau of the Paris *Police judiciaire*, made no reference to the controversial nature of the Italian's theories, beyond noting in passing that Lombroso's ideas had been 'somewhat wide of the mark'. The long-running dispute between the Italian and Lacassagne on the subject of atavism referred to above was apparently forgotten. Indeed, Delarue noted in his book that criminals shared with certain 'primitive' peoples an ape-like anatomy ('excessively long arms' were mentioned), a 'rudimentary mind', 'latent primitivism' and behavioural traits 'the coarseness of which could go as far as brutality' (Delarue and Giraud 1950, 54). In short, the kind of descriptions not unlike those provided by the criminal anthropologists themselves.

In the middle of the 1960s, a French book on cybernetics went as far as claiming that criminology *was* Lombroso (Aurel 1965). Was this a sign that the Turin professor was making something of a come-back in the country? Well, yes and no. Certainly, after the First World War, the detailed critical response to Lombroso in France we have charted began to give way to a recognition of his insights by the country's specialists in positivist penology and social defence theory. In this sense, Lombroso's theories continued to influence medical practice and even the legal profession in the inter-war period. A more recent example of his continuing influence is provided by a conference organised by the Paris Institute of Criminology in 1976 to mark the centenary of the publication of the first edition of *L'Uomo delinquente*. While distancing themselves from the claims of the criminal anthropologists, those involved in the centenary event acknowledged that Lombroso had played a key role in the emergence of their discipline. The jurist Marc Ancel, for example, a theorist of the New Social Defence school, argued that *Criminal Man* had 'created shock-waves' on its publication, and he paid the work the supreme compliment of equating its influence with that of Beccaria's *On Crimes and Punishments* (Ancel 1977). Other speakers at the conference also sought to rehabilitate Lombroso's reputation. Thus, Jean Dupreel, chair of the International Penal and Penitentiary Foundation, argued that the French *Milieu Social* School had been unduly critical of the criminal anthropologists (Dupreel 1977, 540), while Pietro Nuvolone described *Criminal Man* as having heralded 'a veritable turning point in intellectual history' (Nuvolone 1977, 291). As for the magistrate Jean Pinatel, he suggested that 'Lombroso's great achievement was to have founded the discipline of criminology as an independent and autonomous science' (Pinatel 1977, 549).

This recognition of Lombroso's work as having played a role as important of that of Beccaria can be seen as something of a posthumous triumph for the Turin professor. That being said, this apparent victory, like everything linked to his legacy in France, is paradoxical in more than one respect. First of all, the compliment is generally paid by jurists, the same profession which generated Lombroso's most vociferous critics during the Italian's lifetime. Further, this vision of Lombroso as the founding father of criminology is based on a highly selective reading of the man's work; reducing in effect his legacy to an objective (judge the criminal rather than the crime), a method (the scientific study of the offender) and a consequence: the need to reform the criminal justice system according to the principles of social defence theory. Indeed, it is above all for his allegedly pioneering status as a champion of social defence that the name Lombroso continues to be cited in France, whether in medical and legal circles (Robert 2008) or in the realm of political debate.

However, there are clearly limits to the rehabilitation of Lombrosian theory in France, as a last example, this time from January 2008, makes clear. In a debate in the French parliament on a bill concerning the incarceration of the criminally insane, Elizabeth Guigou, a former Justice Minister, addressed Rachida Dati, the current occupant of the post, with the following words:

> Madame Minister, ... you are in the process of turning your back on Beccaria and the heritage of the Enlightenment in favour of Lombroso and his 'Criminal Man', while you know full well that it was this very positivist philosophy which led to the worst excesses of Nazi Germany.[3]

That attempt to tar official policy with the Lombrosian brush prompted howls of protest on the government benches, but the resulting controversy did nothing to challenge that erroneous historical interpretation which sees a direct line of descent from Lombroso to Nazism. In other words, the legacy of Cesare Lombroso is selectively – and often inaccurately – remembered but is certainly alive and kicking. Indeed, in France that memory has retained a vitality which the Italian's contemporary adversaries (including home-grown ones like Alexandre Lacassagne) lost a long time ago. His name continues to be evoked outside the narrow circle of academic history, a situation which reveals the extent to which the ideas with which he is (rightly or wrongly) associated continue to resonate with the preoccupations of our time.

Acknowledgement

The author would like to thank Neil Davie for his translation of this work.

Notes

1 Gabriel Tarde, 'Le type criminel', *Revue philosophique*, 1885, vol. 19, pp. 593–627. This article was republished in 2000 in a special issue of the *Revue d'Histoire des Sciences Humaines*: 'Gabriel Tarde et la criminologie au tournant du siècle', 2000, n 3, pp. 89–116.
2 The complete run of the *Archives d'anthropologie criminelle* (1886–1914) is available online on the Criminocorpus website (http://www.criminocorpus.cnrs.fr).
3 'Rétention de sûreté et déclaration d'irresponsabilité pénale pour cause de trouble mental. Assemblée nationale. XIIIe legislature', Ordinary Session, 2007–8, Verbatim Report, Third session, 8 January 2008 http://www.assemblee-nationale.fr/13/cri/2007-2008/20080094.asp.

Bibliography

Ancel, M. (1977) 'Le centenaire de l'*Uomo delinquente*. Exposé introductif', *Revue de science criminelle et de droit pénal comparé*, 285–301.
Actes du premier congrès d'anthropologie criminelle (biologie et sociologie). Rome. 1885. (1887). Torino-Roma-Firenze: Bocca frères.

Aurel, D. (1965) *La cybernétique et l'humain.* Paris: Gallimard.
Becker, C. (2005) 'Zola et Lombroso. A propos de *La Bête humaine*', in *Cesare Lombroso e la fine del secolo: la verità dei corpi*, Atti del Convegno di Genova 24–5 Settembre 2004, Publif@rum 1. http://www.farum.it/publifarumv/n/01/becker.php.
Blanckaert, C. (1994) 'Des sauvages en pays civilisé. L'anthropologie des criminels (1850–1900)', in L. Mucchielli (ed.) *Histoire de la criminologie en France*. Paris: L'Harmattan, pp. 55–88.
Bordier, A. (1879) 'Etude anthropométrique sur une série de crânes d'assassins', *Revue d'anthropologie* 2: 265–300.
Borlandi, M. (2000) 'Tarde et les criminologues italiens de son temps (à partir de sa correspondance inédite ou retrouvée)', *Revue d'Histoire des Sciences Humaines*, no. 3, 7–56.
Bosc, O. (2007) *La foule criminelle. Politique et criminalité dans l'Europe du tournant du XIXe siècle. Scipio Sighele (1868–1913) et l'école lombrosienne*. Paris: Fayard.
Brouardel, P. (1890) 'Le criminel', *Gazette des hôpitaux*: 313–14, 341–2, 368–70, 469–71, 493–5, 529–30, 577–9, 669–70, 698–9.
Coffin, J. C. (2003) *La transmission de la folie. 1850–1914*. Paris: L'Harmattan.
Dallemagne, J. (1896) *Les stigmates biologiques et sociologiques de la criminalitéi.* Paris: Masson.
Debierre, C. (1895) *Le crâne des criminels*. Paris: Masson.
Delarue, J. and Giraud, R. (1950) *Les tatouages du 'milieu'*. Paris: La Roulotte.
De Rolandis (1835) 'Lettre à M le docteur Fossati, sur un criminel convaincu de plusieurs viols, suivis de meurtre', *Journal de la Société phrénologique de Paris*, April 1835: 244–7.
Dupreel, J. (1977) 'Lombroso et la pénologie', *Revue de science criminelle et de droit pénal comparé* 535–40.
Espinas, A. (1879) 'La philosophie expérimentale en Italie', *Revue philosophique* 131–53.
Féré, C. (1888) *Dégénérescence et criminalité (essai physiologique)*. Paris: Alcan.
Houzee, E. (1890) 'Normaux et dégénérés: les erreurs de Lombroso', *Clinique*. Bruxelles: 385–9.
Kaluszynski, M. (1988). *La criminologie en mouvement. Naissance et développement d'une science sociale en France à la fin du XIXe siècle. Autour des 'Archives de l'Anthropologie criminelle d'Alexandre Lacassagne'*. Lille: Atelier de reproduction des thèses.
Lacassagne, A. (1876) 'consanguinité', Dechambre *Dictionnaire encyclopédique des sciences médicales* 19: 652–714.
Lacassagne, A. (1882) 'L'homme criminel comparé à l'homme primitif', *Bulletin du Lyon médical*, 210–17, 244–55.
Lacassagne, A. and Martin, E. (1906) 'Etat actuel de nos connaissances en anthropologie criminelle pour servir de préambule à l'étude analytique des travaux nouveaux sur l'anatomie, la physiologie, la psychologie et la sociologie des criminels', *Archives d'anthropologie criminelle* 104–14,
Laurent, E. (1908) *Le criminel, du point de vue anthropologique, psychologique et sociologique*. Lyon: Storck.
Legrain, P. (1894) 'La médecine légale du dégénéré' *Archives d'anthropologie criminelle* 1–26.
Magnan, V. (1893) *Recherches sur les centres nerveux (alcoolisme, folie des héréditaires dégénérés, paralysie générale, médecine légale)*. Paris: Masson.
Maupaté, L. (1893) *Recherche d'anthropologie criminelle chez l'enfant: criminalité et dégénérescence*. Lyon: Storck.
Maury, A. (1879) 'L'homme criminel', *Journal des savants*, July: 389–99.
Mayet, L. (1902) *Les stigmates anatomiques et physiologiques de la dégénérescence et les pseudo-stigmates anatomiques et physiologiques de la criminalité*. Lyon: Storck.

Noiray, J. (2005) 'La réception de *L'Homme criminel* dans la "Revue des Deux Mondes"' in *Cesare Lombroso e la fine del secolo: la verità dei corpi*, Atti del Convegno di Genova 24–5 Settembre 2004 Publif@rum 1.

Nuvolone, P. (1977) 'Lombroso et le droit pénal', *Revue de science criminelle et de droit pénal comparé* 291–301.

Pinatel, J. (1977), 'Lombroso et la criminologie', *Revue de science criminelle et de droit pénal comparé* 541–49.

Rakowsky, K. G. (1896–7) *De la question de l'étiologie et de la dégénérescence précédée d'un aperçu sur les principales théories de la criminalité*, Medicine thesis Montpellier no. 75.

Renneville, M. (1994) 'La réception de Lombroso en France (1880–1900)', in L. Mucchielli (ed.) *Histoire de la criminologie française*. Paris: L'Harmattan, pp. 107–35.

Renneville, M. (1997) 'Rationalité contextuelle et présupposé cognitif. Réflexion épistémologique sur le cas Lombroso', *Revue de Synthèse*, no. 4 497–528.

Renneville, M. (2004a) 'Le printemps des sciences du crime', in G. Tarde, *La criminalité comparée*, Les Empêcheurs de penser en rond 7–23.

Renneville, M. (2004b), 'Gabriel Tarde. L'hirondelle de la criminologie', in G. Tarde, *La criminalité comparée*, Les Empêcheurs de penser en rond 207–17.

Rétention de sûreté et déclaration d'irresponsabilité pénale pour cause de trouble mental. Assemblée nationale. XIIIe législature. Session ordinaire de 2007–2008. Compte rendu intégral. Troisième séance du mardi 8 Janvier 2008.

Robert, J. H. (2008), 'La victoire posthume de Lombroso et Ferri', *Droit pénal. Revue mensuelle du jurisclasseur*, February, 1–2.

Sanson, A. (1893) *L'hérédité normale et pathologique*. Paris: Asselin et Houzeau.

Tarde, G. 2004 (1886) *La criminalité comparée*. Paris: Les Empêcheurs de Penser en rond.

Thulié, H. (1907) *L'école d'anthropologie de Parigi (1876–1906)*. Paris: Alcan.

17

LOMBROSO IN CHINA

Dong Xue Wei Ti, Xi Xue Wei Yong?[1]

Bill Hebenton and Susyan Jou

Beginning with Liu Lin-Sheng's landmark translation *Criminology of Lombroso*, published in Shanghai in 1922, this essay addresses how and in what ways Lombroso's work has been received and variously reflected in the development of criminological and penological thinking in China in the Republican, New China and Post-Tiananmen periods.[2] The 'controlled renewal' and 'guided discussion' of contemporary criminology in China also forms part of the broader context against which we examine Lombroso's legacy (Mei and Wang 2007). As we elucidate, matters of translation have a significance in any consideration of national impact of criminal anthropology in China. Mary Gibson's work on the historiography of Lombroso's published material is pertinent here. She observes:

> Lombroso's daughter, Gina, issued a short synopsis of her father's work in 1911 [partial], two years after his death, also under the title *Criminal Man*. Because this posthumous volume is the only one to have been translated into English, many readers do not have access to the original formulation of Lombroso's theory or to the evolution of his ideas during the height of his popularity... Gina's synopsis, as well as a compendium produced by Lombroso for foreign audiences, *Crime: Its Causes and Remedies*, lack the wealth of detail and broad scope of the last editions of *Criminal Man*. They also synthesise a rambling and often contradictory set of observations into a falsely compact and coherent theory.
>
> (Gibson 2006, 141–2)

Accordingly, establishing exactly what of Lombroso's writings have actually ever been translated in China is of importance in outlining his legacy (of course this point applies indeed in other countries, see generally, Rafter and Gibson 2006).

FIGURE 17.1 Portraits of Chinese emigrants. Staits Settlements (British Colonies in South-East of Asia, 1930)

Source: Archivio storico del Museo di Antropologia criminale "Cesare Lombroso" dell'Università di Torino (Italia).

Traditional approaches to the study of crime and punishment – what, in the West, would now be the domain of 'criminology' – have ancient origins in China. At the core, the underlying approach was always to see violation of law ('crime') as part of a problem of normative governance. This can be illustrated with reference to the case of the imperial dynasties, and the writings of Zhou Gong of the Western Zhou dynasty (1100 BC–771 BC). His handbook for rulers known as *Zhouli* makes him a kind of Machiavelli of his day. Zhou's idea for enlightened rulers of *ming de sheng xing* can best be translated as 'develop kindness and punish sparingly' (Kang 1998, 227–51; see Wong 2008 for commentary). The *Zhouli* reveals an implicit causal model in understanding crime: benevolent governance reduces crime and indiscriminate punishment increases criminality; second, a distinction of criminals (habitual) and crimes (intentional) are more blameworthy and dangerous than others; and third, Zhou Gong shifted the focus of crime and punishment study, from exclusively focusing on the conduct of the offender to wider duties of the state (or in modern parlance 'social policy'). Instead of asking why individuals commit crime, the focus was on how the Emperor could avoid disorder and maintain peace within his state. This was consistent with ancient Chinese philosophy of seeking the cultivation of the self (by the emperor), instead of seeking to regulate the conduct of others. Alongside the influence of Confucius, one can discern in the *Zhouli* the importance of 'example' and pedagogic instruction, inculcating certain useful dispositions and practices for successful governance.[3] In this sense, and importantly, the traditional approach in China to matters of crime and punishment was not a scientific endeavour, but a moral enterprise of good governance. In contrast, modern social sciences, the self-styled consciously 'scientific' scholarly disciplines devoted to investigating and generalizing about society, are Western innovations (Freedman 1962).

Late Qing/Republican period (1890s–1949)

This period in China's past can be characterized by the rise of a new intellectual class educated along modern lines, the proliferation of the periodical press and of mass publishing in the vernacular (as opposed to the classical language), and above all, an extraordinary openness to Western intellectual influences. As Dikötter (2002) points out in relation to criminology *qua* discipline in China, crime and punishment assumed radically different meanings in the late Qing period, as part of larger forces at work, internal and external, which shaped legal reform in China. More than just a familiar tale of 'progress' told in the context of a different national history, these reforms reveal a deeply felt need to secure Western recognition of China's social and political transformation and of its commitment to the project of 'modern civilization', itself also a product of an organic conception of nationalism emerging after defeat in the Sino-Japanese war of 1894–5.[4] And it is no coincidence that the example of crime and punishment should be taken up for this purpose. In many ways, how to understand 'criminology' (*fanzuixue*) and to deal with prisoners (*jianyuxue*) were interdependent; penology offering a scientific treatment of punishment that would ensure the transformation of the offender into a decent citizen, and criminology identifying the causes of crime in a preventive fashion in order to promote social harmony and order. While in parts of Europe disillusionment with the prison was accompanied by biological and social deterministic frames of reference, a reformative model in China produced criminological knowledge that stressed human agency (and responsibility). As such, criminology was suffused with moral sentiment; indeed it could claim to be the premise on which the legitimacy of such knowledge was based.

In 1895, Bei-yang University (later renamed Tianjin University), China's first 'modern' university, introduced lectures on legal method and penology. Shen Jiaben (1840–1913) was very influential in promoting the concept of offender rehabilitation, carefully mixing classical Confucian and Mencian texts with up-to-date material from international sources. At his behest, the Board of Justice in Beijing introduced new ways of doing things with prisoners, and promoted formal study of penology as well as attendance at international penitentiary congresses. Shen also oversaw numerous translations of important European and Japanese texts. Another key figure of the period was Ogawa Shigejiro, an appointed Japanese envoy and penology expert, who drafted a new criminal code (1908), which would eventually enter into force in 1911. Liu Fan (1905) produced a translation of Ogawa's lectures with sections including 'crime and criminals' and 'penal statistics'. Modernizing elites at the Qing court did not merely respond to Western impact, they actively appropriated globally circulating ideas and technologies, like the new penology, from within their own cognitive and moral traditions. In late Qing and the early Republic, work on what we would term criminology, together with the prison and the study of the prison, illustrate how modern tools were used to pursue a more traditional vision of an ordered and cohesive social body governed by virtue and both 'radically new and remarkably traditional' (Dikötter 2002, 7). There appears to have been only limited efforts at translation of foreign authors before 1930 and it is against this general backdrop that a translation of Lombroso's work by Liu Lin-Sheng (Liu 1922/9) appeared (some twenty years after Lombroso's death).

Liu's translation, published in Shanghai in October 1922 by Sheng-Wu Yin Shu Guan Publishers, was the first Western criminology book ever translated into Chinese (Yao 2007). Liu's book contained three parts: the origins of criminology, Lombroso and his work, and Lombroso's theories on crime and their critiques. In that book, there was no information or acknowledgement of the original source, nor did Liu himself make clear the source of ideas. For many years, most readers and (indeed criminologists in China) mistakenly thought it was translated from Lombroso's *Criminal Man* of 1876. However, if we compare the contents of the translated book, it is clear that it is from Lombroso's *Crime: Its Causes and Remedies*. This mistake was clarified by Liu when the second edition of his translation (Lombroso's *Crime: Its Causes and Remedies*) was published in 1929 by Wan Yao Wen Koo Publishers. In this two-volume version, the publisher revealed the source for the translation. Liu's translations were from English to Chinese, using Gina Lombroso-Ferrero's existing English translations. As Mary Gibson has recently noted

> the final edition of *Criminal Man*, then, Lombroso had recognized a spectrum of deviant types outside of the born criminal. Some were comprised of individuals with few anomalies ... proliferation of categories increased the weight of sociological factors in Lombroso's explanation of the causes of crime. Indeed as early as the first edition, he argued that there is no crime that is not rooted in multiple causes, including education, hunger and urbanization.
> (Gibson 2006, 144)

Yet this multi-causal discourse is largely elided in the existing translation.

In 1929, Xu Tian-Yi did his own translation of Lombroso's *Crime: Its Causes and Remedies*. Unlike Liu's version, Xu translated his book from the Japanese. Using Seiichi Terada's (1884–1922), 1914 translation, itself based on Gina Lombroso-Ferrero's English version (Nakatani 2006, 282; see Yao 2007). The Japanese translation included seven chapters: an introduction, types of criminal man, causes of crime, preventions and remedies of crime, investigation of criminals, the implications of criminal anthropology, and a conclusion. Xu's translation from the Japanese into Chinese was published by Le-Fan Yuan Bien Yi Chu Publishers (Legislation Yuan Compile and Translation Division). In the preface of Xu's translation, a former Vice-chancellor of Sun Yat-Sen University in Guangzhou, Dai Ji Tao (1891–1949) expressed the hope that Xu's translation of Lombroso's work would bring at least two changes in China:

> first, by understanding that some criminals may have biological, psychological and social deficiencies, the public should not resent criminals they deem to be evil. Criminal justice policy could then search for other new ideas or knowledge instead of focusing on punishment and retaliation. Secondly, we can improve our legal and moral standards by exercising the virtues of forgiveness and pardon
>
> (Xu 1929, ii)

Indeed, throughout this period, there was a strong resonance with notions of reformation; itself embedded within the traditional Mencian view of human beings as inherently good and highly malleable. The father of the Republic, Sun Yat-Sen, in his *Three Principles of the People* aimed to create a new Republic through information and example of what he termed *ganhua* (Sun 1956). This broadly based moral education was also the mission in dealing with criminal offenders. At the level of crime causation, criminological discourse remained open, embracing a multi-factorial approach, and bowing to neither simple sociological nor biological determinism. As Dikötter (2002) rightly points out, criminologists in this period undertook little empirical work, instead acting as 'cultural brokers', conduits disseminating their own personal views on Western theories. There were notable exceptions, especially in the later Republican period, including Zhao Chen, Li Jianhua and Yan Jingyue (for example, Li 1931, 1937; Yan 1928, 1930, 1934; Zhao 1931).

Both Li and Yan conducted empirical studies suffused with moral values; both drew on social and economic inequalities as sources of crime. (Li indeed drew explicitly on the work of the European Marxist criminologist Willem Bonger.) Zhao Chen found Lombroso's criminal anthropology fascinating, but dismissed its central tenets as 'prejudiced'. In his classic 1931 treatise on penology, he acknowledges that certain physical characteristics are more prominent in the criminal population compared with the general population: large jaws, high cheekbones, prominent superciliary arches, large orbits, a flat nose, a corpulent body, thick hair, insensitivity to pain, acute sight, incapacity for sustained work, lack of forethought, lack of self-control, a tendency to violence and a love of alcohol. Yet he opines that Lombroso's central idea is likely to invalidate any attempt to improve society and reform the criminal; thus for Zhao Chen, any preventive policy, derived from Lombroso, would require the extermination of criminals physically in order to pre-empt any deviant offspring (Zhao 1931). Li (1937) echoes this sentiment and distrust; a perception of criminal anthropology's biological determinism which not only negated the possibility of reforming the criminal, but also in the wider scheme. Such a determinism could be seen as a denial that the Chinese nation itself stand 'undetermined' (free-willed) in the struggle for international political survival. Nevertheless, one can still see aspects of Lombroso's influence even in Li's writings. For example, drawing on Lombroso's notion that education could act to increase 'perverted skills of born criminals', Li presents a variety of data from the Ministry of Justice in Beijing and opinion linking elementary education to higher crime rates (Li 1937, 70–81).

Another criminologist, Xu Pengfei (1934), himself trained in France and something of a Francophile, in his *Outline of Criminology*, specifically compares and contrasts Lombroso's ideas with those of the Durkheimian school of sociology. Xu argues for the obviousness of an eclectic or middle-way approach, invoking both anthropological and sociological explanations of crime causation. Heredity and environment are not seen here as exclusive; instead as something like an 'inner' and 'outer' set of forces that interact to produce criminogenic circumstances. Yet Xu was also convinced, drawing on Lombroso, that eugenic measures could prevent the spread of the hereditary components of criminality. Citing vasectomy and ovariotomy as options, Xu merely echoes calls from medical science in the China of the time (Xu 1934, 256). Criminal tendencies were seen as not only located at a genetic level; in line with criminal anthropology, the shape of the skull was not without significance. Fei Xiaotong, best known for his study of culture, turned towards anthropometrics, laboriously measuring criminals in Beijing prisons for his MA thesis at Qinghua University. In a short article, Fei found that most grave robbers could be classified as 'delta types', a term coined by his Russian supervisor at Qinghua (see Fei 1935; also Arkush 1981, 37–40). The work involved callipers and an 'anthropometer' with which to measure, including twenty-three absolute measurements, then derive relative measurements such as cephalic index.

Yet, although very limited in numbers and scope, fieldwork studies in prisons did produce data that argued against a simple mono-causal approach to understanding the offender: notably the research of University of Chicago trained Yan Jingyue (1905–76). His doctoral thesis, entitled *Crime in Relation to Social Change in China* (Yan 1934), interpreted crime as a result of an inability to adapt appropriately to rapid social change, rather than as a biological defect. His survey of Beijing Prison No. 1 inmates in 1926 led him to note the lack of education among this group; he administered the Binet-Simon intelligence test, finding little difference between the offenders and general population. Other examples of prison fieldwork include empirical studies by Liang (1932) and Wang (1935), which also failed to produce evidential support for central tenets of Lombroso's account. Liang studied fifty violent robbers in Zhejiang, interviewing and measuring them. Results showed them to be, in the main, illiterate, young, male and poor. Neither physical features, which were unevenly distributed accounted for their criminal careers. Wang in his research, also including measuring the heads and bodies of prisoners in

Jiangsu, found similar results: the main criminogenic factors appeared to be social and economic.

To sum up, cruder versions of criminal anthropology – especially on inheritance – were seen as insufficiently 'flexible' to the modernizing intellectuals of the period. There is no doubt that an evolutionist vocabulary existed in the criminological discourse of the time; yet, only in the interstices. Inheritance had to be a more flexible process that could be improved by human intervention; in other words capable of being tempered by faith in human potential. Indeed, this critical note was sounded by Lombroso's Chinese translator himself, in the introduction to the translation pointing to a need to recognize that both heredity and environment could be contained by the power of morality (Liu 1922/9).

New China period (1949–89)

Yin Jiabao (1997) describes the development of criminology in post-liberation China. Lombroso and criminal anthropology, like all bourgeois 'pseudo-sciences' were rejected by Mao and the Chinese Communist Party line. The early period of 1949–57 mainly dealt with the 'crime' of anti-revolutionary groups and class struggles between the working class and capitalists. Not recognized as an independent discipline, 'crime and punishment' was taught as part of criminal law, crime investigation and labour reform law. Most of the published criminology material consisted of lecture notes produced by law schools in key universities.[5] Like Soviet criminology of an earlier period (see Solomon 1974), the study of 'crime and punishment' became tied to an emergent socialist legal system, and (as we shall see), this has a continuing resonance.

Mao's crime-free society of this period was achieved with an all-embracing ideology, totalitarian state, and paternalistic government by means of ideological indoctrination, economic planning, social administration for the believers, and political education and labour reform for the *refuseniks* (Wong 2008). Mao's theory of corrections was grounded in Marxist analysis, particularly that a person's thinking is conditioned by society, material base and economic relationship (Wu 2003). People can be made to change their mind by education and indoctrination, and society has a responsibility in removing corrupting ideas and correcting unwholesome ideology. Thus Mao's correctional theory is very much 'environment' (macro change in social structure and material condition) and 'mind' work (individual change of mental state and ideology). In 1952, criminology, along with other social sciences, was formally declared as 'bourgeois pseudo science' and abolished (Wong 1979). Doctrinally, Chinese leaders believed that social issues should be studied from a Marxist perspective, which was the only source of the 'truth' (*zhen li*). The role and functions of (social) science is not to dispute (political) 'truth' but to validate its principles and help to put them in practice. For example, Yan Jingyue's work of the 1920s was cited as demonstrating that crime and economy are intimately linked. Or, put another way, any attempt to explain crime solely or deterministically in biological or social terms was deemed as lacking in the appreciation for the true nature and ultimate cause of crime.

The period between 1958 and 1966 has been called the 'interruption period', an era in which the political struggles within the Chinese Communist Party intruded into the development of criminology. Research was harnessed to the political agenda. The atmosphere fostered by central economic development plans supplied momentum for the establishment of an orthodox line in most fields of study. No criminology publications appeared in this period. The period between 1966 and 1976 is acclaimed by Yin and other commentators as the 'destruction period'. In this period of the Great Proletarian Cultural Revolution, social researchers, like many others, were politically denounced as members of counter-revolutionary groups (the 'Black Five' groups).

Finally, the period between 1976 and 1989 can be characterized as the 'recovery period'. In fact, Liu and Xu's two translations of Lombroso's works were re-introduced in this period during a renaissance of criminology due to the serious juvenile delinquency problem, itself a result of the Great Proletarian Cultural revolution (Wong 2008). Many criminologists in the 1970s were inspired by these two books.[6] Until Huang Fen's translation of Lombroso's *Criminal Man* in 2000, these two books remained the key textbook reference point on understanding Lombroso. In making a case for criminology in this period, scholars returned to both of the issues dominating the politics of criminology's demise in the Mao years, namely ideological acceptability and the practical utility of the field. The theories and methods of the field had to be still broadly compatible with Marxian assumptions about crime, and the study of crime had to support, rather than undermine claims of the party and the state. Crime causation, seen as part of historical material processes, had been the orthodoxy, but now criminologists examined a variety of social, psychological and indeed biological factors that seemed to influence crime with references to crime as a 'remnant of the past' itself receding further into obsolescence. Integration of theory and practice to develop and enrich criminology and the enhancing of social order were understood as the main goals of the discipline. In this way, the discipline advanced the modernization of socialist society. Thus, crime could only be adequately explained and effectively controlled by looking at it as a social (structural, process, material and/or cultural) as well as a personal (psychological, biological, experiential and mental) problem. Crime is caused by objective social factors, for example, class oppression or cultural corruption, as well as subjective factors, for example, biological constitution, and motivational factors. Consequently, prevention or reform, it is argued, must take all criminogenic factors into account. Anti-crime measures in China, called comprehensive crime 'management' (*zhonghe zhili*), include such formal and informal elements (see Kang 1998; Zhong 2009).

Post-Tiananmen period (1989 – present)

The events of Tiananmen hang heavily over the development of the general social scientific enterprise in China (see Sleeboom-Faulkner 2007). On the one hand, it cut short the period of intellectual blooming of the 1980s, when reformist academics nursed ideals for which they sought the support of politicians.

On the other hand, it persuaded China's leadership of the need to promote academic pluralism to prevent the ideological vacuum created by economic marketization and thereby encouraged the move to 'selectively appropriate' foreign ideas (Bakken 2000). At the same time, controls and regulations were increased. The creativity of the 1980s was simply replaced, as one of our criminology respondents put it, by an 'atmosphere of controlled renewal and guided discussion'. As the power of ideology became diluted as a control mechanism, so the regulation of institutions was enhanced to replace it. Such regulation touches on all aspects, including professional activities and research funding, and takes the form of controls on salary, housing, pension, and other financial incentives for individuals in socialist state organization. Here, concepts such as 'freedom of research' and 'expertise' need to be viewed in their institutional *locale* (not as abstractions) and should be seen against a background of increased research regulation, organizational steering, but decreased ideological pressure. The official line on scholars' theoretical resources (*lilun ziyuan*) remains, but it is evident from criminology publications of this period that crime continues to be seen in multifaceted and nuanced ways and as a social as well as individual phenomenon. From this perspective, crime can only be adequately explained and effectively controlled by looking at it as a social (involving structural, material and cultural factors) as well as an individual problem (involving psychological and physiological factors). In this regard, crime is caused by objective social factors, for example, class oppression or cultural corruption, as well as subjective factors, such as biological constitution, and individual motivation. Any approach to control of crime and criminals, be it prevention or reform, must take all criminogenic factors into account.

Fanzuixue Da Cidian (Big Dictionary of Criminology) published in 1995 is seen as an important collaboration between 200 criminology and criminal law experts (see also Chen 1994); Lombroso's four contributions to Chinese criminology are re-stated there as:

1. the introduction of empirical methodology to Chinese criminology (where the traditional focus had been on the legal/moral perspective)
2. an inspiration for Chinese criminologists to focus on 'the criminal' as a human being, rather than simply the 'crime', which had been part of the traditional normative approach.
3. bringing an individual's physical constitution into criminological focus
4. the introduction of the idea of individualized treatment for recidivist criminals which can be applied through penological mechanisms of parole, probation, and sentencing reduction policies.

In relation to Lombroso, Chen and other contributors of this period were prepared to put to one side the broader question about whether or not empirical evidence validated central claims. The utility of Lombroso's ideas of prevention and rehabilitation of criminals is key to understanding his modern claim among contemporary Chinese criminologists, especially in reconsidering their approach to penal reform, which itself is a continuing intellectual thread from the Republican period. In particular, we can point to modern textbooks emphasis on the lessons to be drawn from Lombroso's consideration of the Irish system of 'good time' credit and early release from prisons.

Textbooks can play an important part in the reproduction of a discipline. They can do so in two senses: first, they reproduce and synthesize the ideas that set that discipline apart; in addition, they can have a role in reproducing and renewing the people who work in the discipline, helping to recruit and socialize, or perhaps even 'discipline' new personnel (Israel 1997). Lombroso's presence in key textbooks of this period can tell us much about the state of a discipline by revealing whether or not there exists a strong informal consensus about what his legacy is and should be for future 'students' of the discipline. Furthermore, what may be revealed in textbooks is the flow of ideas and the perceived status of research (in essence demonstrated by what work is cited and how it is evaluated). Current textbook representation of Lombroso's significance stresses his recognition that criminology could become a science: one that can accumulate empirical data, use control groups, test theories and so on.[7] Indeed Wei's *Crime and Prevention Policy in a Market Economy* (1995), dealing with the empirical implications of fast moving marketization for crime and crime policy, and Zhou Lu's collected edition of empirical research *Contemporary Empirical Criminology* (1995; reprinted in 2004) are testaments to this renewed Lombrosian-'scientism' in the modern period.

Refracted through the prism of contemporary criminologists' concerns in China, perhaps one can gain an insight into Lombroso's lasting legacy in a recent textbook by Wang M. (President of the Chinese Society of Criminology). For Wang, Lombroso's work is portrayed as both liberating and challenging for criminologists in China (Wang M. 2010, 348). Liberating, to the extent that it provided and does still provide a counterpoint to criminal law experts' attempt to claim exclusive ownership of criminology by claiming that historically, criminology is a secondary subject and theoretically, a derivative discipline of criminal law. Liberating also, according to Wang M., in the more significant sense that it displaces the object-of-inquiry of criminology, from the moral to the natural domain. Yet, challenging in that, in contrast to the study of dogmatic criminal law, which can be pursued in all kinds of societies, 'the pursuit of criminological research requires a particular kind of social, political and moral climate' (Radzinowicz 1994, 103). Current concerns about lack of transparency in the Chinese criminal justice process, problems with independent data gathering, development of critical research skills and funding pose real challenges for empirical research in modern China. To use a culinary metaphor, for Chinese criminologists, Lombroso's work is akin to Chinese attitudes to the 'salad', a Western dish full of exciting and refreshing ingredients, but culturally, it will never be acceptable to be served as a daily meal on a Chinese dinner table. In the same way, Lombroso's work has only limited connectivity to core values of the Chinese intellectual world. He opens Chinese criminologists' eyes to utility of empirical methodology but his key ideas on the criminal have limited purchase on transforming the focal concerns of Chinese criminology.

Conclusion

Arguably, Lombroso, more than any other nineteenth-century scholar, 'initiated a worldwide conversation about the origins of criminal behaviour' (Knepper 2010, 160). In this essay we have sought to shed light on the reception, dissemination and furtherance of debate which his work engendered in China, alongside the architecture of resistances it met along the way. Paul Rock (2007), in his assessment of Lombroso for British criminology, argues that Lombroso may have been credited with lending the discipline of criminology its name and its preoccupation with the born criminal man and woman, but that otherwise, and except for its worked impact as a negative example, criminal anthropology did not make a lasting impact on the substance and development of British criminology; he quotes Gordon Rose who opined that Lombrosianism was 'an approach alien to English modes of thought' (Rose 1958, 53). Rose's conclusion is perhaps not that far adrift in any comprehensive assessment of Lombroso's long-term strategic impact in China. Part of this can be accounted for by historical modes of governance in China, part explained by the empirical evidence adduced by its own scholars (and referenced earlier in this essay). As Kenny pointed out, following the death of Lombroso 'in the cooler latitudes of Leipzig or London or Boston, there is less reluctance to test the brilliant Italian theories by the results of old experience, and to discount their sweeping generalisations by patient analysis' (Kenny 1910, 220).

There was certainly, as we have documented, no lack of empirical critique in China. Yet, we know that in science, amassing evidence to refute claims is never quite enough. So while Charles Goring's (1919) statistical approach is said to have demolished the specifics of Lombroso's theory, yet, it seems it is necessary to replay this more than once (see criminology's need for another version of Goring's patient 'empirical science' in Robert Sampson and John Laub's work: 'We believe that statistical approaches for data reduction have seduced some ... by giving the appearance of distinct and predictable groupings ('super-predator', 'life-course-persistent offender') that are amenable to direct policy intervention. Substantively meaningful [offender] groups or types do not, in fact, exist' (Sampson and Laub 2003, 590).

Portrayed as he is in textbook 'accounts' as the father of a scientific approach to the study of crime and punishment, where observable and measurable facts are the hallmark of a scientific criminology that seeks to tackle the problem of crime,

Cesare Lombroso has a sharper significance in contemporary criminological discourse in China. As an uneasy potpourri of explanatory, descriptive, political and normative discourses, criminology in the West has always been a hotly contested terrain; then as now, this contestation is to be expected because, criminology is ultimately a site for the division of expert professional knowledge. In contrast, in thinking of Lombroso's legacy in China one is reminded of the observation by American novelist, William Faulkner that 'the past is never dead. It's not even past' (Faulkner 1951).[8] Lombroso, as it were, is indeed still in China, like the unequal treaties of old China and the West, his presence exists in all its ambiguity. There in revered translations and rendered textbook 'accounts' of the historical development of criminology, and indeed, in the debate about the sustained moral commentary that remains stubbornly central to the criminological enterprise. To understand the gap between this textbook acknowledgement and actual research practice, we argue that intellectuals in China today, including criminologists and other social scientists, still largely embrace the principle of '*dong xue wei ti, xi xue wei yong*'. This principle was advocated originally by Zhang Zhi-Dong (1837–1909) in the late Qing period who believed that Western wisdom had great merit in relation to technology and methodology, whereas Eastern wisdom had to remain as the core of Chinese ontology.[9] Contemporary criminologists in China are no less aware than their predecessors in earlier periods, that in defining crimes and in punishing transgressors, societies always attempt more than a mere practical task. Albeit with vision distorted by power and special interests, they are trying also to delineate or re-consecrate 'sacred ground'.

Nicole Rafter points to the receptivity of Lombroso's ideas in the late nineteenth-century USA, citing four situational factors: socioeconomic context, specifically growing industrialization and unease at migration; intellectual context, including early eugenics; growth in criminal justice professionalization; and finally societal consolidation of medico-psychiatric expertise. In short, like some people, she argues 'some theories are lucky, appearing at the right place at the right time' (Rafter 2006, 159). In contrast, our brief overview of Lombroso in China provides one in a growing number of national studies of criminal anthropology's other entanglements with very different historical forces; specifically the bookends of a revolutionary China (1920s–late1970s) and now within a society where political life is no longer painted in such rich binary colours but has taken on a very different and complex hue. Lombroso in China is a tale of how ideas and things have multiple uses; a variegated set of clashes with a vision of an ordered and cohesive social body governed by virtue. Recent calls for greater cross-national research on the impact of criminal anthropology are indeed to be welcomed, as is further more detailed work on the role of 'translation' itself in aiding us in understanding 'making criminology' (Rafter 2011, 153).

Finally, a caveat. Time changes our perception of all things; the historical time-frame of this essay largely focuses attention, inevitably, on a period when China's historical development was intimately bound to the adventures of Western foreign powers and where, in particular, the Chinese elites saw lessons to be drawn from 'Western knowledge'. It had not always been thus. Indeed leading figures of the eighteenth-century European Enlightenment, Leibniz, Voltaire, among others, 'looked to China for moral instruction, guidance in institutional development, and supporting evidence for their advocacy of causes as varied as benevolent absolutism, meritocracy, and an agriculturally based national economy' (Adas 1989, 79; see also Hung 2003). As Giovanni Arrighi (2007) has recently reminded us, the East–West wheel of geopolitics continues to turn even now.

Notes

1 Pinyin romanization of the Chinese written script is used throughout this paper. The question of how to transliterate Chinese into English is a vexed question. The 'pinyin' system developed in the People's Republic of China. (PRC) has now become the scholarly standard, so we use this in preference to the older Wade-Giles system which, for various reasons, has become somewhat archaic. Our subtitle, *dong xue wei ti, xi xue wei yong*, can be translated as 'Using Eastern wisdom as substance, and Western wisdom as technique'.
2 On the background rationale for this periodization see Hebenton and Jou (2010).
3 For the background and consequences of this see Bakken (2000) and Wang (2006); for cross-cultural reflections see Cao and Cullen (2001) and Chen (2004).
4 See, generally, Botsman, (2005), Dikötter (2002). But for a counter-narrative see the celebrated monograph by Wang (1966).
5 That is, *PRC Criminal Law Lecture Notes* by Chinese People's University 1956, and *PRC Criminal Codes Outlines* by Southwest Political and Law School, 1957.
6 See Hebenton and Jou (2010) for interview data with criminologists of the period.
7 Lindesmith and Levin (1937) provide the counter-argument.
8 The quote appears in Faulkner (1951). *Requiem for a Nun*, Act 1: Scene 3, New York: Random House.
9 See Zhang Zhi-Dong, *Quanxue Pien* ('An Exhortation to Learning'), 1898; translated into English by an American missionary Samuel Woodbridge in 1901, under the title *China's Only Hope*.

References

Adas, M. (1989) *Machines as Measure of Men: Science, Technology and Ideologies of Western Dominance*. Ithaca, NY: Cornell University Press.
Arkush, R. D. (1981). *Fei Xiaotong and Sociology in Republican China*. Cambridge, MA: Harvard University Press.
Arrighi, G. (2007) *Adam Smith in Beijing*. London: Verso.
Bakken, B. (2000) *The Exemplary Society: Human Improvement, Social Control, and the Dangers of Modernity in China*. Oxford: Oxford University Press.
Becker, P. and Wetzell, R. F. (eds) (2006) *Criminals and Their Scientists: The History of Criminology in International Perspective*. Cambridge: Cambridge University Press.
Botsman, D. (2005) *Punishment and Power in the Making of Modern Japan*. Princeton, NJ: Princeton University Press.
Cao, L. and Cullen, F. (2001) 'Thinking about Crime and Control: a Comparative Study of Chinese and American Ideology', *International Criminal Justice Review* 11(1): 58–81.

Chen, X-L. (1994) 'Lombroso: Slave of the Gene', *BiJiaoFaYanJiu (Comparative Law Research)* 1:43–8.
Chen, X-L. (2004) 'Social and Legal Control in China: a Comparative Perspective', *International Journal of Offender Therapy and Comparative Criminology* 48 (5): 523–36.
Dikötter, F. (2002) *Crime, Punishment and the Prison in Modern China*. London: C. Hurst & Co.
Faulkner, W. (1951) *Requiem for a Nun*, Act 1: Scene 3, New York: Random House.
Fei, X-T. (1935) 'Anthropometry and Social Selection', *Shehui yanjiu*, No 56.
Freedman, M. (1962) 'Sociology in and of China', *British Journal of Sociology, 13*, 106–16.
Gibson, M. S. (2006) 'Cesare Lombroso and Italian Criminology: Theory and Politics', in Becker, P. and Wetzell, R. F. (eds) (2006) *Criminals and Their Scientists: the History of Criminology in International Perspective*. Cambrige: Cambridge University Press, pp. 137–58.
Goring, C. (1919) *The English Convict*. London: HMSO.
Hebenton, B. and Jou, S. (2010) 'Criminology in and on China: Discipline and Power', *Journal of Contemporary Criminal Justice*, 26(1): 7–19.
Huang, F. (2000) *Fan Zui Zen Lun* (Essays on Criminals). Beijing: Zhongguo fazche chubanshe.
Hung, H.-F. (2003) 'Orientalist Knowedge and Social Theories: China and European Conceptions of East–West Differences from 1600–1900', *Sociological Theory* 21: 3–30.
Israel, M. (1997) 'Reproducing Criminology: The Art of Reading Criminology Textbooks for Australians', *Australian and New Zealand Journal of Criminology* (30:3), 312–29.
Kang, S. (1998) *Fanzui Xue: Lizhi, Xianzhuang, Weilai* (Criminology: History, Status, Future). Beijing: Qunzhong chubanshe, pp. 206–9.
Kenny, C. (1910) 'The Death of Lombroso', *Journal of the Society of Comparative Legislation* 10(2): 220–8.
Knepper, P. (2010) *The Invention of International Crime: A Global Issue in the Making 1881–1914*. Basingstoke: Palgrave Macmillan.
Li, J. (1931) *Fanzuixue* (Criminology). Shanghai, China: Shanghai faxue bianyshe.
Li, J. (1937) *Fanzui Shehuixue* (Criminal Sociology). Shanghai, China: Huiwentang xinji shuju.
Liang, S. (1932) *Wushi Ge Aiangdao: Zhejiang Sheng Di'er Jianyu Fanzui Diaocha Zhi Fenxi* (Fifty Robbers: an analysis of an investigation of criminals in Zhejiang No2 Prison). Shanghai: Fozi shuju.
Lindesmith, A. and Levin, Y. (1937) 'The Lombrosian Myth in Criminology', *American Journal of Sociology* 42(5): 653–71.
Liu, L. (1922/29) *Langboluosuo Zhi Fanzuixue* (The Criminology of Lombroso). Shanghai, China: Shangwu yinshuguan.
Mei, J. and Wang, M. (2007) 'Social Change, Crime, and Criminology in China', *Crime & Justice International*, 23, No. 97: 14–21.
Nakatani, Y. (2006) 'The Birth of Criminology in Modern Japan', in Becker, P. and Wetzell, R. F. (eds) (2006) *Criminals and Their Scientists: the History of Criminology in International Perspective*. Cambridge: Cambridge University Press, pp. 281–98.
Radzinowicz, L. (1994) 'Reflections on the State of British Criminology', *British Journal of Criminology, 34*, 99–104.
Rafter, N. H. (2006) 'Criminal Anthropology: its Reception in the United States and the Nature of its Appeal', in Becker, P. and Wetzell, R. F. (eds) *Criminals and Their Scientists: the History of Criminology in International Perspective*. Cambridge: Cambridge University Press, pp. 159–81.

Rafter, N. H. (2011) 'Origins of Criminology', in Bosworth, M. and Hoyle, C. (eds) *What is Criminology?* Oxford: Oxford University Press, pp. 143–54.

Rafter, N. H. and Gibson, M. (2006) *Criminal Man: Lombroso, Cesare 1835–1909.* (Translated from the Italian). Durham, NC: Duke University Press.

Rock, P. (2007) 'Caesare Lombroso as a Signal Criminologist', *Criminology and Criminal Justice* 7(2): 117–33.

Rose, G. (1958) 'Trends in the Development of Criminology in Britain', *British Journal of Sociology* 9(1): 53–65.

Sampson, R. and Laub, J. H. (2003) 'Life-course Desisters? Trajectories of Crime Among Delinquent Boys Followed to Age 70', *Criminology*, 41, 555–92.

Sleeboom-Faulkner, M. (2007) *The Chinese Academy of Social Sciences: Shaping the Reforms, Academia and China 1997–2003.* Leiden, Netherlands: Brill.

Solomon, P. H. (1974) 'Soviet Criminology: Its Demise and Rebirth, 1928–1963', in R. Hood (ed.) *Crime, criminology and public policy: Essays in honour of Sir Leon Radzinowicz.* Newton, MA: Butterworth-Heinemann, pp. 571–93.

Sun, Z. (1956) *Sun Zhongshan Xuanji* (Selected works of Sun Zhongshan). Beijing: Renmin chubanshe.

Wang, L. (1935) *Jiangsu Diyi Jianyufan Diaocha Dhi Jingguo Ji Qi Jieguo zhi fenxi* (Process and analysis of the results of an investigation into Jiangsu No. 1 Prison inmates). Nanjing: Tongjiju.

Wang, M. (2006) 'Questioning the Theoretical Premise and Study Object of Criminology', *Asian Journal of Criminology* 1: 85–7.

Wang M. (2010) *Fanzuixue Jichu Lilun* (Research on Basic Theory of Criminology). Beijing: Zhou-Gou Jen Chia Publisher.

Wang, Y. C. (1966) *Chinese Intellectuals and the West, 1872–1949.* Chapel Hill, NC: University of North Carolina Press.

Wei, P.-X., Ouyang, T., and Wang, X.-A. (1995). *Shichang Jingji Tiaojianxia fanzui yu dui ce* (Crime and Prevention Policy in a Market Economy). Beijing, China: Qunzhong Chubanshe.

Wong, K. C. (2008) 'The Study of Criminology in China, part 1', *China Report* 44(3): 213–31.

Wong, S. L. (1979) 'Sociology and Socialism in Contemporary China', Boston, MA: Routledge and Kegan Paul.

Wu, Z.-X. (2003) 'Western Prisons and Chinese Prisons: Focusing on Differences', *European Journal of Crime, Criminal Law and Criminal Justice*, 11(1): 93–113.

Xu, P.-F. (1934) *Fanzuixue Dagang* (Outline of Criminology). Shanghai: Shanghai daxue shudian.

Xu, T.-Y. (1929) *Gina Lombroso's On Criminal Man.* Nanjing: Legislative Yuan, Translation Department (in Chinese).

Yan, J. (1928) *Beijing Fanzui Zhi Shehuixue Fenxi* (Sociological Analysis of Crime in Beijing). Beijing, China: Yanjing daxue shehuixuexi.

Yan, J. (1930) 'Crime and Economic Conditions in China', *Howard Journal of Penology*, 3(1), 28–32.

Yan, J. (1934) *Crime in Relation to Social Change in China.* PhD dissertation, Department of Sociology, Chicago University.

Yao, J.-L. (2007) 'Reconsider Modern Criminology Seriously', *Xien Dai Fu Xue* (Modern Law Study) *Vol* 6.

Zhang, Z.-D. (1898) *Quanxuepian* (Essays on Learning).

Zhao, C. (1931) *Jianyuxue* (Prison Study, 1st edition). Shanghai: Shanghai faxue bianyishe.

Zhong, L. Y. (2009) *Communities, Crime and Social Capital in Contemporary China*. Devon, UK: Willan Publishing.

Zhou, L. (ed.) (2004). *Dangdai Shizheng Fanzuixue* (Contemporary empirical criminology). Tianjin, China: Tianjin Academy of Social Sciences (Originally published 1995).

18

LOMBROSO BUT NOT LOMBROSIANS?

Criminal anthropology in Spain[1]

Ricardo Campos and Rafael Huertas

Introduction

The influence of the work of Cesare Lombroso first became apparent in Spain in the early 1880s. It spread quickly and, in very little time, became popular in scientific, legal, journalistic and cultural fields across the country until it reached its 'moment of maximum discussion and timeliness' (Maristany 1983, 362) in 1985. However, the rapid spread of Lombroso's doctrines did not lead to the formation of a group of orthodox followers or the creation of a Spanish school of criminology, like the Italian one. In Spain, Lombroso's ideas were turned around and provoked more social, scientific and cultural debate on the figure of the criminal rather than the creator of a school of criminology. For almost two decades, the works of Lombroso, Ferri, Garofalo and other representatives of the Scuola Nuova were translated, reviewed and discussed, without any real Lombrosian trend developing, strictly speaking. Italian criminal anthropology talked and wrote about numerous issues related to the great sense of unease felt by Spanish society at the end of the century in order to repress anarchism, justify crime prevention policies and extend the application of the concept of social danger to new individuals and groups.

One element which is important in understanding the impact of the new theories on criminality in Spain is the previous controversy over scientific positivism and evolutionism, both in scientific circles and according to public opinion. The most conservative sectors, with the support of the Catholic Church and the Bourbon Restoration regime, rejected these scientific trends, even exiling certain professors from the University in 1876 for defending them (Nuñez 1975; Nuñez 1977; Glick 1982). Therefore, it is no surprise to learn that the majority of the defenders of criminal anthropology were Liberals, Republicans, Socialists and Anticlericals.

The way that Italian criminal anthropology arrived in Spain was different. Throughout the 1880s, psychiatrists played an essential role in disseminating Lombrosian theories and, most importantly, 'language', in their capacity as experts before the courts. However, some of the main supporters of the ideas of the Scuola Nuova were lawyers and criminologists who, although they were critical of its principles, played a significant role in disseminating them as, in order to critique them, they had to clearly explain them. Another important factor which affected the spread of Lombroso's ideas was the almost simultaneous explosion of the ideas of French criminal sociology. The two would end up being combined, making it very difficult to identify their respective influences on various Spanish authors, although at the turn of the century (from the nineteenth to the twentieth), sociological perspectives were more influential. We will see below the main characteristics and distinguishing features of how Lombroso's work was received in Spain, as well as its scientific and cultural impact.

Between medicine and law – the reception and popularisation of the Italian School

Psychiatry and criminal anthropology

In 1883, the lecture 'Locos Delincuentes' by Ángel Pulido (1850–1936) confirmed that Lombroso was beginning to become known in Spain, despite *L'uomo delinquente* (1876) not yet having been translated into Spanish. Pulido was part of a group of doctors led by José María Esquerdo (1842–1912) who were trying to show lawyers and public opinion the advances of alienism, in order to grant it scientific and social legitimacy (Álvarez Uría 1983; Campos *et al.* 2000; Huertas 2002). The importance of forensic psychiatry in the wider field of legal medicine had been previously noted, particularly Pedro Mata (1811–77), but the emergence of degenerationism was greatly significant in the discourse of psychiatrists after the 1880s, as it dealt with factors such as biological inheritance and physical and mental stigmas, which were apparently more plausible than the questionable concept of monomania. In this way, psychiatrists could explain the pathological condition of the accused more easily and claim a scientific jurisdiction once they had proved the link between crime and insanity, which they were denied.

Criminal cases such as that of Otero, who attacked King Alfonso XII in 1878, and, in particular, that of José Garayo, known as 'El Sacamantecas', who raped and murdered women in a rural area in northern Spain between 1870 and 1879, marked the beginnings of this 'offensive' by psychiatrists in the courts. Esquerdo acted as an expert in the trial of 'El Sacamantecas', arguing his lack of criminal responsibility due to his unstable mental condition. The judge did not take Garayo's conclusions into account; he was sentenced to death and executed in 1880. The following year, Esquerdo gave a series of lectures entitled 'Locos que no lo parecen' (1881), intended to prove that a miscarriage of justice had taken place. Numerous elements of degenerationism featured in these lectures but with important points tying in with new Lombrosian theories and practices (Huertas 2002). The anthropometric description that Esquerdo gave of the murderer is significant enough – 'deformed, twisted head', broad 'at the base, narrow vault, narrow at the forehead'. His face, consistent with this deformity, was characterised as having prominent cheekbones, small, sunken, uneven, unequal eyes and heavy eyebrows. He also suffered from a squint and had a hoarse voice. All these signs, he wrote, 'gave him a dark quality' and a fierce and intense stare (Esquerdo 1881). Esquerdo linked these physical stigmas with mental illness, leading to the conclusion that Garayo was not criminally responsible.

Although he did not mention Lombroso and he did mention Morel, it is very likely that Esquerdo knew the Italian doctor's work, given that some of his followers and close friends seem to have been familiar with and directly inspired by it. This is also true of José María Escuder (1856–1921) in his book *Quemas y crímenes* (1881), Ángel Pulido in the 1883 lecture mentioned above and Victoriano Garrido in the series of articles entitled 'La cárcel o el manicomio', which was published in the *Revista de Legislación y Jurisprudencia* and revised two years later in a book with a prologue by Esquerdo himself. Garrido was opposed to 'that metaphysical concept', 'that impediment to progress' that was 'belief in the existence of free will' and he showed his opposition by rallying against the 'anachronistic beliefs' of the 'Correctionist school of law' to the 'clear water of the Positivist school' (Garrido 1888, 6–9), stating that the works of Ferri and Lombroso were grabbing the attention of lawyers, doctors and legislators of the day to such an extent that it was impossible to get away from the 'general trend which is permeating contemporary consciousness like a drop of sweet dew' (Garrido 1888, 230).

In addition to this dissemination in certain media, Esquerdo and his followers continued to act as experts in the courts, aided by oral trials which, from 1882, allowed the presence of journalists and the general public. The press allowed ideas linking insanity with criminality, as well as the anthropological and anthropometric arguments used by the experts to justify them, to become widespread through its articles. The trials of Manuel Morillo (1884), accused of murdering his girlfriend's mother (Rios-Font 2005; Campos 2008), of the priest Galeote, who murdered the Bishop of Madrid (1886) (Varela and Álvarez-Uría 1979; Campos 2003), of Hillairaud (1887) who tried to assassinate the French Marshal Bazain in Madrid and of writer Remigio Vega Armentero (1889), who killed his wife out of jealousy (Fernández 2001), came one after the other and gave Jaime Vera (1859–1918), Luis Simarro (1851–1921) and José María Escuder – all of whom were linked to Esquerdo – the opportunity to take part as experts, invariably defending the link between insanity, criminality and abnormal organic form. Escuder, in particular, stands out in his defence of these positions and his expert reports in the Morillo, Galeote and Hillairaud cases are an example of the dogmatic use of degenerationist positions and Lombrosian theories at the time, constituting an attack on the traditional penal system. His expert reports were characterised by reconstructing the family trees of the accused, which were always full of mental and unusual illnesses which had been passed down generation-by-generation until they reached the insane criminal being tried. Escuder also took care to explain physical stigmas in great detail in order to irrefutably prove the mental trauma of the criminal in question. These fluent descriptions showed his knowledge of criminal anthropology. In his report on Galeote, he remarked 'these investigations may repulse certain people but without mud, there would be no agriculture, without corpses, no medicine and without the criminally insane, criminal anthropology would not have been born' (Escuder 1895). Years later, in his book *Locos y anómalos* (1895), he would dedicate many pages to the relationship between crime and insanity and reveal himself as a follower of Lombroso.

Simarro, too, in his interventions as an expert in the trials of Galeote and Hillairaud, proved to be knowledgeable on the latest psychiatric, anthropological and criminal trends which he had learned about during a long stay in Paris between 1880 and 1885 (Vidal 2007). In his expert report on the priest Galeote, he linked the description of the external somatic features to the state of his mental faculties, indicating that both were part of the same clinical study and were mutually complementary. This is how, Simarro claimed, he had known from the start that Galeote was suffering from 'a degenerative mental illness', in a case which 'offered two highly important aspects – one anthropological and one clinical', information on which 'had to be determined'. With regard to the former, he wrote:

> I will reduce these somatic disturbances down to common expressions. The measurements of the cranium, compared to his size, reveal that the cranium is smaller, in general, than the minimum normal cranial size and is consistent with the cranial measurements of imbeciles and idiots – he is microcephalic. Galeote's cranium presents one anomaly which is that although its front half is less developed than the back half, it is not so to the extent that it would offer any compensation in terms of development. The base of the cranium seems as though it should be higher and there are two reasons to support this argument – the placement of the ear canals, which is irregular, and the elevation of the palatal vault. The cranium is small and particularly defective in the frontal section.
>
> (Varela and Álvarez-Uría 1979, 100)

After this thorough description, Simarro continued to describe Galeote's physical stigmas such as 'the vicious set of teeth and the presence of four wisdom teeth, each with four roots' – unequivocal signs of his atavistic degeneration. However, the role of psychiatrists in the introduction of criminal anthropology in Spain was limited. Their contribution was important in helping to familiarise Spaniards with the terminology and practices of the Positivist school, as well as sparking lively debate in different circles including the Ateneo Científico, Literario y Artístico, the Academia Médico Quirúrgica and the Real Academia de Legislación y Jurisprudencia. But praise for the Italian School and use of some of its concepts did not lead to full acceptance of its positions. It was rather a partial and instrumental appropriation (Maristany 1983; Maristany 1985). One indication of this situation is that no psychiatrists in the 1880s used the concept of the born criminal, as their reports and writings aimed to prove the existence of insane criminals who must be declared not responsible for their acts and locked up in an asylum. Also, one of their objectives was to institutionalise psychiatry as a science and obtain recognition and social legitimacy for the field. The work and efforts of Spanish psychiatrists in the forensic field were carried out in the context of an intense ideological and political battle. The majority of psychiatrists and doctors around Esquerdo were against the death penalty and publicly advocated its abolition. In this context, the potential danger of the criminal or the existence of the born criminal was not one of their main concerns and was barely taken into account. In fact, an 'appropriation of oratory resources on behalf of science' took place in order to defeat its opponents and win over public opinion to the cause (Maristany 1985, 22).

Luis Maristany believes that Esquerdo and his group opened up the way for Lombroso. The Italian school had exploded into Spain at the opportune moment, making the vague idea of the 'monster' or criminal 'savage' take shape and scientific form. However, while it benefitted from the climate created by the Alienist forensic campaigns in Madrid, 'it put aside their isolated, timid and somewhat antiquated attempts, in favour of doctrines which gave a much more emphatic explanation of criminal conduct' (Maristany 1985, 24).

The role of lawyers

Another means of introduction of Lombroso's doctrines into Spain was by penal law. Throughout the 1880s, the *Revista General de Legislación y Jurisprudencia* published notes and articles which echoed the works of Lombroso and Ferri (González 1994, 180), including the articles of Luis Morote 'El Derecho Penal, capítulo de las ciencias naturales' (Morote 1884), 'El primer congreso internacional de Antropología criminal' (Morote 1886a) y 'Las anomalias en los criminales (antropología criminal)' (Morote 1886b), in which he revealed himself to be very much a supporter of Lombrosian doctrines.

Between January and May 1887, an important discussion on criminal responsibility, entitled 'Los médicos Alienistas y los tribunales de justicia' (Alienist doctors and the courts), was held at the Academia Médico-Quirúrgica in Madrid. On this occasion, the traditional clash between doctors and lawyers included debate on what new aspects the Positivist school was presenting to judges and lawyers.

In September of the same year, the President of the Tribunal Supremo finished his opening speech on behalf of the courts, vowing that the latter would reject the new Positivist doctrines, specifically because they would destroy all social order (Maristany 1973). However, there were more intelligent criticisms levelled, such as those made by the Professor of Penal Law at the Universidad de Oviedo, Feliz Aramburu (1848–1913). As a supporter of Correctionist theories, he gave five critical lectures on the Lombrosian school in 1886, which were published under the title *La nueva ciencia penal (exposición y crítica)*. The work aimed to refute Lombrosian ideas but also constituted a thorough exploration of criminal anthropology. Aramburu defended traditional penal law and claimed that criminal anthropology was not a science, opposing biological determinism and the penal innovations made by

Garófalo and Ferri, the existence of free will and proportionality of sentences. In fact, Aramburu saw criminal anthropology as 'a dangerous de-naturalisation of the law and the functions of a lawyer' and an attempt by science to intrude in the field of criminal law. The work was widely debated in Spain and, to a certain extent, had an impact at international level as Ferri himself referred to it in the prologue of the Spanish edition of his work *Los nuevos horizontes del derecho penal y el procedimiento* (Ferri 1887).

However, there is a historiographical consensus in saying that the first methodical introduction of Lombrosian doctrines to Spain was by Pedro Dorado Montero (1861–1919). A lawyer and professor of criminal law at the Universidad de Salamanca, Dorado Montero was able to familiarise himself with the Italian Positivist school directly during his time at the University of Bologna between 1885 and 1887. In 1886, he published the article 'Sobre el estado de la ciencia jurídica italiana en los momentos presentes' (On the state of Italian legal science at the present time), followed by two important books – *La Antropología Criminal en Italia* (1889) and *El positivismo en la ciencia jurídica y social italiana* (1891). Although he did not share all the principles of the Italian school and rejected the idea of the born criminal, Dorado Montero made a significant contribution in terms of disseminating the theories of Lombroso and his followers. In the following years, he continued to write numerous articles which were directly or indirectly related to criminal anthropology and translated various works by E. Sighele and, most importantly, in 1902, Lombroso's *La medicina legal* into Spanish (Peset and Peset 1975). Dorado Montero made an insightful critique of the Italian school, refining many aspects related to it. From a Correctionist point of view, although presenting a certain syncretism, he came to believe that criminal science in the future would be a 'union of the Correctionist and Positivist schools, the infusion of the spirit of the former into the disorganised body of data of the latter' (Maristany 1973, 44). Dorado Montero advocated the reform of the criminal more than punishment, as he was convinced of their moral deterioration and believed that the contributions of medicine and psychiatry should be incorporated into criminal studies. In the future, there would be a deepening of Correctionism and use of scientific advances in order to rehabilitate. To put it otherwise, Dorado considered the criminal to have a sickness of the soul (which distanced him from Lombrosian theories) and suggested that prisons should be clinics for the soul, where they would receive the appropriate therapy. The idea of sentencing would disappear and be replaced by protection, shelter and treatment. Society would not have the right to dispose of criminals but rather the obligation to educate them and protect them as crimes were created by society (Trinidad 1991, 327–33).

The institutionalisation of criminal anthropology

Rafael Salillas, 'the little, Spanish Lombroso', according to writer Pio Baroja, was, for years, the biggest supporter of the Italian in Spain. With a degree in medicine, his professional career was closely linked to penal institutions. In 1880, he enrolled as a civil servant at the Dirección General de Prisiones and, in 1885, he became head of the department of Hygiene and Anthropology at the Ministerio de Gobernación, where he worked alongside Simarro to pen a Judicial Asylums Law. In 1886, he published a series of articles entitled 'La vida penal en España' (Criminal life in Spain) in the *Revista General de Legislación y Jurisprudencia*, which were later compiled in a book (Salillas, 1888) which was praised by Lombroso himself (Galera 1991, 54–6). In 1888, he took charge of organising the penitentiary department of the Exposición Universal in Barcelona and gave a lecture at the Ateneo de Madrid entitled 'La Antropología y el derecho penal' (Anthropology and Criminal Law), which was published a year later (Salillas, 1889). In this text, he hotly defends criminal anthropology in what is considered to be the first true Lombrosian text published in Spain (Maristany 1973, 33; Galera 1991).

In the following years, Salillas remained an orthodox supporter of Lombrosian theories, making an important contribution to the attempt to institutionalise criminal anthropology by founding the *Revista de Antropología Criminal y Ciencias Médico-Legales,* which was quickly renamed the *Revista Internacional de Antropología Criminal,* along with legist Ángel María Álvarez Taladrid. The launch of the journal was met with an excellent international reaction, with Lombroso, Ferri, Garofalo, Lacassagne and Tarde sending congratulations cards and offering to publish in it. In 1888, the journal was the official publication of the Second International Criminal Anthropology Conference in Paris and the International Legal Medicine Conference in New York. Without doubt, this publication contributed to establishing criminal anthropology in Spain and to the spread of its ideas. Its collaborators included Salillas, Álvarez Taladriz, Macias Picavea and figures from European criminology such as Lacassagne and Puglia, who were members of the editorial board. In its pages, numerous articles by representatives of the Nuova Scuola and the French school were published (Galera 1991, 105–10). In 1892, *La Nueva Ciencia Jurídica* was launched, with Lombrosian theories behind it and the collaboration of Rafael Salillas. Although it was only published for two years, it brought Spanish and foreign texts to people's attention and contribution to the spread of new ideas in the field of criminal law. Salillas was responsible for the 'Spanish Criminology Museum' section which was 'the first, and only, systematic attempt to apply Lombrosian methodology to the examination and study of the Spanish criminal' (Maristany 1973, 36).

However, after getting very close to being an orthodox Positivist, in the mid-1890s, Salillas would move drastically away from this school of thought and develop his own theory in his books *El delincuente español. El Lenguaje* (1896) and *El delincuente español. Hampa* (1898). Faced with the endogenuous and personal factors which were predominant in Lombroso's theory, Salillas suggested in *Hampa* that a nutritional deficiency could be the main cause of degeneration and criminal behaviour (Bernaldo de Quirós 1898; Maristany 1973, 39–40; Galera 1991, 68–75). The sociological aspect of his theory focused on the individual's nutritional deficiencies, which he directly linked with poverty and therefore with a specific social context. In this respect, the criminal was the result of nutritional deficiency suffered during childhood, which caused a state of organic degeneration, which would be reflected in their morphological features and behaviour. In short, a lack of food would cause alterations in personal development which would give way to the emergence of the anthropological criminal. Salillas did not move away entirely from certain essential concepts of Lombrosian theories such as atavism, degeneration and epilepsy, but he gave them a new significance by integrating them into a different theoretical body (Bernaldo de Quirós 1898, 80–90; Galera 1991, 72–3). Salillas himself stated that he was not using 'the concept of degeneration, or atavism, or epilepsy, or hysteria as a starting point, nor can we explain the fundamental facts with arrested development, and yet all of these things are related to the basic issue we are studying' (Salillas 1898, XIV). In addition, as with other European authors, he also devoted his attention to studying criminal's tattoos, writing numerous articles from 1888 onwards which led to the publication of the book *El tatuaje* in 1908.

Salillas' attempts to institutionalise criminology continued over the following years, establishing, in 1899, the Laboratorio de Criminología, a seminar with the objective of studying criminals from a morphological and sociological perspective in relation to criminal anthropology. In 1906, as the director of the Carcel Celular in Madrid, he created the School of Criminology within its walls. Headed by Salillas himself, the school had a museum displaying collections of photographs of criminals, criminals' skulls, tattoos, skeletons, prison attire, artistic objects from the prisoners and anthropometric tools. It also had a library of criminal and criminological materials, including collections of foreign journals, particularly French, Italian, British and German ones. The topics it covered included law, physical anthropology, anthropometry, ethnic anthropology, ordinary and abnormal psychology, general and correctional pedagogy, criminal anthropology and criminal sociology. Its professors, other than Salillas, included, most notably, Simarro, Aramburu, the anthropologist Federico Oloriz (1855–1912) and pedagogue Bartolomé Cossio (1857–1935). The school encountered various institutional difficulties from 1913 onwards and, in 1936, it was absorbed by the Instituto de Estudios Penales, which had been established years earlier.

Constancio Bernaldo de Quirós (1873–1959) was another noted connoisseur in the field of criminal anthropology and he contributed to the spread of knowledge of this field in Spanish society, even though he was not a Lombrosian supporter. After earning a degree in law, he soon became interested in criminology. In 1898, he published *Las nuevas teorías de la criminalidad*, an excellent summary of the thinking of the different schools of criminology. The book was informational but also critical and weighed up different trends, especially the Lombrosian trend. In 1908, he published a second edition, which was translated into English in 1911 (Modern theories of criminality), from which any reference to criminal anthropology had disappeared, reflecting a clear loss of interest. However, the best-known work of Bernaldo de Quirós is perhaps *La mala vida en Madrid*, which he wrote in 1901 with José Maria Llanas Aguilaniedo, and which was translated into German in 1911 under a different title, *Verbrechertum und prostitution in Madrid* (Criminality and prostitution in Madrid). This edition included an article by Lombroso on criminality in Spain as the prologue. It also earned a long and highly favourable review in *L'Année Sociologique* (Richard 1901). *La mala vida en Madrid*, although not a Lombrosian work, was inspired by the work by Shigele and Nicéforo entitled *La mala vita a Roma*, which Bernaldo de Quirós translated into Spanish in 1902. However, Bernaldo de Quirós' book was scientifically superior to those of his Italian peers, which were limited to mere description of criminal and dangerous activity in the Roman underworld. On the other hand, *La mala vida en Madrid* was a good combination of anthropological fieldwork with reading and knowledge of the appropriate criminological literature, allowing its authors to carry out an interesting analysis on the causes of petty crime and ways of life, as well as suggesting ways to combat it (Campos 2009). The use of the work of Lombroso and his followers is clear in this work but, despite the points of convergence, its conclusions are very different, especially in terms of the existence of the born criminal (denied by the Spaniards) and the methods proposed to combat crime, rooted in Correctionism and against the increase of repressive measures defended by Shigele and Nicéforo (Maristany del Rayo 1998; Campos 2009). Other works of interest by Bernaldo de Quirós were *El alcoholismo* (1903), *La criminalidad de sangre en España* (1906), and *El bandolerismo andaluz* (1931).

In addition to the work carried out by all these writers, it is also fitting to point out the enormous translation task carried out by Spanish editorials, translating numerous works by Lombroso and his followers into Spanish.

Criminal anthropology and anarchism

The impact of criminological theories in Spain at the end of the century went beyond the small circle of specialists, penetrating various fields throughout the country and provoking interesting controversies. One example of this phenomenon was the debate caused by anarchism with representatives of criminal anthropology. One of Lombroso's works which had the biggest social impact in Spain was *Gli Anarchici* (1894) which was immediately translated into Spanish. The work appeared at an opportune moment, as terrorist attacks rooted in anarchism were a constant occurrence in Europe. In Spain, the phenomenon of terrorist violence was very similar, although the anarchist movement as an organised branch of the workers movement was strongly rooted in different areas of the country, especially in Western Andalusia and Catalonia. Since the 1880s, agrarian anarchism in Andalusia, which gave a revolutionary character to the traditional forms of peasant mobilisation, had reared its head on various occasions, causing strong government repression. One of the culminating moments of this phenomenon was the riots in Jerez de la Frontera at the beginning of 1892 in which thousands of peasants attacked the city, crying 'Long live anarchy!'. Rafael Salillas condemned these events in his article 'Manada de locos' (1892), which was published in the daily publication, *El Liberal*. Salillas dubbed the peasants who took part in these riots ill and insane. The article received a strongly worded response from Ricardo Mella in the anarchist newspaper *El Productor,* analysing the social problems in peasant Andalusia and opposed Salillas' pathologised arguments.

In Catalonia, anarchism was rooted in industrial and urban factors and, from the 1890s onwards, gave way to individual acts of terrorism, which were not always condoned by anarchist leaders, although never openly condemned. Lombroso's book was published at a time when attacks were frequent. In this context, his ideas about anarchists, who he classed as born criminals and mentally ill, linking anarchism, crime and madness, drew much attention from conservative lawyers and sociologists, who quickly rejected the ideas of criminal anthropology. In fact, they continued not to accept them but used them to battle anarchism (Maristany 1973, 78). In this way, anti-anarchist works, which made partial use of Lombroso's theories and mixed them with conservative and traditional thinking, became common. Books such as *El Socialismo y los anarquistas* (1895) by Cristobal Botella and *El anarquismoen España y el especial de Barcelona* (1897) by Manuel Gil Maestre were the trend during those years, in which special laws were also enacted to combat the attacks.

Lombroso's arguments were not met with silence. In 1896, two important figures in Spanish anarchism, Federico Urales (1864–1939) and Ricardo Mella (1861–1925) refuted the Italian professor's arguments in *Sociología anarquista* and *Lombroso y los anarquistas* respectively, and tried to popularise the libertarian ideology that anarchists were not a race of abnormal beings who were distinguished from the rest of humanity by a series of physical and mental traits (Girón 2002). However, Mella's response was much more elaborate, denouncing Lombroso's mediocre scientific basis, denying the existence of the born criminal and calling criminal anthropology into question. Influenced by French criminal sociology and reusing its arguments, as well as other anarchist and socialist authors, he denied the inevitability of inheritance as the origin of crime and shifted the focus of attention to social conditions, denouncing the unfair socio-economic order as he did so. In this respect, he went into greater detail on the issue of physical and mental stigmas, affirming that they are 'the result of the social structure which promotes the degeneration of the working masses' (Girón 2002, 101). Therefore, stigmas did not indicate a special class of men but rather constituted a factor of condemnation of bourgeois society, as they represented the flaws of a 'vicious, absurd and unfair social structure' (Mella 1896, 117). With regard to the same topic, he also recalled Salilla's declarations on the Jerez riots, saying

> the little Caesar of anthropology, like many other men who study men of the people from the greatest possible distance, has surely not seen the type of man who is to be found all over the Andalusian countryside. He has not seen how these farmers are a bundle of bones, protruding from under a layer of rough, dark, almost black skin, bodies deformed by continuous work and insufficient nutrition.
>
> (Mella 1896, 116)

Lombroso's heritage – from lack of criminal responsibility to danger

At the beginning of the twentieth century, degenerationism and ideas originating from criminal anthropology were losing validity and beginning to be revised. In the mid-1890s, an attempt to modify the application of degenerationist doctrine in the courts had been made by certain psychiatrists. The obvious excesses of the Alienists and the numerous refusals of judges to take expert reports into account led them to gloss over the most controversial aspects which could represent a major inconvenience, preventing them from achieving their objectives, defending the existence of diminished responsibility in many degenerates. This doctrine basically consisted of rejecting a total absence of responsibility among the insane and defending the existence of total or diminished responsibility in criminal acts committed by certain mentally ill people. This means that an individual committing a crime in the area of their morbid impulse would not be held responsible, but if they committed it outside of this, they would be responsible as their act could be deemed to be rational.

However, at the beginning of the twentieth century, an interesting redefinition took place which would give way to a new emergence of social defence in the face of crime and insanity. The debate on responsibility – absence of responsibility of the criminally insane or degenerate and discussions on whether or not free will existed – would give way to the idea of the potential social danger that these individuals could pose to society and the means of detecting them before they committed a crime. The legist doctor Lecha-Marzo presents an especially interesting case within the context of this redefinition. A devout degenerationist, in 1906, he published a work entitled 'Las anomalías de Mateo Morral', in which he tried to provide some information on the frequency and importance of the alterations, which were revealed by the autopsy of the corpse of this anarchist, who had attacked the wedding procession of Alfonso XIII and Victoria Eugenia. Although Lecha-Marzo maintained that 'progenism, the prominence of the frontal sinuses and the crookedness of the nose ... make Morral a Lombrosian criminal', he indicates that Morral was not free from responsibility as they did not find 'any atavistic anomalies' in his skull (Lecha-Marzo 1906, 87–8). Although Lecha-Marzo was following in the footsteps of Lombroso in his work on anarchists, the possibility of declaring that Morral was free from responsibility made him uncomfortable. The issue he was researching was hugely important in establishing a new social defence doctrine which was consistent with the thinking of Spanish society. Lecha-Marzo was aware that if he pathologised Mateo Morral, then Morral's act and other similar acts would go unpunished. So he tried to discredit him as a mere criminal who should receive the corresponding sentence, with no excuses. There was a limit, as Lecha-Marzo was aware, to how much degenerationism and criminal anthropology could be brought to social defence. In 1911, he would suggest a new social defence under which these doctrines would be adapted, pointing out the dangers that poor application of the latter would provoke (Lecha-Marzo 1911a, 99–100). In his opinion, while the principle of free will and the issue of responsibility remained a fundamental element on which to base sentences, a large number of criminals could benefit from psycho-forensic reports proving that they suffered from mental trauma and therefore from diminished responsibility and a reduction in their sentence. Therefore, the time spent locked up in prison would be reduced. Thus, he advocated, along with proper application of anthropological criminal knowledge, not reducing sentences in the cases of partial absence of responsibility, as 'when dealing with subjects less able than ordinary people to weigh up the pros and cons of the acts that they commit, possessing *a completely unstable will*' it was appropriate to strengthen this will by increasing the sentence 'in direct proportion' to the degree of instability in order to 'produce an effective impact in the brain' (Lecha-Marzo 1911b, 101).

This line of thinking must be put in the context of the efforts being made by Lombrosian doctors and jurists to obtain significant reform of penal codes, leading to a substitution of the concept of 'responsibility' with that of 'social danger' (Foucault 1981). In a 1915 work on 'medical proof of discernment', Lecha-Marzo and Antonio Piga pursued the idea that courts had to discover 'whether or not the accused is "fearsome" in the society in which they live'. The concept of 'fearsomeness', as a substitute for the concept of free will, rapidly gains ground (Lecha-Marzo and Piga 1915).

Knowing the degree of moral liberty with which an individual acted when committing a crime was not yet the fundamental question being debated by the courts. What was important to the safety of the community was establishing if 'dangerous' could be classed as 'fearsome'. Only thus could an appropriate social defence be put in place, which characterised the criminal both somatically and mentally, to identify subjects suspected of attacking the established order, using the same processes.

Epilogue

All these ideas, which came into being in the last few decades of the nineteenth century and early twentieth century, lived on into the 1920s and 1930s, in a different context. Psychiatry was immersed in a revision process of asylum institutions, caused by the mental hygiene movement. This movement promoted the emergence of open services and the creation of mental hygiene dispensaries as part of a health system which sought to prevent mental illness as a main objective. The chronically ill and dangerous were the only ones who would be confined to what are now known as closed services. However, despite the fact that this would be a minority group, the interest that the danger posed by the mentally ill piqued among psychiatrists was considerable, to such an extent that it became the keystone of the psychiatric reform. This danger went beyond that shown in committing a crime. The interest, in the framework of mental prophylaxis, centred on the potential danger posed by individuals. This was no trivial matter as it involved adopting a concept that was not strictly medical, extremely difficult to define and which had much more to do with social defence policies. Psychiatrists discussed the issue of the danger posed by the mentally ill at length and advocated crime prevention measures, based on the principles of mental hygiene. The need to adopt pre-crime measures against certain individuals became one of its main objectives and was consistent with the interests of sectors of the judiciary and, of course, executive powers.

The broadness and ambiguity of the concept of danger which psychiatrists were defending saw them faced with a dual challenge. Firstly, they must scientifically discover that individuals were prone to move on to action and, therefore, foresee the danger posed by said individuals, obliging them to offer some kind of prevention technology. Secondly, they were obliged to suggest therapeutic, security and isolation measures to be applied to dangerous individuals who were considered to be ill. Their suggestions mainly involved carrying out a psychological assessment of the entire population, with a view to discovering the potential danger posed by each individual and being able to prevent it, creating judicial asylums in which criminals suffering from mental illnesses would be held and, lastly, changing penal codes by introducing crime prevention measures.

Along with this, psychiatric reports became more technical. New techniques to define the danger posed by individuals exploded into the fields of criminal endocrinology and even criminal psychoanalysis. In this context, various countries set to work on promulgating new penal codes to include the new parameters. In Spain, the Primo de Rivera dictatorship would partially echo these demands by promulgating a new Penal Code in 1928, which would be harshly criticised by psychiatrists for not clearly taking into account the potential danger or pre-crime danger posed by individuals. However, this type of reasoning was incorporated into the Ley de Vagos y Maleantes of 4 August 1933, inspired by the jurist and socialist Jiménez de Asúa and the application of which left such a tragic mark during Franco's regime (Campos 2007). In a country like Spain where there were barely any Lombrosians, the work of Lombroso was disseminated and used for different purposes, the Italian ended up triumphing in ways very different from those which he would have imagined.

Note

1 This work was carried out under Proyecto de Investigación n° HAR2009-13389-C03-02 financed by The Ministerio de Ciencia e Innovación (Spain).

References

Álvarez-Uría, F. (1983) *Miserables y locos. Medicina mental y Orden social en la España del siglo XIX*. Barcelona: Tusquets.
Aramburu Zuloaga, F. (1887) *La nueva ciencia penal*. Madrid: Est. tip. de Ricardo Fe.
Bernaldo de Quirós, C. (1898) *Las nuevas teorías de la criminalidad*. Madrid: Imp. Revista de Legislación.
Bernaldo de Quirós, C.(1903) *El alcoholismo*. Barcelona: Juan Gili.

Bernaldo de Quirós, C. (1906) *La criminalidad de sangre en España*. Madrid: P. Apalategui.
Bernaldo de Quirós, C. and Ardila, L. (1931) *El bandolerismo andaluz*. Madrid: Gáfica Universal.
Bernaldo de Quirós, C. and Llanas Aguilanieda, J. M. (1901) *La mala vida en Madrid. Estudio psico-sociológico con dibujos y fotograbados del natural*. Madrid: B. Rodríguez Serra Editor.
Campos Marín, R. (2003) 'Criminalidad y locura en la Restauración. El proceso del cura Galeote (1886–1888)', *Frenia* 3 (2): 111–45.
Campos Marín, R. (2007), '¿Psiquiatría para los ciudadanos o psiquiatría para la represión? El problema de la peligrosidad del enfermo mental en España (1920–1936)', in Ricardo Campos, Olga Villasante and Rafael Huertas, *De la Edad de plata al exilio. Construcción y reconstrucción de la psiquiatría española*. Madrid: Frenia, pp. 15–36.
Campos, R. (2008) 'De la cárcel al manicomio: el caso del doctor Morillo', in José Martínez Pérez, Juan Estévez, Mercedes del Cura and Luis Victor Blas *La gestión de la locura: conocimiento, prácticas y escenarios (España, siglos XIX–XX)*. Cuenca: Ediciones de la Universidad de Castilla-La Mancha, pp. 311–42.
Campos, R. (2009) 'La clasificación de lo difuso: el concepto de 'Mala Vida' en la literatura criminológica de cambio de siglo', *Journal of Spanish Cultural Studies* 10 (4): 399–422.
Campos Marín, R., Martínez Pérez, J. and Huertas, R. (2000) *Los ilegales de la naturaleza. Medicina y Degeneracionismo en la España de la Restauración (1876–1923)*. Madrid: CSIC.
Dorado Montero, P. (1886) 'Sobre el estado de la ciencia jurídica italiana en los momentos presentes', *Boletín de la Institución Libre de Enseñanza* 10: 137–9.
Dorado Montero, P. (1890) *La Antropología criminal en Italia*. Madrid: Imp. de la Revista de Legislación.
Dorado Montero, P. (1891) *El positivismo en la ciencia jurídica y social italiana*. Madrid: Imp. de la Revista de Legislación.
Escuder, J. M. (1895) *Locos y anómalos*. Madrid: Establecimiento Tip. Sucesores de Rivadeneyra.
Escuder, J. M. (1881) *Quemas y crímenes (causas)*. Valencia: Imp de E. Pascua.
Esquerdo, J. M. (1881) 'Locos que no lo parecen. Garayo el Sacamantecas', *Revista de Medicina y Cirugía Prácticas* 5: 101–9; 153–9; 211–17; 303–12; 358–65; 402–9.
Fernández, P. (2001) *¿Loco o delincuente? Novela social contemporánea (1890)*. Madrid: Celeste.
Ferri, E. (1887) *Los nuevos horizontes del Derecho y del procedimiento penal*. Madrid: Centro Editorial de Góngora.
Foucault, M. (1981) 'L'évolution de la notion d'"individu dangereux" dans la psychiatrie legale', *Déviance et societé* 5 (4): 403–22.
Galera, A. (1991) *Ciencia y delincuencia. El determinismo antropológico en la España del siglo XIX*. Sevilla: CSIC.
Garrido y Escuín, V. (1888) *La Cárcel o el Manicomio. Estudio Médico Legal sobre la locura*. Madrid: Administración Casa Editorial de don José María Faquineto.
Girón, Á. (2002) 'Los anarquistas y la criminología de Cesare Lombroso (1890–1914)', *Frenia* 2 (2): 81–108.
Glick, T. (1982) *Darwin en España*. Barcelona: Ediciones Península.
González, J. (1994) *La imputabilidad en el Derecho Penal Español. Imputabilidad y locura en la España del siglo XIX*. Granada: Comares.
Huertas, R. (2002) *Organizar y persuadir. Estrategias profesionales y retóricas de legitimación de la medicina mental española (1875–1936)*. Madrid: Frenia.
Lecha-Marzo, A. (1906) 'Antropología criminal. Las anomalías de Mateo Morral'. *Revista de Medicina y Cirugía prácticas* 72: 84–9,
Lecha-Marzo, A. (1911a) 'Sobre los ligeramente locos', *Protocolo Médico-Forense* 13: 99–100.

Lecha-Marzo, A. (1911b) 'Más sobre los fronterizos', *Protocolo Médico-Forense* 13: 101–2.
Lecha-Marzo, A. and Piga, A. (1915) 'La prueba médica del discernimiento', *Los Progresos de la Clínica* 5: 352–61.
Maristany, L. (1973) *El gabinete del doctor Lombroso (Delincuencia y fin de siglo en España)*. Barcelona: Anagrama.
Maristany, L. (1983) 'Lombroso y España: nuevas consideraciones', *Anales de Literatura Española* 2: 361–81.
Maristany del Rayo, L. (1985) *El artista y sus congéneres. Diagnosticos sobre el fin de siglo en España*. Tesis doctoral. Facultad de Filología. Universidad de Barcelona.
Maristany del Rayo, L. (1998) 'Situación y contexto de La mala vida de Madrid', in C. Bernaldo de Quirós and J. M. Llanas de Aguilaniedo *La mala vida en Madrid. Estudio psicosociológico con dibujos y fotografías al natural*. Huesca: Instituto de Estudios Altoaragoneses, Justo Broto Salanova (ed.), pp. XXXI–LVIII.
Mella, R. (1896) *Lombroso y los anarquistas*. Barcelona: Ciencia Social.
Morote, L. (1884) 'El Derecho penal, capítulo de las ciencias naturales', *Revista General de Legislación y Jurisprudencia* 65: 439–68.
Morote, L. (1886a) 'El primer congreso internacional de Antropología criminal', *Revista General de Legislación y Jurisprudencia* 68: 261–72.
Morote, L. (1886b) 'Las anomalias en los criminales (antropología criminal)' *Revista General de Legislación y Jurisprudencia* 68: 334–61.
Nuñez, D. (1975) *La mentalidad positiva en España; desarrollo y crisis*. Madrid: Túcar.
Nuñez, D. (1977) *El darwinismo en España*. Madrid: Castalia.
Peset, J. and Peset, M. (1975) *Lombroso y la Escuela Positivista italiana*. Madrid: CSIC.
Pulido Fernández, Á. (1883) 'Locos delincuentes', *Discursos pronunciados en la Sección de Ciencias Naturales del Ateneo científico y literario de Madrid sobre el tema: Estado actual de la Ciencia Frenopática y sus relaciones con el derecho penal*. Madrid: Imprenta de la Revista de Legislación.
Richard, G. (1901) 'Milieux Criminogènes, les sociétés de malfateurs et leurs moeurs', *L'Année Sociologique* 5: 461–6.
Rios-Font, W. (2005) 'El crimen de la calle de San Vicente: Crime Writting and Bourgeois Liberalism in Restoration Spain', *MLN* 120 (2): 335–54.
Salillas, R. (1888) *La vida penal en España*. Madrid: Imprenta de la Revista de Legislación y Jurisprudencia.
Salillas, R. (1889) 'La Antropología y el derecho penal', *Revista de Legislación y Jurisprudencia* 73: 603–29.
Salillas, R. (1892) 'Manada de locos', *El Liberal* (8 February).
Salillas, R. (1896) *El delincuente español. El Lenguaje*. Madrid: Imprenta de V. Suárez.
Salillas, R. (1898) *El delincuente español. Hampa*. Madrid: Imprenta de V. Suárez 1898.
Salillas, R. (1908) *El tatuaje en su evolución histórica, en sus diferentes caracterizaciones antiguas y actuales y en los delincuentes franceses, italianos y españoles*. Madrid: Imp. Eduardo Arias.
Trinidad Fernández, P. (1991) *La defensa de la sociedad. Cárcel y delincuencia en España (siglos XVIII–XX)*. Madrid: Alianza Editorial.
Varela, J. and Álvarez-Uría, F. (1979) *El cura galeote asesino del obispo de Madrid.-Alcalá. Proceso médico legal reconstruido y presentado por...* Madrid: La Piqueta.
Vidal, A. (2007) *Luis Simarro y su tiempo*. Madrid: CSIC.

19
THE INFLUENCE OF CESARE LOMBROSO ON PHILIPPINE CRIMINOLOGY[1]

Filomin C. Gutierrez

The criminal anthropology of Cesare Lombroso (1835–1909), which argued that crime was rooted in human biological makeup, has been "discredited" as a pseudo-science. During the twentieth century, textbooks and syllabi in criminology courses dismissed it as problematic and misguided, or included it to demonstrate how pseudo-sciences in the past made false starts to explain criminal behavior. But no matter how far Lombroso's work has "fallen from grace," it cannot be denied that his ideas have gripped not only the scientific quarters but also the cultural imagination of many societies for decades.

Scholars have expounded on the influence of Lombroso's ideas in the intellectual and cultural contexts of Western societies (notably, Horn 2003; Gibson and Rafter 2006). Beyond the West, the diffusion of Lombroso's thought has started to be mapped; in Japan, for example (Nakatani 2006). This chapter deals with how Lombroso's criminal anthropology came to the Philippines through the waves of colonization in the late nineteenth and early twentieth centuries. The discussion points to Lombroso's influence in the work of Sixto De Los Angeles, a physician who became an expert in legal medicine. He produced *Legal Medicine* (1934), a reference that has guided generations of students in law and medicine in the Philippines. The work of De Los Angeles can be considered among the treatises of local Filipino scholars who attempted to participate in nation-building by way of scientific knowledge.

Toward the close of the nineteenth century, scientific paradigms competed for hegemony in explaining criminality. Social sciences, such as anthropology, psychology, and sociology, were sought to take root in the academy. Simultaneously, political transitions erupted among colonial empires and states, including the Philippines. The production of scientific knowledge is not only determined by the logical progress, but is also shaped by intellectual contingencies in the social and political milieu (Kuhn 1996). Colonization projects transferred certain scientific ideas from Western empires to colonies which could verify or challenge their viability outside their Eurocentric origin.

The colonial background

During the last years of the 1890s, when positivist criminology and criminal anthropology received enormous attention in Europe, the Philippines was in the throes of a revolution against Spain's more than 300 years of colonial rule. Spanish was then the official language of government and of formal education, which was mostly limited to members of the local elite. It continued to be the spoken and written language among local intellectual elites, in addition to the eventual introduction and concurrent use of English in the early 1900s. Thus, it was likely the 1899 Spanish edition of *The Criminal Man* (*Los Criminales*, published by Centro Editorial Presa in Barcelona), that brought criminal anthropology to the wider consciousness of Filipino scholars. The political transition following the revolution provided them with the impetus to build the Philippines as an independent nation through scientific knowledge and its application to their society.

The revolt against Spanish rule culminated in a declaration of independence in June 1898 and placed revolutionary leader Emilio Aguinaldo as president of the Philippines. The independence was short-lived, however, as the Treaty of Paris was signed in late 1898. Spain ceded the Philippines, along with its other colonial territories (Cuba, Puerto Rico and Guam), to the United States. The new situation jeopardized the achievements of the Philippine revolution against Spain and resistance against the new colonial power ensued. The United States initially responded with force, quelling the rebellion and criminalizing many acts of resistance to its rule. Later, with the promise of granting the Philippines its own independence after establishing a democratic system, the United States deployed less forceful strategies. The Americans incorporated members of the local elite in the lower tiers of leadership of the state bureaucracy and the rest of the native population in the lower ranks of military and police forces. Intellectuals were assimilated into the new academic machinery that vowed to fuel national development through scientific knowledge.

The new strategy included an educational campaign that began in the 1900s. Access to secondary and university education beyond members of the higher socioeconomic status boosted the literacy rate in the Philippines from an estimated 8 percent of the population in the late nineteenth century (Agoncillo and Guerrero 1970) to 49 percent by end of the First World War (Census Office 1921). State-sponsored academic colleges specializing in medicine, law, and education, eventually including a wider range of fields, were established leading to the foundation of the University of the Philippines in the capital city of Manila. To occupy the required academic posts, scholars from the United States came to the Philippines on government service. Filipino intellectuals who had been educated in either Europe or Philippine colleges established by Spanish friars were recruited to collaborate with them (Gillet 1995; Anderson 2007).

A rising class of Filipinos called *ilustrados* (meaning, enlightened) played a crucial role in the political and cultural changes in this period. Regarding one as an *ilustrado* precluded considerations of race or economic class. Prestige was accorded to the "nobility" of intellectual status and political beliefs. Identified chiefly by their being highly educated in Philippine or European universities, *ilustrados* consisted of a mix of individuals belonging to the rising middle class drawn from prosperous peasant and merchant classes, or from the more progressive families of the native, Chinese or Spanish *mestizo* upper classes. Possessing modernist, progressive, and scientific worldviews, *ilustrados* were typically anti-clerical, critical of Spanish and Filipino traditions, and patriotic. They had campaigned for the national autonomy of the Philippines from Spain, and this political aspiration extended during the American period. They presented an eager, if not impatient, anticipation of the promised independence of the Philippines from the United States.

Early Filipino "criminologists"

To grasp the production of knowledge or science in a particular historical period, it is useful to examine the biographical contingencies of intellectuals. Who were the people who became interested in the study of crime? What questions about crime did they want to answer? What social or intellectual background did they come from? With whom did they work? Whose work did they read, and how were these ideas interpreted in their own work? Scholars of Lombroso's work have shown the importance of recognizing the biographical interplay of Lombroso's work and the intellectual conditions of his social milieu in the culmination of criminal anthropology (Gibson and Rafter 2006). In the early 1900s, two Filipino scholars could be regarded as "criminologists": Ignacio Villamor and Sixto De Los Angeles. In the fields of law and medicine, they sustained interest in studying crime and its causes and pursued this interest through research and publication.

Ignacio Villamor was a lawyer by training and profession who rose to prominent positions in the state judiciary system, later becoming an associate justice alongside American justices appointed to the Philippine Supreme Court. He devoted many years of his career to the study of crime statistics, most of which were collated under his supervision as attorney general and as director of the Bureau of Census at one point. Using official crime records covering the years 1903 to 1918, Villamor published his analyses of crime in *La Criminalidad en las Islas Filipinas* (1909) and *Crime and Moral Education* (1924), as well as in numerous abridged versions of his written work in popular magazines and serials. Although judicial crime statistics and criminal cases were his main sources of empirical data, Villamor stepped out of the classical school's adherence to rational choice and criminal liability as principles behind criminal behavior. He regarded crime as an outcome of the confluence of varied factors, ranging from social, economic, and political to the physical environment, and did not contest the contribution of biological factors. Prior to the criminal anthropological work of De Los Angeles, Villamor (1915, 220) already referred to Lombroso's atavism theory, stating that criminal offenders carry "the tendency to revert to the 'primitive type' as generally recognized by criminologists, and that it occupies a preeminent place in the study of the causes of crime."

In his review of various criminological theories, Villamor (1915, 221; 1924, 45–50) cited Lombroso along with hereditary theories on crime based on genealogy and family studies by such authors as Paul Aubry, Arthur Griffiths, and Richard Dugdale. Villamor's publications also confirm the trend of embracing biologically oriented theories of crime causation among scholars and practitioners in the judicial system who generally came from an academic background in law. These scholars offered statements of judges and prison directors in their subscription to such theories, for example, the article of New York county judge Warren Foster titled "Hereditary Criminality and Its Certain Cure" (1901), and recognized the role of heredity in criminal behavior (Villamor 1915, 220–1).

The scholar mainly responsible for bringing criminal anthropology to the Philippines, Sixto De Los Angeles, was born to a landed family in San Mateo, Rizal, a town northeast of Manila. He rose to prominence as professor of medicine, the country's medico-legal expert and member of the Philippine Congress. His father was a teacher and his mother a businesswoman. Educated by Spanish friars, De Los Angeles finished his Bachelor of Arts degree at Colegio de San Juan de Letran, which was established by Dominicans in 1620, making it one of the oldest colleges in the Philippines. He acquiesced to his father's wishes for him to take up law and studied the course for two years before pursuing medicine, which he believed to be his true calling. He finished his medical degree at the University of Santo Tomas, which was also established by Dominicans in the seventeenth century and recognized as an institution of higher learning in the Philippine colony by the Spanish monarchy and by the Vatican. De Los Angeles obtained his medical license at the age of 23 in 1898. Appointed as Military Chief of Health by revolutionary president Aguinaldo, he used his medical training to attend to wounded revolutionary fighters in Lucena, Tayabas Province (Artigas 1917).

Nation-building through addressing crime

The shift from the Spanish to the American political regime unsettled and divided members of the Philippine elite. They had to choose whether to acquiesce to the new colonial power or to continue the fight of the revolutionary government. They weighed the risk of losing or gaining positions in the coming order.

The arrest and incarceration of Aguinaldo by United States forces weakened the bid of the revolutionaries for supremacy and made uncertain the positions that supposedly awaited the *ilustrados* in Aguinaldo's government. Villamor, who was originally drafted as a cabinet member in Aguinaldo's government, and De Los Angeles, who would likely hold an important medical post, might have reconciled themselves to working with the United States. Notwithstanding subordination to American "mentors," this appeared to be the more rational path to sustaining their own careers and remaining in patriotic service to the Philippines. The project of building a modern democratic state, fueled by education, science-based policies for economic development, and the promise of later independence for the Philippines seemed to be a more proactive route when compared to the "independent nation" agenda of the defeated and beleaguered revolutionary government. In effect, the American administration co-opted the *ilustrados* to participate in efforts of nation-building by offering them positions in government bureaus, including teaching posts in newly instituted state colleges. For the *ilustrados*, cooperating with the United States' effort to build the nation of Philippines through education and science could be justified as an extension of their resistance to the Spanish regime: the "old order."

De Los Angeles spent the interim period of regime change in hibernation in his hometown in San Mateo in 1899, where he turned his energies instead to literature, writing a Spanish *sainete* (comic opera) and a Tagalog *zarzuela* (musical play). He returned to public service three years later, when he was appointed president of the Board of Health of Rizal Province in 1902 under the American administration. This integration into the American-led bureaucracy continued when he became a physician at government hospitals, San Pablo and San Juan de Dios hospitals, and professor at the Philippine Medical School (Artigas 1917).

Politics and political change provided a decisive background to the quest to address criminality. Political turbulence often framed politically motivated dissent and aggressive actions which were deemed crimes against the state or against public order, such as sedition, rebellion, insurrection, and even political "banditry," and were routinely and aggressively pursued by the authorities. The call to establish peace and public order and end "the rising criminality and lawlessness" was a key rhetoric in the project of building the democratic Philippine state. This call to "address crime" appealed strongly to Filipino "criminologists" Villamor and De Los Angeles.

Lombroso's criminal anthropology

Criminal anthropology, particularly Lombroso's principles of atavism, pertaining to those inferior or aberrant physical characteristics found among criminal offenders, made an impression on De Los Angeles. Lombroso's work compelled him to conduct clinical studies of convicts at the Bilibid Prison[2] in 1916 and publish the results in *Estudios sobre criminal anthropologia en las Islas Filipinas* in 1919.

The rise of criminal anthropology benefited from the widespread success of Charles Darwin's evolution theory in the late nineteenth century. Darwinism rippled through the biological sciences and renewed interest in enterprises such as physiognomy and phrenology that were already on the brink of being regarded as pseudo-sciences. It revived the curiosity of the public and the scientific world in the human body and its evolution, improvement, or degeneration, and provided the study of Philippine racial and ethnic types.

In the Philippines, curiosity about the body was first directed at human types, at demystifying the human bodies that peopled the new colonies. Thus, scientists such as anatomists, physical anthropologists, and ethnologists who studied the Philippine colony with a basic interest in cataloguing the racial or ethnic stock paved the way wider for Lombrosian-inspired inquiries in the Philippines in the early 1900s. But in as early as the 1800s, European scientists had already included the Philippines in their scope of study. German scientists such as Carl Semper (*The Philippine Islands and Their Inhabitants, Six Sketches*, 1869), Fedor Jagor (*Travels in the Philippines*, 1875) and Rudolf Virchow (*The Peopling of the Philippines*, 1899) had investigated and written on the physical ancestry of Filipinos based on studies of skulls and hair, notably of the Negritos in the Philippines. French ethnologist Joseph Montano documented his observations of the Philippines in 1880 and reported this in *Rapport á M. Ministre de L'Instruction Publique sur une Mission aux Iles Philippines et en Malaisie, 1879–1881* (Montano 1885). The report included the anthropometric measurements of the bodies of various ethnic groups in the archipelago. Montano's data set was to become one of the three data sets later tapped by De Los Angeles as non-criminal Filipino population in comparison with the criminal population of prison convicts.

This interest in the Philippines as a scientific field of observation increased in the early 1900s when American scientists arrived to perform civil service. They also taught at the newly established University of the Philippines and conducted research at the Philippine Bureau of Science. One of these, Robert Bennett Bean, would later become a renowned physical anthropologist in the United States and president of the Anthropological Section of the American Association of the Advancement in Science in 1928. He trained in anatomy and anthropology at Virginia Polytechnic State Institute, Johns Hopkins Medical School, and the University of Michigan. He also trained in anthropometrics under Leon Manouvrier at the Ecolé d' Anthropologie in Paris. From 1907 to 1910 he was appointed Director of the Biological Laboratory of the Philippine Bureau of Science and the University of the Philippines College of Medicine (Bean 1945). Bean studied the various racial and ethnic characteristics of peoples in the Philippines, including their anthropometric measurements. Among his known books was *The Racial Anatomy of the Philippine Islanders* (1910), which was based on his studies of different groups of the Philippine population, including students, various individuals, and inmates of the Bilibid Prison.

Another American scholar sent to perform civil service in the Philippines was anthropologist Daniel Folkmar, a prominent member of the Anthropological Society of Washington. He served as Lieutenant Sub-governor of Bontoc Province in the Philippines. In documenting the Philippine types, he gathered the anthropometric measurements of Filipinos drawn from Bilibid Prison inmates in 1903 (Folkmar 1904). The main output of his work was a collection of 1,024 photographs and 128 body casts of Bilibid inmates presented at the World Exposition in St Louis, Missouri, in 1904. The accompanying book, *Album of Philippine Types Found in Bilibid Prison in 1903, Christians and Moros, Including a Few Non-Christians* (1904), published photographs of some 80 prisoners and their corresponding anthropometric data such as height, weight, cephalic index, length of head, breadth of nose, span of arms and shoulders.

De Los Angeles and Lombroso

The reluctance to engage Lombroso's criminal anthropology might have arisen from the perception of Lombroso's ideas as static in their assertion of criminals being born with an unavoidable disposition to crime. However, although biologically deterministic to some extent, Lombroso's scholarship embraced the sociological causes of crime (Gibson and Rafter 2006, 2) and must be credited for a wider view of crime beyond biological factors, which he was known for emphasizing. It was this inclusive approach of Lombroso to understanding crime that was appropriated by De Los Angeles in his study of Filipino criminals. In his work, *Estudios sobre antropología criminal en Las Islas Filipinas*, he argued for a criminal anthropology characterized as

> [T]he systematic study of criminal individuals, their relationship with the physical and socio-economic environment in which they live, in order to know the causes of their delinquency and crime, and to propose from a positive basis the practical means for their correction and prevention.
> (De Los Angeles 1919, 24)

The writings of De Los Angeles, as well as those of Villamor, appear to have been extensively informed by the proceedings of the first two International Congresses of Criminal Anthropology held in Rome in 1885 and Paris in 1889. Both authors cite the works of leading criminologists, with Lombroso as the central figure in the published proceedings.

However, De Los Angeles (1919, 14) also subscribed to the idea that criminal behavior was not limited to organic causes discernable through anatomic and physiological peculiarities. Criminality for him could also come from the economic, social, and physical environment, and from illnesses arising from congenital or acquired conditions. Appropriately, his version of criminal anthropology derived from an amalgamation of theories within positivist criminology consisting of ideas from both biological and sociological schools of thought that had come to increasingly interconnect by the early 1900s. De Los Angeles framed the epistemological parameters of his study by expounding on the merits of positivism, saying that various empirical sciences, both natural and social, had culminated in making the scientific study of crime possible through criminal anthropology. He noted how medicine, his professional base, and sociology, anthropology, and psychiatry combined various modern knowledge to identify the causes of crime and determine its cure and prevention (De Los Angeles 1919, 20–4).

The empirical aspect of positivism could not have received greater emphasis from De Los Angeles. He relied extensively on Lombroso's Italian adherents, Raffaele Garofalo and Enrico Ferri. He references, for example, Garofalo's declarations in *Criminology* (2nd edition, 1914) about the precedence of empirical research over theory and reflection in any scientific undertaking. He also draws on the works of Lombroso's Spanish interpreters, Bernaldo de Quirós and Pedro Montero, as well as the English criminologist Charles Goring among a list of European and American criminologists. To anchor the arguments linking human behavior to biological causes, De Los Angeles mentioned prominent scientific works: Darwin's theory of evolution, Karl Ernst von Baer on embryology, Ernst Haeckel on morphology, Francis Galton's work on heredity, and Rudolf Virchow's cell theory (De Los Angeles 1919, 13–15).

De Los Angeles hardly recognized the rift and competition between the biologically oriented (Lombroso's Italian School) and the sociologically oriented (Lacassagne's French School) criminological paradigms. For him, modern biological and social sciences shared a common ground in their empiricism and combined to challenge the vacuity of traditional doctrines of penology drawn from legal-philosophical reflections. At this point, De Los Angeles joined the modern scientific criminology's claim to impact government policy and the judicial system and emacipate them from the "cruelties of penology which have been based only on philosophy" through treatment rather than punishment (De Los Angeles 1919, 14–16).

De Los Angeles's call for the unity of the sciences and the coordinated collaboration among Filipino scholars reflects his position as one of the institution-builders of the University of the Philippines. A few years after the Americans established the university, its Filipino academic members eagerly anticipated the turnover of its leadership to them. However, the American leaders of the University, distrusting the abilities of Filipino scholars to conduct original and independent research, hesitated in relinquishing full leadership of such scientific institutions (Anderson 2007). The efforts of Filipino scholars finally came to fruition in 1915, when Ignacio Villamor became the University's first Filipino president and Sixto De Los Angeles the first head of the newly created Medical Jurisprudence and Ethics Department of the University's College of Medicine.

De Los Angeles could be interpreted as urging Filipino scientists to demonstrate a deservedness to take over the academic and national leadership from the Americans. In their respective works, together with Villamor, they asserted expertise in crime in their respective fields of law and medical jurisprudence, emphasizing that theories coming from abroad need to be empirically grounded in the local field (Gutierrez 2010). In other words, Lombroso's empiricism offered a means for indigenizing scientific traditions originating overseas.

Lombroso's atavism: cranial anomalies

De Los Angeles recapitulated the idea of Lombroso that criminal offenders, at least a distinct portion of their population, have atavistic characteristics. They have inferior or less evolved physical states, especially their cranial features, and have poor hereditary history compared to non-criminals. While acknowledging the effect of social factors on generating criminal behavior, he recognized that there were "instinctive criminals." He noted this category to be similar to Lombroso's "born criminal," whose pathology stemmed from their organic physical constitution and congenital or acquired physiological anomalies, and to whom the effect of environmental factors was secondary. Their mental and moral degeneracy enslaved them to their instincts and made it difficult for them to adapt to the rules of advanced civilization. Like Lombroso, De Los Angeles (1919, 24) deemed education useless, if not dangerous, to this type of criminal.

To test out the atavism thesis, De Los Angeles set out to Bilibid Prison with a comprehensive study plan. He clinically examined 100 male and 8 female inmates and anthropometrically measured their bodies and features, such as the length of their ears, pelvic bones, and fingers; the maximum circumference of their thorax and abdomen; the amount and distribution of their hair and blood pressure rate. He also took their craniometrical measurements: length, width, index, depth, and circumference of the skull. De Los Angeles carried out autopsies and examinations of the skulls of some 44 deceased convicts to verify further the link between cranial anomalies and criminal behavior. Moreover, he used psychometric tests to determine mental abilities, intelligence, memory, moral character, emotional suggestibility, and physiological responses, such as sensitivity to touch, temperature and pain, muscular, visual, and auditory responses. De Los Angeles further noted the tattoos of some inmates, echoing in his own studies Lombroso's fascination with the tattoos and writings of criminal offenders.

Following the atavism hypothesis, the criminal population in the Bilibid study of De Los Angeles was expected to manifest inferior or regressive anthropometric features, such as smaller brain capacity indicative of impaired ability to regulate propensity to criminal behavior. To establish their inferior biological state, De Los Angeles needed to compare his data with non-criminal populations. For this, he tapped the anthropometric data of Bean, Folkmar and Joseph Montano (see Figure 19.1).

Most anthropometric measures of the criminal population, such as height, weight and nasal index, did register lower figures but the difference was not significant enough to merit a definite conclusion (De Los Angeles 1919, 87). Mindful of the strict tenets of scientific observation, De Los Angeles refrained from making inferences. He found only one significant difference between the criminal and non-criminal populations: the former had smaller cephalic index compared to the latter. This one important finding bolstered the stake of Lombroso's atavism hypothesis with lower and less-evolved brain capacity. Moreover, De Los Angeles's scrutiny revealed the skulls of deceased inmates convicted of serious crimes, such as murder, homicide, robbery, and rape, to possess cranial and brain anomalies. These defects prominently presented in a series of photographs (see Figure 19.2).

De Los Angeles recognized the limited comparability of criminal and non-criminal groups, noting that Bean's data were based on Filipino and *mestizo* students aged 18 years and above who went to Manila schools and came from different parts of the archipelago. Bean (1909, 264) himself pointed out that his samples were of students presumably from better classes and *mestizos* (possibly of mixed foreign blood and nurture) compared to Montano's and Folkmar's measurements, which were of common people in the Philippines. What escaped De Los Angeles's better

Lombroso and Philippine criminology 333

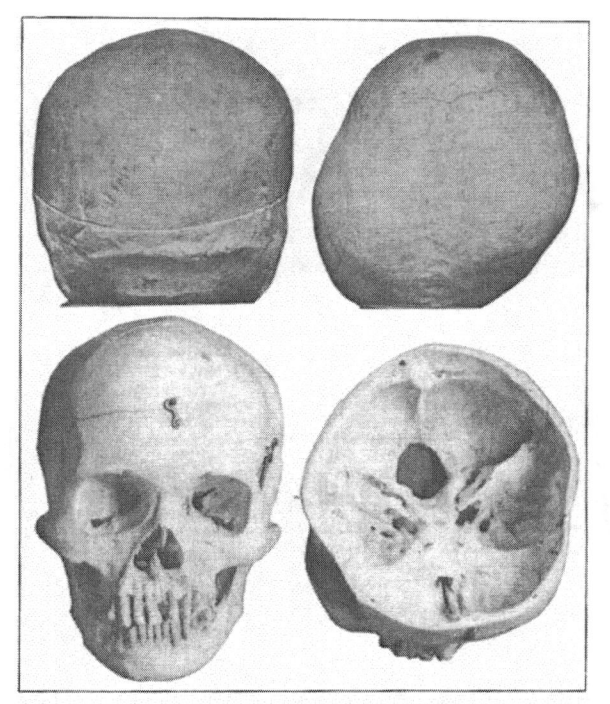

Cráneo del P. No. 10596. Mesaticéfalo. Capacidad craneal, 1,596 cc. Edad, 67 años. Crimen, asesinato. Sentencia, cadena perpetua y P1,000 de indemnización. Sinóstosis prematura, sub-escafocefalia, asimetría craneal, asimetría facial, desviación del tabique nasal, foseta occipital vermiforme y anomalías dentarias.

LÁMINA I. COMBINACIÓN NOTABLE DE SIETE ANOMALÍAS CRANEALES EN UN MISMO INDIVIDUO.

FIGURE 19.1 A series of images showing seven notable anomalies in the skull of a Bilibid prison inmate convicted of murder based on the clinical analysis of Sixto De Los Angeles

Source: De Los Angeles 1919.

judgment was that Folkmar's data were in fact not those of non-criminals as he had presumed but were of Bilibid Prison convicts presented in the *Album of Philippine Types* by Folkmar (1904). Verification of this blunder could be found in an article on Filipino types written by Bean and published in the *Philippine Journal of Science* in 1909, where Folkmar's data were also used and appropriately labeled as those of Bilibid Prison convicts (Bean 1909, 291).

Heredity, criminality, and social hygiene

The interest in linking the behavioral with the biological could be seen not only in the clinical-anthropometric core of De Los Angeles's study but in the examination of the hereditary family history of inmates, which was incorporated in his study plan.

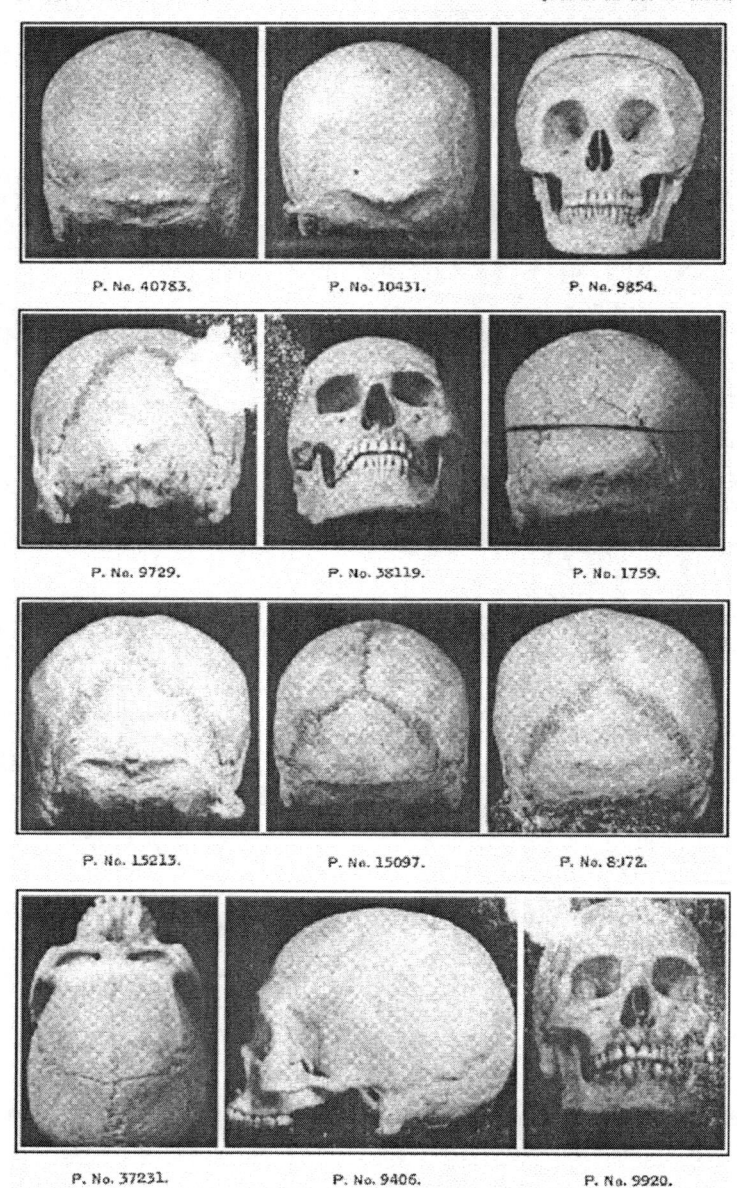

FIGURE 19.2 A sampling of cranial anomalies of criminals based on the autopsies of 44 deceased convicts

Source: De Los Angeles 1919.

De Los Angeles's belief in the link between biological characteristics and antisocial traits and behaviors, including criminal ones, was maintained throughout his later works; for instance, his attempt to contribute to legislative debates on population management from a science perspective. In an article on the need for a scientific study of the population which he wrote for the *Journal of Philippine Islands Medical Association* in 1936, he states:

> In the anthropological, medical and biological fields, we may be able to determine the various racial types of the population, the peculiar traits, taints, and diseases that are inherited; the number and causes of defective marriage selection and breeding; the number and family origin of psychopaths, criminals, professional swindlers, vagrants, and other antisocial groups with relation to heredity.
>
> (De Los Angeles 1936, 266)

De Los Angeles extended his expertise in criminal anthropology to the eugenics movement, which could also be traced to Lombroso and like-minded biological scientists in the 1920s and 1930s. In a brief article calling for the scientific study of "population problems," De Los Angeles echoed the views of scholars of the eugenics movement about monitoring the development of not only the quantity but also the quality of a population, as this would "improve the physical, mental, and moral efficiency of our individual citizens . . . for a full, progressive, and happy nationhood" (De Los Angeles 1936, 267). He cited a range of scientists associated with the ideas of mental hygiene, social hygiene, and eugenics, such as Francis Galton, Adolph Pinard, Achille Guilliard, and particularly Alois Scholz who had completed research at the Boarding Technical Training Institute at Modling in the 1920s.

De Los Angeles, moreover, proposed to link government institutions such as national defense units, presumably referring to the military and the police, schools, prisons, reformatories, and health institutions in the country to coordinate and collaborate with one another to "penetrate deeper in to the roots of the peculiarities of our race and population" (1936, 269). It is not clear to what extent this proposal was implemented. Nor is it clear if eugenic solutions, such as the radical measure of sterilization of convicted serious criminals, was considered or carried out in the Philippines.

Inquiries on hereditary factors influencing social behavior such as crime, among others, became an anathema to most scholars after the Second World War and the Nazi extermination of the Jews at death camps (Gibson and Rafter 2006, 5). This led to the decline of theoretical and research projects associated with the eugenics movement, following that of criminal anthropology. But it must be recognized that criminal anthropology and social hygiene's socio-biological perspective were widespread enough to have thrived for several decades and permeated the social sciences in the Philippines. Social hygiene, for example, is prominently referred to in the sociology textbook *Social Problems*, by Serafin Macaraig[3] as social efforts associated with the eugenics movement in its aim toward the "improvement of the human race" (Macaraig 1929, 147). The discussion of social hygiene in Macaraig's work, however, is limited to how the problem of prostitution and venereal disease could be addressed in the Philippines.

Cultural practices and crime

De Los Angeles's *Estudios sobre antropología criminal en las Islas Filipinas* (1919) mostly deals with aspects that go beyond the physical traits of inmates, including cultural, moral, and economic conditions that "contribute to criminality." In about 20 out of 120 pages of exposition on criminality, De Los Angeles, much like Lombroso's attempts to link criminal behavior to the social environment, extended the reach of his expertise as physician to dabble in anthropology and sociology. He offered his insights on the influence of the social environment on criminality. De Los Angeles recognized the diverse opinions of authors on the "psychological constitution" or the "moral sensibility" of Filipinos. He cited impressions of British writer John Foreman (1906) in the late 1800s, for example, who described the Filipinos as "inclined to disputes and quarrels" and "lacking in the noble sentiments of honor and magnanimity." He also cited the positive comments of J.P. Sanger, director of the Bureau of Census of 1903, on the criminal statistics of the Philippines: "Filipinos as a race are not particularly inclined to crime" (De Los Angeles 1919, 106–7).

De Los Angeles (1919, 110) expounded on several cultural traits and practices linked to criminal behavior among Filipinos. These included the "traditional Malayan practice or disposition of *amok*, an uncontrollable aggression or rage provoked by things of small importance." To bolster his argument, De Los Angeles referred to the authoritative work on tropical medicine by Castellani and Chalmers (1913), particularly the malady called *tropical fury* studied by Albert Plehn, as highly similar to the phenomenon of *amok*. De Los Angeles then attempted to relate aggressive behavior to more organic causes by presenting a few cases of inmates who had committed violent crimes. He argued that such violent, irrational behavior was an expression of *amok* and that one of the perpetrators he examined had corresponding problematic hereditary and family history. He cited the case of a convict who killed several people over a "senseless dispute" related to the ownership of a rooster. The convict came from an impoverished background where the alcoholic father abandoned his family. He adjudged the anthropometric data of the person as showing a few cranial anomalies, seemingly falling within Lombroso's classification of the *occasional criminal* (De Los Angeles 1919, 112).

De Los Angeles also enlisted the supporting arguments forwarded by authors who had written about the customs, traditions, and predispositions of indigenous populations in the Philippines, such as Soncuya (1917), De Mas (1843), and De La Gironiere (1854). The positive traits of Filipinos identified included being pleasant and agreeable, respect and care for elders, honesty, protectiveness over family members, courage, hospitality to strangers, and patience but with the tendency to be driven to fury when triggered by insults, especially when intoxicated (De La Gironiere 1854 quoted in Bureau of the Census 1905). The negative dispositions of Filipinos, as pointed out by Soncuya, were laziness, dishonesty, ingratitude, and cruelty.

De Los Angeles (1919, 113) attempted to integrate diverse and often opposing views on the behavior temperament of Filipinos, citing the difficulty in ascertaining the character of any society or community, given its many dimensions. He finally drove his main point: "it is however not difficult to observe the miseducation passed on by parents to children," referring to vices such as alcohol and gambling.

The presentation of "empirical evidence" was primary in De Los Angeles's approach in defending his arguments, his central tool for adhering to positivism. When numbers were unavailable to sustain the arguments, he often cited case studies culled from his long experience as a medico-legal practitioner. He extended his observations of these anecdotal cases to conjecture and infer about the cultural practices of Filipinos. In his book *Legal Medicine* (1934), he presented these field observations as "true reflections of the local conditions" which could significantly differ from cases presented by books based on foreign societies. In the foreword to the book, De Los Angeles writes that his

> principal objective [was] ... to publish a book [on legal medicine] so adapted to local needs, conditions and peculiarities that it might be of some practical use not only to classroom instructors and their students but to medical men, jurists, police officers, and social workers as well.
> (De Los Angeles 1934, v)

Crime, culture and science

The work of De Los Angeles could be considered among the treatises of local Filipino scholars who attempted to participate in nation-building in their own way as intellectuals, by way of scientific knowledge. These intellectuals viewed criminality as both a biological and a social problem that could be addressed using scientific scrutiny and, as much as possible, by intervention. The interventions they had in mind involved creating and strengthening legislation that prevented criminality or mitigated its known causes, and securing societal support for academic, interdisciplinary, and coordinated scientific projects that attempted to gain a better understanding of criminality and ways to control it. In effect, De Los Angeles, and to a great extent Villamor, justified their personal and professional involvements as intellectuals in a period of Philippine history when "men of science" or "men of letters" took active role in politics and state matters.

De Los Angeles saw positivism as a call for a culture of research among various fields and professions, more reliable data, and the working together of scholars from various disciplines. He further argued that criminal anthropology must work with related fields such as law, medicine, psychology, sociology, and statistics. He committed considerable lapses in his study, however. Many variables in his study plan, including hereditary family history, criminal history, psychometric measures, and physiological responses, were not processed nor presented in research. Moreover, pronouncements of the cultural practices and social-environmental correlates of criminality were not based on some systematic empirical observation but were rather opportunistically harvested from a combination of anecdotal impressions in the course of his work as medico-legal practitioner, common-sense knowledge, and public opinion. More significantly, there was the crucial error of assuming the non-criminality of the comparison population (Folkmar's data) when this was in fact comprised of convicted criminals.

But focusing on the procedural or methodological errors of De Los Angeles's work is not the point. It is more important to ask the broader question of how much impact did Lombrosian criminology or criminal anthropology make on the scientific, cultural, and policy landscape of the period. It had a significant academic impact on scholars who did "criminology," such as De Los Angeles and Villamor, their associates and students. Criminal anthropology was indelibly included in the knowledge reservoir of generations of medical doctors under the tutelage of De Los Angeles and lawyers under Villamor. Thus for medicine, law, and the social sciences in the early 1900s up to as late as the 1930s, it was a theory to reckon with.

It is equally important to recognize the cultural impact of the theory. De Los Angeles and Villamor wrote some of their ideas in popular magazines. The public gravitated to the notion of a fearsome biologically aberrant and culturally backward criminal type. The controversial early 1900s American writer Katherine Mayo, for example, drew from De Los Angeles's ideas about the criminality of Filipinos in her critique of the cultural superstitious beliefs and practices in the Philippines in her book *The Isles of Fear: The Truth about the Philippines* (1924).

As a member of the Philippine Legislative Assembly, De Los Angeles contributed to improving nutrition, infant mortality, and diseases, and health and sanitation, taking into account their effects on behavior. He blamed the overarching impact of poverty on the Philippine population as the root cause of criminality. De Los Angeles pointed out the lack of education and poor nutrition resulting from poverty, superstition, and so forth, as factors influencing criminality in the Philippines. These ideas, however, were not related uniquely to Lombroso or to criminal anthropology, nor even to biological or sociological criminologists, but to the general wisdom carried by scholars and the general public. Policies based on the analysis of cultural practices and social-environmental factors included in De Los Angeles's study were more feasibly turned into legislation, that is, improvement in education and moral education to combat "ignorantism," "superstition," and "idleness and vices" that led to crime (De Los Angeles 1919, 117–21).

Conclusion

By the 1920s, criminal anthropology began its decline, and sociological criminology rose as the dominant paradigm. Lombroso's influence waned in the 1920s and 1930s in the Philippines, as it did in the United States and in Europe. But criminal anthropology left enough trace in the intellectual imagination of societies for them to consider the possibility that criminality is rooted not in human choice nor in social conditions but in things beyond the control of social policy, such as human biology. It has also left a relegated discourse among social sciences with their ambivalence on socio-biological propositions. Contemporary scientists, biocriminologists in particular, now recognize a small inner circle of very serious, habitual offenders as a distinct group from the numerous run-of-the-mill offenders (Gibson and Rafter 2006, 31).

Criminal anthropology gripped the intellectual and imagination of the Philippines in the early twentieth century, foreshadowing the reception of biologically oriented criminological theories, most recently of behavioral genetics, which propose that certain antisocial behaviors that could lead to crime are linked to genetic predispositions (Gibson and Rafter 2006, 32). Lombroso's propositions about crime did decline but the indelible trace of his original propositions manifests in many other criminological theories that have developed in most parts of the world. In the 1940s, for example, another wave of biological theory on crime, somatotyping, surfaced in the work of William Sheldon in the United States (Rafter 2007). Shortly after its rise, somatotyping ignited several studies of the link between delinquency and body types in the Philippines and generated another wave of interest in the human biological makeup among scholars of crime in the Philippines.

Notes

1 The author wishes to thank the funding support provided to this research by the Office of the Vice Chancellor for Research and Development, University of the Philippines Diliman.
2 Bilibid Prison, the national penitentiary, presented an opportunity to many scientists who needed to tap into a representative sample of the population that included various ethnic groups spread across the 7,000-plus islands of the Philippine archipelago. It was established by the Spanish government in 1865, and its physical layout comprised of dormitory buildings radiating from a panoptic surveillance tower (Gutierrez 2006, 88–90). It covered an area of 17 acres in Santa Cruz, a district of Manila. Bilibid was "the largest prison [that came] under the control of the American Government and [was] said to be the largest prison in the world" (Bureau of Prisons 1927, 20). At the time of the study of De Los Angeles in 1917, it confined 2,495 inmates (1919, 58). The Bureau of Science Biological Laboratory, established by the United States in the early 1900s, was virtually annexed to the Bilibid Prison hospital as a satellite laboratory, where American scientists conducted biomedical experiments on vaccinations against various tropical diseases (Gutierrez 2010, 362–363).
3 Serafin Macaraig was the first Filipino known to have obtained a PhD in Sociology (University of Wisconsin); he also taught sociology at the University of the Philippines.

References

Agoncillo, T. and Guerrero, M. (1970) *History of the Filipino People*. Quezon City: Malaya Books.

Anderson, W. (2007) "Science in the Philippines," *Philippines Studies* 55 (3): 287–318.

Artigas, M. (1917) *Galeria de Filipinos ilustres: biografias á uspic desde las primeros tiempos de la dominacíon Hispana, de los hijos del pais que en sus respectivas profesiones descollaron ó hayan alcanzado algun puesto de uspicious en sociedad*. Manila: Imp. Casa Editora Renacimiento.

Bean, R. B. (1909) "The Filipino Types: Manila Students, an Attempt to Classify the Littoral Population of Luzon and Adjacent Islands," *Philippine Journal of Science* 4 (4): 263–366.

Bean, R. B. (1910) *The Racial Anatomy of the Philippine Islanders: Introducing New Methods of Anthropology and Showing their Application to the Filipinos with a Classification of Human Ears and a Scheme for the Heredity of Anatomical Characters in Man*. Philadelphia: J.B. Lippincott Co.

Bean, W. B. (1945) "Robert Bennett Bean: 1874–1944," *Science, New Series* 101 (2623): 346–8.

Bureau of the Census. (1905) *Census of the Philippine Islands, Taken under the Direction of the Philippine Commission in the Year 1903*, Vol. 4, No. 1. Washington: Government Printing Office.

Bureau of Prisons. (1927) *Catalogue of Products of the Industrial Division of Bilibid Prison and General Information*. Manila: P. W. C.

Castellani, A. and Chalmers, A. (1913) *Manual of Tropical Medicine*, 2nd edn. London: Bailliere, Tindall and Cox.

Census Office (1921) *Census of the Philippine Islands Taken Under the Direction of the Philippine Legislature in the Year 1918*, Vol. 1, No. 2. Manila: Bureau of Printing.

De La Gironiere. (1854) *Twenty Years in the Philippines*. New York: Harper and Brothers.

De Los Angeles, S. (1919) *Estudios sobre sntropología criminal en las Islas Filipinas*. Manila: Bureau of Printing.

De Los Angeles, S. (1934) *Legal Medicine*. Manila: Pobre Press.

De Los Angeles, S. (1936) "The Scientific Study of Population Problems," *Journal of the Philippine Islands Medical Association* XVI (5): 265–70.

De Mas, Sinibaldo (1843). *Informe sobre el estado de las islas Filipinas en 1842*. Madrid: Imprenta Sancha.

Folkmar, D. (1904) *Album of Philippine Types Found in Bilibid Prison in 1903, Christians and Moros, Including a Few Non-Christians*. Manila: Bureau of Printing.

Foreman, J. (1906) *The Philippine Islands: a Political, Geographical, Ethnographical, Social and Commercial History of the Philippine Archipelago*. London: T. Fisher Unwin.

Gibson, M. and Rafter, N. H. (2006) *Criminal Man: Cesare Lombroso*, trans. with a new introduction. Durham and London: Duke University Press.

Gillet, M. C. (1995) *The Army Medical Department, 1865–1917*. Washington, DC: Center of Military History.

Gutierrez, F. C. (2006) *Intersections of Gender and Social Status: Exploring Records and Documents on Criminality in the Philippines*, unpublished dissertation, University of the Philippines at Diliman, Quezon City.

Gutierrez, F. C. (2010) "Studying Criminality and Criminal Offenders in the Early Twentieth Century," in Shlomo Giora Shoham *et al.* (eds) *International Handbook of Criminology*, 343–74, Boca Raton: CRC Press.

Horn, D. (2003) *The Criminal Body: Lombroso and the Anatomy of Deviance*. New York and London: Routledge.

Jagor, F. (1875) *Travels in the Philippines*. London: Chapman and Hall.
Kuhn, T. S. (1996) *The Structure of Scientific Revolutions*, 3rd edn. Chicago: Chicago University Press.
Lombroso, C. (1899) *Los Criminales*. Barcelona: Centro Editorial Presa.
Macaraig, S. (1929) *Social Problems*. Manila: The Educational Supply Co.
Montano, J. (1885) *Rapport aì M. le Ministre de L'Instruction Publique sur une Mission aux Iles Philippines et en Malaisie, 1879–1881*. Paris: Impremerie Nationale.
Nakatani, Y. (2006) "The Birth of Criminology in Modern Japan," in P. Becker and R. Wetzell (eds) *Criminals and Their Scientists: the History of Criminology in International Perspective*, New York: Cambridge University Press, pp. 281–99.
Rafter, N. (2007) "Somatotyping, Antimodernism, and the Production of Criminological Knowledge," *Criminology* 45 (4): 805–33.
Semper, C. (1869). *The Philippine Islands and Their Inhabitants: Six Sketches*. Wurzburg: A. Stuber.
Soncuya, J. (1917) *Historia prehispana de Filipinas, contenida en la conferencia sobre la isla de Panay, los bisayas y la monarquia, explicacion del uspicious de reyes en Manila, dada por Jose Soncuya en el Centro escolar de senoritas el dia 30 de junio de 1917 bajo los uspicious de la Sociedad historico-geografico de Filipinas*. Manila: n.p.
Villamor, I. (1909) *La Criminalidad en Las Islas Filipinas*. Manila: Bureau of Printing.
Villamor, I. (1915) "The influence of Hereditary Tendencies on Criminal Acts," *Philippine Law Journal* 2 (5): 119–226.
Villamor, I. (1924) *Crime and Moral Education*. Manila: Bureau of Printing.
Virchow, R. (1899) *The Peopling of the Philippines*, trans. O.T. Mason. Washington, DC: Smithsonian Institution.

20
LOMBROSO AND THE 'MEN OF REAL SCIENCE'

British reactions, 1886–1918

Neil Davie

In August 1896, the Home Office dispatched prisons inspector and former deputy governor of Millbank, Arthur Griffiths, to the fourth International Congress on Criminal Anthropology in Geneva. Interestingly, the lion's share of the report submitted by Griffiths on his return to London comprised a detailed discussion and evaluation of Lombrosian criminology. Griffiths had gone to Geneva a sceptic, and the five days of debates there evidently did not lead him to revise his opinions. 'Criminal anthropology', he wrote, '... has never seriously taken root in this country, the seeming extravagance of its momentous deductions and from such imperfect premises has tabooed it among men of real science, and its consideration has been left exclusively to those little qualified or competent to deal with it' (Griffiths 1896, 12).

'Tabooed' it might have been, but criminal anthropology was clearly considered a subject worthy of discussion for the prison doctors, psychiatrists and Home Office officials who comprised Britain's medico-penal Establishment, those self-proclaimed 'men of real science' to whom Griffiths had referred. In his report, the latter cited a talk given the previous year by the president of the Medico-Psychological Association, Dr David Nicolson, a career prison doctor, and now superintendant of Broadmoor Asylum for the Criminally Insane. An Establishment figure in every sense of the word, Nicolson had used his presidential address to the association to deliver a withering attack on criminal anthropology, calling into question the very idea of looking for common physical traits in criminals. If the term 'criminology' could be given to such an enterprise, he suggested, 'the terms doctorology, parsonology, [and] shoe-maker anthropology could be applied to similar studies on other groups of men who follow special occupations in life'. Not only were the criminal anthropologists' basic precepts flawed, Nicolson argued, the statistical foundations were also unsound, with sweeping generalisations made on the basis of insufficient data, the result being that it was 'impossible to regard its conclusions or assumptions to be either authentic or authoritative.' '[I]t is not for us', he told his colleagues, 'to stamp "criminals" as lunatics or quasi-lunatics, or to place them on a special morbid platform of mental existence, merely because they prefer thieving, with all its concomitant risk, to more respectable, if more laborious, modes of maintaining themselves.' Nicolson ended his talk with a warning:

> I hope the day will never come when, in our official examination into the medical condition of suspected persons, or persons lying in prison upon a criminal charge, we as medical men will be expected to produce our craniometer for the head measurements, and to place reliance upon statistical information as to the colour, size, or shape of any organ.
> (Nicolson 1895, 579–81)

In place of the clip-board and the craniometer, Nicolson urged that 'each case must be taken on its own merits'. This would become a common refrain in the following twenty-five years among Britain's criminological mainstream (Davie 2005, ch.3–4). Indeed, Sir Bryan Donkin, as medical commissioner, the country's most senior prison doctor, went as far as declaring in 1919 that 'even the most correct generalizations ... concerning convicted criminals in the mass are not likely to be of much positive value in the study or treatment of individuals' (Donkin 1919, 96).

Thus eschewing the kind of lofty theorising they associated with the criminal anthropologists, British prison doctors and psychiatrists favoured at most tentative generalisations after lengthy clinical experience with individual criminals. Not for them the deductive reasoning and shoddy methodology they associated with the 'grave professors', as leading forensic psychiatrist Charles Mercier called them; men whose 'eager gullibility' meant that they would swallow doctrines 'without any attempt to examine them critically' (Mercier 1918, 40). This was the basis of the scornful rejection by the British of the Lombrosians' scientific credentials. There was no substitute, they argued, for hands-on experience on the prison block or in the doctor's consulting rooms. If their own case-histories revealed physical and mental abnormalities, then that needed explaining of course, but Lombroso's cardboard cut-out criminal type was seen as a pitifully inadequate tool for the purpose. It was a bit like expecting to understand the complexities of bridge construction with a child's set of wooden building blocks (Davie 2005, 166).

We shall see in this chapter, however, that the foregoing account, based on the words of articulate spokesmen of the late-Victorian and Edwardian criminological Establishment like Griffiths, Nicolson, Donkin and Mercier, tells us only part of the story regarding British reactions to Lombroso in this period. This is not to deny the significance of these actors. Indeed, the body of work they generated would play a crucial role in the construction of British criminology's Lombrososceptic self-image at the turn of the nineteenth and twentieth centuries. However, it shall be argued here that for all its persistent appeal (cf. Rock 2007), this account of British reactions to the theories of Cesare Lombroso is misleading on a number of levels. First, it underestimates the extent of explicit support for Lombroso and criminal anthropology in Britain in this period, notably among asylum-based psychiatrists. Indeed, it was precisely an awareness of that support, and what were seen as its potentially harmful consequences, that prompted Britain's medico-penal Establishment to devote so much time and energy at the turn of the century to combating the Italian School in print. Second, and more importantly perhaps, we shall see that the conventional account fails to acknowledge the many points in common between British mainstream practice and that of the Italian school. In reality, the former accepted, despite frequent protestations to the contrary, that hereditary defects condemned certain offenders to a life of crime, and moreover that those defects were identifiable by means of standardised anatomical and physiological stigmata. Where most British practitioners differed from Lombroso and the criminal anthropologists (as well as from home-grown eugenicists) was on the size of this group of incorrigible offenders, and the implications for criminal justice policy.

* * * * * *

It is difficult in fact to speak about 'British reactions to Lombroso' before the latter part of the 1880s, a full ten years after the publication of the first edition of *L'Uomo delinquente*. Although the increasing availability of French and German translations of the work no doubt accounts in part for this belated interest, there is some evidence to suggest that it was the publication of Gabriel Tarde's *La Criminalité comparée* in 1886 that first brought Lombroso's work to the attention of British specialists (Tarde 1886). It was a review of Tarde's book in January 1887 in the pages of the *Journal of Mental Science* by Daniel Hack Tuke that provided the occasion for the first detailed discussion of Lombroso's work in Britain, and Havelock Ellis would equally cite Tarde's book as having been the catalyst for his own investigations in the field, published in 1890 as *The Criminal* (Tuke 1887; Ellis 1890).

Some nine months after Tuke's review, Lombroso's work was introduced to a larger audience via an article in the *Pall Mall Gazette*. The article, called 'The Science of Crime', referred to the 'remarkable work' of 'a clever Italian scholar' and provided translations of several key passages from *L'Uomo delinquente*. The author concluded his discussion by citing Lombroso's theory of the born criminal, observing that here was a group of lawbreakers 'whom no house of detention, no penal servitude will change, and to whose existence the public had better accustom themselves' (*PMG* 1887). How far the public did 'accustom themselves' to Lombroso's theories in these years is, however, a moot point. It is likely that beyond the specialised readerships of publications like the *Journal of Mental Science* and the *British Medical Journal*, few were aware of their existence, and thus when in September 1889 *The Times* devoted a lengthy article to 'The Italian School of Criminal Jurisprudence', its content would have come as a surprise to most, probably even to those versed in criminal matters (*Times* 1889).

Within eighteen months, however, the situation had been transformed. Havelock Ellis's survey of criminal anthropology, *The Criminal*, had been published, as had *Crime and its Causes*, the work of Wandsworth prison chaplain, William Douglas Morrison (Morrison 1891). Both authors claimed to distance themselves from some of the 'impetuous' methods and lack of 'solid conclusions' of the Italian school, but ended up endorsing positions very close to those of Lombroso himself (Davie 2005, 155–60). Ellis, for example, argued that criminals 'present a far larger proportion of anatomical abnormalities than the ordinary European population', adding that 'our own criminals frequently resemble in physical and psychical characters the normal individuals of a lower race. This is that "atavism" which has been so frequently observed in criminals and so much discussed' (Ellis 1890, 206–7, 209).

While Leon Radzinowicz and Roger Hood are broadly correct in their assessment of Ellis's *The Criminal* as 'a slight publication, with no originality and little critical acumen' (Radzinowicz and Hood 1990, 12), the book nevertheless did much to bring criminal anthropology to a wider audience, prompting reviews in a number of the leading newspapers and scientific and literary journals of the day. Ellis's dictum that 'We cannot punish a monstrosity for acting according to its monstrous nature' (Ellis 1890, 233) was widely quoted, prompting a sharp reaction from the conservative press. In the *Scots Observer*, for example, Ellis was mocked for appearing to suggest that the criminal 'ought not to be punished, poor fellow, but rather cherished and soothed, and taught, and drilled, and fed, until he is purged of his "anti-social" weaknesses and converted into a happy and useful member of the human family'. The author added that 'the prophets of "criminal anthropology" ... come to be as fond of their criminals as a biologist is of his amoebas and his centipedes' (*Scots Observer* 1890, 401–2). *The Saturday Review* criticised *The Criminal* in similar fashion, pointing out that the book risked 'creating or fostering the idea that crime is a matter of course'. Quoting Ellis's remark that he had found little interest in Britain in the subject of criminal anthropology when researching his book (Ellis 1890, 47–8), the *Review* observed that 'it is certainly to the credit of such remains of national sanity as we may possess that it is so', before reiterating its support for the whip and the gallows (*Saturday Review* 1890, 255–6). Other reviewers also noted with approval the apparently low level of support in Britain for what one called 'the sham speculations of Lombroso and the Lombrosians'. Unlike the Americans, Italians, French and Germans, who had, it was alleged, 'poured out' books and articles on the subject 'by the score', the United Kingdom had contributed 'little or nothing' to this 'rubbish heap' of 'pseudo-scientific' research (*National Observer* 1893, 21).

Such reactions were far from universal, however. The *Pall Mall Gazette* would continue to offer favourable coverage of the criminal anthropologists in the coming decade (*PMG* 1890, 1895), as did the *Westminster Review* and *The Scotsman* on occasion (Chapman 1892; Foard 1898, 1899; *Scotsman* 1896, 1897), while in a series of lengthy and detailed articles, translator and Italophile Helen Zimmern provided articulate support for the tenets of Lombrosian criminology (Zimmern 1891, 1891a, 1895, 1898). Particularly significant for our purposes, however, was the support from the scientific community. This was not limited, as previous accounts have often implied (Radzinowicz and Hood 1990, 11–15; Rock 2007, 118), to a handful of mavericks like Francis Galton or Havelock Ellis (who continued to publicise the researches of European and US criminal anthropologists in his annual reviews for the *Journal of Mental Science*), but extended, as we noted earlier, to a significant number of doctors and psychiatrists.

Indeed, in the first half of the 1890s, the country's two leading medical journals, *The Lancet* and the *British Medical Journal*, both voiced their support for the criminal anthropologists, albeit support of a qualified kind (Davie 2005, 145–6). In a typical piece from the *Lancet* published in August 1892, the sceptical attitude of British jurists towards Lombroso's theories was noted, before adding that 'Between the cautious attitude of the British law and the confident procedure of the Italian there is surely a *via media.*' After all, was it not true that 'Criminals ... generally come far short of a high or ideal standard of brain, body and mind'? The article concluded that more research was needed before firm conclusions could be reached (*Lancet* 1892, 371). By the latter part of the 1890s, however, both journals had abandoned the search for a 'via media' in criminological matters, and had joined the chorus of mocking criticism of Lombroso and his works (*Lancet* 1896; BMJ 1898, 1900).

Yet this was by no means a universal stance in the medical profession in these years. In particular, British psychiatry would generate a steady stream of advocates of Lombrosian criminology in the period up to the First World War. Thus, when the distinguished anatomist and archaeologist Dr Alexander Macalister noted with approval in his presidential address to the Anthropological Institute in 1894 that 'the practical subject of the Anthropology of crime ... has been lately taken up by many of the distinguished alienists in this country', this was only a partial exaggeration (Macalister 1894, 415). *The Journal of Mental Science*, the influential organ of the Medico-Psychological Association, continued to give Lombroso and the criminal anthropologists a generally positive press, despite David Nicolson's strictures from the president's chair in 1895. The journal's written response to the findings of the 1895 Departmental Committee on Prisons, chaired by Home Office Minister Herbert Gladstone, provides a good example of this. Noting its approval for the report's recommendation that prison staff should be trained in the theories and techniques of criminal anthropology, the journal added that it had '... no sympathy with those connected with asylums and prisons in this country who deride the work of Lombroso and his pupils'. Although acknowledging that it parted company from the Italian School on certain points, the article concluded that it 'accept[ed] such investigations as being in the proper spirit, and should deem it evidence of progress if the same lines of inquiry were systematically followed in this country' (*JMS* 1896, 604).

In this context, it should come as no surprise to learn that both of the asylum-based psychiatrists called before the Gladstone Committee defended the view that crime could be largely explained in terms of inherited constitutional defects. Thus, when Dr Bevan Lewis, medical superintendent of Wakefield Asylum in Yorkshire was asked by the committee if he agreed with the proposition that 'crime is always, or very nearly always, connected with mental unsoundness', he replied: 'Well, I go very far in that view. I would not emphasise it so strongly as Lombroso and Krafft-Ebing and others have done, but they all have some kind of physico-psychical basis.' In a reply to a subsequent question, Lewis added:

> The habitual criminal I regard as simply a degenerate offspring of a very degenerate stock; and if I may be allowed to express my opinion more freely, I would say that both insanity and crime are simply morbid branches of the same stock ... [;] on the borderline between insanity and crime a very large proportion of the criminal class stand.
>
> (Lewis 1895, 303)

The other asylum practitioner questioned by the committee was Dr Thomas C. Shaw, principal of the Banstead Asylum in Middlesex. His evidence was if anything even more unequivocal than that of Dr Lewis. Shaw stated that *all* criminals 'should be regarded as patients' and that punishment should consequently be 'of a very limited character'. In reply to a further question as to whether the simple fact of having committed a criminal act like a burglary could be counted as scientific evidence of insanity, Shaw declared himself 'pretty confident' that in examining an offender, he 'should come to something which, in the great majority of instances, would justify me in signing a certificate'. The doctor added that 'measurement of the head and sundry other tests' would no doubt provide the necessary proof of 'bodily instability' (Shaw 1895, 195–6).

The published work of Scottish psychiatrist Thomas Clouston, superintendent of the Royal Edinburgh Asylum and like Nicolson a former president of the Medico-Psychological Association, provides further evidence of this strain of crypto-Lombrosianism in the late-Victorian psychiatric profession. In a paper read to the Anthropological Institute in 1894 on 'The Developmental Aspects of Criminal Anthropology', Clouston suggested that the time was 'very near' when some knowledge of the subject would 'be required by all medical men, and especially of all lawyers and the higher officials of our prisons'. While acknowledging that the discipline had thus far often been in the hands of 'enthusiasts' who 'have seen perhaps both more and less than the men of cooler judgement who will follow them', Clouston followed Lombroso in explaining hereditary defects among criminals chiefly in terms of atavism and arrested development (Clouston 1894; see also Clouston 1911, 24–5, 181–2).

In similar fashion, a paper given in 1891 to the British Association for the Advancement of Science by Dr Samuel Strahan of the Northampton County Asylum, entitled 'Instinctive Criminality, Its True Character and Rational Treatment', argued that a *full two-thirds* of the prison population was composed of 'instinctive criminals'. The latter, Strahan suggested, were 'drawn to such a course by an instinct which is born in them, which is too strong to be resisted by their weak volitional power had they the desire to resist, which they have not.' In a passage that could have come straight out of *L'Uomo delinquente*, the Northampton psychiatrist listed the physical traits of such instinctive criminals, which included 'a small, overlarge and ill-shapen head', 'asymmetrical features', 'heavy misshapen jaws', 'outstanding ears' and other 'deformities'; not to mention 'a restless, animal-like or brutal expression' (Strahan 1891, 811).

Men like Lewis, Shaw, Clouston and Strahan were in many ways the heirs of Henry Maudsley, and evidently shared the gloomily fatalistic attitude to criminal aetiology expressed by the latter in a series of influential works published a quarter of a century earlier, shot through with references to 'evil ancestral influences' and 'the tyranny of organisation' (Maudsley 1867, 1870, 1874). What is ironic in this context is that by the beginning of the 1890s, Maudsley himself had retreated somewhat from the unalloyed determinism of his younger years. In an 1888 article for the *Journal of Mental Science*, he argued that much wrongdoing was in reality the work of 'occasional criminals', free of any constitutional defects; simply ordinary men and women placed in a situation of great temptation or provocation (Maudsley 1888, 160). Although he conceded the existence of 'instinctive criminals', Maudsley stressed the existence of a wide spectrum of types of offending. There was no substitute, he cautioned his colleagues, for 'the laborious observation of particulars', and concluded, in stark contrast to his earlier views, that 'there is no general criminal constitution predisposing to and, as it were, excusing crime' (164–6).

Although Lombroso is not mentioned by name, it seems clear that the intended target of Maudsley's admonitions were the Italian's British followers in the psychiatric profession, apparently drawn to the 'empty generalities, . . . barren disquisitions and pretentious speculations' of their mentor (Maudsley 1888, 166–7). In the second edition of *Pathology of Mind* (1895), Maudsley would return to the point, warning that it was 'easy to make too much of criminal instincts or dispositions and tempting to be content with them as a sufficient explanation of crime.' No criminal, he added, 'is really explicable except by an exact study of his circumstances as well as his nature' (Maudsley 1895, 82).

This brings us back full circle to David Nicolson's presidential address to the Medico-Psychological Association referred to earlier, which dates from the same year as the publication of Maudsley's book. Nicolson's and Maudsley's emphasis on, respectively, taking 'each case on its own merits' and 'the exact study of his circumstances' would turn out to be the characteristic responses to criminal anthropology in this period from within Britain's medico-penal Establishment. We shall consider this mind-set in more detail presently, but first let us turn to the question raised earlier of why the country's criminological mainstream should have devoted so much time, energy and column inches at the turn of the century to combating the Lombrosian creed.

There was clearly widespread distaste in official circles for what the *British Medical Journal* referred to in 1894 as that 'morbid love of notoriety fostered by the cheap newspapers of the present day with their blood-curdling "bills" and their puffing paragraphs'. Indeed, the article goes on to suggest, seemingly only partly in jest, that this 'morbid love of notoriety' was 'responsible for more crime and is a greater danger to society than "atypical confluence" of the fissures of the brain and the other signs relied upon by criminological Zadigs' (*BMJ* 1894, 427). Evelyn Ruggles-Brise, who succeeded Edmund Du Cane as chairman of the Prison Commission in 1895, developed this point in a book of memoirs published in 1921. Looking back on the circumstances surrounding Dr Charles Goring's large-scale anthropometric study of English convicts in the early 1900s (more on which later), Ruggles-Brise acknowledged that Lombroso had brought 'much acumen, a great diligence, and imagination to the examination of the subject'. However, in his view the theory of the born criminal had had a deleterious effect on public opinion:

> [L]ike all sensational dogmas, based on untested observation, it affected the public imagination prone to believe that the criminal is a sort of 'bogey-man'— the stealthy enemy of peaceful persons, ever ready to leap in the dark. This uneasy feeling encouraged the idea that the criminal was a class by himself— an abnormal being, the child of darkness, without pity and without shame, and with the predatory instincts of a wild beast. Thus gradually the common belief has taken root that there is a criminal-type, and that it is persons of this particular brand or species who commit crime, and go to prison.

Yet for the chairman of the Prison Commission, such a conception of the criminal represented far more than a simple *faute de goût*:

> This belief ... stands in the way of Prison reform, which darkens counsel in dealing with crime, which renders rehabilitation difficult, and which stifles and discourages the zeal of the philanthropist, to whom the 'criminal' is a man of like passions with himself, and amenable to the same influences; and not predestined to crime and anti-social conduct, from which no human effort could save him.
>
> (Ruggles-Brise 1921, 199–200)

While liberal penologists like Ruggles-Brise and Bryan Donkin worried that popular beliefs about predatory criminal 'bogey-men' would hold back dispassionate debate about crime and penal reform (including their own projects for dealing with habitual offenders), others feared that painting offenders as the passive victims of defective heredity would end up placing responsibility for their actions solely on their 'criminal brains', thereby undermining the whole philosophy of individual responsibility which underpinned Britain's classical tradition of criminal jurisprudence (Davie 2005, 150; Radzinowicz and Hood 1990, 16–19).

H.B. Simpson, a senior official in the Home Office's criminal department, entered the fray on this issue in 1896 with an article for the *Contemporary Review* written to mark the publication of Douglas Morrison's English translation of *La Donna delinquente* the previous year. After a long, highly critical evaluation of Lombroso's theories, Simpson stated that it was 'not moral monsters or "degenerates" that English legislators and administrators have to consider, but men whose passions are a little stronger, whose wills are a little weaker than those of their respectable fellow-citizens' (Simpson 1896, 99–100). He was clearly worried, like the author from the *Scots Observer* quoted earlier in this chapter, that if the criminal anthropologists had their way, Britain would be heading for an Elmira-style prison regime, 'with its lectures and discussions, its Turkish baths, massage and gymnastics for prisoners, its reading clubs, [and] its daily newspaper'. With inmates allegedly carefully protected from 'anything that may hurt a sensitive prisoner's feelings, or remind him that he has done anything to be ashamed of', there was a real danger, according to Simpson, that the deterrent effect of the prison would be seriously undermined (103).

British criminologists would return time and again to this argument, often lacing their comments with heavy irony. Charles Mercier's comments, from his 1918 textbook *Crime and Criminals*, is typical:

> You are a criminal, it is true, but the fault is not yours. It is not in the habit you have formed of yielding to your passions. It is not in your self-indulgence; your laziness; your slavery to impulse; your selfishness; your cultivated lack of control. No! It is impressed on you by your inheritance. You, poor fellow, are visited with the sins of your father and grandfather. ... In a word, you are a degenerate; and since your crimes are no fault of yours, you shall not be punished for them.
>
> (Mercier 1918, 210)

An article published in August 1891 in the Conservative-leaning *Saturday Review*, in the form of a review of the paper by Dr Samuel Strahan referred to earlier, adopts a similar tone to Mercier's:

> The hereditary criminal is an object of pity. All criminals are more or less hereditary – measure their noses and you will see it, says Dr. LOMBROSO. Let us seclude them kindly, says Dr. STRAHAN, work on their higher nature, as is done at Elmira; let their instinctive criminality be held to qualify them for the receipt of a gratuitous university education, and when we have blunted the edge of their evil passions let us turn them loose and see what will happen. This, Dr. STRAHAN thinks, will be cheaper than our present prison system – and infinitely more worthy of the loving kindness we owe our brother the instinctive criminal.
>
> (Saturday Review 1891, 241)

For this dominant strain in turn-of-the-century British criminological thought, the criminal was to be considered, as H.B. Simpson put it, as 'after all, a man of like passions with ourselves, swayed by similar motives, aiming at the same ultimate ends, recognising for the most part the same maxims of morality, imbued with the same social traditions as other members of his class' (Simpson 1896, 96). For many British prison doctors, the conclusion to be drawn was obvious. As David Nicolson told the Gladstone Committee, 'a very large proportion' of criminals were sane, could be considered responsible for their actions, and punished as such. 'The exceptions', he added, 'form a small minority' (Nicolson 1895a, 312).

On the face of it, the foregoing discussion might suggest that a fundamental distinction needs to be drawn between the officials and medical specialists of Britain's medico-penal Establishment and the views held by those on the fringes of the criminal justice system, often with links to asylum-based psychiatry or anthropology, with support for Lombroso and his theories confined uniquely to the latter group. As we have noted, this was the self-image British criminology carved out for itself in these years, and one which later historians of the discipline have on the whole been content to follow (Garland 1988; Radzinowicz and Hood 1990; Rock 2007). This description of late-Victorian and Edwardian criminology in Britain certainly fits the emphasis we have noted among the members of the mainstream discipline from that period; one which stresses the value of white-coated medical expertise and the need to base diagnosis on 'patient inquiry' and 'common sense' rather than ticking boxes from some predetermined check-list of born-criminal stigmata. The alternative, as the British never tired of pointing out, was that 'The mildest and most blameless curate may be branded to the world as a sleeping volcano of criminal tendencies by the mere fact of his possessing a Mongolian cast of feature, large-lobed ears, or a misshapen skull' (BMJ 1900). And then there was the problem that 'some of our greatest criminals are men who were born of respectable and estimable people, and who are free from all hereditary taint of crime' (Anderson 1902, 568).

However, despite the rhetorical force of such statements, things are not quite as clear-cut as they appear. An illuminating illustration of this is provided by an impromptu exchange at the end of David Nicolson's 1895 address to the Medico-Psychological Association. Among those in the audience for the talk was Edinburgh psychiatrist Dr Thomas Clouston. Clearly surprised by what he had just heard, Clouston made the following comment:

> I am certain that most of us will scarcely agree with you in your optimistic view of criminology and its psychological relations. No doubt most of us who have looked through the books of Lombroso and Havelock Ellis and others are inclined to admit that it is a little overdone by some of our continental brethren, but to say that the mass of criminals in this country are merely criminals by want of opportunity of doing good, by want of education, and not by their organisation, is absolutely contrary to the results of psychological investigation for the last fifty years.
>
> (quoted Nicolson 1895, 589)

In his reply, Nicolson countered that Clouston was mistaken in implying that he rejected outright the findings of the criminal anthropologists:

> I wish to take this earliest opportunity of saying that I am entirely in agreement with much of the phraseology and the descriptions of the criminologists, but

I repeat – and this is the point which I wish to make quite clear – that these descriptions only apply to a minority of criminals. What I object to is that a description – honest, true, verbose if you like – applicable to the few should be held up to the world as being applicable to the whole criminal class.

(Nicolson 1895, 590)

This off-the-cuff exchange provides a revealing insight into just what separated the British medico-penal Establishment from its crypto-Lombrosian critics in the psychiatric profession. As Nicolson's comments make clear, when pressed, the former conceded that the physical and mental traits associated with Lombroso's born criminal type could be found among a certain category of prisoners. What they objected to in the Lombrosian method was that the born criminal type, conceived by its inventor after the study of a few atypical cases, was then applied indiscriminately to a whole range of offenders; a case of all manner of different-sized pegs being forced into the same round hole. Such a method went, they argued, against the whole inductive ethos of Victorian empirical science (Davie 2005, 140–67; Rock 2007, 121).

However, despite their vocal rejection of Lombrosian labels, British criminologists would make regular use of their own alternative generic terms in the ensuing period, notably in connection with the ongoing debate on how to tackle habitual crime, what one Edwardian commentator would describe as 'Britain's blot' (Sutherland 1908). Here was a group of apparently 'incorrigible' recidivists, stubbornly resistant, as Mercier put it, both to 'the ancient method of brutal severity [... and to] the modern method of providing him with beer and skittles, with newspapers to edit and lectures on Sophocles to listen to' (Mercier 1918, 280). Arthur Griffiths had come to similar conclusions. His paper read at the 1896 Geneva congress, entitled 'The Practical Treatment of Habitual Crime', had evoked those habitual criminals 'against which the law fights more or less strenuously, but generally in vain.' Here was 'a pariah, hardened and generally irreclaimable, who still remains the *crux* of criminology' (Griffiths 1896, 32–3).

Griffiths had declared himself little interested in the 'curious traits and anomalies elucidated by the criminal anthropologists', preferring to focus on what he called the 'concrete criminal' (29). Others within the prison regime clearly did not share Griffiths' lack of interest. Among their number was Dr James Scott of Holloway Prison, who accompanied Griffiths to Geneva, and had evidently been conducting his own anthropometric research on the criminals in his charge (Griffiths 1896, 8). From the scattered evidence which survives, it is clear that Scott was not the only British prison doctor to be engaged in empirical research into the mental and physical traits of habitual and weak-minded prisoners in this period (Baker 1892, 1901; East 1901).

Although the scale of such research is difficult to determine with precision, what does seem clear, at least as far as convicts are concerned, is that the categories 'habitual' and 'weak-' or 'feeble-minded' were coming to be seen by many experts as essentially synonymous (Wiener 1990, 248, 354). Thus, medical commissioner Sir Bryan Donkin was able to state with confidence in a speech in 1908 that 'a very large proportion' of the inmates of the country's convict prisons were congenitally feeble-minded (*Lancet* 1908), echoing a viewpoint voiced by Evelyn Ruggles-Brise in his testimony to the Gladstone Committee (Ruggles-Brise 1895, 346).

With this category of prisoner apparently stubbornly immune to conventional penal remedies, the hunt for alternative solutions was on. Given, as Mark Jackson (2000, 95) has shown, that the mentally deficient were often considered in this period both as 'a pathological and dangerous sub-section of the population' and as a group 'sharing a peculiar set of physical, mental and moral defects', it is not surprising that such individuals and such defects should have been a focus of interest for practitioners within the prison medical service. Indeed, the oral evidence provided by a number of prison doctors called before the Royal Commission on the Feeble-Minded (1904–8) indicates a belief in the existence of a generic type of habitual, mentally-deficient offender complete with 'stigmata' identical in their essentials to those of Lombroso's born criminal type (Davie 2005, 213–4).

Despite such apparent common ground with the tenets of Lombrosian criminology, most British specialists, certainly those within the criminal justice system, remained determined to distance themselves from the Italian School and its British supporters. Indeed, a major motivation behind the Home Office decision in 1901 to commission a large-scale anthropometric survey of Britain's convict population was, as Ruggles-Brise later put it, to 'fire the last shot' at the 'deserted ship' of Lombrosianism (quoted Bailey 1997, 314). But if 'the Lombrosian theories of the criminal-né' had indeed been 'exploded' by this period, as was alleged, was it really necessary to undertake a lengthy, highly complex and presumably costly statistical study to prove what was already widely accepted?

There was indeed some opposition to the proposed anthropometric study on these grounds from within the Home Office (Forsythe 1991, 36), but the project went ahead anyway, under the supervision of Dr Charles Goring, medical officer of Parkhurst Prison (Beirne 1988). Clearly, the Lombrosian 'bogey-man' was still felt to be poisoning public debate on criminal subjects, and correcting this view was seen as an important objective of the Goring study. Bryan Donkin expressed this view forcefully in a lecture before an audience at the Royal College of Physicians in 1910, arguing that the project was of vital importance

> not because any serious students of this subject now accept the doctrine of the so-called science of 'criminology', ... but because this doctrine, so much emphasised by Lombroso, Max Nordau, and others, of the hereditary nature of crime, or, in other words, of the criminal being a racial 'degenerate', is still very dominant over the public mind. It is widely popularised at the risk of producing practical effects, not only by writers of fiction, but also by philanthropists, journalists, and public speakers on social questions.
>
> (quoted Ruggles-Brise 1913, 8)

This was no mere abstract intellectual issue then, to be resolved purely to satisfy scientific curiosity. If accepted, it was argued, Lombroso's born criminal theories risked bringing about a fundamental shift in Britain's criminal justice policy, the logical result of which, according to Ruggles-Brise, 'would be either [the] elimination of the unfit, or the translation into the province of medicine of all legal procedure' (Ruggles-Brise 1921, 199).

Is there any evidence that Lombrosian doctrine was indeed 'very dominant over the public mind' in Edwardian Britain? A study of contemporary press coverage points to a mixed picture. One important strand of reporting gave the impression that Donkin had little to worry about. Lombroso's interventions at the beginning of the decade on such subjects as the Boer War and the criminal ramifications of bicycling – which had provoked responses of, respectively, self-righteous indignation (*BMJ* 1900a, b) and mirth (*Punch* 1900; *BMJ* 1900c) in the British press – had tended to reinforce an earlier reputation for eccentricity and unreliability acquired at the time of the publication of *The Man of Genius* (1891), and the tone of the majority of articles written to mark the Italian's death in 1909 indicated that earlier objections to Lombroso's method and findings had lost none of their force either (*Times* 1909; *Guardian* 1909). But this is only part of the picture. Lombrosian criminology continued to be treated with respect by proponents of the hereditarian theory of criminal causation, and consequently received favourable coverage in some sectors of the press, as did the works of criminal anthropologists like Henry M. Boies, Gina Lombroso-Ferrero and Hans Kurella (*Speaker* 1902; *Guardian* 1911; Parkyn 1911). As in the previous decade, asylum-based psychiatry furnished a number of vocal exponents of this approach, particularly among those claiming expertise in the fashionable speciality of 'feeble-mindedness' (Jackson 2000, ch.4). Perhaps the most influential of these was Dr A.F. Tredgold, author of a much-reissued textbook on the subject first published in 1908, whose dire warnings of a 'tide' of feeble-minded degeneracy were taken seriously enough in official circles to be circulated to the Liberal cabinet in 1911. Tredgold's 'morally perverse or habitual criminal type' owed much to Lombroso's born criminal (Tredgold 1908, 1909; Wiener 1990, 354–5).

Less alarmist, but also indicative of the influence of Lombrosian reasoning in Edwardian psychiatry was the work of Dr J.F. Sutherland, deputy commissioner in lunacy for Scotland, and author of a detailed study of the causes and characteristics of habitual crime (Sutherland 1908). Although Sutherland rejected Lombroso's criminal stigmata as an unreliable guide to identifying criminals (much as Morrison and Ellis had done in the previous decade), he did argue for the usefulness of the techniques pioneered by the criminal anthropologists 'as a means of identification and of revealing accurately the degree of physical degeneration to be met with among recidivists'. His own measurements of 370 Scottish and English criminals provided the basis for his claim that there existed physical traits peculiar to certain categories of criminals (habitual offenders convicted of murder and assault were found for example to have longer heads than other inmates). He also found evidence of 'an elusive yet unmistakeable criminal physiognomy, ... as real as the facial types met with in asylums' (39–45).

As far as Ruggles-Brise's warnings about 'the elimination of the unfit' were concerned, there certainly were calls for such a policy in the Edwardian period, but these remained exceptional (Radzinowicz and Hood 1990, 332–35). More common, though still controversial even in eugenics circles, was support for a policy of sterilising certain categories of incorrigible offenders, as part of a wider campaign to 'prevent "degenerates" from propagating their like', as one advocate put it in 1905 (quoted Sim 1990, 140). Galton had come round to this position by 1909, and other supporters included Havelock Ellis and A.F. Tredgold, though Sutherland's unequivocal hostility towards this 'drastic remedy' (Sutherland 1908, 94) indicates that support for Lombrosian criminology could co-exist with a rejection of the eugenicist agenda.

The official position of the prison authorities was to firmly reject the sterilisation of criminals for practical as well as moral reasons. After all, as we have seen, mainstream British criminology refuted the proposition advanced by eugenically-minded specialists in feeble-mindedness that crime and irreversible mental defect were largely synonymous (Davie 2005, 257, 272). However, this robust stance – vigorously defended in public by Establishment figures like Bryan Donkin, Charles Mercier and Dr W.C. Sullivan of Holloway Prison – did not prevent Charles Goring from breaking ranks and arguing for just such a policy in the conclusion to his anthropometric study of 3,000 convicts, published as *The English Convict: A Statistical Study* (Goring 1913). Goring noted that the main alternative to sterilisation, the segregation of all criminals, would have the advantage of reducing crime 'to nothing' in the short term, but he argued that this would not stop 'parents with the least social proclivities [. . . from] begetting offspring who, on the average, would commit the greatest number of anti-social offences'. Thus, sterilisation alone offered the prospect of 'regulat[ing] the reproduction of those degrees of constitutional qualities – feeble-mindedness, inebriety, epilepsy, deficient social instinct, etc. – which conduce to the committing of crime' (373).

As expected by those who had commissioned the study, Goring found no evidence of the predictive capacity of the stigmata associated with Lombroso's criminal type and he proclaimed the 'anthropological monster' duly slain, but he did produce statistical evidence purporting to prove that 'the criminal of English prisons is markedly differentiated by defective physique ...; by defective mental capacity ...; and by anti-social proclivities' (Goring 1913, 370). However, Goring went further than simply describing the distinctive physical and mental traits of the prison population, arguing that these traits were to be explained principally in terms of defective heredity, which was consequently given a key role in the genesis of criminal behaviour. Environmental factors, in contrast, were considered of only 'trifling' importance (288). Ironically then, a study which had been commissioned to fatally undermine the Lombrosian thesis ended up providing partial succour to the Italian School (Beirne 1988; Leps 1992); a fact not lost on supporters of the latter like

Gina Lombroso-Ferrero, whose well-known judgement on *The English Convict* was that Goring was 'more Lombrosian than Lombroso' (Lombroso-Ferrero 1914).

A number of those associated with the project publicly disowned themselves from Goring's eugenicist recommendations (Donkin 1917, 1919), and in private Home Office officials complained that *The English Convict* would generate 'a superstition as difficult to eradicate as was Lombroso's' (quoted in Forsythe 1991, 36). Indeed, official opposition was such that publication was repeatedly delayed, much to the frustration of the author (Davie 2005, 240). Sir Evelyn Ruggles-Brise, for his part, played down the more controversial of the book's conclusions, warning readers in his preface to the book that the physical and mental defects Goring had found to characterise the convict population 'must not be pressed so far as to affect the liability to punishment of the offender for his act' (Ruggles-Brise 1913, 8).

So while opinion in the eugenics movement welcomed *The English Convict* for apparently providing copper-bottomed scientific confirmation for its hereditarian vision of the causes of habitual crime (Darwin 1914–15; Pearson 1919), the majority view in Britain's criminological community remained, as Dr Sullivan put it in a 1909 article in the *Eugenics Review*, that 'criminal conduct is usually the outcome of the action of the environment on an organisation of normal aptitudes'. Arguing that the relation of crime to eugenics was 'limited', Sullivan stated his conviction that 'we cannot speak of a special innate disposition to crime except in connection with a small minority of offenders [...for whom] the power of inhibition is so weak that the individuals are more prone to criminal conduct than are other weak-minded persons' (Sullivan 1909, 112, 117).

Sullivan's last comment is significant, however, indicating that behind the combative rhetoric there was in reality a measure of common ground between the eugenicists, Lombrosians and mainstream criminologists of Edwardian Britain. Although there remained fundamental differences of opinion as to the scale of the problem and the measures to be adopted to deal with it, all sides agreed that there existed types of incorrigible habitual offender for whom the prisons had 'lost their power of deterrence and become nothing else than costly shelterhouses'. In the face of what Ruggles-Brise privately admitted was the penal regime's 'powerlessness' in the face of habitual crime, the only viable solution appeared to be long-term, possibly, permanent, incarceration under medical and/or penal supervision (Ruggles-Brise 1900).

A series of laws passed in the period 1908–13 attempted to address this problem, putting in place a range of parallel institutions to provide specialised medico-penal segregation either in addition to, or in the place of, a regular prison sentence, whether it be for 'professional' criminals (1908 Prevention of Crime Act) or feebleminded offenders (1913 Mental Deficiency Act). Many commentators on both sides of the eugenics debate argued that such institutions held out the prospect of at once protecting the community from rapacious criminals and preventing the latter from transmitting their degenerate seed to future generations (Radzinowicz and Hood 1990, 268–87, 316–38). In this limited respect, it is possible to detect a leakage of eugenicist assumptions into mainstream criminology, despite the latter's insistence that it was hermetic to such influences (Davie 2005, 230).

Several historians have rightly drawn attention to the limited scope and muddled thinking involved in the framing and implementation of this legislation, and pointed out that a combination of vacillating political will, administrative inertia and judicial resistance to any challenge to classical notions of criminal responsibility limited its effect once on the statute book. The result was that no more than a tiny fraction of the country's convicted criminals ever found themselves on the receiving end of an 'indeterminate' prison sentence or interned in an institution for feeble-minded delinquents. There was clearly no thoroughgoing Lombrosian turn in British penal policy in this period (Bailey 1997, 302–5; Forsythe 1995, 266–7). Indeed, one exponent of this view goes as far as suggesting that 'old fashioned early Victorian moralism was more important than the new positivistic science in formulating discourse about prisoner reformation at the end of the [nineteenth] century' (Forsythe 1995, 268).

However, it is important not to take this post-revisionist argument too far. If we adopt a broad definition of criminological debate in Britain in this period – in other words do not limit ourselves to the positions adopted by those self-proclaimed 'men of science' working within the criminal justice system – then Lombroso's theories can be seen to have played an important role in setting the terms of the debate in the country during the period 1880–1918. In this sense, Paul Rock's statement that Lombroso and the Lombrosians had been 'effectively dispatched' in Britain by the outbreak of the First World War fails to appreciate this wider picture (Rock 2007, 124). Dyed-in-the-wool Lombrosians were never very thick on the ground of course either before or after the publication of *The English Convict*, but throughout the period there were a significant number of commentators, both in the medical profession and the press, who acknowledged the veracity and relevance of the Italian's criminological research, if not necessarily its ready application to every type of crime and criminal. Even within the Lombrososceptic halls of the medico-penal Establishment, it could be argued (*pace* Forsythe and Rock) that it was the criminal anthropologists who set the agenda for discussion of habitual and weak- or feeble-minded offenders throughout the Edwardian period, with inherited mental and physical defects increasingly seen as the principal cause of the compulsive lawbreaking which characterised this type of offender. Indeed, the fact that that the Home Office should have considered it necessary to commission a large-scale anthropometric study to prove Lombroso wrong may be considered as something of a back-handed compliment to the influence of the Italian School in Britain in these years.

The positivist discourse was never in a position to dethrone long-standing moralistic assumptions about personal guilt and responsibility within the British criminal justice system. However, the various laws aimed at tackling the problems of habitual and feeble-minded crime, damp squibs though they might have turned out to be, nevertheless represented, as *The Times* astutely observed in 1909, 'a striking recognition of some of the principles for which Lombroso contended' (*Times* 1909). This was a long way of course from the wholesale segregation or mass sterilisation of the country's criminal classes called for by the eugenics movement and certain members of the Italian School, but it does lend some credence to Lombroso's observation in 1899 that the British, unlike those 'less advanced peoples ... lingering over the utopias of the old jurists and, believing that reform is possible for all criminals', had indeed 'recognised that although they have been able by their efforts to eliminate the accidental criminal almost entirely, the born criminal still persists' (Lombroso 1911 [1899], 432). More advanced or not, British criminology had found a place for Lombrosian theory, albeit a limited one, at the heart of its practice, and this strand of criminological thought would continue to exert its influence over the development of the discipline in the country well into the new century (Sim 1990, 64–5).

References

Anderson, R. (1902) 'More About Professional Criminals', *The Nineteenth Century and After: A Monthly Review*, 52, 308: 562–75.
Bailey, V. (1997) 'English Prisons, Penal Culture and the Abatement of Imprisonment, 1895–1922', *Journal of British Studies*, 26, 3: 285–324.
Baker, J. (1892) 'Some Points Connected with Criminals', *Journal of Mental Science*, 38: 364–9.
Baker, J. (1901) 'Epilepsy and Crime', *Journal of Mental Science*, 47: 260–77.
Beirne, P. (1988) 'Heredity vs. Environment: A Reconsideration of Charles Goring's *The English Convict* (1913)', *British Journal of Criminology*, 28: 315–39.
BMJ (1894) 'Criminals And Criminal Anthropology', *The British Medical Journal*, 1, 1730, (Feb. 24): 427.
BMJ (1898) 'A Murderer and his Marks', *The British Medical Journal*, 2, 1975 (Nov. 5): 144.
BMJ (1900) 'The Fallacy of the Criminal Type', *The British Medical Journal*, 1, 2051 (Apr. 21): 980.
BMJ (1900a) 'Professor Lombroso on the Boers', *The British Medical Journal*, 1, 2059 (Jun. 16): 1486–7.
BMJ (1900b) 'The Training of an Imperial Race', *The British Medical Journal*, 2, 2082 (Nov. 24): 1517–18.
BMJ (1900c) 'The Criminal Anthropology of the Bicycle', *The British Medical Journal*, 1, 2049 (Apr. 7): 859.
Chapman, J. (1892) 'Contemporary Literature', *Westminster Review*, 138, 1: 436–8.
Clouston, T. S. (1894) 'The Developmental Aspects of Criminal Anthropology', *Journal of the Royal Anthropological Institute of Great Britain and Ireland*, 33: 215–25.
Clouston, T. S. (1911). *Unsoundness of Mind*. New York: Dutton & Co.
Darwin, Major L. (1914–15) 'The Habitual Criminal', *The Eugenics Review*, 6: 214–18.
Davie, N. (2005) *Tracing the Criminal: The Rise of Scientific Criminology in Britain, 1860–1918*. Oxford: Bardwell Press.
Donkin, H. B. (1917) 'Notes on Mental Defect in Criminals', *Journal of Mental Science*, 63: 16–35.
Donkin, H. B. (1919) 'The Factors of Criminal Actions', *Journal of Mental Science*, 65: 87–96.
East, W. N. (1901) 'Physical and Moral Insensitivity in the Criminal', *Journal of Mental Science*, 47: 737–58.
Ellis, H. (1890) *The Criminal*. London: Walter Scott.

Foard, I. (1898) 'The Criminal: Is He Produced by Environment or Atavism?', *Westminster Review*, 150, 1: 90–103.
Foard, I. (1899) 'The Power of Heredity', *Westminster Review*, 151, 5: 538–53.
Forsythe, W. J. (1991) *Penal Discipline, Reformatory Projects and the English Prison Commission*. Exeter: Exeter University Press.
Forsythe, W. J. (1995) 'The Garland Thesis and the Origins of Modern English Prison Discipline', *The Howard Journal*, 34,3: 259–73.
Garland, D. (1988) 'British Criminology Before 1935', *British Journal of Criminology*, 28, 2: 1–18.
Goring, C. (1913) *The English Convict: A Statistical Study*. London: HMSO.
Griffiths, A. (1896) *Report to the Secretary of State for the Home Department on the Proceedings of the Fourth Congress of Criminal Anthropology, Held at Geneva in 1896*. London: Eyre & Spottiswoode for HMSO.
Guardian (1909) 'Lombroso', *The Guardian*, (Oct. 20): 6.
Guardian (1911) 'Criminal Man', *The Guardian*, (July 4): 5.
Jackson, M. (2000) *The Borderland of Imbecility: Medicine, Society and the Fabrication of the Feeble Mind in Later Victorian and Edwardian England*. Manchester: Manchester University Press.
JMS (1896) 'Crime and Insanity', *Journal of Mental Science*, 42: 602–4.
Lancet (1892) [Untitled], *The Lancet*, (Aug. 13): 370–1.
Lancet (1896) [Untitled], *The Lancet*, (Oct. 31): 1243.
Lancet (1908) 'The Feeble-Minded Criminal', *The Lancet*, (Feb. 15): 511.
Leps, M.-C. (1992). *Apprehending the Criminal: The Production of Deviance in Nineteenth-Century Discourse*. Durham & London: Duke University Press.
Lewis, B. (1895) Oral Evidence in 'Report from the Departmental Committee on Prisons' [Gladstone Committee], *Parliamentary Papers* 56: 302–8.
Lombroso, C. (1911 [1899]) *Crime: Its Causes and Remedies*. Boston: Little Brown & Co.
Lombroso-Ferrero, G. (1914) 'The Results of an Official Investigation Made in England by Dr. Goring to Test the Lombroso Theory', *Journal of the American Institute of Criminal Law and Criminology*, 5: 207–23.
Macalister, A. (1894) 'Presidential Address', *Journal of the Anthropological Institute of Great Britain and Ireland*, 23: 400–17.
Maudsley, H. (1867) *The Physiology and Pathology of Mind*. London: Macmillan.
Maudsley, H. (1870) *Body and Mind: An Inquiry into Their Connection and Mutual Influence, Specially in Reference to Mental Disorders*. London: Macmillan.
Maudsley, H. (1874) *Responsibility in Mental Disease*. London: Henry King.
Maudsley, H. (1888) 'Remarks on Crime and Criminals', *Journal of Mental Science*, 34: 159–67.
Maudsley, H. (1895) *The Pathology of Mind*, 2nd edn. London: Macmillan.
Mercier, C. (1918) *Crime and Criminals: Being the Jurisprudence of Crime, Medical, Biological and Psychological*. London: University of London Press.
Morrison, W. D. (1891) *Crime and its Causes*. London: Swan Sonnenschein.
National Observer (1893) 'Almost Precipitous', *National Observer*, 11, 261, Nov. 18: 21.
Nicolson, D. (1895) 'Presidential Address', *Journal of Mental Science*, 41: 567–91.
Nicolson, D. (1895a) Oral Evidence in 'Report from the Departmental Committee on Prisons' [Gladstone Committee], *Parliamentary Papers* 56: 311–16.
Parkyn, E. A. (1911) 'Criminal Anthropology', *Man*, 11: 187–8.
Pearson, K. (1919) 'Preface' in Charles Goring, *The English Convict: A Statistical Study* (abridged edn.). London: HMSO.
PMG (1887) 'The Science of Crime', *Pall Mall Gazette*, (10 Oct).

PMG (1890) 'Crime: Its Causes and Cure', *Pall Mall Gazette*, (Sept. 16–17).
PMG (1895) 'Scientific Treatment of Crime', *Pall Mall Gazette*, (Sept. 17, 20; Oct. 2, 11, 23; Nov. 2).
Punch (1900). 'A Cycle of Crime', *Punch*, (March 7).
Radzinowicz, L. and Hood, R. (1990) *The Emergence of Penal Policy in Victorian and Edwardian England*. Oxford: Clarendon Press.
Rock, P. (2007) 'Caesare Lombroso as a Signal Criminologist', *Criminology and Criminal Justice*, 7: 117–33.
Ruggles-Brise, E. (1895) Oral Evidence in 'Report from the Departmental Committee on Prisons' [Gladstone Committee], *Parliamentary Papers* 56: 337–52.
Ruggles-Brise, E. (1900) 'Measures to Deal With Habitual Criminals, 1899–1904' [memo], *National Archives*: PCOM/7/286.
Ruggles-Brise, E. (1913) 'Preface' in Goring (1913).
Ruggles-Brise, E. (1921) *The English Prison System*. London: Macmillan.
Saturday Review (1890) 'Criminal Literature', *Saturday Review of Politics, Literature, Science and Art*, 70, 1818 (Aug. 30): 265–6.
Saturday Review (1891) 'Jukes Again', *Saturday Review of Politics, Literature, Science and Art*, 1870, (Aug. 29): 241–2.
Scots Observer (1890) 'Bleat about Malefactors', *Scots Observer*, 4, 94 (Sept. 6): 401–2.
Scotsman (1896) 'Criminal Anthropology: Its Fourth Congress', *The Scotsman*, (Aug. 31, Sept. 3–4).
Scotsman (1897) [Untitled], *The Scotsman*, (Jan. 18).
Shaw, T. C. (1895) Oral Evidence in 'Report from the Departmental Committee on Prisons' [Gladstone Committee], *Parliamentary Papers* 56: 192–9.
Sim, J. (1990) *Medical Power in Prisons: The Prison Medical Service in England 1774–1989*. Buckingham: Open University Press.
Simpson, H. B. (1896) 'Crime and Punishment', *Contemporary Review*, 70, July: 91–108.
Speaker (1902) 'Elimination of the Crime Factor', *Speaker*, (Apr. 19): 74–5.
Strahan, S. A. K. (1891) 'Instinctive Criminality: Its True Character and National Treatment', *Report of the British Association for the Advancement of Science*. London: John Murray.
Sullivan, W. C. (1909) 'Eugenics and Crime', *The Eugenics Review*, 1, 2: 112–20.
Sutherland, J. F. (1908) *Recidivism: Habitual Criminality and Habitual Petty Delinquency: A Problem in Sociology, Psycho-Pathology and Criminology*. Edinburgh: William Green.
Tarde, G. (1886) *La Criminalité comparée*. Paris: Félix Altan.
Times (1889) 'The Italian School of Criminal Jurisprudence', *The Times*, (Sept. 11): 8.
Times (1909) 'Professor Lombroso's Work', *The Times*, (Oct. 21): 9.
Tredgold, A. F. (1908) *Mental Deficiency (Amentia)*. London: Ballière, Tindall & Cox.
Tredgold, A. F. (1909) 'The Feeble-Minded—A Social Danger', *The Eugenics Review*, 2, 2: 97–104.
Tuke, D. H. (1887) 'Psychological Retrospect', *Journal of Mental Science*, 32: 597–601.
Wiener, M. J. (1990) *Reconstructing the Criminal: Culture, Law and Policy in England, 1830–1914*. Cambridge: Cambridge University Press.
Zimmern, H. (1891) 'Professor Lombroso's New Theory of Political Crime', *Blackwood's Edinburgh Magazine*, 149, 904: 202–211.
Zimmern, H. (1891a) 'The Palimpsests of Prison', *The New Review*, 5, 31: 537–45.
Zimmern, H. (1895) 'An Indictment of Parliaments', *Blackwood's Edinburgh Magazine*, 158, 958: 227–33.
Zimmern, H. (1898) 'Enrico Ferri', *The New Century Review*, 3 (17 May): 352–9.

INDEX

Adorno, Theodor 83
Africans 165, 236, 244
Albertani case 137–9
alcoholism 21, 178–9, 286, 317
American Institute of Criminal Law and Criminology 119, 124
Americanization 116, 119–20
anarchists 47–60; body characteristics of 52; geography of violence 60–2; ideology of 57, 61; in Chicago 52; in London 219; in opera 236; in Spain 317–18; martyrdom 57, 63; most not poor 49; prevention of 62–5; religious fanaticism 54; women as 54
Ancel, Marc 289
Annenberg, Moses 255
anthropometry: chapter in *Criminal Man* 34; criminal anthropology and 269; Jewish social science and 173, 175; in Chinese prisons 298; in Philippine prison studies 329, 332; Lombroso's doubts 76; measurement of 151, 203; Spanish study 310–11
anti-Semitism 5, 114, 127, 171–2, 180–4, 260
assassination 51–2, 54–5, 58–9
atavism: American reaction to 116; anti-Semitism 180–1; before Lombroso 282; criminal anthropology and 17, 215; criticism of 123; De Los Angeles and 331; Ellis and 345; evolutionary hierarchy 155; experience and 218; ghosts and 82; Lacassagne's view of 284; Mantegazza and 116–17; opposite of 204; prison studies and 34, 35, 40;

prostitution and 190; racial theory of 285; revealed in skulls 101; Salillas and 316; Villamor and 326–7; savages and 141, 155–6; social conditions and 160
atavistic criminality 178
atavistic psychic legacy 26
Auburn penitentiary 42

banditry 13–14, 26, 103, 254, 258–9, 358
Bayout case 135–8
Bean, Robert 329, 332
Beccaria, Cesare 11, 14, 127, 153, 289–90
Beethoven, Ludwig 332, 243
Bell, Daniel 255, 265
Bellezza, Paolo 231–3
Beltrani Scalia, Martino 14, 33, 43
Bendikt, Moritz 133
Berenini, Agostino 2–3
Bernardo de Quiros, Constancio 317–18, 330
Bertillon, Alphonse 17
Bianchi, Leonardo 24
biocriminology 147, 153–5, 158, 163, 165
biological criminology 148–8, 153, 271, 338; *see also* contemporary biological criminology
biological determinism *see* determinism
biological stigmata 35
biosocial criminology 149–52, 154, 160–4, 166
Bistolfi, Leonardo 1, 19, 24
black number 21
Bocca, Giuseppe 16
Body: Aristotle on 268; Caserio's 57; criminal's 34–5, 297, 346; criminality

within 150; evolution of 174, 328; Jewish 175; ghosts and 79; hysteria and 76; Lombroso's 104; machines and 83; measurements 79, 176, 203, 269–70, 329; neuroscience and 142; parts of 103; photography of 74; science of 4, 84; spirits and 89, 93; stigmata 117; types of 272, 339
Boito, Arrigo 243
Bordier, Arthur 283
born criminal: Albertani case 139; anarchism and 318; as the 'other' 164; atavistic 155; British views 254; coined by Ferri 150; criminal anthropology and 102; De Los Angeles view of 331–2; Dreyfus Affair and 180; economic crime and 17; French reaction 283–4, 287; ghosts 76, 82, 88, 92; Italian prisoners and 39; Jewish self-hatred and 260; juvenile 42; Lombroso's concept of 132, 141, 227; Lombroso's view of 155–6; not Lombroso's term 147; political crime and 52, 56, 63–4; Ruggles-Brise and 349; Spanish psychiatrists 312; social conditions and 123; Tolstoy's reaction to 277; women and 188
born prostitute 35, 189, 190–1, 248
brain: Bordier's research 282–4; biosocial criminologists and 162; brain waves 134; psychic communication 87; criminal atavism and 101; fingerprinting of 134; neuroscience and 133; Lombroso v modern views 150; museum collection 98; phrenology and 269
brain overclaim syndrome 140
Broca, Paul 133
Brouardel, Paul 287

capital punishment *see* death penalty
Capuana, Luigi 237–9
Carduci, Giosue 233
Carli, Andrea 234
Carrara, Francesco 22, 140
Carrara, Mario: dismissed from chair 127; Lombroso museum 101–6; Lombroso's legacy 26; Lombroso's son-in-law 11; scientific reputation 18; strong personality 21
Caserio, Sante 48, 53, 56–9
Catholic Church 132, 181, 268, 309
cephalic index 173
classical school 38, 127, 131, 141, 326

classification of criminals 17, 23, 25, 114, 242, 336
Chamblerlain, Houston Stewart 171
Charcot, Jean-Martin 286
Chinese criminology 301, 303
Clouston, Thomas 347–8, 351
Cohen, Jonathan 139
Colajanni, Napoleone 21, 283
comprehensive crime control 300
congenital degeneracy 206
congress of criminal anthropology: at Brussels 287; at Geneva 342, 352; at Paris 25, 87, 111, 286, 315, 330; at Rome 25, 39, 100, 103, 284, 330; at Turin 22, 24, 34, 275
Conrad, Joseph 219–22, 260
contemporary biological criminology 149, 151–3
Corday, Charlotte 52, 56
cranial physiognomy 151
cranium 19, 270, 312; *see also* skull
craniometry 175
Crime: Its Causes and Remedies 47, 124–5, 296
crime-free society 299
crime of passion 55–6, 76, 121, 239
crime prevention 123, 272, 297, 309, 321
criminal anthropology: anti-Semitism and 180; born criminal and 102, 269; controversy about 114; cross-national research 304; dangerous de-naturalisation of the law 314; De Los Angeles and 330; exhibition about 107; first classes in 32; gothic imagination 94; Griffiths and 342; in China 293, 297, 299; in Spain 309, 312, 315; in the Philippines 324–5, 330, 338–9; Italian School of 20, 75–6; literature and 230; Lombroso museum 4; Lombroso's conception 212–23, 268; opera and 246–7; popular among prison directors 43; punishment and 153; renewal of 105
criminal class 273
criminal justice: American 126, 193; biocriminology 153, 155; British 358; Chinese 297, 302, 304; eugenics and 210, 344; fascists and 190; Italian 119, 272; Marx on 259, 264; neuroscience and 132; political cases in 48; positivism and 272, 354; prisoners on 37; reform of 11, 119 289
criminal language 276

Criminal Man: According to the Classification of Cesare Lombroso 113, 121
Criminal Man: criminals in literature 236; crimes of passion 239; Dante in 228; Durkheim and 91; English translation 113; fifth edition 4–5, 47, 218; first edition 32–3, 99, 122, 227, 296; Korean translation 197; literary types 240; many editions of 34; policy prescriptions in 44; Spanish translation 325; second edition 216; third edition 215–16; *see also L'uomo delinquente*
criminal profiling 269–73
criminal psychology 42, 81
criminal sciences and spirit world 74–6, 86, 88–9; *see also* sciences of crime.
criminal sociology 11, 24, 26, 310, 316, 319
criminal type: definition of 216; diagnosis of 83; French reaction 24, 283; intuition of 270; mediums and 79; Topinard and 24
Criminal Woman 194–6; influence on opera 250; Korean translation of 197; no female convicts 32; Rafter translation 187; Shakespeare in 228; *see also La donna delinquente, The Female Offender*
criminology: as bourgeois pseudo-science 299; as Jewish sect 261–2; Ferrero's contribution 20; British 351, 358; French criminal sociology 310, 318; in China 294; Lombroso as father of 6; science of 4, 302; study of spirit world 75
Croce, Benedetto 116, 132
Cesare Lombroso Institute for Psychic Research 95
CSI effect 134
cultural criminology 23–6, 277
culture: American 119; ancient Greek 207; criminal 37, 276; European 18, 93, 231; Italian 26, 50, 126, 227; of positivists 15, 337; popular 164–5; nature and 202, 274; primitive 92; Russian 276; scientific 116; subculture 30

dangerous classes 21, 43, 190
dark figure of crime 38
dark figure of female crime 205, 207
Darwin, Charles 10–11, 61, 156, 176, 328
Darwinism 35, 156, 159, 164, 166, 189
D'Annunzio, Gabriele 239
De Amicis, Edmondo 234–5
De Gobineau, Arthur 282

death penalty 58, 62, 141, 153, 157
Debierre, Charles 286
decadent movement 239
Dega, Edgar 288
degeneracy 153, 180, 206, 230–1, 332, 354
degenerate race 172, 174, 353
degeneration: mass-democracy 165; atavism and 157; Britain and 349–50; France and 161–2, 285–7; in *Criminal Man* 216; Jewish self-hatred and 260; Lombroso's concept 16; Lombroso-Ferrero's concept 19; mental 286; paradigm of 202; Spain and 310–11, 316, 319; traits 54
dehumanizing 163
Delarue, Jacques 288
delinquent type 215
Derrida, Jacques 90
De Los Angeles, Sixto 324, 326–8, 330–2, 335–9
De Sanctis, Francesco 227, 230–1, 233
De Sanctis Sante 24
descriptive naturalism 217
determinism: appeal of 153; biological 121, 138–9, 147, 166, 218, 242, 297, 298, 313; free will and 141; hard 152, 348; Lombroso on 142, 152, 217; positivism and 116; soft 140
DiIulio, John 160
Di Tullio, Benigno 20, 25
Dohm, Christian Wilhelm von 256
Donkin, Brian 343, 349, 353
Dostoyevsky, Fyodor 56, 226, 275
Dreyfus affair 180–1
Dugan, Brian 134
Dupreel, Jean 289
Durkheim, Emile 450, 91, 286, 288

eclecticism 204
Efron, John 184, 262
Ellis, Havelock: Lombroso and 204; *The Criminal* 192–3; Elmira 122; eugenicist 161, 355; female sexuality 209; links between French and Lombroso 288; Lombroso's methods 202; *Man and Woman* 193; squabbles over words 288; survey of criminal anthropology 344–6; translates Lombroso 119
Ellis, L, 158–60, 164
Elmira reformatory 121–2, 350
emotions 276
Englander, Martin 180

Enlightenment 304; criminal anthropologists as heirs 231; legal theories 188; philosophers 89; rationalism 92; Lombroso in opposition 153
ennoblement 196
epilepsy: anarchists and 53; Caserio 57; criminal behaviour 355; delinquent behaviour 35, 223; extremism 49, 59; Lombroso and 316
Escuder, Jose 311
Espinas, Alfred 283
Esquerdo, Jose 310
ethical responsibility 140
eugenics: biocriminoloy 147–50, 154; British views 355–7; Chinese views 298; Galton coins word 176: Nazi policy 335
evil gene 135
evolution: antisocial behaviour and 150; born criminals 269; evolution of the psyche 87–8; evolutionary hierarchy 154, 157, 165; genius and madness 229; national health 162; of women 189; through revolution 51
evolutionary psychology 151, 158, 162, 271

Female Offender 118, 187, 191–4; *see also La donna delinquente, Criminal Woman*
feminists 188, 194
Fen, Huang 300
Fere, Charles 286
Ferrero, Guglielmo: co-author of *Female Offender* 118; co-author of *La donna delinquente* 188; Lombroso's son-in-law 10, 20; Lombroso ceremony 24; political crime 48, 50; legal training 18; well-known intellectual 17–18
Ferri, Enrico: coins 'born criminal' term 150; crime classification of 121, 217–8; criminal anthropology 44; *Delinquents in Art* 231; focus on criminal 21–2; influence in Spain 309, 311; influence in the Philippines 330; legal training 18; Lombroso museum 104; Lombroso's prison studies 33; *L'uomo delinquente* 12; methodological error 38; Modern Criminal Science series 119, 124; official triad 23; on anarchists 62–3; on Lombroso's starting assumptions 264; penal substitutes 43; popularises Lombroso 1–2, 11–12; positive school 27, 271; Radzinowicz and 261; Tarde and 283

Finot, Jean 182
Fishbein, Diana 154–5
Fishberg, Maurice 173, 179–80, 183–4
Folkmar, Daniel 329, 332–3, 338
Ford, Henry 171
Forgacs, David 183–4
Foucault, Michel 31, 43–4, 206, 210
four musketeers 9–10
Franchetti, Alberto 250
Franklin, Benjamin 61
free will: criminal sciences and 88; denial of 14, 137, 141, 188; government and 51; positivists and 192; principle of 22, 117, 139–40, 311, 314, 320
Freud, Sigmund 85–8, 92, 120, 126–7, 202, 261–2
Fumero family 73–4
functional magnetic resonance imaging 134

Gadebusch, Mariacarla 260
Gage, Phineas P. 133
Gall, Franz Joseph 120, 133, 269
Galton, Francis: biometric method 271; coins 'eugenics' 176; criminal anthropology and 346; De Los Angeles 331; eugenics views 149, 161, 355; forensic science pioneer 17; studies with Jacobs 177
Gambelli, Aristide 23
Gans, Eduard 258–9
Garafalo, Raffaele: criminal anthropology 43; *Dizionario di Criminalogia* 27; first criminology text 10–11; influence in Spain 309; influence in the Philippines 330; methodological error 39; Modern Criminal Science series 119; official triad 23; socialist 19; *Sociologia criminale* 21; positive school 271
Garland, David 163, 210
Gazzaaniga, Michael 140
Genius: criminal and 81, 86, 164; insanity and 9, 179, 223, 230, 277; Jacobs and 176; Jews and 182, 260; literary 16, 235, 241; Lombroso as 10, 11, 31, 78, 89, 221; Lombroso on 172, 180, 243; men and 230; revolution and 51
Genius and Degeneration 232
Genius and Madness 277
Gemelli, Agostino 26, 270
geography 60, 93, 208
ghost hunting 74
ghosts 75, 84, 90, 93
ghost trials 85

Gibson, Mary: *Crime: Its Causes and Remedies* 293; *Criminal Man* 113, 296; *Criminal Woman* 194, 196; Ingrasci and 197; *La donna delinquente* 190; Lombroso and anti-Semitism 260; Lombroso and prostitutes 190; Lombroso's negative image 118; Lombroso's methods 203; Lombroso's reception in the USA 125; Lombroso's self-promotion 227; positivism and literature 228; revisionist pioneer 5–6; translating Lombroso 188
Giordano, Umberto 248
Gladstone Committee 346–7, 350, 353
Gli Anarchici 47, 59, 65, 103, 317
Gluecks, Sheldon and Eleanor 125, 209
Gong, Zhou 294
Goring, Charles 303, 349, 353, 355
gothic criminology 163
gothic romance 187
Gould, Stephen J. 270
Graf, Arturo 16, 18, 230
Grandi, Carlo 117
graphology 268
Greene, Joshua 139
Griffiths, Arthur 327, 342, 352
Grispigni, Filippo 25
Grunhut, Max 262
GxE metaphor 152–3
gypsies 178, 247, 260

habitual crime 354–6
Hamon, Frederic 59
Harrowitz, Nancy 183, 226, 260
Hart. Mitchell 181, 183–4
haunted houses 72
Healy, William 125–6
Hegel, G.W.F. 90
Heidensohn, Frances 193
Heine, Heinrich 232, 243, 258
Henry, Emile 54, 59–60
Hirschi, Travis 165
history of crime 6
Hitchcock, Alfred 214
Hitler, Adolf 171
Hobsbawm, Eric 253–6, 265
Hollinger, David 262
homosexuality 205, 211
Hood, Roger 345
Horton, Henry P. 124
human genome project 148, 151
human sciences 5, 23, 86, 107, 115, 127, 201–4
hypnotism 74, 87

ideology 22, 51, 57, 108, 149, 260, 318
Il Delitto Politico 47, 52, 60
incorrigibles 41, 141, 160–1, 352
Ingrasci, Ombretta 197
insane asylums 42–3
insanity: alcoholism a cause 179; anarchists and 48; born criminals 318–19; degenerative mental illness 312; genius and 229; museum of madness 103; legal definition 135; partial insanity 138
Institute of Forensic Medicine 101
interdisciplinarity 277
Italian positivism 116
Italian Socialist Party 40

Jackson, Mark 353
Jacobs, Joseph 172–3, 175–6, 180
James, Henry 4
James, William 85, 119
Jeffrey, C. Ray 272
Jewish nose 172, 175
Jewish social science 171–2, 184
Jews: as a race 172–5; criminality and 178–9, 255–6; criminology 261–2; fantasy of Jewish crime 258; London study of 177; mental illness and 179–80; robbers 254, 258
Jiaben, Shen 295
juvenile born criminals 42

Kafka, Franz 84
Kardec, Allen 75
Kemp, Martin 260
Krafft-Ebing, Richard von 189, 193, 202–3, 205–7
Kropotkin, Peter 50–2
Kuliscioff, Anna 18, 188–9
Kurella, Hans 89, 119, 124, 354

Lacassagne, Alexandre: criminal anthropology critic 288, 290; degeneration concept 287; De Los Angeles and 331; French criminology 282, 284–5
La donna delinquente 21; original version 188–90, 194–5, 223; 2009 reprint 197; *see also The Female Offender, Criminal Woman.*
L'antisemitismo e le science modern 103, 182–3
Lamarck, Jean Baptiste 174
Laplace, Pierre-Simon 140
Laurent, Emile 287
left-handedness 34, 35, 156
Lenz, Adolf 271

Leoncavallo, Ruggero 248–9
Leopardi, Giacomo 231–3
lesbian 189–90, 199, 204–10
liberating discourse 174, 302
Lin-Sheng, Liu 293
Lombardi, Giovanni 26
Lombroso Carrara, Paola: arguments with Lombroso 189; family life 18; Kuliscioff and 189; Lombroso's daughter 9–10; marriage to Carrara 101
Lombroso Ferrero, Gina: arguments with Lombroso 189; author of *Criminal Man* 121–3, 125; Chinese version of Lombroso 296; father as 'born collector' 98; family life 17–18; Kuliscioff and 189; *La donna delinquente* 188; Lombroso's daughter 9–10; museum collection 105; on Lombroso as prison director 32; on Lombroso's prison studies 32–4
Lombroso Museum: Carrara as director 104–6; Grandi exhibit 117; laboratory link 15; mythical status 10; opening of 4, 99–101; origins of collection 33–4; period of decline 105–6; reaction to opening of 114; re-organisation of 106–8
Lombroso school 16–17, 234, 288, 313
Lombrosian type 215, 217, 219, 221
Lucchini, Luigi 22–3
L'Uomo delinquente: first edition 99, 113, 310, 344; fifth edition 113; French translation 281; ignored 9; Lombroso's reputation 66; second edition 12, 178; themes in 51; *see also Criminal Man*
Luzzato, Simone 263

MacDonald, Arthur 260
madness *see* insanity
mafia 13, 26, 53, 197
magic 75, 84, 87, 92–3
Magnan, Valentin 287
Majorana, Angelo 48
Mannheim, Hermann 262
Man of Genius 231, 354
Manouvrier, Leonce 285, 288
Mantegazza, Paolo 9, 116
Marro, Antonio 20, 21, 24, 32–3
Marx, Karl: alienation concept 84; criminology founder 265; ghost metaphor 90; Hobsbawm and 253–8; Lombroso and 260; religion 264
Marzolo, Paolo 12

Mascagni, Pietro 243, 245–7
mattoids 54
Maudsley, Henry 132, 348
Maupate, Leon 287
Maurey, Alfred 282
Mayhew, Henry 208
medium 75, 77–80, 82, 87, 90, 120, 156
Mella, Ricardo 318
Melossi, Dario 162, 274
Mendelssohn, Moses 256–7, 264
mental illness *see* insanity
Mercier, Charles 350
Merlino, Francesco 50
Mesmer, Franz 120
mesmerism 74, 87
Minority Report 142
misogyny 142, 260
misoneism 51
Moleschott, Jakob 6–7
monster: criminals as 141, 165, 282, 313; female criminal as 187; gothic 76; moral 84, 349, 355; science of 4, 83; theory of 90; true 36, 94, 235
moral education 297
moral poverty 160
Morillo, Manuel 311
Morrison, W. Douglas 191, 345
Morse, Stephen 139–40
Morselli, Enrico 24, 78–9, 116
multi-causal approach 296–7, 326
museum 5, 10, 34, 39, 86, 270, 315
museum of madness 103
Mussolini, Benito 2, 241, 242

Nazi Germany 115, 120, 147, 272, 290
National Institute of Health conference 154
Neppi Modona, Guido 34
neuroscience 114, 120, 131–42
new lombrosianism 139
Niceforo, Alfredo 21, 27–8, 230, 317
Nicolson, David 342–3, 348, 350–2
Nitti, Francesco 20
Nordau, Max: cultural critic 83; degeneration concept 202; Lombroso dedication 123; science of criminology 353; well-known intellectual 49; Zionist leader 172–4
nutritional deficiency 315–16, 318

occasional criminal 121
opera 243–50
Oriani, Alfredo 240–1

organized crime 41, 255, 265
Ottolenghi, Salvatore 20, 24, 25, 33, 103, 272

Paladino, Eusapia 78–82, 120
palmistry 268
parapsychology 77–8
Parent-Duchatelet, A.J.B. 208, 210
Parmelee, Maurice 122–4
Patrizi, M.L. 231–2
Pearson, Karl 161, 271
pellagra 8, 36, 38, 49, 57–8, 66, 98
penal science 14, 32
penal substitutes 42
Pende, Nicola 27
Penta, Pasquale 103
Philadelphia penitentiary 39–40
photographs: beautiful prostitutes 36; criminal women 188: Jewish boys 176; ghost images 74, 77, 84; museum collection 100, 270; scientific evidence 79–81; Russian prisoners 202; reveals anarchist's disposition 55
phrenology 12, 35, 133, 202, 268–9, 328
physiognomy 214, 219, 234–5, 241–2, 268
Pick, Daniel 260
pigmentation 174
Pinatel, Jean 289
police: Heine on 258; Italian 271; legal medicine 337; Lombroso on 272; Marx on 259; political criminals and 50, 65; prostitutes and 190, 208; scientific 273; women as 211
political crime 51, 160, 165, 328; *see also* anarchism
political criminal 47, 52, 60
Pollak, Otto 205
positive school: denies freewill 140; dispute within 22; Facism and 190; in Italy 132; Lombroso's view 30–3; opposes jury trial 65; scientific discourse 155; separate from religious view 264; Spanish lawyers 313; views of capitalism 264
positivism: crisis of 10; ghosts and 74; Italian 115–16, 226; literature and 236; parapsychology and 78
positron emission tomography 134
postmodern 207
prisons: as a laboratory 31, 34, 202, 270; as 'special theatre' 34; born criminals 39; clinics for the soul 314; cellular design 40–1; communication among prisoners 40; doctors in 33, 100, 202, 350; encouraging prostitution 208; in Britain 346–7; in China 295, 298; in Spain 316; in the Philippines 328–9, 332; inmate subculture 37; in Italy 14; Lombroso's view of 141; signs of atavism in 40; studies in 298, 316, 329, 332
Prison palimpsests 30, 36, 41, 58
probation 122
prostitutes: beautiful 36; debate in Italy 188; in Paris 208; Lombrosian type 217; Lombroso's view 189–90; Jewish 260; Jewish procurers 262; opera themes 243
pseudo-science 114, 269, 299, 324, 328, 345
psychiatry 81, 85, 102, 312, 320
psychoanalysis 321
psychopathy 203
public hygiene 6
Pulido, Angel 310

racism 142
racist 108, 115, 127, 136, 149, 155, 183
race science 171–2, 174
racial theories 235, 282
Radzinowicz, Leon 11, 261–2, 345
Rafter, Nicole: *Criminal Man* 113; disagreement with Lombroso 196; diffusion of Lombroso's ideas 304; Ingrasci and 197; Jae Lee and 197; on biocriminology 148; on biosocial model 143, 152, 159; on Lombroso and anti-Semitism 260; on Lombroso's contribution 275; on Lombroso's methods 118, 203; on Lombroso's reception in the USA 125; positivism and literature 228; translation of Lombroso 113, 195–6, 199; revisionist pioneer 5–6
Raine, Adrian 162
rape 15, 159, 191, 310, 332
rational mediation 218
Regina Coeli prison 101, 104
regression theory 284
Renneville, Marc 115
revisionist historians 5, 6
Rock, Paul 303, 357
Ruggles-Brise, Evelyn 349, 353, 356
Ruppin, Arthur 177–8, 180–1

Sackville-West, Vita 210
Salillas, Rafael 314–17
sapphism 204

savages 35
science of born criminal 3, 223
science of literature 237
sciences of crime 13
scientificity 12
scientific criminology 118–19, 126, 192, 303, 331
scientific objectivity 137, 171
scientific police 273
scientific study of society 295, 324–5, 337–8
Scuola Nuova 309–10, 315
Scuola Positiva 23, 27
séances 86
selfish gene 158–9, 163, 165
Sergi, Giuseppe 100, 230, 233
Servi, Flaminio 182
sexual deviancy 36
sexual inversion 202
sexual psychopathy 203
sexual sensitivity 199, 203
sexology 188, 189, 208–10
Shaw, Thomas 347
Shockley, William 150
Simarro, Luis 311, 314–15
Simon, Jonathan 125–6
Simpson, H.B. 349–50
skull 97; anarchist Caserio's 57; criminal atavism and 101; collection of 103; 151, 173–4, 269–70, 281; degeneration and 286; neuroscience and 133; *see also* cranium
Smart, Carol 194
social defence 12, 210, 262, 289, 320–1
social hygiene 210, 333, 335
social progress 161
socialism 5, 10, 20, 60, 80, 165
socialists 19, 41, 53
Societa di Cultura 20
Societa Italiana di Criminologia 25
sociobiology 151
Spanish criminology museum 315
spiritualism 75, 238
Spiritualism? 238
Spencer, Herbert 51
Spurzheim, Johann 133
statistic seriality 217
Stein, Gertrude 210
Stigmata: atavistic 275; born criminal 114, 351, 353–4 physical 35, 117, 286–8, 344; religious 91; sign of abnormality 137
Sull'incremento del delitto in Italia 272
superhuman 163

superpredator 160, 303
supervillain 163

Tarde, Gabriel 271, 282–4, 344
tattoos 12, 151, 210, 270, 283, 316
Techini, Lorenzo 133
technology 83, 151
Thiele, A.F. 260
Thon, Jakob 177–8
Tolstoy, Leo 49, 277–8
Topinard, Paul 24, 271, 287
translation effects 195–6
tribadism 204–9
Turin murder case 281
Turati, Filippo 18, 283

Ulrichs, Karl Henrich 205
urban anthropology 37

Valliant, Auguste 53, 55, 58
vampires 90, 163–5, 239–40
Verga, Giovanni 236
Villamor, Ignacio 326–8, 331
Villella, Giuseppe 11, 98, 114, 121, 141
violence gene 135–6
Virchow, Rudolf 9, 11, 329, 331

Wagner, Richard 242–3, 249
Walsh, A. 158–60, 164
warrior gene 136
Weber, Max 92
West, Donald 81
The White Man and the Man of Colour 235, 244
Wigmore, John 118, 120, 124–5
Wilson, James Q. 154
women: as criminals 35, 36, 193; as anarchists 56; as inferior to men 189; as spirit mediums 85; born criminals 188; criminal physiognomy 219; Jewish walk 175; lesbian 189; masculine traits 193; Wulffen and 271; *see also* prostitutes
World of Occult 239
Wulffen, Eric 271
Wyzewa, Teodor 234

x-rays 77

Zanardelli code 103
Zimmern, Helen 117, 345–6
Zionism 172, 180–3
Zini, Zino 18–19
Zola, Emile 288
Zuccarelli, Angelo 103

eBooks

eBooks – at www.eBookstore.tandf.co.uk

A library at your fingertips!

eBooks are electronic versions of printed books. You can store them on your PC/laptop or browse them online.

They have advantages for anyone needing rapid access to a wide variety of published, copyright information.

eBooks can help your research by enabling you to bookmark chapters, annotate text and use instant searches to find specific words or phrases. Several eBook files would fit on even a small laptop or PDA.

NEW: Save money by eSubscribing: cheap, online access to any eBook for as long as you need it.

Annual subscription packages

We now offer special low-cost bulk subscriptions to packages of eBooks in certain subject areas. These are available to libraries or to individuals.

For more information please contact webmaster.ebooks@tandf.co.uk

We're continually developing the eBook concept, so keep up to date by visiting the website.

www.eBookstore.tandf.co.uk